GENERAL JOHN A. RAWLINS

GENERAL
JOHN A. RAWLINS

NO ORDINARY MAN

Allen J. Ottens

Indiana University Press

This book is a publication of

Indiana University Press
Office of Scholarly Publishing
Herman B Wells Library 350
1320 East 10th Street
Bloomington, Indiana 47405 USA

iupress.org

Manufactured in the United States of America

First printing 2021

Library of Congress
Cataloging-in-Publication Data

Names: Ottens, Allen J., author.
Title: General John A. Rawlins :
  no ordinary man / Allen J. Ottens.
Description: Bloomington, Indiana :
  Indiana University Press, [2021] | Includes
  bibliographical references and index.
Identifiers: LCCN 2020057366 (print)
  | LCCN 2020057367 (ebook) |
  ISBN 9780253057303 (hardback) |
  ISBN 9780253057310 (ebook)
Subjects: LCSH: Rawlins, John A. (John
  Aaron), 1831-1869. | Grant, Ulysses S.
  (Ulysses Simpson), 1822-1885—Friends and
  associates. | Generals—United States—
  Biography. | United States. Army—
  Biography. | United States—History—Civil
  War, 1861-1865. | Cabinet officers—United
  States—Biography. | United States—
  Politics and government—1865-1877. |
  Galena (Ill.)—Biography.
Classification: LCC E467.1.R25 O88 2021
  (print) | LCC E467.1.R25 (ebook) |
  DDC 355.0092 [B]—dc23
LC record available at https://
  lccn.loc.gov/2020057366
LC ebook record available at https://
  lccn.loc.gov/2020057367

CONTENTS

Illustrations follow page 236.

FOREWORD

THE LAST SEVERAL YEARS HAVE seen a renaissance in book-length studies of General and President Ulysses S. Grant. New books have sought to provide insight into the quiet man's personality and character, striving to illuminate aspects of his life that might help explain the traits and motivations that made the victorious general and two-term president the man that he was.

Although many insightful treatments of Grant have been published, it is important to remember that Grant did not live in a vacuum. He was a product of the era in which he lived and was influenced by those around him. Acknowledging that context is vital to understanding the man himself and the momentous times in which he lived.

One of the most influential figures in Grant's life was John A. Rawlins. Rawlins was a lifelong resident of Galena, Illinois, who identified politically with the Democratic Party leading up to the Civil War. Yet at the outbreak of the war, he quickly distinguished himself as a strong supporter of the Union. He entered the Federal army and went on to serve his country alongside Grant, playing a key role in the preservation of the nation.

Early on, Rawlins saw in Grant someone who shared his ideas and one to whom he could provide unwavering support. He proved to be a superb staff officer whom Grant could always trust. He had the skills to assist Grant in managing the day-to-day operations of massive armies in the field, whether the Western Theater's Army of the Tennessee or the Army of the Potomac in the East. Rawlins knew how to ensure that Grant did not fall victim to ambitious and vindictive generals, sensationalistic reporters, and all sorts of other people who wanted to take advantage of him. Like Grant's wife, Julia, Rawlins recognized that Grant had unique talents and was just the leader who could win the war.

Rawlins was no stock figure in the drama of the war years. Instead, he grew and changed with the times and understood the importance of the moment in which he lived. Like so many others caught up in the turmoil of the prewar period and the Civil War itself, Rawlins went from being someone who believed that the preservation of the Union was the major aim of the war to recognizing that civil rights for African Americans were also crucial.

Rawlins remained close to Grant after the conflict and became the new president's first secretary of war in 1869. Although his life was cut short, he loomed large in the ascendancy of Grant to national prominence. His early death leaves us to ponder what impact he might have had on Grant's presidency since he had become such a trusted confidant of Grant during the war.

Despite Rawlins's importance, his role and influence in the Grant story have been frequently caricatured or otherwise misunderstood. Too many studies have viewed Rawlins only as a teetotaling crusader against alcohol, ignoring other facets of his life. He has usually been portrayed as a man who showed Grant the straight and narrow, who regularly warned him about drinking, and whose influence held Grant back from self-destructive behavior. These characterizations of Grant and Rawlins diminish the truth about both men.

On the other hand, there has been another common misinterpretation of Rawlins's role that overemphasizes his authority. He has been cast as the man who actually made the great decisions that pushed Grant forward to the front of the military and, after the war, to the head of American politics—all for his own benefit. Rawlins has been described as the great person behind the supposedly weak man, with some writers going so far as insisting that Grant accomplished what he did only because of Rawlins's drive, intelligence, and watchfulness.

This is certainly unfair and inaccurate. Rawlins was more than just a watchdog who kept Grant sober, but he was certainly not a puppet master manipulating Grant to further a personal agenda. He was Grant's good friend, a bright person in his own right, and someone whom Grant could trust. The renaissance in Grant studies is providing a more accurate portrait of the Civil War general and Reconstruction president, but Rawlins also deserves a place in this reevaluation.

Until now, the dearth of in-depth studies on Rawlins himself has kept us from knowing all that we need to know about him, Grant, and the Civil War itself. But through this new book about Rawlins, a clearer picture of the true nature of Rawlins and his impact emerges. Allen J. Ottens, a retired professor emeritus of adult counseling and higher education at Northern Illinois University and a longtime student of the Civil War, has written a book that clarifies the key role that Rawlins played. Ottens's book contributes to a more nuanced understanding of the broader picture of both Rawlins as an individual and the context that helped shape Grant's decisions at a pivotal moment in American history.

The publication of this book on John A. Rawlins is a major step toward increasing our knowledge of the Civil War and of one of its major players. To know John A. Rawlins is to know Ulysses S. Grant better, and Ottens's book provides this insight.

John F. Marszalek, David S. Nolen, and Louie P. Gallo,
Ulysses S. Grant Presidential Library

PREFACE

THE GENERAL U. S. GRANT Highway that leads into Galena, Illinois is a short jaunt from my front door. In the course of my life, I've made dozens of visits to that quaint town that time appears to have left behind. On one of those visits over ten years ago, I spent half an afternoon chatting with an old friend, Bill Butts, proprietor of Main Street Fine Books and Manuscripts. "Why don't you do a bio of John Rawlins?" he asked. "It's high time another one appeared." He was right. The most serious biography of General John Rawlins, Grant's fellow Galenian, adjutant, chief of staff, and first secretary of war, was written by his wartime friend General James "Harry" Harrison Wilson and published almost a century before. Bill knew of my lifelong study of the Civil War, dating back to early elementary grades. Before I turned ten, for example, I had devoured the four volumes of *Battles and Leaders of the Civil War*.

"You know, I just might take you up on that idea," I replied, thinking ahead to my looming retirement from academia and the time I would soon have to dedicate to such a task. And while I pursued that task, a number of significant biographical works about Grant were published that have served to smartly burnish his image. Their publication underscored the timeliness of a biography of the man who teamed with Grant on the journey from Galena to Cairo, Illinois, and ultimately to the Executive Mansion.

Accomplishing a biography of the staff person and friend Grant regarded as "no ordinary man," I soon learned, is fraught with complications, beginning with what to make of him. To those relatively few familiar with him, John Rawlins has come to be known as a one-dimensional or stereotyped character, perhaps described as Grant's alter ego or conscience or dismissed as the profanity-spouting staff officer who labored to keep Grant sober. In this regard, one early Grant biographer said of Rawlins, "Perhaps his greatest service was keeping him from drink."[1] Rawlins even fashioned himself as the only one, besides Grant's wife, who could "stay" him from drink. In contrast to the role of temperance fanatic, not too long after Rawlins's death, some of his prominent associates who had issues against Grant attributed a significant amount of his military success to Rawlins's wiser counsel. That leaves the question of how much of Rawlins's influence on Grant was spuriously augmented.[2] Those inaccuracies and overgeneralizations about Rawlins complicate the task of unraveling his accomplishments and contributions to Grant the general and the politician. The challenge, then, for a biographer of Rawlins is to understand him apart from these overwrought points of view.

Another complicating factor is that a good deal of the paper material created by Rawlins has disappeared, perhaps destroyed. He left no diary. Much of the content of his war-dated letters to his wife is factual material that might have been found in newspapers—he eschewed discussing sensitive material lest the letters fall into the wrong hands. Moreover, it's impossible to ascertain to what extent the orders or reports that went out under Grant's name contain input generated by Rawlins.

Besides attempting to maintain a balanced view of Rawlins, I constantly had to be on guard so that Grant's looming presence did not eclipse him. I had to provide enough background and information about Grant to allow Rawlins's actions and decisions to become understandable. I hope I have succeeded in achieving that balance.

So who was John Rawlins? Above all, Rawlins would have regarded himself as a patriot, one who loved the Union and detested those who would tear it asunder. He was hardworking, disapproving of the slackers on Grant's staff, and committed to his cabinet responsibilities until succumbing to the ravages of tuberculosis. An impoverished upbringing, meager educational attainments, and lack of military training left him at times questioning whether he was competent to be of use to Grant on his ascent to ever greater responsibilities. Yet he was arguably Grant's best personnel choice because he helped administer the country's most complex military apparatus prior to the Second World War.

A recent Grant biographer perceived a thread running through his life: "Strength of character—an indomitable will that never flagged in the face of adversity. . . . He saw his goals clearly and moved toward them relentlessly."[3] I think Rawlins quickly apprehended Grant possessed these qualities of strength and steadfastness, thereby inspiring his decision to give him his trust and loyalty. Grant and Rawlins formed a team, but one in which Rawlins would submerge his needs and ambitions in the service of Grant. Rawlins was devoted to Grant, allied with him in the face of rival generals endeavoring to spoil his reputation, opportunists wishing to take advantage of his mild nature, strategists hoping to make political hay from his popularity, and profiteers who were angered by his commitment to prevent corruption.

And what about his seemingly vital service as the curb on Grant's drinking? In truth, Grant had more control over his drinking than most of his contemporaries realized or cared to know. Rawlins's value was in his reputation as a sworn enemy of drink, one who was known to keep a watchful eye over headquarters. His role as the guardian was more important to individuals such as Abraham Lincoln and powerful Illinois congressman Elihu Washburne, who had invested in Grant so much responsibility. If Grant failed, they would suffer grave political consequences. They could therefore rest easier knowing that the alert Rawlins was "on the job."

What I regard as one of Rawlins's most noteworthy achievements is the personal growth he evidenced as a vigorous proponent of personal and citizenship rights for those formerly enslaved. This was a remarkable step forward for the erstwhile Galena Democrat and ardent supporter of Stephen Douglas, a politician who did not regard Blacks as full-fledged human beings.[4] As secretary of war, Rawlins, in his last few months, desired to see slavery brought to an end in Cuba and the oppressed there liberated from their Spanish rulers.

Above all, John Rawlins was beloved by many, from his friends in Galena to his fellow officers in the Army of the Tennessee. Washington, DC, was awash in grief following his death on September 6, 1869, at age thirty-eight. Rawlins counted Ulysses Grant as his greatest friend, and Grant reciprocated that friendship. In 1864, Grant presented Rawlins his Vicksburg battle sash on which he had inscribed his appreciation to the man he regarded "an officer and friend."[5] That Grant expressed such sentiments only deepens the mystery of why his remarkable *Memoirs* are virtually bereft of accolades to Rawlins.

NOTES

1. Louis A. Coolidge, *Ulysses S. Grant* (Boston: Houghton Mifflin, 1917), 125.

2. E. B. Long, "John A. Rawlins: Staff Officer Par Excellence," *Civil War Times Illustrated* 12, no. 9 (1974): 4.

3. Jean Edward Smith, *Grant* (New York: Simon and Schuster, 2001), 15.

4. *New York Tribune*, December 6, 1858.

5. *Galena Daily Gazette*, May 14, 1864.

ACKNOWLEDGMENTS

I COULD NOT HAVE COMPLETED this book without the help of numerous friends, librarians, archivists, historians, curators, and researchers who graciously offered their time and assistance to attend to my many requests, make helpful suggestions, and provide much needed feedback. Those individuals in Galena, Illinois, are Nancy Breed, Lori Garcia, Shelby Miller, Karen Sieber, and Ray Werner of the Galena-Jo Daviess County Historical Society; Claire Bersbach, Guilford Township clerk; Bill Butts, Main Street Fine Books and Manuscripts; attorney Louis Nack; and a special thanks to Scott Wolfe of the Galena Public Library for his insights, information, and humor.

Librarians and library staff who made this book possible are John Millhorn and Gary Weishaar at Northern Illinois University; Clare Murphy and Mel Smith, Connecticut State Library; Claude B. Zachary, Doheny Memorial Library at the University of Southern California; Melinda Hayes, Special Collections, University of Southern California Libraries; John Muller, District of Columbia Library; Margaret Kieckhefer, Library of Congress; Debbie Hamm, Meghan Harmon, and Hannah Jellen, Abraham Lincoln Presidential Library; Dr. Stacy Pratt McDermott, assistant director of the Papers of Abraham Lincoln; Lauren Rogers, Special Collections, University of Mississippi; Ann Roche, Goshen, New York Public Library; Maggie Grossman, University of Chicago Library; Anne Causey and Penny White, Special Collections Library at the University of Virginia; Kellie Clinton, University of Illinois, Urbana-Champaign; Dr. Tom Kanon, Tennessee State Library and Archives; and Erika Gorder and Fernanda Perrone, Special Collections, Rutgers University Libraries.

I owe much gratitude to these historians, researchers, curators, and archivists: Ellen Keith, Chicago History Museum; Jeanine Wine, Manchester College; Jerry Stauffer, Mt. Morris, Illinois, Historical Museum; Frank Crawford, Belvidere, Illinois; Ann Roche, Goshen, New York History Museum; Shawna Mazur, River Raisin Battlefield Park; Brian Baxter, LaSalle County, Illinois, Historical Society; Alicia Mauldin-Ware, US Military Academy; Gail Lelyveld, independent researcher; Kerck Kelsey, Washburne family historian; Vicki Catozza, Western Reserve Historical Society; Brigid Guertin and Patrick Wells, Danbury, Connecticut, Museum; Ellen Bridenstein and Sheri Stelling, State Historical Society of Iowa; Christine Ruggere, Institute of the History of Medicine, the Johns Hopkins University; Jamie Cassel, attorney at law; Norma Vinchkoski, Wooster Cemetery, Danbury, Connecticut; DeAnn Blanton and Dennis Michael Edelin, National Archives and Records Administration; Sarah Minegar, Morristown National Historical Park; Carl Hallberg, Kathy Marquis, and Suzi Taylor, Wyoming State Archives; and Terry Reimer, National Museum of Civil War Medicine.

I owe special thanks to Dr. John Marszalek for his encouragement, feedback, and assistance and to his staff members Louie Gallo, Ryan Semmes, and Rebecca Houston at the Ulysses S. Grant Presidential Library at Mississippi State University; Dr. Michelle Krowl, Manuscript Division of the Library of Congress; and Marie Kelsey, professor emerita, the College of St. Scholastica, for her unflagging assistance, comments, feedback, and suggestions.

For help with obtaining photos and illustrations I am indebted to Melissa A. Winn; for maps, I thank Ray Boomhower, Indiana Historical Society Press, and Hal Jespersen, the most "obedient servant." Sarah Forgey, art curator at the Center for Military History, provided assistance with options regarding the cover art.

I have valued the assistance of the professionals at Indiana University Press, especially Ashley Runyon, who saw potential in my raw manuscript as well as the helping hand provided by her assistant, Anna Francis.

While writing this book, I benefited from comic relief provided by three green-cheek conures: Smokey, Mango, and Cisco. Lastly, this book could not have been completed without the patience, love, support, and help of my bride, Amy. She read every word and even shed a tear over Rawlins's death.

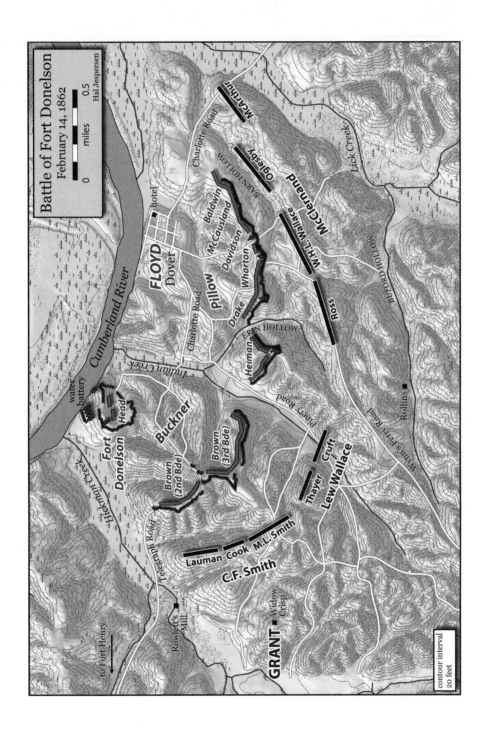

Battle of Fort Donelson
February 14, 1862

Hal Jespersen

0   0.5
miles

contour interval
20 feet

MARCH OF LEW WALLACE'S DIVISION TO SHILOH, APRIL 6, 1862

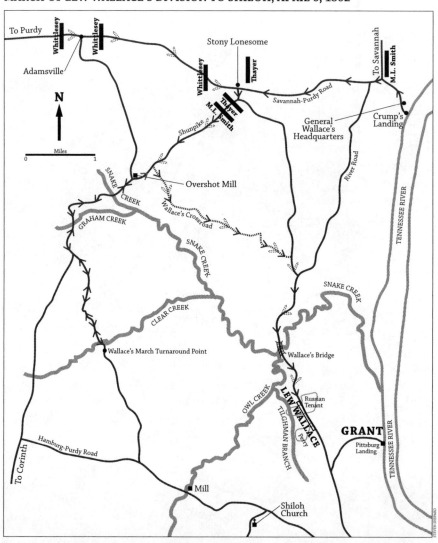

Map by Steven Shepard from Gail Stephens, *Shadow of Shiloh:
Major General Lew Wallace in the Civil War*
(Indiana Historical Society Press, 2010).

Vicksburg Campaign
December 1862–March 1863

0   miles   50

Hal Jespersen

TENNESSEE
- Bolivar
- Memphis   Grand Junction
- Corinth

(2) Holly Springs • Ripley

GRANT (1)

- Oxford
- Tupelo

ARKANSAS   Helena

Coldwater R.

(7)

- Panola

White R.
- St. Charles

McCLERNAND (4)

Arkansas Post

Arkansas River

Tallahatchie R.

Mississippi River

Yalobusha R.
- Grenada

MISSISSIPPI DELTA

(8) **Fort Pemberton**
- Greenwood

- Columbus

- Greenville

Big Sunflower R.

Yazoo R.

MISSISSIPPI

- Macon

LOUISIANA

Lake Providence (6)

- Yazoo City

(3)

(9)

Steele's Bayou

Big Black R.

- Canton

Pearl R.

SHERMAN

(10) Chickasaw Bayou

- Duckport
- **Vicksburg**
- Warrenton • **JACKSON**
- New Carthage • Raymond

- Meridian

- Grand Gulf
- Port Gibson

- Bruinsburg

- Natchez

(1)	Central Mississippi Advance: November 14–December 21	(7)	Yazoo Pass Expedition: February 3–April 10
(2)	Holly Springs: December 20	(8)	Fort Pemberton: March 11–April 5
(3)	Chickasaw Bayou: December 27–29	(9)	Steele's Bayou Expedition: March 14–27
(4)	Arkansas Post (Fort Hindman): January 9–11	(10)	Duckport Canal: March 31–April 11
(5)	Grant's Canal: January 24–March 27		
(6)	Lake Providence Expedition: February 3–March 29		

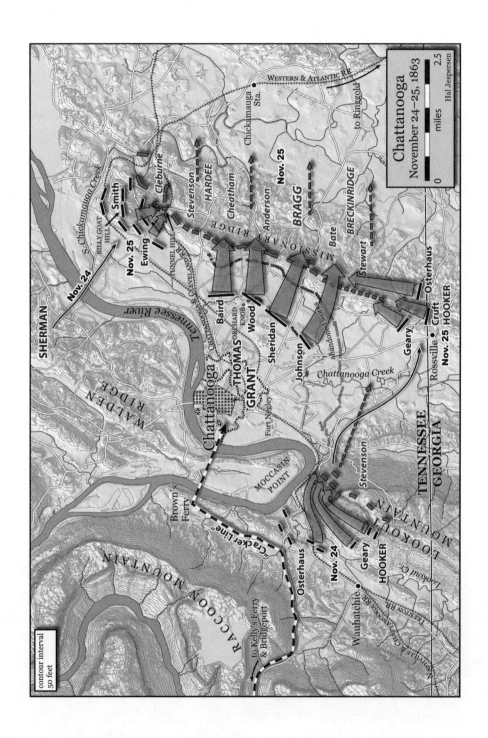

Chattanooga
November 24–25, 1863

Hal Jespersen

0 miles 2.5

contour interval 50 feet

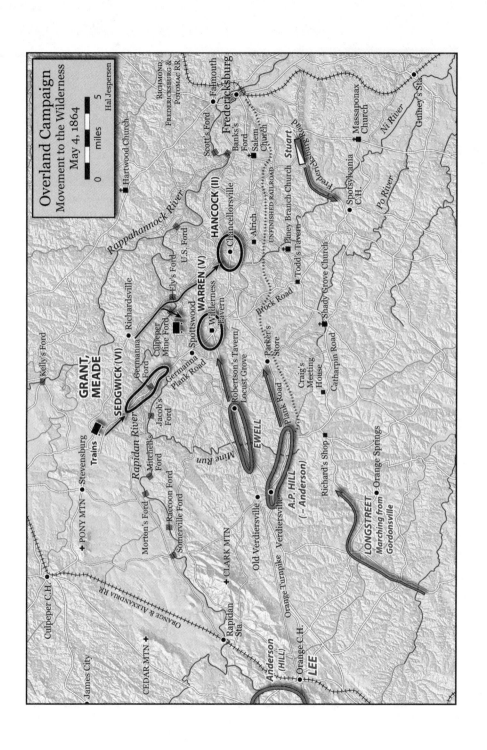

Overland Campaign
Movement to the Wilderness
May 4, 1864

Hal Jespersen

0   miles   5

Culpeper C.H.

James City

CEDAR MTN

Rapidan Sta.

Orange C.H.
LEE
Anderson (HILL)

ORANGE & ALEXANDRIA RR

PONY MTN

Stevensburg

Kelly's Ford

Trains

GRANT, MEADE

Rapidan River

Morton's Ford
Mitchell's Ford
Raccoon Ford
Somerville Ford

CLARK MTN

Old Verdiersville

Verdiersville
A.P. HILL (–Anderson)

Orange Turnpike

Mine Run

Plank Road

LONGSTREET
Marching from Gordonsville

Orange Springs

Richard's Shop

SEDGWICK (VI)

Germanna Ford

Jacob's Ford

Culpeper Mine Ford

Spottswood

Germanna Plank Road

WARREN (V)

Wilderness Tavern

EWELL

Robertson's Tavern/ Locust Grove

Parker's Store

Craig's Meeting House

Catharpin Road

Shady Grove Church

Richardsville

Ely's Ford

U.S. Ford

HANCOCK (II)

Chancellorsville

Alrich

UNFINISHED RAILROAD

Brock Road

Todd's Tavern

Rappahannock River

Hartwood Church

Scott's Ford

Banks's Ford

Salem Church

RICHMOND, FREDERICKSBURG & POTOMAC RR

Falmouth

Fredericksburg

Piney Branch Church

Fredericksburg Road

Stuart

Spotsylvania C.H.

Po River

Massaponax Church

Ni River

Guthey's Sta.

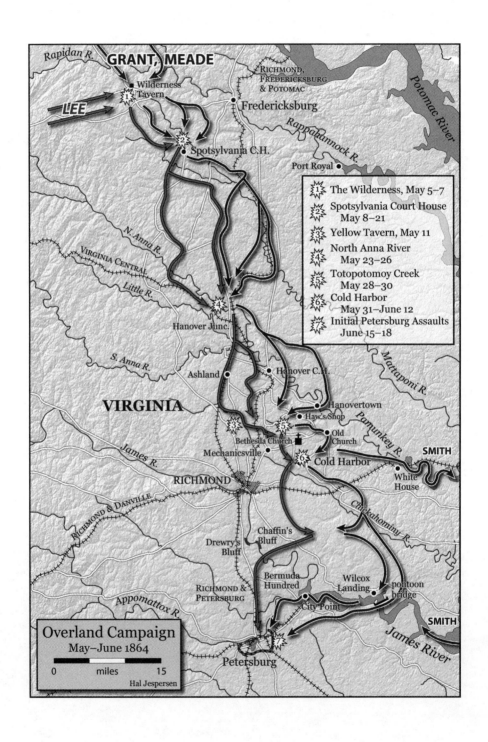

Overland Campaign
May–June 1864

0 — miles — 15

Hal Jespersen

Legend:

1 The Wilderness, May 5–7
2 Spotsylvania Court House May 8–21
3 Yellow Tavern, May 11
4 North Anna River May 23–26
5 Totopotomoy Creek May 28–30
6 Cold Harbor May 31–June 12
7 Initial Petersburg Assaults June 15–18

GENERAL JOHN A. RAWLINS

Prologue

DURING THE LAST HALF OF December 1861, allegations buzzed in the western war theater about Brigadier General Ulysses S. Grant's uncontrolled drinking. No one was sure who started the malicious rumors. Perhaps it was some of the crooked contractors and suppliers who wanted to retaliate because Grant thwarted their schemes to defraud the government. Perhaps the stories were planted by detractors who second-guessed Grant's decision in November to pick a fight with Confederates at Belmont on the Missouri side of the Mississippi River across from Columbus, Kentucky. Whoever was responsible knew resurrecting suspicions about his drinking would strike him where he was most vulnerable. The commotion precipitated a miniflurry of correspondence—three letters from three people—urging an uncovering of the facts and ascertaining whether the general might prove too incapacitated to carry out duties at his district headquarters at Cairo, Illinois. In succession the correspondents were an alarmed businessman, who alerted a congressman, who aroused a staff officer, who in turn assured the congressman. All three of the correspondents, as well as the subject of their correspondence, had ties to Galena, Illinois, a town in the lead-mining region of northwest Illinois.

The businessman was Benjamin H. Campbell, originally from Virginia and residing in Galena since 1835. A prosperous merchant and owner of a packet line doing trade on the upper Mississippi, Campbell had just returned from a trip to St. Louis where worrisome stories circulated about Grant. On December 17, he sent a letter to his congressman with dire news: "I am sorry to hear from good authority, that Gnl Grant is drinking very hard, had you better write to Rawlins to know the fact."[1]

The congressman, Republican Elihu Washburne, had come west and in 1840 settled in Galena, where he became a prominent lawyer and was elected in 1852 to his first term in Congress. He was a flinty, ascetic New Englander by birth who didn't drink, smoke, or chew; who spurned attendance at theatrical performances; and who was a foe of any swindler out to hoodwink the US government. Washburne was also an intimate of President Lincoln—so close that when plots against President-Elect Lincoln's life forced a change in his train schedule through Baltimore, Washburne was the only one to greet him at the Washington railroad platform.[2] The congressman was understandably interested in these drinking rumors because earlier in the year, he was influential in having Grant, a fellow Galena resident, included in the first batch of newly minted brigadiers appointed from Illinois. On receipt of Campbell's letter, Washburne immediately dashed off his own on December 21 to Captain John A. Rawlins, Grant's assistant adjutant general in Cairo, requesting an explanation.

Rawlins was also a Galena lawyer—he had lived in or near Galena all his life—and the town's most prominent Democrat. It is telling that despite their differing political perspectives, Rawlins was the person Washburne should first consult. He knew well of Rawlins's patriotic fervor and that Rawlins was steadfastly abstemious, a man of unquestioned probity and uncompromising values. If Grant were tippling, Rawlins would know, and it would not sit well with him. However, Washburne's letter "astounded" Rawlins, and he took several days before penning his reply, which was a lengthy and impassioned defense of his commanding officer.

Rawlins made several points in his letter, among them a categorical denial of Benjamin Campbell's statement about General Grant's hard drinking ("ut[t]erly untrue and could have originated only in malice"); a tally of virtually each of the few instances in which alcohol in strictly modest amounts touched Grant's lips since Rawlins had joined him at Cairo (e.g., "on one or two occasions he drank a glass of [champagne] with his friends"); testimony to Grant's resolute attention to the duties of his command (e.g., "Ever since I have been with Genl. Grant he has sent his reports in his own hand writing to Saint Louis daily when there was a matter to report"); and an allusion to scurrilous cheats who wanted to strike back at Grant and cause him injury ("That General Grant has enemys [sic] no one could doubt, who knows how much effort he has made to guard against & ferret out frauds in his District").[3]

Rawlins ended the letter with a heartfelt self-disclosure and then a pledge to Washburne: "No one can feel a greater interest in General Grant than I do; I regard his interest as my interest, all that concerns his reputation concerns me; I love him as I love a father, I respect him because I have studied him well, and the more I know him the more I respect and love him." Rawlins disclosed his devotion to Grant and that he had come to regard Grant as a man worthy of his personal investment. This was meant to assure Washburne that Rawlins was a man who had Grant's best interests—which were his interests as well—at heart. It was not hero-worshipping, nor was it Rawlins viewing Grant as a father figure. It was definitely not Rawlins engaging in a repudiation of his own father for his presumed shortcomings.

In closing, Rawlins pledged "that should General Grant at any time become an intemperate man or an habitual drunkard, I will notify you immediately, will ask to be removed from duty on his staff (kind as he has been to me) or resign my commission." There would be no cover-up by Rawlins if Grant wavered. When he vowed to be Washburne's eyes and ears in the field, he was not making an empty promise: Rawlins was almost like a divining rod in detecting the presence of ardent spirits in camp, and as he showed in this letter, he could recite chapter and verse of each instance when Grant hoisted a glass.[4]

To his credit, Rawlins shared his reply with Grant before sending it to Washburne. There would be no colluding with a congressman behind Grant's back. Moreover, this written show of support helped assuage some of the mortification Grant was feeling as a result of the spurious allegations. A grateful Grant pored over the letter and then nodded his assent. "Yes, that's right; exactly right. Send it by all means."[5]

Rawlins's powerful letter succeeded in defusing this threat to Grant's character and fitness to command. It wasn't the first threat, and there would be more.

—⁓⁓—

The story of John Aaron Rawlins is intertwined with the history of Galena and the man Ulysses S. Grant, whom he loyally served as assistant adjutant general, chief of staff, and finally secretary of war. Grant had lived in Galena for a year before the Civil War commenced. There, he came into contact with a number of men, and after receiving a general's commission, he invited several of them to complement his staff. These were men with whom Grant felt comfortable and whom he could trust, Rawlins above all. Regarding his feelings for Rawlins, Grant in later life revealed in his *Memoirs*, "I became very much attached to him."[6] Years earlier, in a letter to Congressman Washburne, he shared his opinion regarding Rawlins's capabilities as an officer: "Rawlins especially is no ordinary man. The fact is had he started in the Line there is every probability he would be today one of our shining lights. As it is he is better than probably any other officer in the Army who has filled only staff appointments. Some men, to[o] many of them, are only made by their Staff appointments whilst others give respectability to the position. Rawlins is of the latter class."[7]

Rawlins performed a host of invaluable tasks for Grant besides writing reports and handling and organizing his files and documents. These included issuing orders for Grant, serving as his emissary on certain delicate missions, offering input on strategy decisions as well as staff business, and possessing the vehement assertive qualities in making personnel and policy choices that his confrontation-averse commander avoided. Rawlins's value to Grant as confidant, administrator, adviser, and loyal staffer cannot be denied. Ely Parker, Grant's military secretary who knew both men dating back to prewar Galena, once told Washburne that Rawlins was "absolutely indispensible [*sic*] to General Grant.... I am also very confident that General Grant's continued success, will, to a great extent, depend upon his retaining General Rawlins as his privy counsellor or right hand man."[8]

Although Rawlins is not well known today, he was a near constant presence at Grant's command headquarters. Theirs was a trusted friendship as well as close working relationship. As historian E. B. Long noted, "They were quite inseparable during much of the war, and this was undoubtedly not entirely because of their relationship in the army command."[9] Regarding how connected they were, Long went on: "When one studies and records the rise of Grant through the winter of 1861–1862, through the capture of Fort Donelson, the controversial Battle of Shiloh, the area command in the summer of 1862, and the early abortive but important moves against Vicksburg, one is studying simultaneously the career of John Aaron Rawlins."[10]

However, to many Rawlins is known as Grant's protector—the staffer who insulated him from untrustworthy aides, grafters, and fellow general officers who wished to promote themselves at Grant's expense—or as the adviser who functioned as an alter ego, providing a counterbalance to some of Grant's natural tendencies: where Grant eschewed conflict, Rawlins had no trouble expressing his displeasure or laying down the law, and where Grant could be trusting at times to a fault, Rawlins's initial inclination was often to be suspicious of motives. Rawlins's reputation as the scold who kept Grant sober is unwarranted.

Grant, the general, did drink on occasion during the war—and he did not hold his drink well. But he rarely drank to excess and not in a way that would blemish his record. Much more often, the problem of Grant's drinking revolved around the stories that circulated about his overfondness for alcohol and gossip about the trouble it brought him during his pre–Civil War military career; those rumors and doubts hung over him like a cloud and made for ammunition that could be used by men who disliked him or who could profit if he failed. Given that reputation, Grant operated as if under a microscope: Were his military decisions made while under the influence? Were troublemakers abetting his taste for alcohol? At every social event at which drinks were served, attendees kept close watch to see (and often report) whether he abstained or imbibed.

John Rawlins did not control Grant's drinking—it could be argued that Grant did not need a nag or scold to maintain his sobriety while fighting Confederates. But Rawlins provided two things that benefitted Grant: the shield of a "temperance zone" that enveloped Grant and a loyalist's zeal. The presence of a temperance zone reassured Grant's supporters ("If Rawlins is policing the camp, it must be as dry as the Sahara") and kept critics at bay. Rawlins, as the loyal staffer, ran stout downfield interference to keep Grant moving to the goal line. Whether Rawlins proved more helpful to Grant as protector and alter ego than as a hardworking adjutant and chief of staff is open to debate. Grant would have agreed more with the latter.

—◦◦◦—

Despite Grant's expressed appreciation, fondness, and respect for John Rawlins, it remains a mystery why Grant barely made mention of Rawlins in his famed *Memoirs*. Perhaps it was a simple omission on Grant's part, or he could have done it intentionally to keep from stirring up old stories about Rawlins as his protector.[11] At the time of the publication of *Memoirs*, mutual friends struggled to explain the oversight and found it hurtful to Rawlins's memory. Ely Parker was one such mutual friend who felt for Rawlins and wondered whether the omission could be attributed to Grant harboring a grudge against Rawlins for having supposedly opposed William Sherman's campaign

through Georgia and even going to Washington behind Grant's back to sabotage it.[12] Parker expressed his feelings to John C. Smith, then lieutenant governor of Illinois and a fellow Galenian:

> [Rawlins] certainly did conspicuous and meritorious services to his Chief
> and his country as A.A.G. [Assistant Adjutant General] and Chief of Staff. He
> builded [sic] and saved much for which no credit is awarded him. No one could
> have been more true and loyal to his Chief and country than he, and yet he gets
> only faint praise from Grant in his Memoirs . . . he almost charges him with dis-
> loyalty to himself, an imputation, which, even if true should have been omitted
> or not referred to. . . . It was, in my judgment, a grave and serious error, which
> the true friends of both will never cease to regret. If Rawlins was opposed to
> Sherman's campaign to the sea, it was from conscientious motives with no de-
> sire or intent to thwart Grant in his plans or wishes.[13]

In truth, Rawlins did have some initial misgivings about Sherman's plan, misgivings that had ample face validity. However, he did not play the role of an
obstructionist, and it was not his style to do an end run around his superior.
Rawlins's gesture to share with Grant the letter he sent to Washburne illustrates that point.

———

Rawlins and Grant established a geographic connection at Galena, a river
town in a mining region that produced a bevy of politicians, jurists, wealthy
entrepreneurs, high-ranking military officers, and memorable personalities
far out of proportion to its size. John Rawlins was one of Galena's most revered
sons. He spent his first thirty years, or about three-quarters of his brief life, in
Galena and surrounding Jo Daviess County, rarely venturing beyond its borders. At the outbreak of the Civil War, Rawlins was a rising political and professional figure. He was a successful lawyer and civic leader who towered over
the reticent and generally reclusive Grant. But before achieving prominence,
Rawlins was a product of the Jo Daviess hills and its hardwood forests, mean-
dering streams, and rich mineral deposits. He burned the wood to produce the
charcoal that smelted the ore that yielded fortunes in pig lead. To a generation
of townspeople, John Rawlins was known as the "Galena Coal Boy." Where he
came into the world, who brought him into it, and how he came by that sobriquet is where the story begins.

NOTES

1. John Y. Simon, ed., *The Papers of Ulysses S. Grant* (Carbondale: Southern Illinois University Press, 1972), 4:116.

2. John Y. Simon, "From Galena to Appomattox: Grant and Washburne," *Journal of the Illinois State Historical Society* 58, no. 2 (1965): 170.

3. John Y. Simon, ed., *The Papers of Ulysses S. Grant*, 4:116, 117.

4. Ibid., 118.

5. Albert D. Richardson, *A Personal History of Ulysses S. Grant* (Boston: D. L. Guernsey, 1885), 187.

6. U. S. Grant, *Personal Memoirs of U. S. Grant* (New York: Charles L. Webster), 1:256.

7. John Y. Simon, *The Papers of Ulysses S. Grant*, U. S. Grant to Elihu B. Washburne, August 30, 1863, 9:218.

8. Ely Parker to Elihu B. Washburne, April 12, 1864, Box 37, Elihu B. Washburne papers, Library of Congress.

9. E. B. Long, "John A. Rawlins: Staff Officer Par Excellence," *Civil War Time Illustrated* 12, no. 9 (January 1974): 43.

10. Ibid., 8–9.

11. Ibid., 43.

12. See U. S. Grant, *Personal Memoirs of U. S. Grant*, 2:376.

13. Ely Parker to John C. Smith, February 15, 1887. SC 1143, Abraham Lincoln Presidential Library, Springfield, IL.

1

Anxious to "Strike a Lead"

JOHN AARON RAWLINS WAS BORN in a topographically unique area—a geological anomaly—astride the Upper Mississippi. It encompasses a patch of southeast Minnesota, the western shank of Wisconsin, a swath of northeast Iowa, and the northwestern beak of Illinois. Here, one encounters a landscape of ravines, ridges, and bluffs that qualifies as rugged. This pocket of the Midwest was mostly unscathed by encroaching glaciers of the past two million years. Because no glacier worked its shearing, leveling effect, geologists refer to the region as the Driftless Area. No mounds of drift—sand, rock, and clay, the detritus from a melting glacier—were left behind. What's more, embedded in the terrain were massive deposits of lead sulfide. The area's history has unfolded from the richness of this ore known as galena. Specifically, John Rawlins was born nearby the town named after the ore, Galena. He was homegrown to the core—the only lawyer in town and the only one of its Civil War generals born and bred right there.

Decades before John's birth, the ore deposits had been exploited by the French, especially the canny Julien Dubuque, who arrived in Prairie du Chien in 1785. Dubuque, who possessed "all the suavity and grace of the typical Frenchman,"[1] ingratiated himself with the Meskwaki tribe and obtained their permission to prospect thousands of acres in eastern Iowa. Dubuque quickly applied himself to the mining, smelting, and shipping of lead downriver to St. Louis, establishing a virtual monopoly. However, the Louisiana Purchase signaled the end of the French domination in the region, and the US government's issuance of mining leases in 1822 sealed the demise of Native Americans' control of their land.

The government soon advertised for miners and settlers, and the floodgates burst open. The little Illinois settlement of Galena became one of America's earliest boomtowns. Thus began in 1827 an influx of emigrants, many of them eager prospectors anxious to "strike a lead." Some arrived from far-flung locations like Ireland, Cornwall, and Switzerland. But most hailed from the mid-south—Kentucky, southern Illinois, and Missouri. The Southern Illinoisans were fair-weather residents, coming up the river in spring to work the mines and heading home in the fall. Their seasonal migration coincided with the runs of the Mississippi fish known as suckers. As a derisive nickname, it was applied to the Southern Illinois boys—and it stuck. To get even, they scoffed at the uncouth Missourians who gushed into the lead region as if the Show-Me State had spewed forth the worst of her population.[2] "So, if we're Suckers, you ruffians are the 'Pukes,'" is the way the name-calling went.

In September 1827, one of those Missourians, a twenty-six-year-old wayfarer named James Dawson Rawlins, arrived in Galena on a scouting mission. He wanted a look-see at what Galena and surrounding Jo Daviess County—named for a militia officer killed at Tippecanoe—had to offer a man with marriage in his plans. James's journey likely started in Howard County, hunched on the north bank of the Missouri River, about smack-dab in the middle of the state. Howard County was settled by pioneers who were mostly from the upper South and were pro-slavery, and James Dawson Rawlins was cut from that geographic bolt of cloth. His father, John Holladay Rawlins or Rawlings—the g was probably lost to local dialect—was born in Spotsylvania County, Virginia. John's first wife was a cousin named Nancy Holladay, by whom he had eight children: Thomas, Polly, Benjamin, Levi, John, Susan, Robert, and Owen. All were born before the family moved in 1795 to Kentucky. James Dawson Rawlins's half brother Robert who had served in the Fifth Kentucky during the War of 1812, was killed at the Frenchtown massacre on property owned by Jean Baptiste Jerome.[3] Half brother Owen achieved political prominence in Missouri, serving terms as president pro tempore of the state senate.

The Rawlingses' Kentucky farm was large—John Holladay is said to have owned forty to fifty slaves—and its main crop was tobacco.[4] Wife Nancy passed away about 1800. Shortly thereafter, the widower married a widow, Jane Bush Embree, who had three children herself. John and Jane raised their own brood of six. The first was James Dawson, born February 28, 1801, in Madison County, Kentucky. The blended family, or what was left of it, moved to

Howard County, Missouri, in 1817. There, John bought farmland but died in 1820 before putting it to work.

James Dawson Rawlins's northwest Illinois sojourn lasted twelve months. He was impressed by what he found in Galena, a humble village but one on the rise. It offered an active social life with plenty of dances, turkey shoots, and horse races, and he connected with some of the unrefined Southrons like himself, who swapped salty stories while hoisting a glass. As he discovered, Galena was becoming a popular destination. An end to hostilities with the Ho-Chunk Indians had ushered in a sense of security, and more liberal access to the mineral riches increased the flow of settlers and seekers. The improving conditions also meant higher quality immigrants, including a clutch of men of estimable character like Thomas Ford and Henry Dodge, later Illinois governor and Wisconsin senator, respectively.[5] Of course, as a wide-open river town, it drew its share of thirsty keelboat men, rowdy prospectors, and "quick-buck" artists. It also attracted men such as Yale-educated Reverend Aratus Kent, who relished the challenge of ministering to the stubbornly impious. During the winter of 1828–29, Kent applied to the American Home Missionary Society "for a place so hard that no one would take it."[6] The society obliged and packed him off to Galena.

During his yearlong stay, James became acquainted with Lemon Parker, a founder of the Galena Mining Company. The company, located on the east side of the Fever River (later renamed the Galena River)[7] in an enclave once known as Ottawa, did a brisk lead-smelting business. Parker and his partners' furnaces were a handful of the many in the county that consumed an enormous amount of fuel. It occurred to James that he might make a living providing the charcoal to keep those furnaces fed. Failing that, there was agricultural potential in the county. Native Americans did well cultivating corn, pumpkins, beans, and even tobacco—the latter of interest to James, who was raised on a Kentucky tobacco farm.

James, fortified with glowing reports about Galena, returned to Howard County in September 1828 and wasted little time taking twenty-five-year-old Lovisa Collier as his bride. They were married on October 5, 1828. Like James, Lovisa Collier was Kentucky born, near Crab Orchard, a hamlet off a slender branch of the Wilderness Road. Her father, Aaron, had moved there from Ohio. Her paternal grandfather was not only a Revolutionary War veteran but a Valley Forge survivor. Lovisa had five siblings: Mortimer, Develcourt, Nancy, Laura, and Mehitabel. By November the newlyweds made a home just east of Galena in a double log cabin owned by Lemon Parker. There, they embarked on their first year in Jo Daviess County with sixty more to follow.

———⟊ℳⱰ⟊———

Lemon Parker's commodious cabin boasted two sixteen-square-feet rooms connected by a passageway and was the birthplace of the couple's first two children. The low-roofed dwelling was purported to be the first frame building erected in Galena.[9] Thirteen months after moving in, they welcomed their first child, Jarrard Owen, born December 15, 1829. John Aaron came right behind on February 13, 1831. Motivated by the need to give his swelling family—Lovisa would give birth again in less than eighteen months—a more permanent residence, James erected another cabin about three hundred yards from the double-wide cabin. However, the family's stay there was brief. While Lovisa was pregnant with a third child in 1832, an Indian War erupted, throwing the mining district into panic. The leader of a band of Sauk refused resettlement on the west side of the Mississippi and became unruly about it. That Sauk leader was the venerable Black (Sparrow) Hawk. Twenty years earlier, Black Hawk had cast his lot with the British during the War of 1812, and ironically, he was present at the Battle of Frenchtown, where Robert Rawlings was killed.

In the spring of 1830, the US government forced Black Hawk to vacate from northwest Illinois, which meant giving up ancestral lands and the village of Saukenuk, located at the mouth of the Rock River. Because the winter of 1831–32 was exceptionally bitter, the members of Black Hawk's band desired to risk a return to Saukenuk and make a spring planting. In early April 1832, Black Hawk and his followers, including women, children, and elderly, crossed the Mississippi. On May 14, Black Hawk clashed with a battalion of Illinois rangers under Major Isaiah Stillman and put them to rout. Perhaps a dozen rangers were killed and mutilated by celebrating Sauk warriors. So ended the Battle of Stillman's Run—*run* as in skedaddle. A gangly Illinois militia captain named Abe Lincoln later assisted in the burial.

The news of Stillman's debacle arrived swiftly in Galena. The *Galenian* of May 23, 1832, acquainted any who were still oblivious to the ominous situation that "the tomahawk and scalping knife have again been drawn on our frontier. Blood of our best citizens has been spilt in great profusion within the borders of Illinois." Nervous Galena officials proclaimed martial law. To thwart an attack, all able-bodied men were ordered to begin building a stockade and blockhouses. Residents were advised to be on the ready. Their preparedness was tested in the dead of one June night. Colonel J. M. Strode, a militia officer, authorized the firing of cannon for what might be called a surprise massacre drill. The booming guns announced what everyone believed to be an imminent Indian attack. Galena's postmaster leaped out of bed and rushed into the stockade, sans trousers and wrapped in a bedsheet. He pleaded for anyone to bring him a pair of pants. A matron who was in the stockade calmly assembling cartridges shoved a musket at him and said, "Here, take this gun, and don't be scared to death."[10]

With violence threatening to erupt anywhere at any time, residents of northwestern Illinois fled to safer ground. Several hundred men, women, and children evacuated to Chicago. Many women and children were put on steamboats and sent downriver. Pregnant Lovisa Rawlins, with her two sons, toddler Jarrard and infant John, sought refuge with the Collier family in Howard County. At her parents' home, she gave birth to son number three, the nobly named Mortimer Cherbury Rawlins, on September 19, 1832, while James remained in Galena. A noncombatant, James hauled provisions and equipment (e.g., saddles, bridles) to troops at Fort Union, a militia headquarters, in southwestern Wisconsin. Half a century after the war, it was said that he "was not actively engaged fighting Indians, but was fully as much exposed . . . often within hearing distance of the guns of the combatants, not knowing at what moment he would fall into an ambush; has an inexhaustible fund of reminiscences of those early days." It cannot be ascertained to what extent James's exposure and bravery might have been embellished in his frequent reminiscing about his Black Hawk War adventures.[11]

After months on the run and facing annihilation, Black Hawk and his followers were pinned against the bank of the Mississippi. With surrender his only choice, Black Hawk faced the ignominy by dressing in a regal attire of white deerskin. He was brought to Fort Crawford in Prairie du Chien for transfer to Jefferson Barracks at St. Louis. The military retinue accompanying Black Hawk made a brief stop in Galena, where a curious crowd was barred from getting a glimpse of him. Perhaps the proud Sauk's most agreeable moments of this entire tragedy were provided by the leader of his escort, recent West Point graduate and Mississippian Lieutenant Jefferson F. Davis, "who treated us all with much kindness. He is a good and brave young chief, with whose conduct I was much pleased."[12]

With Black Hawk subdued, it was time for James to reunite with Lovisa and their three sons.

NOTES

1. Johnson Brigham, *Iowa: Its History and Its Foremost Citizens* (Chicago: S. J. Clarke, 1918), 24.

2. Thomas Ford and Milo Milton Quaife, eds., *A History of Illinois, from Its Commencement as a State in 1818 to 1847* (Chicago: Lakeside, 1945), 85–86.

3. G. G. Clift, *Remember the Raisin! Kentucky and Kentuckians in the Battles and Massacre at Frenchtown, Michigan Territory, in the War of 1812* (Frankfort, KY: Kentucky Historical Society, 1961), 193.

4. Cora Monnier Rawlins, letter of April 2, 1909, addressed To Whom It May Concern, James Harrison Wilson Papers, Box 22, Library of Congress.

5. Augustus L. Chetlain, *Recollections of Seventy Years* (Galena, IL: Gazette, 1899), 7.

6. *The History of Jo Daviess County Illinois* (Chicago: H. F. Kett, 1878), 502.

7. One explanation traces the origin of the Fever River name to the Meskwaki language. When some of the Meskwaki living on the site of present-day Galena and its river and by a much smaller stream to its south traveled eastward around 1760 to come to the aid of stricken tribesmen, they discovered on their return that they had brought back an unknown disease (smallpox). To describe it, they coined the term *mah-cau-bee*, or "fever that blisters." The French applied their translation, naming the larger river Rivière de la Fièvre. In 1854 this "Fever River" was rechristened the Galena River. The smaller stream is still known as Small Pox Creek. In its infancy, the town of Galena was called the Fever River Settlement. See *The History of Jo Daviess County Illinois*, 227–28, for speculation concerning how the Fever River acquired its name.

8. Cora Monnier Rawlins, April 2, 1909, JHWP.

9. *Galena Daily Gazette*, October 5, 1895. This house, the birthplace of John Rawlins, was razed in 1895.

10. *The History of Jo Daviess County Illinois*, 288

11. Cora Monnier Rawlins, April 2, 1909, JHWP; *The History of Jo Daviess County Illinois*, 713.

12. Black Hawk, *Life of Black Hawk*, ed. M. M. Quaife (Mineola, NY: Dover, 1994), 69.

2

"He Ought to Get Out of the Woods"

WITH A FAMILY OF FIVE, James needed roots and a steady income. On March 24, 1834, he claimed 320 acres of woodland and prairie about eight miles east of town on Smallpox Creek in what later became Guilford Township. The 1839 township map shows "Rollins" property across sections 15 and 22.[1] There, James erected a house that he and Lovisa occupied for their entire lives.

What Jarrard, John, and Mortimer discerned beyond their doorstep were distant mounds—tree-covered hillocks and little else. The township was thinly settled, with not a single town or village inside its borders. Roads were cow paths or were demarcated by wagon ruts. There was some mining in the township, but agriculture was primary. Farmers had success with livestock as well as field crops like wheat, corn, and timothy. A few enterprises dotted the landscape, such as a feed and grist mill and an axe-handle manufactory. E. T. Isbell's general store carried groceries and a few necessities. The smelting furnace in the township flamed out in 1839.

For Guilford's socially starved settlers, an opportunity to extend hospitality qualified as a special event. H. S. Townsend, of nearby Rush Township, described a social call: "Game was plentiful, such as deer, turkeys, and a few bear. . . . If you visited a settler, you would have had a hearty welcome, and would have been received in the most friendly manner. In their log cabins a bountiful meal would have been set before you, of venison and corn bread, or mush, the meal for which was ground on a tin grater."[2]

These frontiersmen thirsted for information about the world beyond. Townsend recollected, "We received a newspaper about once in two weeks, and such was the interest produced by its advent that no one would think of sleep until every word of the paper had been read aloud."[3] For those wanting spiritual uplift, "Uncle Billy" Johnson delivered a sermon and then sold pins, thread, and notions to defray travel expenses.

Not all in Jo Daviess County's hinterland were so hospitable. Newcomers needed to steer clear of the Daves family, notorious for their sociopathic tendencies. The Daveses' homestead on a branch of the Apple River became known as Hell Branch. When the Daves brothers had a claim dispute with Alexander McKilips, they tied him to a stump and meted out a near fatal whipping.[4]

———

Under the guidance and examples of James and Lovisa, John's informal education began. One of John's earliest chain of memories was watching his father wring a living out of the hardwoods on their land. It was as a collier, a charcoal burner, that James Rawlins earned his income—how coincidental that he married a Collier!—and he imparted this craft to John. The process of distilling wood to its carbon content requires strenuous labor, attention to detail, and risk of immolation. The labor started with felling timber—one cord yielded forty bushels of charcoal—and continued with the building of the pile or kiln in which the burn occurred. After erecting a split-wood chimney, James ringed it with billets (lengths of wood placed at a proper pitch) and then filled in chinks around the billets. Once he ignited it, he had to ensure a proper burn—downward and out—and be ready to quickly seal any blowout. Sometimes a collier had to "jump the pile," climbing on top of the smoldering heap to compact it for an even burn. As the burn progressed, James raked out the charcoal, listening for a sound like broken crystal that indicated a finished product. The charcoal was then loaded onto an oxcart for delivery to a smelter in Galena.[5]

To a preschooler, transforming hardwoods into charcoal must have seemed like a fascinating art. James probably brought John along slowly: first the ride into Galena, lessons in raking the charcoal, tips on kiln building, and how to tend to the burn. But the fascination lapsed into drudgery. As John gained in strength, he did more woodchopping, burning, and hauling. Grimy John and his oxcart were in town so often that he became known as Galena's "Charcoal Boy." In those days, children performed heavy lifting to ease the burden on parents. James had no compunctions with unburdening himself of responsibilities; he was so successful in foisting the farm's operations on John that eventually he referred to his son as "the Governor."[6] This arrangement allowed James to roam the woods and shoot game.[7]

James's interest in community life and politics transferred to John. James freely spouted his Democratic views about national issues such as presidential candidates, slavery, and westward expansion. Locally, in January 1847, James was involved with arbitrating the conflicting claims between farmers and miners in Jo Daviess County. Up to the organization of the county in 1827, there had been no statutes governing the differences between the two.[8] Later, he was one of a three-person committee charged with choosing a name for the township.[9] The first annual Guilford Township meeting was held on April 5, 1853, at the Rawlinses' farm, one of several local governmental meetings that James hosted during the 1850s.[10] Their home also served for a while as the location of the township's post office.[11] As a staunch Jacksonian Democrat, James was probably proudest of his stint as chairman of the township's Democratic Party. John acquired his father's penchant for civic-mindedness and Democratic politics. Eventually, he became engaged in Galena's civic affairs, rose in Galena's prewar Democratic circle, and campaigned for Stephen A. Douglas.

James displayed other personal preferences that John declined to emulate. For example, for most of his married years—with a notable exception—James's low personal drive kept him hunkered on his land, and he rarely ventured into Galena. This lifestyle was part of James's culture: he fit in with the Upper South settlers of Illinois, regarded as "mostly a simple, neighborly, unambitious people, contented with their condition, living upon plain fare, and knowing not much of anything better."[12] John disdained this listless approach to life; he sought an outlet for his ambition and an escape from a hardscrabble existence.

Little is known about Lovisa. A niece of John's, Cora Monnier Rawlins, provided a brief description of her grandmother. Cora said Lovisa possessed honor and morality, reached out to the needy, was an extensive reader, and grew up in an antislavery family. A grandson termed her "very strict and puritanical."[13] Cora recalled that Lovisa was "a strong advocate of temperance" and held the first local temperance meeting in her house, an event she deemed "a matter of special pride." Lovisa likely understood that slavery and sectionalism threatened the country's stability, and according to Cora, she valued patriotism: "At the breaking out of the war she was earnest in her pleas for the Union and encouraged her sons to fight for that cause."[14]

Lovisa was born one county removed from and two years after the massive 1801 revival meeting at Cane Ridge in Bourbon County, Kentucky. There, thousands of penitents were exposed to animated stump preaching, with many being overtaken by "jerking" tremors or trancelike states.[15] Cane Ridge ushered in the Second Great Awakening—a burst of evangelical sentiment marked by a quest for moral reform—on the Kentucky frontier and helped sow seeds for both temperance and antislavery movements.[16] It is likely the Colliers were significantly affected by the teachings of the revivalist preachers and the spiritual impacts of Cane Ridge.

John held affection for both parents, but his bond with Lovisa was the stronger, as exemplified by how much of her personality found expression in him, often to an amplified degree, such as his keen tendency to cast issues in right-or-wrong dichotomies. As staff officer to Ulysses Grant, he became notorious for rooting out corruption and troublemakers. Encouragement to better himself through education came mostly from Lovisa. Regarding slavery, John adopted a hybrid opinion that spanned his parents' views on the institution: he believed slavery protected by the Constitution, yet "his very soul revolted against the idea of property in human beings."[17] Whereas Lovisa advocated temperance, John was a sworn enemy of drink, and his antipathy toward it was legendary. He was heard to declare "that he would rather see a friend of his take a glass of poison than a glass of whiskey."[18] In some way the dynamics in John's family fostered his abhorrence for alcohol. But was his attitude about drinking based on the examples set by mother or by father—or both?

—◦◦◦—

John grew up during a time when "drinking had reached unparalleled levels."[19] The volume of alcohol consumed was staggering due to its versatility as a medicinal tonic, a lubricant at social and political gatherings, and a stimulant for field laborers, mechanics, or anyone needing a pick-me-up during the workday. One could hardly ignore the connection between rampant drinking and epidemics of gambling, fighting, job injuries, and domestic abuse. Convinced that something must be done to staunch the flow of alcohol, a million and a half Americans had joined the American Temperance Society by 1835, in eight thousand affiliated associations.[20] The Galena Temperance Society, organized in 1838, was founded on a platform of "total abstinence."[21]

The temperance movement strived to recruit women to the cause. As exemplars of purity, they could, through compassion and gentle suasion, guide husbands along the path to reform while instructing the children about the perils of drink. Mothers were counted on to drive rum sellers out of business because "temperance reformers expected the first line of defense against alcohol to be erected during childhood by maternal influence."[22] Although there is no proof that John's commitment to temperance resulted from Lovisa's remonstrations, that he adopted a teetotaler lifestyle fulfilled the movement's expectations of her.

James imbibed, but to what extent alcohol troubled his life is not precisely established. Some historians have unsympathetically concluded James was a besotted failure. He has been depicted as "a ne'er-do-well charcoal burner who had never quite been able either to control a taste for frontier whiskey or to support his family adequately"; "a shiftless, ne'er-do-well farmer who managed to eke out an existence as a charcoal burner when not too busy being indolent"; "a failed, and reportedly drunken, lead miner"; and "an improvident charcoal burner who had died at last of the alcoholism that had kept him and his large family in poverty all his life."[23]

Lloyd Lewis gave a more balanced depiction, saying of James, "He loved his bottle as he did his gun, but few people thought him a sodden drunkard. . . . Ignorant of books, he was wonderful company for children who liked to hear about red-eyed bears coming out of hibernation in the spring."[24] Grandson Edward Rawlins, who knew James only in James's later years, wrote, "He hit the bottle liberally, wasn't a drunkard at all, but drank freely."[25] However, granddaughter Jennie Rawlins Sheean challenged widely held assumptions about James's self-indulgent drinking. Her recollections fit with James as the beloved children's storyteller: "During the last twenty-five years of his life," she said, "his grandchildren with whom he lived had no reason to suspect that he had ever been a drinking man."[26]

John Rawlins's biographer and Civil War comrade James "Harry" Harrison Wilson described James as "a man of determined will, but of unsettled purpose and roving disposition." Here, Wilson hints at how John came to abhor alcohol by sharing what sounds like a snippet of local gossip: "It is said that it was the knowledge of this [the 'unsettled purpose and roving disposition'] that early caused his son John to adopt and live up to the rule of total abstinence, except when his doctor ordered otherwise."[27] The reader must assume it was drink that left James unable to stay focused. But why was Wilson so coy?

John Rawlins's former law partner David Sheean provided Wilson with material for his biography of Rawlins. In a February 25, 1885, letter to Wilson,

Sheean wrote, "It is true that his father was addicted to drinking for many years prior to 1856 and during that time was shiftless and his conduct in this respect was a source of annoyance and trouble to the rest of the family *but I think they would not desire to have anything said about it.*"[28] It appears that in respect to the Rawlins family, Wilson avoided derogatory terms like *shiftless* and substituted less disparaging ones (e.g., *unsettled*) to explain James's presumed lack of resoluteness.

Sheean's revelations raise numerous questions. Did James's drinking qualify as an addiction as we understand it today? Was Sheean equating long-term use of alcohol with addiction to alcohol? Was James's drinking more disturbing (a worrisome sign to others) than it was disturbed (problematic to the drinker)? To what degree was James's low need for achievement the result of alcohol abuse or addiction? Was John propelled to personal ambition or to abstinence by the example set by James?

In the same letter, Sheean stated that after 1856, James "became more temperate" and that "since 1860 I do not think he has tasted liquor." In the next chapter, a conjecture is offered about what motivated James to curb his drinking. Sheean also recognized James's positive character, adding, "He is a good hearted man." We might expect that someone with a history of hard drinking would qualify as a "dry drunk," a person who no longer drinks but sits on a mountain of unresolved issues. How could his good-hearted constitution after 1856 and social-mindedness prior thereto be reconciled with a serious addiction problem?

John's personal repudiation of liquor was more than advocating for the eradication of a social evil, more than a moralist's refusal to surrender himself to his baser appetites, and more than escaping the grip of that which could bind him to a life of drudgery and penury. Evidence for this is found in a cryptic but revealing passage within a letter he wrote to his soon-to-be second wife, Emma Hurlburt, about ten years after leaving his parents' farm. In an anguished voice, he wrote, "I tell you, my dearest Emma, unless the blighting shadow of intemperance had hung like a pall over one's pathway all his life and the consummation of his fondest hopes, and made him, from its continuous presence, fear to ask himself the question—'Am I to die a drunkard?'— he can poorly appreciate my feelings on this subject."[29] This is the voice of one struggling against the inescapable suction of the downward, swirling whirlpool and beset by a horrifying thought: "What if I lose that struggle?" Perhaps the only way to respond to that question is to do all it takes to stave off that catastrophe and to be on constant guard against the rupture of one's moral defenses.

The notion that the father's intemperance may result in the son dying a drunkard's death raises another issue. During that era, many espoused a theory, based on phrenology, that excessive drinking (or eating or sexual activity) could lead to morally depraved (i.e., criminal) behavior. In the 1850s, the phrenological view would be challenged by a competing theory that held that degenerative traits and vices are passed to offspring. Moreover, the expression of those vices intensified with each succeeding generation to the point where a family loses its ability to proliferate. In this pre-Darwinian scheme known now as progressive hereditary degeneration, alcoholism was one of the diseases or conditions believed to be heritable. The scheme also appears to have a theological underpinning, with its predication that the sins of the father redound to the destruction of the son. John's disclosure to Emma suggests that he may have believed he was grappling with irresistible, unknowable forces operating to destroy him and his issue. Thus, is it any wonder he took aggressive steps to protect himself—and others he held in esteem—from a catastrophic fate?[30]

In sum, whether John was drawn to an abstemious life more by his mother's temperance teaching or was repelled from alcohol by his father's example remains a moot point. His choice in the matter may also have been shaped by experiences during his few years of formal education.

—⁂—

John attended grammar school on a sporadic basis beginning in 1838 and ending with the winter of 1849–50. All told, he attended eight quarters of three months each.[31] There wasn't money to afford more than that. Before John was old enough to begin school, James and Lovisa had two more mouths to feed. Lemmon Parker was born in December 1834. In February 1837 came Robert Jerome, named for James's half brother, who was killed in the War of 1812. John began his education in a country school that had just opened its doors in 1838 and was located about four miles south of Millville, in Rush Township. This was the first school in the eastern region of the county and was probably a private or subscription school—hence the problem with affordability. Architecturally, it would have been the equivalent of a small log house. Its location made it a long trek for some students. Young John may have had to board with a family given the distance from his home.

We don't know John's reactions to his first day of school; however, Lovisa would have sent him off with some encouraging words. She probably saw a measure of educational potential in John, along with a willingness on his part to give book learning a fair trial. On the other hand, the edifice in which this instruction was delivered was more likely to test his capacity for discomfort than to challenge his intellect, if it resembled a typical county school of the day:

> Stoves and such heating apparatus as are in use now were unknown. A mud and stick chimney in one end of the building, with earthen hearth, with a fire-place wide enough and deep enough to take in a four-feet log, and smaller wood to match, served for warming purposes in Winter and a kind of conservatory in Summer. For windows, part of a log was cut out in either side, and may be a few panes of eight-by-ten glass set in, or, just as likely as not, the aperture would be covered over with greased paper. Writing benches were made of wide planks or, may be, puncheons, resting on pins or arms driven into two-inch augur-holes, bored into the logs beneath the windows. Seats were made out of thick planks or puncheons. Flooring was made of the same kind of stuff. Every thing was rude and plain.[32]

Instruction consisted mostly of arithmetic, reading and grammar, and memorization and recitation.

John supplemented his spotty grammar school education by reading poetry, history, and biography. His self-study proved valuable because as he matured, he was forced to sacrifice formal schooling and devote more time to work. Circumstances increased the need to ramp up charcoal production. One reason was that the Rawlins family kept increasing. Four more children arrived in seven years: Mary ("Laura") in 1839, Benjamin Thomas in 1841, James Sidney in 1844, and William DeVelcourt in 1846. Fortunately for a family that depended on income from charcoal, the production of lead in the district was reaching all-time highs. Over fifty-four million pounds were produced in 1845 alone, and smelting furnaces voraciously consumed charcoal. Coming into his teen years, John was responsible for more of the chopping, kiln building, and tending to the burn. An old Galena acquaintance recalled John's mature work ethic and positive attitude of that time: "I knew John A. Rawlins as a boy working on his father's farm in Guilford, and as a coal burner, hauling the product of his labor and skill in that line, himself, begrimed and sooty from the dust, to market ever cheerful and independent feeling and manifesting the inherent manliness of his nature among all classes and surroundings."[33]

When not in school, John soaked up much incidental learning on his business between Guilford and Galena. One thing he acquired—by imitating either his father or the vulgar boatmen on the Galena levee—was a prolific vocabulary of profanity, which he used to shocking effect. While on Grant's staff, he could color the air Union blue when upbraiding drunks or troublemakers. Assistant Secretary of War Charles Dana noted John possessed "a rough style of conversation" that qualified him as "one of the most profane men I ever knew."[34] For now, he was limited to cussing his pair of oxen as they staggered up the county's undulating hills.

—∿—

Trips into town gave John a hankering for a life beyond the charcoal pit. His coming of age coincided with the halcyon days of Galena. The business district was booming. Tradesmen and small businessmen found eager customers for hardware, dry goods, livery services, and building construction. In 1848, Galena boasted over five dozen groceries, sixteen butchers, six brewers, and three printers.[35] It was the center of river commerce between St. Paul and St. Louis. One former resident recalled the problems posed by all the traffic: "The little narrow levee was crowded with boats coming in, and going out in all direction. Main street and along the levee was so crowded in the busy season, that it was difficult to pass along the side walk. The ladies generally deserting it and taking to the upper street. Goods would often lie on the levee all night."[36] The wealth being created followed its typically unequal path of distribution, allowing for an upper crust of society to separate itself from the lower strata.

One way to escape the charcoal pit was to enlist and join the war against Mexico. John ached to get in on the adventure. "I was sixteen when it broke out," he said years later, "and was almost crazy to get permission to enlist." Parental permission was denied. He was in awe of the local Mexican War veterans, although they weren't the kind to wear epaulets: "Up our way we had a great idea of a Mexican war soldier, the extent of our heroes being private soldiers of that war."[37]

John had to be familiar with success stories about interesting personages about town. There was Captain David Smith Harris, who in 1845 piloted the steamboat *War Eagle* from St. Louis to Galena in under forty-four hours, and the wealthy Captain Orrin Smith, who owned a fleet of steamboats. Eccentric Billy Hamilton, son of Founding Father Alexander, had a profitable lead mine in Wisconsin and was well known as a former militia officer and Illinois State legislator.[38] The greatest rags-to-riches story belonged to Hezekiah Gear, a miner who was once nearly destitute. In 1833, his pick cracked into a drift lined with sparkling galena ore. It was the biggest lode in the lead-mining district. "When the sight of this great wealth met his eye, he wept like a child, threw down his pickaxe with which he had dug to this wealth, and ran home to the dear ones, mounted his horse, rode into Galena" and announced his discovery to his creditors.[39] Just a few years later, this once almost played-out miner would be host to Martin van Buren and Elizabeth Schuyler Hamilton, Alexander's widow.

Although John had no capital to launch a steamboat or start a mining operation, there was one respectable career path, the law, that he could embark on by way of borrowed books, self-discipline (which he possessed in abundance), and a willing mentor. John would have noticed the host of attorneys, many from the East, practicing in town. They were young "immigrant lawyers," drawn to a frontier commercial hub for adventure and "an opportunity immediately to rise to some prominence either in his chosen profession, or in business, or in politics."[40] They included two "intensely partisan" Democrats, Marylander Joseph P. Hoge, "tall, of symmetrical figure, and dressed with exquisite taste," and Ireland-born and Pennsylvania-bred Thompson Campbell, "the wit of the bar."[41] Both had lucrative practices, and both had represented Illinois's Sixth District in Congress. The dean of the bar was Elihu Washburne, a Maine native and Harvard Law graduate, who was soon to become a towering figure in the House of Representatives and possessed "indomitable will, forceful energy and untiring industry, keen discrimination and sturdy integrity."[42]

By midadolescence, John was no doubt aware he had the makeup for success. He didn't carry the characterological baggage—vanity, sluggishness, intemperance, deceitfulness—that prevent many from realizing their potential. Moreover, others saw potential in this hardworking youth and offered encouragement. As friend David Sheean surmised, "It is probable that his ambition . . . was spurred on by his neighbors in the country where he lived who regarded him as being fit for some other calling than a farmer or collier and would talk about him in that regard."[43]

We do not know whether John aspired to a law career and a fling at politics in his late teens. For the former, he would need, beyond the compulsory book learning, the adroitness to think on his feet, the perspicacity to see through to the nub of an issue, and the verbal fluency to argue persuasively. For the latter, he needed to establish familiarity with viable opinions—not just the Democratic screed he heard at home—on the questions roiling the country at that time, such as Texas annexation, abolition, internal improvements, the Wilmot Proviso, Mexican cession, and the national bank. There is anecdotal evidence that at that age, he displayed some of those lawyerly verbal skills and had acquired a degree of knowledge about hot topics of the day.

Shortly after John's death, Cyrus B. Denio recollected how the teenaged John held his own against him in a local debate in 1849. Denio, known as the "Mississippi Bricklayer," represented Jo Daviess, Carroll, and Stevenson counties in the Illinois State House and was regarded as a shrewd but well-liked Whig politician.[44] One day, Denio attended a debating club meeting, where he encountered a formidable opponent.

> The first speaker was a Baptist preacher, a man of considerable talent, and he opened the question handsomely, and was followed by the schoolmaster. The question was a political one. It became my duty to answer the schoolmaster; and I congratulated myself on having made a fair impression on my log cabin audience. You can judge then of my surprise when a mere boy arose and commenced a reply to my speech, and I am not the least ashamed to say that he triumphantly answered all my arguments, one by one as he came to them. At this distance of time it would be hard for me to tell which feeling was uppermost in my mind, that of chagrin at my own failure, or admiration for the boy who had answered me; and that boy was Gen. John A. Rawlins, the late Secretary of War.
>
> As soon as the debate was over I lost no time in getting acquainted with him, and asked what he was doing. I learned from him that he was cutting cordwood and burning charcoal, and that his name was Rawlins. I told him to go home and tell his father that Mr. Denio said he ought to get out of the woods; go to school; and then come into Galena and practice law.[45]

As the 1840s ended, so did John's bare-bones primary school education. His education was supplemented by parental influences, independent study, observational learning, growing self-awareness, and positive feedback from within and without the family. But at this moment, events occurring two thousand miles away were to impact the Rawlins family. John would manage to further his education in dribs and drabs, but he would be hindered by his penurious circumstances and increased responsibilities caring for family and managing the charcoal production.

NOTES

1. Tract Book 25, August 1842.
2. *The History of Jo Daviess County Illinois*, 577.
3. Ibid., 577.

4. Ibid., 565.

5. This charcoal-burning process is described in Timothy Crumrin, "Fuel for Fires: Charcoal Making in the Nineteenth Century," *Chronicle of the Early American Industries Association* 47, no. 2 (1994): 35–38.

6. David Sheean to James H. Wilson, February 25, 1885, James Harrison Wilson Correspondence, File S(1), Box 14, Series 2, Ulysses S. Grant Presidential Library, Mississippi State University.

7. Statement of Edward Rawlins, Series 2, Box 21, Folder 18, U. S. Grant Presidential Library, Mississippi State University.

8. *The History of Jo Daviess County Illinois*, 535.

9. *Portrait and Biographical Album of Jo Daviess County* (Chicago: Chapman Brothers, 1889), 558.

10. Guilford Township, Jo Daviess County, Illinois. Township Record Book from 1853 through 1863.

11. *The History of Jo Daviess County Illinois*, 604.

12. John G. Nicolay and John M. Hay, *Abraham Lincoln: A History* (New York: Century, 1890), 1:51–52.

13. Statement of Edward Rawlins, Series 2, Box 21, Folder 18, U. S. Grant Presidential Library, Mississippi State University.

14. Cora Monnier Rawlins to "To Whom It May Concern," April 2, 1909, James Harrison Wilson Papers, Box 22, Library of Congress.

15. A description of the emotional effect on the multitude attending can be found in W. P. Strickland, ed., *Autobiography of Rev. James B. Finley* (Cincinnati: Cranston and Curts, n.d.), 367–68.

16. For a perspective on revivalism in late eighteenth-century Kentucky, see Ellen Eslinger, *Citizens of Zion: The Social Origins of Camp Meeting Revivalism* (Knoxville: University of Tennessee Press, 1999).

17. James H. Wilson, *The Life of John A. Rawlins* (New York: Neale, 1916), 43.

18. Ibid., 25.

19. Mark Edward Lender and James Kirby Martin, *Drinking in America: A History* (New York: Free Press, 1982), 47.

20. See ibid., 41–71.

21. *The History of Jo Daviess County Illinois*, 257.

22. Scott C. Martin, *Devil of the Domestic Sphere: Temperance, Gender, and Middle-Class Ideology, 1800–1860* (DeKalb: Northern Illinois University Press, 2008), 61.

23. Bruce Catton, *Grant Moves South* (Boston: Little, Brown, 1960), 67–68; G. Perret, *Ulysses S. Grant: Soldier and President* (New York: Modern Library, 1999), 151; William S. McFeely, *Grant: A Biography* (New York: Norton, 1982), 85; Shelby Foote, *The Civil War: A Narrative* (New York: Penguin, 1963), 2:416. Foote writes that John A. Rawlins was deeply affected by the death of his father; however, James survived John by almost a quarter century.

24. Lloyd Lewis, *Captain Sam Grant* (Boston: Little, Brown, 1950), 380.

25. Statement of Edward Rawlins, Series 2, Box 21, Folder 18, U. S. Grant Presidential Library, Mississippi State University.

26. Fragment of a letter written by Jennie Rawlins Sheean, no date, no addressee, in James Harrison Wilson Papers, Box 22, Library of Congress.

27. James H. Wilson, *The Life of John A. Rawlins*, 24.

28. James Harrison Wilson, Correspondence File, Series 1, Box 14, Series 2, U. S. Grant Presidential Library, Mississippi State University Libraries; emphasis added.

29. John A. Rawlins to Emma Hurlburt, November 16, 1863, Rawlins file, Chicago History Museum.

30. Perspectives on alcohol and degeneration can be found in W. F. Bynum, "Alcoholism and Degeneration in 19th Century Medicine and Psychiatry," *British Journal of Addictions* 79, no. 1 (1984): 59–70; K. Mann, D. Hermann, and A. Heinz, "One Hundred Years of Alcoholism: The Twentieth Century," *Alcohol and Alcoholism* 35, no. 1 (2000): 10–15; A. Lewis, "Fertility and Mental Illness," *Eugenics Review* 50, no. 2 (1958): 91–106.

31. Sheean to Wilson, January 10, 1885, USGPL.

32. *The History of Jo Daviess County*, 358.

33. John C. Spare to John Beadle, March 29, 1899, J. C. Spare Folder SC 1442, Abraham Lincoln Presidential Library.

34. Charles A. Dana, *Recollections of the Civil War* (New York: D. Appleton, 1989), 63.

35. *The Galena Directory and Miner's Annual Register for 1847–8* (Galena, IL: E. S. Seymour, 1847).

36. S. W. McMaster, *60 Years on the Upper Mississippi: My Life and Experiences* (Rock Island IL, 1893), 140.

37. "How Grant Got to Know Rawlins" [interview with John A. Rawlins], *The United States Army and Navy Journal and Gazette of the Regular and Volunteer Forces*, September 12, 1868 (New York: n.p.), 6:53.

38. Larry Gara, "William S. Hamilton on the Wisconsin Frontier: A Document," *Wisconsin Magazine of History* 41, no. 1 (1957): 25–28.

39. R. G. Hobbs and C. E. G. Hobbs, "Autobiography of Clarissa Emily Gear Hobbs," *Journal of the Illinois State Historical Society* 17, no. 1 (1925): 625.

40. Anton-Hermann Chroust, *The Rise of the Legal Profession in America* (Norman: University of Oklahoma Press, 1965), 2:115.

41. Ibid., 31.

42. Ibid., 38–39.

43. D. Sheean to J. H. Wilson, February 25, 1885, USGPL.

44. Augustus L. Chetlain, *Recollections of Seventy Years* (Galena, IL: Gazette, 1899), 35.

45. This description of Rawlins's debating skills is found in the handwritten manuscript "Reminiscences, 1896," by Sylvanus Cadwallader, at the Abraham Lincoln Presidential Library, ALPS-ZCH, 866–67.

3

"Speeches That Would Have Done Credit to a Statesman"

IT WAS THE DISCOVERY ONE January morning in 1848 of shiny grits in a Northern California millrace that "triggered the most astonishing mass movement of peoples since the Crusades." Soon word broke that gold had been found at John Sutter's mill on the American River. The news drew a flood of "farmers and merchants and sailors and slaves and abolitionists and soldiers of fortune and ladies of the night."[1] Across the United States, fortune hunters would descend in a feverish rush on the Sacramento Valley. Call them argonauts or forty-niners—all wanted a share of the chimerical riches.

James Dawson Rawlins contracted the fever in a roundabout way from Thomas O. Larkin, the US consul appointed to California. In two letters to Secretary of State James Buchanan in June 1848, Larkin attested to the stupendous gold find, describing how gold flakes could be found in a shovelful of dirt. Larkin's letters were published in the *New York Herald* and widely disseminated. When Larkin died in 1858, he was eulogized for having spawned the Gold Rush: "Probably no one who was in the country at that time took a greater interest in the development of the gold discoveries of 1848, and in spreading before the Eastern world early, reliable and full particulars of the new El Dorado than the subject of our memoir."[2]

The "full particulars" reached Jo Daviess County in October. The *Galena Daily Advertiser* of October 7, 1848, printed a July 1, 1848, letter from Larkin out of Monterey to the Navy Department (Larkin was also a navy agent) that said, "This part of California is at present in a state of great excitement from the discovery of an extensive gold region on the Sacramento River. The gold is obtained on the surface of the earth to three feet deep—the workmen needing only a pickaxe and shovel to dig up the dirt, and a tin pan to work it in. All our towns are being vacated." For the prairie dwellers eager to stake a claim, the approaching winter meant it would be six months before one could safely embark on a two-thousand-mile trek, a galling wait for scuffling miners in the lead district who possessed the skill to work the gold fields for all they were worth. After all, "For a lead miner, gold mining was a signal promotion."[3]

On March 5, 1849, the *Galena Daily Advertiser* printed the recommended routes to California and counseled gold seekers to start "early in the spring." Many heeded this advice because on March 14, the newspaper contained this bittersweet opinion: "There is not a village that we hear from where there are not those who are making serious arrangements for the long journey. . . . We are sorry to see so many of our old friends go; but the object might be worse, and the right is certainly theirs. . . . In the world which will be represented in California, no section, turning out the same number of men, will be better represented than the mining region of Illinois, Wisconsin, and Iowa."

For James Rawlins who embraced Jacksonian democracy, it might be expected that he'd be bitten by the gold bug. As historian Laurence Seidman remarked, the Gold Rush had it all for a man like James: "The dream of the Jacksonian Americans was interwoven with the frontier—a dream of land, independence, self-reliance, and human equality. It was also interwoven with the ideas of abundance and of the freedom that comes from being the possessor of property, emancipated from poverty and want. By 1849, all the facets of the dream were symbolized by gold. Men abandoned everything in their rush to get to the diggings."[4] James must have hoped gold would set him free.

⁓⁓⁓

James left for California with eldest son Jarrard, now twenty, in the spring of 1850. We have few details of their adventure other than James's niece noting that they left with an ox team, James returned by himself two years later,[5] and Jarrard chose to stay in California. However, it's possible to speculate about their preparations and trip.

Historian Malcolm Rohrbough discussed several separation issues facing the families of prospective argonauts. First, the man must have compelling reasons for leaving. Often these were variants on the argument, "I'll endure the hardships for the ultimate economic welfare of the family." Second, argonauts often failed to grasp the burden their leaving placed on the family. This actually made perfect sense: if the prospective prospector did "get it," then he'd be obliged to stay home. Third, it's no surprise that most wives were initially opposed to the idea, "but many women seem to have given their consent in exchange for the best possible terms, of which the most significant was a promise that the future 49er would return home at a specified time."[6] That James was gone for only two years may have been a promise Lovisa extracted from him.

Wives also feared they might never see their husbands again—a real fear given the shorter life expectancy of that era and hazards of an overland journey.[7] It was not unusual for men to leave young children, even infants, at home. Perhaps this was allowable in part due to male privilege and in part to how missing the children could count as one more hardship to endure. Finally, before departure, a male would be designated as supervisor. That lot fell to John, who at nineteen would be assisted by Mortimer (seventeen), Lemmon (fifteen), and Robert (thirteen).

James was in the second wave of forty-niners, many of whom from the upper Mississippi River Valley used Council Bluffs, Iowa, as their launching pad to the West. It's likely that James and Jarrard followed suit. They probably joined a party along the route for safety and socializing. With so many making the trek, they would often be within sight of other pods of wagons. Optimism would have been unbounded as the emigrants joined in robust song around campfires:

> I soon shall be in Frisco
> And there I'll look around,
> And when I see the Gold lumps there
> I'll pick them off the ground.
> I'll scrape the mountains clean, my boys,
> I'll drain the rivers dry,
> A pocketful of rocks bring home—
> So brothers don't you cry.[8]

James and Jarrard faced countless obstacles and constraints, especially time. They needed to average about fifteen miles a day before the weather deteriorated. When not mindful of the Donner party's experience, an argonaut might worry about attacks by a Plains Indian tribe. But perhaps the most insidious enemy was cholera, which contaminated western rivers. That fifty-year-old James survived the round-trip ordeal was testimony to his toughness. Other lead mine region argonauts were not so lucky. Ira Bowker of Rush Township died on the return trip; Jasper Rosencrans and Ira Townsend, both from Rush, started home together but were never heard from again.[9] Irrepressible Billy Hamilton of Wisconsin died a miserable death in Sacramento in 1850, probably from cholera.[10]

James had little to show for his California adventure. Those coming up empty like James Rawlins who had no alternative but to retrace their steps eastward sung a different tune:

> It's four long years since I reached this land,
> In search of gold among the rocks and sand;
> And yet I'm poor when the truth is told,
> I'm a lousy miner,
> I'm a lousy miner in search of shining gold.
>
> I've lived on swine till I grunt and squeal,
> No one can tell how my bowels feel,
> With flapjacks swimming round in bacon grease.
> I'm a lousy miner,
> I'm a lousy miner; when shall my troubles cease?[11]

When he returned to his Guilford cabin in the latter part of 1852 and shook the dust (not the gold variety) out of his shoes, he would have received a report from John about the status of the charcoal production and perhaps a mixed reception from Lovisa. At this point, recall David Sheean's observation that James's drinking dropped markedly in the mid-1850s. Could a chastened James have been cowed into making amends to Lovisa by adopting a more abstemious lifestyle?

—◦◦◦—

Besides burning charcoal and assuming the surrogate paternal role, John furthered his education during James's absence. In the winter of 1850–51, he attended a term of high school in Galena.[12] He stayed at the home of Eunice Hallett, becoming a schoolmate of her son Moses. The Rawlins and Hallett families knew each other in Howard County, Missouri. Young Moses Hallett, once described as a "bright-eyed, large-headed, quiet boy,"[13] was one of that remarkable cadre of Galena men who went on to impressive public service careers. Prior to the Civil War, he moved to Colorado, where he practiced law and was a justice of the Colorado Territorial Supreme Court.

High school whetted John's appetite for advanced study. His choice was the Rock River Seminary, which had opened in November 1840. The seminary, established by the Illinois Conference of the Methodist Episcopal Church,

was in Mt. Morris, about seventy miles southeast of Galena. The town's found-
ers passed ordnances prohibiting gambling, drunkenness, horse racing, and
the sale of liquor, and the Seminary enforced moral behavior in its students,
forbidding "games of chance; the use of intoxicating drinks."[14] The Seminary
charged $1.50 per week for board.[15] Tuition varied from $5.50 to $7.75 per term
depending on course of study.[16] The curriculum favored classical and mathe-
matical training and emphasized moral instruction. John matriculated in 1851,
with his name appearing on the roll as a student from Galena.[17] Against the
leading Eastern institutions, the seminary "was not even a third-class college,"
as one of John's classmates allowed, but at the time "it was the leading institution of higher learning in Northern Illinois."[18] The Seminary was coeduca-
tional, with a student body of 113 men and 60 women.[19]

John's attendance at the seminary was sporadic, necessitated by having to
withdraw to earn money burning charcoal. After eight months of attendance,
he left college for good in June 1853, short of earning a degree. He made the
most of his studies, enjoyed close friendships, and left a lasting impression.[20]
He and Moses Hallett occupied room 13 in the seminary, which became "the
scene of many hot controversies" and political debating.[21] John was a member
of the college's Amphictyon Society, an organization that encouraged student
debates. Topics for debate included the issues of internal improvements, the
Fugitive Slave Law, and boundary disputes with England.[22] Its president was
Shelby Cullom, later governor of Illinois and US senator. Cullom recollected
that "Rawlins was a Democrat, and a strong one, during his school days, and
I believe remained one until the Civil War. Robert Hitt and his brother John,
together with Rawlins and myself, formed a sort of four-in-hand, and we were
very intimate. We would take part in the discussions in our society, and Rawlins was especially strong when a political question was raised. I have always
heard him, during his school days, make speeches that would have done credit
to a statesman."[23] Robert Hitt became well known to Abraham Lincoln, who
relied on him to make shorthand drafts of his debates with Stephen Douglas.
He spent years in politics, serving briefly as assistant secretary of state in the
Garfield-Arthur administration and as a member of the US House of Representatives. Rawlins, Hallett, Cullom, and Hitt—quite an assortment of notables from a less than third-class college perched on the prairie.

Regarding John's academic performance, few facts exist. From the Rock
River Seminary Exhibition Exercises held on June 24, 1852, John is listed as
one of the speakers. He chose the topic "Catholicism as It Is." Others that

afternoon weighed in on similarly profound subjects such as "The English Language" and "Life—Its Object."[24] Among the courses John took were geometry, political economy, and moral philosophy.[25] According to the seminary's 1852 catalogue, the textbook used for the moral philosophy course was written by Francis Wayland, which meant that John was exposed to *The Elements of Moral Science*, one of the most influential college textbooks of the nineteenth century. Moral philosophy was considered the capstone course of the curriculum, "the binding glue that held all the other subjects together."[26] It is possible that this text mirrored and influenced John's antebellum political stances.

Wayland took a middle ground on slavery, one of the reasons his *Elements* was such a best seller. Although he was no proponent of slavery as a system— he concluded that "slavery thus violates the personal liberty of man as a *physical*, *intellectual*, and *moral* being"[27]—he thought the wrong of slavery could be righted only by a moral change in society, not by edict. However, Wayland underwent a profound moral and political metamorphosis: he turned Free Soiler, then ardent Lincoln supporter. Of Wayland, it can be said that "his life was a microcosm in the transition from moderate antislavery sentiment to full-b[l]own Unionism and emancipation."[28] Rawlins also saw slavery as a blemish but believed it safeguarded by the Constitution until that document might be amended. Like Wayland, when the tipping point came, Rawlins threw himself full force behind Lincoln and the Union.

On March 19, 1854, the young women of the Goshen, New York, Female Seminary staged a "Programme of Evening Entertainment."[29] The Goshen Seminary, an academy of higher learning, provided women with an education similar to what men might receive. At a time when women were excluded from most colleges, the female seminary movement advanced the cause of women's equality. The "Programme" was an evening filled with merrymaking and music such as the "Katy-did Polka" and the "Repertoire" from the opera *La Favorita*.

One of the students, the comely twenty-year-old Emily Smith, sang a rendition of Edgar Allan Poe's hauntingly lovely poem *Eulalie*, which begins:

> I dwelt alone
> In a world of moan,
> And my soul was a stagnant tide,
> Till the fair and gentle Eulalie became my blushing bride—
> Till the yellow-haired Eulalie became my smiling bride.

It is thought that the poem, first published in 1845, is a paean to Poe's wife, Virginia, for turning his sadness into happiness. Three years earlier, Poe had written the short story "The Masque of Red Death," perhaps a metaphor for the illness known as consumption then afflicting Virginia. During the course of the illness, a consumptive's face takes on a red tint or flush; the "fever often lent a ruddiness to the complexion of consumptives, giving them the appearance of good health."[30] That disease, tuberculosis, took Virginia's life in 1847. The sad irony was that of all the poems she could have sung, Emily sang this one on that gay evening.

—◦◦◦—

On Tuesday, April 5, 1853, the Rawlinses hosted Guilford Township voters at their farm to elect its officers. After a long winter, neighbors had gossip to share along with plugs of chewing tobacco. Eventually, the meeting was called to order, and stoop-shouldered Black Hawk War veteran Samuel Hathaway was chosen moderator. Once Hathaway had people's attention, John A. Rawlins was appointed clerk in order to record the proceedings and votes. This was the first time he penned a report for submission, and it would be the first of many. In a legible but slightly sprawling hand, he confirmed that "the following named persons received the number of votes annexed to their respective names, for the following described offices to wit[:] John W. Taylor had ninety-one votes for Supervisor. John A. Rawlins had ninety votes for Town Clerk. James D. Rawlins had fifty-nine votes for commissioner of highways. Samuel W. Sherrill had fifty-five votes for commissioner of highways. John Combellick had thirty-nine votes for commissioner of highways."[31] Attesting to the veracity of the record, he applied his signature, "Jno. A. Rawlins," his title of "Clerk," and a double-looped flourish thereunder.

After garnering ninety votes for the office of town clerk, John may have had the feeling that regardless how minor this election, it was an indication he was primed to make a mark for himself. In his first spring back from California, with his gold fever reduced, it was fitting that James's neighbors elected him one of the commissioners of highways after he spent two years tramping them. In less than three months, James and his fellow commissioners presented a plan to divide the township into four road districts.

In late June, John finished his last term at the seminary. That was not his plan. He expected to resume studies—he had by this time spent eight months in attendance—after another stretch burning charcoal. That summer a Galena lawyer, Richard H. Jackson, visited John by his parent's "rude log cabin," performing "hard manual labor." Jackson recollected that John spoke about his intent to study law "as soon as he could acquire something of a Western education."[32] His decisions to study law and to quit wood-burning occurred almost simultaneously. On a hot day in September 1854 while hauling a charcoal load into Galena, his ox team gave out. He spent the night resting and set out in the morning when, outside of town, the oxen faltered near where construction was underway on a branch of the Illinois Central Railroad. One of the contractors on the site made him an offer for the wagon and the oxen; John's counteroffer included the charcoal in a package deal. With about $250 in hand, John continued into Galena feeling, much like James must have felt on the way to the gold fields, an emancipated man.[33]

—•∕∿∕•—

It is not known why John selected this moment to take up law, but it was as propitious a time to do so as any. Legal business was sagging due to a decline in land titles being processed, and mining operations slowed due to the mass emigration to California, but these regressions were compensated by a spate of openings at the bar. Elihu Washburne went to Congress, and several lawyers headed to California to advance their careers. Furthermore, Galena was awash in capital and boasted more banks than any city in the west other than Chicago and St. Louis. Galena's prospects looked bullish.[34]

John had gained confidence in his rhetorical skills during debates at the seminary. He no doubt knew that in the courtroom, homespun common sense and passionate disputation counted more than one's legal pedigree or splitting hairs over legal precedent. Simply put, "It was the oratory which swayed those frontier juries, not legal distinction."[35] It's also likely that he figured he could learn more by apprenticing himself to a practicing attorney than by absorbing lectures. After a stretch of reading law under the tutelage of a preceptor, John's combination of higher education and law office apprenticeship would have been on par with the backgrounds of the typical lawyer of the day. For example, of the forty-four lawyers in Chicago admitted to practice between 1831 and 1850, twenty-six had some college education, and thirty-nine had studied in a law office.[36]

Apprentices' legal training varied widely in quality. There were no standards or prescribed requirements. John could have begun and terminated his studies whenever he wanted. He could be expected to spend a good portion of office time reading treatises such as Timothy Walker's *Introduction to*

American Law and Joseph Chitty's *Practical Treatise on Pleading*. If lucky, his preceptor would supplement this reading with occasional instructive comments on various points of law. Another chunk of time would be devoted to clerical duties like copying material out of legal form books. Perhaps John was expected to compensate the preceptor for his time and use of his law library.

When John deemed himself ready for admission to the bar, he faced absurdly low entrance requirements. Attestations of good moral character and the passing of an exam—which might range from nothing more than exchanging pleasantries to an agonizing grilling—were the major hurdles. "Standards for admission to the bar remained low even when Illinois changed from an oral examination given by judges to an oral examination given by attorneys in 1850. The ease of the examination remained the same."[37] One examinee, Jonathan Birch, recalled his oral examination at the hands of attorney Abraham Lincoln: "Lincoln's first question was 'What books have you read?' When Birch told him, he said, 'Well, that is more than I had read before I was admitted to practice.' Lincoln then told a story about trying a case against a 'college-bred lawyer who apparently had studied all the books.' . . . Lincoln rapidly asked Birch a series of questions that appeared to Birch to be but faintly related to the practice of law. Lincoln abruptly stopped, declaring that he had asked Birch enough, and wrote the requisite certificate of recommendation."[38]

That individuals at this time needed only minimal preparation to qualify as lawyers was one result of the leveling effect of Jacksonian democracy. "The advent of 'Jacksonian democracy,'" wrote legal historian Anton-Herman Chroust, "probably dealt the death blow to any organization of the legal profession. Statutes throwing the practice of law wide open to all citizens were the common result."[39] Relaxed standards were in keeping with "Western egalitarian views," the notion that upright young men with rudimentary familiarity of the law ought to have an opportunity to practice in the sparsely populated frontier.[40] To traditionalists claiming the law profession was at risk of becoming vulgarized, James Rawlins could respond that his son was a beneficiary of Old Hickory's liberal legacy that expanded freedom of choice.

—⁓—

John commenced reading law in November 1854 under the tutelage of Isaac Perrin Stevens. Stevens was a staunch Whig, but he and John were able to negotiate their political divide. His law office was on Hill Street, aptly named because it rises in a steep incline from Main Street. Stevens was born in Ohio in

1814 and arrived in Galena in 1836, hoping to cash in on the booming lead production. No one could gainsay Stevens's great energy, but that energy caused him to veer in tangential directions. His first foray was in the lumber business, supplying siding for local construction. He acquired part ownership in the *Galena Gazette and Advertiser*, which lasted until 1841, when he detoured into law. In 1840, he became so fascinated by the pseudoscientific theory of phrenology after attending lectures delivered by a "Dr. Burhans"[41] that he helped organize a phrenological society. Interest in it waned rapidly, and "nothing further is known of the society."[42] It's not difficult to imagine that during a lull in the law office's workday, Stevens acquainted John with the principles of phrenology and perhaps used them to expound on the adverse effects on the cranium of habitual alcohol use.

Although he was not a luminous beacon at the Galena bar, Stevens had a sizeable practice and a reputation as "a prominent attorney."[43] Stevens could lay claim to having been one of perhaps as few as eleven attorneys to have been examined by Abraham Lincoln. A three-person examining committee consisting of Lincoln, Jonathan Young Scammon (later a law mentor of Robert Todd Lincoln), and Thompson Campbell (added perhaps to provide a friendly Galena connection) found Stevens worthy of a passing mark.[44]

While an apprentice, Rawlins boarded with Reverend Hooper Crews of the Methodist Episcopal Church on Bench Street;[45] Crews was later a trustee of the institution that became the Garrett Theological Seminary. Rawlins cut an impressive physical presence at this time. Manual labor had contributed to his "strong, robust body, [and] vigorous constitution."[46] At first acquaintance, one would be struck by John's dark countenance, black hair, and thick brows, but then attention would fasten on the eyes beneath. "His flashing black eyes," recalled schoolmate Moses Hallett, "were more eloquent than his tongue."[47] Fellow Galenian John M. Shaw provided a dense description of John during his apprenticeship:

> My own personal acquaintance with Rawlins commenced during the year 1853, while he was still a law student. I well remember the first time I ever saw him. I was then a clerk in a store in the same city. I passed him upon the sidewalk. A strong, sturdy looking young fellow, swarthy in complexion, with hair and eyes black as night, eyes which, when they looked at you, looked through you; but in those youthful days they had in them a merry and kindly twinkle, which at once impressed you with the notion that they were the windows of a large and generous soul. After he had passed I turned around and looked at him, and my mental comment was: "There goes a fellow worth knowing."[48]

John was aware of the gaps in his schooling, but he would overcompensate by immersing himself in the law books. That drive paid off because by October 1855, after one year of preparation, he had passed his examination and been admitted to the bar. Isaac Stevens must have been impressed by his potential, because he took John into his practice that same month. Their partnership lasted less than a year. In August 1856, Stevens split to take up lead mining in Apple River. In seemingly no time, John had evolved from charcoal boy to proprietor of an income-producing law practice, becoming the only born and bred Jo Daviess County resident at the Galena bar. With a practice providing a secure base, John was positioned to branch out socially, professionally, and politically.

NOTES

1. H. W. Brands, *The Age of Gold: The California Gold Rush and the New American Dream* (New York: Doubleday, 2002), 18.

2. *Sacramento Daily Union*, October 29, 1858.

3. H. W. Brands, *The Age of Gold*, 132.

4. Laurence I. Seidman, *The Fools of '49: The California Gold Rush 1848–1856* (New York: Alfred A. Knopf, 1976), 36.

5. Cora Monnier Rawlins to "To Whom It May Concern," April 2, 1909, James Harrison Wilson Papers, Box 22, Library of Congress.

6. Malcolm J. Rohrbaugh, *Days of Gold: The California Gold Rush and the American Nation* (Los Angeles: University of California Press, 1997), 36.

7. Although James returned, Lovisa effectively lost Jarrard, who stayed in California, and that loss was aggravated when brothers Mortimer and Robert later joined him there. Lovisa suffered the deaths of sons John and Jarrard, which occurred within months of each other. Jarrard died as a result of an explosion at the Golden Gate Sugar Refinery plant on October 26, 1869. Jarrard and several coworkers were in the drying room, which used centrifugal pans for drying the sugar. The *Daily Alta California* of October 27, 1869, describes the event: "Mr. J. O. Rawlins, one of the proprietors, went into the room and stood near the pans, holding his watch to time the revolutions. . . . After the work had gone on but seven minutes . . . a sudden crash was heard and the four men were thrown around the room. . . . The accident was caused by one of the centrifugal pans giving way while in motion. . . . The pans burst into fragments, the pieces striking the men in the lower portions of their bodies."

8. Malcolm J. Rohrbaugh, *Days of Gold*, 285.

9. *History of Jo Daviess County*, 576.

10. Larry Gara, "William S. Hamilton on the Wisconsin Frontier: A Document," *Wisconsin Magazine of History* 41, no. 1 (1957): 25.

11. Laurence I. Seidman, *The Fools of '49*, 148.

12. James Harrison Wilson, *The Life of John A. Rawlins* (New York: Neale, 1916), 29.

13. Augustus L. Chetlain, *Recollections of Seventy Years*, 40.

14. Rock River Seminary Catalogue 1866, Manchester University Archives.

15. H. G. Kable, *Mount Morris: Past and Present*, 2nd ed. (Harry G. Kable, 1938).

16. *The Catalogue of the Officers and Students of Rock River Seminary for the Year Ending June 29, 1848*, 12, Manchester University Archives.

17. Manchester University Rock River Student Record Book, in the Mount Morris College cabinet.

18. Shelby M. Cullom, *Fifty Years of Public Service: Personal Recollections of Shelby M. Cullom Senior United States Senator from Illinois* (Chicago: A. C. McClurg, 1911), 6.

19. *The Catalogue of the Officers and Students of Rock River Seminary for Year Ending June 24, 1852*, Manchester University Archives.

20. John's brief but successful tenure at the seminary blazed a trail for two brothers. Lemmon Parker (listed as "L. P.") is entered on the Rock River Seminary student roll for the winter term ending March 6, 1856; brother William is listed in the 1866 catalogue. Manchester University Archives.

21. James Harrison Wilson, *The Life of John A. Rawlins*, 29.

22. Isabel Wallace, *Life & Letters of General W. H. L. Wallace* (Chicago: R.R. Donnelley and Sons, 1909), 6.

23. Shelby M. Cullom, *Fifty Years of Public Service*, 11.

24. Manchester University Archives, General File.

25. James Harrison Wilson, *The Life of John A. Rawlins*, 29.

26. Matthew S. Hill, "God and Slavery in America: Francis Wayland and the Evangelical Conscience" (PhD diss., Department of History, Georgia State University, 2008), 32.

27. Francis Wayland, *The Elements of Moral Science*, 4th ed. (Boston: Gould, Kendall, and Lincoln, 1844), 208.

28. Matthew S. Hill, "God and Slavery in America: Francis Wayland and the Evangelical Conscience," 17.

29. Goshen Public Library and Historical Society Archives.

30. Sheila M. Rothman, *Living in the Shadow of Death: Tuberculosis and the Social Experience of Illness in American History* (Baltimore: Johns Hopkins University Press, 1994), 16.

31. Guilford Township, Jo Daviess County, Illinois. Township Record Book from 1853 through 1863.

32. September 11, 1869, communication to the Washington *Daily Morning Chronicle*. The letter to the chronicle is signed with the initials "RHJ," which suggests that it was almost certainly written by Richard H. Jackson.

33. James Harrison Wilson, *The Life of John A. Rawlins*, 30–31.

34. R. H. Jackson, Washington *Daily Morning Chronicle*, September 11, 1869.

35. Jack Nortrup, "The Education of a Western Lawyer," *American Journal of Legal History* 12 (1968): 304.

36. The statistics on Chicago lawyers are found in Mark E. Steiner, *An Honest Calling: The Law Practice of Abraham Lincoln* (DeKalb: Northern Illinois University Press, 2006), 29.

37. Ibid., 39.

38. Ibid., 39.

39. Anton-Herman Chroust, *The Rise of the Legal Profession in America*, vol. 2, *The Revolution and the Post-Revolution Era* (Norman: University of Oklahoma Press, 1965), 156.

40. Ibid., 106.

41. "Dr." Burhans was Kelly E. Burhans (1811–43), originally born in Albany County, New York, and then farming in Tazewell County, Illinois; S. Burhans Jr., *Burhans Genealogy* (New York: Private Distribution, 1894), 193, 226. His lecture series electrified the imagination of the Galenians in attendance, who were impressed by the potential of applying phrenological principles "to the education of youth, to legislation, jurisprudence, and the treatment of the insane"; *Northwestern Gazette and Galena Advertiser*, August 14, 1840.

42. *History of Jo Daviess County*, 482.

43. John M. Shaw, "The Life and Services of General John A. Rawlins," in *Glimpses of the Nation's Struggle*, ed. Edward D. Neill (New York: D. D. Merrill, 1893), 383.

44. Martha L. Benner, Cullom Davis, et al., eds., *The Law Practice of Abraham Lincoln: Complete Documentary Edition*, 2nd ed. (Springfield: Illinois Historic Preservation Agency, 2009), File ID N05308, Document ID 130286, July Term 1842, http://www.lawpracticeofabrahamlincoln.org.

45. *The Galena City Directory* (Galena, IL: H. H. Houghton, 1854), 112.

46. James Harrison Wilson, *The Life of John A. Rawlins*, 31.

47. Ibid., 30.

48. John M. Shaw, "The Life and Services of General John A. Rawlins," 385.

4

"He Was a Powerful and Earnest Talker and Masterful in All His Efforts at the Bar"

AFTER COMPLETING SCHOOLING AT THE Goshen seminary, Emily Smith pondered her options. The most tempting was a trip to the vast and flourishing west, to the tall grass prairie states where one might find "a newer garden of creation."[1] Her destination would be Galena, pride of the upper Mississippi, where she was to reside with her father's brother, Bradner, and his wife, Mary. For Emily, the scale of such adventure could hardly be overestimated. Her family had been rooted for decades in central Orange County, New York. Emily's mother, Sally Jane Bull Smith, descended from William Bull, who in the early eighteenth century was one of that area's first settlers.[2] William and his fellow colonizers were so captivated by "the native beauty of the place" that "they stood upon the wooded hills and looked with glad eyes upon the fertile, fruitful valley. All around about them lay the land of their desire, and they called it Goshen, the 'promised land' of the Scriptures."[3] Emily's grandfather, Jesse Smith, was a Revolutionary War veteran of the Second New York Regiment. He was captured at Fort Montgomery, where in 1777 the British hoped to wrest control of the Hudson River.[4] Father Hiram Smith, a tanner, was one of Goshen's solid citizens.

Uncle Bradner had been in Galena since 1843 and had probably sent reports to his Goshen-bound relatives crowing about his adopted city's vitality. He started out as a carpenter and then kept the hotel in the little village of Elizabeth, east of Galena. He ran a successful livery stable in Galena, built a brick home on fashionable Bench Street, and moved within a sizeable circle of friends.[5] His stable boasted "a large and well selected stock of horses and carriages ready at all times."[6] Once in Galena, Emily could be assured of a comfortable place to reside, exposure to cultural amenities, and access to society.

Emily was perhaps as captivated by Galena's charms as were her ancestors by the terrain of Upstate New York. On approaching town by rail from Chicago, a traveler espied "a varied scene of churches, dwellings, hills, valley, rock and river, all beautifully blended," which in "contrast with prairie scenery . . . may awaken emotions that were enkindled in his childhood among the peaks of the Alleganies [sic] or the beautiful hills of New England."[7] Bustling Main and Commerce Streets tracked the curve of the Galena River. The residential streets, on terraced bluffs above town and connected by steeply pitched wooden stairs, presented an impressive panorama: "The streets rise one above another, and communicate with each other by flights of steps, so that houses on the higher streets are perched like an eagle's eyrie overlooking the rest and communicating an extensive prospect."[8] The red brick Italianate and Greek Revival mansions boasted of the wealth created by mining, timber, and steamboats. Anchoring the downtown was the newly built De Soto Hotel, finest in the West, whose dining hall seated three hundred. Ladies' parlors were decked out "with velvet carpets, rosewood furniture, four large gilt mirrors, sofas, divans, marble-top tables, satin damask curtains, and one of Munn & Clark's best double round, seven octave, carved rosewood Piano Fortes."[9]

However, Emily was captivated most by John Rawlins, with the flashing black eyes, shock of black hair, and "sonorous bass voice,"[10] whose drive and earnestness bespoke potential for professional advancement and connubial stability. John was smitten by her "amiability of manner, gentleness, sweetness of disposition and virtue" and soon secured permission for her hand.[11] The Goshen and Galena Smiths were pleased to welcome John into their family. On June 4, 1856, he and Emily were married in Bradner's home, with Reverend F. A. Reed officiating[12] and Aunt Mary and Mary's four-year-old niece, Hattie, beaming happily.[13] Nothing was about to spoil the Rawlinses' nuptial bliss, not even the misspelling of their name in the county's record book.[14]

On April 12, 1857, John and Emily welcomed their first child, a son. They named him James Bradner, after the two most important men in John's life. That John honored his father in this fashion suggests the fundamental affection he had for him. James Bradner would be John's only son to survive to adulthood; however, James never married due to chronic health problems.

These health problems (e.g., seizures, eventual blindness) were likely complications resulting from being infected with tuberculosis as an infant. In November, the Rawlins family suffered the loss to tuberculosis—the leading cause of death in mid-nineteenth-century America[15]—of sixteen year-old Benjamin Thomas Rawlins, one of John's younger brothers who still lived at home in Guilford Township.[16] It was the disease that would check John Rawlins's ascent to greater prominence and devastate his family.

Emily was exhibiting signs of chronic illness; she might have been symptomatic during the courtship—probably chest or joint pains, fatigue, cough, or fever. J. C. Spare, a husky Galena businessman with a black shovel-shaped beard who became acquainted with Rawlins, recollected that "Mrs. Rawlins was not a strong healthy woman and would often be quite poorly, when Mrs. Spare would often take her some little delicacies which I think knit closer and strengthened the friendship that subsisted between the husbands, and during these times 1856–1861 there was hardly a day passed when I did not call at his office."[17]

Her symptoms might have been attributed to bronchitis and anticipated to spontaneously remit. But even if the symptoms had been correctly diagnosed as incipient tuberculosis, that would not have necessitated calling off the marriage. As medical historian Sheila Rothman noted, individuals of that era lived out their lives despite the uncertain course of illness, which meant that "in the 1840s the community expected those with consumption to marry and bear children." Despite the risks facing pregnant women with consumption, physicians eschewed "counsel[ing] female patients to avoid pregnancies. Bearing children was a woman's duty, and medicine had no business in abrogating it."[18] Emily's intensifying symptomatic burden did not prevent the Rawlinses from rapidly augmenting their family. Daughter Jane "Jennie" Lovisa Rawlins was born on October 20, 1858, and second daughter Emily Smith Rawlins arrived on April 21, 1860. Thus, consumption-wracked Emily was pregnant for almost half her married life.

Today, one is shocked that John and Emily could expose infants to a devastating illness. Yet just as societal norms sanctioned consumptives to marry and procreate, the medical establishment tended to regard consumption as hereditary, not contagious. However, many physicians were baffled by the epidemiological puzzle consumption presented. The eminent Dr. Henry Bowditch presented arguments in favor of both views. After careful analyses of cases he treated, he abandoned his belief that consumption was contagious: "Let me say that I commenced this investigation strongly possessed with the idea . . .

of the essentially contagious nature of phthisis, under certain circumstances. The force of my own facts, when thoroughly examined, has led me materially to doubt the correctness of my former impressions."[19]

Treatment in mid-nineteenth-century America varied depending on gender. Men of means sought cures in salubrious climates such as the southern seacoast or the island of Madeira. Women were to improve their health within the confines of domestic life and among family, relatives, and friends. There is the possibility—although no evidence has been discovered to confirm it—that Emily's trip to her western relatives might have been arranged to benefit her health. It is not known when her latent tuberculosis infection became active, thus making her communicable.

Galena physicians would have recommended Emily to maintain a rapacious appetite, take medications (often opiate-laced), and exercise. Horseback riding was thought to promote respiratory health, and the rocking motion was thought to strengthen chest muscles. In Emily's case, Uncle Bradner probably had a carriage from his livery stable to provide gentle rolling and pitching exercise. Galena newspapers, like many others, carried advertisements for medicines touting cures for lung diseases. It is quite possible that Emily tried Dr. Hoofland's German Bitters and Balsamic Cordial or Dr. Carter's Cough Balsam, the latter available for one dollar per bottle at J. Dodge & S. Crawford in Galena.[20]

—◊◊◊—

The newlyweds settled into 517 Hill Street, a very modest board and batten house featuring twin arched windows below a peaked roof. John acquired the home and the mortgage to purchase it on February 14, 1857, from another Galena attorney, Wellington Weigley,[21] who had bought it in April 1854 for $750. The Rawlinses were flanked by staunch Republican neighbors. William Reuben Rowley lived at 515. Originally from Lawrence County, New York, Rowley had started as a schoolteacher in Scales Mound Township before opting for a public service career, which included a term as sheriff and two decades as clerk of the circuit court in Galena. Swiss-born John Eugene Smith, proprietor of a Main Street jewelry store, was briefly the other neighbor. Smith, with his European bearing and salt-and-pepper beard, looked every inch the imposing army colonel, a rank he achieved as organizer of the "Lead Mine Regiment."

The Rawlinses' home was convenient to John's downtown law office at the corner of Hill and Main and above the Saint Louis Store, a dry goods establishment just down from the J. R. Grant leather goods store at 145 Main Street.

Jesse Grant's second oldest son, Simpson, managed the leather goods store, which carried harnesses, saddlery, shoe findings, and assorted hardware.[22] The eldest son, Ulysses, had been in Galena briefly in 1856, probably not long after John was hired to do the legal work for the store. "Soon after entering the bar, I got, by some luck or good word, the law business for the leather and hardware store of Jesse Grant," is how John remembered it years later.[23]

John's legal career spanned only about five years. His law practice kept him busy but never made him wealthy. As a generalist, he took jobs such as real estate transactions, settlement of debts, and property disputes. Newspaper accounts provide glimpses into types of cases he handled. Prior to his June 1856 wedding, he represented the plaintiff in a divorce petition; in *Brobson v. Rosebrough*, he unsuccessfully represented the defendant, who had to pay $42.12 to the plaintiff.[24] The proceedings of the circuit court indicated that in August 1857, Rawlins won his client an award of $329.63.[25] During the October 1858 circuit court term, Rawlins represented three clients in criminal cases but failed to get any acquitted: Robert Campbell was found guilty of petit larceny, fined twenty-five dollars, and given three days in the hoosegow; Jeremiah Lynch got four years in the penitentiary for robbery; and John Beatty was sentenced to a year and a day for larceny.[26]

Just as Isaac Stevens had served as his legal mentor, so John extended the favor to David Sheean, an acquaintance from Guilford Township who was just returned to Jo Daviess County from a five-year odyssey to California. Sheean's father, James, emigrated from County Cork to Boston, where he married and sired three children, which included David in 1833. The Sheeans gambled on finding success out in the west. A steamboat disgorged them in Galena in 1837, and the next spring James Sheean filed a squatter's claim on farmland in Guilford Township. In the winter of 1851, at age eighteen David bade farewell to his parents and embarked on his Gold Rush adventure. Unlike James and Jarrard Rawlins, David took the water and land route, braving the dangers of the seventy-mile trek across the Isthmus of Panama. Compared to the Rawlinses, he had some success in placer mining in California. On returning home in May 1856, he absorbed himself in reading law under John's tutelage.[27] Rawlins, now in the role of the young mentor, had been practicing law himself for barely a year and a half. Replicating his own experience with Stevens, John formed a partnership with David in January of 1858 after David passed his bar exam.[28]

Mentor and mentee shared more than friendship and a youth spent on Guilford farmland: they were ardent Democrats. Only a few months returned from California, Sheean attended a fête on December 2 at the De Soto House celebrating the election of James Buchanan. The legal apprentice brashly disparaged the town's foremost Republican when he rose to commend his fellow Democrats for having "resisted the contaminating influence of [Congressman] Washburne" and causing him to suffer "a rebuke."[29] The Rawlins law office became the venue for frequent "bull sessions" regularly attended by the quartet of Rawlins, Sheean, Philip McQuillan, and John M. Shaw.[30] Shaw, who in 1860 began a law practice in Galena and later became a judge in Minnesota, recounted how the discussions veered into national affairs. The foursome never lacked for topical material, what with the dire complications arising from the questions of whether and how to permit or bar slavery in the territories. "They were all Democrats but me, and all but me also very bright fellows," Shaw recollected. "I was a dyed-in-the-wool Abolitionist. You may naturally suppose that I was sometimes pretty hard pushed, and I verily believe that in that office I received the most valuable lessons of my life in the act of logical fencing."[31]

Shaw might have been describing Rawlins's demeanor as a lawyer as much as the tenor of the office parleys: "As a lawyer Rawlins was very strong and able. While in those earlier years his learning could not, in the nature of things, have been so exhaustive as that of many of the older men whom he met at the bar, his strong *forte* was a transparent and sturdy integrity of mind and character, accompanied by a powerful logic and a masterful and impressive style of delivery, which inspired confidence and commanded assent."[32] Richard Jackson, another legal contemporary of Rawlins, regarded him a tough courtroom opponent: "Possessing but a limited education, with no classical knowledge, literary resources, or profundity in the law, yet in ordinary jury trials he soon became a formidable adversary." According to Jackson, this was due to Rawlins being a trusted local product: "The country people regarded him with peculiar pride and affection—as their chosen son—as one of themselves. While in the trial of a cause they might mistrust a brilliant and accomplished advocate, they had the most unlimited confidence in 'John.' Here was the secret of his power and success at the bar. His simple assertion was to them oracular authority, and frequently dissipated the most exhaustive and conclusive arguments."[33] Besides his verbal prowess, Rawlins was also remembered for being well prepared: "He was a powerful and earnest talker and masterful in all his efforts at the bar. He tried his cases so well that those who heard him would say nothing was left undone on his side of the case."[34] On the other hand, he was not the deepest thinker, lacked a memory for legal facts and cases, was no slick courtroom operator, and possessed no more than ordinary academic and legal training. Forcefulness, common-sense logic, compulsive preparation, and rock-solid integrity were his attributes, and all transferred well to his success as a staff officer.

—◦◦◦—

Rawlins's status in the community of attorneys provided a natural avenue into his role as contributor to the civic life of Galena. Besides being an outlet for his natural civic-mindedness, a prominent public profile could bring legal business his way—and provide a platform when he was ready to assert his passion for Democratic politics. He even helped his town in ways that didn't require wearing a white collar: he was a member of the Galena Volunteer Fire Department's Neptune Number 2 company.[35]

Four years after his election as Guilford town clerk, Rawlins scored a more significant win by besting Wellington Weigley 698 votes to 292 in the race for Galena City attorney. Weigley was a well-to-do legal powerhouse, and Rawlins's trouncing of him—John carried all five wards—was a phenomenal upset. Rawlins was sworn in at a city council meeting on March 7, 1857.

Galena's city council tackled its share of routine obligations. For example, the *Galena Daily Advertiser* of June 18, 1857, reported on a council meeting of June 16 that dealt with such issues as the Spring Street culvert caving in; the Bridge Committee procuring two new signs; the Committee on Streets contracting for a new horse, cart, and driver; and a demand for restitution from a woman, represented by Rawlins's friend Richard H. Jackson, who claimed injury due to a sidewalk in disrepair. The latter problem was referred to city attorney John Rawlins.

Jackson, in a tribute to Rawlins immediately after his death, chose one case in particular to review that Rawlins had handled while city attorney. Jackson represented a plaintiff in a suit in trespass *vi et armis*—a trespass by force against an individual—against several of Galena's policemen, whom Rawlins represented. To Jackson, "the case on the part of the defendants was a most outrageous one," and "their conduct was without extenuation." Rawlins, Jackson thought, had "gone beyond professional requirements" in defending them and raised this point to him after the trial. Rawlins said he submitted to representing them because he "had been instructed by the City Council to defend them as officers of the city; otherwise they would have had to employ other counsel." The officers may have engaged in misconduct we would now call "unlawful force." Perhaps they roughly handled someone who was only suspected of a crime. If the police had acted properly as agents of the city, then it would have been appropriate for Rawlins to represent them. Jackson suggested that the policemen acted so egregiously that their behavior went beyond their charge of authority. Rawlins represented them out of duty to the established authority and perhaps out of sympathy to spare them the expense of retaining their own attorneys.[36]

As a prominent attorney and civic leader, it was virtually de rigueur that Rawlins hold membership in fraternal organizations. He was a member of the local Miners' Lodge 273, chartered on October 15, 1858. His fellow Masons included court clerk William Rowley, jeweler John E. Smith, master carpenter and builder John Corson Smith, engineer Ely Parker, and attorney Madison Y. Johnson.[37]

Of Madison Johnson, it could be stated almost unequivocally that "he was not popular." As one of the most cantankerous attorneys in Jo Daviess County, Johnson's approach to trial law as blood sport drew clients to him and made him wealthy: "He was fearless in maintaining what he believed to be right, even if it involved personal inconvenience and danger."[38] On introduction, one's attention would be drawn to the nose that hung from his swarthy face like a sock, but it was his return squint that gave pause to anyone foolhardy to joust with him: "From the glance of his eye—deep-set, dark and penetrating—the coward invariably slinks away."[39] Politically, he was an old-line Whig, proud of his southern heritage, and rabidly negrophobic. By the close of the 1850s, "he harbored a deep and abiding hostility to the . . . party of Lincoln and particularly to the organization and person of Congressmen Elihu Washburne."[40]

Ely Parker (or Do-ne-ho-ga-wa, the name bestowed on him after installation as a sachem of the Iroquois Confederacy) was an engineer sent to Galena to oversee construction of two federal buildings, one to accommodate a customs house and post office and another to serve as a hospital for river boatmen. On arriving in April 1857, Parker's perspective of Galena was not so much a panoramic one from the "eagle's eyrie" but a close-up of dingy alley, raucous saloon, and congested levee. For the educated and dignified Parker, Galena was bereft of recreations "unless it be drinking whiskey, and plugging one's fist into somebody el[s]es mug."[41] Although many residents still remembered the threat posed by Black Hawk a quarter century past, Parker, a Native American, received a respectful if not warm acceptance. He was a founder of the Miners' Lodge and its first worshipful master. On December 27, 1859, the lodge's dress ball was held at the De Soto Hotel, and the evening's highlight was Parker's entrance in Knight Templar regalia.[42]

Rawlins was also an Odd Fellow of Lodge No. 17. To celebrate the fortieth anniversary of the founding of the Odd Fellows on April 26, 1859, Rawlins and John Spare were chosen to give speeches. Four days before the celebration, Rawlins begged out, telling Spare he had too much work to do to prepare for the May term, so it would fall to Spare to do all the speechifying. Spare reluctantly agreed, saying he had some ideas jotted down. Could John come to dinner the next evening and give his opinion as to their suitability? After a turkey dinner, Spare auditioned his address. Rawlins declared it "worthy." However, within minutes of Rawlins leaving, Spare became violently ill, took to bed, and stayed there until May 10. Now Rawlins had to deliver the address that Spare could not. On April 25, Rawlins came to Spare's house to borrow the speech. However, as Spare explained, "On the 25 I became delirious it seems . . . & utterly refused to let Rawlins read it." Undaunted, the resourceful Rawlins dug up a printed address that former Illinois Congressman Richard Yates had once delivered and read it at the Odd Fellow event. No one seemed the wiser.[43]

This glimpse of Rawlins is intriguing because he was so much the upright fellow who would never resort to plagiarizing a speech or deceiving an audience. It is also interesting for the out-of-character action he took to solve a problem. Customarily, if Rawlins's initial attempts at fixing a problem did not work, he would double down and force the issue—that is become more confrontational, display a hotter temper, work all the harder, or more strictly invoke the rules. Lifting Yates's speech was problem-solving by demonstrating flexibility, by outflanking that which frustrates rather than battering through it. Doing more of the same is known as first-order change; switching gears with a different approach is second-order change. Many of Rawlins's most obvious contributions as Grant's close aide came about because of the former—his habitually confrontational style. These are the contributions that won Rawlins gratitude. Rarer are instances when he perceived the wisdom in taking a different, even paradoxical tack, but when he did, these secured for him his singular niche in the historical record.

While reading law, Rawlins had little time to attend to the partisan events shaking the republic, let alone become an entrant into the political arena. As a fellow member of the Galena bar recalled, "Upon the passage of the Kansas and Nebraska bill, in 1854, Rawlins was too inexperienced and too deeply engaged in his professional studies to take any part in the fearful political excitement that swept over the Northwest."[44] And what excitement there was!

In May 1854, a bill was signed into law allowing the settlers of the Kansas and Nebraska Territories to decide whether slavery should be established there. The bill meant the demise of the Missouri Compromise's 36°30' line demarcating the boundary above which slavery was not permitted. Many Northerners railed against the bill, believing it a sop to slave power and predicting that White laborers would resist moving into territories where they could not compete against slave labor. Southerners were initially gratified by the Kansas-Nebraska Act, which, with its removal of the Missouri prohibition, allowed them to freely migrate with slaves in tow.

The politician most responsible for shepherding the bill through Congress was convinced that the solution to the slavery predicament was to let voting— the fundamental principle of self-government—decide the issue. Let people in territories, through their territorial legislatures and without interference from Washington, determine what institutions they prefer based on local needs and agricultural conditions. *Popular sovereignty*, he called it. And he had two quick retorts for the act's critics: first, the Missouri Compromise was no sacred cow; second, critics were nothing but nigger-loving abolitionists.

That politician was Senator Stephen Douglas, the face of the Democratic Party in Illinois. When Douglas came to Illinois as a young adult, he readily assimilated Western tastes, including one for corn liquor, and a preference for utilitarian clothing as coarse as his language. He unabashedly admired Andy Jackson, a believer in national expansion and improvement of rail and river transport. Support for waterway commerce made Douglas a favorite in river towns like Galena. John Rawlins was an ardent Douglas devotee for all those reasons and stood behind him on Kansas-Nebraska and popular sovereignty.[45]

By spring 1855, the popular sovereignty experiment in Kansas deteriorated as anti- and proslavery agitators flooded in to wrestle for control. Soon the situation erupted into violence. Border Ruffians from Missouri targeted Free State settlers. In May 1856, a proslavery contingent attacked and looted Lawrence, Kansas. Days later, abolitionist John Brown and a small band retaliated by killing five men by Pottawatomie Creek. Despite such violence, Douglas maintained his faith in popular sovereignty but failed to appreciate the fact that "if the majority rules one way, the minority must accept the verdict. If no one is willing to lose, a democracy is impossible."[46]

Almost coincidental with the raid against Lawrence, Massachusetts Senator Charles Sumner inflamed sectional passions with his "Bleeding Kansas" speech condemning the politicians abetting slavery. For those remarks, he was brutally caned by Preston Brooks, a South Carolina congressman. To the general public and politicians of every stripe, it seemed only a matter of time until there was a death on Capitol Hill. As if the nation needed more discord, in March 1857, the Supreme Court decided in *Dred Scott v. Sandford* that neither court edict nor legislation could exclude slaves from a territory. The decision was fraught with implications, including popular sovereignty's sustainability: Southerners interpreted the Supreme Court's pronouncement as validation for their stance that territorial legislatures could not prohibit slavery.

In Kansas, a constitutional convention attended mostly by proslavery men was held in the town of Lecompton. The conveners adopted a proslavery constitution and hastily put it to a vote largely boycotted by the free-soil faction. Buchanan embraced the sham Lecompton constitution and urged congressional action to admit Kansas as a slave state. Douglas took umbrage with the fraudulent manner in which the Lecompton constitution was rammed through and argued that the voters in Kansas had been denied the right to exercise popular sovereignty. Thus, on December 9, 1857, Douglas engaged in a three-hour anti-Lecompton harangue from the Senate floor. In truth, as much as Douglas appeared to take the high ground by opposing Lecompton, it was also the more politically advantageous position with Illinoisans. Debate in the House of Representatives on Lecompton became so contentious that on February 5, 1858, a fists-flying sectional donnybrook featuring Elihu Washburne occurred during the wee morning hours.

The Kansas tumult wrought deep fissures in the political landscape: "The split between the Buchanan-dominated Lecomptonites and the Douglas-led anti-Lecomptonites was fast disintegrating the national Democratic party."[47] Southern Democrats distrusted Douglas's popular sovereignty because it provided no guarantees to slavery's expansion into territories. They demanded legal sanction for the spread of slavery, and the fire-eaters among them howled that without protection of their interests, there was little incentive to remain in the Union. Douglas Democrats assailed the *Dred Scott* decision because it was at odds with popular sovereignty. As Democrats bifurcated into Northern and Southern factions, the Whig Party wheezed its last. Many Southern Whigs affiliated with Democrats, and Northern Whigs gravitated to the rising Republican Party. The Republicans were for holding the line against territorial expansion of slavery—no casting ballots for or against it—a stance in opposition to the Supreme Court's *Dred Scott* ruling.

After passing the bar exam, "Rawlins took little or no part in political discussion up to 1858. . . . He was too poor pecuniarily to sacrifice his profession upon the altar of political devotion, and had too much to contend with to engage in the pursuit of politics."[48] Presumably, he was too preoccupied contending with profession and marriage—and, soon, parenting. The Rawlinses' June 1856 wedding coincided with the Democratic convention in Cincinnati. During those first days of matrimony, Emily would have had to vie for John's attention as he devoured newspaper accounts of Douglas's attempts over sixteen ballots to overtake Buchanan as the presidential nominee.

With a pregnant wife and fledgling law practice, Rawlins was so "pecuniarily" challenged that his political involvement was mostly limited to office bull sessions and monitoring local Democratic Party activities. Evidence for the latter is in a letter he wrote to Senator Douglas in 1857 explaining that he had recently signed a petition to retain Ely Parker as Galena's superintendent of government buildings. Now, Rawlins wished to renege on that endorsement and to "recommend to your favorable consideration, the appointment of Robert W. Carson Esq. as such Superintendent aforesaid, in the place of Mr. Parker who is neither citizen nor resident of our State." Among Carson's top qualifications, according to Rawlins, was "his sound and consistent Democracy." Rawlins disingenuously explained he retracted support for Parker because he hadn't read the contents of the petition "being at the time engaged in professional duties."[49]

Galena Democrats were miffed that newcomer Parker was made superintendent without their input and got Douglas's support. Carson, an Odd Fellow and former second ward alderman, lacked Parker's civil engineering qualifications, so it was fortunate that Parker had his own supporters like Congressman Washburne who succeeded in retaining him. Parker's supporters were rewarded because his handsomely designed customhouse and post office is in use 160 years later as Galena's post office.[50]

While Rawlins watched from the Democratic sideline, Galena was a destination of prominent representatives of the nascent Republican Party. Senator Sumner arrived during the summer of 1855 on his exploration of the West. Desiring to descend an operational mine, he was escorted to the Marsden diggings, known for yielding collectible specimens of galena, blackjack spar, and iron pyrites. Outfitted with candle and pick, Sumner dug out some fine pieces of ore.[51]

A year later, Abraham Lincoln came campaigning on behalf of the Republican ticket of John C. Frémont and William Dayton. Lincoln had already gained prominence by garnering votes as Frémont's running mate. On the evening of July 23, 1856, Lincoln addressed a "large and attentive audience" from the De Soto Hotel balcony. The local Republican paper reported, "In a clear, connected and masterly manner he traced the history of slavery aggression from the commencement to the present time and pointed out, like a true statesman, the consequences of permitting the curse to spread itself over immense territories."[52] Around 11:00 p.m., Lincoln rolled toward a rousing conclusion:

> But the Union, in any event, won't be dissolved. We don't want to dissolve it, and if you attempt it, *we won't let you*. With the purse and sword, the army and navy and treasury in our hands and at our command, you *couldn't do it*. This Government would be very weak, indeed, if a majority, with a disciplined army and navy, and a well-filled treasury, could not preserve itself, when attacked by an unarmed, undisciplined, unorganized minority.
>
> All this talk about the dissolution of the Union is humbug—-nothing but folly. *We* won't dissolve the Union, and *you* shan't.[53]

Lincoln's warning of the foolhardiness of secession brimmed with such confidence as to make it unimaginable that in five years, his words would ring eerily miscalculated.

—◦◦◦—

The year 1858 saw Rawlins advance into local political prominence. He followed his election as city attorney by capturing one of the two third ward aldermanic seats in Galena's March 1 election. In a four-man race (with the top two vote getters sharing aldermanic duties), he came in runner-up (158 votes) to John Packard (179 votes), wealthy owner of a mercantile business. Rawlins's seat on the city council buttressed Mayor Robert Brand, a Democrat with

Southern roots. During his single term, Rawlins served on five standing committees: Finance, Depot, Contracts, Police, and Salaries.[54]

City aldermen addressed those customary maintenance functions—tax collection, granting licenses, equipping fire companies, authorizing bridge repairs—that kept a municipality whirring, as well as the occasional "human resources" issue. For example, in a September 1858 city council meeting, Mayor Brand announced that Galena's marshal, James Gallaher, who had been suspended for intemperance, must either be reinstated or replaced. Alderman Rawlins voted for reinstatement, suggesting he believed in a drinker's capacity to reform.[55] Looming over the council were other, more significant developments that offered few easy solutions, even as their portents were difficult to divine: slumping lead production, the silting of the Galena River, and the dubious wisdom of favoring river over rail commerce and thus passing on the opportunity to serve as the western terminus of the Illinois Central. However, these concerns receded in importance in the face of a humdinger of a US Senate race. In fact, it would be the most momentous Senate race in American history.

About a month after being sworn in as alderman, Rawlins took part in a "Grand Rally" of local Democrats showing their support for President Buchanan against the Know-Nothings and Black Republicans.[56] But the signal event of the year was the visit to Galena by Stephen Douglas on August 25. Douglas had just finished the first senatorial debate with Lincoln at Ottawa, Illinois, on August 21 and was girding for the second at Freeport on August 27. This diversion in Galena gave Douglas opportunities to glad-hand Jo Daviess Democrats, gloat about the pummeling he had just inflicted on Lincoln, and deflect some recent Republican allegations against him.

Douglas pitched into the debates with gun blazing—literally. He traveled aboard a private train that included a flat car on which a mounted artillery piece boomingly announced his arrival. In the Ottawa debate, Douglas took the offensive and delivered some below-the-belt rhetorical blows. He rebuked Lincoln for inciting "sectional conflict" with the remark he had made two months before in Springfield, when accepting the Republican nomination for senator, that the nation could not continue to exist half free and half slave. He played the race card, ridiculing Lincoln for talk about Black equality. He also wanted to brand Lincoln a political extremist and resorted to shifty sleight of hand to connect him with some radical Republican resolutions. As "proof" of

Lincoln's extremism, Douglas read from portions of an antislavery Republican platform he claimed Lincoln helped write in 1854 in Springfield. The resolutions called for repealing the Fugitive Slave Act and abolishing slavery in Washington, DC

Soon thereafter, Robert Hitt, Lincoln's stenographer clerk and Rawlins's seminary friend, noticed that Douglas quoted from a radical platform drawn up in Aurora in Kane County, Illinois, and not the more moderate one endorsed in Springfield. In fact, Lincoln had not even been in Kane County at the time. How was it that Douglas had gotten his sources crossed? The suspicious Republicans cried foul and forgery. Today, in his Galena remarks, Douglas was prepared to throw a bone of an explanation to the whining Republicans.

A crowd estimated in the local Democratic paper as between five and seven thousand assembled to hear Douglas's address. It was a smaller draw than anticipated, perhaps because many planned to attend the next debate on Friday in Freeport. Rawlins was chosen to introduce the "Little Giant," an indication of the importance he had achieved so quickly among Galena Democrats. As "an ardent admirer" of Douglas, to stand with him on the speaker's platform was a signal honor of Rawlins's young life.[57] With his bass voice reaching the edge of the crowd, Rawlins effused a reverential greeting:

> To me has been assigned by the Democracy of this city and county, the proud position of welcoming you to our city and county. The great principles with which your efforts have been, and we doubt not ever will be identified, find welcome for you in our hearts. As our representative, and as a statesman, we welcome you as citizens of this State, for which your exertions have proved so beneficial, and whose present high, noble and prosperous position is directly traceable to your untiring efforts in her behalf. (Cheers). I have now the honor, sir, of introducing you to the audience here assembled.[58]

Amid prolonged applause, Douglas took center stage and launched into a two-hour speech. It was a recapitulation and a defense of his Ottawa remarks.

He blamed abolitionists for tearing the country asunder and Republicans, with their "all slave or all free" pronouncements, for inciting sectional conflict. "Our fathers never dreamt of this new-fangled doctrine that the domestic institutions of all States must be uniform," he said, making the inevitable case for popular sovereignty. "Our fathers were so simple-minded as to suppose that in a Republic so extensive as ours, having a variety and diversity of climate, soil and interests, there would be a corresponding variety of local institutions. . . . But Lincoln and the black Republican party, wiser than the statesmen who founded this wonderful Republic, say that it cannot endure as now constituted; hence they must change it, or it will fall to pieces."[59]

Douglas saved some of his choicest repartee for the charges that he quoted the wrong set of resolutions. Pumping his fist, he gave his explanation:

> When I read these resolutions at Ottowa [sic], I tried to get an answer from Lincoln whether he stood upon that platform. He wouldn't answer. When now you put the question to the Republicans whether they are in favor of an unconditional repeal of the fugitive slave law, whether they would be willing to admit a State into the Union where the people have a resolve to permit slavery, when you ask them these questions, they say, "Oh, those resolutions were not adopted at the right spot." Before I get through, I will show you that they were adopted at the right "spot."[60]

Here, Douglas got in a lick regarding Lincoln's "Spot Resolutions" brouhaha during his term in Congress when he pressed President Polk to establish the precise spot where Mexican soldiers had invaded Texas. Instead of apologizing, Douglas pardoned himself for making a wholly understandable assumption that this was the Republican platform. In truth, Douglas was making "a lame excuse," because he had been set straight on this matter in 1856 by Illinois Senator Lyman Trumbull. As historian Michael Burlingame argued, "Clearly, Douglas had not made an honest mistake, his protestations to the contrary."[61]

—⁓⁓⁓—

Before the last Lincoln-Douglas debate in Alton on October 15, a team of Democrats, including Rawlins and his partner David Sheean, was dispatched to various Jo Daviess County locations to give speeches and incite voters to cast ballots for Democratic candidates for the state legislature. The speeches occurred between October 4 and November 1 in several county locations. At Hanover on October 11, Judge Mathew Marvin warmed up the crowd with a ninety-minute harangue, and Rawlins "followed in a speech of nearly two hours, sound in argument, and replete with eloquence. . . . Both speakers dealt unsparingly with Republican doctrines. They indulged in no low slang or personal epithet."[62]

Ohio's antislavery governor, Salmon Chase, came to Illinois on Lincoln's behalf and made stops in Jo Daviess County. With his balding pate, clean-shaven face, and statesman's wardrobe, he cut a patrician figure. However, Chase was a lumbering speaker with a slight lisp and looked better from the stump than he sounded.

On the evening of October 26, the town of Dunleith, across the river from Dubuque, hosted a large Democratic rally. A torchlight procession of one thousand converged on the ferry crossing, where the Germania Band tooted patriotic airs. "The famous 'Jo Daviess Coal Boy'" gave one of the addresses,[63] on which J. B. Dorr, editor of the *Dubuque Express and Herald*, lavished praise:

> One of the most powerful political speeches by John A. Rawlins, Esq. we have ever heard. This gentleman . . . has attained a high reputation in the legal profession, and as one of the most powerful political speakers in Illinois. Like the Great Senator whose cause he so eloquently advocates, he has made his way through poverty and obscurity, to rising and well deserved fame by his own industrious talent and determined efforts. With a fine distinct clear voice, pure and faultless pronunciation and grammatical correctness, with unusual powers of logical argument, joined to a fine flow of eloquence, he adds a well knit powerful frame, dark flashing eyes, and a countenance that bears the impress of genius and power.[64]

A by-product of the Lincoln-Douglas drama was that Rawlins, playing only a bit part, emerged as a political entity and with an augmented reputation as an influential speaker.

Election Day, November 2, saw strong voter turnout across Illinois despite gloomy weather. Overall Republicans garnered more votes, but Democrats came up the majority in the state legislature—thus ensuring Douglas's third Senate term.

Between Hanover and Dunleith, on October 20, Rawlins became a father again when Emily gave birth to a daughter, Jane ("Jennie"), who would become their longest-lived child.

—✑—

Because the status of Blacks and of slavery's expansion or containment were such salient election issues, it is worth considering how Rawlins may have viewed them during this period of his life. Two close associates of Rawlins agreed that he was opposed to slavery but that he raised no objection to it. John Shaw recollected, "His instincts and opinions were such to make him a pronounced opponent of slavery, but, in common with many others of his political faith, he looked upon it as an evil protected by the Constitution of the United States."[65] James Wilson, who also served on Grant's staff, claimed that although Rawlins found slavery repugnant, he never denounced it, preferring a solution to the slavery question that could protect the constitutional rights of slave owners and find concordance with most everyone else:

No precept or statement ... could convince Rawlins or the people that slavery itself, mild and mitigated as it might be, was essentially right, or could ever be regarded as beneficial to either slave or master. His very soul revolted against the idea of property in human beings. ... Yet it does not appear that he denounced it in its moral aspects in any public speech. But on the other hand, I have failed to find a single word ever uttered by him in its favor. ... Indeed, so far as can be discovered, he never felt called upon to consider or discuss it as an abstract question of morals, or even of economics, much less to uphold it as an ideal condition of society. It was a concrete fact, for which neither he nor any living citizen of the Republic could be held primarily responsible. He therefore considered it merely as an established institution, which it was his duty as a citizen to assist in protecting by such means and in such way as would not interfere with vested and established rights, but which should best promote the peace and prosperity of the whole country as well of the people more immediately concerned.[66]

To Rawlins, the best option for maintaining this tricky balance regarding slavery was popular sovereignty. Popular sovereignty, as Douglas espoused it, was "in a sense his professed attitude of indifference and moral neutrality toward the institution of slavery transformed into a principle and a device," the moral neutrality portion of which Rawlins appeared to share. As Douglas conceived it, popular sovereignty allowed slavery to be protected as far as local voters were inclined to protect it, and Rawlins was complacent with the "established institution" being guaranteed certain legal protections. Rawlins and Douglas found slavery repulsive, but Rawlins kept mum about slavery just as "Douglas would neither praise nor condemn slavery openly."[67]

Although one can find no examples of Rawlins's expressed racial attitudes about Blacks during this time, it is likely they would have been similar to those held by Douglas and Rawlins's Jo Daviess Democratic contemporaries. At Ottawa, while speaking about the Black man, Douglas said,

He belongs to an inferior race, and must always occupy an inferior position. ... I hold that humanity and christianity both require that the negro shall have and enjoy every right, every privilege, and every immunity consistent with the safety of society in which he lives. ... You and I are bound to extend to our inferior and dependent being every right, every privilege, every facility and immunity consistent with the public good. The question then arises what right and privileges are consistent with the public good. This is a question which each State and each Territory must decide for itself—Illinois has decided it for herself. We have provided that the negro shall not be a slave, and we have also provided that he shall not be a citizen, but protect him in his civil right, in his life, his person and his property, only depriving him of all political rights whatsoever, and refusing to put him on an equality with the white man.[68]

In early September 1858, delegates were named to the Democratic convention to nominate a candidate for the First Congressional District, which included Jo Daviess County, and to adopt a number of resolutions, among them a "willingness to protect the negroes resident among us in their persons and property and to extend to them all the rights, privileges and immunities which they can safely exercise . . . [but] we are not willing to make them our equals under the law, or to confer upon them the privilege of citizenship."[69]

Thus, it was not the lot of Blacks to remain forever in bondage; manumitted or "resident" Blacks could be entitled to property and personal protection but not citizenship that would grant them equal status. It behooved Whites to provide Blacks with paternalistic guidance, doling out only those privileges and rights that they could safely exercise. If this summed up Rawlins's racial attitudes, they would have been typical of Whites at the time in northern Illinois.

Meanwhile in St. Louis, an erstwhile hardscrabble farmer, Ulysses Grant, was grappling with his own attitude about slavery in general and what to do with one slave in particular. Grant now worked as a rent collector in a real estate agency that shared office space with a law firm. He was not engaging in abstract political or economic theorizing about slavery but was pondering a decision to manumit a family slave, thirty-five-year-old William Jones. This was a puzzling action to take given that Grant was in financial straits, and Jones could fetch a high price. Nonetheless, with his signature and the witness of two of the lawyers (one was William Hillyer, who later joined Grant's staff), he officially declared, "And I do hereby manumit, emancipate & set free said William from slavery forever."[70]

NOTES

1. Walt Whitman, "The Prairie States," *Leaves of Grass* (New York: Modern Library, 1993), 500.

2. Josephine C. Frost, *Ancestors of Hiram Smith and His Wife Sarah Jane Bull: Compiled for Their Grand Daughter May Smith Pfeiffer* (Brooklyn, NY: J. C. Frost, 1927).

3. George F. Gregg, "Town of Goshen," in *The History of Orange County New York*, ed. Russell Headley (Middletown, NY: Van Deusen and Elms, 1908), 220.

4. James A. Roberts, *New York in the Revolution as Colony and State*, 2nd ed. (Albany, NY: Brandow, 1898), 37.

5. Obituary of Bradner Smith (1806–1887) in the *Galena Daily Advertiser*, April 1, 1887.

6. *Galena Directory* (Galena, IL: H. H. Houghton, 1854), 47.

7. *Galena City Directory 1858–9* (Galena, IL: W. W. Huntington), 130.

8. George W. Hawes, *Illinois State Gazetteer and Business Directory for 1858 and 1859* (Chicago: George W. Hawes), 91.

9. *Galena Daily Advertiser*, April 9, 1855.

10. B. P. Thomas, ed., *Three Years with Grant as Recalled by War Correspondent Sylvanus Cadwallader* (New York: Alfred A. Knopf, 1961), 208.

11. James Harrison Wilson, *The Life of John A. Rawlins* (New York: Neale, 1916), 399.

12. David Sheean to James H. Wilson, October 24, 1887, Wilson Papers, Box 22, Library of Congress.

13. It would have appeared that Hattie, the child Bradner and Mary Smith doted on, was their daughter. In fact, the Smiths were childless. Mary Smith was Hattie's aunt. Mysteriously, Hattie, shortly after the marriage of John and Emily, went missing for half a year. Born in 1852, she was the daughter of Marshal Pierce and his first wife, Mary Smith's sister. When Hattie's biological mother died in May 1854, Marshal arranged for Hattie to be taken into the Smiths' home. Hattie resided there until Marshal Pierce remarried in July 1856, when she was returned to her father and stepmother at their residence in Savannah, Illinois. But her stay there was short-lived. Within months, Hattie was back in Galena with the Smiths. The Smiths and the Pierces arranged a deal whereby Marshal turned over Hattie to the Smiths in exchange for their promise to raise her as their daughter and to provide her a good education. At the time, Pierce was struggling to raise a large family on his steamboat clerk salary and saw this exchange as a way to lighten his burden. The child transfer was made, and for the next twenty-five years, the Smiths proved devoted surrogate parents. At age twenty-nine, Hattie's future was secured with her marriage to a successful physician, Frederick Pond. After Bradner and Mary died, Hattie and her stepmother made a claim for the remainder of the Smith estate. They argued that as part of the agreement for unofficially adopting Hattie, she would inherit their property. Bradner, who outlived Mary, executed a codicil to his will shortly before he died depriving Hattie of his property. Hattie contended that Bradner was mentally incompetent when he executed it. The case came before the Illinois Supreme Court, which ruled against Hattie. David Sheean, John Rawlins's former law partner, represented the Smith estate against Hattie Pond. See William A. Keener, *A Selection of Cases on Equity Jurisprudence* (New York: Baker, Voorhis, 1896), 715–21.

14. *Jo Daviess County Marriage Records, Vol. B: 1855–1865* lists the name as "Rawlings."

15. Sheila M. Rothman, *Living in the Shadow of Death: Tuberculosis and the Social Experiences of Illness in American History* (Baltimore: Johns Hopkins University Press, 1994), 2.

16. Letter of Cora Monnier Rawlins to "To Whom It May Concern," April 2, 1909, John Harrison Wilson Papers, Library of Congress.

17. J. C. Spare March 29, 1899, letter to "Friend [John] Beadle," Abraham Lincoln Presidential Library, SC 1442.

18. Sheila M. Rothman, *Living in the Shadow of Death*, 7, 107.

19. Henry I. Bowditch, *Is Consumption Ever Contagious, or Communicated by One Person to Another in Any Manner?* (Boston: David Clapp, 1864), 13. However, Dr. Bowditch hedged by recommending avoiding sleeping in the same bed with a consumptive, using disinfectant agents in the spittoon, and avoiding inhaling the consumptive's breath. He recommended not letting a sister or wife care for the consumptive; instead, "let a regular hired

attendant assume all the harder work, and sleep in the room, if need be, at night, or still better, in an adjacent room" (14).

20. *Galena Daily Advertiser*, July 13, 1860; *Galena Evening Courier*, March 15, 1859. The Balsamic Cordial was sure to cure "without fail" the most severe and long-standing bronchitis, pneumonia, and incipient consumption "and has performed the most astonishing cures ever known of confirmed consumption." The Cough Balsam "never fails to relieve a cough in twenty-four hours and always cures the worst cases of Colds, Coughs, and diseases of the Throat and Lungs in a few days."

21. Jo Daviess County Courthouse Recorder's Office, Mortgage Book M, p. 1.

22. *Galena City Directory 1858–9*, 48.

23. Interview of John A. Rawlins in *The United States Army and Navy Journal and Gazette of the Regular and Volunteer Forces*, September 12, 1868, 53.

24. *Galena Daily Advertiser*, June 3, 1856; *Galena Daily Advertiser*, June 4, 1856.

25. *Galena Daily Advertiser*, September 1, 1857.

26. *Daily Courier*, November 13, 1858.

27. *Portrait and Biographical Album of Jo Daviess County, Illinois* (Chicago: Chapman Brothers, 1889), 191–92.

28. John M. Palmer, ed., *The Bench and Bar of Illinois. Historical and Reminiscent* (Chicago: Lewis, 1899), 517.

29. *Galena Courier*, December 4, 1856.

30. Philip McQuillan, at age twenty-three, left Galena in the late 1850s and moved to St. Paul, Minnesota, where he became a well-to-do wholesale grocer. His oldest daughter, Mollie, married Edward Fitzgerald in 1890. In 1896 the couple became the parents of a boy known as F. Scott; see James L. W. West III, *The Perfect Hour: The Romance of F. Scott Fitzgerald and Ginevra King, His First Love* (New York: Random House, 2005), 13–14. This connection to Galena may shed light on Fitzgerald's reference to Grant in Galena found in *Tender is the Night*.

31. John M. Shaw, "The Life and Services of General John A. Rawlins," in *Glimpses of the Nation's Struggle. Third Series*, ed. Edward D. Neill (New York: D. D. Merrill, 1893), 386–87.

32. Ibid., 384.

33. Richard H. Jackson [R.H.J.], *Washington Daily Chronicle*, Washington, DC, September 11, 1869.

34. John M. Palmer, ed., *The Bench and Bar of Illinois*, 515–16.

35. Ledger Book, Galena Fire Department.

36. Richard H. Jackson, *Daily Morning Chronicle*, September 11, 1869.

37. J. C. Smith, *History of Freemasonry in the City of Galena, Illinois* (Galena, IL: Gazette, 1874).

38. John M. Palmer, *The Bench and Bar of Illinois*, 515.

39. *Portrait and Biographical Album of Jo Daviess County, Illinois*, 205.

40. Gene Edwin Arnold, "Without Due Process: Madison Y. Johnson and the Civil War" (master's thesis, DePaul University, 1967), 96.

41. William H. Armstrong, *Warrior in Two Camps: Ely Parker Union General and Seneca Chief* (Syracuse: Syracuse University Press, 1978), 62.

42. J. C. Smith, *History of Freemasonry in the City of Galena, Illinois*.

43. J. C. Spare March 29, 1899, letter to "Friend [John] Beadle," Abraham Lincoln Presidential Library, SC 1442.

44. A letter from "R.H.J." dated September 10, "Reminiscences of the late General John A. Rawlins," in the *Daily Morning Chronicle*, Washington, DC, September 14, 1869. "R.H.J." is almost certainly Rawlins's former friend and fellow attorney from Galena, Richard H. Jackson.

45. James L. Huston, *Stephen A. Douglas and the Dilemmas of Democratic Equality* (Lanham, MD: Rowman and Littlefield, 2007); Damon Wells, *Stephen Douglas: The Last Years, 1857–1861* (Austin: University of Texas Press, 1971).

46. James L. Huston, *Stephen A. Douglas and the Dilemmas of Democratic Equality*, 119.

47. Reinhard H. Luthin, "The Democratic Split during Buchanan's Administration," *Pennsylvania History*, 11, no. 1 (1944), 22.

48. "R.H.J.," in the *Daily Morning Chronicle*, Washington, DC, September 14, 1869.

49. John A. Rawlins to Stephen A. Douglas, August 7, 1857, Stephen A. Douglas Papers, University of Chicago, Box 8, Folder 12. Rawlins had a connection to Douglas through Joseph B. Chandler, Douglas's personal secretary. Chandler was one of Rawlins's friends at the Rock River Seminary. See D. Sheean to J. H. Wilson, December 16, 1884, File, S(1), Box 14, Series 2, Ulysses S. Grant Presidential Library, Mississippi State University Libraries.

50. William H. Armstrong, *Warrior in Two Camps*, 64–65; *History of Jo Daviess County*, 521, 528.

51. Augustus L. Chetlain, *Recollections of Seventy Years* (1899), 60. Chetlain recollected erroneously that Sumner visited Galena in 1856; however, that summer, Sumner was recovering from the caning inflicted on him by Congressman Brooks.

52. *Weekly Northwestern Gazette*, Galena, IL, July 29, 1856.

53. Roy P. Basler et al., eds., *The Collected Works of Abraham Lincoln* (New Brunswick: Rutgers University Press, 1953), 2:355.

54. *Galena City Directory 1858–9*, 7.

55. *Daily Courier*, Galena, IL, September 9, 1858.

56. *Galena Daily Advertiser*, April 12, 1858.

57. John M. Shaw, "The Life and Services of General John A. Rawlins," 384.

58. *Daily Courier*, Galena, IL, August 26, 1858.

59. Ibid.

60. Ibid.

61. M. Burlingame, *Abraham Lincoln: A Life* (Baltimore: Johns Hopkins University Press, 2008), 1:490; see pages 489–90 for details regarding Douglas's Galena remarks.

62. Letter signed by "A Citizen" to the Editors of the *Daily Courier*, October 13, 1858.

63. *Daily Courier*, Galena, IL, October 28, 1858.

64. In the *Daily Courier*, Galena, IL, October 29, 1858.

65. John M. Shaw, "The Life and Services of General John A. Rawlins, 384.

66. James Harrison Wilson, *The Life of John Rawlins*, 43.

67. Damon Wells, *Stephen Douglas: The Last Years, 1857–1861*, 127; 109.

68. Roy P. Basler et al., eds., *The Collected Works of Abraham Lincoln*, 2:355.

69. *Daily Courier*, Galena, IL, September 4, 1858.

70. John Y. Simon, ed., *The Papers of Ulysses S. Grant* (Carbondale: Southern Illinois University Press, 1967), 1:348.

5

"The 'Coal Boy's' Grape Shot Puts the Republicans to Flight!"

THE 1850S CLOSED IN GALENA on a grand scale. On December 27, the Masonic and Citizens' ball was held at the opulent De Soto House. Hissing gas jets reflected in the hotel's ballroom mirrors, transforming the De Soto into a blaze of illumination. The prominent of Galena turned out with their ladies attired in the latest fashions. The ball served as a farewell for Brother Ely Parker, recently appointed superintendent of construction on the Dubuque custom-house. With his stout frame enveloped in Masonic regalia, he made a striking appearance weaving among the guests, shaking hands, and receiving thanks for his contributions to the community's progress.

December 1859 may have ended on a gracious note, but the month began with Galenians aroused by the execution of fanatical John Brown. The past twelve months had given John Rawlins and David Sheean plenty of grist for their late afternoon law office bull sessions. The partners had to wonder whether the Union could stand much more strain. Agitating on one side were the fire-eaters of the Deep South, advocates for extending slavery everywhere and into perpetuity. In the opposite corner were militant abolitionists who encouraged disunion and relished war because, as they saw it, only blood could wash clean the stain of slavery.

Even as Rawlins feared for the Union's fate, he had to be dismayed that discord continued to plague Democrats. Some of that played out in the rough treatment Stephen Douglas had been receiving at the hands of President James Buchanan and the southern "Ultras" of the party. While the vindictive Buchanan shrank Douglas's patronage pool, powerful Deep South politicians grew distrustful of Douglas as a result of his performance in the second debate with Lincoln in Freeport. There, the Little Giant appeared to gainsay that the *Dred Scott* decision in any significant way voided his cherished popular sovereignty. In what was dubbed his Freeport Doctrine, Douglas responded to Lincoln that slavery's existence in a territory could not be vouchsafed unless there were "local police regulations" in place, and those "can only be established by the local legislature."[1] For his failure to be "right" on this issue, Douglas, soon after reelection, was stripped of his chairmanship of the Committee on Territories, a move spearheaded by John Slidell of Louisiana and Jefferson Davis of Mississippi.

In June 1859, J. B. Dorr, editor of the Dubuque *Express and Herald*, asked Douglas for his positions at the next Democratic convention in Charleston, South Carolina. In his reply, known as the Dorr Letter, Douglas said he could not accept the nomination if the convention endorsed such issues "as a congressional slave code for the territories, the revival of the African slave trade, or the doctrine that the Constitution either establishes or prohibits slavery in the territories beyond the power of the local population legally to control it."[2] This last point finds Douglas doubling down on his Freeport Doctrine. With this letter, Douglas played to his Northern base at the expense of shedding support in the slave states. Here was a harbinger of the bifurcation that would dismantle the Democratic Party in 1860.

Although the Dorr Letter smacks of sectionalism, Douglas desired that the sections put aside their self-interests and collaborate on a common purpose, such as westward expansion. Douglas believed that popular sovereignty was the solution to extremists' clamoring for or against federal intervention on the issue of slavery in the territories. Rawlins shared Douglas's belief in the Union's indivisibility and believed in the merits of popular sovereignty.

In the spring and summer of 1859, Douglas consulted history texts to fashion his argument for why popular sovereignty was the practical way to address slavery.[3] He attempted to make two arguments, the first, "that popular sovereignty was firmly based on historical precedent, that the 'fathers of the Revolution' had recognized the inalienable right of dependent political communities to local self-government, and that the slavery question was considered by them to be a matter of domestic and internal concern; and second, to provide a constitutional justification for popular sovereignty."[4] Despite his efforts, this treatise on popular sovereignty is bad history badly written. In tortuous prose, he fairly elevated popular sovereignty to the principle for which the Revolution was fought. Douglas's history lesson won few converts and offered nothing to Southerners.

One person impressed by Douglas's scholarship was John Rawlins. It is almost inconceivable that he was not influenced by the article because in 1860, as he canvassed northern Illinois on behalf of presidential candidate Douglas, Rawlins larded his speeches with words of the Founding Fathers to edify audiences with historical justifications for popular sovereignty.

Although Rawlins and Sheean approached the coming year with trepidation, there were positive events to plan for. Sheean planned to run for Galena city attorney and was elected to that office in March. Rawlins anticipated the birth of his third child—if Emily's health prevailed. That child, also named Emily, was born on April 20, 1860, practically coinciding with the arrival into town of the family Grant.

———

On the day the Grants—Ulysses, Julia, and their children—disembarked from the steamboat *Itasca*, Ulysses stepped gingerly down the gangplank, carrying some chairs as evidence he intended to stay awhile. As he surveyed the bustling wharf and glanced at the residences on the town's crest, Ulysses could have been forgiven if he had a moment of existential crisis: *So this is what it has all come to.* Since graduating West Point, his endeavors could fit in a nutshell: an army career that ended on a sour note, a stretch of hardscrabble farming, and most recently a job in the St. Louis real estate office of Julia's cousin, which exposed his lack of business acumen. Add to that a cascade of bad luck that had dogged him during his military career—dead livestock, faulty investment schemes, loans made to fellow officers gone unpaid—that had left him strapped. He was thirty-eight and needed to be rescued by his father, Jesse, who hired him for the family's leather goods store on Galena's Main Street.

Ulysses tried to prevent this day from occurring. While in St. Louis two months earlier, he had made a last attempt to find employment by requesting the president of the Board of St. Louis County Commissioners to reconsider his application for County Engineer if the office became vacant.[5] In the summer of 1859, he had made a bid for it but was passed over because of his presumed Democratic political leanings. Add rejection to the list of failed opportunities.

But if Ulysses felt resigned to his fate, Julia put a cheery construction on their life's new chapter: "After a journey of four or five days, we arrived at Galena, a charming, bustling town nestled in the rich ore-laden hills of northern Illinois. The atmosphere was so cool and dry, the sun shone so brightly, that it gave us the impression of a smiling welcome."[6]

Ulysses's younger brother Simpson was in charge of the shop, but the youngest brother, Orvil, had been on site for a year because Simpson was ill with consumption. Ulysses was to work behind the counter, fill orders, buy raw cowhides for shipment down to Jesse's tanneries, and look in on customers in the region. The Grants rented a snug brick home on High Street—still extant and privately occupied to this day—for about one hundred dollars per year, or approximately 15 percent of their annual income. It was a good two hundred feet above Main Street, which required a grueling climb of dozens of wooden steps each night after work.

If clerking at his father's leather and saddlery store was not what Ulysses had envisioned at this life stage, the position offered several consolations. First, he was surrounded by his family. At the end of the day, he could look forward to a romp on the carpet with his children and a home-cooked meal. In contrast, his last months in the army at Ft. Humboldt on the northern California coast were filled with loneliness bordering on hopelessness. "You do not know how forsaken I feel here!" he began one letter to Julia.[7] A month later, he was on the verge of leaving the army: "I sometimes get so anxious to see you, and our little boys, that I am almost tempted to resign and trust to Providence, and my own exertions, for a living where I can have you and them be with me.... Whenever I get thinking on the subject however, *poverty, poverty*, begins to stare me in the face and then I think what would I do if you and our little ones should want for the necessities of life."[8] His longing for family must have outweighed the fear of failing to provide for them because five weeks later, Ulysses resigned his commission as an officer.

He found satisfaction in his new job. If he stuck at it, he might escape his mound of debt. Only four months after arriving in Galena, he could report, "Since leaving St. Louis I have become pretty well [initiated] into the Leather business and like it well. Our business here is prosperous and I have evry reason to hope, in a few years, to be entirely above the frowns of the world, pecuniarily."[9] Living frugally helped. He wore a battered hat and threadbare army overcoat. It might draw stares, but, as he was quoted, "I suppose people think it strange that I should wear this old army coat, but the fact is, I *had* this coat, it's made of good material, and so I thought I'd better wear it out."[10]

A stay in Galena would afford Grant space to take stock of himself and time to regroup emotionally. In the army, his psychological and physical miseries—which included a recurring toothache—left him so unnerved he used alcohol as medication. Unfortunately, one or two drinks left him reeling. He ran afoul of the crusty post commander at Ft. Humboldt, Robert C. Buchanan, who had little regard for Grant. Speculation spread down the army grapevine that Grant resigned his commission to head off a court-martial, and the rumor mill churned out chaff about his alleged weakness for drink. Even among Galenians, whispers swirled about his struggles with alcohol, but as the townsfolk learned, there was no hint that Captain Grant was anything but a stone sober citizen. The merchant Augustus Chetlain recollected that Grant kept to himself "but was highly esteemed by all who knew him. With his family, he was a regular attendant at the Methodist Episcopal church."[11] Words that aptly described him were "patient," "diligent as a clock," and "abstemious."[12] Lawyer John Shaw, a casual observer of Grant, remarked that "during all his residence in Galena his habits in this respect were, to all appearances, most exemplary, and I have never heard it hinted that while he lived there, there was the slightest lapse from perfect sobriety."[13]

Grant kept a low profile, and the only business he minded was the store: "During the eleven months that I lived in Galena . . . I had been strictly attentive to my business, and had made but few acquaintances other than customers and people engaged in the same line with myself."[14] There was one unusual exception, when he found himself at the center of a barroom altercation. Perhaps a political discussion overheated, or someone in his cups took umbrage at a remark—there was no evidence that Grant had been imbibing—and some toughs set upon him. Fortunately, Ely Parker was in town that day and passing by the saloon when he heard trouble. The burly Seneca chief burst in and helped Grant make an escape.[15]

The right topic could coax Grant out of his shell. Then the "shy and undemonstrative" Grant, who was usually "silent and taciturn to a degree,"[16] became an entertaining narrator. On business trips, he might discuss current events with the locals. "These generally knew I had been a captain in the regular army and had served through the Mexican war," Grant wrote. "Consequently, wherever I stopped at night, some of the people would come to the public-house where I was, and sit till a late hour discussing the probabilities of the future."[17] He had tales of garish San Francisco and the travails of crossing the Panama Isthmus, which would have resonated with David Sheean, who had also been on that trail of misery. His Galena acquaintances were probably most riveted by his Mexican War exploits. Years earlier at remote Ft. Vancouver, Grant regaled his comrades with these war narratives, leaving them to remark, "How clear-headed Sam Grant is in describing a battle! He seems to have the whole thing in his head."[18]

As Grant, in storytelling mode, leaned on the leather store's counter, the person most enthralled by the battle details was the store's attorney, John Rawlins, who had to be restrained from enlisting in that war by his parents. Rawlins was among a few Galenians who knew Grant as slightly more than a passing acquaintance. David Sheean thought it hardly went that far: "The only remarks I heard from Rawlins about Grant before the war were that Grant was a queer, peculiar kind of man—these remarks were made jocularly. If he was impressed with any superiority of Grant I feel very confident he would mention it to me."[19] For unknown reasons, the reserved Grant and the fiery Rawlins found points of congruence. Perhaps both saw in each other elements of special talents. It took a while before they realized an affiliation between them was evolving. In the year before his death, Rawlins reflected on that affiliation: "I looked cautiously at Grant, and under his simplicity saw the marks of power given him by nature and command. . . . He sometimes at solicitations, sat on the store counter and related incidents of Mexico . . . I got to know General Grant slowly and respectfully, and it was not till after the beginning of the war that I found out that he had any specific liking for me."[20]

⸺⸺⸺

While John Rawlins divided his attention between three-day-old Emily and his wife's delicate condition, his political spirit was pulled toward Charleston, South Carolina, where the Democratic Party's nominating convention convened. Senator Stephen Douglas appeared to have the inside track—if the party's center held and there were enough men who could put aside sectional partialities and recognize Douglas as the best choice to sustain the party. But on those scores Douglas had no luck. The Buchananites and Ultras scuttled his chances. Deep South delegations staged a convention walkout, and when the bolters were removed from the balloting arithmetic, it appeared to favor Douglas's path to the nomination. However, a resolution passed by those remaining required a successful nominee to receive the votes of two-thirds of all delegates present at the outset of the convention. Rawlins must have been incensed by reports of a deadlocked convention. After fifty-seven ballots, the sweat-soaked delegates adjourned to reconvene the next month in Baltimore. The Democrats would find no solace nor gain any traction in Baltimore; the traumatic fracture became compounded. There was more bolting—this time from Upper South and border state delegates. The Southern Rights zealots staged a rival convention in Baltimore, nominating John C. Breckinridge. The remnants of the party's mainstream met in late June to nominate Douglas. Events in Baltimore salvaged nothing for Douglas and the Democrats. It had been all over at Charleston. As one historian remarked, "In a move wholly in keeping with the suicidal predisposition of the times, many of the delegates had turned their backs on the one man who might have led them to victory in November. The old Democracy died at Charleston and the bolt that killed it was, in retrospect, the first overt act of secession by the South from the rest of America."[21]

Compared to Douglas's difficult route to the nomination, Abraham Lincoln's third ballot triumph in Chicago was a cakewalk. The Republicans caucused in a frame megastructure, the Wigwam, which accommodated thousands. With a month's head start over the Douglasites, the Republicans stitched together a grassroots organization that scheduled rallies and recruited men into marching clubs known as the Wide Awakes. During the next four months, many clubs became established in villages across northern and central Illinois; even Galena had its own.

The Wide Awake marching clubs appealed to young men fascinated with martial display. They were a paramilitary organization—members were assigned rank—trained in marching drill, clad in uniforms, caped in shiny oilcloth, and outfitted with torches or lanterns that made a soul-stirring sight during an evening procession. When not marching or singing party songs, the Wide Awakes passed out political leaflets, maintained discipline at rallies, and served as attendants for the invited speakers. The Democrats had political clubs, but they weren't as numerous as the Wide Awakes. The Douglasite clubs went by various names such as Rockford's "Douglas Invincibles," Fulton County's "Ever-Readies," and Springfield's "Douglas Rangers," with the Douglas Rangers resplendent in red jackets, black pants, and tricornered hats.[22]

In Galena, politics was customarily a source of contention, and the 1860 election featuring two favorite sons of Illinois figured to be a barnburner.

Democrats and Republicans were about evenly matched, but Democrats had gained strength from the influx of Irish and Germans and from tradesmen who feared that Republican antislavery rhetoric meant competition from free Blacks. In the larger first congressional district, however, Republicans predominated.[23] Given the tight local political situation, it was natural that any new arrival would be sounded out for his political proclivity, especially if the newcomer was a former army captain, West Point graduate, and family employee of a downtown business.

If asked about his political leaning, Grant might have looked askance, scratched his beard, and replied with a question: "Do you mean would I be voting less in support of one candidate and more in opposition to the other?" This was how he voted in the 1856 election: more a vote against the Republican Frémont than an endorsement of Buchanan, of whom the best Grant could say was that four years of Buchanan might buy time for "the passions of the people" to cool.[24] He was once partial toward the Whig Party but couldn't abide the anti-immigrant Know-Nothings. Of course, it was known that Ulysses's father and Orvil were staunch Republicans, but no one had a reading where Ulysses stood—not that nobody was trying.

William Rowley, the clerk of the circuit court in Galena and a Republican, became acquainted with Grant through a minor business transaction: a leather cover for his office desk. After Rowley thought he heard Grant speaking critically of Douglas, he tried to convince Grant that technically he had resided in town long enough to be eligible to vote. Grant demurred, probably feeling uncomfortable with stretching the truth about his residency and also relieved that he had an excuse to duck the issue. However, as the campaign heated up, both sides made overtures to secure his vote and exploit his military expertise.

⸺

By late afternoon on August 1, a huge crowd was assembling in downtown Galena. The night marked the appearance of the Galena Wide Awakes, the headliners of the evening's rally. The Wide Awakes had been drilling secretly inside their Wigwam and under the eye of their captain, jewelry shop owner John E. Smith. Other Wide Awakes included lawyer John Shaw, court clerk Rowley, and merchant Augustus Chetlain. Each man in the 240-strong company was pledged to the purpose of "securing the transcendancy and perpetuity of the Republican party, and the election of its candidates for office to all places of honor and trust in the Government."[25]

When the Wide Awakes burst from their Wigwam, the Republican faithful erupted. Resplendent in new uniforms, toting burning lanterns, and carrying banners ("Old Abe, the Giant Killer," "Lincoln and Hamlin"), they "presented a most magnificent appearance" and thrilled the five thousand onlookers with "the most magnificent torch light procession ever before witnessed in Galena." Apparently, the watchword of the day, from the perspective of the *Daily Advertiser*, a Republican organ, was *magnificent*. At the De Soto House, the Wide Awakes encircled the speakers' platform, erected out of split rails. Galena's Republican women had stitched a banner "made of white satin upon one side and red upon the other, trimmed in gold and silver braid, and edged with the finest linen lace." On one side gold letters proclaimed, "Eternal Viglance [*sic*] the price of Liberty," and the other side stated, "Galena Wide Awakes."[26] Austrian expatriate Friedrich Hassaureck sustained the cause of Republicanism in both English and German—perhaps prying away some of the German vote. Music and cheering preceded closing remarks by Congressman Washburne. With their mission having been magnificently accomplished, the Wide Awakes tramped back to the Wigwam.

The Republican rally completely upstaged the Galena Democrats. In an interview after the Civil War, Rawlins seemed still taken aback: "Some time during the campaign, John E. Smith, a soldier of the Mexican War, burst upon the town with a magnificent display of Wide-Awakes, whom he had drilled secretly. This mortified our side a good deal, and we resolved to get up a similar organization." Rawlins was a member of a committee that paid Grant a call, expecting to find him warm to their overture: "We counted on him as a Douglas Democrat, though all his brothers were Republicans." Would the captain be amenable to being elected marshal of the future Democratic marching club? Grant retreated to nonaligned ground. "He said he was beginning business," Rawlins recollected, "and should have to decline entering into politics."[27] Mexican War veteran Jasper Maltby was chosen in Grant's stead.[28]

A committee of influential Republicans also courted Grant. John C. Smith, who then ran a construction business and was later a brevet brigadier general, said Grant was offered the position of orderly sergeant in the Wide Awakes. He graciously declined: "My reason for declining is that, having held a commission as Captain in the Army of the United States, I do not think it becoming in me now to serve a citizen body, though semi-military, as its Orderly Sergeant." However, he "occasionally met with the 'wide awakes'—Republicans—in their rooms, and superintended their drill."[29]

While the rival marching clubs paraded for supremacy, Stephen Douglas was on the hustings fighting for his political life. He was in a four-way tussle: besides Lincoln and Southern Democrat Breckinridge, there was creaky John Bell heading the Constitutional Union Party ticket and hoping to attract former Whigs in Dixie. Douglas knew that he could be elected only if things broke just right: if he could maintain strength in the Great Lakes states; if there were enough voters of moderate stripe in the Deep South; if he could count on support in the Border and Middle Atlantic States; and if his health and stamina held out. He had cast aside tradition and decided to take his case for popular sovereignty directly to the voters. It was a decision borne of desperation. The cross-country travel and hours of speechifying left him hoarse, exhausted, and, some feared, close to death.

———

In this watershed election year, Rawlins received the highest honor of his political life. He was chosen as the presidential elector on the Democratic ticket for Illinois's First Congressional District. The twenty-nine-year-old Rawlins was moving up the party ladder. That summer, Rawlins boned up on history in preparation for debates against his Republican counterpart. Such debates had become customary in Illinois by 1860, and a candidate would be foolish to shirk his opponent's challenge to debate. Up and down the state, there would be dozens of minor debates, often called "joint discussions," between local personalities and politicians. Quite a few of these would pit the district's presidential electors against each other. Rawlins was eager to set the record straight on popular sovereignty and to serve as Douglas's hard-punching proxy in his own string of debates.

Rawlins drew a formidable opponent in Republican elector Allen C. Fuller —he of the luxurious beard that overlaid his cravat and the half-bald pate across which he slicked down strands of hair—a prominent lawyer in Boone County. Rawlins and Fuller agreed to meet once during September and October in each of the district's counties. Besides engaging Rawlins across northern Illinois, Fuller teamed up with gubernatorial candidate and antislavery activist, Richard Yates, to campaign across most of the state that fall on behalf of the Republican ticket. After Yates won the governor's race, he appointed Fuller adjutant general of Illinois.[30]

The first Rawlins-Fuller debate took place on September 29 at Warner's Hall in Rockford. Other discussions were to follow in short order at Freeport,

Oregon, Galena, and Mt. Carroll. Rawlins was escorted to the hall by the local Douglas Invincibles, who could provide security for him if the event got out of hand. The audiences were known to get rowdy, but the worst that happened that evening was "several of the most rampant Black Republicans tried their utmost to disturb and distract the speaker. They even went so far (be it said to their shame) as to hiss him repeatedly. But in this characteristic procedure of the hypocritical crew they were completely failed. For every time the blackies would hiss, the Democrats would cheer."[31]

Rawlins was the first to speak and allotted sixty minutes. He carefully laid out Douglas's position on popular sovereignty and showed how it was "in perfect harmony with the Fathers of our country."[32] He read excerpts from Jefferson, Madison, and Clay to corroborate his points—as Douglas had done in his dense disquisition for *Harper's Magazine* the year before. He elaborated on the argument that there was never an attempt to legislate slavery in the territories until the passage of the Missouri Compromise with its demarcation line, above which slavery was banned. The compromise, Rawlins pointed out, was regarded by Jefferson and Madison as "unwise and unjust, and dangerous to the peace and union of the country."[33]

Fuller spoke from 8:20 p.m. until 10:15, and then Rawlins rebutted until the debate concluded at 11:00. While the Rockford Band played "Hail Columbia," the crowd dispersed, satisfied that "Mr. Rawlins has won golden opinions in this neighborhood."[34] Did Rawlins come out the winner in this debate over a heavily favored Fuller? The Galena *Daily Courier* thought so, but it slanted heavily Democratic, and "the outcome of these debates depended on the viewpoint of the person or newspaper reporting them."[35] Galena Democrats surely reveled in the *Courier*'s reporting that Rawlins, within the initial sixty minutes of the debate, delivered a combination of rhetorical blows that reduced Fuller to jelly:

> At the conclusion of Mr. Rawlins' speech, Mr. Fuller came upon the stand and commenced his reply. Poor man, after listening to the preceding scathing and truthful speech, he was perfectly dumfounded.—He wandered about for the space of fifteen minutes, in every word he uttered making himself appear ridiculous in the extreme, and disgusting every republican in the room with his miserable apology for a reply. When he announced to his *friends* that he was SICK! and almost went down upon his knees praying that the meeting would be merciful enough to adjourn till half past seven in the evening.[36]

The Jo Daviess County debate was held on October 20 at the Galena Court House. Rawlins's strategy was probably similar to the ones he used in each debate. He began with the general argument that the Douglas Democrats disdained congressional intervention in the territories with regard to slavery, whereas both the Republicans and Breckinridge Democrats were in favor of it: the former wanted legislation against slavery, and the latter were for congressional intercession if the people in the territory wanted to exclude it. He followed with an historical discourse on Congress's decisions regulating slavery in the territories and the critical misjudgment, according to some, of prohibiting slavery north of the Missouri Compromise line:

> [Rawlins] then proceeded to show that the Ordinance of 1787 was a compact between Virginia and the Congress of the Confederation—that among the first acts of Congress under the Federal Constitution was one making the Ordinance conform to the Constitution, and to carry out the compact in good faith, as the Congress of the Confederation was pledged to do. He showed conclusively that the policy of the Fathers, under the present Constitution, had been to organize Territories without restricting citizens of the Slave or Free States from settling therein with any particular class of property; that up to 1820, no Territory was organized with a restriction with regard to the African Slave Trade, except in Territories covered by the Ordinance of 1787, which Congress always recognized as of binding force. The first departure from this policy was the establishment, in March, 1820, of the Missouri Compromise line, which prohibited Slavery north of 36 degrees 30 minutes. This is the first prohibition ever imposed by Congress. He then read from the letters of Jefferson and Madison to show that they were opposed to the adoption of the Missouri Compromise, and also exposed how Judge Fuller had dodged in former discussions on the subject of Jefferson's opinions on this point.[37]

When Rawlins was declared the winner in Rockford, the *Daily Courier* gloated, "The 'Coal Boy's' Grape Shot Puts the Republicans to Flight!" and added that Fuller had been "annihilated" in Galena.

Even after dispatching Fuller, Rawlins had no time to rest. More voters had to be steered into the Douglas column. With the election coming down to the final days, Rawlins made a push to get out the popular sovereignty message. He gave six more addresses throughout Jo Daviess County between October 29 and November 3. The other side was not taking anything for granted either, and the *Galena Daily Advertiser* made a last-minute plea to its readership: "We appeal to Republicans in the most earnest and urgent manner . . . to devote the succeeding thirty-six hours to the service of their country! Spend this day in preparation—Tomorrow, till the last Republican Vote that can be deposited is cast, in action."[38]

Galenians on Wednesday awoke to read the *Daily Advertiser* exulting, "We enjoy the high satisfaction of informing our readers this morning that the People yesterday elected Abraham Lincoln of Illinois to be President of the United States." Early estimates gave Lincoln a thousand-vote majority in Jo Daviess County. Elihu Washburne was reelected by over twelve thousand votes, the largest margin in his five runs for Congress.[39] An exhausted John Rawlins had fought hard for the Democratic slate, and although his party was defeated, he had emerged a prominent figure and forceful speaker among northwest Illinois Democrats. He had also earned a share of political capital, but with Republicans holding major patronage-bearing positions, it would be some time before he could reap benefits. Now, he was left watching the Republicans celebrate.

The celebrations had started on Tuesday night. Young Republicans, including Grant's brothers, stayed up waiting for the returns over the telegraph wire. Once news came in, the brothers hosted a "jollification" in the leather store with oysters and liquor for all the celebrants—except for Ulysses, who passed on the alcohol. To those present, Ulysses "seemed as much gratified as any one at the result, and from that time was regarded by his friends as a moderate republican."[40]

Galena partied with a grand illumination and fireworks. Candles and oil lamps shone from almost every window. Colored lanterns swung from porches and dotted backyard gardens. Along the levee, torches lit up the river, leaving a trail of illumination. From atop the *Advertiser* building, rockets and roman candles were set off, treating spectators to what looked like spouts of liquid fire. Cannon placed on the brow of a hill boomed frequently and deafeningly. The Wide Awakes were out in force, marching through the streets on both sides of the river, accompanied by two bands that provided a constant beat of music. After the Wide Awakes cheered the success of the Republican ticket, they fired more roman candles as an exclamation point to the evening's pyrotechnic extravaganza.[41]

But celebrations had to be tempered by the perception in the South that Lincoln's election signaled the threat of "sectional domination." Fearing subjugation by the North, "the South [was] prepared to go out of a Union which no longer afforded any guaranty for her right or any permanent sense of security, and which had brought her under the domination of a section, the designs of which, carried into legislation, would destroy her institutions, and even involve the lives of her people."[42] Preparations were underway in South

Carolina to establish itself as an independent state. Would others follow suit? Would military force be necessary to curb their rebellious actions?

During Rawlins's leather store visits, it was impossible to keep politics from spilling into business discussions. Grant's predictions were pessimistic, but given the fulminating in the South, perhaps he was realistic. By December his impression from news reports was that multiple states would secede: "I have no doubt at least five of them will do it."[43] He was also candid about the seceding states' reaction if coerced: they would fight. Rawlins shuddered to imagine such an outcome. "I could not bring my mind to contemplate this," he said after the war, "but the captain seemed to be positive, and from that day began to speak oftener of his military education, his debt therefor to the country, and talk with me upon the capacities of the North to raise troops."[44] The ballots had hardly been counted, and Grant was coolly apprising Rawlins about girding for war.

Grant set circuit court clerk Rowley straight on the matter of Southern resistance. One day Rowley downplayed the potential for conflict. "There's a great deal of bluster about the Southerners," he opined, "but I don't think there's much fight in them."

Grant, who had trained with Southerners at West Point and served with them in Mexico, knew better. He corrected Rowley, "You are mistaken; there is a good deal of bluster; that's the result of their education; but if they once get at it they will make a strong fight. You are a good deal like them in one respect—each side under-estimates the other and over-estimates itself."[45]

Shortly after Lincoln's election, the South Carolina General Assembly called for a convention to draft secession plans. It took a month for the deed to be done. John Rawlins followed the news out of Carolina with dismay and simmering anger. Secession was a traitorous affront to the Constitution, a breaking of hallowed bonds, an insult to his love for the Union. Rawlins had little love left for Charleston, where Douglas's chance for the presidency was scuttled by southern Ultras and resentful Buchananites. They could present no positive alternative to Douglas or countenance any compromise. Their intention had been to disrupt, tear down, and (in the case of the Ultras) push the nation to the brink.

Rawlins's pessimistic mood, intensified by Emily's deterioration, was news throughout town. As the signers of South Carolina's Ordinance of Secession were poised to sign that fateful sheet of parchment, the Galena *Gazette* editorialized that the situation looked hopeless: "We cannot, for ourselves, see how any compromise can be made that both sections can accept, or that would not lead to greater difficulties hereafter. . . . But, we doubt if any plan can be contrived that will be of any lasting utility."[46]

News out of South Carolina reached Galena late on December 20. Rawlins and his friend J. C. Spare had attended an Odd Fellows meeting and were walking home up Bench Street. They heard commotion from a billiard hall, with people inside shouting and expressing great excitement. Rawlins and Spare went in and learned about the ordinance's passage. They were too stunned to react, but Rawlins was churning inside. "Rawlins seemed to be very much effected [sic] by what he had heard," Spare wrote years later, "but said nothing till after we got to his office and would have said nothing then I think but a gentleman & I got into a controversy over the action of South Carolina." This sent Rawlins into a profanity-laced invective. "At first Rawlins said nothing but as we were warming up Rawlins . . . joined in taking my place. The discussion was of short duration but Rawlins['s] position was very strongly defined, and on his way home he expressed himself very freely and with much warmth."[47]

Secession left the *Gazette*'s editor feeling warm as well: "This news . . . mediates rebellion, if it be not actually the thing itself. . . . If the South Carolinians lift a hostile hand against our arsenal and forts, at or near Charleston, Buchanan should at once be brought to trial for impeachment, in refusing to take measures to defend them."[48] When that hostile hand was raised against Fort Sumter, John Rawlins galvanized Galenians into taking offensive measures.

NOTES

1. Robert W. Johannsen, ed., *The Lincoln-Douglas Debates of 1858* (New York: Oxford University Press, 1965), 88.

2. Robert W. Johannsen, *Stephen A. Douglas* (New York: Oxford University Press, 1973), 704. A treatment of the Dorr letter can be found in Johannsen, *Stephen A. Douglas*, 704–6, and in Damon Wells, *Stephen Douglas: The Last Years, 1857–1861* (Austin: University of Texas Press, 1971), 174–79.

3. Stephen A. Douglas, "The Dividing Line between Federal and Local Authority: Popular Sovereignty in the Territories," *Harper's New Monthly Magazine* 19, no. 112 (September 1859): 519–37.

4. Robert W. Johannsen, *Stephen A. Douglas*, 708.

5. U. S. Grant to J. H. Lightner, February 13, 1860, in *The Papers of Ulysses S. Grant*, ed. John Y. Simon, 1:354–55.

6. John Y. Simon, ed., *The Personal Memoirs of Julia Dent Grant (Mrs. Ulysses S. Grant)* (Carbondale: Southern Illinois University Press, 1975), 83.

7. U. S. Grant to Julia, February 2, 1854, in *The Papers of Ulysses S. Grant*, ed. John Y. Simon, 1:316.

8. U. S. Grant to Julia, March 6, 1854, in *The Papers of Ulysses S. Grant*, ed. John Y. Simon, 1:322–23.

9. U. S. Grant to Mr. Davis, August 7, 1860, in *The Papers of Ulysses S. Grant*, ed. John Y. Simon, 1:357.

10. Hamlin Garland, *Ulysses S. Grant: His Life and Character* (New York: Doubleday and McClure, 1896), 150.

11. Augustus L. Chetlain, *Recollections of Seventy Years* (Galena, IL: Gazette, 1899), 66.

12. Hamlin Garland, *Ulysses S. Grant: His Life and Character*, 151.

13. John M. Shaw, "The Life and Services of General John A. Rawlins," in *Glimpses of the Nation's Struggle*, ed. Edward D. Neill (New York: D. D. Merrill, 1893), 392.

14. U. S. Grant, *Personal Memoirs of U. S. Grant* (New York: Charles L. Webster, 1885), 1:216.

15. William H. Armstrong, *Warrior in Two Camps: Ely S. Parker Union General and Seneca Chief* (Syracuse: Syracuse University Press, 1978), 74.

16. John M. Shaw, "The Life and Services of General John A. Rawlins," 392.

17. U. S. Grant, *Personal Memoirs of U. S. Grant*, 1:222.

18. Albert D. Richardson, *A Personal History of Ulysses S. Grant* (Boston: D. L. Guernsey, 1885), 132.

19. David Sheean to James H. Wilson, December 16, 1884, Mississippi State University Libraries, Ulysses S. Grant Collection, James Harrison Wilson Correspondence File, S(1), Box 14, Series 2.

20. "Interview with John A. Rawlins," *The United States Army and Navy Journal and Gazette of the Regular and Volunteer Forces* (September 12, 1868), 53.

21. Damon Wells, *Stephen Douglas: The Last Years, 1857–1861*, 231.

22. Jon Grinspan, "Young Men for Far: The Wide Awakes and Lincoln's 1860 Presidential Campaign," *Journal of American History* 96, no. 2 (2009): 357–78; H. Preston James, "Political Pageantry in the Campaign of 1860 in Illinois," *Abraham Lincoln Quarterly* 4, no. 7 (1947): 313–46.

23. Kenneth N. Owens, *Galena, Grant, and the Fortunes of War: A History of Galena during the Civil War* (DeKalb: Northern Illinois University, 1963), 23, 30.

24. U. S. Grant, *Personal Memoirs of U. S. Grant*, 1:215.

25. *Galena Daily Advertiser*, Galena, IL, August 2, 1860.

26. Ibid.

27. "How Grant Got to Know Rawlins," interview with John A. Rawlins, *The United States Army and Navy Journal and Gazette of the Regular and Volunteer Forces* 6 (September 12, 1868): 53.

28. Norman C. Delaney, *The Maltby Brothers' Civil War* (College Station: Texas A&M University Press, 2013), 9–10.

29. John C. Smith, "Personal Recollections of General Ulysses S. Grant," before U. S. Grant Post No. 28, Dept. of Illinois, Grand Army of the Republic, February 11, 1904, 7.

30. *Belvidere Illustrated: Historical, Descriptive and Biographical* (Belvidere, IL: Daily Republican, 1896), 70–77; H. Preston James, "Political Pageantry in the Campaign of 1860 in Illinois," 344.

31. *Daily Courier*, Galena, IL, October 5, 1860; excerpted from a story about the Rawlins-Fuller debate that ran in the Chicago *Times and Herald*.

32. Ibid.

33. *Daily Courier*, Galena, IL, October 11, 1860; excerpted from a story about the Rawlins-Fuller discussion that ran in the Rockford *Standard*.

34. *Daily Courier*, Galena, IL, October 5, 1860.

35. H. Preston James, "Political Pageantry in the Campaign of 1860 in Illinois," 344.

36. *Daily Courier*, Galena, IL, October 5, 1860.

37. *Daily Courier*, Galena, IL, October 22, 1860.

38. *Galena Daily Advertiser*, November 5, 1860.

39. *Galena Daily Advertiser*, November 7, 1860; Gaillard Hunt, *Israel, Elihu and Cadwallader Washburn: A Chapter in American Biography* (New York: MacMillan, 1925), 173.

40. Albert D. Richardson, *A Personal History of Ulysses S. Grant*, 167. Grant may have appeared gratified, but he later revealed that if he had been eligible, he would have felt "compelled" to vote for Douglas; see U. S. Grant, *Personal Memoirs of U. S. Grant*, 1:216.

41. *Weekly Northwestern Gazette*, November 13, 1860.

42. Edward A. Pollard, *The Lost Cause* (New York: E. B. Treat, 1867), 80.

43. U. S. Grant to unknown addressee, sometime in December 1860, in *The Papers of Ulysses S. Grant*, ed. John Y. Simon, 1:359.

44. "How Grant Got to Know Rawlins," interview with John A. Rawlins, *The United States Army and Navy Journal and Gazette of the Regular and Volunteer Forces* 6 (September 12, 1868): 53.

45. Albert D. Richardson, *A Personal History of Ulysses S. Grant*, 168.

46. *Weekly Northwestern Gazette*, December 17, 1860.

47. J. C. Spare to "Friend [John] Beadle," March 29, 1899, Abraham Lincoln Presidential Library, SC 1442.

48. *Weekly Northwestern Gazette*, December 24, 1860.

6

"We Will Stand by the Flag of Our Country, and Appeal to the God of Battles!"

In rapid order, six states—Mississippi, Florida, Alabama, Georgia, Louisiana, and Texas—followed South Carolina out of the Union. By the end of February 1861, the scaffolding of a Confederate government had been erected at Montgomery, Alabama. Whether the sections of the fractured country resorted to hostilities hinged on events unfolding in the harbor of Charleston, South Carolina. There inside Fort Sumter, a small garrison under Major Robert Anderson was resisting capitulation to the Confederate commander, Brigadier General P. G. T. Beauregard. Years earlier, Anderson had served during the war against Black Hawk and had mustered in Abraham Lincoln as a private in a company of rangers after his tenure as a militia captain had expired.

With supplies dwindling, surrender appeared imminent, but Confederate authorities discerned prevarication in Anderson's communications with them, perhaps to allow a nearby relief fleet to resupply him. Unwilling to wait out Anderson, Beauregard began bombarding Sumter into submission. The shelling started early morning on April 12 and lasted for almost a day and a half. Hot shot set the fort ablaze, and with the defenders down to their last barrels of gunpowder, Anderson realized further resistance was futile. Dejected, he watched as Old Glory was lowered and the Confederate and Palmetto flags were hoisted above Sumter's ramparts.[1]

Lincoln reacted swiftly to the aggression. A day after Sumter fell, he called for seventy-five thousand state militia to serve ninety days, enough time needed, most believed, to suppress the rebellion. That same day, April 15, Galena's Republican *Weekly Northwestern Gazette* urged the nation to take defensive military measures: "Civil War, in its most ferocious aspect, has been forced upon the United States. It has not been the result of any sudden outburst of passion ... but of a cool and deliberate purpose carefully elaborated in all its parts. .... Self defence is the sacred duty of a nation. .... A war has been commenced on us, the most shameful in its object of any that disgraced civilized man." Reaction among Democrats was also swift but mixed. Some cautioned against taking precipitous action against the departed states. Others decried Lincoln's call for volunteers as an unconstitutional usurpation of power. There were those allied with Stephen Douglas, who also on April 15 stated, "We must fight for our country and forget our differences. There can be but two parties—the party of patriots and the party of traitors. We belong to the first."[2]

—◦◦◦—

Sumter's surrender stunned the citizens of Galena, who were not quite sure what to do except to gesture patriotically by flying flags. Lincoln's call for volunteers instilled in everyone a sense of purpose and caused them to deliberate how best to respond. A meeting was hastily arranged at the Galena courthouse for April 16, a Tuesday. As Ulysses Grant recalled, "As soon as the news of the call for volunteers reached Galena, posters were stuck up calling for a meeting of the citizens at the court-house in the evening. Business ceased entirely; all was excitement."[3] The Wide Awakes were summoned to lead the march to the courthouse.

Who knew what political scuffling to expect when Galena's Republicans and Democrats faced off on the issue? One optimistic sign was that in the crush of citizens squeezing into the courthouse was the quintet of John C. Smith, John Spare, Jasper Maltby, William Rowley, and John Rawlins. That this amalgam of Democrats and Republicans arrived in a show of solidarity portended that bipartisanship might win out. As Rawlins elbowed his way in, someone, perhaps a political crony, tugged his sleeve and warned him not to enter the courtroom where the meeting would be held: "John, you don't want to go up there and talk to that crowd; it is a ------- Black Republican meeting." Rawlins, his face contorted into a glower, pulled away and retorted, "I am going to the court room, and I intend to make a speech. We are going to have a great war, and in time of war there are no Democrats or Republicans; there can be but two parties now, one of patriots and the other of traitors."[4] Rawlins's words echoed Douglas's from the day before.

After Charles Hempstead, the dean of Galena's bar, gaveled the meeting to order, he moved that Mayor Robert Brand assume the chair. As Brand sidled his way to the front, a murmur rippled through the courtroom that bespoke anticipation and apprehension: Hempstead had turned the gavel over to a "stanch Democrat." Brand was also a Southerner, born in New Orleans and educated at Kentucky's Transylvania College. There, he was a classmate with John Breckinridge, the Southern Democrats' choice over Douglas.[5]

Aware of the gravity of the moment, Brand wanted his remarks to set the proper tone. He chose a conciliatory middle ground, saying in part, "I am in favor of any honorable compromise that will again unite our whole country. I am in favor of sustaining the President so long as his efforts are for the peace and harmony of our country.... Yet I am opposed to warring on any portion of our beloved country, if a compromise can be effected."[6] He was not prepared for the furor that erupted.

Leading the verbal assault was the First District's congressman, Republican Elihu Washburne, Hempstead's law partner and a granite-hewn New Englander. Washburne sprang from his chair, his voice ringing out in protest: "Mr. Chairman, any man who will try to stir party prejudices at such a time as this, is a traitor!"[7] Shouts and applause sustained Washburne as he thundered that he would never submit to the idea that when "when our flag was assailed by traitors and conspirators, that the government should be thus dealt with"—that is, with compromise and adjustments as Brand had just advised.[8]

When Washburne spoke, men listened. As some Deep South congressmen had learned firsthand, he was capable of using his fists to uphold his convictions. Proof of that was the incident—still fresh in the minds of his constituents—that occurred on the US House floor early on February 3, 1858. While debate raged about the admission of Kansas under the Lecompton Constitution, Galusha Grow of Pennsylvania crossed to the Democratic side of the House to confer with a colleague. Lawrence Keitt, a South Carolinian fire-eater, confronted Grow and told him he had no business there. After an exchange of insults, Keitt grabbed Grow and hissed, "You are a d----d black, Republican puppy!"

Struggling to loose himself, Grow countered, "No nigger driver shall crack his whip over me." As Grow and Keitt grappled, Washburne waded into the fracas, doing such damage that afterward it was said, "Mr. Washburne, of Illinois, was conspicuous among the Republicans dealing heavy blows." Hulking William Barksdale of Mississippi, thinking that Elihu had slugged him, retaliated by catching him in a suffocating clinch. Just then Elihu's younger brother, Cadwallader Washburn,[9] a representative from Wisconsin, came to

his rescue and took a roundhouse swing at Barksdale that knocked off his tou-
pee. Barksdale indignantly retrieved his hairpiece and slapped it on—back-
side first. Barksdale was such a ridiculous sight, that the melee abruptly ended
with everyone bent over laughing.[10]

After denouncing Brand's introductory remarks, Washburne moved to
have him ousted as chair. Sensing that the situation was about to disintegrate,
former mayor Frederick Stahl pleaded for harmony and chided the throng
for its partisan display. After the subdued Washburne withdrew his motion,
he presented resolutions that included forming two companies immediately
in case the governor called for troops and pledging "that having lived under
the Stars and Stripes, by the blessing of God we propose to die under them."
The resolutions, after sustained cheering and applause, were unanimously
adopted.[11]

Washburne was barely seated before the crowd began a rhythmic chant:
"Rawlins! Rawlins!" The Republican had had his say, and now Galena's leading Democrat should have his. He threaded his way up to the platform where
a tiny island of space was reserved for the speakers. He sized up his audience
as they took measure of him. They saw a lithe lawyer with raven-black hair
and pale face alternating between expressions of fury and determination.
John Rawlins was about to give the speech that not hell, high water, or hostile
"Black Republicans" could prevent.

Rawlins started slowly. His full-bodied voice enveloped the hall. He started
with a history lesson. Listeners who were in this room six months before recollected how Rawlins, as a self-assured debater, used a similar approach when
confronting Allen Fuller. Now, he harkened the audience back to the sacrifices
made by the patriots of the Revolution and the blood they had shed to defend
their country. He reminded everyone about the American way: minority factions yield peaceably to the opinion of the majority—even on contentious issues like the Missouri Compromise and Kansas-Nebraska Act.

He spoke for forty-five minutes. The great speech seemed to build on itself,
to gather momentum, and the audience was carried along. Rawlins was reaching a crescendo. Now was no time for partisanship. The moment required una-
nimity. Leaning into the audience, Rawlins's voice quavered with emotion. "I
have been a democrat all my life; but this is no longer a question of politics. It
is simply country or no country. I have favored every honorable compromise;
but the day for compromise is passed." He had his listeners in an emotional
clinch. In anticipation of a rousing conclusion, many began to lift themselves

from their chairs. "Only one course is left for us," he intoned, pausing briefly for effect. "We will stand by the flag of our country, and appeal to the God of battles!"[12] That brought them all to their feet. They cheered for Rawlins. They cheered for the Union, for the flag, and for Major Robert Anderson. It was the night when "the Court House rang with such a tempest of applause as was never before heard within its walls."[13]

—◦◦◦—

Other speakers followed to the platform, men like Isaac Stevens, Rawlins's mentor, and former postmaster and Democrat Bushrod Howard. But their words hardly registered. The audience still buzzed about Rawlins's electrifying speech. The meeting closed with more cheering and a plan to reconvene on the evening of April 18 to recruit a company of volunteers. Strangely, no one thought to take names of recruits at the meeting just ended, with patriotic fervor sky-high.

Ulysses Grant was present but in low profile, just like he had comported himself during his year in Galena. Rawlins handled the leather store's legal matters, but beyond that role, he and Grant were merely acquaintances and hardly equals on the scale of local renown. Something in Rawlins's message resonated with Grant, perhaps providing the words for the feelings that secession had aroused in him. Orvil also attended, and they left the courthouse together. They weaved wordlessly past knots of other men still animated by the proceedings, with Ulysses lost in thought. Suddenly, their silence was broken when Ulysses burst forth with a firm decision. "I think," he announced to Orvil, "I ought to go into the service." The decision seemed to represent the point at which his stream of thought had just arrived.

Orvil registered no surprise. "I think so, too," he replied. "Go, if you like, and I will stay home and attend to the store."[14]

If Grant teetered on the edge of rejoining the army, Rawlins's speech could have nudged him over. This matches what Grant later told Rawlins's biographer General James Wilson: "that it had stirred his [Grant's] patriotism and rekindled his military ardor."[15] Evidence for that is also in a letter Grant wrote to his father soon after the speech in which he expressed an obligation to repay the government: "We are now in the midst of trying times when evry [sic] one must be for or against his country, and show his colors too, by his every act. Having been educated for such an emergency, at the expense of the Government, I feel that it has upon me superior claims, such claims as no ordinary motives of self-interest can surmount."[16] In truth, the deftly worded letter also served as Grant's exit strategy from the tedium of working in his father's store.

Years later, Rawlins's former law partner, David Sheean, shared with Wilson a collection of Rawlins's letters and newspaper clippings. One topic Sheean researched was the impact of Rawlins's speech on Grant. Sheean was not aware of any, but he corresponded with a bookkeeper employed in 1861 in the leather store who might know the answer. The bookkeeper responded, "John A. Rawlins['s] speech did not change his, Grant's, views at all as he was an ultra Union man from the start, but their acquaintance commenced from that date and Rawlins'[s] speech endorsed Grant's sentiments so strongly that without doubt it had considerable to do with their further relations."[17] Not only did the speech launch their relationship, but consider how similarly both men had compressed the complexity of the historical moment into an understandable dichotomy: Rawlins boiled the crux of the matter down to, "It is simply country or no country." Grant, only days later, summed up the situation in like fashion: "There are but two parties now, Traitors & Patriots and I want hereafter to be ranked with the latter, and I trust, the stronger party."[18] Moreover, when Rawlins cancelled politics out of the present debate ("I have been a democrat all my life; but this is no longer a question of politics"), Grant echoed this sentiment in a letter to his "secesh" father-in-law, saying, "But now all party distinctions should be lost sight of and evry [sic] true patriot be for maintaining the integrity of the old *Stars & Stripes*, the Constitution and the Union."[19] In sum, the relationship was facilitated by the two men sharing the same emotional frequency in response to the crisis facing their country and by sharing a similar opinion regarding the response now required of them.

———∽∾∾∼———

On the evening of April 18, an even larger crowd jammed into the courthouse for the raising of the first company of ninety-day volunteers. It was likely because of Congressman Washburne that a flabbergasted Ulysses S. Grant found himself summoned to below the judge's desk at the front of the court room to serve as the meeting's chair.[20] His inexperience speaking before audiences was readily apparent. His recruiting pep talk sounded more like dissuasion: "Before calling upon you to become volunteers, I wish to state just what will be required of you. First of all, unquestioning obedience to your superior officers. The army is not a picnicking party, nor is it an excursion. You will have hard fare. You may be obliged to sleep on the ground after long marches in the rain and snow. Many of the orders of your superiors will seem to you unjust, and yet they must be borne. If an injustice is really done you, however, there are courts martial, where your wrongs can be investigated and offenders punished."[21] Realizing that his audience was uneducated about military organizations, he added facts about the size of a typical company and regiment, the duties of the unit's officers and men, and what kind of pay to expect. When he closed with his own pledge to reenlist, that gave many incentive enough to sign the roster.

Washburne followed by lobbing derogatory remarks at the rebels, scoffing that the old women of the North could whip the Southerners with broomsticks. But the throng wanted to hear Rawlins and called his name. Despite repeated urging, he didn't respond. Jasper Maltby and John Spare appealed to Rawlins, but he still declined. Spare pleaded to Rawlins's sense of duty, claiming that he owed it to his friends and the citizens of Galena. Rawlins shook his head, explaining, "My wife is sick and I can[']t leave her and go in the army." Spare understood: "we all know the circumstances, John, and you can allude to it in such a way that you will be rel[ie]ved from embarrassment and friends and the whole audience will appreciate your position and honor you the more."

From the center of the courtroom, Rawlins made a brief and poignant testimonial. He spoke about the danger facing the nation, and the duty owed it by every able-bodied man. However, his responsibility was with his grievously ill wife. "I cannot stand up here before you, young men and say 'go your country calls, go do your duty.' My friends all know that my young wife is sick, with little or no hope of being better. I cannot go and leave her. If she were the rosy cheek girl she was when I married her, with her consent, I would go, and I know she would give it." If Rawlins's worry was that he'd be seen as a shirker, it dissolved under a volley of applause.[22]

Augustus Chetlain was the first to volunteer, and he was followed by two dozen more. Rawlins suggested preserving the list of enlistees' autographs for its historical value. Before adjourning, it was decided that recruitment teams should fan out the next day, April 19, to cover Dunleith (East Dubuque), Galena, and Hanover, located about sixteen miles south of Galena. Rawlins, Rowley, and Grant, along with Orvil, agreed to ride down to Hanover.

—◊◊◊—

The Hanover recruitment meeting was held in a schoolhouse. Rawlins gave a speech, as did Grant, who used a straightforward approach: "I don't know any thing about making speeches; that is not my line; but we are forming a company in Galena, and mean to do what we can for putting down the rebellion. If any of you feel like enlisting, I will give you all the information and help I can." When the meeting ended at 11:00 p.m., a dozen recruits had been signed up. While riding back to Galena, the men discussed what secession might mean for the country's fate. Rowley held a sanguine opinion about quashing the rebellion: "I guess the seventy-five thousand troops the President has called for will stop all the row." Grant was more cautious. "I think this is a bigger thing than you suppose. Those fellows mean to fight, and Uncle Sam has a heavy job on his hands." And he told his companions, just as he had said to his father, "If I am needed I shall go."[23]

Rawlins, trying to lighten the mood, joked, "Captain Grant, suppose we get up a company for the war; you shall be captain, and Rowley and I will toss up to see which shall be first lieutenant and which second." Grant agreed that he had the qualifications to command a company—he didn't tell them he was over-qualified to lead one.[24]

On April 22, the company, christened the Jo Daviess Guards, was capped at 103 men and officers, with Chetlain elected captain. Grant had graciously declined the captaincy, figuring his experience and West Point education suited him for a colonelcy and regimental command. A telegram was sent to Governor Yates formally offering the Guards to the service of the State. Yates gladly accepted and, under the urgent circumstances, pleaded to get them uniformed and delivered to Springfield as soon as possible.

A large quantity of suitable fabric was discovered, enough to outfit the recruits in handsome blue frock coats and dark gray trousers with blue cords. Every available tailor cut out the pieces of cloth, and the women of Galena got stitching furiously. With Grant supervising, the uniforms were finished in just three days. Grant also volunteered to give some of the recruits rudimentary drill instruction on Congressman Washburne's front lawn. This seemed appropriate, given the heavy Republican makeup of the Guards.[25]

There was no time to alter the uniforms, because the company was to entrain for Springfield on the twenty-fifth. There, the Jo Daviess Guards would become Company F of the Twelfth Illinois, a ninety-day regiment. Everyone turned out this Wednesday to see their men off to war. Two brass bands and four fire companies led the procession to the Illinois Central station. Grant marched along, but in the rear guard. There was something different, a bounce of vitality, in his stride and carriage. Rawlins noticed it right off. The old "Captain"

Sam Grant looked suddenly energized. "He dropped a stoop-shouldered way he had of walking," Rawlins said, "and set his hat forward on his forehead in a less careless fashion." Rawlins attributed Grant's sharper bearing to the unfolding military crisis: that because of it, "A larger career had opened before him." *Larger* in this instance is a relative term—Grant was not fantasizing about wearing a brigadier's star—for as Rawlins could determine, Grant to this point "never seemed to have an ambition above regimental rank."[26]

Grant planned to accompany the Guards to Springfield and stay a few days at Washburne's behest to see they got fed and organized. And who knew but that an opportunity might arise for a West Point–trained, Mexican War–tested former infantry captain while at the state capital?

At the station, the men were given a rousing send-off punctuated by speeches and prayers and the presentation of a silk flag. Rawlins watched as Grant hoisted his carpetbag onto the railcar and, before swinging aboard, shouted, "Rawlins, if I see anything that will suit you, I'll send you word."

"Do, Captain!" Rawlins replied with a gush of enthusiasm that perhaps surprised him. Who knew, but that there might even be opportunity for a die-hard Democrat and erstwhile charcoal burner?[27] With all safely aboard, the train chugged off "amid the huzzas, waving of hats and handkerchiefs and the tearful farewell of the great crowd."[28]

—⁂—

April found Rawlins finalizing plans to take Emily to her parents' home in Goshen, where a climate change might restore her health.[29] Tragically, her consumption had progressed to its final stage. No longer could any diminution of symptoms be considered cause for optimism. This had become a deathwatch. Now Emily's eyes peered at John and the children as from the bottom of a lead mine, her face pinched by the impoverishment of her physical reserves. The weaker Emily got, the heavier became the burden on John's meager support system. Being helpless against Emily's pain and sustaining her through bloody coughing fits was more than Uncle Bradner's wife, Mary, could possibly manage alone. And the children—James, Jennie, and Emily—needed some buffer against the trauma of witnessing their mother's wraithlike transfiguration.

Spring 1861 was the most difficult period thus far of Rawlins's life. He would have been strapped to set aside even a moment to rehearse how he might manage as a widower caring for three young children. With Emily transported to

Goshen, John returned to Galena to see to his law practice. He also partook in one noteworthy event by serving as the speaker at Galena's memorial service for Stephen Douglas, who had died on June 3. Two days later, with city bells tolling, a procession of fire companies, city supervisors, and mourners all led by John E. Smith formed before the De Soto House. It was appropriate that Rawlins was chosen to deliver the eulogy, which in tone and gravity was deemed "eloquent."[30]

During the courthouse and recruiting meetings following Sumter's surrender, Rawlins had been conflicted about choosing between service to his country and devotion to Emily. However, as Emily's end drew closer, John seemed freer to cast his lot with the military. He had been intrigued by Grant's offer to consider him for some fitting position. As the weather warmed, Rawlins assisted recruiting men for a regiment being organized in the upper counties of Illinois by John E. Smith, with Maltby's help. The regiment, mustered in as the Forty-Fifth Illinois, would later achieve an enviable reputation as the Lead Mine Regiment. Smith was commissioned as a colonel on July 23, 1861, and Maltby made lieutenant colonel. Rawlins received consideration as the regiment's major, but he bowed out when another opportunity arose.[31]

—⁓—

On August 5, 1861, the United States Senate confirmed Ulysses S. Grant as brigadier general to rank from May 17.[32] Two days later, Grant wrote to Rawlins at Galena inviting him to accept a position that might suit him.[33] In an August 10 letter to Julia while he was at his district headquarters at Ironton, Missouri, Ulysses stated, "I have envited [sic] Mr. Rollins of Galena to accept a place on my Staff. I wish you would tell Orvil to say to him that I would like to have him come as soon as possible if he accepts the position."[34] Grant had two aide-de-camp positions to fill. He made his first offer to Rawlins, and on August 11 he appointed First Lieutenant Clark B. Lagow, a merchant from Palestine, Illinois, to the other.[35]

Now Rawlins had two possibilities to consider. Because it was his intention to enlist at some point, it became a matter of which choice was preferable. He consulted David Sheean, and both agreed it was more advantageous to serve as Grant's staff officer than as a line officer under John E. Smith.[36] An excited Rawlins jumped at Grant's offer. From Galena, on August 12 he wrote:

> Your letter bearing date St. Louis, Missouri, August 7th, A. D. 1861, tendering
> me the position of aid-de-camp on your staff is before me. It is a compliment

unexpected; but fully appreciating your kindness and friendship for me, and believing from your long experience in and knowledge of the military service, and its duties, you would not have offered me the position were you not satisfied it is one I could fill, gladly and with pleasure I accept it and whatever the duties and responsibilities devolved upon me by virtue of the same, I will with the help of God discharge them to the best of my ability.[37]

The offer quickly became even more advantageous. Grant's acting assistant adjutant general, Montague Hasie, left the staff, opening a higher-ranking position for Rawlins. On August 30, Rawlins was officially appointed captain and assistant adjutant general to Grant.[38]

From all of Grant's available choices, he first tapped the volatile young attorney who enthralled with his passionate speeches and moved audiences with his powerful emotional appeals. Rawlins was a man Grant felt drawn to, and Rawlins could say the same about Grant. Rawlins was flattered by the offer and seemed to bank on Grant's "long experience" and "knowledge of the military service" because Rawlins understood he knew nothing about military affairs. It had to be to Rawlins's advantage that he arrived on the coattails of a formally trained officer, as opposed to being on the staff of a politician-general who was also naïve about military affairs.

Before Rawlins could plan to join Grant in Missouri, word reached him in Galena that Emily was failing rapidly. He left on the evening of August 19, and on arriving at his in-laws' home on the evening of the twenty-first, he "found Emily very low . . . and confined to her bed." In a sorrowful letter to Aunt Mary, John lamented, "Her lamp of life is nearly gone out. It scarcely seems possible that one so calm, so amiable, so gentle, so lovely and so beautiful, whose stay on earth is so much needed and desired should so young be cut down by death."[39] He was able to spend over a week with her before she passed at age twenty-eight on August 30.[40]

Near the end, Emily expressed a fear that whoever became John's next wife would not be kind toward the children. To prevent that, at some point he approached Emily's sister, Sarah, with the suggestion of marriage, one that Rawlins thought "was not entirely displeasing to her." However, he was even more lukewarm about the idea than she and backed off because he could not summon enough affection for her.[41]

While at his in-laws' home, Rawlins received a forwarded letter from Galena. It was from Grant, indicating his staffing needs had changed. "I am entitled to a captain and acting adjutant general," he said. "I guess you had better come take it." If Rawlins had had any misgiving about the wisdom of forego-ing joining Smith's regiment as a major, Grant's latest offer sealed the deal, especially given Rawlins's doubts about his "capacity to be independently use-ful" and the fact that he was "so inexperienced." [42]

Now it became a race to return to Illinois in order to decide what to do about the children, the law practice, and his house on Hill Street.[43] There was also a matter of his personal debt, between three and four thousand dollars. It would take him almost three years of penny-pinching to pay it off.[44] Moreover, he had no time to mourn for Emily or to feel sorry for himself, so compelling seemed the urgency of the crisis facing Unionists in Missouri. From Galena, he would hightail it down to Cairo at the southernmost tip of Illinois and hook up with Grant there.

Grant was pleased as punch about the men he chose to round out his staff. He crowed to his father, "I have filled all the places on my Staff and, flatter my-self, with deserving men. Mr. J. A. Rawlins of Galena is to be my Adj't. Gen. Mr. Lagow of the Regt. I was formerly Colonel of and Mr. Hillyer of St. Louis, Aides. They are all able men, from five to ten years younger than myself."[45] On August 29, Grant formally requested Lorenzo Thomas, adjutant general of the army, to confirm his appointments to Rawlins and Hillyer.[46]

Two days after requesting Rawlins's appointment, Grant wrote a newsy let-ter to Julia in which he commented about how his staff was taking shape. "Mr. Hillyer is with me. When I get Dr. Sharp and Mr. Rawlins I will have a clever set about me."[47] Grant had only earlier that day appointed his brother-in-law, Dr. Alexander Sharp, to his staff as brigade surgeon—an appointment that subsequently was not confirmed by Adjutant General Thomas.[48] Grant was constructing a staff of men with whom he was familiar and around whom he felt at ease. Rawlins's special standing in Grant's estimation was already emerging, as he indicated to Julia in this same letter: "Tell the friends of Mr. Rawlins that I have never had an idea of filling his place with anyone els[e]. I have received four or five letters from different friends of his on the subject."

At this moment, Grant was grappling with significant military, adminis-trative, and staffing challenges. He had just received some "important special instructions" assigning him to command the District of Southeast Missouri, a sketchily drawn geographic region that also included southern Illinois and, later, parts of western Kentucky. Moreover, even as his scope of duties grew, he still had the services of but one available staff officer, Clark Lagow, causing Grant himself to do "all the detail work usually performed by an adjutant general."[49] Anxious for help to arrive, Grant inquired of Julia regarding Rawlins's whereabouts: "Has Mr. Rawlins got back to Galena? I hear nothing of him."[50] But what occupied more of Grant's attention and patience was a combined military expedition he now commanded, coordinating with other troops under Brigadier General Benjamin Prentiss, to capture Meriwether "Jeff" Thompson, a brigadier general of the Missouri State Guard.

Known as the "Swamp Fox of the Confederacy," Thompson led a mobile assortment of semi-irregular foot soldiers and cavalry in the swamps of southeast Missouri and northeast Arkansas. The colorful Thompson was "famous for his eccentricities, his theatrical air, and his appreciation of strong liquor."[51] Grant's attention should have been focused on Thompson, but his patience was being tried by Prentiss, who was squabbling over who held higher rank; technically, Grant outranked Prentiss. However, because Prentiss balked at responding to Grant's orders, the Swamp Fox eluded capture. Grant threatened Prentiss with arrest; Prentiss, in a snit, tendered his resignation. Things got smoothed out in fair order as Grant took the high-minded step of writing Prentiss, "I have no personal feeling . . . [and] am perfectly willing to see the charges quashed and the whole matter buryed [sic] in oblivion."[52]

In the immediate aftermath of this botched expedition against Thompson, Grant expressed to Washburne his commitment to Rawlins: "In regard to the appointment of Mr. Rawlins I never had an idea of withdrawing it so long as he felt disposed to accept no matter how long his absence. Mr. Rawlins was the first one I decided upon for a place with me and I very much regret that family affliction has kept him away so long." Then to provide an educational context for the events of the last few days, he remarked to Washburne, "The past would have been a good s[c]hool of instruction for him in his new duties."[53] Too bad, Grant was saying, that his greenhorn assistant adjutant had not been on hand for lessons in how to organize a military expedition and deal with an obdurate subordinate.

Thankfully, Grant did not have much longer to wait for his staff to come together. On September 8, he issued from his district headquarters at Cairo General Orders No. 4, announcing the appointments of Rawlins as captain and assistant adjutant general, Lagow as captain and aide-de-camp, and Dr. James Simons as medical director. One week later, on September 15, John Rawlins arrived.[54]

NOTES

1. Samuel W. Crawford, *The Genesis of the Civil War: The Story of Sumter 1860–1861* (New York: Charles L. Webster, 1887), 443.

2. John W. Forney, *Anecdotes of Public Men* (New York: Harper and Brothers, 1873), 225.

3. U. S. Grant, *Personal Memoirs of U. S. Grant* (New York: Charles L. Webster, 1885), 1:230–31.

4. John C. Smith, February 11, 1904, *Personal Recollections of General Ulysses S. Grant,* address before U. S. Grant Post, No. 28, G.A.R., 8.

5. *Portrait and Biographical Album of Jo Daviess County, Illinois* (Chicago: Chapman Brothers, 1889), 747.

6. *Weekly Northwestern Gazette,* Galena, IL, April 23, 1861.

7. Albert D. Richardson, *A Personal History of Ulysses S. Grant* (Boston: D. L. Guernsey, 1885), 170.

8. *Galena Daily Advertiser,* April 17, 1861.

9. As a young man, Elihu added *e* to his surname to make it consistent with the spelling used in England; Gaillard Hunt *Israel, Elihu, and Cadwallader Washburn: A Chapter in American Biography* (New York: Macmillan, 1925), 155.

10. Galusha A. Grow, "The Last Days of the Duello in Congress," *Saturday Evening Post,* June 23, 1900, 1194–95; *The New York Times,* February 6, 1858.

11. *Weekly Northwestern Gazette,* Galena, IL, April 23, 1861.

12. Albert D. Richardson, *A Personal History of Ulysses S. Grant,* 171.

13. *Galena Daily Advertiser,* April 17, 1861.

14. Albert D. Richardson, *A Personal History of Ulysses S. Grant,* 171.

15. James H. Wilson, *The Life of John A. Rawlins* (New York: Neale, 1916), 49.

16. Ulysses S. Grant to Jesse Root Grant, April 21, 1861, in *The Papers of Ulysses S. Grant,* ed. John Y. Simon (Carbondale: Southern Illinois University Press, 1969), 2:6.

17. David Sheean to J. H. Wilson, January 10, 1885, James Harrison Wilson Correspondence File, S (1), Box 14, Series 2, Ulysses S. Grant Presidential Library, Mississippi State University Libraries.

18. Ulysses S. Grant to Jesse Root Grant, April 21, 1861, in *The Papers of Ulysses S. Grant,* ed. John Y. Simon, 2:6.

19. Ulysses S. Grant to Frederick Dent, April 19, 1861, in *The Papers of Ulysses S. Grant,* ed. John Y. Simon, 2:3.

20. See John Y. Simon, ed., *The Papers of Ulysses S. Grant,* 2:7n1.

21. Hamlin Garland, *Ulysses S. Grant: His Life and Character* (New York: Doubleday and McClure, 1898), 157–58.

22. J. C. Spare to "Friend" [John] Beadle, March 29, 1899, Abraham Lincoln Presidential Library, Spare Folder SC 1442.

23. Albert D. Richardson, *A Personal History of Ulysses S. Grant,* 173.

24. Ibid.

25. The county's second company of recruits, the cleverly named Anti-BeaureGards, was formed just days after the Jo Daviess Guards. It was mostly Democratic in makeup and was assembled by Bushrod Howard, who was elected captain. The Anti-BeaureGards became part of the Nineteenth Illinois. During the evening of September 17, 1861, the

regiment was aboard two trains heading to Cincinnati when a bridge gave out, causing one train to crash. Captain Howard and seventeen men were killed. Dozens were injured. Mayor Brand was charged with proceeding to Cincinnati to return the bodies to Galena. See *History of Jo Daviess County*, 413.

26. "How Grant Got to Know Rawlins," interview with John A. Rawlins, *The United States Army and Navy Journal and Gazette of the Regular and Volunteer Forces* 6 (September 12, 1868): 53.

27. Ibid.

28. Augustus L. Chetlain, *Recollections of Seventy Years* (Galena, IL: Gazette, 1899), 73.

29. *Galena Daily Gazette*, September 9, 1861.

30. *Daily Advertiser*, Galena, IL, June 6, 1861.

31. "How Grant Got to Know Rawlins," interview with John A. Rawlins, 53.

32. John H. Eicher and David J. Eicher, *Civil War High Commands* (Stanford: Stanford University Press, 2002), 722.

33. That August 7, 1861, letter from Grant to Rawlins has never been found. See John Y. Simon, ed., *The Papers of Ulysses S. Grant*, 2:97n5.

34. Ulysses S. Grant to Julia Dent Grant, August 10, 1861, in *The Papers of Ulysses S. Grant*, ed. John Y. Simon, 2:96.

35. Grant to John C. Kelton, August 11, 1861, in *The Papers of Ulysses S. Grant*, ed. John Y. Simon, 2:98. Clark Lagow was then an officer in the Twenty-First Illinois, the regiment commanded by Grant before he became brigadier general. Grant wanted to appoint someone to his military district staff from his old regiment. Grant had advised Rawlins to let himself be commissioned a lieutenant in John E. Smith's regiment and then report to Grant.

36. D. Sheean to J. H. Wilson, December 16, 1884, James Harrison Wilson Correspondence File, S (1), Box 14, Series 2, Ulysses S. Grant Presidential Library, Mississippi State University Libraries.

37. James H. Wilson *The Life of John A. Rawlins*, 53.

38. John Y. Simon, ed., *The Papers of Ulysses S. Grant*, 2:126n.

39. John A. Rawlins to Mary E. Smith, August 22, 1861, John A. Rawlins File, the Galena & U. S. Grant Museum. Copy.

40. *Galena Daily Advertiser*, August 20, 1861.

41. John A. Rawlins to Laura Rawlins Sheean, October 12, 1863, typescript of letter in U. S. Grant Presidential Library, Mississippi State University, John A. Rawlins Subject File, Series 2, Box 13, Folder 1.

42. "How Grant Got to Know Rawlins," interview with John A. Rawlins, 53.

43. It is not clear what arrangements Rawlins made at this time for his three children. Later in the war, the two older children were in the care of Rawlins's mother-in-law and an aunt in Goshen. The youngest child, Emily, and the one who, in John's estimation, needed "the most attention," was cared for by Rawlins's parents in Guilford Township; see John A. Rawlins to "Emma" [Mary E. Hurlburt], November 2, 1863, Rawlins Collection at the Chicago History Museum. Eventually, Rawlins found a renter for his house, but he was concerned whether it was being kept properly. See ibid.; John A. Rawlins to Mary E. Hurlburt, November 23, 1863. Rawlins and David Sheean agreed to have the latter manage their law practice in John's absence.

44. James H. Wilson, *The Life of John A. Rawlins*, 400.

45. Ulysses S. Grant to Jesse Root Grant, August 27, 1861, in *The Papers of Ulysses S. Grant*, ed. John Y. Simon, 2:145. William Hillyer was the lawyer in the law firm who shared space in the real estate office in which Grant was once employed.

46. Ulysses S. Grant to Brigadier General Lorenzo Thomas, August 29, 1861, in *The Papers of Ulysses S. Grant*, ed. John Y. Simon, 2:148.

47. Ulysses S. Grant to Julia Dent Grant, August 31, 1861, in *The Papers of Ulysses S. Grant*, ed. John Y. Simon, 2:161.

48. See ibid., 157n.

49. U. S. Grant, *Personal Memoirs of U. S. Grant*, 1:260–61.

50. Ulysses S. Grant to Julia Dent Grant, September 3, 1861, in *The Papers of Ulysses S. Grant*, ed. John Y. Simon, 2:181.

51. Bruce S. Allardice, *More Generals in Gray* (Baton Rouge: Louisiana State University Press, 1995), 219.

52. Ulysses S. Grant to Brigadier General Benjamin M. Prentiss, September 3, 1861, in *The Papers of Ulysses S. Grant*, ed. John Y. Simon, 2:177.

53. Ulysses S. Grant to Elihu B. Washburne, September 3, 1861, in *The Papers of Ulysses S. Grant*, ed. John Y. Simon, 2:182.

54. General Orders No. 4, September 8, 1861, in *The Papers of Ulysses S. Grant*, ed. John Y. Simon, 2: 206. Grant scholar John Y. Simon places Rawlins's arrival coincident with the issuing of General Orders No. 4. Others place Rawlins's arrival a bit later. For example, Albert D. Richardson, *A Personal History of Ulysses S. Grant*, 185, gives September 15 as the date Rawlins reported for duty at Cairo; James H. Wilson, *The Life of John A. Rawlins*, 55, says it was September 14. September 15 is the date given by Henry Coppée *Grant and His Campaign: A Military Biography* (New York: Charles B. Richardson, 1866), 457. Because Rawlins himself probably supplied Coppée with this date and other personal biographical information, September 15 is given here as the date Rawlins joined Grant.

7

"A Good Looking Set, Aint They?"

WHILE JOHN RAWLINS CONTEMPLATED LIFE as a widower and weighed his military options, Ulysses Grant experienced four months of uncertainty, disappointment, rejection, exhilaration, pride, embarrassment, and anxiety. He also staggered under a mountain of administrative tasks, engaged in various military operations, and reined in undisciplined recruits—before Rawlins arrived at his Cairo, Illinois, headquarters on September 15.

Grant had accompanied Captain Chetlain and the Jo Daviess Guards to Springfield, where on April 25 they were sent to nearby Camp Yates. Grant was enticed to stay over because, as Congressman Washburne told him, Governor Yates might need someone to manage the surplus volunteers pouring into Springfield. Grant met with Yates, who, instead of offering him a military appointment, hired him to carry out minor jobs such as inventorying recently captured muskets and performing clerical tasks in the state's adjutant general's office. As Grant sarcastically admitted to Julia, he was "on duty with the Governor, at his request, occupation principally smoking and occationally [sic] giving advice as to how an order should be communicated &c."[1] On May 2, a curious Chetlain checked on Grant at the adjutant general's office. Although he and Grant shared a room in Springfield, Grant had not disclosed a word to Chetlain about his work. All Chetlain could surmise was that his roommate "was not in the best of spirits." He found Grant copying orders at a small table in a tiny, dimly lit office. He looked disgusted. "I am going back to the store tonight. I am of no use here," he complained. "You have boys in your company who can do this work."[2]

Maybe he should wait in Galena for Lincoln to make another appeal for volunteers than suffer in Springfield, where, he had to admit, "I don't see really that I am doing any good."[3] But Yates convinced him to stay. Around this time, Chetlain claimed he recommended Grant for the colonelcy of the Twelfth Illinois, but an unnamed bigwig politician who wanted that slot objected, citing Grant's reputation for intemperance, and Chetlain could not press the issue. Then came a break: Captain John Pope, the West Pointer who was overseeing Camp Yates and mustering in the Illinois regiments, left in a huff after failing to be elected to head a brigade that was being formed. Yates turned to Grant to command the camp and to assume the mustering duties. He would remain a civilian, but this inched him closer to leading his own regiment.

An early mustering trip was to Belleville, allowing Grant to cross to St. Louis to confer with dynamic Nathaniel Lyon, an acquaintance from academy days, and other officials about an appointment to lead Missouri state volunteers. Same disheartening story: nothing available. On the trek back to Springfield, Grant stopped at Caseyville, where the Twelfth Illinois was stationed, to reconnect with some Galena friends. He dropped by Chetlain's headquarters on May 11. Chetlain saw that Grant was "blue as a whet-stone."[4] "He seemed depressed in spirits," Chetlain said, "and seemed to feel keenly his lack of success in obtaining some suitable appointment in the volunteer service." As Chetlain recollected, Grant pinpointed the source of his dejection: "During his visit he more than once alluded to the singular fact that an educated military man who had seen service could not get a position in the volunteer army, when civilians without military education or experience could easily obtain them."[5]

When the mustering work concluded on May 22, Grant returned to Galena. There, it occurred to him he might directly apply to the adjutant general himself, Lorenzo Thomas, at Washington, DC. In a politely worded letter, he wrote,

> Having served for fifteen years in the regular army, including four years at West Point, and feeling it the duty of evry [sic] one who has been educated at the Government expense to offer their services for the support of that Government, I have the honor, very respectfully, to tender my services, until the close of the War, in such capacity as may be offered. I would say that in view of my present age, and length of service, I feel myself competent to command a Regiment if the President, in his judgement, should see fit to entrust one to me.[6]

But Grant could wait into old age for a reply from General Thomas, because the letter was misplaced and lay for years undiscovered.[7]

A week home in Galena yielded the same old results—no military appointment in the offing, more time to while away. So he returned to Springfield to wait out Governor Yates. Deeply frustrated, he wrote Julia: "I am still here and uncertain about what I shall do. The Governor has just returned and as I have had nothing to do in his absence I might just as well be at home up to this time."[8] On obtaining a leave from Yates, Grant traveled to Covington, Kentucky to visit his parents, arriving on June 9. There was a larger motive to the Covington trip: Major General George McClellan, Grant's acquaintance from West Point and Mexico, was in Cincinnati. Although McClellan was four years younger, he was off to a meteoric start with organizing Ohio troops. "In reality I wanted to see him," Grant wrote. He made an unannounced visit at McClellan's headquarters. "I was in hopes that when he saw me he would offer me a position on his staff. I called on two successive days at his office but failed to see him on either occasion, and returned to Springfield."[9] It was a callous snub.

Between Cincinnati and Springfield, Grant stopped at Lafayette, Indiana, to see West Point friend Joe Reynolds, now colonel of an Indiana volunteer regiment. The only thing to spoil the visit was the news that Indiana had no use for more colonels. Springfield, St. Louis, Cincinnati, Lafayette—the story was the same. To a dismayed Ulysses Grant, the situation appeared just as he had explained it to Chetlain: "The politicians have got everything[;] there is no use of my trying to do anything, here."[10]

The news Grant had been waiting for arrived in Covington just after he left. On June 15, Governor Yates appointed him colonel of the Seventh Congressional District Regiment, which was ordered to report to Springfield. That was the good news. The bad news was that the Seventh District Regiment was an unruly mob that seemed within days of dissolving. Grant, on May 15 at Mattoon, Illinois, had mustered this regiment, 1,250 strong, into state militia service for a thirty-day hitch. The colonel whom Grant was replacing was Simon Goode, a flamboyant dandy who proved incompetent at disciplining these recruits. Their first month of service was an anarchy of drunken carousing, disregard for regulations, and raids on farmers' henhouses. With the expiration of their thirty-day stint, fewer than half extended their service by another month. On June 28, this remainder would be asked to volunteer for up to three years in the Federal army. It was expected that most of the Seventh District Regiment would prefer to go home rather than re-up.

When Grant assumed command on June 18, he scheduled drill and cracked down on rule breakers. "He stopped all drinking.... He put an end to foraging, arresting every insubordinate and making him understand that lawlessness was past."[11] Furthermore, being absent from camp "will not be received as a paliation [*sic*] for any absence from duty, on the contrary will be regarded as an aggravation of the offence, and will be punished accordingly."[12] To encourage reenlistment, Grant had two Illinois congressmen, Democrats John McClernand and John Logan, address the regiment. The combination of the congressmen's patriotic exhortations and Grant's strictness paid off: 603 men, almost all, volunteered and were mustered in as the Twenty-First Illinois Volunteers.[13]

———

In mid-July 1861, the Twenty-First found itself in northeast Missouri among secessionists. Missouri was deeply divided in sentiment, and keeping it in the Union was paramount. The regiment had shaped up under Grant's hand—and none too soon—as it drew its first assignment. Grant was to march southward from its encampment about twenty miles to snare a Confederate force under Brigadier General Thomas Harris, a member of the Confederacy's Provisional Congress.[14] Harris's men were said to be positioned along a creek bottom near Florida, Missouri. The route taken by the Twenty-First wound through almost deserted countryside, giving the run-up to the confrontation an eerie foreboding. The last few hundred yards to the Confederate position were the worst. As Grant led his men up the crest of the bluff abutting the creek, wondering whether he would discover a substantial enemy, he recalled, "My heart kept getting higher and higher until it was in my throat."[15] To everyone's relief, the Illinois boys discovered that Harris had withdrawn several hours earlier.

Colonel Grant had been in Missouri only a few weeks when, unbeknownst to him, Lincoln nominated him for promotion to brigadier general. The Senate confirmed Grant's promotion on August 5. Grant attributed his promotion to behind-the-scenes work of Elihu Washburne and thanked him warmly: "In conclusion Mr. Washburn allow me to thank you for the part you have taken in giving me my present position. I think I see your hand in it and admit that I had no personal claims for your kind office in the matter."[16] Grant acted quickly to complete his staff when, on August 7, he offered Rawlins a position as aide-de-camp.

Shortly after the promotion, the Western Department commander, Major General John C. Frémont, ordered Grant to Ironton, seventy miles south of St. Louis, to check a rebel force supposedly in the area. What he found instead in Ironton was a detachment of ill-trained troops, broken-down transportation, and deficient artillery. Grant was in the midst of drilling the troops, acquiring fresh horses, and making camp improvements when, on August 17, four regiments arrived led by Brigadier General Benjamin Prentiss. Prentiss explained he was in Ironton, under Frémont's orders, to take command in southeastern Missouri. A perplexed and disappointed Grant was unsure what to make of Prentiss's orders other than that he had been relieved. Grant had no recourse but to entrain for St. Louis and confer with Frémont about what his next assignment, if any, might be.

With scant explanation, Frémont dispatched Grant to take command at Jefferson City. There, instead of a Confederate military threat, Grant found "a great deficiency in everything for the comfort and efficiency of an army. Most of the troops are without clothing, camp and garrison equipage. Ammunition was down to about ten rounds of cartridges and for the artillery none is left."[17] There was a horde of needy Unionist refugees spilling into town to avoid depredations by their secessionist neighbors. Without a proper staff, Grant was forced to assume the roles of drillmaster, ordnance officer, and commissary, often toiling until 2:00 a.m. to complete all the paperwork. Yet he seemed to be thriving. "I stand it first rate however," he wrote Julia, "and never enjoyed better health in my life."[18] Grant was barely eight days into his new assignment when he received a visit from Colonel Jefferson C. Davis (no relation to Confederate President Jefferson F. Davis). Davis came bearing orders from Frémont that relieved Grant from command and directed him to "report at department headquarters at St. Louis without delay, to receive important special instructions."[19] Grant left behind his lone staff officer, Clark Lagow, to brief Davis.

What awaited Grant was another new assignment: command of the newly created District of Southeast Missouri, about thirteen thousand troops. He was to proceed to Cape Girardeau, Missouri, almost due west of Cairo, and coordinate several Union forces in order to sweep Confederates out of southeastern Missouri in preparation for a move across the Mississippi into Kentucky. It amounted to a sweep of Jeff Thompson and his irregular "Swamp Rats," the only Rebels in the vicinity. But the operation fizzled in large measure because General Prentiss would not abide by Grant's orders. Prentiss believed himself to be senior in rank, but because Grant had been an officer in the regular army, he was technically Prentiss's superior. Perhaps it mattered little, because the elusive Swamp Rats dissolved safely into the Missouri wetlands.

The new district commander established his headquarters at Cairo, where he anxiously inquired about the arrival of his assistant adjutant general, John Rawlins. It was from Cairo that Grant good-naturedly mentioned to Washburne how these recent events would have been good schooling for newcomer Rawlins. By the time Rawlins arrived a few days later in Cairo, Grant would have made one of his "more monumental decisions during the Civil War."[20]

———∿∿∿———

At the war's onset, Kentucky adopted a posture of neutrality. Its politicians, figuring it safer to stay out of the fray, even forbade troops of either side to march into the state. However, both North and South saw advantages in controlling strategic positions in Kentucky, so it seemed likely that neutrality would be violated. One strategic point was at Columbus, situated south of Cairo astride lofty bluffs on the Mississippi's eastern bank. Whichever side controlled Columbus held a commanding presence over Mississippi River traffic. Another such point was Paducah, about forty-five miles almost due east of Cairo, at the confluence of the Ohio and Tennessee Rivers, a waterway into the heart of the mid-South.

While Grant moved into his district headquarters at Cairo, Confederate General Leonidas Polk descended on Columbus. Grant understood the threat posed by a Confederate takeover there. Moving with alacrity and on his own initiative, Grant cobbled together a small force and wired Frémont that, if he had no objection, Grant was fixed to occupy Paducah, which he soon entered virtually unopposed. Rawlins applauded this thrust into Kentucky. He regarded that state's "conditional neutrality as absolute hostility to the Government" and urged Grant to ignore it.[21] The "monumental" aspect of occupying Paducah was that Grant established a counterforce in the rear of the Confederates in Columbus, blocked them from having a staging area into southern Illinois, and gained access to the vital Tennessee River. Not bad work for having been in district command so brief a time. Moreover, Grant demonstrated an ability "to recognize the advantages of seizing and maintaining the initiative. Forcing the enemy to react to his own moves shifted the burden of uncertainty to the Confederates, leaving them to ponder, to speculate, and to make mistakes."[22]

John Rawlins's first experience under enemy fire occurred two months later at Belmont on the Missouri side of the Mississippi opposite Columbus. Rawlins would emerge from that fight "convinced that it was always best to strike the first blow. Afterward, whenever Rawlins thought Grant hesitant, he pushed for immediate action."[23] Thus, both the army veteran and his neophyte staffer shared the perspective that action and initiative trumped wait and see.

———∿∿∿———

The incoming assistant adjutant general was aware of Grant's difficulties in the regular army and heard the gossip that Grant had resigned due to his weakness for the bottle. It could be said that John Rawlins therefore came to his staff position with an agenda. Certainly, for Rawlins's own sake and for the good of country, he hoped Grant had the wherewithal and single-mindedness to succeed. But lessons from Lovisa, his deep-seated beliefs, and his education at the Rock River Seminary would have cautioned him that there is no such thing as a safe level of drinking or a "safer" kind of alcohol. Grant's success would depend on the only alternative: abstinence. In a widely circulated treatise on intemperance and one with which Rawlins was likely familiar, Reverend Lyman Beecher, cofounder of the American Temperance Society, offered remedies for this societal affliction. He warned, "It is in vain to rely alone upon self-government and voluntary abstinence." The drinker lacks the capacity to restrain his appetite for alcohol. The true remedy, according to Beecher, was the "banishment of ardent spirits" from society—outlawing its sale.[24] Telescoping Beecher's assertions down to military command level, this could take several shapes: if the drinker cannot govern himself, then some responsible other should keep close watch; a responsible other can banish alcohol from camp and restrict the drinker's access to fellow drinkers; and if the drinker cannot voluntarily abstain, then some responsible other might threaten the drinker with a penalty or extract a pledge of sobriety. John Rawlins could perform all these functions.

What one should bear in mind is that during those muddled four months before Rawlins joined him, there is no evidence that Grant resorted to abusing or using alcohol. This seems noteworthy. Apparently, he did not turn to drink to assuage the disappointment after unsuccessful efforts to obtain a commission. Or to massage the blow to his pride when assigned to a clerk's desk. Or to dilute the dose of humiliation he felt after cooling his heels in McClellan's anteroom. Or to raise a self-congratulatory toast on his promotion to brigadier. Or to brace himself against the challenges of reining in a regiment of undisciplined troops. Or to occupy the idle hours while simply waiting. Or to embolden himself with a nip of bottled courage when approaching a creek bed believed full of Rebels. Quite the contrary. While facing frustrations and adversity, he persevered and met circumstances head-on. Perhaps General Grant could exert more self-control than many would allow themselves to believe.

Certainly, these few months in Illinois and Missouri were qualitatively different from his difficult period on the remote Pacific coast. While Frémont bounced him from assignment to assignment, Julia was only a few days' journey away, and Grant had his son, Fred, by his side during part of June 1861. In California, he was a half continent removed from family, stuck in what seemed a dead-end career, and facing ruin from failed investment schemes. Augustus Chetlain recollected Grant told him, "I don't know whether I am like other men or not, but when I have nothing to do I get blue and depressed, I have a natural craving for drink, when I was on the coast I got in a depressed condition and got to drinking."[25] Although Grant was at situational risk for abusing alcohol during the four months after leaving Galena and assuming command at Cairo, his dedication to the service was stronger than the competing force exerted by idleness and depression, and this augured well for his success.

Coincidentally, on the same day, September 8, that Grant issued General Orders No. 4 announcing the appointments of Captains Rawlins, Lagow, and Hillyer as his personal staff and Dr. Simons to his special staff,[26] he also issued sternly worded General Orders No. 5:

> It is with regret the Genl Comdg sees and learns that the closest intimacy exists between many of the officers and soldiers of his command; that they visit together the lowest drinking and dancing saloons; quarrel, curse, drink and carouse generally on the lowest level of equality, and neglect generally the interests of the Government they are sworn to serve . . .
>
> In future it will be the duty of every Commanding officer of a Regiment or detachment to at once arrest any one of their commands guilty, of such conduct and prefer charges against them, and the duty of all officers who have a decent respect for themselves and the service they have entered into to report everything of the kind.[27]

On September 8, Grant wrote Brigadier General McClernand, one of the commanders in his district, to recommend the appointment of a provost marshal to clean up the drunkenness, gambling, and prostitution endemic in Cairo.[28] Rawlins would have seen this correspondence on arrival and would have endorsed Grant's preemptive efforts. Unfortunately, McClernand appointed a Democratic politician and crony, Major Andrew Jackson Kuykendall, as provost marshal. Kuykendall established a corrupt police force that ran roughshod over Cairo. It was claimed that "They were blackmailers, clothed with power to compel terms from their victims. The people had to appease these sharks by frequent *voluntary* subscriptions to buy presents from their *admirers,* in the way of fine swords, horses, watches, and champagne, cigars and whisky."[29] On February 1, Rawlins issued orders to temporarily relieve Kuykendall of his duties.[30]

—∿∿∿—

Grant's personal staff was coming together. At his level of command, Grant would have been allowed one assistant adjutant general (AAG) and two aides-de-camp (ADCs) for his personal staff. He began with what historian Steven Jones called "a ragged collection of civilians with little military knowledge" and molded them into a professional and efficient body.[31] Thirty-two-year-old ADC Clark Lagow was the first of this collection to join Grant, who thought it "proper" that one of his aides should be an officer from the Twenty-First Illinois.[32] Lagow entered service on May 7, 1861, as first lieutenant in the unruly Seventh Congressional District Regiment that became the Twenty-First.

Aide-de-camp William S. Hillyer became acquainted with Grant in St. Louis when Hillyer and his law partners shared space with Boggs and Grant. Hillyer, a Republican and former member of the Indiana state legislature, and Grant, a Democrat, discussed politics in such a way that Hillyer impressed Grant as being "very brilliant."[33] Around mid-August 1861, Grant and Hillyer met at the Planter's Hotel in St. Louis. Grant invited him to join his staff on the spot. "Come, Hillyer, here's your horse all ready. I have kept a steamer waiting for you for three hours. I am going to Cape Girardeau, and want you to go with me on my staff."

Hillyer was taken aback: "Why, I haven't enlisted!" Furthermore, he had no money, no clothes, unfinished business to attend to, and a wife waiting at home.

Grant waved off those minor impediments. "We're ordered to the field, and expect a fight with Jeff Thompson. If you survive it, I'll give you a leave of absence to come home and settle your business." That sold Hillyer. Shortly after embarking on the steamboat, Hillyer inquired about his rank and a commission. Grant assured him that Frémont would attend to that. "For the present we will call you captain."[34]

When brand-new army captain John Rawlins reported for duty, he found Grant at his Cairo headquarters on the third floor of Alfred Safford's City National Bank, located near the Ohio River levee. Right off, Rawlins was impressed by the methodical way Grant made short work of piles of paperwork. As Rawlins remembered, "I was amazed at the quiet, prompt way in which he handled the multitude of letters, requisitions, and papers, sitting behind the cashier's window-hole, with a waste basket under him, and orderlies to dispatch the business as he did."[35] This coming together was more than just a reunion of two Galena acquaintances. Rawlins described how the moment was fraught with potential: "Beyond my friendship of Grant, I felt that I was going to be attached to a man equal to the enlarging situation."[36] The feeling turned out to be mutual, and Grant deemed Rawlins "a very useful officer" and a person to whom he "became very much attached."[37] The AAG would provide his commander with invaluable service. Although it was still too early to know, historical perspective suggests that "Perhaps the best appointment Grant ever made to his staff was that of assistant adjutant general John Aaron Rawlins."[38]

After welcoming the three men to his personal staff, Grant made two special staff appointments. For medical director, Grant named Dr. James Simons, a full surgeon in the regular army, whose commission dated back to 1839. A South Carolinian, Simons married into a Baltimore family loyal to the Union. His immediate worry was the burgeoning number of men being felled by disease. The fetid backwaters surrounding Cairo were breeding grounds for the mosquitoes described as "very powerful and bloodthirsty . . . huge and insatiate," resulting in an "overwhelming" problem with malaria.[39] The squalid soldiers' camps were sources of rampant typhoid fever, measles, and dysentery. Fifty-year-old Joseph Dana Webster was appointed chief of engineers. He had served in the Topographical Engineers before resigning in 1854. When war broke out, Webster volunteered and quickly found himself in Cairo. On September 7, Grant sent Webster to Paducah to oversee construction of fortifications.[40]

—◈—

During his first two months as district commander, Grant kept an eye on the Confederates at Columbus, augmented the Federal presence at Paducah, built defensive works between Cairo and Columbus, tracked enemy movements, positioned infantry or naval craft at various locations, and relayed information to subordinates. He moved troops into Smithland, Kentucky, which sat strategically at the mouth of the Cumberland River just east of Paducah. The Cumberland, like the Tennessee River, was a navigable invasion route into the center of the Confederacy. To facilitate all this activity, Grant's personal staff was involved in drafting his orders and transmitting military correspondence. However, much of the army's activity was routine, and as Grant himself put it, "From the occupation of Paducah up to the early part of November nothing important occurred with the troops under my command."[41] This allowed Grant time to break in his staff.

He expected Lagow, Hillyer, and Rawlins to take some burden off his shoulders. By the time of Rawlins's arrival, Grant was feeling the effect of having worked too long without proper staff assistance: "My duties are very laborious and have been from the start," he groaned to his sister. "It is a rare thing that I get to bed before two or three o'clock in the morning and am usually wakened in the morning before getting awake in a natural way. Now, however, my staff are getting a little in the way of this kind of business and can help me."[42] Not only were they sharing the workload, but members of the staff shared quarters with Grant in back of his office.[43]

As personal staff learned their jobs and soaked up military protocol, Grant was figuring out, ad hoc, how to use them to proper advantage. When war began, army regulations failed to specifically define the responsibilities of various military officers, including staff members.[44] There was latitude in Union and Confederate armies as to how commanders utilized personal staff, especially in the duties performed by aides-de-camp. "There is no distinct and positive duty for an Aide-de-Camp; he is to do whatever may be required of him by the General," wrote General August Kautz, "and his services will be in proportion to the amount of knowledge, ability and experience that he may possess."[45] ADCs processed paperwork, served as couriers, and wrote out instructions as directed by the commander. When a "go-fer" was needed, an ADC was summoned.

The typical Civil War ADC was a young lieutenant (in his twenties or early thirties) and a friend (or relative) of the commander, a profile Hillyer and Lagow mostly fit. Nepotism was an acceptable practice. Grant was besieged by requests for a staff appointment. Even Jesse Grant troubled Ulysses to appoint a cousin. "Father asks for a position for Albert Griffith," he wrote to his sister. "I have no place to give and at best could only use my influence. I receive letters from all over the country for such places, but do not answer them."[46] It was routine for generals to augment their personal staffs with volunteer aides-de-camp (VADCs). Early in the war, John Riggin served Grant as a VADC with honorary rank.[47]

Hillyer issued orders and prepared written directives for Grant as instructed. However, Grant used his personal staff for more than simple clerical functions. In late September, when troops at Cairo had yet to be sworn into service, Grant had Rawlins issue special orders to appoint Hillyer as mustering officer.[48] A month later, Grant sent Hillyer on a prisoner exchange mission to return a Confederate captain. The mission brought Hillyer face-to-face with the Confederate department commander, Major General Leonidas Polk, described as "a rather tall, thin fellow, toothless, and bland to a degree."[49] Grant was not above using his ADCs for mundane tasks like running errands. When Hillyer was in St. Louis at the beginning of September, Grant asked him to bring down to Cairo a package of clothing and a horse that was being boarded at a stable.[50]

The AAG acted as the commander's main assistant. He was the hub through whom command information was processed and records were archived. This in itself was a daunting task. According to Kautz, the AAG's scope of responsibilities was all-inclusive: "All orders of the General, and every matter of detail affecting the command, should be executed through the Assistant Adjutant General's office; all orders affecting the command in any way, all details for detached service, details for guard, all change in the position or condition of the troops, all accessions to the command, all reports and communications from subordinates to the General, in fact, everything essential to the command should be transacted through his office."[51] Orders, reports, and information were funneled through the AAG. He was keeper of the records: the books containing general and special orders, as well as the letter book that held a record of letters sent. He prepared status reports on number of casualties suffered, prisoners captured, and property seized. He was the custodian for reports such as courts-martial proceedings. Besides carrying out these informational functions, the AAG, depending on the predilections and flexibility of his commander, might assume more independent responsibilities such as ascertaining that the commander's orders had been properly executed; providing advisement to the commander; and when necessary, giving orders in the name of the commander, as such orders were consistent with the AAG's understanding of the commander's intent. As the war unfolded, Grant entrusted such responsibilities and more to Rawlins.

For now, Rawlins was getting acquainted with military etiquette and the forms for filing reports. He learned the scope of duties performed by special staff officers in the quartermaster, medical, commissary, engineering, and ordnance departments. Rawlins also took measure of the men serving Grant. Some were given staff positions because Grant had been too busy to make careful personnel decisions—Andrew Jackson Kuykendall being one example. As it turned out, "During their connection with the staff several gave much trouble and were the source of constant anxiety."[52] Whereas Grant tended to overlook staffers' troublemaking potential or failed to deal assertively with them, Rawlins noted those who displayed indolence, illicit behavior, or fondness for drinking.

Rawlins, with Hillyer's help, handled the correspondence flowing out of headquarters. The first time that Ulysses S. Grant and John A. Rawlins were linked on an official military document occurred with the printed issuance of General Orders No. 6 on September 16, 1861. The order aimed to curtail the abuse of leaves of absence and free passes:

> Hereafter no furloughs to soldiers, or leaves of absence to officers, will be considered valid, unless first receiving the approval of the Commanding Officer of the Post where the applicant is stationed.

> Furloughs, or leaves of absence, will, in no case, entitle the soldier, or officer, to a free pass, by any conveyance, at the expense of the Government.

> The system of granting leaves of absence, and free passes, having been so much abused, hereafter no passes will be received by steamboats, railroads, or other public conveyance, except by order of the Commanding Officer of the Post where granted; and each pass must state that the officer or soldier is traveling on public service.

> Quartermasters will provide transportation for Government stores, and troops, on an order from the Commanding Officer having authority to give such order.

> By order
>
> > Brigadier General U. S. GRANT,
> > Commanding
> > [SIGNED]
> > *JOHN A. RAWLINS,*
> > Captain, and Assistant Adjutant General [53]

General Orders No. 6 was typical of the paperwork that occupied Rawlins during the fall of 1861. He received reports or queries from commanders in the field and dispatched orders for such things as providing forage or sending out troop details, even issuing special orders stipulating that quarters be erected in anticipation of the inclement fall weather.[54] His duties as assistant adjutant general at this time could be boiled down to "issuing orders, sending out instructions and making returns. These orders announced the staff, the creation of brigades and divisions, and the assignment of regiments thereto, but the greater number of them were dictated verbally by Grant from his own personal experience, and related to the discipline of the troops in camp and on the march, prohibiting them from leaving camp or going outside of the line of sentinels except upon duty, forbidding them to straggle, maraud, or fire away ammunition upon any pretext except in battle."[55]

One of the noteworthy set of orders issued by Grant through AAG Rawlins at this time was General Orders No. 11, which specified the commander and unit composition of each of the five brigades comprising the District of Southeast Missouri. Brigadier General John McClernand, Colonel Richard J. Oglesby, Colonel William H. L. Wallace, Colonel John Cook, and Colonel Joseph B. Plummer were designated commanders of the First through Fifth Brigades, respectively.[56]

—⁓—

During September and October, there were diversions from business as usual in the District of Southeast Missouri. Grant and Rawlins, Lagow, Hillyer, and Simons donned dress uniforms to pose for photographs. Grant appears in the full-dress of a brigadier general. He sports an odd beard, short at the chin but luxuriantly long on the neck. Dr. Simons strikes a doughty pose with eyes at half squint and a clenched jaw. Rawlins stares into the camera with an almost vacant expression, perhaps a residue of melancholy lingering from his wife's recent death. He has a close-trimmed beard, wears a plumed Hardee hat turned up on the left side, and holds a sword across his lap. Grant sent a set of the photos to his sister and couldn't help commenting, "A good looking set aint they?"[57]

Elihu Washburne corresponded with Rawlins in Cairo. The congressman, who was virtually unacquainted with Grant in Galena, took great interest now in advancing his career: "Sponsorship of Grant was part of Washburne's political program of picking successful generals or furthering the military careers of useful men."[58] Rawlins showed Grant a letter he received from Washburne in which Washburne indicated he was working to get Grant promoted to major general. On October 6, Grant wrote Julia about this great news, trying to accept it in stride. However, he urged Julia to act as an emissary and cozy up to Mrs. Washburne: "I want you to lay aside the rule of society which would require Mrs. W. to pay you the first visit and call upon her and make known the many obligations I feel to her husband. Say that I shall endeavor not to disappoint him."[59]

Washburne was on a fact-finding congressional committee that traveled to Cairo at the end of October. The committee investigated questions concerning government contracts. Grant testified about problems with contractors supplying unsuitable muskets, scrawny cattle, and poor-quality forage. Grant left the committee feeling satisfied that there was no evidence of mismanagement within his department. Thus, Washburne felt even freer extolling Grant to Washington. He wrote a favorable report to Lincoln's Treasury Secretary, Salmon Chase, in which he heaped praise on his fellow Galenian: "Genl. Grant, who is in command of this whole section, is one of the best officers in the army, and is doing wonders in bringing order out of chaos. He is as incorruptible as he is brave."[60] Washburne seemed so taken by Grant's ability and convinced he was the "coming man" of the war that his friends joked he had "Grant on the brain."[61]

October brought family visitors. Jesse Grant made a brief visit to Cairo at the beginning of the month to see Ulysses.[62] Hillyer's son, Willie Jr., was in camp and making a big hit at headquarters. In a moment of lighthearted fun, Grant "officially" appointed "Master Willie" a "Pony Aid de Camp with the rank of major to be attached to my staff. All stable boys will take due notice and obey him accordingly." The commanding general's "orders" were duly attested to by John A. Rawlins.[63] The Hillyer family visit must have been especially poignant for Rawlins, who was separated from his three motherless children.

October ended with Rawlins writing a letter to a concerned mother interceding on behalf of her son. Rawlins's response reveals his courtesy to plain folks or to the disempowered, likely because they reminded him of his humble roots. In the body of the letter he spouts the standard inflexible military line, but in the postscript he abandons his military persona and provides her with warm lawyerly advice. To "Mrs. Williams" Rawlins wrote:

> Unless the Captain of the company in which your son is enlisted, desires he should be discharged, General Grant can not well do any thing toward having him discharged. He is informed your son was enlisted upon your written consent. And furthermore, by express order from the War Department, "No discharges will be granted to volunteers in the service of the United States on the ground of minority["] P. S. If you are desirous he should be discharged you must see a Lawyer & get out a writ Habeas Corpus, that will determine the question [o]f his right to a discharge.[64]

During September and October, Grant's personal and special staffs were striving to deal with the burgeoning sick roll, equip the troops, tighten discipline, fortify the Federal presence around Paducah, and manage the flow of supplies. Increasingly, Grant's attention fixed on the Rebel stronghold in

Columbus. From Columbus, it was possible for Leonidas Polk to ferry troops into Missouri. In but one week after Rawlins offered his legal assistance to Mrs. Williams, he would join Grant in a clash with Rebel forces across from Columbus and get a first taste of battle. Soon his life as a Galena attorney would feel as if he had left it far behind.

NOTES

1. Ulysses S. Grant to Julia Dent Grant May 1, 1861, in *The Papers of Ulysses S. Grant*, ed. John Y. Simon (Carbondale: Southern Illinois University Press, 1969), 2:16.

2. Papers read before the Commandery of the State of Illinois, Military Order of the Loyal Legion of the United States, in *Recollections of General U. S. Grant in Military Essays and Recollections*, ed. Augustus L. Chetlain (Chicago: A. C. McClure, 1891), 1:14.

3. Ulysses S. Grant to Julia Dent Grant, May 3, 1861, in *The Papers of Ulysses S. Grant*, ed. John Y. Simon, 2:19.

4. Notes from a talk by General Chetlain [ca. 1890], Hamlin Garland Collection, Collection no. 0200, Special Collections, USC Libraries, University of Southern California, 3.

5. Papers read before the Commandery of the State of Illinois, Military Order of the Loyal Legion of the United States, in *Recollections of General U. S. Grant in Military Essays and Recollections*, ed. Augustus L. Chetlain, 1:16.

6. Ulysses S. Grant to Brevet Brigadier General Lorenzo Thomas, May 24, 1861, in *The Papers of Ulysses S. Grant*, ed. John Y. Simon, 2:35.

7. Ibid., 36.

8. Ulysses S. Grant to Julia Dent Grant, June 6, 1861, in *The Papers of Ulysses S. Grant*, ed. John Y. Simon, 2:38.

9. U. S. Grant, *Personal Memoirs of U. S. Grant* (New York: Charles L. Webster, 1885), 1:241.

10. Notes from a talk by General Chetlain, 3.

11. Hamlin Garland, *Ulysses S. Grant: His Life and Character* (New York: Doubleday and McClure, 1898), 174.

12. Ulysses S. Grant Orders No. 8, June 19, 1861, in *The Papers of Ulysses S. Grant*, ed. John Y. Simon, 2:46.

13. Lloyd Lewis, *Captain Sam Grant* (Boston: Little, Brown, 1950), 430.

14. Bruce S. Allardice, *More Generals in Gray* (Baton Rouge: Louisiana State University Press, 1995), 121; Ezra J. Warner and W. B. Yearns, *Biographical Register of the Confederate Congress* (Baton Rouge: Louisiana State University Press, 1976), 109.

15. U. S. Grant, *Personal Memoirs of U. S. Grant*, 1:250.

16. Ulysses S. Grant to Elihu B. Washburne, September 3, 1861, in *The Papers of Ulysses S. Grant*, ed. John Y. Simon, 2:183.

17. U. S. Grant to Speed Butler, August 22, 1861, in *The Papers of Ulysses S. Grant*, ed. John Y. Simon, 2:128.

18. U. S. Grant to Julia Dent Grant, August 29, 1861, in *The Papers of Ulysses S. Grant*, ed. John Y. Simon, 2:140.

19. U. S. Grant, *Personal Memoirs of U. S. Grant*, 1:260.

20. William B. Feis, *Grant's Secret Service: The Intelligence War from Belmont to Appomattox* (Lincoln: University of Nebraska Press, 2002), 22.

21. James H. Wilson, *The Life of John A. Rawlins* (New York: Neale, 1916), 64.

22. Ibid., 24.

23. Peter Cozzens, "General Grant's 'Living and Speaking Conscience,'" *Civil War Times* 48, no. 5 (October 2009): 30.

24. Lyman Beecher, *Six Sermons on the Nature, Occasions, Signs, Evils, and Remedy of Intemperance*, 4th ed. (Boston: T. R. Marvin, 1828), 62.

25. Notes from a talk by General Chetlain, 3, 4.

26. The personal staff was one component of a headquarters staff. Size of personal staff was positively correlated with rank. A brigade commander in the Union army was entitled to one assistant adjutant general (AAG), who served as the main assistant, and two aides-de-camp (ADCs). A general commanding an independent army had a chief of staff as main assistant, two AAGs, two military secretaries, perhaps as many as seven ADCs, and an inspector general. The other component of a headquarters staff was the special staff, which included "a chief of engineers, chief of ordnance, quartermaster general and assistant quartermaster general, chief and assistant chief of commissaries, provost marshal and assistant provost marshal, chief surgeon, and chaplain." R. Steven Jones, *The Right Hand of Command: Use and Disuse of Personal Staffs in the American Civil War* (Mechanicsburg, PA: Stackpole, 2000), viii.

27. General Orders No. 5, September 8, 1861, in *The Papers of Ulysses S. Grant*, ed. John Y. Simon, 2:207–8.

28. U. S. Grant to Brig. Gen. John A. McClernand, September 8, 1861, in *The Papers of Ulysses S. Grant*, ed. John Y. Simon, 2:210–11.

29. H. C. Bradsby, "History of Cairo," in *History of Alexander, Union and Pulaski Counties*, ed. William Henry Perrin (Chicago: O. L. Baskin, 1883), 66.

30. John Y. Simon, ed., *The Papers of Ulysses S. Grant*, 4:143n1.

31. R. Steven Jones, *The Right Hand of Command*, xv.

32. U. S. Grant, *Personal Memoirs of U. S. Grant*, 1:254.

33. Ibid., 255.

34. A. D. Richardson, *A Personal History of Ulysses S. Grant* (Boston: D. L. Guernsey, 1885), 182.

35. "How Grant Got to Know Rawlins," interview with John A. Rawlins, *The United States Army and Navy Journal and Gazette of the Regular and Volunteer Forces* 6 (September 12, 1868): 53.

36. Ibid.

37. U. S. Grant, *Personal Memoirs of U. S. Grant*, 1:256.

38. R. Stephen Jones, *The Right Hand of Command*, 67.

39. John H. Brinton, *Personal Memoirs of John H. Brinton* (New York: Neale, 1914), 52–53.

40. U. S. Grant to John C. Frémont, September 7, 1861, in *The Papers of Ulysses S. Grant*, ed. John Y. Simon, 2:203.

41. U. S. Grant, *Personal Memoirs of U. S. Grant*, 1:269.

42. U. S. Grant to Mary Grant, September 11, 1861, in *The Papers of Ulysses S. Grant*, ed. John Y. Simon, 2:238.

43. U. S. Grant to Julia Dent Grant, September 20, 1861, in *The Papers of Ulysses S. Grant*, ed. John Y. Simon, 2:290.

44. General August V. Kautz fulfilled a professional goal by writing a comprehensive training manual for officers, *Customs of Service for Officers of the Army* (Philadelphia: J. B. Lippincott, 1868). But it was not published until the war was over and most officers had left the army. For background regarding Kautz's manual, see Lawrence G. Kautz, *August Valentine Kautz, USA: Biography of a Civil War General* (Jefferson, NC: McFarland, 2008), 162–63.

45. A. V. Kautz, *Customs of Service for Officers of the Army*, 196.

46. Grant to Mary Grant, September 11, 1861, in *The Papers of Ulysses S. Grant*, ed. John Y. Simon, 2:238.

47. Some VADCs were young men of privilege, anointed with staff officer rank, and invited to become part of a general's entourage. VADCs commonly swelled the staffs of political generals or "men who brought pomp and parade to their duties" (Robert E. L. Krick, *Staff Officers in Gray: A Biographical Register of the Staff Officers in the Army of Northern Virginia* [Chapel Hill: University of North Carolina Press, 2003], 12). Confederate General Milledge Bonham surrounded himself with at least eight VADCs at the Battle of First Bull Run. Grant eschewed such pretentious display.

48. John Y. Simon, ed. *The Papers of Ulysses S. Grant*, 2:323n1.

49. John H. Brinton, *Personal Memoirs of John H. Brinton*, 57. About a week earlier, Dr. James Simons and Dr. John H. Brinton took a steamer toward Columbus to retrieve wounded soldiers. While on their medical mission, they too met General Polk. The description of Polk is Dr. Brinton's.

50. U. S. Grant to Charles Ford, September 1, 1861, in *The Papers of Ulysses S. Grant*, ed. John Y. Simon, 2:168.

51. August V. Kautz, *Customs of Service for Officers of the Army*, 190.

52. James H. Wilson, *The Life of John A. Rawlins*, 60.

53. General Orders No. 6 from author's private collection; an earlier, written version of General Orders No. 6 was issued by order of Grant and under the signature of Acting AAG William Hillyer. General Orders No. 6, September 14, 1861, in *The Papers of Ulysses S. Grant*, ed. John Y. Simon, 2:256.

54. John Y. Simon, ed. *The Papers of Ulysses S. Grant*, 3:65n.

55. James H. Wilson, *The Life of John A. Rawlins*, 72.

56. General Orders No. 11, October 14, 1861, in *The Papers of Ulysses S. Grant*, ed. John Y. Simon, 3:38–39.

57. U. S. Grant to Mary Grant, October 25, 1861, in *The Papers of Ulysses S. Grant*, ed. John Y. Simon, 3:76–77.

58. John Y. Simon, "From Galena to Appomattox: Grant and Washburne," *Journal of the Illinois State Historical Society* 58, no. 2 (1965): 188.

59. U. S. Grant to Julia Dent Grant, October 6, 1861, in *The Papers of Ulysses S. Grant*, ed. John Y. Simon, 3:23.

60. John Y. Simon, ed. *The Papers of Ulysses S. Grant*, 3:98n.

61. Albert D. Richardson, *A Personal History of Ulysses S. Grant*, 186.

62. U. S. Grant to Julia Dent Grant, October 6, 1861, in *The Papers of Ulysses S. Grant*, ed. John Y. Simon, 3:23.

63. U. S. Grant to William S. Hillyer, November 1, 1861, in *The Papers of Ulysses S. Grant*, ed. John Y. Simon, 3:102.

64. John Y. Simon, ed. *The Papers of Ulysses S. Grant*, 3:395.

"Collect Your Men at Once;
We Must Get Out of This"

IN SEPTEMBER AND OCTOBER, THE department commander, John C. Frémont, and his district commander, Grant, were preoccupied with his set of
perceived threats and opportunities. An apprehensive Frémont focused attention primarily on western Missouri, where secessionist forces, the Missouri
State Guard, under silver-haired Sterling Price, held sway. In Cairo, Grant cast
his eyes southward toward Columbus, Kentucky, trying to discern the intentions there of Leonidas Polk and making appeals to move against that strategic stronghold.

Price followed up his victory at Wilson's Creek on August 10 over a small
army led by Nathaniel Lyon with the siege and capture on September 20 of the
thirty-five-hundred-man garrison at Lexington, Missouri. The outnumbered
Federals held out for eight days without any reinforcements from Frémont.
Lexington's fall reinvigorated secessionist sentiment in Missouri and subjected Frémont to such criticism that he took to the field with over thirty thousand men to bag Price. By purging Price's ragtag militia from Missouri, Frémont hoped he could send his sagging reputation soaring. Moving cautiously,
Frémont's force retook Lexington on October 21, but Price easily slipped into
the Ozarks. What unnerved Frémont was the thought that Price's State Guard
might be reinforced by wily Jeff Thompson and Leonidas Polk at Columbus.

What nettled Grant was the failed opportunity to seize Columbus after
the Federals had moved into Paducah.[1] But Frémont, looking westward, had
other priorities. On September 10, he ordered Grant to "confine yourself to
holding the positions we have taken in Kentucky."[2] Grant tried persuading

Frémont, suggesting, "If it was discretionary with me with a little addition to my present force I would take Columbus."[3] Two days later from Cairo, Grant proposed how its capture could be effected: "I am of the opinion that if a demonstration was made from Paducah towards Union City supported by two columns on the Kentucky side from here. The Gun Boats and a force moving upon Belmont the enemy would be forced to leave Columbus leaving behind their heavy ordnance."[4] Grant's proposals did not merit a reply from Frémont. With movement against Columbus stymied, Grant bided time by sending out reconnaissance patrols, dispatching naval vessels to study the placement of Confederate batteries on the Kentucky bluffs, and gauging the strength of Rebel troops at their Belmont, Missouri, camp across from Columbus. He worked sources for intelligence that led him to conclude Polk was content to stay on the defensive, which only strengthened Grant's desire to take the offensive. He shared this desire and frustration with Julia: "I am very sorry that I have not got a force to go south with, at least to Columbus, but the fates seem to be against any such thing.... What I want is to advance."[5]

The frustration was about more than losing an opportunity to seize a strategic Confederate fortress: he sensed his budding military career was threatened, again telling Julia, "I would like to have the honor of commanding the Army that makes the advance down the river, but unless I am able to do it soon cannot expect it. There are to[o] many Generals who rank me that have commands inferior to mine for me to retain it."[6] In other words, he feared being replaced soon by someone who might reap the glory that could have been his.

Grant made one last appeal late in October when he presented Frémont's adjutant, Captain McKeever, with the tantalizing item that Polk had had troops drawn away from Columbus. Now was the time, Grant pressed, "that if Genl [C. F.] Smith, and my command were prepared it might now be taken."[7] This pitch, like the earlier two, elicited no response from Frémont. However, before the week ended, Grant's desire to advance would come closer to realization.

—❦—

Out in southwest Missouri, Frémont fretted that Price might be reinforced from Columbus. To forestall that possibility, on Friday, November 1, he dispatched an order to Grant to "hold your whole command at an hours notice" and "to make demonstrations with your troops along both sides of the river ...

without, however, attacking the enemy."[8] In other words, Grant was only to make some martial bluster to put Polk on the defensive so he dared not release any troops. On Saturday, Frémont followed with another order to have Grant detach troops to oppose Jeff Thompson, whose Swamp Rats were said to be at Indian Ford on the St. Francis River, about sixty miles west of Columbus.[9] Frémont feared that Thompson's cavalry might serve as a screen for any reinforcements being sent to Price. From Grant's District of Southeast Missouri, Colonel Richard Oglesby's and Colonel Joseph Plummer's commands were sent off against Thompson. As for Frémont, these should have been among his last acts as department commander. Patience in Washington had worn so thin over corruption in his department and his proclamation to emancipate slaves of Missourians abetting the rebellion that he was relieved on November 2. He was temporarily replaced in the field the next day by Major General David Hunter.

At district headquarters in Cairo, John Rawlins sensed the military drumbeat was picking up tempo. Preparations had to be made double-quick for any chance to drive off Jeff Thompson. Rawlins dispatched orders expediting Oglesby's regiments. He directed that the Eighteenth and Twenty-Ninth Illinois have ready ammunition, rations, and forage to move out by 4:00 p.m. on November 3. A similar order went out under Rawlins's name to mobilize a section of Oglesby's artillery.[10]

Activity at Grant's headquarters suddenly escalated after Frémont's removal. Grant alerted McClernand on November 5 that he would be embarking on a "reconnoisance [sic] in force" on the evening of the sixth. Orders went out to General Charles F. Smith at Paducah to make a demonstration toward Columbus while Grant, acting on supposed instructions from headquarters, outfitted an expedition to "menace Belmont." Smith's demonstration, as Grant explained, was to keep Polk from sending any more troops over to Belmont "than they now have there, and might enable me to drive those they have now out of Missouri."[11] Significantly, Grant was using the words "menace" and "drive out," which connote a more aggressive attitude than "to make demonstrations." But the main reason, Grant told Smith, for his move downriver against Belmont was to prevent Polk from sending a pursuing force against Oglesby or Plummer.

In addition, on Wednesday, November 6, Grant recalled Oglesby from chasing Thompson and instructed him to move toward New Madrid, Missouri, and, when arriving "at the nearest point to Columbus from which there is a road to that place, communicate with me at Belmont."[12] Grant scholar John Y. Simon speculated that Oglesby's order to return to Grant might indicate that at this moment, Grant could have been contemplating assaulting Columbus or turning its flank.[13]

How to account for this sudden surge in activity and preparation? In his revised report on Belmont written almost two and a half years later, Grant professed to the arrival on November 5 of a telegram from department head-quarters in St. Louis, which allegedly stated "that the enemy was reinforcing Price's Army from Columbus by way of White river, and directing that the demonstrations that had been ordered against Columbus, be immediately made."[14] Responding as if this were the long-awaited permission to advance, Grant sprang into action.

The sunny morning of November 6 was devoted to making all prepara-tions to ship out on "reconnaissance." Because Grant kept his plans closely concealed, much speculation abounded among officers and men as to where they were headed and for what purpose. The men had been straining for weeks to get into a fight, so the physical activity of preparation—packing knapsacks, frying rations, filling cartridge boxes, cleaning rifles, loading supplies onto wagons—helped drain energy arising from anticipation.

McClernand's brigade, the Twenty-Seventh, Thirtieth, and Thirty-First Il-linois and a cavalry company, was encamped at Cairo. Around midafternoon, they started embarking onto troop transports. As darkness approached, the transports shoved off southward to nearby Bird's Point, Missouri, where a small brigade consisting of two regiments, the Seventh Iowa and Twenty-Second Il-linois, boarded the plush *Memphis Belle*, Grant's headquarters steamer. It was dark before all men, horses, artillery, and ordnance were stowed on board and nine o'clock when the five transports steamed downriver in the wake of the two leading gunboats, *Tyler* and *Lexington*. All told, Grant counted a com-bined force of about thirty-one hundred infantry, cavalry, and artillerymen.

Because the steamers were flowing with the current, the soldiers erupted in cheers, excited that Columbus would be their destination. Finally, a fight was in the offing! It seemed more certain that Columbus was the destination when around 11:00 p.m., the boats tied up on the Kentucky shore. Instead of turning in, most men talked animatedly, rehearsing for what was to come. There would be little sleep for Grant's staff. As 2:00 a.m. approached, AAG John Rawlins was bent over a desk in the headquarters office of the *Memphis Belle* scratching out an order from Grant intended for immediate delivery:

On Board Steamer Belle Memphis
November 7, 1861—2 o'clock a.m.

The troops comprising the present expedition from this place will move promptly at 6 o'clock this morning. The gunboats will take the advance, and be followed by the First Brigade, under command of Brig Gen. John A. McClernand, composed of all the troops from Cairo and Fort Holt. The Second Brigade, comprising the remainder of the troops of the expedition, commanded by Col. Henry Dougherty, will follow. The entire force will debark at the lowest point on the Missouri shore where a landing can be effected in security from the rebel batteries.[15]

Rawlins handed a copy to Colonel Dougherty, which was the first he learned he would command Second Brigade. The thrill of assuming command would be tempered by the three grievous wounds he suffered later that day—and would never recover from.[16]

During this early hour, a messenger, never identified and allegedly sent from Colonel W. H. L. Wallace, was brought on board. He possessed important intelligence gleaned recently from an unnamed "reliable union man." The Union man reported he had seen Confederates "crossing troops from Columbus to Belmont the day before, for the purpose of following after and cutting off the forces under Col. Oglesby."[17] As Grant said later, this intelligence instantly focused his expedition: "I knew there was a small camp of Confederates at Belmont, immediately opposite Columbus, and I speedily resolved to push down the river, land on the Missouri side, capture Belmont, break up the camp and return."[18]

—⁓⁓⁓—

So this was the plan: hustle downriver, tussle with the Rebels, inflict as much damage as possible, and hustle back upriver. It seemed straightforward, but questions, mostly unanswered, have been raised as to why this fight at Belmont occurred, how it was officially reported, and whether Grant won or lost it. For example, was Grant's decision to turn a demonstration into combat made on the fly or concocted in advance? What about the orders and intelligence that brought Grant to a face-off against Polk? With Frémont having been sacked on November 2, who issued those November 5 orders from department headquarters in St. Louis directing Grant to demonstrate against Columbus? And there was the unorthodox manner in which a revised official report of the fight at Belmont was later compiled and submitted—and the hand John Rawlins had in writing it. These issues will be developed later in the chapter.

At dawn on November 7, the fleet of seven Federal vessels departed the Kentucky shore and edged down the Missouri side looking for a secure landing place, one out of sight of the Confederate gunners on the Columbus bluffs. A suitable spot was found about three miles as the river bends above Belmont.

Belmont, or a handful of simple structures, was "a steamboat landing rather than a town."[19] Separated from Columbus by one-half mile of river, it made an excellent point from which the Confederacy could ferry troops between Kentucky and Missouri. A small contingent of Confederates—an infantry regiment, a bit of cavalry, and an artillery battery—was encamped on an open stretch that fronted against the Mississippi. This observation post, which consisted mostly of tents and a drill field, was named Camp Johnston in honor of Albert Sidney Johnston, who commanded all Confederate troops west of the Alleghenies. Behind Camp Johnston lay formidable woodland through which ran a couple of roads that provided access to the camp. On this back side of the camp, a defensive obstacle called an abatis had been erected. It was created by sharpening limbs of felled trees and pointing them in the direction of a likely attack.

After Grant and his staff got the troops disembarked, the five regiments were formed in columns by 8:30 a.m. for a southerly tramp down a country lane through cornfields, wetland, and woodland and eventually around to the rear of Camp Johnston. If all went well, Grant had the advantages of surprise and numerical superiority.

—◦◦◦—

Almost as soon as the Federal transports touched the Missouri bank, Leonidas Polk was alerted, and he sent an aide beating across the river to warn Camp Johnston. So much for the element of surprise. Polk had to make a quick judgment: was this just a Yankee ruse? Would the Federals' main attack come from Paducah? Polk couldn't risk waiting to find out. He called on Brigadier General Gideon Pillow, his second in command, to take four reinforcement regiments over to Belmont. That negated Grant's numerical advantage. Pillow was a wealthy planter-politician from Tennessee and an owner of vast tracts of land and multitudes of slaves. As a general during the Mexican War, he earned a reputation for arrogance and foolish tactical judgment. Pillow was reviled by some career military men and considered a laughingstock by most; Grant was in the latter group.

Pillow arrived about 9:00 a.m. His untrained military eye allowed him to set up a defensive line northwest of the camp in an exposed cornfield facing thick woods. In the meantime, the Union troops worked their way inland through a muddy slough, dense undergrowth, and large sycamore trees. Knots of Rebel skirmishers in thickets or behind trees kept up a ragged fire that hindered the Federals' progress. Grant's acting medical director, Dr. John Brinton—Dr. Simons was on leave in Baltimore visiting his wife's relations—was absorbed by the escalating drama of combat and rode at a distance behind the advancing infantry, but close enough to feel the warmth of the musketry: "About this time I learned for the first time the sound of a bullet. . . . I could hear all around me the whiz of the bullets, and the dry pat as they cut through the dead leaves. At first I could not think what the noise was, but soon one fellow came unpleasantly near my ear, and as I saw and heard the dry leaves rip and fly, and saw the holes which were left, I then knew what it all meant. Then, too, men were hit near me and I began to feel uncomfortable."[20]

The Federals returned fire in kind. They took cover behind trees and peppered away, with little effect, at an enemy mostly concealed from view. Grant, accompanied by his staff, rode among the men, yelling words of encouragement and trying to coax them from their shelter. The thin line of Rebel skirmishers gradually melted before the oncoming Federal regiments. Grant shouted to Rawlins, "Stop the men, they are wasting ammunition." Not even Rawlins's deep, booming voice could be heard over the racket. His order was drowned out by "the thunder of the captains and the shouting." While Grant rode among the men, exhorting them not to fire until they saw a target, his horse was taken down by a shot in a hind leg. Rawlins was with Grant at this precise instant. He described this situation a week later in a letter to his mother: "I was by the side of General Grant when his horse was shot under him. Just the moment before he was trying to urge his horse up to the ranks of our men, and his horse not being very bridle-wise, refused to go ahead, and my horse being one that will go any place, I rode ahead, the General following. Just then I turned to look towards him, when the General said his horse was shot so severely that it was necessary to leave him on the field."[21] Luckily, Hillyer was also on the scene to give Grant his horse.[22]

Once the Rebel skirmishers were pushed aside, the Union attacking column emerged from the woods at about 11:00 a.m. and discovered the Confederates in the cornfield. They were greeted by a volley from the Rebel artillery that chased them back into the woods. Pillow sent his men forward into the woods in an old-fashioned bayonet charge, but a Yankee counterattack hurled them back into the cornfield and beyond. The Federals brought up their own cannon as the Rebels fled back to the safety of Camp Johnston. As if sensing a wounded prey, the Federals pursued them to the camp perimeter. There was little but the abatis to slow them down.

Up to this point, Grant had been fighting with only four regiments. A fifth, the Twenty-Seventh Illinois, had somehow gone unaccounted for. The Twenty-Seventh was commanded by Colonel Napoleon Bonaparte Buford, a Kentuckian and former West Point classmate and friend of Leonidas Polk. The Twenty-Seventh had started the operation on the right end of the Union line, but as it marched along, the regiment kept veering farther right. Buford's men had to bypass a shallow slough that took them south and onto unfamiliar roads. At a fork in the road, Buford decided a left turn would bring them to the fighting. It was a serendipitous choice. "Acting without the knowledge of his superiors, dangerously separated from the main body, indeed, threatening to jeopardize Grant's entire mission," Buford was marching toward the lightly defended rear of Camp Johnston and sidling into position to land a telling blow.[23] The boys of the Twenty-Seventh linked up with the Seventh Iowa and Twenty-Second Illinois to tangle with the abatis.

The Union regiments picked their way through the abatis and flooded into Camp Johnston. Volleys of musket fire chased Pillow's men through rows of tents, out of the camp, and north up a road to the safety of the riverbank. Near 2:00 p.m., the firing ceased. Grant's troops felt flushed with victory and commenced celebrating. Some company musicians started tooting patriotic airs; other Yankees, famished from the morning's fight, dug into Johnny Reb breakfasts still in the frying pans. General McClernand, ever the politician, saw an opportunity to arouse patriotic ardor in constituents and launched into speechifying. "Some of the higher officers were little better than the privates," Grant wrote later in his *Memoirs*, in a not very veiled dig at McClernand: "They galloped about from one cluster of men to another and at every halt delivered a short eulogy upon the Union cause and the achievements of the command."[24] Meanwhile, clouds of gun smoke swirled over the camp, panicked horses raced to and fro, and the soldiers became a mob of looters, gathering up abandoned weapons and poking through tents for trophies. Grant, satisfied his mission to smash Belmont was accomplished and figuring it time to withdraw, ordered his aides to torch the Rebels' tents. This was done more to impede the looters than to punish the Rebels.

While the Yankees caroused inside Camp Johnston, Polk unleashed a furious artillery barrage. Shot and shell arced over the Mississippi, mostly harmlessly over the heads of the Federals. However, a shell from the Confederates' largest gun, a 128-pound Whitworth called the Lady Polk, slammed into the drill field. While Rawlins nervously appraised the mounting danger, he saw a soldier lift a canvas-covered trunk onto his horse and gallop off. Another soldier, a sergeant, stood near Rawlins by the flap of a Rebel's tent, calmly rolling up a bundle of pilfered clothing. Infuriated, Rawlins barked, "Collect your men at once; we must get out of this." The sergeant, unaware of the hit-and-run objective of the operation, replied, "What and give up the position?"[25]

Meanwhile, an officer of the Thirtieth Illinois returned from a scouting party alerted Grant that Confederate reinforcements were coming from the opposite side of the river.[26] Dr. Brinton spied the stacks of two steamers heading upriver and pointed them out to Grant, who saw them brimming with enemy troops.[27] Polk had committed the last of his reserves. These reserve regiments were led by Brigadier General Benjamin Franklin Cheatham, a hard-drinking secessionist Democrat from Nashville. Cheatham came ashore north of Camp Johnston where Pillow's beaten men found safety. Cheatham's force merged with Pillow's stragglers, and the combined forces marched southward and inland to take another crack at the Yankees.

With effort, Grant got his exhausted men into a column to retrace the route back to their transports. The column hadn't progressed too far when Cheatham's men appeared on its right flank and fell on Henry Dougherty's brigade. A few volleys were exchanged, and then Cheatham ordered a bayonet charge. After an interval of fierce fighting, the Union line crumbled. Meanwhile at the head of the column was one of the regiments of McClernand's brigade, the Thirty-First Illinois under Colonel John "Black Jack" Logan. With Confederates pressing the right flank, Logan, to his horror, discovered that the path ahead was blocked by gray-jacketed infantry. It was the Eleventh Louisiana, part of Polk's second batch of reinforcements, and they were not in a conciliatory mood. Panic suddenly gripped the Federal line, and cries of "surrounded" rang out. At this moment of crisis, Grant's cooler head provided the needed leadership: "At first some of the officers seemed to think that to be surrounded was to be placed in a hopeless position, where there was nothing to do but surrender. But when I announced that we had cut our way in and could cut our way out just as well, it seemed a new revelation to officers and soldiers."[28] With the help of an artillery battery and the orders to cut their way through, the men of Logan's Thirty-First Illinois forced a breakout.[29]

From this point, it was every man for himself. The retreat turned into a rout as the Louisiana boys, strung along the Yankee flank, peppered their fleeing targets with impunity. The way back was littered with discarded knapsacks, rifles, blankets, and even wounded comrades—anything that hampered the dash to the transports. Luckily for the Federals, the Confederates' pursuit was tardy, giving Grant a window to get his men reembarked. A squirming mass of officers and men elbowed for position, forced to make way for the occasional artillery piece or frightened horse being loaded aboard. The Union regiments might get off in time, but it would be close.

Grant and Rawlins rode down the riverbank a quarter mile to retrieve a battalion that had been posted to guard the boats. However, they found no one there—the battalion, without orders, had vacated the post. This left Grant and Rawlins well outside their lines, fully exposed. As they headed back, a contingent of Rebel infantry emerged from a nearby cornfield. Grant, wrapped in an enlisted man's overcoat, slowed his horse to a walk to avoid attention. But the Confederates were more interested in shooting at the docked Union transports.

Once the general and his adjutant thought that they were out of the Rebels' sightline, they spurred their horses to a gallop. Rawlins's horse was the faster. As Rawlins clambered up the gangplank of the *Memphis Belle*, Grant trailed at a distance, an easy target.[30] He barely made it aboard, as he later described:

> I was the only man of the National army between the rebels and our transports. The captain of a boat that had just pushed out but had not started, recognized me and ordered the engineer not to start the engine; he then had a plank run out for me. My horse seemed to take in the situation. . . . My horse put his fore feet over the bank without hesitation or urging, and with his hind feet well under him, slid down the bank and trotted aboard the boat, twelve or fifteen feet away, over a single gang plank. I dismounted and went at once to the upper deck.[31]

Under withering fire from the Confederates on the riverbank and with covering fire from the gunboats, the transports, with the regiments aboard—well, almost all the regiments—churned upriver.

—◈—

Most of Napoleon Buford's Twenty-Seventh Illinois regiment was unaccounted for. It had fallen out of the retreating column and drifted westward during Cheatham's attack. McClernand had gone out himself to look for them, without success, because this time Buford had gotten badly disoriented. His troops endured an exhausting march before they arrived at the river's edge and discovered the transports and gunboats had already left. All that saved Buford and his men from a long trek back to their base was a quick decision by McClernand to turn around a transport and watch for their emergence along the riverbank. Somewhat miraculously, the men of the Twenty-Seventh began assembling on the bank, and by 6:00 p.m., the last of the strays had been picked up.

Napoleon Buford was saved, but his performance at Belmont sank his career. When his name appeared on the promotion roll fifteen months later, Grant and Rawlins hoped to scuttle Buford's promotion. In his succinct writing style, Grant gave Lincoln a scathing appraisal of Buford's fitness for more responsible command: "I see the name of N. B. Buford for Maj. Gen. He would scarsely make a respectable Hospital nurse if put in petticoats, and certain is unfit for any other Military position. He has always been a dead weight to carry becoming more burthensome with his increased rank."[32] The more verbose Rawlins made about the same point in a letter to Congressman Elihu Washburne:

> I see by the papers the name of Napoleon Bonaparte Buford before the Senate for confirmation as Major General, which confirmation would be so unjust to the many brave and deserving men and officers of the "Army of the Tennessee" that I feel it my duty to call your attention, "as friend of this Army" and the one to whom it owes so much for the proper representation at Washington, to the fact, that if so possible so great a calamity if it has not already fallen, may be prevented. . . . His disobedience of positive orders given him on the field of Battle at Belmont came near losing to the country his entire Regiment which was only saved from such fate by the fire from our gun boats driving him off of the main road, and thereby avoided meeting the enemy. . . . As it was, it was the merest accident he was saved. For his conduct at Belmont he was never afterwards trusted by Genls. Grant or McClernand. He was left behind on the expedition into Kentucky, and also against Forts Henry and Donelson.[33]

Grant and Rawlins got the desired result: the Senate failed to confirm Buford as major general. It would not be the only time that Rawlins would vent his wrath against a general who had lost his bearings.

—⁓—

In the wake of combat, an interval is reserved to mend the broken survivors and inter the dead; convey news, hopefully reassuring, to those back home;

appraise the outcome of that combat; construct, in each combatant's mind, a personal story or narrative to give meaning to his harrowing experience; and submit a final report. So it was with the battle of Belmont.

As soon as practicable, Union and Confederate details, working under flags of truce, combed the battlefield tending to the wounded and arranging burials. In the war's early days, few were inured to the horrific aftermath of battle. Dr. Brinton was not prepared for a grisly discovery:

> The next day I saw a fearful case; a shell had exploded behind, but close to, the back of a soldier. He was dying when I saw him and evidently in a dreadful condition, so I dismounted to render him what help I could. I have never seen a worse wound, before or since. The whole of the skin and muscles of the back from the nape of the neck to the thighs and on both sides of the spine had been torn away, as if the tissues had been scooped out by a clean-cutting curved instrument. . . . In a moment or two he expired, and I remounted and rode on.[34]

For a small battle, Belmont was particularly sanguinary. Union losses were reported as 120 men killed, 383 wounded, and 104 missing or captured, and Confederate losses as 105, 409, and 117, respectively. Considering that Grant's force was little more than 3,100, the casualty rate of almost 20 percent is substantial.[35]

Grant dispatched Major Joseph Webster the day after the battle to confer with General Polk about tending to casualties. Over the next two months, Webster would play a key role in prisoner exchange. Soon after, Grant, accompanied by a retinue of staff and senior officers, met with Polk and his command to congenially discuss the finer points of prisoner exchange and principles of civility that should obtain during the exigencies of war. General Cheatham proposed a more sporting way to decide the war's winner by staging "a grand, international horse-race over on the Missouri shore," to which proposal "Grant laughingly answered that he wished it might be so."[36]

In the aftermath of the battle, folks in Galena were eager for news about favorite sons Grant and Rawlins. In Cairo, C. H. Pendleton of Galena reported he "saw General Grant and Adjutant Rawlins after their return from Belmont. They were in excellent health and spirits, having accomplished in their expedition about all that they expected." And what had Grant expected to accomplish? According to Pendleton, Grant had heard that "three or four regiments of rebels were in a fortified camp at Belmont, [and] Gen. Grant concluded to go down with about an equal number of men and clean them out." During the cleansing process, Grant lost "2 or 3 horses under him," and "at one time [during the battle] Adjutant Gen. Rawlins was the only officer of the staff to be found on horseback."[37] This was the horse that outran Grant's mount to the *Memphis Belle* and the one recently presented to Rawlins by the townsfolk of Galena, who would be relieved to know the horse "was in the fight of the battle of Belmont and escaped with its rider without a scratch. It is a popular animal in the army, and is as fearless as its owner."[38]

Regarding the battle's outcome, opinions in the first few weeks were mixed—not unexpected given that the Federals were chased off the field and back to their boats. Congressman Washburne's early take on the result heaped praise on all: "We have only meagre details of the battle of Belmont, and all concur that the most brilliant fighting was done there that has been done during the war, and that our troops covered themselves with glory, and, further, that you and McClernand have won undying laurels. My regards to Capt. Rawlins."[39] Replying to the congressman, Grant wholeheartedly agreed: "The battle of Belmont, as time passes, proves to have been a greater success than Gen. McClernand or myself at first thought. The enemies loss proves to be greater and the effect upon the Southern mind more saddening."[40] The Republican *Galena Daily Advertiser* crowed, "If this is not a victory to our arms, we do not know the meaning of the expression."[41] However, the *Chicago Tribune* blasted the Belmont operation as a "disastrous termination of the Cairo expedition to Columbus. . . . Our troops have suffered a bad defeat."[42] A week barely passed before the *Daily Advertiser*'s editor criticized both the *Tribune* for printing "malicious flings" against Grant and the Springfield *Journal* for claiming "that the attack at Belmont was not a success" and for finding "great fault with the generalship there."[43] Even some soldiers in Grant's command were unconvinced that a victory had occurred. Conrad Betts, a private and musician in the Twenty-Ninth Illinois of Oglesby's brigade, wrote his sweetheart that "The Boys . . . had a desperate Battle Nov. 7th at Belmont Missouri. They were defeated and many who I had formed acquaintances with were hurried to their long home."[44]

When congratulations were meted out by the chief executive in Washington, they were directed to McClernand, the subordinate, and not the commander of the expedition. Two days after the battle, Lincoln wrote McClernand, "You have had a battle, and without being able to judge as to the precise measure of its value, I think it safe to say that you, and all with you have done honor to yourselves and the flag and service to your country. Most gratefully do I thank you and them."[45] Rawlins's feelings about McClernand were quite the opposite. "God damn it, it's insubordination!" Rawlins allegedly exclaimed. "McClernand says—. McClernand did—. After his great victory McClernand—. The bastard! The damned, slinking, Judas bastard!"[46]

Belmont was Rawlins's first exposure to combat, and he had not kept out of harm's way, as he described his experience to Lovisa: "I have been in one battle, heard the whistling of bullets and the whizzing of cannon balls, and I tell you I thought no more of the first than of the last; still I never thought of running. . . . Your mind is filled more with a desire of winning victory than of personal safety, and this is felt more strongly when the chances appear against you. Success is the paramount feeling. I was in the midst of danger and within the reach of rebel fire more than once during the day."[47] In this letter, Rawlins put into context the confusing and dangerous event he had just survived. Being exposed to fire seemed to stir, even embolden Rawlins. If he had wondered whether he would stand or run when tested, he had his answer: he learned he had the makeup to hold his ground and even blot out thoughts of danger.

If Rawlins entertained doubts beforehand about the strength of his courage, he must surely have wondered how intensely his fellow Democrats would demonstrate their battlefield fervor. Belmont gave him an answer: "We had three thousand men all told, the effective and well men of five regiments, commanded by Colonels Buford, Logan, Fouke, Dougherty and Lauman, the three first under General McClernand, the other two under Colonel Dougherty, while all were under the command of General Grant. All of the above mentioned officers, except Colonel Lauman, whose politics I do not know, are Democrats. I mention this to show that Democrats will fight (I mean Union Democrats) for the country, Washington and the stars and stripes."[48]

Here, he saw a manifestation of the impassioned plea he made during the great Galena speech seven months earlier: that this crisis transcends party politics and requires steadfastness to the Union. He closed the letter to Lovisa with rhetoric that underscored this point: "I am glad old Guilford is for the Union. I am as you are a Democrat, but I am also for the Union of the States and the triumph of my country in arms against whomsoever may oppose us."[49]

As historian John Y. Simon put it, "Once the battle ended, Grant faced the problem of explaining it."[50] If the aphorism that a job is not completed until the paperwork is submitted is true, Grant wasn't finished with Belmont until much later. His first explanation, or official report, was sent in shortly after returning to Cairo. However, a second official report, revised and backdated, which Rawlins assisted in preparing, was not sent to the War Department until almost three years after the battle.[51] The authenticity of the November 5 telegram from Department Headquarters and unnamed messenger contained in that second report that was composed by Rawlins and used by Grant to justify the attack against Camp Johnston have complicated historians' attempts to understand the battle at Belmont.

—◦◦◦—

Grant's first report of the Belmont affair, dated November 10, was relatively light on details. It includes, among a few topics, his two reasons for the expedition: to prevent Price from being reinforced and Plummer's and Oglesby's columns from being cut off as they pursued Jeff Thompson. His description of the battle is brief but mentions charging through an enemy attempting to surround him. And there is an encomium reserved for his personal staff: "To my staff, Capts. Rawlins[,] Lagow & Hillyer, and volunteer Aides, Capts. Hatch & Graham I am much indebted for the assistance they gave.—Col. Webster, acting chief Engineer also accompanied me and displayed highly soldierlike qualities."[52]

Then, for reasons known to himself only, Grant allowed a second report to be prepared in the spring of 1864 and backdated to November 17, 1861. Perhaps Grant, who had weathered criticism for Belmont, had grown more defensive about it.[53] Perhaps he was concerned that the reasons he cited earlier simply wouldn't pass muster long-term—for example, Polk was known to have been dug in at Columbus and not about to part with any troops on Price's behalf— and a revision was in order.[54] Perhaps when Commander-in-Chief Lieutenant General Grant pondered his momentous move against Lee and Richmond in spring of 1864, he did not want questions about his first military operation to resurface.

The revised report was finished on April 26, 1864. Rawlins wrote it with the assistance of another staffer, Theodore "Joe" Bowers.[55] Rawlins spoke about the revision in a letter written the next day to his second wife: "Colonel Bowers and myself finished yesterday General Grant's report of the battle of Belmont. It is a very creditable one and places that engagement in its true light for transmittal to posterity, so far as could be known to our side. I have long since learned than an action creditable in itself can be best presented in the garb of real facts. So whenever you see any report with which I have had anything whatever to do, depend upon it, the historian who accepted it as true will most certainly not deceive the searchers after truth."[56]

Unlike the original version, the revision contains two critical items that appear to give a rationale for Grant's decision to attack Belmont. There is that claim of a November 5 telegram arriving from department headquarters in St. Louis ordering an immediate demonstration against Columbus, because Price was being reinforced from Columbus by way of the White River. However, this telegram has never been found, and there is doubt that it ever existed. Moreover, Frémont, who had been sacked three days earlier, was not around to issue it. John Simon speculated that Grant's staff "extrapolated" the existence of this telegram from those bona fide telegrams dispatched from St. Louis on November 1 and 2 that ordered Grant "to make demonstrations along both sides of the Mississippi and to send troops in order to disperse Brig. Gen. M Jeff Thompson who reported to be at Indian Ford on the St. Francis river."[57] If this speculation holds, Rawlins and Bowers probably made a good-faith error.

The second questionable item in the revision concerns the mysterious 2:00 a.m. messenger sent from Colonel W. H. L. Wallace, who was bearing intelligence gleaned from the "reliable union man" who allegedly saw Confederate troops crossing from Columbus to Belmont and thereby posing a threat to Oglesby. None of Grant's early accounts of the battle include any mention of such a message or messenger. No record of the message has ever turned up. Furthermore, no Confederate force was sent to intercept Oglesby. W. H. L. Wallace was not available in 1864 to add his perspective to the story because he was mortally wounded at the Battle of Shiloh in 1862.[58] Nonetheless, both the telegram and 2:00 a.m. message came to be included later in Grant's personal narrative—in his *Memoirs*—of the Belmont campaign.[59]

To construct the revised report, Rawlins and Bowers borrowed, or perhaps extrapolated from, documents and records from fall 1861. Rawlins would have relied also on his recollections—Bowers would have had none, because he wasn't on staff at that time—of an early November morning fraught with last-minute combat preparations and details, recollections that may have become imprecise over time. Was Rawlins purely motivated to provide historians with the "real facts" about Belmont and to shed a "true light" on the operation? Or, "judging from the rough treatment given Grant over Belmont," was the Rawlins and Bowers account "an effort to deflect further criticism from their boss, now [in 1864] commander of all Union armies"?[60] Given Rawlins's loyalty to and protectiveness of Grant, this latter motive cannot be ruled out. There is also evidence that when a situation called for it, Rawlins was not above offering a narrative that a historian would have trouble accepting as true—recall John Spare's story that Rawlins presented as his own one of Richard Yates's speeches to the Odd Fellows, and no one was the wiser.

Initially, Grant was to make only a demonstration toward Columbus, but it is now believed "that Grant had in mind more than mere saber rattling."[61] This was perhaps his only chance to take the offensive and a calculated risk. As biographer William McFeely put it, "Grant had set out to fight and to take the fort—not to demonstrate."[62] Following Frémont's departure, department command was in flux, so there was no one to stop Grant from attacking. Belmont was lightly defended and a less risky target than Columbus.[63] Later, the references to the November 5 telegram and the 2:00 a.m. intelligence report would establish that Grant was justified to make the advance he had been hankering to make and give the appearance he was taking properly aggressive action to protect Union troops. But as historian William Feis concludes, "Unfortunately, in their attempt to set the record straight, Rawlins and Bowers only confused the issue further by offering unsubstantiated evidence to demonstrate that their chief had exhibited wisdom and prudence, not reckless insubordination."[64]

—⁓—

Belmont was a fight between raw adversaries. As Rawlins noted, Grant went into battle with men "some of whom had had arms issued to them for the first time only two days before."[65] The rawness extended to the way in which Grant underutilized his personal staff who, during the battle, "functioned more as a headquarters escort than they did as instruments of command."[66] That one of the escorts included Grant's Black servant, Bob, revealed the informality of the operation. Grant had not yet progressed to cultivating a staff that could serve as his arm on the battlefield. Later, as battles grew in size, trained staff would be needed to coordinate action on the field.[67]

John Rawlins did not emerge from Belmont humbly thanking Providence for having sustained him. On the contrary, he emerged feeling like a conqueror—"the great majority of men and officers engaged in it felt they were the victors."[68] Rawlins, as he told his mother, had taken part in the defeat of an elite enemy "consisting of Tennessee, Arkansas and Louisiana troops, the flower of Southern chivalry."[69] And a magnificent victory it was too. "We met and defeated them on their own ground, took possession of and burnt all their tents and camp equipage, captured six pieces of artillery and brought two with us, all under the guns of the strongest fortified position on the Mississippi River."[70]

However, there was more to take from Belmont than these spoils of battle. A lesson had been learned. The success achieved there had been due to "the advantage of taking the initiative, and made [Rawlins] always afterward the earnest advocate of striking the first blow."[71] Belmont could only have strengthened the bond between Rawlins and Grant. Facing enemy fire together tempered their mutual trust. Rawlins came away with renewed respect for his commander. He saw a leader who had the strength to will his men through the pincers of the enemy. He saw a man of action, not equivocation.

NOTES

1. U. S. Grant, *Personal Memoirs of U. S. Grant* (New York: Charles L. Webster, 1885), 1:269.
2. *The War of the Rebellion: A Compilation of the Official Records of the Union and Confederate Armies*, series 1 (1881), 3:484.
3. U. S. Grant to J. C. Frémont, September 10, 1861, in *The Papers of Ulysses S. Grant*, ed. John Y. Simon (Carbondale: Southern Illinois University Press, 1969), 2:225.
4. U. S. Grant to J. C. Frémont, September 12, 1861, in *The Papers of Ulysses S. Grant*, ed. John Y. Simon, 2:242.
5. U. S. Grant to Julia Dent Grant, October 20, 1861, in *The Papers of Ulysses S. Grant*, ed. John Y. Young (Carbondale: Southern Illinois University Press, 1970), 3:63–64.
6. U. S. Grant to J. C. Frémont, September 10, 1861in *The Papers of Ulysses S. Grant*, ed. John Y. Simon, 2:300.
7. U. S. Grant to Chauncey McKeever, October 27, 1861, in *The Papers of Ulysses S. Grant*, ed. John Y. Simon, 3:78.
8. Ibid., 143–44.
9. Ibid., 144.
10. Ibid., 109n, 110n2.
11. U. S. Grant to J. A. McClernand, November 5, 1861, in *The Papers of Ulysses S. Grant*, ed. John Y. Simon, 3:113; U. S. Grant to C. F. Smith, November 5, 1861, in *The Papers of Ulysses S. Grant*, ed. John Y. Simon, 3:114.
12. U. S. Grant to R. J. Oglesby, November 6, 1861, in *The Papers of Ulysses S. Grant*, ed. John Y. Simon, 3:145.
13. John Y. Simon, "Grant at Belmont," *Journal of Military History* 45, no. 4 (1981): 16–64.
14. U. S. Grant to Seth Williams, November 17, 1861, in *The Papers of Ulysses S. Grant*, ed. John Y. Simon, 3:145.
15. *Official Records of the Union and Confederate Armies*, series 1 (1881), 3:270.
16. Nathaniel Cheairs Hughes Jr., *The Battle of Belmont: Grant Strikes South* (Chapel Hill: University of North Carolina Press, 1991), 234n52; ibid., 216.

17. John Y. Simon, ed. *The Papers of Ulysses S. Grant*, 3:146.

18. U. S. Grant, *Personal Memoirs of U. S. Grant*, 1:271.

19. Nathaniel Cheairs Hughes Jr., *The Battle of Belmont*, 82.

20. John H. Brinton. *Personal Memoirs of John H. Brinton* (New York: Neale, 1914), 79.

21. James H. Wilson, *The Life of John A. Rawlins* (New York: Neale, 1916), 66.

22. Albert D. Richardson *A Personal History of Ulysses S. Grant* (Boston: D. L. Guernsey, 1885), 191.

23. Nathaniel Cheairs Hughes Jr., *The Battle of Belmont*, 111.

24. U. S. Grant, *Personal Memoirs of U. S. Grant*, 1:274.

25. Albert D. Richardson, *A Personal History of Ulysses S. Grant*, 192.

26. *Galena Daily Advertiser*, November 11, 1861.

27. John H. Brinton, *Personal Memoirs of John H. Brinton*, 77.

28. U. S. Grant, *Personal Memoirs of U. S. Grant*, 1:276.

29. Nathaniel Cheairs Hughes Jr., *The Battle of Belmont*, 153.

30. Albert D. Richardson, *A Personal History of Ulysses S. Grant*, 194.

31. U. S. Grant, *Personal Memoirs of U. S. Grant*, 1:277–78.

32. U. S. Grant to Abraham Lincoln, February 9, 1863, in *The Papers of Ulysses S. Grant*, ed. John Y. Simon (Carbondale: Southern Illinois University Press, 1979), 7:301.

33. J. A. Rawlins to E. Washburne, n.d., in *The Papers of Ulysses S. Grant*, ed. John Y. Simon, 7:302n.

34. John H. Brinton, *Personal Memoirs of John H. Brinton*, 75.

35. William M. Polk, "General Polk and the Battle of Belmont," in *Battles and Leaders of the Civil War*, eds. Robert Underwood Johnson and Clarence Clough Buel (1887; repr., New York: Thomas Yoseloff, 1956), 1:355–56. Some twenty years or more after the battle, one source reported that one of the casualties on the Confederate side was a Lieutenant Bob Hitt. Robert Hitt was John Rawlins's college friend from the Rock River Seminary and an Illinois congressman. That Robert Hitt served in the Confederate army seems a preposterous claim, and subsequent investigation proved it to be false; see Nathaniel Cheairs Hughes, *The Battle of Belmont*, 251n28.

36. William M. Polk, "General Polk and the Battle of Belmont," 357.

37. *Galena Daily Advertiser*, November 11, 1861.

38. Ibid., December 24, 1861.

39. John Y. Simon, ed., *The Papers of Ulysses S. Grant*, 3:206n1.

40. Ulysses S. Grant to Elihu B. Washburne, November 20, 1861, in *The Papers of Ulysses S. Grant*, ed. John Y. Simon, 3:205.

41. *Galena Daily Advertiser*, November 15, 1861.

42. *Chicago Tribune*, November 9, 1861.

43. *Galena Daily Advertiser*, November 18, 1861.

44. Conrad W. Betts to Ellen Sherman, November 15, 1861, collection of the author.

45. Roy P. Basler, ed., *The Collected Works of Abraham Lincoln* (New Brunswick: Rutgers University Press, 1953), 5:20.

46. Helen Todd, *A Man Named Grant* (Boston: Houghton Mifflin, 1940), 29–30.

47. James H. Wilson, *The Life of John A. Rawlins*, 65–66.

48. Ibid., 66.

49. Ibid., 67.

50. John Y. Simon, "Grant at Belmont," 165.

51. U. S. Grant to Seth Williams, November 10, 1861, in *The Papers of Ulysses S. Grant,* ed. John Y. Simon, 3:143n.

52. Ibid., 143.

53. Brooks D. Simpson, *Ulysses S. Grant: Triumph over Adversity* (Boston: Houghton Mifflin, 2000), 102.

54. John Y. Simon, "Grant at Belmont," 165.

55. Bowers was the twenty-nine-year-old editor of the Mount Carmel, IL, *Register* when brought onto Grant's staff as an aide-de-camp after the battle of Shiloh.

56. J. A. Rawlins to Emma, April 27, 1864, transcription in Wyoming State Archives, Bender Collection, James H. Wilson Papers, Microfilm Reel 61b.

57. John Y. Simon, ed., *The Papers of Ulysses S. Grant,* 3:149n1.

58. See ibid., 150n1, for a discussion of the enigmatic message; see ibid., 152, for a discussion of how several of Grant's biographers juxtapose his motives for attacking Belmont given these revelations contained in the revised report.

59. See U. S. Grant, *Personal Memoirs of U. S. Grant,* 1:270–71.

60. William B. Feis, *Grant's Secret Service: The Intelligence War from Belmont to Appomattox* (Lincoln: University of Nebraska Press, 2002), 48.

61. Ibid., 50.

62. William S. McFeely, *Grant* (New York: W. W. Norton, 1982), 92.

63. John Y. Simon, "Grant at Belmont," 163.

64. William B. Feis, *Grant's Secret Service,* 48.

65. General Rawlins's Address, November 14, 1866, in *Report of the Proceedings of the Society of the Army of the Tennessee at the First Annual Meeting* (Cincinnati: Author), 28.

66. Brooks D. Simpson, *Ulysses S. Grant,* 99.

67. Michael B. Ballard, *U. S. Grant: The Making of a General, 1861–1863* (Lanham, MD: Rowman and Littlefield, 2005), 21.

68. General Rawlins's Address, November 14, 1866, in *Report of the Proceedings of the Society of the Army of the Tennessee at the First Annual Meeting,* 28.

69. Ibid., 66.

70. Ibid., 67.

71. Ibid.

9

"His Eye and Intellect Are as Clear and Active as Can Be"

AFTER BELMONT, JULIA AND THE children arrived in Cairo for an extended visit. The Grants settled into the upper floors of Safford's bank, where it soon felt like old times, even extending to the children singing their Sunday school hymns.[1] Grant and his staff were in the headquarters office on the second floor. There, Rawlins culled through requisitions, while Grant, seated facing a window, fretted about equipping his troops, contemplated his next military movement, and braced for the new department commander, Major General Henry Halleck. Halleck appeared about two weeks after Belmont to assume command of the new Department of the Missouri.

With his high forehead and protruding eyes, Halleck looked more the scholar or fussy bureaucrat. Indeed, he graduated near the top of his West Point class, authored the *Elements of Military Art and Science*, and pushed papers to greater effect than he ever led troops in battle. His first challenge was addressing the corruption engulfing the department under Frémont's mismanagement. Halleck's superior, George McClellan, put it bluntly in a November 11 communication: "You have not merely the ordinary duties of a military commander to perform, but the far more difficult task of reducing chaos to order . . . and of reducing to a point of economy . . . a system of reckless expenditure and fraud, perhaps unheard of before in the history of the world."[2] The townspeople of Galena were alert to this corruption. The *Galena Daily Advertiser* of November 7 copied a report from the Cincinnati *Enquirer* that declared, "As to the military management of the army in Missouri . . . [p]rominent men there must love money more than they love their country, and if our

army is defeated in the impending battle, we shall fear that we have been literally, *sold*."

The situation was complicated by the fact that those (e.g., Halleck, Washburne, General C. F. Smith, and especially Grant) who were trying to clean
up the messes—not just fraud but backbiting among officers, and misapplied
patriotism—came under vicious attack. The attacks were played out inside
the political arena, in personal vendettas that leaked into the newspapers, and
even as charges of intoxication and lack of fitness for duty.

—⁓—

One of Halleck's first orders forbade runaway slaves from being harbored
at Federal military camps. In a tense border state like Missouri it was risky
to jeopardize the support of Unionist slave owners. His predecessor, back in
August, took the political misstep of emancipating the slaves of secessionists
within his department. Halleck's order "was as good as declaring that Fré-
montism was dead."[3] The runaway slave order and his crackdown on corruption brought Halleck much negative press from Frémont loyalists. General
Charles F. Smith, a regular army officer to the core and a staunch Unionist,
became the target of hurtful rumors of disloyalty. He was suspected of being
soft on secessionists and slave owners, but he was really a disciplinarian who
restrained his volunteer troops from acting aggressively against suspected
Rebel sympathizers. Some rumors were likely spread by a subordinate, Brigadier General Eleazar Paine, who had provoked Smith's ire during maneuvers
associated with Belmont. Smith requested department headquarters to convene a court of inquiry into what he called Paine's "unjustifiable departures
from my orders." Smith asserted that Paine had taken independent action that
put his men at risk for the "fixed purpose from the start to attempt to gain notoriety without reference to the public interests or his plain duty as a soldier."[4]
With Halleck's support, Smith was sustained. Newspapermen in Grant's
district circulated stories back to the North that accused Smith of returning
fugitive slaves to the purported owners. One of Rawlins's duties was supervising outgoing newspaper telegrams. Grant instructed Rawlins to expunge
any derogatory stories going over the wires about Smith. Rawlins replied that
correspondents could still send their rumors through the mail. Grant insisted
Rawlins do what he could to impede the inevitable: "Never mind. Any report
against Smith must be a lie. Stop it anyhow; that will make it twenty-four
hours later in seeing the light."[5]

Smith and Grant were connected by a nasty charge that made for lurid reading. In the latter part of October 1861, Grant and his staff visited Smith at Paducah. Smith's house was too small to accommodate the entire party, so his subordinate, Brigadier General Lew Wallace, made his lodging available to Grant and Rawlins. After enjoying dinner and cigars, Grant and Smith took a walk to talk business—probably Grant's ideas for dealing with the Rebels across from Columbus. The rest of the evening was spent telling Mexican war stories, puffing cigars, singing tunes off-key, and sipping a libation to stoke the coals of camaraderie. To Wallace's embarrassment, newspapers soon trumpeted this modest event as "an orgie [sic], a beastly drunken revel led by both Grant and Smith." Wallace traced this false story to a regimental chaplain who later resigned. Over the next several months Grant became the target of other false charges of intoxication, and Wallace regretted that these slanders originated in his house.[6]

One of the biggest fraud-busters was Elihu Washburne. He was part of a congressional committee charged with investigating crooked government contracts. The committee traveled to several cities, took testimony, and filed thick reports. Frémont's Western Department headquarters in St. Louis was heavily scrutinized. The committee was there from October 15 to October 29 and at Cairo on October 31, where Grant gave testimony. Washburne quickly uncovered gross irregularities in Fremont's department. As he wrote Lincoln on October 17, "We find things in the most deplorable condition imaginable. . . . The robberies, the frauds, the peculation in the gov't which have already come to our knowledge are absolutely frightful."[7] Surprisingly, there was no evidence that Frémont lined his pockets; he simply failed to rein in the crooks.

For all the waste the committee cleaned up, they took heat from the Radical Republicans, especially from powerful Thaddeus Stevens of Pennsylvania. Because the investigating committee contained moderate Republicans, they were criticized for being biased against Frémont from the start. The Radicals hailed Frémont as a political balancing weight in the west to General McClellan, a stalwart Democrat, in the east.

Even acting medical director Dr. Brinton came under the gun. During a brief absence by Grant, General McClernand assumed temporary command and ordered that all able-bodied men convalescing in hospitals should be returned to their command without regard to the duties they were performing in the hospitals. In that era, some physically able convalescing soldiers served as male nurses. These men played important roles because female nurses were in short supply. If Brinton had complied, "The order . . . would have instantly paralyzed the whole hospital department of the entire district of Cairo." When Grant returned, Brinton admitted his disobedience and was prepared for the consequences. To his astonishment, Grant penned an endorsement sustaining him. Brinton later said, "I doubt if another officer of his rank in the army would have supported a medical officer under like circumstances."[8]

As the year ended, Grant would find himself in the crosshairs of men determined to bring him down. He might have weathered the attacks on his own, but the help he got from John Rawlins improved his chances of survival.

—◦◦◦—

Illinois attorney Leonard Swett champed at the opportunity to share in the Cairo profiteering. Swett was politically connected, a recent Republican presidential elector, and a behind-the-scenes maneuverer for Lincoln at the Chicago nominating convention. Swett pushed Grant to appoint a person of his choosing to be the official post sutler[9] at Cairo. Figuring that this sutler would have unfair advantage, Grant refused to be buffaloed by Swett and rejected the plan. After some bitter exchanges, Swett took his complaint to the White House, but Lincoln upheld Grant.[10]

In late 1861, a Pennsylvanian named William Kountz was in Cairo and about to stir trouble for Grant. Kountz, a steamboat transportation expert, had developed close ties to McClellan during his western Virginia campaign when he was in charge of operating river vessels. Kountz also fashioned himself a reformer. During the summer of 1861, he investigated possible bribery in issuing transportation contracts at Cincinnati. The bribery charges were substantiated, but Kountz made enemies in the process. He bothered Montgomery Meigs, quartermaster general of the US Army, with plans to cut river freight costs. Kountz had some valid ideas, but he was too meddlesome by half. Meigs warned him, "You show one defect. You are too apt to quarrel with the officers of the United States. If you can not work harmoniously with those above you, you will be obliged to quit the service."[11] On receiving an army commission, Kountz was sent to St. Louis, where he began looking for inefficiencies in the supply system.

On about December 19, Kountz was in Cairo at General McClernand's post. McClernand told Quartermaster Reuben Hatch to allow Kountz to inspect all books and records in order to carry out his orders to analyze the needs of the command. Without much trouble, Kountz found evidence of alleged inefficiencies and irregularities, and McClernand recommended that he should see General Grant. Kountz met with Grant and told him of his findings. To Kountz's surprise, Grant came down hard on him: "You will desist from further investigation, until you have reported to me, and shown your authority . . . you have acted in a manner displaying great ignorance of Military usage in not reporting to the Commanding Officer the object, and authority of your visit."[12] Hardly chastened, Kountz frequented Grant's headquarters with drafts of his ambitious plans and was such a bother that Grant moved his office into the family quarters. Even Julia found Kountz's personality "malignant." During one visit, Rawlins's patience snapped. He unleashed a verbal rebuke against Kountz, blaming him for chasing the general out of his office. When Kountz took umbrage, an enraged Rawlins made a physical rush toward Kountz, expelled him from the room, and ordered him to stay away.[13]

Kountz couldn't keep from overstepping his bounds. Within weeks he discharged a steamboat from government service, thereby interfering with troop movements. It was too much for the usually mild-mannered Grant. To Halleck, he complained that Kountz "has caused so much trouble and shown such a disregard for my orders that I have been compelled to order his arrest."[14] Hillyer seized him and placed him in confinement. "As a result, Captain Kountz declared a personal war on the man who invaded his special field of operations," and he knew where this man was most vulnerable.[15]

On January 29, 1862, Kountz wrote Rawlins requesting reasons for his arrest and a copy of the charges.[16] Meanwhile, Kountz filed his own charges against Grant, alleging he was "beastly drunk" and intoxicated to the point of "setting an evil example to the officers and soldiers under his command."[17] On February 8, he filed a series of even wilder charges, including one that Grant had received a harlot on board a steamer and another of him being drunk and vomiting on the floor of a steamer.[18] Considering that Kountz purported to have witnessed events allegedly occurring two weeks before his arrival in Cairo, his charges could be dismissed as simple retaliation. Grant assured Julia, "He can do me no harm. He is known as a venimous [sic] man whose hand is raised against every man and is without friends or influence."[19] Grant was right: Kountz was gone within two months. But graver threats were stirring.

An informal group of wealthy citizens in Cairo had managed to rig the system for awarding contracts. They had prospered under Frémont's lax control. Grant called the group the Cairo Ring. Its members kept outsiders from making successful bids "by bidding just under the highest bid offered from any

outside person and then pulling out all lower bids."[20] These crooked speculators claimed to have power to topple any general in the Cairo District who
failed to play their game. In a bold move, Grant foiled the Ring contractors
by initiating a voucher system. Contractors could only be paid by voucher—
there was not enough cash to cover costs—and the voucher had to be signed
by Grant. If a contractor charged too much, Grant refused to sign.

Grant's quartermaster at Cairo, Captain Reuben Hatch,[21] was deeply involved in corruption. The scandal exploded on December 12 when the *Chicago
Tribune* broke a story that an unnamed quartermaster or agent had been buy-
ing lumber for Cairo at one price and invoicing it at a higher price.[22] Grant
quickly communicated to Halleck's headquarters that he was sending Captains Hillyer and Hatch to Chicago to investigate. Hillyer had not yet suspected Hatch.[23]

On December 22, Hillyer wrote Grant explaining his method of investigation and findings. In Chicago, a witness told Hillyer that Hatch "with a full
knowledge of the facts paid the parties for the December purchases an excess
above what they had sold and delivered the lumber for."[24] Hatch followed up
Hillyer's letter eight days later with his own, in which he shifted blame to dis-
honest clerks. On January 12, 1862, Rawlins issued Grant's General Orders No.
2 appointing Captain Algernon Baxter as district quartermaster and Special
Orders No. 13 placing Hatch under arrest.[25]

The year 1861 ended with more bad news for Grant. On December 30, William Bross of the *Chicago Tribune* wrote a letter to Secretary of War Simon
Cameron in which he denounced Grant as an "inebriate."[26] Apparently, this
was retribution for slights Bross received at the hands of Grant and his aide
Clark Lagow. Bross's letter was ill timed for Grant: word of his alleged alcohol
troubles percolated inside the cabinet, within earshot of Lincoln.

Washburne had received news regarding rumors of Grant's drinking problem in a December 17 letter from Galenian Benjamin Campbell. There was no
containing the allegations, which could have sprung from multiple sources.
Some on Grant's staff suspected Brigadier General Lew Wallace (not to
be confused with William H. L. Wallace), who was known to be jealous of
Grant. Reuben Hatch was a logical culprit.[27] Rawlins figured the sources were
crooked contractors frustrated by the voucher system. Also, Kountz would
be piling on with his shocking charges a month into the new year. Having

consistently defended Grant's reputation, Washburne was eager to know the facts, and he wrote Rawlins for them.

Rawlins penned Washburne a lengthy and impassioned reply. He felt compelled to stand up for Grant, a man he saw growing in stature. In this remarkable letter, Rawlins does not defend Grant's abstemious ways but rather portrays Grant as a man of temperate character. Shortly into the letter, he calls Grant "a strictly total abstinence man." Oddly, just one sentence later, we find this is not true. Rawlins has exaggerated that claim: Grant has been obligated to drink recently, albeit sparingly and infrequently. Rawlins explains there were a few extenuating occasions where Grant was obliged to tip a glass, and he had been under doctor's orders to consume beer to treat dyspepsia. Rawlins got around this apparent contradiction by assuring Washburne that the amount Grant consumed was "[not] enough to in the slightest unfit him for business, or make it manifest in his words or actions."[28] Therefore, although Grant was not truly abstinent, he didn't display the unfitness suggestive of intemperance. This seems a clever distinction, and perhaps Rawlins owed credit to one of Reverend Lyman Beecher's widely circulated sermons on intemperance. In his second of six sermons, Beecher described seven "symptoms of intemperance."[29] If Rawlins could demonstrate that Grant was "symptom-free," he would have succeeded in protecting Grant by reassuring Washburne.

Rawlins's second assurance to Washburne was that an intemperate individual would not have been assiduously attending to paperwork or spearheading fraud investigations. For example, Rawlins mentioned Grant's swift response to charges in the *Chicago Tribune* of crooked lumber contracts. Clearly, Grant showed no impairment in carrying out the responsibilities of command. Third, Rawlins emphasized how Grant's appearance and manner bespoke sobriety: "his eye and intellect are as clear and active as can be."[30] Reverend Beecher warned that "redness of eyes" is a guaranteed indicator of intemperance as is "the extinction of all the finer feelings of the soul."[31] On this latter point, Beecher wrote that alcohol strips away one's soul or identity—one is no longer the same friend, husband or, it might be presumed, commanding general. According to Rawlins, Grant passed the "eye test" and retained his customary cognitive acuity.

As a fourth assurance, Rawlins suggested Washburne inquire of character references such as Colonel Joseph Webster and Flag Officer Foote. The previous week, Grant had named Webster his chief of staff. Rawlins described him as "a man of unquestionable habits" who "has seen [General Grant] daily and has had every opportunity to know his habits." And Foote, the commander of the flotilla of gunboats, Rawlins reminded Washburne, was "a strict and faithful member of the Congregational Church."[32] Foote's scorn for drink was legendary. While commanding a fleet in the Far East before the war, "he converted every officer and man in the fleet to the principles of temperance, and had every one of them sign a pledge."[33] Webster and Foote would not countenance intemperance in their commander.

Rawlins saved his most potent assurance for last. He too had been observing Grant's habits and sizing him up, and he felt he knew the real man. "I respect him because I have studied him well," Rawlins said, "and the more I know him the more I respect and love him." So certain is Rawlins of Grant's character that "I am willing to trust my hopes of the future upon his bravery and temperate habits." Moreover, Rawlins promised Washburne that should Grant prove "an intemperate man or an habitual drunkard, I will notify you immediately" and request removal from his staff or even "resign my commission."[34] With this powerful endorsement: Rawlins, a paragon of temperance, placed all his chips on Grant's character.

Rawlins's letter is a masterly and well-timed stroke. Rawlins could not deny Grant had been drinking; there were too many witnesses to conceal that fact. Instead, he made a lawyerly argument that Grant appeared free of the symptoms of intemperance. "This letter probably arrived just in time to ease Washburne's mind," wrote Grant biographer Brooks Simpson, because the allegations made by the *Chicago Tribune's* William Bross would be reaching Washington soon.[35]

William Rowley's January 30 letter to Washburne provided Grant additional defense just as Kountz began wreaking vengeance. "I have no hesitation in saying," he told Washburne, "that any one who asserts that he is becomeing [sic] dissipated is either misinformed or else he lies."[36] In truth, Rowley's main purpose in writing was to seek Washburne's influence in helping him get appointed to Grant's personal staff.

—⁂—

When not clearing out crooks, Grant and his staff were occupied with more typical military matters. Halleck felt sufficiently satisfied with Grant's performance that he increased the size of Grant's district of command and renamed it. The new District of Cairo included "all the Southern part of Illinois, that part of Kentucky west of the Cumberland River, and the southern counties of Missouri south of Cape Girardeau."[37] This meant that General Charles F. Smith's small district encompassing the mouths of the Cumberland and Tennessee Rivers was folded into the District of Cairo. Smith had been commandant of cadets at West Point while Grant was a student there, and Grant held him in utmost respect. Now Grant was his superior, and he felt considerable diffidence giving him an order.[38] Smith took the rank differential in stride.

On December 23, Grant announced the composition of his personal staff. John Rawlins remained as assistant adjutant general, and Colonel Joseph D. Webster, the chief engineer, became Grant's first chief of staff.[39] Webster was the only military professional on the staff and could provide advice on engineering matters and artillery tactics. For his work during the Belmont battle, Webster had gained Grant's trust and respect. A boyhood friend of Grant, Absalom Markland, recalled in later years an incident at Cairo in 1861 involving Grant, Webster, and Rawlins. A young officer was found derelict in some sensitive duty and incurred Grant's wrath. Grant ordered Webster to bring the handcuffed miscreant to headquarters. Rawlins scoffed, "What is the use of Gen. Grant giving Webster such an order as that? If Webster brings that man here in irons Grant will reprimand Webster and recommend the officer for promotion." It transpired almost as Rawlins prophesized: the officer's offense had been misrepresented; Grant apologized and later recommended him for promotion.[40] The incident illustrates how Rawlins (as the "heavy") would provide a counterbalance to Grant (as one less likely to take offense).

During the early winter, how the war in the West was to be waged was being decided levels above Grant's District of Cairo. In Washington, Lincoln and general-in-chief McClellan argued for an advance through the Cumberland Gap and into east Tennessee in order to liberate the pro-Union population there. The general in place for that job was Don Carlos Buell, commander of the Department of the Ohio and headquartered at Louisville. Buell was an aloof personality, hard to warm up to, and slow to take action. Instead of spearheading such an advance, he dragged his feet, fretting that his adversary, Albert Sidney Johnston, outnumbered him. He complained that he was not getting any cooperation from General Halleck in the adjacent Department of the Missouri. Buell was not just taking precautions—he was displaying passive-aggressiveness. He balked because he thought his superiors' Cumberland Gap plan was unwise. He favored striking the enemy more centrally at Bowling Green, Kentucky, and Nashville, but that was unfeasible unless Halleck cooperated by blocking the Confederates from sending reinforcements to Bowling Green. Halleck groused that he had no men to spare and that his hands were full keeping Missouri secessionists subdued. The two department chiefs eyed each other warily, knowing that whoever achieved success would likely be promoted to command in the West.

The impasse was broken in early January 1862. On the third, McClellan ordered Halleck to make demonstrations to prevent Rebel troops from being sent from Columbus, Kentucky, to reinforce those already opposing Buell at Bowling Green.[41] For this work, Halleck tapped Grant, who was eager for activity even if he was expressly forbidden from picking a fight with the Rebels. Rawlins was busy organizing river transportation. On January 8, he ordered Captain Kountz, whose days were numbered, to ready vessels for six thousand infantry, one thousand cavalry, and land transportation. A day later, Rawlins issued Special Orders Number 11 instructing Kountz to properly man the transports required to move the troops.[42] Flag Officer Foote dispatched his few gunboats to prowl the Tennessee and Cumberland Rivers, General Smith went up the west bank of the Tennessee to menace the Confederates at Fort Henry, and Grant accompanied McClernand's column into western Kentucky.

Grant could claim that he accomplished the object of the weeklong demonstrations because no reinforcements reached the enemy at Bowling Green. The expedition was carried out in bad weather, with everyone "splashing through the mud, snow and rain."[43] Despite the bad roads, Grant, his staff, and a company of cavalry made a thirty-five-mile reconnaissance on January 16.[44] John Rawlins had endured rough days while burning charcoal, but few as arduous as this.

Perhaps the expedition's most valuable intelligence was gathered by reliable Charles Smith. He saw that Fort Henry, erected on low ground, looked exceedingly vulnerable. Foote thought so too. Smith's report confirmed Grant's opinion that there was great military advantage in advancing up the Tennessee and Cumberland Rivers. Such a move would force the Confederates to abandon Kentucky and could take the war into Alabama. Both Smith and Foote urged Grant to present this idea to Halleck.

Grant took their advice and met with Halleck on January 24 in St. Louis. He barely stated his purpose before Halleck testily interrupted. Late in life, Grant recalled the experience: "I was received with so little cordiality that I perhaps stated the object of my visit with less clearness than I might have done, and I had not uttered many sentences before I was cut short as if my plan was preposterous. I returned to Cairo very much crestfallen."[45] In fairness to Halleck, none of this information was news to him. He was cognizant of the existence and usefulness of such an invasion route.[46] Word got back to Washburne about Grant's rough handling through a letter Rawlins wrote to Washburne's friend, J. Russell Jones, business partner of Ben Campbell and a former Galena alderman. Rawlins said he would resign rather than tolerate the scorn Halleck heaped on Grant.[47]

Despite the rebuff, Grant tried again four days later. He telegraphed Halleck, "With Permission I will take Fort McHenry [sic] on the Tennessee and hold & establish a large camp there."[48] And in his message the next day, Grant was more assertive: "In view of the large force now concentrating in this District and the present feasibility of the plan I would respectfully suggest the propriety of subduing Fort Henry, near the Ky. & Tennessee line."[49] In an abrupt turnaround, Halleck dashed off the go-ahead: "You will immediately prepare to send forward to Fort Henry . . . all your available forces. . . . Fort Henry should be taken and held at all hazards."[50] Grant, Rawlins, and staff were exuberant. But it wasn't so much Grant's plea that convinced Halleck to take the offensive: he had just received intelligence that General Beauregard was heading west to Bowling Green with fifteen Rebel regiments. Thus the urgency to strike first before the enemy was reinforced.[51]

It was this military expedition that vaulted Grant into the public forefront and stationed Rawlins at his side.

NOTES

1. H. Sherman, "Personal Recollections of General Grant," *Midland Monthly,* 9, no. 4 (1898): 326.

2. *The War of the Rebellion: A Compilation of the Official Records of the Union and Confederate Armies,* series 1, 5:37.

3. Geoffrey Perret, *Ulysses S. Grant: Soldier & President* (New York: Random House, 1997), 155.

4. *The War of the Rebellion: A Compilation of the Official Records of the Union and Confederate Armies,* Series 1, 3:300.

5. Albert D. Richardson, *A Personal History of Ulysses S. Grant* (Boston: D. L. Guernsey, 1885), 202.

6. Lew Wallace, *An Autobiography* (New York: Garrett, 1969), 352. Originally published in 1906.

7. Quote in Mark Washburn, *A Biography of Elihu Benjamin Washburne: Congressman, Secretary of State, Envoy Extraordinary* (self-pub., Xlibris, 2001), 2:73.

8. John H. Brinton, *Personal Memoirs of John H. Brinton* (New York: Neale, 1914), 103–4.

144 | GENERAL JOHN A. RAWLINS

9. A sutler was a civilian who sold wares, usually out of a wagon or tent.

10. T. K. Kionka, *Key Command: Ulysses S. Grant's District of Cairo* (Columbia: University of Missouri Press, 2006), 155–56.

11. Theodore R. Parker, "William J. Kountz, Superintendent of River Transportation under McClellan, 1861–62," *Western Pennsylvania Historical Magazine* 21, no. 4 (1938): 243–44.

12. U. S. Grant to William J. Kountz, December 21, 1861, in *The Papers of Ulysses S. Grant*, ed. John Y. Simon (Carbondale: Southern Illinois University Press, 1970), 3:320–21.

13. John Y. Simon, ed., *The Personal Memoirs of Julia Dent Grant* (New York: G. P. Putnam's Sons, 1975), 96.

14. U. S. Grant to J. C. Kelton, January 14, 1862, in *The Papers of Ulysses S. Grant*, ed. John Y. Simon (Carbondale: Southern Illinois University Press, 1972), 4:54.

15. Theodore R. Parker, "William J. Kountz, Superintendent of River Transportation under McClellan, 1861–62," 251.

16. John Y. Simon, ed., *The Papers of Ulysses S. Grant*, 3:110n.

17. Ibid., 112n.

18. Ibid., 113n.

19. U. S. Grant to Julia Grant, February 16, 1862, in *The Papers of Ulysses S. Grant*, ed. John Y. Simon, 4:229.

20. T. K. Kionka, *Key Command*, 161.

21. Reuben Hatch avoided court-martial for his shady dealings in Cairo in part because of the intercession of his brother, Ozias, who was the Illinois secretary of state and well-known to Lincoln. Lincoln requested a commission be appointed to investigate charges against Hatch and even suggested individuals for the commission. In July 1862, the commission acquitted Hatch. See John Y. Simon, ed., *The Papers of Ulysses S. Grant*, 4:83–84n. In April 1865, while quartermaster at Vicksburg, Hatch had a hand in overcrowding ex-prisoners of war on board the *Sultana*, perhaps receiving kickbacks from the fee paid to the steamboat operator for each soldier boarded. The sickly ex-POWs had been released from Confederate prison camps Cahaba and Andersonville. As many as twenty-three hundred were crammed together, and perhaps eighteen hundred perished when the boat exploded. See William O. Bryant, *Cahaba Prison and the Sultana Disaster* (Tuscaloosa: University of Alabama Press, 1990); Jerry O. Potter, *The Sultana Tragedy: America's Greatest Maritime Disaster* (Gretna, LA: Pelican, 1992).

22. John Y. Simon, ed., *The Papers of Ulysses S. Grant*, 3:290n1.

23. U. S. Grant to John C. Kelton, December 15, 1861, in *The Papers of Ulysses S. Grant*, ed. John Y. Simon, 3:289.

24. John Y. Simon, ed., *The Papers of Ulysses S. Grant*, 3:326n.

25. John Y. Simon, ed., *The Papers of Ulysses S. Grant*, 4:43n, 44n.

26. Ibid., 118n.

27. Bruce Catton, *Grant Moves South* (Boston: Little, Brown, 1960), 95, 98.

28. James H. Wilson, *The Life of John A. Rawlins* (New York: Neale, 1916), 68–69.

29. Lyman Beecher, *Six Sermons of the Nature, Occasions, Signs, Evils, and Remedy of Intemperance*, 4th ed. (Boston: T. R. Marvin, 1828), 25–46.

30. Ibid., 70.

31. Lyman Beecher, *Six Sermons of the Nature, Occasions, Signs, Evils, and Remedy of Intemperance*, 32, 35.

32. James H. Wilson, *The Life of John A. Rawlins*, 70.

33. James B. Eads, "Recollections of Foote and His Gunboats," in *Battles and Leaders of the Civil War*, eds. R. U. Johnson and C. C. Buel (1887; repr., New York: Thomas Yoseloff, 1956), 1:346.

34. James H. Wilson, *The Life of John A. Rawlins*, 71.

35. Brooks D. Simpson, *Ulysses S. Grant: Triumph over Adversity* (Boston: Houghton Mifflin, 2000), 107.

36. John Y. Simon, ed., *The Papers of Ulysses S. Grant*, 4:277n.

37. John Y. Simon, ed., *The Papers of Ulysses S. Grant*, 3:330.

38. Ezra J. Warner, *Generals in Blue: Lives of the Union Commanders* (Baton Rouge: Louisiana State University Press, 1993), 455.

39. General Orders No. 22, in *The Papers of Ulysses S. Grant*, ed. John Y. Simon, 3:330–31.

40. *The Ulysses S. Grant Association Newsletter* 10, no. 3 (April 1973): 21.

41. George McClellan to Henry W. Halleck, January 3, 1862, in *The War of the Rebellion: A Compilation of the Official Records of the Union and Confederate Armies*, series 1, 7:527–28.

42. John Y. Simon, ed., *The Papers of Ulysses S. Grant*, 4:7n, 20n.

43. U. S. Grant, *Personal Memoirs* (New York: Charles L. Webster, 1885), 1:286.

44. U. S. Grant to J. C. Kelton, January 17, 1862, in *The Papers of Ulysses S. Grant*, ed. John Y. Simon, 4:62–63.

45. U. S. Grant, *Personal Memoirs*, 1:287.

46. See Bruce Catton, *Grant Moves South*, 125–27.

47. J. R. Jones to Elihu Washburne, January 17, 1862, Washburne Papers, Library of Congress.

48. U. S. Grant telegram to Henry W. Halleck, January 28, 1862, in *The Papers of Ulysses S. Grant*, ed. John Y. Simon, 4:99.

49. U. S. Grant to Henry W. Halleck, January 29, 1862, in *The Papers of Ulysses S. Grant*, ed. John Y. Simon, 4:103.

50. H. W. Halleck to U. S. Grant, January 30, 1862, in *The War of the Rebellion: A Compilation of the Official Records of the Union and Confederate Armies*, series 1, 7:121.

51. Ibid., 122.

10

"[A] Silent And Determined Purpose to Strike Swiftly"

WHEN HALLECK'S ORDER TO ADVANCE arrived at Grant's headquarters, it set off pandemonium. The staff cheered, and some danced a Highland fling. The customarily restrained Rawlins merrily kicked over several chairs and pounded his fists against a wall. Grant let them exult before waving for their attention. As he gazed across the room, he gave everyone a solemn mandate: no one must whisper a word about the imminent expedition. Then he set them to work.[1]

Abiding by Halleck's imperative to make immediate preparations, Grant exploited every second for the complicated arrangements required to coordinate an army and navy operation. The scattered forces in the district had to be consolidated. Rations, ammunition, winter clothing, wagons, and teams had to be ready. The untried troops were required to comport themselves with honor and discipline. Rawlins issued a general order that prohibited plundering of private property and held regimental commanders accountable for their men's behavior.[2]

Freed from confinement in Cairo, Grant planned to strike the enemy by the most promising invasion corridor: up the Tennessee and Cumberland Rivers. Eager for battle, Grant had a force of seventeen thousand men—twelve thousand from Cairo and five thousand of C. F. Smith's troops from Paducah—ready to depart in three days. Flag Officer Foote's gunboats led the way, followed by the troop transports. A giddy Julia Grant recalled watching them depart: "How pretty the steamers looked as they swing out into the stream laden with troops and bright with flags! My enthusiasm almost amounted to a delirium. I never once expected to hear bad news from my General."[3]

Aboard a transport, Grant paced the deck, occasionally peering through field glasses at the Tennessee River behind. When the steamer passed an imaginary point of no return, his face showed a glimmer of satisfaction: he was beyond Halleck's reach. Rawlins noticed the look and said later that "Grant seemed a new man." The "new" Grant suddenly turned affable. He laid a hand on Rawlins's shoulder and said, "Now we seem to be safe, beyond recall by either electricity or steam. I am glad. I am thankful. We *will* succeed, Rawlins; we *must* succeed." Grant knew the heady implications of his success upriver: "If we cut the enemy's spinal column up here in Tennessee," he explained to Rawlins, "Buell will not have much trouble with the head up his way, *when he gets ready to move next summer,* and the tail over at Columbus will not do much signalling." The dig at Buell's dilatory approach to campaigning was not lost on Rawlins. He recalled that he and Grant clasped hands in a grip of solidarity, one that Rawlins said "expressed a silent and determined purpose to strike swiftly, and to *succeed* or *perish* in a courageous attempt."[4] At that moment, it seemed a team was formed not just for the impending conflict at Fort Henry but for battles beyond.

—◦◦◦—

Much of February 4 and 5, Tuesday and Wednesday, was spent reconnoitering around Fort Henry and disembarking troops. McClernand's division landed about three miles north of the fort on the east bank of the Tennessee River. In the operation to start on the sixth at 11:00 a.m., Foote's gunboats aimed to shell the fort into submission, with McClernand's troops ready to storm it or cut off the enemy's escape.

To Fort Henry's commander, Brigadier General Lloyd Tilghman, the Federal buildup beyond the walls looked powerfully impressive: "Far as the eye could see, the course of the river could be traced by the dense volumes of smoke issuing from the flotilla."[5] Against this might, Tilghman commanded about 3,400 men, "mostly raw regiments armed with shot-guns and hunting rifles."[6] Tilghman's problems went beyond being outnumbered and outgunned. It hardly required his West Point engineering background to see that Fort Henry was poorly sited on low ground, susceptible to flooding, and virtually indefensible. Tilghman had to decide how to cut his losses. On the evening of the fifth, he convened his senior officers and told them his plan: he and a skeleton crew would man the fort's artillery pieces, absorb the attack, and delay the attackers to allow the rest of the garrison to escape eastward to Fort Donelson.

A cold rain fell Wednesday evening, perhaps an ominous indication for Thursday's battle. Whether John Rawlins spent that night pondering his fate or his children's, one cannot say, but such thoughts filled the mind of his fellow staffer, William Hillyer. To his twenty-nine-year-old wife, Annie, Hillyer penned a farewell letter:

> *My dear wife—*
> This is the eve of battle. Twelve thousand of our men are sleeping on their arms—all anxious for the morrow. To many doubtless to morrow will be their last waking. Some of us must die. . . . Who shall it be? Whose wife will be a widow, whose children orphans, whose home made desolate God only knows. If it should be your husband & your childrens father, bear the blow bravely my darling. . . .
>
> I have a thousand things to say to you, and yet I hardly know what to say. I desire that you should *know* & *feel* how entirely my heart [and] my thoughts are yours—and if you never hear from me again, Annie, know that my *last thoughts* will be of you. Forgive all my weaknesses [and] remember only my love. . . . Good night and good bye. . . . I will go and dream of home and happiness & wife & children . . . and I will see you and fold you to my bosom and whisper in your ear a thousand words of tenderness and love.[7]

At 10:30 p.m., Grant found a moment to write Julia. He felt almost sanguine about his chances: "I am well and in good spirits yet feeling confidence in the success of our enterprise . . . I have just written my order of battle. . . . Kiss the children for me. Kisses for yourself."[8]

The next day's attack was delayed to allow McClernand's division to deploy. Mud-caked roads and poor planning slowed his advance, allowing most of the Confederate garrison to flee. It was up to Foote's gunboats to reduce the fort. During the lively artillery exchange, several of the Confederate pieces malfunctioned or exploded, artillery crews were decimated, and even General Tilghman manned a gun. It was over in about two hours. Tilghman surrendered himself and about eighty officers and men. Dr. Brinton, now medical director in the field, surveyed the carnage: artillery carriages "were broken and stained with blood. Here and there too, were masses of human flesh and hair adhering to the broken timbers. The interior of the fort was a mass of mud, the back water from the stream having flowed in from the rear."[9]

While Halleck and Buell sputtered and sparred, Grant had won a stunning victory. Within hours Grant telegraphed Halleck, "Fort Henry is ours," and warming up for the second act, he added, "I shall take and destroy Fort

Donaldso[n] on the eighth and return to Ft Henry."[10] The day after Fort Henry fell, Grant took the staff and a cavalry contingent on a reconnaissance to within a mile of Fort Donelson's outer works. Although the recon mission didn't reveal the size of the garrison there, Grant believed it undermanned and less formidable than Fort Henry. Word was that pompous Gideon Pillow was in command, but he would be superseded by Brigadier General John B. Floyd, Buchanan's former secretary of war. To Grant, it mattered little whether Floyd or Pillow held top spot. He thought both inept.

Grant's message of victory might have had Halleck rubbing his hands in glee. However, the department chief seemed to be feeling on tenterhooks. With Cairo short on troops, he fretted it could be vulnerable to attack from Columbus. He worried that Fort Henry was vulnerable too, so on the eighth, Halleck ordered Grant to "Hold on to Fort Henry at all hazards" and promised to send him picks and shovels to strengthen its entrenchments.[11] At the same time, Halleck urged moving boldly toward the Cumberland River, telling Foote, "It is of vital importance that Fort Donelson be reduced immediately."[12] Grant himself posed a question mark. Halleck doubted Grant had the fitness to lead, believing he was going off half-cocked on this river campaign. Such misgivings motivated Halleck to go behind Grant's back for a replacement. Halleck favored someone with experience, specifically Brigadier General Ethan Allen Hitchcock. But the ancient Hitchcock, West Point class of 1817, was experienced to the point of ossification. The ultimate dissolution of the Union may have been averted because the plan to replace Grant failed.

On the other hand, Fort Henry's fall gave Rawlins more proof that his decision to pin his future on Grant was paying off. Rawlins could see that with Grant came results, not boasts; aggressiveness, but without recklessness. Moreover, Rawlins's respect for him grew daily. For example, even in the midst of a thousand details, Grant failed to overlook those deviations from proper military comportment that undermined discipline. On February 9, Grant learned there had been pillaging by men of the Fiftieth and Seventh Illinois regiments of matériel captured at Fort Henry. Such behavior was in disregard of the previous week's order and its promise to hold people accountable. The next day, Rawlins was authorized to release General Field Orders No. 7 warning that "if the guilty parties are not punished promptly the Company officers will be at once arrested, or if they are not known the punishment will have to fall upon the Regimental or Brigade Commander. Every offence will be traced back to a responsible party."[13]

Grant's pledge to capture Fort Donelson by February 8 was too optimistically stated. Foul weather and the absence of Foote's gunboats delayed the attack. For the busy staff, this might have been just as well. Captain Hillyer was on the steamer *Iatan* accompanying the Fort Henry prisoners to Paducah. There was a new special staff member on board. Lieutenant Colonel James Birdseye McPherson, a whipsaw sharp West Pointer with a twinkling eye, was now chief engineering officer. He had been sent by Halleck to "obtain special information," that is, to determine whether the rumors circulating around St. Louis about Grant's drinking were true.[14] Surgeon Brinton denounced them as unfounded. The affable McPherson would soon become closely attached to both Grant and William T. Sherman. Chief of Staff Webster was aboard one of the gunboats making an incursion up the Tennessee River to take out key railroad bridges. Rawlins, cooped up at the staff headquarters on the steamer *Tigress*, was occupied with issuing instructions and orders, most of which were dictated by Grant. This paperwork included field orders that directed certain troops be left behind at Fort Henry, organized various regiments into brigades, and shifted regiments into existing brigades.

The decisive General Field Orders No. 12, issued by Grant through Rawlins on February 11, announced the deployment of troops for the next day's advance on Donelson. According to those orders, the movement was to proceed along two roughly parallel roads. The northerly one, Telegraph Road, led toward Fort Donelson; the southerly one, Ridge Road, led to the town of Dover on the Cumberland's west bank below the fort. One brigade from McClernand's First Division was to move along Telegraph Road. McClernand's remaining brigades would take Ridge Road, accompanied by two brigades from C. F. Smith's Second Division.[15]

Grant and his staff would take Ridge Road too. Weather for Wednesday, February 12, promised to be mild, almost springlike.

—◦◦◦—

The divisions of McClernand and Smith were on the march by 8:00 a.m. Meanwhile, Foote with six gunboats was steaming up the Cumberland to assist. There were expectations that the gunboats alone could pummel Donelson into submission as they had against Fort Henry. On the lower road, Grant and staff were virtually unencumbered by baggage: Grant stuck a toothbrush in his waistcoat; a small satchel contained a few articles—clean collars, combs and brushes, and toilet articles—for staff. Dr. Brinton kept a flask of spirits in his pocket. Grant's orders were to use it only for medicinal purposes "and not to furnish a drink under any pretext to any member of the Staff, except when necessary."[16]

The troops had a march of about ten miles to their designated bivouac ground. Balmy weather caused many to shed their heavy coats. The country they traversed was not conducive to growing crops, so farmers took to raising pigs. The oak-forested hollows kept the pigs well fed with acorns. On the evening of the twelfth, the encamped Union soldiers sang and danced while purloined porkers roasted over glowing fires. As the fires died down and night temperatures plunged, many of the soldiers who had cast away coats and blankets found scant protection beneath mounds of leaves. The Grant party, on the other hand, had appropriated for their headquarters a log house owned by a Mrs. Crisp that lay west of Dover on the Ridge Road. An open fireplace kept the downstairs toasty. Grant claimed the kitchen with its double featherbed, leaving the staff to crowd into smaller rooms.

The Confederates only lightly contested the Union advance to Donelson's doorstep. Floyd seemed content to let Grant be the attacker, which played right into the latter's hand. On the thirteenth, Grant deployed two divisions in an investing semicircle around the west, with the Cumberland River enveloping Donelson on the east. McClernand's division made up the right, with C. F. Smith's on the left. During the day, Confederate artillery bothered the men on the Union right, and McClernand, ill-advisedly flexing his combat muscle, sent forward a brigade to silence the guns. He did so without authorization from headquarters. Their assault up a steep rise and into an abatis was repulsed with heavy loss.

Toward evening, two soldiers wounded in that assault were hobbling toward a field hospital when they passed Grant and Rawlins. One had a shattered arm, the other a disabled leg, but despite their pain, they heartily acknowledged Grant. Good-naturedly, Grant called out to them, "Men, you seem disfigured. Been hunting bear?"

"We've got 'em treed, General," they laughed. "We'll bring 'em down to-morrow."

The soldier with the useless arm said, "You see, General, I couldn't load my gun, but I could shoot with my right hand, so Jack and me we got behind a big stump below them cannon over on the point of that ere hill, and he loaded both guns and I kept a shootin'. Every time a reb would start to load the cannon I'd shoot and the feller'd drop, and I kept them cannon cool all afternoon."

Taking this repartee a little further, Grant asked, "You didn't hurt any one, did you?"

When the soldier saw Rawlins crack a smile, he caught on and said, "Why, General, I dunno; I reckon I just scared 'em and they fainted."[17]

Grant needed reinforcements to augment his line, so regiments at Fort Henry under Brigadier General Lew Wallace were summoned.[18] Around 1:00 a.m. on the fourteenth, he received an order from Rawlins to bring up his troops. Lew Wallace, a Hoosier with a Van Dyke beard, was born the son of a former Indiana governor and possessed a gift for writing. In 1880, his historical novel *Ben-Hur* became an instant classic. In the early morning hours and in the teeth of a snowy wind, Wallace set out with two regiments, the Eleventh Indiana and Eighth Missouri, and an artillery battery, leaving behind on the Tennessee River his cavalry and one regiment of infantry.

This first full day opposite Donelson ended with spring reverting back to winter. Snow, wind, sleet, and ten-degree temperatures made conditions life-threatening. While the infantrymen of Smith's and McClernand's divisions already in place flailed their bodies to forestall frostbite, more help was on the way: Foote and the gunboats were en route and due for action on the fourteenth, and Lew Wallace's men would arrive at Grant's headquarters before noon.

———

At 11:00 a.m., Wallace presented himself at the headquarters shack. He cooled his heels while Grant finished dictation to Rawlins. Then with barely a nod, Grant ordered Wallace to have his two regiments sent over to General Smith. Allowing Wallace not a moment to recover from this shock, Grant explained that a batch of regiments, seven total, from up the Cumberland was soon to arrive on transports, and these were to be brigaded to constitute the third division, which Wallace was to command. Wallace's newly created division would become the center of the Union line, between Smith's division, which made up the top (or left) of the Federal arc and McClernand's division which constituted the bottom (right). With Wallace holding the center, McClernand would be able to extend himself farther east toward the Cumberland, thus narrowing the enemy escape route in that direction. With this business finished, Wallace was invited to stay for lunch: hard biscuits, boiled beans seasoned with salt pork, and pickles so sour they could "parboil the throat."[19]

Rawlins escorted Wallace's division to its place in line. Rawlins was somewhat familiar with the ground from the reconnaissance of several days before. For a good part of the march, the column of regiments was screened by forest, but once they emerged into view, they drew fire from the fort's artillery. Before long Rawlins called the column to a halt at a gaping hole between C. F. Smith, perhaps three-quarters of a mile off to the left, and McClernand, about a half-mile to the right. The gap left Wallace astonished. "Why hasn't the enemy come in here and cut you in two?" he asked Rawlins.

Rawlins laughed. "Because there's but one soldier among them; and he is third in rank." Rawlins was referring to Brigadier General Simon Bolivar Buckner, a West Pointer and a subordinate to Floyd and Pillow. Suddenly, the conversation was interrupted by a shell exploding down the road. Wallace had time for one last question for Rawlins: "And to get by me Mr. Floyd must come through the woods on the left or down this road?"

"Yes," Rawlins replied, and as he turned to ride off, he bid Wallace adieu. "I will see you in the morning, if not sooner."[20]

—◦◦◦—

Foote needed the morning to prepare his warships. By midafternoon the four ironclads were underway, with the two wooden gunboats trailing a respectable distance. Although the vessels were a mile and a half above Donelson, enemy shells found their mark. Not content to duel at this range, Foote, hoping to repeat his success at Fort Henry, steamed to within a few hundred yards of the fort. Foote's guns were unable to damage Donelson. Instead, the little fleet began taking a terrific pounding. The flagship, *St. Louis*, took dozens of hits, and *Louisville*'s rudder was damaged. Foote was struck by debris and suffered a painfully contused ankle. The battered boats, drifting out of control or in danger of sinking, fled downstream. Despite gaining this advantage, the Confederate high command elected not to follow up by attacking the Union line. As the enemy held fast in the fort, Grant pondered his options, including laying siege to it.

Just after dark on the fourteenth, an event lightened the gloom at headquarters in the Crisp house. A lanky, mud-stained prisoner was escorted into a room for an interrogation with Rawlins. The Johnny Reb said he had just deserted, was tired of the war, and aimed to relocate to Illinois. But before he did, he said he had information he'd like to pass along to Grant. He claimed to have overheard at Confederate headquarters that General Polk was to arrive from Columbus with twenty thousand men. What was more, Albert Sidney Johnston was bringing another twenty thousand from Nashville. Rawlins's legal nose smelled something fishy: this "deserter" was planting disinformation to convince Grant to withdraw. While the Rebel recounted this story to Grant, Rawlins and chief of staff Webster concocted their own plan to feed him false information and then let him escape. Rawlins scripted and choreographed it to perfection. The deserter was put in an adjoining room, placed under guard, and told he was under arrest as a spy. Rawlins returned to the other room to attend to duties, but he left open the connecting door. After an interval of suitable length, the announcement of an important incoming dispatch interrupted Rawlins's clerical work. The spy and his guard heard the staff erupt in exuberant exclamations that turned into cheers as Rawlins read the news in his loud voice: Sherman had just captured Columbus and Polk's entire army! Thirty minutes later, more "news" arrived: General Buell was on the way with twenty-five thousand men, and fifteen thousand more were expected from Cairo and St. Louis! Now that the spy was fortified, he needed to be sprung. Webster ordered the guard to move the prisoner outdoors on the pretext that the interrogation room was needed. An hour or so later, Rawlins called the guard inside for a moment, allowing the spy to bolt. A few desultory rounds fired into the darkness added to the realism. It is not known whether the plant returned to the Confederate lines or whether Rawlins's deception had any bearing on the decision made by the Confederate command to break out of Fort Donelson the next day.[21]

General Floyd had been at Fort Donelson less than forty-eight hours, but late on the fourteenth, in consultation with his senior officers, he called for evacuation. The plan was to assail McClernand's division on the Union right and, by turning it back, reach the road connecting Nashville. There they would link up with Albert Sidney Johnston. Gideon Pillow, with a majority of troops, was picked to engage McClernand. Third-in-command Simon Buckner had about four thousand men to restrain Lew Wallace's division in the Union center and cover Pillow's flank. A nominal force—and the last to leave—was to keep occupied General Smith's division on the left.

While the Confederates massed for the breakout, Grant left headquarters at dawn to meet with Foote aboard his flagship. With Foote disabled, Grant was forced to make a precarious two-mile ride to the river landing over a frozen rutted path. Before he left, Grant told Rawlins to direct the three division commanders to hold their positions and not precipitate any engagement with the enemy until ordered. This directive reflected Grant's disfavor with McClernand for having initiated the day before that costly charge against the Rebel line. After discussing with Foote the need for repairs to the gunboats, he was preparing to return when an ashen-faced Captain Hillyer rode up with dire news that the enemy had struck McClernand and that his line was disintegrating.

Pillow had fallen hard against Colonel Richard Oglesby's brigade at the extreme right end of the Union line. By 10:00 a.m., a desperate Oglesby was running out of ammunition and almost cut off. McClernand sent urgent appeals for reinforcements to Lew Wallace, whose division buttressed his on the left. Wallace was unsure whether he should comply because the order to hold his position had not been countermanded. Seeking clarification, Wallace dispatched a messenger to headquarters, but the staff, in Grant's absence, balked at taking independent action. In what might have been a fatal act of omission, Grant had failed to authorize a staff officer to act in his absence. The staff were still learning their way, and Grant had not figured out how best to use them. However, Wallace took matters into his own hands and sent a brigade to McClernand. Rawlins, actuated by Wallace's message, rode out to find him.

Consider it an uncanny coincidence, but there was Rawlins joining Wallace in midmorning as he had called it the previous day. While Wallace informed him about the threat against McClernand and the decision to reinforce him, Rawlins noticed a growing stream of stragglers heading his way and behind them a cacophony of shouting that grew steadily louder. Suddenly, a terrified officer rode past, shouting repeatedly, "We're cut to pieces!" Where Wallace witnessed an officer overcome by emotion, Rawlins saw disgraceful cowardice. He drew his sidearm, intending to shoot the shirker, but Wallace intervened. That earned Wallace a gust of Rawlins's profanity, which might have erupted into a gale if an orderly had not galloped up. "The road back there is jammed with wagons, and men afoot and on horseback, all coming towards us," he reported. "On the plains we would call it a *stampede*." Rawlins broke off, feeling compelled to take this news back to headquarters. Wallace collected his staff and ordered his regiments forward. He would bring up his battery, regroup the remnants of shattered units clogging the road, and assemble all into a defensive line to meet the enemy head-on.[22]

Wallace's makeshift line held against three separate Confederate attacks. This heroic defensive stand probably was the turning point in the battle. The next day, Captain Hillyer sent Wallace a note acknowledging as much: "*I speak advisedly*. God bless you! You did save the day on the right!"[23] Then a strange thing happened. It was only early afternoon, and despite Wallace's efforts, the Confederates' evacuation routes were still open. Pillow could have led everyone in an orderly procession to safety, but instead he dithered—perhaps he believed his men were exhausted and the Union forces on the right had been effectively neutralized—and pulled his men back to regroup. Floyd and Buckner were astonished by Pillow's returning to the trenches. Meanwhile, Grant, accompanied by Webster, appeared on the beleagured Union right around 2:30 p.m. He found McClernand and Wallace engaged in conversation, with their bewildered troops clustered around company officers waiting for instructions. McClernand's salute to his superior was followed with the remark, "This army wants a head"—a swipe at Grant for his morning's absence.[24] There was truth to McClernand's remark. Grant should have designated someone to act on his behalf while he met with Foote. Webster, his most experienced staff person, might have been trusted to remain at headquarters to direct operations or handle crises.[25]

The odds were stacked against Grant at that moment. The right of the line had almost caved in, McClernand's division had taken a licking, and the road out of Donelson remained open. But Grant deduced something significant from comments made by McClernand's men that the Confederates' knapsacks were filled with rations. To Grant, this was the clue "that the enemy had started to march out with his entire force." Now was the time to attack. "I directed Colonel Webster to ride with me and call out to the men as we passed: 'Fill your catridge-boxes, quick, and get into line; the enemy is trying to escape and he must not be permitted to do so.'" Leaving Wallace and McClernand to send their men into action, Grant and Webster rode up to see General C. F. Smith.[26]

Having had his fill of fighting for the day, McClernand deferred the leadership of the counterattack to Wallace. In his official report, Wallace described what happened next: "Well aware of the desperate character of the enterprise, I informed the regiments of it as they moved on, and they answered with cheers and cries of 'Forward!' 'Forward!' and I gave the word. My directions as to mode of attack were general, merely to form columns of regiments, march up the hill which was the point of assault, and deploy as occasion should require."[27] By 5:00 p.m., Wallace's counterattack had driven the Confederates three-quarters of a mile and forced them back into their entrenchments.

When Grant found General Smith, his charge to his old West Point commandant boiled down to three words: take Fort Donelson. Smith's reply was adamantly succinct: "I will do it!"[28] By midafternoon he was leading his division up a brush-tangled slope, through an abattis, and into the right of the Confederate line. Erect in the saddle, Smith manifested a fearless presence. He urged the men with goads and curses: "Damn you, gentlemen, I see skulkers, I'll have none here. Come on, you volunteers. Come on."[29] By dusk his division was within Donelson's defenses.

On returning to headquarters in late afternoon, Grant and staff rode over ground hotly contested hours before by Wallace and McClernand. They came on two horribly wounded soldiers, a Union lieutenant and Confederate private. The lieutenant was sharing his canteen with the enemy, now a comrade in suffering. The scene touched Grant deeply. He requested a flask of brandy and gave each man a taste. He told Rawlins, "Send for stretchers, send for stretchers at once for these men." After ascertaining both would receive equal care, the general and party rode on, only to encounter more casualties. Grant shared with Webster and Rawlins how such sights always left him depressed. Although hardly one to quote poetry, the solemnity of the moment moved Grant to recite a Robert Burns couplet:

Man's inhumanity to man
Makes countless thousands mourn.[30]

Very early in the morning of Sunday, February 16, a messenger under a truce flag was brought to see Smith. He carried a note from General Buckner who wished to negotiate terms for Donelson's surrender. Overnight, command had devolved on Buckner during a testy squabble among the Confederate leadership. They had argued various options, hold fast or break out, but these were dismissed as too perilous or infeasible. Floyd and Pillow opted out rather than face the ignominy of surrender. Floyd's motive to flee ran deeper than sparing himself a modicum of ignominy. Many Northerners believed him responsible for transferring weapons before the war to arsenals in the South. If captured, he might face charges of treason. Floyd absconded on a steamboat. Pillow crossed the Cumberland on a little flatboat.

Now Smith was in the Crisp house headquarters, unthawing before the hearth. Grant left the featherbed to pull on some clothes. Dr. Brinton was asleep on the floor, saddle for a pillow. While Grant read Buckner's message, Smith requested a drink. Dr. Brinton handed him the flask, from which he took a medically approved swig. "What answer shall I send to this, General

Smith?" Grant asked. "No terms to the damned rebels," was Smith's reply.[31] Grant chuckled and selected a sheet on which he wrote a succinct answer: "No terms except an unconditional and immediate surrender can be accepted." Beneath that he added, "I propose to move immdiately upon your works."[32] He read it aloud and got muted approval from Smith, "Hm! It's the same thing in smoother words."[33] While Smith delivered the "no terms" terms to Buckner, Grant dispatched Riggin to Wallace and McClernand, alerting them to attack the Confederate line on signal if Buckner rejected the ultimatum.[34]

Buckner swallowed hard and accepted the inevitable. He invited Grant and staff to the tavern in Dover for breakfast that included vile, ersatz Confederate coffee. By noon, Old Glory flew over Fort Donelson. Next came broadcasting the news of this momentous victory, reaping the rewards, extending words of appreciation, wrapping up details, and moving forward.

The electrifying news went over the wires from Grant to Halleck: "We have taken Fort Donelson and from 12,000 to 15,000 prisoners, including Generals Buckner and Bushrod Johnson."[35] On the seventeenth, Charles Dana's *New York Tribune* made the Donelson capture its lead story.[36] Northerners, eager for battlefield successes, celebrated the victory. Elihu Washburne reminded his colleagues in Congress, "I want . . . to state that General U. S. Grant, who commanded the land forces that captured the fort, is from Galena, my district."[37] Also on the seventeenth, Halleck excitedly broke the news to General William Rosecrans: "Johnston & Buckner & it is said by some Pillow, & fifteen thousand prisoners taken."[38] It seems Halleck was so elated that he believed briefly the Confederacy's top field general, Albert S. Johnston, had been captured, which would have been the military coup of the war.

Fort Donelson was the prize that could leapfrog Halleck over Buell and into command of Union forces in the West. From St. Louis, Halleck telegraphed McClellan to push his personal agenda: "Make Buell, Grant and Pope Major-Generals of Volunteers, and give me command in the West. I ask this in return for Forts Henry and Donelson."[39] On February 19, a grateful Senate confirmed Grant, but neither Buell nor Pope, as major general. Moreover, Grant announced that Halleck had just assigned him to command of the newly formed Military District of West Tennessee.[40] Halleck would have to wait until March 11 for an executive order that would elevate him to full command in the West and put Buell under his control.[41] However, this eventual promotion came only after Halleck was rebuffed by McClellan and Secretary of War Stanton, which caused him much anxious frustration.

There were more dividends forthcoming. Grant wrote Washburne on the twenty-first that he had offered his brother, Cadwallader, a position on his staff, a move that could only strengthen ties between the general and the congressman.[42] Shortly after Donelson, William Rowley, Rawlins's neighbor, got his wish when, with Washburne's help, he was appointed aide-de-camp with rank of captain. Grant gave him a hearty welcome: "Well, Rowley, our speculations have come true. Rawlins and you and I are all in the service."[43] Rowley became Rawlins's assistant, and they worked closely together.

Halleck sent congratulations to Foote, Grant, and all the men under their commands "on the recent brilliant victories on the Tennessee and Cumberland."[44] Curiously, Halleck did not send a separate personal tribute to Grant. The significance of that snub was not yet evident.

In his report of February 16, Grant distributed words of commendation to his personal staff—Webster, Rawlins, Riggin, Lagow, Hillyer, and McPherson—"for their gallantry and service."[45] Apparently, one staff officer felt those few words were not enough. Soon after Wallace submitted his own battle report, he was visited by Hillyer, who had lauded him for saving the day on the Union right. Hillyer carried a copy of the report and said, "On reading it, I saw you had omitted mention of a point of importance which I doubt not you will see the propriety of inserting. . . . You omitted to mention that you had seen Captain Lagow and myself delivering orders during the fight." Hillyer, it seems certain, was trying to work Wallace for a reciprocal favor. Wallace had seen neither Hillyer nor Lagow near the fighting or delivering orders, but he felt pressure was being applied by "two aides [who] had the ear of the commanding general night and day." Wallace told Hillyer to leave the report and return in an hour. In the interim Wallace checked with his staff, but none recalled seeing either aide during the battle. When Hillyer returned, Wallace handed him the report unchanged. Thereafter Wallace noticed he was icily received at headquarters, although Grant's demeanor was friendly. The Hillyer incident, Wallace admitted, was "trifling in itself" but "the origin of a trouble that was to go with me through life."[46]

Hillyer, sometimes too clever for his own good, wrote a multistanza lampoon of Wallace. The doggerel savaged Wallace for cowardice during the battle and praised as the real hero Colonel Morgan Smith, one of Wallace's brigade commanders:

With general orders to advance
To pitch in rough and take his chance
Smith with my men dashed bravely through
I expect he did—I told him to.
All other troops were in the rear
I know that well for I was there

Hillyer also accused Wallace of hustling to get into the captured Confederate fortifications in order to cash in on the glory due Grant and McClernand, whose name Hillyer coyly altered:

Through forest and thicket o'er hill and glen
Reckless and fearless I dashed ahead
Heeding not wounded, trampling the dead
Over the rifle pit over the ditch
Federal or Rebel I didn't care which
All that I cared for was to get over
And under the white flag capture [of] Dover
In that perilous charge but one fear came o'er me
Grant or McFadden might get there before me.[47]

The lampoon undoubtedly circulated among Grant's staff, and Grant probably read it too. When Wallace learned of its existence, he seethed with anger.[48] There has never been an adequate explanation why Hillyer's feeling toward Wallace took such a malicious turn.

Attending to countless details subsequent to the campaign kept Rawlins fully occupied. For example, an influx of reinforcements necessitated adding a division and assigning brigades. Brigadier General Stephen Hurlbut, a Belvidere, Illinois, attorney with virtually no military qualifications, was given command of the new fourth division.[49] Rawlins issued Grant's orders to return two of Wallace's brigades to Fort Henry and to begin transporting thousands of Confederate prisoners to Cairo.[50]

It was Grant's nature to press the enemy—no resting on past accomplishments. Thus, on February 19, Grant sent Webster to accompany Foote and two of his gunboats on a reconnaissance up the Cumberland to Clarksville, a strategic rail center northwest of Nashville. Webster discovered the Confederates had abandoned nearby Fort Defiance, and he received intelligence that General Albert S. Johnston had evacuated Nashville.[51] The Tennessee capital,

Grant now thought, seemed ripe for taking. On the twenty-first, he wrote Halleck's chief of staff, "It is my impression that by following up our success Nashville would be an easy conquest."[52] Flag Officer Foote concurred: "The Cumberland is in a good stage of water, and General Grant and I believe we can take Nashville."[53] But Halleck insisted that Foote's gunboats were not to pass higher up the Cumberland than Clarksville, and he preferred that "everything must remain *in statu quo*."[54] In a letter to his wife, Foote displayed his frustration: "I am disgusted that we were kept from going up and taking Nashville. It was jealousy on the part of McClellan and Halleck."[55] Meanwhile, Buell, always fearful of a surprise attack by Johnston, brought his troops southward ever so slowly from Bowling Green, Kentucky, toward Nashville.

On the twenty-fourth, Grant with his staff visited Clarksville, a town now occupied by General C. F. Smith and mostly deserted by its White citizens. On the next day's steamer trip upriver back to Donelson, Rawlins and Grant were at a table in cabin headquarters when they spied transports loaded with Federal soldiers. Grant slammed his hand on the table and exclaimed, "Rawlins, I have it; this is probably Nelson and his command. I will order him to report to Buell at Nashville."[56] Indeed, it was a division under huge William "Bull" Nelson finally arriving after having been sent by Buell to reinforce Grant at Donelson—reinforcements that obviously were no longer needed. After conferring with Nelson, Grant sent him to Nashville, ordering him to await Buell. Nelson's men entered Nashville uncontested—Grant figured that would happen—but when Buell finally arrived, he was furious that Grant had exposed Nelson to possible attack. What Grant had accomplished, by hook and a little crook, was to use Buell's men to capture Nashville, when Grant had been ordered to proceed no farther than Clarksville.

With Nashville secured, Grant traveled there with staff to meet Buell and see the city. On the twenty-fifth, Grant informed Halleck he would soon leave for Nashville "should there be no orders to prevent."[57] On receiving none, Grant's party hopped on a steamer, delighted in the fine weather, and rejoiced to see the Stars and Stripes atop the capitol building. Grant and Rawlins ambled through the streets and were joined by Colonel W. H. L. Wallace and General McClernand on a visit to President James K. Polk's widow. The Polks' brick mansion sat on a large yard amid blooming magnolias and daffodils. Polk's tomb occupied a corner of the yard.[58] Colonel Wallace snatched a daffodil from the former first lady's garden and mailed it to his beloved wife.[59] The only thing to mar a lovely day was the edgy meeting with Buell. He thought Grant had taken needless risks at Nashville. Grant dismissed the criticism: the enemy was falling back, not poising to strike.

Grant and staff returned to Donelson late in the day on the twenty-eighth. Grant was laid low with a bad cold and not in top form as a firestorm was about to commence.

The communication exchange between Grant and Halleck had failed for some reason, and now Halleck learned that the situation in Tennessee was not what he thought it was. He was shocked that Grant had been in Nashville and not at Fort Henry, where Halleck wanted him to embark on an expedition up the Tennessee River to destroy bridges and rail connections toward Corinth and Eastport, Mississippi. Orders and reports between Halleck and Grant were not being received. Unbeknownst to them, the telegraph system was dysfunctional. There may even have been a telegraph operator sympathetic to the Confederacy, as Grant suggested in his *Memoirs*, who absconded south with military dispatches.[60] Even a legitimate reason for the communication disruption wouldn't have mollified Halleck: his plea for top command in the West had been rejected, and he was already distrustful of Grant's style of generalship. On March 4, an angry Halleck ordered Grant to place C. F. Smith at the head of the Tennessee River expedition and told Grant to stay put at Fort Henry. Then in a petulant voice, he asked Grant, "Why do you not obey my orders to report strength & positions of your command?"[61] Grant could only deny the charges: "I am not aware of ever having disobeyed any order from Head Quarters . . . I have reported almost daily the condition of my command and reported ev[e]ry position occupied."[62]

Halleck directed Smith to take the expedition upriver to Savannah, Tennessee, not far from the railroad, which Smith occupied on March 11. The significance of Smith's departure was keenly noted at Grant's headquarters. With all the troops gone, Dr. Brinton noticed dejection had descended on headquarters: "The General was depressed, Rawlins was out of spirits, and everyone, down to the very orderlies, was feeling below par."[63]

Halleck vented his frustration to McClellan, overall commander of US troops: "I have had no communication with General Grant for more than a week. . . . It is hard to censure a successful general immediately after a victory, but I think he richly deserves it. . . . I am worn-out and tired with this neglect and inefficiency. C. F. Smith is almost the only officer equal to the emergency."[64] McClellan, a thousand miles removed, offered a bold suggestion: "Do not hesitate to arrest him at once if the good of the service requires it, and place C. F. Smith in command."[65] A day later, Halleck wired McClellan again, attributing the communications failure to that old character flaw: "A rumor has just reached me that since the taking of Fort Donelson General Grant has resumed his former bad habits. If so, it will account for his neglect of my often-repeated orders."[66]

During this wrangle, Rawlins was in Paducah on March 7 delivering a report to General Sherman, who was preparing to join Smith on the river expedition. Halleck's vituperative behavior against Grant puzzled Rawlins, and he asked Sherman if he knew "the real trouble with General Grant at Department Headquarters." Sherman first said no but then assured Rawlins, "I will tell you it will be all right with Grant in a few days. Tell him to give himself no anxiety."[67]

But before everything turned out all right, there was more damaging innuendo to follow. At about this same time, a Bloomington, Illinois, judge and Lincoln intimate, David Davis, forwarded an anonymous letter to Halleck alleging misappropriation of captured food and equipment from Donelson. The scheme supposedly involved Colonel John Cook, a brigade commander in Smith's division, and Cook's quartermaster. They arranged that captured goods were turned over to a group of sutlers who sent them north. Halleck shared the letter with Grant, whose angry reaction was understandable given his efforts to combat graft and punish plunderers.[68] There were other rumors that Grant authorized the destruction of valuable Fort Donelson property.

Grant's staff rose to his defense, aware he was getting abused by Halleck and sniped at by detractors. Regarding destruction of property, Dr. Brinton said what got destroyed was a pile of insufficiently salted pork the Confederates left under a bluff, rotten goo Rawlins referred to as "that pork."[69] Colonel Cadwallader Washburn joined the staff briefly as aide-de-camp on March 2.[70] He apprised Elihu about the travesty underway: "The pretense was that [Grant] had no business to have gone to Nashville, and he had not furnished daily reports of the strength of his command. The pretense is frivolous and contemptible, and the last I am assured is destitute of truth."[71]

Over a year later and after the capture of Vicksburg, McPherson was quoted: "There were very few hours between the beginning and the end of the Donelson campaign that I was not personally present with Grant. . . . He was never intoxicated during that time, and did not at any time during that campaign, or since, drink to excess."[72]

Rawlins said as much—and more:

> I dislike to think, much less speak, about it. No baser calumny was ever uttered against any man than the insinuation at that time as to Grant's "bad habits." I was near him all the time. We were seldom an hour apart. He was never drunk. He did not drink to excess. He worked every day and much of the nights in that laborious and glorious campaign. He was never idle. Reports were sent to Halleck or to his Chief of Staff, General Cullum, every day.... There was no reason under heaven for Grant's suspension or supersedure; none whatever.[73]

Halleck's agitation lasted less than two weeks before he yielded. What forced his hand was a wire from Adjutant General Lorenzo Thomas requesting all the facts about Grant's improper actions.[74] Halleck realized this affair could land in a military court and turn ugly. Moreover, he had just received his coveted promotion to command in the West, and this eased his tension considerably. His answer to Lorenzo Thomas was of the "all's forgiven" variety: "General Grant has made the proper explanations and has been directed to resume his command in the field."[75]

But all was not easily forgotten. Grant was hurt and humiliated by this episode. And some changes would be necessitated.

—◦◦◦—

Halleck's eruption over the absent reports made maintaining order and regularity at headquarters top priorities, especially with regard to precise record-keeping. On March 15, Rawlins issued Grant's General Orders No. 21 assigning staff specific responsibilities. Rawlins, assisted by Rowley, "will have special charge of the books or records, consolidating returns, and forwarding all documents to their proper destinations." Hillyer was to ensure that all commanders furnished their returns to headquarters. Lagow and Riggin oversaw passes and tracked supplies for both commissary and quartermaster departments. Chief of Staff Webster would serve as Grant's adviser and attend "to any portion of duties that may not receive proper attention."[76] The aftermath of the Fort Donelson operation provided Rawlins a clear lesson: tighter control must be exerted over the entire flow of communications from headquarters upward to Halleck (and beyond) and down to officers and troops in the field. Here was likely the genesis for what was later termed Rawlins's "cast-iron rule that no scrap of correspondence should ever leave the office until it had passed under his personal supervision."[77]

Other changes were employed. Given the corruption and rumormongering perpetrated by men surrounding Grant, there was, as one historian described it, "the narrowing of the circle of those whom he chose to regard as friends, and a growing distrust, not at all innate, of the motives and actions of every one outside that circle."[78] A ceremony held in a cabin on board Grant's head-quarters steamer, *Tigress*, brought this issue of "whom should you trust" into perspective. A few days before his reinstatement, Grant was feted by some of his field commanders and staff officers by being presented with an exquisite sword. Four names were inscribed on the sword, signifying it as a gift from George W. Graham, Captain Clark Lagow, Colonel John Cook, and Colonel C. Carroll Marsh. Marsh, of the Twentieth Illinois, spoke for the group and said the sword "affords us an opportunity to express our renewed confidence in your ability as a commander" at a time when "the jealousy caused by your brilliant success has raised up hidden enemies who are endeavoring to strike out in the dark." Grant, disconsolate over losing his command, was so over-taken by grateful emotion that Hillyer had to acknowledge the gift.[79]

Consider the taint associated with several of the ceremonial delegation. Cook and his quartermaster were subjects of concern in the anonymous let-ter Judge David Davis forwarded to Halleck regarding goods captured at Fort Donelson. Graham, a steamboat superintendent, was also mentioned in that letter as the one who facilitated their shipment upriver to Cairo. Incidental-ly, Graham was fingered by Captain Kountz in his second series of bizarre charges as the person who allegedly provided a harlot for Grant on board a government steamer.[80] Lagow, a member of the unrestrained Seventh District Regiment, had long been in Rawlins's sights. Lagow and Hillyer were con-spicuous as "good old boys, partial to good food, strong drink and poker."[81] Rawlins had doubts about their trustworthiness and influence on Grant. They were also the staffers who had teamed to pressure Lew Wallace into embel-lishing their roles during the Donelson fighting. One wonders whether this quartet was motivated to use the gift to soften up Grant.

With the singular successes in the field at Henry and Donelson and Grant's advancement to major general, this was time for another change: promo-tions for staff. Back in Halleck's good graces, Grant wrote Secretary of War Stanton to recommend promotions to brigadier general for several of his "subcommanders," including Colonel Webster.[82] Two weeks earlier—and before Grant was relegated to Halleck's doghouse—Grant requested Stanton to arrange for promotions for staff. Rawlins sent a copy of that request letter to Washburne, asking the congressman for his assistance in securing colonelcies for Hillyer and Lagow and in appointing Rowley ("our mutual Friend") assistant adjutant general with rank of captain. Grant's request also included promoting Rawlins to major, allowable under an act of Congress that entitled a major general to one AAG with rank of major. Now Rawlins beseeched "Friend Washburne" to influence Lincoln on his behalf. Rawlins felt assured that "whatever you may deem necessary to my interest without injury to the public good you will cause to be done."[83]

On March 18, the War Department informed Grant that Rawlins's promotion was the only one that by law could be allowed.[84] Rowley, who was on more cordial terms with Washburne than Rawlins, wrote frankly to the former, clarifying the situation: having himself and Hillyer and Lagow denied advancement was not a bitter disappointment for Grant; Rawlins's promotion, according to Rowley, "was really more desired by the Gen (in my opinion) than any portion of it." And he put in a strong plug for Rawlins. "Rawlins is justly entitled to the promotion for if any one ever earned it he has. He works night and day and probably performs as much or more hard labor than any other Staff officer in the service of the United States."[85]

That was Rawlins: dedicated, conscientious, compulsive—and always with a grip on circumstances at headquarters and on himself.

—◦◦◦—

Changes in staff duties and rank were trifling issues when compared to the shifting military situation. The losses of Forts Henry and Donelson ruptured the Confederate line, forcing General Albert S. Johnston to abandon Columbus and Bowling Green, Kentucky, as well middle Tennessee, and to withdraw his remaining forces to northern Alabama. Meanwhile, General P. G. T. Beauregard, hero of Ft. Sumter and Bull Run, was sent west to assist Johnston. Beauregard, soon to be joined by Johnston, was receiving reinforcements and growing an army at Corinth, a strategic rail center in northwest Mississippi. Simultaneously, Halleck entertained a movement southward against them, but it would occur at Halleck's pace. While Halleck prevaricated, Grant and C. F. Smith only grew frustrated waiting for the chance to strike now rather than later.

In mid-March, the Federals were concentrating most of their divisions at Pittsburg Landing, perched on the west bank of the Tennessee River about twenty-five miles from Corinth. Sherman's division had occupied the Landing on March 15. There, Grant was ordered to await Buell's army, marching overland from Nashville. Once conjoined, the combined force would be unleashed against the Beauregard and Johnston tandem. On March 17, Grant was reunited with his army as he arrived on his steamer *Tigress* to establish headquarters at Savannah, Tennessee, in the mansion owned by William H. Cherry, a wealthy farmer, businessman, staunch Unionist, and slaveholder. The Cherry Mansion lies about nine miles downstream (that is, north) of Pittsburg Landing. Grant and staff would commute by steamer to the Landing in the morning and return to overnight at Savannah.

Even as the staff established headquarters at the mansion, one of Grant's divisions under Brigadier General William Sherman moved out a few miles west of the Landing to establish its position in the vicinity of a log house of worship called Shiloh Church.

NOTES

1. John W. Emerson, "Grant's Life in the West and His Mississippi Valley Campaigns," *Midland Monthly* 9, no. 5 (May 1898): 417.

2. General Orders No. 7, February 2, 1862, in *The Papers of Ulysses S. Grant*, ed. John Y. Simon (Carbondale: Southern Illinois University Press, 1972), 4:138–39.

3. John Y. Simon, ed., *The Personal Memoirs of Julia Dent Grant* (New York: G. P. Putnam's Sons, 1975), 97.

4. John W. Emerson, "Grant's Life in the West and His Mississippi Valley Campaigns," 419.

5. Jesse Taylor, "The Defense of Fort Henry," in *Battles and Leaders of the Civil War*, ed. Robert Underwood Johnson and Clarence Clough Buel (1887; repr., New York: Thomas Yoseloff, 1956), 1:369.

6. Ibid., 370.

7. Hillyer Papers, Special Collections, University of Virginia Library.

8. U. S. Grant to Julia Dent Grant, February 5, 1862, in *The Papers of Ulysses S. Grant*, ed. John Y. Simon, 4:153.

9. John H. Brinton, *Personal Memoirs of John H. Brinton* (New York: Neale, 1914), 114.

10. John Y. Simon, ed., *The Papers of Ulysses S. Grant*, 4:158n.

11. H. W. Halleck to U. S. Grant, February 8, 1862, in *The War of the Rebellion: A Compilation of the Official Records of the Union and Confederate Armies*, series 1, 7:595.

12. H. W. Halleck to A. H. Foote, February 11, 1862, in *The War of the Rebellion: A Compilation of the Official Records of the Union and Confederate Armies*, series 1, 7:603.

13. John Y. Simon, ed., *The Papers of Ulysses S. Grant*, 4:177n.

14. John H. Brinton, *Personal Memoirs of John H. Brinton*, 131.

15. John. Y. Simon, ed., *The Papers of Ulysses S. Grant*, 4:191–92.

16. John H. Brinton, *Personal Memoirs of John H. Brinton*, 116.

17. John W. Emerson, "Grant's Life in the West and His Mississippi Valley Campaigns," 511.

18. Wallace, in a February 11, 1862, letter to his wife, was outraged at being left at Fort Henry, blaming General C. F. Smith. "I have been sick from rage since yesterday. . . . My patience with old Smith is now 'played out,'" he wrote. On the same day, Hillyer sent Wallace a conciliatory letter, urging him to keep mum and to be advised that Grant would award him "a good position in the next fight"; John Y. Simon, ed., *The Papers of Ulysses S. Grant*, 4:192–93n.

19. Lew Wallace, *An Autobiography* (New York: Harper and Brothers, 1906), 1:388.

20. Ibid., 392–93.

21. John W. Emerson, "Grant's Life in the West and His Mississippi Valley Campaigns," 516.

22. Lew Wallace, *An Autobiography*, 1:402.

23. W. S. Hillyer to Lew Wallace, February 16, 1862, Indiana Historical Society, Wallace Collection.

24. "Battle of Fort Donelson," *Daily Gazette*, Galena, IL, September 18, 1865.

25. R. S. Jones, *The Right Hand of Command: Use and Disuse of Personal Staffs in the Civil War* (Mechanicsburg, PA: Stackpole, 2000), 78.

26. U. S. Grant, *Personal Memoirs of U. S. Grant* (New York: Charles Webster, 1885), 1:307–8.

27. Lewis Wallace's Report of February 20, 1862, in *The War of the Rebellion: A Compilation of the Official Records of the Union and Confederate Armies*, series 1, 7:238.

28. "Battle of Fort Donelson," *Daily Gazette*, Galena, IL, September 18, 1865.

29. J. H. Brinton, *Personal Memoirs of John H. Brinton*, 131.

30. John W. Emerson, "Grant's Life in the West and His Mississippi Valley Campaigns," 523.

31. John H. Brinton, *Personal Memoirs of John H. Brinton*, 129.

32. U. S. Grant to Simon B. Buckner, February 16, 1862, in *The Papers of Ulysses S. Grant*, ed. John Y. Simon, 4:218.

33. John H. Brinton, *Personal Memoirs of John H. Brinton*, 130.

34. General Smith took a copy of the "unconditional surrender" in Grant's hand to deliver to Buckner. The original was retained by John Rawlins, who kept it until his death. After the surrender was consummated, Rawlins found the copy on the floor of Buckner's headquarters. Rawlins later gave it to a relative of his second wife. See John Y. Simon, ed., *The Papers of Ulysses S. Grant*, 4:218–19nn.

35. U. S. Grant to H. W. Halleck, February 16, 1862, in *The War of the Rebellion: A Compilation of the Official Records of the Union and Confederate Armies*, series 1, 7:625.

36. *New York Tribune*, February 17, 1862.

37. Mark Washburne, *A Biography of Elihu Benjamin Washburne: Congressman, Secretary of State, Envoy Extraordinary* (self-pub., Xlibris, 2001), 2:102.

38. H. W. Halleck to W. S. Rosecrans, February 17, 1862, author's personal collection.

39. H. W. Halleck to General McClellan, February 17, 1862, in *The War of the Rebellion: A Compilation of the Official Records of the Union and Confederate Armies*, series 1, 7:628.

40. General Orders No. 1, February17, 1862, in *The Papers of Ulysses S. Grant*, ed. John Y. Simon, 4:230.

41. Abraham Lincoln, Executive Order—President's Special War Order No. 3, March 11, 1862, online by Gerhard Peters and John T. Woolley, *The American Presidency Project*, https://www.presidency.ucsb.edu/documents/executive-order-presidents-special-war -order-no-3.

42. U. S. Grant to E. B. Washburn, February 21, 1862, in *The Papers of Ulysses S. Grant*, ed. John Y. Simon, 4:263–64.

43. A. D. Richardson, *A Personal History of Ulysses S. Grant* (Boston: D. L. Guernsey, 1885), 232.

44. General Orders No. 43, Department of the Missouri, February 19, 1862, in *The War of the Rebellion: A Compilation of the Official Records of the Union and Confederate Armies*, series 1, 7:639.

45. U. S. Grant report, February 16, 1862, in *The War of the Rebellion: A Compilation of the Official Records of the Union and Confederate Armies*, series 1, 7:160.

46. Lew Wallace, *An Autobiography*, 1:435–36. Two months later, Hillyer wrote a letter that said in part, "True [Grant] was absent in the necessary discharge of duty at the gunboats at the time of the terrible conflict between McClernand's division and the enemy on our right on Saturday morning. But he had so dispersed his forces as to enable McClernand, as he eventually did, to check and repulse the advance of the enemy there, and had sent a portion of his staff, with authority and instructions to represent him"; John Y. Simon, ed., *The Papers of Ulysses S. Grant*, 5:82n. Hillyer was protecting Grant by falsely augmenting the role the staff played that morning.

47. Papers of William S. Hillyer, University of Virginia Special Collections, MSS 10645, Box 3.

48. Gail Stephens, *Shadow of Shiloh: Major General Lew Wallace in the Civil War* (Indianapolis: Indiana Historical Society, 2010), 62.

49. General Orders No. 6, February 21, 1862, in *The Papers of Ulysses S. Grant*, John Y. Simon, 4:253–54.

50. Special Field Orders No. 6, District of Cairo, February 16, 1862, in *The War of the Rebellion: A Compilation of the Official Records of the Union and Confederate Armies*, series 1, 7:626.

51. John Y. Simon, ed., *The Papers of Ulysses S. Grant*, 4:258n.

52. Ibid., 257.

53. A. H. Foote to Gen. Cullum, February 21, 1862, in *The War of the Rebellion: A Compilation of the Official Records of the Union and Confederate Armies*, series 1, 7:648.

54. John Y. Simon, ed., *The Papers of Ulysses S. Grant*, 4:260n; H. W. Halleck to G. W. Cullum, February 21, 1862, in *The War of the Rebellion: A Compilation of the Official Records of the Union and Confederate Armies*, series 1, 7:648.

55. *Official Records of the Union and Confederate Navies in the War of the Rebellion*, February 23, 1862, series 1, 12:626.

56. J. H. Brinton, *Personal Memoirs of John H. Brinton*, 138–39.

57. U. S. Grant to G. W. Cullum, February 25, 1862, in *The Papers of Ulysses S. Grant*, ed. John Y. Simon, 4:286.

58. *New York Times*, March 5, 1862.

59. John Y. Simon, ed., *The Papers of Ulysses S. Grant*, 4:298n1.

60. U. S. Grant, *Personal Memoirs of U. S. Grant*, 1:325.

61. John Y. Simon, ed., *The Papers of Ulysses S. Grant*, 4:319n1.

62. U. S. Grant to H. W. Halleck, March 5, 1862, in *The Papers of Ulysses S. Grant*, ed. John Y. Simon, 4:318.

63. J. H. Brinton, *Personal Memoirs of John H. Brinton*, 150.

64. *The War of the Rebellion: A Compilation of the Official Records of the Union and Confederate Armies*, March 3, 1862, series 1, 7:679–80.

65. Ibid., 680.

66. Ibid., 682.

67. James H. Wilson, *The Life of John A. Rawlins* (New York: Neale, 1916), 446.

68. Bruce Catton, *Grant Moves South* (Boston: Little, Brown, 1960), 208–9; John Y. Simon, ed., *The Papers of Ulysses S. Grant*, 4:353–54n.

69. John H. Brinton, *Personal Memoirs of John H. Brinton*, 142–43.

70. General Orders No. 19, March 2, 1862, in *The Papers of Ulysses S. Grant*, ed. John Y. Simon, 4:307; Cadwallader Washburn took command of the Second Wisconsin Cavalry Regiment, telling his brother, "I had rather have command of a Regt. than be on anybody's staff." Cadwallader Washburne to Elihu Washburne, April 9, 1862, Washburne Papers, Library of Congress.

71. Cadwallader Washburn to Elihu Washburne, March 7, 1862, Washburne Papers, Library of Congress.

72. John W. Emerson, "Grant's Life in the West and His Mississippi Valley Campaigns," 227–28.

73. Ibid., 228.

74. L. Thomas to H. W. Halleck, March 10, 1862, in *The War of the Rebellion: A Compilation of the Official Records of the Union and Confederate Armies*, series 1, 7:683.

75. H. W. Halleck to L. Thomas, March 15, 1862, in *The War of the Rebellion: A Compilation of the Official Records of the Union and Confederate Armies*, series 1, 7:683.

76. General Orders No. 21, March 15, 1862, in *The War of the Rebellion: A Compilation of the Official Records of the Union and Confederate Armies*, series 1, part 2, 10:41.

77. James H. Wilson, *The Life of John A. Rawlins*, 80–81, 431.

78. Arthur L. Conger, *The Rise of U. S. Grant* (New York: Century, 1931), 212.

79. John Y. Simon, ed., *The Papers of Ulysses S. Grant*, 4:376n.

80. Ibid., 354n; ibid., 113n.

81. Edward G. Longacre, *General Ulysses S. Grant: The Soldier and the Man* (New York: Da Capo, 2006), 95.

82. U. S. Grant to Edwin M. Stanton, March 14, 1862, *The Papers of Ulysses S. Grant*, ed. John Y. Simon, 4:356–57. Webster had to wait until November 29, 1862, for confirmation; ibid., 357n.

83. Ibid., 444n1.

84. Ibid., 445n1.

85. Ibid.

11

"Rawlins Is a Maj. and Ought to Be a Brig. Gen."

MARCH 1862 COULD BE REMEMBERED at headquarters as the month of misery. Besides the Halleck trouble, Grant, Rowley, and Rawlins—and much of the Federal army—were wracked by intestinal miseries from polluted river water. Yet there could be no respite from attending to administrative details as Grant marshalled his troops for what he believed could be the pivotal (and last) big fight in the West.[1] The army was concentrating at Pittsburg Landing on the west bank of the Tennessee River, a site Sherman chose because of the roads leading from it to Corinth, Mississippi. Beginning in mid-March, transports disgorged Federal troops at this nondescript landing situated at the base of yellow clay bluffs. From the fifteenth through the twentieth of the month, a crush of transports jostled for space. Sherman's Fifth Division of green recruits was the first to arrive. It was followed by Hurlbut's Fourth Division, the Second Division under C. F. Smith, and McClernand's First Division. As unattached units—mostly raw recruits—disembarked, they were melded into a new Sixth Division and, by an order issued through Rawlins, placed under Brigadier General Benjamin Prentiss, the officer who had sparred with Grant over seniority.[2] Lew Wallace's Third Division was off by its lonesome, stationed upstream on the west bank at Crump's Landing, about midway between Pittsburg Landing and Savannah. As the divisions assembled into what would be known as the Army of the Tennessee, Rawlins routed incoming troops to proper destinations.[3]

While Grant's army disembarked at Pittsburg, Buell learned that Beauregard might strike toward Savannah.[4] Halleck relayed this intelligence to

Grant on March 18, saying that if Buell was correct, "General Smith should immediately destroy railroad connections at Corinth."[5] Grant usually looked to start a fight, and he was eager to act on Halleck's recommendation. There might be enough troops at the Landing, he told Halleck, to move on March 23 or 24.[6] Halleck blanched and then sent a reply to rein in Grant: "By all means keep your forces together until you connect with General Buell, who is now at Columbia [TN]. . . . Don't let the enemy draw you into an engagement now. Wait until you are properly fortified and receive orders."[7] Grant sent Hillyer to St. Louis to meet with Halleck and plead the case for demolishing the railroad. Halleck received him frigidly, listened impassively, and issued a peremptory order not to bring on a general engagement.[8]

Halleck's order contained the noteworthy word *fortified*. Curiously, the Federal encampment beyond Pittsburg Landing was not fortified against enemy attack. Sherman's division, posted three miles west of the Landing and Prentiss's division on Sherman's left, would bear the brunt of such an attack—although none was expected. The divisions of McClernand and Smith formed to their rear. The Federal encampment was deemed secured by streams that protected the Union flanks, Owl Creek on Sherman's right and Lick Creek to the south, on the left. These unfordable creeks provided about a two-mile-wide space through which an enemy attack could be funneled. Why weren't fortifications erected along the Federal front? Grant's explanation was that the Union encampment was only temporary, a staging ground for the proposed offensive against Corinth: "When all reinforcements should have arrived I expected to take the initiative by marching on Corinth, and had no expectation of needing fortifications. . . . The fact is, I regarded the campaign we were engaged in as an offensive one and had no idea that the enemy would leave strong intrenchments to take the initiative when he knew he would be attacked where he was if he remained."[9] Because many of the regiments were hastily organized, Grant felt the men "needed discipline and drill more than they did experience with the pick, shovel, and axe."[10] The absence of entrenchments suited General Smith: "By God, I ask nothing better than to have the Rebels to come out and attack us! We can whip them to hell. Our men suppose we have come here to fight, and if we begin to spade it will make them think we fear the enemy."[11]

While Grant's attention fixed on offensive prospects, Rawlins closed holes on the defensive front, as it were, at headquarters. On March 19, he issued orders to safeguard captured enemy materiel. This was to prevent corrupt officers from profiteering and to protect Grant from the kind of criticism that erupted over the letter Judge Davis had passed to Halleck. Rawlins's order also appealed to a shared patriotic sensibility: "While [the property] is being collected brigade guards will be detailed to prevent pillage, and all commanders will use their utmost endeavor to restrain those under them from the improper appropriation of captured property. For one person to take possession for himself what has been gained by the united bravery and exertion of all is nothing less than pilfering."[12] Combined with General Orders No. 21 issued four days before, authorizing greater oversight of communications, Grant and Rawlins were moving to address vulnerable areas.

—⁓⁓—

While awaiting Buell and Halleck—the latter presumably would appoint himself head of the combined army and lead it against Johnston—there were decisions concerning General C. F. Smith. On March 26, through Rawlins, a special order was issued that placed Smith in command at Pittsburg Landing while Grant was at headquarters in Savannah.[13] But this appointment soon became "more form than substance."[14] Two weeks earlier, Smith met with Lew Wallace aboard the *John J. Roe*. When Smith attempted to board a skiff to return to his own steamer, the *Continental*, he lost his balance and pitched against the edge of a seat. He slammed against the sharp wood and suffered a bone-deep gash of his right leg from ankle to knee. By March 26, he was feverish and in agonizing pain. A week later, erysipelas set in, and he was sent to the Cherry Mansion to convalesce. Fearing that his mentor might be incapacitated for the coming advance, Grant, on the twenty-second, approached William H. L. Wallace—he had just received his brigadier's star the previous day—about possibly assuming leadership of Smith's Second Division.[15]

Albert Sidney Johnston was determined to strike Grant before Buell joined him. The Confederate army moved out on April 3 but made poor headway due to rain, muddy roads, and confusion regarding the order of march. They were supposed to be in position to launch a surprise attack toward Pittsburg Landing early on Saturday, April 5; however, their columns weren't properly arrayed until midafternoon. Beauregard was concerned that they had lost the element of surprise due to the delays and brisk skirmishing with Federal pickets on the third. Moreover, the march had been hardly carried out in stealth: on Saturday after the rain ended, some Confederate infantrymen fired their muskets to see whether they still worked.[16]

Beauregard need not have feared. Grant believed if an attack were made, it would come against Lew Wallace's isolated division at Crump's Landing, where the army's supplies were guarded. The skirmishing that erupted on the third was sharp enough to warrant Grant's attention, but he merely stayed longer on the field, delaying his commute back to Savannah, until the firing simmered down. There was skirmish fire the next night too, and while Grant was riding back to the boat to return to Savannah, his horse slipped on the mud, fell on him, and almost crushed his ankle. The enemy was out there, somewhere on the periphery, but the Union command expected that the big fight would occur after the march to Corinth.[17] Grant was so unbothered about being attacked that on Saturday, April 5, when the first of Buell's divisions arrived—"Bull" Nelson's consisting of about forty-five hundred troops—it was bivouacked at Savannah on the east bank of the Tennessee River, and the men were told to get comfortable because it would not be until early the next week that they'd be transported down to Pittsburg Landing.[18]

That sanguine outlook was evident in two dispatches sent on Saturday. Sherman told Grant, "I have no doubt that nothing will occur to-day more than some picket firing. The enemy is saucy, but got the worst of it yesterday, and will not press our pickets far. I will not be drawn out far unless with certainty of advantage, and I do not apprehend anything like an attack on our position."[19] Grant telegraphed Halleck that "I have scarsely [sic] the faintest idea of an attack, (general one,) being made upon us but will be prepared should such a thing take place."[20]

With his swollen leg, Grant hobbled around a depleted Savannah headquarters. Colonel Webster was on a reconnaissance mission aboard a gunboat to assess the feasibility of destroying the Memphis and Charleston Railroad near Eastport, Mississippi.[21] Hillyer had been ordered by Rawlins to take two Jessie Scouts, suspected of horse stealing, to St. Louis and deliver them to the provost marshal.[22]

—◦◦◦—

Hillyer returned to the Cherry Mansion at 3:00 a.m. on Sunday, April 6. He made enough noise that Rawlins was unable to fall back to sleep, so the efficiency-minded adjutant made use of the morning light by sorting Grant's pile of mail. There was enough work to warrant the early start: the headquarters office at Savannah was being closed down and moved to Pittsburg Landing; Buell was anticipated momentarily (although he had actually arrived, unbeknownst to the staff, during the evening of the fifth); and there were countless arrangements in preparation for the major operation launching within a week.

While breakfast cooked, Grant perused his mail and conversed with Brigadier General John Cook, just returned from leave. Around 7:00 a.m., a private at headquarters interrupted the meal to report that the thump of artillery fire was emanating from the direction of Pittsburg Landing.[23] The breakfasters scurried outside where they could feel the ground shaking. Colonel Webster, the experienced artilleryman, turned his ear, trying to gauge the exact direction of the cannonading. All agreed this was the sound of battle. What they heard was Prentiss's division being engaged by General William Hardee's corps. Prentiss had been alerted by enemy movement just beyond his camp and had time to shake out a defensive line. However, Hardee's attack was irresistible, and in ninety minutes, Prentiss's division was shattered. As Prentiss struggled to hold, Sherman's division around Shiloh Church absorbed an assault by Leonidas Polk's corps. Sherman made a spirited stand, but his division yielded under unrelenting pressure.

Grant, staff, and their mounts hurried on board the *Tigress* to steam upriver to Pittsburg Landing. Shoving off was delayed briefly in order to transmit last-second dispatches. One went to Buell, alerting him to the heavy firing "indicating plainly that an attack has been made upon our most advance positions."[24] Rawlins told General Nelson to move his division southward down the east bank of the Tennessee to opposite Pittsburg Landing.[25]

Between Savannah and Pittsburg Landing, a rendezvous had to be made with Lew Wallace at Crump's Landing. If the locus of the Confederate main attack was not against Wallace's isolated division, then it would be needed elsewhere—exactly where was to be determined. The *Tigress* sidled up to Wallace's headquarters steamer. From the railing of *Tigress*'s second deck, Grant called out instructions, which Wallace recollected were to "hold yourself in readiness to march upon orders received." The order to stand pat for a while was not what Wallace wanted to hear. He replied that two hours earlier, he had ordered his three brigades to concentrate at aptly named Stoney Lonesome, a barren plot about three miles west of Crump's—and he was ready to move now. Grant paused to consider this adjustment before slightly altering his order: "Very well. Hold the division ready *to march in any direction*." With that, *Tigress* peeled away and, under a powerful head of steam, disappeared upriver to Pittsburg Landing.[26]

—∿∿—

Tigress docked at Pittsburg Landing about 8:00 a.m., as Rawlins later recollected.[27] There, he saw hundreds of cowering stragglers, including officers, taking refuge under the river bluff. From there, Grant and staff headed for the front. All they had to do was follow the crescendo of musketry, plumes of smoke, and howling voices. About one-half mile forward, they met General W. H. L. Wallace, Smith's substitute, whose division was in reserve. Wallace gave Grant a status report: Sherman was hotly engaged and giving ground reluctantly; he would be forced backward about three miles before dark. The divisions of McClernand, Prentiss, and Hurlbut were also being mauled by what felt like an enemy juggernaut. Circumstances required immediate action: the shirker problem had to be addressed;[28] Grant needed to consult with each division commander and bolster their determination; and more than anything else, help had to be summoned.

Trusting a good portion of help could come from Buell's approaching divisions, Grant penned a message addressed to "Comd.g Officer Advance Forces Near Pittsburg, Ten." The cryptic address suggested Grant was unsure whether Buell was at Savannah.[29] "The attack on my forces has been very spirited from early this morning," he began. "The appearance of fresh troops on the field now would have a powerful effect both by inspiring our men and disheartening the enemy. If you will get upon the field leaving all your baggage on the East bank of the river it will be a move to our advantage and possibly save the day to us. The rebel forces is estimated at over 100,000 men. My Hd Qrs. will be in the log building on top of the hill."[30] That Grant so much overestimated the troops opposing him seems an indication of how alarmed he had been by the force of the attack.

Lew Wallace's division was closer than Savannah and could be summoned relatively quickly to strengthen the Federal right. Grant asked Rawlins to go back to the river and engage Quartermaster Algernon Baxter to deliver the order to Wallace to bring up his division and position it behind W. H. L. Wallace's. Baxter was to board *Tigress* and get to Crump's Landing as quickly as possible. As Rawlins stated one year later in his report, he found Baxter near

Pittsburg Landing and conveyed to him Grant's order. Fearing he might get details wrong, Baxter requested it in writing. On board *Tigress*, Rawlins found ink and pen, and with Baxter transcribing, Rawlins dictated what he regarded as substantially the following order: "Major-General Wallace: You will move forward your division from Crump's Landing, leaving a sufficient force to protect the public property at that place, to Pittsburg Landing, on the road nearest to and parallel with the river, and form in line at right angles with the river, immediately in rear of the camp of Maj. Gen. C. F. Smith's division [in the temporary command of W. H. L. Wallace] on our right, and there await further orders."

With the order in his possession, Baxter departed, as Rawlins reported, "not later than 9 o'clock a.m." and returned before noon.[31] After seeing off Baxter, Rawlins, accompanied by a volunteer aide, Douglas Putnam, returned to find Grant. Putnam wondered where he might be found, to which Rawlins replied, "We'll find him where the firing is heaviest." As they rode to the front, signs of battle became increasingly evident. Putnam, who had no combat experience, heard a patter in the leaves overhead and wondered if it wasn't raining. "Those are bullets, Douglas," was Rawlins's terse reply. Farther on, they passed a horse, disemboweled by a cannon ball but still on his feet. Putnam wanted to put him out of his misery, but Rawlins, mindful of protocol, rebuffed the idea: "He belongs to the quartermaster's department; better let them attend to it." They soon found Grant busy dispatching aides and preparing to visit each division commander.[32]

Meanwhile, Captain Baxter had reached Crump's Landing, where he found tied to an elm tree the mount that Lew Wallace left if a messenger needed it. Baxter rode west three miles to Stoney Lonesome where, Wallace recollected, he arrived around 11:30 a.m. and handed him an order. So began one of the most confusing and controversial episodes of the Civil War. It set in motion a chain of events that in a few months would leave Wallace feeling as if "suddenly somebody in the dark gave me a push, and I fell, and fell so far that I could almost see bottom."[33]

———～⁓⁓———

Confusion is evident in the discrepancies reported in terms of departure and arrival times, how Baxter received the order for Wallace, the physical appearance of the order, and what it actually said. Rawlins claimed Baxter left for

Crump's Landing at 9:00 a.m., but Rowley's report states that Baxter received the order at 8:00 a.m., suggesting an earlier departure time.[34] There is also a discrepancy regarding the time the order reached Wallace. Rawlins's report has Baxter delivering Grant's order at 10:00 a.m., whereas Wallace claimed it was delivered an hour and a half later.[35]

According to Rawlins, he dictated Grant's order to Baxter, but Rowley's report suggests that it was Grant who transmitted the order verbally to Baxter. Again, according to Rawlins, the dictated order was accomplished in ink. However, Lew Wallace said that he was handed an unsigned order that had been hurriedly scrawled in pencil on a shabby half sheet of tobacco-stained writing paper that had the print of a boot heel on it. Wallace said that Baxter told him he had received the order verbally from General Grant and, while on the *Tigress* and fearing that he might make an error in transmission, had written it in pencil on a piece of paper he had found on the floor in the ladies' cabin.[36] Some of this confusion might have been cleared up if Baxter had submitted his own report of the events, but he was not required to.[37]

Grant, Rowley, McPherson, and Wallace, besides Rawlins, provided versions of what the order required. Grant emphatically wrote he directed Baxter "to go back and order General Wallace to march immediately to Pittsburg [Landing] by the road nearest the river."[38] According to Rowley, Wallace was instructed "to march with his division up the river and into the field on the right of our line as rapidly as possible."[39] McPherson's report says the order called for Wallace "to move up immediately by the River road and take a position on our right."[40] Wallace provided his own almost verbatim recollection of the order: "You will leave a sufficient force at Crump's Landing to guard the public property there; with the rest of the division march and form junction with the right of the army. Form line of battle at right angles with the river, and be governed by circumstances."[41] A key difference between Wallace's version and what Rawlins and Grant claimed was that the latter two said the order specified the road Wallace was to take, the River Road, and the final destination point, Pittsburg Landing. The River Road lay a bit west of Wallace's headquarters at Crump's and ran roughly southward and parallel to the Tennessee River. Wallace steadfastly claimed the order specified neither road nor Pittsburg Landing destination. Who was right? The answer will probably never be known because the only copy of the order passed to Wallace's adjutant, Frederick Knefler, who tucked it under his sword belt . . . and somehow lost it.

Just before Baxter started on his return to the *Tigress* at Crump's, and almost as an afterthought, Wallace inquired of him, "Now, how is the battle going?"

Baxter replied, "We are repulsing the enemy."[42] Baxter couldn't have been more wrong.

With Wallace operating from the assumption that the choice of route to the right of the army was deferred to him, he had two options. One was the River Road; the other was the Shunpike. The latter was Wallace's choice for several reasons. First, it could be accessed from Stoney Lonesome, where Wallace concentrated his division, thus saving marching distance. The Shunpike ran southwesterly until just past Snake Creek, where it bent to the south, thereby allowing Wallace to bring his division to nestle against Sherman's on the Federal right flank—perhaps even a bit to the rear of Sherman if, as Baxter said, he was pushing the enemy backward. Also, the Shunpike, which Wallace had recently caused to be repaired, was in better condition than the River Road. Actually, it was Wallace's intent to use the Shunpike as the sensible route for moving his troops back to the main army or for reinforcements to reach him at Crump's Landing. Unfortunately, he never communicated this intent to Grant. On the other hand, Grant assumed that the River Road was the preferable route between Crump's and Pittsburg Landing, but he never shared his assumption with Wallace. This failure in communication spawned considerable confusion and led Grant and Rawlins to believe that Wallace must have been lost when his division was discovered later on the Shunpike.[43]

Baxter had barely left Wallace when a contingent of the Second Illinois Cavalry galloped up. Grant had sent them to reinforce the message that Wallace was needed immediately. Wallace allowed his men a half hour to eat lunch—critics excoriated him for this delay—but once on the Shunpike at precisely noon, they marched at a decent pace. Back on the battlefield, Grant nervously anticipated Wallace's arrival. The anticipation gnawed on Grant such that at 12:30 p.m., he dispatched Rowley to press Wallace with the admonition, "Do not spare horseflesh."[44]

——◊◊◊——

While Rowley made his way to Wallace, General Buell arrived by steamer at Pittsburg Landing around 2:00 p.m. There, he was disgusted by the sight of perhaps five thousand shirkers huddling under the river bluff. Buell barked insults at them, hoping to shame some into rejoining the battle, and threatened to have gunboats train their cannons on the cowardly remainder.[45] Rawlins recollected that Buell was received at Grant's log house field headquarters atop a bluff. One of Buell's first questions, possibly inspired by the mob of stragglers, was, "What preparations have you made for retreating?"

Grant optimistically replied, "I have not despaired of whipping them, general."[46] Their brief meeting dealt mostly with arrangements for getting Buell's men across the river.

About this time when Rawlins was near the landing, he saw an officer from Buell's army on the riverbank who was shouting instructions to the captain of a steamer that was hauling a load of pontoon boats: "For God's sake, Captain, land and get those pontoons in position so that the army can cross the river." Rawlins vehemently overruled the officer's order: "You take your boat away from the landing and keep her away or I will burn her up. Do you understand?" Rawlins had surmised that the pontoon bridge would provide the stragglers an escape route to the opposite bank. A few minutes later, Rawlins again intervened. A stern-wheeler, the *Rocket*, had towed two barges of much-needed ammunition to the landing. Suddenly, a shell exploded near a barge, prompting the *Rocket's* captain to order his lines cut so he could head to safety. Rawlins hustled over and ordered the captain to return or else he would shoot everyone on board.[47]

Grant's optimism notwithstanding, the Federal's situation at that moment looked precarious. Sherman and McClernand on the right fought stubbornly but were forced farther and farther rearward. The Union left was enveloped. But the center of the line still held: men from the divisions of Prentiss, W. H. L. Wallace, and Hurlbut were desperately holding out, repulsing multiple Confederate assaults. These Federals occupied a tangle of timber that drew such a stinging fire, it became renowned as the Hornet's Nest. Augustus Chetlain commanded the Twelfth Illinois regiment in W. H. L. Wallace's division. Chetlain had been stricken by that intestinal ailment but had left his hospital bed to rejoin his regiment, which by 1:00 p.m. had been driven back. During the retreat, Chetlain collapsed and was carried to the rear. There, he was received by Grant and staff. "Tomorrow morning with Gen. Lew Wallace's division and the fresh troops of the Army of the Ohio, now crossing the river," Grant told him, "we will soon finish [the enemy] up." [48]

Minutes before Grant offered Chetlain this assurance, he made two more efforts to secure those fresh troops. At 2:30 p.m., a frustrated Grant ordered

McPherson and Rawlins to find Wallace and conduct him to the field. Then Grant ordered Hillyer to take troop transports to Savannah to move one of Buell's divisions, Crittenden's, to Pittsburg Landing.[49]

At almost the moment McPherson, Rawlins, and Hillyer departed, the Confederate commander, Albert S. Johnston, lay bleeding to death on the battlefield.

⸻

At Crump's Landing, Rowley found a wagon driver who pointed him to the road that Wallace had taken—a road Rowley doubted would lead to Pittsburg Landing. After a ride of five or six miles, Rowley reached the rear of Wallace's division between 2:00 and 2:30. The division was on the Shunpike, having just crossed Clear Creek, and the troops were at rest. Some had stacked their arms. Rowley found Wallace at the head of the column, sitting on his horse and surrounded by staff. They may have been waiting for a report from the cavalry that was scouting the road ahead.[50]

When Rowley asked Wallace where he was going, he replied, "To join Sherman." Drawing Wallace aside, a rattled Rowley burst out, "Great God! Don't you know Sherman has been driven back? Why, the whole army is within half a mile of the river, and it's a question if we are not all going to be driven into it."[51] This news left Wallace dumbstruck: if he continued on the Shunpike, he'd march into the rear of the enemy's line.

Wallace had to retrace his steps northward up the Shunpike. However, instead of ordering a simple about-face command, he ordered a countermarch by brigades. This more time-consuming maneuver allowed him to keep his regiments in the battle order he preferred but would negate the order Rowley was conveying from Grant: "he wants you at Pittsburg Landing—and he wants you there like hell."[52] Fortunately for Wallace, his staff found a local who knew a crossroad that linked the Shunpike with the River Road leading to Pittsburg Landing. The crossroad, barely a rough path, intersected the Shunpike about a mile beyond Snake Creek and meandered southeastward.

Rawlins and McPherson rode up River Road expecting, but failing, to link with Wallace. They reached Crump's Landing, turned west to Stoney Lonesome, and then went down the Shunpike before they spied the back end of Wallace's division disappearing onto the little crossroad. They found Wallace and Rowley between 3:30 and 4:00. McPherson delivered Grant's instructions and implored Wallace for "God's sake to move forward rapidly." In his report,

McPherson said Wallace's column didn't seem to march with the alacrity circumstances warranted, but McPherson conceded such a criticism could be attributed to his own "impatience and anxiety."[53]

Rawlins did not give Wallace such benefit of a doubt. Rawlins's report bristles with examples that fault Wallace for taking a too casual approach and that question his leadership and courage. For example, Rawlins described his efforts to make Wallace comprehend the urgency of the situation: "Colonel McPherson, Captain Rowley, and myself represented to him how matters stood when we left. I urged him with all the earnestness I possessed the importance of his presence on the field. . . . He said there was no danger; he would yet reach there in good season." McPherson even suggested that Wallace let his lumbering artillery fall to the rear to quicken the pace, a suggestion Wallace assented to but which caused such a delay that he dismounted and sat down—to Rawlins's consternation. Wallace, Rawlins reported, allowed the regiments time to close up, and even on the march, Wallace had them moving "coolly and leisurely" all the way to Pittsburg Landing. When the column was near Snake Creek, there was heard a crescendo of artillery fire at Pittsburg Landing from the Federal heavy guns. The closeness of the artillery suggested the enemy might be between Wallace and the river. According to Rawlins, Wallace seemed perplexed by this possibility and asked, "What had best be done?"

To which McPherson replied, "Fight our way through until communication can be had with General Grant." Yet Wallace still hesitated, displaying, in Rawlins's terms, "the utmost coolness and indifference."[54]

What the men in the approaching column did not know was that the thunderous artillery barrage was part of the last significant action of the first day's fighting. Around 5:30, the remaining defenders of the Hornet's Nest were forced to surrender. With that pocket of resistance gone, Beauregard, in command since the death of Johnston, could unleash a demolishing thrust against the Federals who were holding onto a slice of real estate by the Landing. After taking precious time to reorganize, Beauregard launched a fierce attack against this last line of Union defense, two thousand yards in length that stretched out from the river, up a slope, and along a ridge. Anchoring this line were Union infantry and dozens of pieces of artillery put in place by Colonel Webster. Backing up Webster were the naval guns of the *Tyler* and *Lexington*. A furious Confederate assault led by Braxton Bragg was met by a hailstorm of shot and shell and finished off by the infantry's musket fire. On seeing that exposure to the cannonade would result in senseless casualties, Beauregard called off

Bragg. With the Federal line intact but pressed almost to the Tennessee River, the last Confederate assault repulsed, and dusk settling over the combatants, Grant's hoped-for help was arriving. Buell's divisions were coming over the river, and Wallace's stray division tramped onto Pittsburg Landing. Then rain began falling.

McPherson found his way to Grant. He reported that perhaps a third of the army were combat casualties, the rest demoralized. To McPherson, prospects looked bleak: "Well, General Grant; under this condition of affairs, what do you propose to do, sir? Shall I make preparations for retreat?"

Grant's blunt reply was, "*Retreat? No!* I propose to attack at daylight, and whip them."[55]

The last of Wallace's division trudged onto the field at 8:00 p.m. Wallace, by himself and in the inky darkness, tried to position his division into the line. McPherson and Rawlins were in the vicinity, but neither guided him nor brought him orders from Grant. Rawlins sought shelter from the lashing rain inside a field hospital tent. There, he bedded down among the dead and grievously wounded. Finally, around 1:00 a.m. Wallace had his division aligned, and he reclined under a tree to sleep.[56] But the tree provided scant shelter from the rain. Through the downpour, he could hear the anguished pleas of a wounded soldier, a drawn-out moan that continued throughout the night.[57]

Wallace's division acquitted itself creditably in the second day's fighting. In fact, two of Wallace's artillery batteries reopened the battle. However, his military career would never fully recover from the roundabout march of April 6 that brought him afoul of both Halleck and Grant. To the end of his days, Grant claimed Wallace had gotten it wrong: "I never could see," he wrote, "and do not now see, why any order was necessary further than to direct him to come to Pittsburg Landing, without specifying by what route. . . . Later in the war, General Wallace would never have made the mistake that he committed on the 6th of April, 1862."[58]

The reports of Rawlins, McPherson, and Rowley with descriptions of their frustrating encounters with Wallace and their criticisms of his lackadaisical pace contributed to the prevailing belief that Wallace was confused or lost on that first day of battle. These reports received Grant's imprimatur. In a dispatch to Halleck, he attested to their veracity: "All these reports are substantially as I remember the facts. I vouch for their almost entire accuracy." In the same dispatch Grant assessed Wallace's generalship as inept: "Had General Wallace been relieved from duty in the morning, and the same orders communicated to Brig. Gen. Morgan L. Smith (who would have been a successor), I do not doubt but the division would have been on the field of battle and in engagement before 10 o'clock of that eventful 6th of April."[59] Rawlins's biographer and close associate, General James Wilson, placed confidence in Rawlins's version: "No one can read Rawlins's clear and convincing account of the efforts made to get Wallace into that battle, without reaching the conclusion that Wallace was not only inexcusable for taking the wrong road, but was culpably slow in all his movements that day. . . . Rawlins gave clear and unequivocal testimony to support this conclusion, and sets it forth in a way which shows that he perfectly understood every military consideration involved in the controversy."[60]

Despite Wilson's certainty of Rawlins's conclusions, his account does not prove that Wallace was on the wrong road or "culpably slow." Wallace was on the Shunpike because it was the road he had had improved—he simply hadn't explained this to Grant earlier. The route taken by Wallace's troops covered almost seventeen miles, and they accomplished that march, much of it on bad roads, in a remarkably fast seven hours.[61] One must also wonder whether Rawlins's tendency to view situations in right or wrong terms inclined him to find Wallace at fault. McPherson entertained the possibility that impatience might have affected the conclusions he drew; Rawlins was not one to give the benefit of doubt. Indeed, Rawlins's opinions about Wallace's competence and courage may have been biased by the circulation of Hillyer's lampoon following Fort Donelson's capture.

Wallace's Shiloh performance received frequent rehashing among Grant and staff. *New York Herald* reporter Sylvanus Cadwallader, a steadfast champion of Rawlins and one who had close access to Grant, remarked about the prevailing attitude toward Wallace: "In common with all the members of his old staff, I knew the esteem—or rather lack of esteem—in which Wallace had ever been held for his conduct at the battle of Shiloh. Every member of Grant's staff at Shiloh were hot and outspoken whenever the subject was introduced. I have heard Gens. McPherson, [William R.] Rowley, [William S.] Hillyer, Rawlins, and others rehearse the affair many times, in Grant's presence. He always assented to their criticisms of Wallace's behavior. More conclusive than all this, he never intrusted him with any important command."[62]

Moreover, Hillyer extended his earlier lampoon of Wallace with stanzas on Shiloh. He called it "Lewellin at Pittsburgh Landing" and ridiculed Wallace for both tardiness and cowardice. Considering the strength of the opposition he faced, it is little wonder that Wallace fought the rest of his life trying to vindicate himself.[63]

—◈—

Daylight on April 7 found the Federals taking the initiative: Buell's fresh troops on the left, Wallace's division perched on the far right, and Grant's bloodied survivors in the middle. Beauregard was rallying an army that was exhausted and wanting better unit organization but hadn't lost its nerve to fight. The second day's battle raged back and forth across the entire field, with neither side able to wrest advantage from the other. But by early afternoon, the Union troops were wearing down the Confederates, who were desperate for reinforcements and more ammunition. Around 2:00 p.m., Beauregard had had enough and called for a general withdrawal. By 4:00 the Confederates had cleared the field and were retreating to Corinth.

The Union army waited until the eighth to pursue—and a vigorous pursuit might have shattered Beauregard—but it amounted to a token effort. So ended the costliest battle of the first year of war. The Union armies' losses were more than thirteen thousand killed, wounded, and missing. Confederate casualties were at least ten thousand. Appalled citizens, North and South, were left wondering what such bloodshed could mean and what conclusions could be drawn from the battle.

Members of Grant's staff also tried to make sense of what they experienced. Shiloh brought aide-de-camp Hillyer into too cozy an acquaintance with death. Writing his wife four days after the battle, he said a cannon ball had whizzed past the head of his horse. He had seen the spectacle of "dead bodies scattered through the woods in every direction"—the unfortunates who somehow slipped through the protective fingers of a divine providence. Hillyer tallied it up, and what it meant was that "I had seen enough of war," and he looked to bow out of it once Corinth fell.[64]

Rawlins's letter home is a mostly fact-laden narration of events, except for one self-disclosure that no doubt caused Lovisa to shudder: "I was on more than one occasion in the thickest of the fight, but remain unharmed." To Rawlins, Shiloh should have been another lesson to the rebellion's leaders: the defeats at Forts Henry and Donelson demonstrated that the Rebels can build no fortification that cannot be taken; now they've learned they cannot prevail in open battle. It was folly, he wrote, for the secessionists to "bring the 'Northern Hessians' into an engagement in the open field" and expect that "there Southern chivalry would surely triumph."[65]

Initially, Shiloh gave cause for celebration in the North; Lincoln set aside a day for giving thanks. But what was regarded as a brilliant military victory would soon be assessed in a different light, and this was due in large measure to a dynamic Ohio war correspondent, Whitelaw Reid, who not only witnessed the battle but was breakfasting with Lew Wallace on his steamboat while he awaited Grant's orders.[66] Under the pseudonym Agate, Reid filed a riveting, nineteen-thousand-word narrative about the battle for the *Cincinnati Gazette*. It contained disturbing allegations and others that were distorted, even spurious. Readers in the North were left to wonder how many of their sons died due to poor preparation or faulty generalship. Sherman, Reid charged, failed to build an abatis or line of breastworks in front of his camps; instead "for three weeks he had lain there . . . without making the slightest preparation for the commonest means of defence!"[67] When the Confederates attacked, the unsuspecting Federals, particularly the officers, were caught literally with their pants down. Many had not gotten out of bed; guns and ammunition lay scattered about. Perhaps Reid's most chilling claim was that the enemy burst into the camps, "springing toward our laggards with the bayonet."[68] Reid came close to charging Grant with dereliction: "Sunday night there was a council of war, but if the Major General commanding developed any plans there beyond the simple arrangement of our line of battle, I am very certain that some of the division commanders didn't find out."[69]

Thanks in large part to the wide dissemination of Reid's story, the adulation for Grant soon turned into a drumbeat of criticism. He was denounced for having recklessly exposed the army, whereas Buell was extolled for having come to its rescue.[70] Ohio Governor David Tod, defending the dignity of two Buckeye regiments that broke and ran, placed the blame on the "criminal negligence" of top command. Tod's lieutenant governor, Benjamin Stanton, opined that "Grant and Prentiss ought to be courtmartialed or shot."[71] Writing to fellow Illinoisan President Lincoln, General McClernand took a behind-the-back swipe at Grant: "It was a great mistake that we did not pursue [the enemy] Monday night and Tuesday."[72] Many congressional Republicans were outspoken in their condemnation of Grant and applied pressure against

Lincoln to relieve him.[73] Then came rumors that liquor was responsible for the bad generalship.

Grant's close supporters rushed to his defense. In sharply worded letters published in the *Cincinnati Commercial*, General Sherman sparred with Benjamin Stanton.[74] Hillyer wrote a long letter to Jesse Grant, which the elder Grant likely leaked to the papers as a response to Reid's account. Hillyer called the criticisms "unjust, untrue and unmanly" and referred to Sherman's claim in his official report that his division was in line of battle two hours before being attacked.[75] In a letter later copied and forwarded to Elihu Washburne, Rowley stated, "As to the story that [Grant] was intoxicated at the Battle of Pittsburg, I have only to say that the man who fabricated the story is an infamous *liar*," and added that the stories about men being bayonetted in their tents were "simply all humbug."[76] Washburne took the floor of the House to salute Grant, whom he characterized as the most temperate man in the army, for bravery and leadership bordering on genius. Washburne used the opportunity to praise the valor of his Galena friends, Chetlain, Rowley, and Rawlins.[77] The ever-loyal Rawlins made sure that after the war, a proper version of events was placed before the public. In his 1866 address to the Society of the Army of the Tennessee, Rawlins reminded those assembled, "It is sufficient to say that we did not expect to be attacked in force that morning, and were surprised that we were, but we had sufficient notice, before the shock came, to be under arms to meet it. There was no capturing of commands asleep in their camps that morning, or bayoneting of men asleep in their tents."[78]

In the final analysis, Grant survived this crisis because of Lincoln's faith in him. After hearing a litany of reasons for sacking Grant, Lincoln mulled them over and concluded, "I can't spare this man; he fights."[79]

—◦◦◦—

If the cacophony of bad press had not cast enough misery over headquarters, the two beloved commanders of the Second Division, William H. L. Wallace and C. F. Smith, passed away inside the Cherry Mansion. Wallace, the Ottawa, Illinois, lawyer, suffered a mortal head wound during the fighting in the Hornet's Nest. His near lifeless body was found on the battlefield and transported to the mansion. Miraculously, he survived for several days. His wife, Ann, was by his side at the last. She described their final moments together: "My darling knew he was going and pressed my hand long and fondly to his heart. Then he waved me away and said, 'We meet in Heaven.'"[80] Those were the hands that had picked for her the daffodil from the garden of Sarah Polk. Soon thereafter, Rawlins issued orders for sending details of officers to accompany Wallace's body back to Ottawa.[81]

On April 25, surgeon John Brinton checked on Smith at the mansion and found him "unconscious and moribund."[82] Within hours, Halleck issued orders announcing Smith's death and honoring him as "a faithful officer, an excellent disciplinarian, an able commander, and a modest and courteous gentleman."[83] As a tribute, Rawlins instructed those orders be read to each regiment.[84]

While turmoil swirled around Grant, he lauded his staff. In his battle report, Grant singled out Rawlins, Rowley, and Hillyer for praise and gave especial commendation to Chief of Staff Webster and Chief Engineer Lt. Colonel McPherson, the former for taking charge of the artillery defense and the latter for leading troops to where they were most needed in the field.[85] With commendations came promotions. Rawlins was made major in mid-April, one year after his electrifying courthouse speech ignited patriotic passions in Galena. Coinciding with Rawlins's advancement, Grant requested Halleck to have aides Hillyer and Lagow made colonels; their promotions were confirmed three months later.[86] Writing to Julia, Grant revealed his honest opinion regarding the recent promotions: "Hillyer & Lagow will be Colonels. Rawlins is a Maj. and ought to be a Brig. Gen."[87] He enlarged on this point a few weeks thereafter: "I think [Rawlins] is one of the best men I ever knew and if another War should break out, or this one be protacted [sic], he would make one of the best General officers to be found in the country."[88] Given that Rawlins had not shown a partiality for operational planning, Grant was making a broad but unsubstantiated claim.[89]

Before April was out, a new aide-de-camp was added to the staff, twenty-nine-year-old Theodore S. Bowers, recently the owner and publisher of the Mt. Carmel (IL) Register, and a lieutenant in the Forty-Eighth Illinois Infantry. When war broke out, Bowers, known familiarly as Joe, helped organize the Forty-Eighth but, declining a commission as captain of Company G, entered service as a private. Bowers would be by Grant's side to Appomattox and beyond—to the moment of Bowers's death in a grisly train accident in 1866.[90]

Grant's staff could take pride in their performances at Shiloh, an improvement over what they had done at Fort Donelson. According to historian Steven Jones, "They acted with an independence of thought and action that enabled them to make spot decisions without specific orders from Grant."[91] Hillyer almost single-handedly facilitated the arrival of Buell's divisions using troop transports. Webster's placement of artillery became the bulwark of the last defensive line. Rowley and Rawlins were forced to make ad hoc decisions to bring Lew Wallace's division onto the field. And on the battle's first day, Rawlins's quick intervention and verbal threats helped prevent panic at Pittsburg Landing.

—⁓⁓—

On April 11, Major General Halleck arrived at Pittsburg Landing from St. Louis to assume field command of the armies within his extensive Department of the Mississippi. The brainy expert on the theory of warfare who had never commanded troops in battle now assumed charge of Grant's Army of the Tennessee, Buell's Army of the Ohio, and John Pope's Army of the Mississippi. Always the stickler, Halleck was appalled by what he encountered: units requiring reorganization, stragglers needing to be rounded up. He minced no words with Grant: "Your army is not now in condition to resist an attack. It must be made so without delay."[92] To his wife, Halleck was blunter: "This army is undisciplined and very much disorganized. The officers being utterly incapable of maintaining order. I have been very hard at work for the last three days endeavoring to straighten things out."[93]

Grant and Rawlins wasted little time complying. Rawlins issued an order that cracked down on troops leaving their brigade grounds without authority and addressed deficiencies in drill and discipline.[94] A day later, Rawlins issued another order appointing a board to investigate officers who had not conducted themselves "with military propriety in recent battles." Sherman himself forwarded charges against five officers.[95]

With a combined force of over one hundred thousand, Halleck was girding for a grand movement against Beauregard at Corinth. He would show his subordinate generals, Grant in particular, how a successful campaign should be carried out. For Grant, it would mean a demoralizing contraction in his role and authority and sorely test his confidence. But in the process, it would bolster his relationship with two men who would become his stalwart allies: William T. Sherman and John A. Rawlins.

NOTES

1. U. S. Grant to Julia Dent Grant, March 29, 1862, in *The Papers of Ulysses S. Grant*, ed. John Y. Simon (Carbondale: Southern Illinois University Press, 1972), 4:443.

2. Special Orders No. 26, March 26, 1862, in *The War of the Rebellion: A Compilation of the Official Records of the Union and Confederate Armies*, series 1, part 2, 10:67.

3. Albert D. Richardson, *A Personal History of Ulysses S. Grant* (Boston: D. L. Guernsey, 1885), 235.

4. *The War of the Rebellion: A Compilation of the Official Records of the Union and Confederate Armies*, series 1, part 2, March 17, 1862, 10:44.

5. Ibid., March 18, 1862, 10:46.

6. Ibid., March 20, 1862, 10:50.

7. Ibid., March 20, 1862, 10:50–51.

8. Albert D. Richardson, *A Personal History of Ulysses S. Grant*, 235.

9. U. S. Grant, *Personal Memoirs* (New York: Charles L. Webster, 1885), 1:332–33.

10. U. S. Grant, "The Battle of Shiloh," in *Battles and Leaders of the Civil War*, ed. Robert U. Johnson and Clarence C. Buel (1887; repr., New York: Thomas Yoseloff, 1956), 1:481.

11. Allen H. Mesch, *Teacher of Civil War Generals: Major General Charles Ferguson Smith, Soldier and West Point Commandant* (Jefferson, NC: McFarland, 2015), 248.

12. General Orders No. 24, March 19, 1862, in *The War of the Rebellion: A Compilation of the Official Records of the Union and Confederate Armies*, series 1, part 2, 10:50.

13. Special Orders No. 26, March 26, 1862, in *The War of the Rebellion: A Compilation of the Official Records of the Union and Confederate Armies*, series 1, part 2, 10:67.

14. Allen H. Mesch, *Teacher of Civil War Generals: Major General Charles Ferguson Smith, Soldier and West Point Commandant*, 249.

15. Larry J. Daniel, *Shiloh: The Battle That Changed the Civil War* (New York: Simon and Schuster, 1997), 109.

16. Ibid., 128–29.

17. Timothy B. Smith, *The Untold Story of Shiloh: The Battle and the Battlefield* (Knoxville: University of Tennessee Press, 2006), 23.

18. Larry J. Daniel, *Shiloh*, 139–40.

19. William T. Sherman to U. S. Grant, April 5, 1862, in *The War of the Rebellion: A Compilation of the Official Records of the Union and Confederate Armies*, series 1, part 2, 10:93–94.

20. U. S. Grant to Henry W. Halleck, April 5, 1862, in *The Papers of Ulysses S. Grant*, ed. John Y. Simon, 5:14.

21. *The War of the Rebellion: A Compilation of the Official Records of the Union and Confederate Armies*, series 1, part 1, April 3, 1862, 10:85–86.

22. Special Orders No. 39, March 29, 1862, in *The Papers of Ulysses S. Grant*, ed. John Y. Simon, 4:440n; Jessie Scouts were Union cavalrymen volunteering as scouts and spies and often operating behind enemy lines while donning Confederate uniforms. They were named after Jessie Frémont, wife of Major General John C. Frémont.

23. Report of John A. Rawlins, April 1, 1863, in *The War of the Rebellion: A Compilation of the Official Records of the Union and Confederate Armies*, series 1, part 1, 10:184.

24. U. S. Grant to D. C. Buell, April 6, 1862, in *The Papers of Ulysses S. Grant*, ed. John Y. Simon, 5:17.

25. Ibid., 18n3.

26. Lew Wallace, *An Autobiography* (New York: Harper and Brothers, 1906), 1:461.

27. Report of John A. Rawlins, April 1, 1863, in *The War of the Rebellion: A Compilation of the Official Records of the Union and Confederate Armies*, series 1, part 1, 10:185.

28. To deal with shirkers, Paymaster Major Isaac Cooke was directed by ADC Lagow "to arrest every Commissioned Officer that shows himself on the Levee near Steamers unless sick or wounded, taking his sword, name, Regiment and Company and order him back to his quarters there to remain until he is regularly relieved." John Y. Simon, ed., *The Papers of Ulysses S. Grant*, 5:19n. Under critical battle conditions, special staff like the paymaster could be pressed into more soldierly roles.

29. Bruce Catton, *Grant Moves South* (Boston: Little, Brown, 1960), 230.

30. U. S. Grant to "Comd.g Officer Advance Force Near Pittsburg, Ten.," April 6, 1862, in *The Papers of Ulysses S. Grant*, ed. John Y. Simon, 5:18.

31. Report of John A. Rawlins, April 1, 1863, in *The War of the Rebellion: A Compilation of the Official Records of the Union and Confederate Armies*, series 1, part 1, 10:185.

32. Douglas Putnam Jr., "Reminiscences of the Battle of Shiloh," in *Sketches of War History, 1861–1865: Papers Prepared for the Ohio Commandery of the Military Order of the Loyal Legion of the United States*, ed. Robert Hunter (Wilmington, NC: Broadfoot, 1991), 3:199.

33. Lew Wallace, *An Autobiography* (New York: Harper and Brothers, 1906), 2:589.

34. Report of W. R. Rowley, April 4, 1863, in *The War of the Rebellion: A Compilation of the Official Records of the Union and Confederate Armies*, series 1, part 1, 10:179.

35. Lew Wallace, *An Autobiography*, 1:463.

36. Ibid., 463–64.

37. Harold Lew Wallace, "Lew Wallace's March to Shiloh Revisited," *Indiana Magazine of History* 59, no. 1963): 27.

38. U. S. Grant, *Personal Memoirs*, 1:336.

39. Report of W. R. Rowley, April 4, 1863, in *The War of the Rebellion: A Compilation of the Official Records of the Union and Confederate Armies*, series 1, part 1, 10:179.

40. Report of J. B. McPherson, March 26, 1863, in *The War of the Rebellion: A Compilation of the Official Records of the Union and Confederate Armies*, series 1, part 1, 10:181.

41. Lew Wallace, *An Autobiography*, 1:463.

42. Ibid., 464.

43. Gail Stephens, *Shadow of Shiloh; Major General Lew Wallace in the Civil War* (Indianapolis: Indiana Historical Society, 2010), 74–75.

44. Report of W. R. Rowley, April 4, 1863, in *The War of the Rebellion: A Compilation of the Official Records of the Union and Confederate Armies*, series 1, part 1, 10:179.

45. U. S. Grant, *Personal Memoirs*, 1:344.

46. Report of John A. Rawlins, April 1, 1863, in *The War of the Rebellion: A Compilation of the Official Records of the Union and Confederate Armies*, series 1, part 1, 10:186.

47. Joseph Mills Hanson, *The Conquest of the Missouri* (Chicago: A. C. McClurg, 1909), 43–44.

48. Augustus L. Chetlain, *Recollections of Seventy Years* (Galena, IL: Gazette, 1899), 87–89.

49. *The Ulysses S. Grant Association Newsletter* 1, no. 2 (January 1964): 11.

50. Report of W. R. Rowley, April 4, 1863, in *The War of the Rebellion: A Compilation of the Official Records of the Union and Confederate Armies*, series 1, part 1, 10:179–80; Gail Stephens, *Shadow of Shiloh*, 87.

51. Lew Wallace, *An Autobiography*, 1:466–67.

52. Ibid., 468.

53. Report of J. B. McPherson, March 26, 1863, in *The War of the Rebellion: A Compilation of the Official Records of the Union and Confederate Armies*, series 1, part 1, 10:182.

54. Report of John A. Rawlins, April 1, 1863, in *The War of the Rebellion: A Compilation of the Official Records of the Union and Confederate Armies*, series 1, part 1, 10:187–88. Writing to Halleck, Wallace countered some of the criticism directed at himself. To the charge he idled along, he explained that he halted his column only long enough to allow it to close up. As a result, he claimed, he brought his division up in "perfect order and without a straggler." Copy of a letter from Lew Wallace to Henry Halleck, March 14, 1863, in the William R. Rowley Papers, SC 1306 (Folder 1), Abraham Lincoln Presidential Library, Springfield, IL.

55. Douglas Putnam Jr., "Reminiscences of the Battle of Shiloh," 205.

56. Gail Stephens, *Shadow of Shiloh*, 90.

57. Lew Wallace, *An Autobiography*, 1:475.

58. U. S. Grant, "The Battle of Shiloh," 1:468.

59. U. S. Grant to Col. J. C. Kelton, April 13, 1863, in *The War of the Rebellion: A Compilation of the Official Records of the Union and Confederate Armies*, series 1, part 1, 10:178.

60. James Harrison Wilson, *The Life of John A. Rawlins* (New York: Neale, 1916), 97–98.

61. In 2005, a group of historians set out to duplicate Wallace's march. A GPS measurement indicated the route covered 16.75 miles. Moving as fast as they could, and taking a thirty-minute lunch, the group made the trek in seven and three-quarters hours, fifteen minutes slower than Wallace's division. See Gail Stephens, *Shadow of Shiloh*, 91–92.

62. Sylvanus Cadwallader, *Three Years with Grant as Recalled by War Correspondent Sylvanus Cadwallader*, ed. Benjamin P. Thomas (New York: Alfred A. Knopf, 1961), 228–29.

63. The long-held idea that Lew Wallace was lost at Shiloh may be passing into a myth. Historian Timothy Smith argues that Wallace was on the Shunpike by intention: he had interpreted the order to march to the right of the army as meaning toward Sherman's division camped by Shiloh Church. Thus, the Shunpike, not River Road, was the appropriate route. See Timothy B. Smith, *The Untold Story of Shiloh* (Knoxville: University of Tennessee Press, 2006), especially chapter 3, "Oft-Repeated Campfire Stories: The Ten Greatest Myths of Shiloh," 25–26.

64. *The Ulysses S. Grant Association Newsletter* 1, no. 2 (January 1964): 10, 13.

65. James Harrison Wilson, *The Life of John A. Rawlins*, 90.

66. Robert E. Morsberger and Katharine M. Morsberger, *Lew Wallace: Militant Romantic* (New York: McGraw-Hill, 1980), 87.

67. James G. Smart, ed., *A Radical View: The "Agate" Dispatches of Whitelaw Reid* (Memphis: Memphis State University Press, 1976), 127.

68. Ibid., 129.

69. Ibid., 160.

70. A. K. McClure, *Abraham Lincoln and Men of War-Times* (Philadelphia: Times, 1892), 178.

71. Bruce Catton, *Grant Moves South*, 254.

72. John A. McClernand to Abraham Lincoln, April 14, 1862, in *The War of the Rebellion: A Compilation of the Official Records of the Union and Confederate Armies*, series 1, part 1, 10:114.

73. A. K. McClure, *Abraham Lincoln and Men of War-Times*, 178.

74. William T. Sherman, *Memoirs* (New York: D. Appleton, 1875), 1:246.

75. John Y. Simon, ed., *The Papers of Ulysses S. Grant*, 5:79n.

76. *The Ulysses S. Grant Association Newsletter* 10, no. 1 (1972, October): 2–3.

77. See Mark Washburne, *A Biography of Elihu Benjamin Washburne: Congressman, Secretary of State, Envoy Extraordinary* (self-pub., Xlibris, 2001), 2:132–38.

78. Proceedings of the Society of the Army of the Tennessee at the First Annual Meeting, Cincinnati, Ohio (Cincinnati: The Society), 37.

79. A. K. McClure, *Abraham Lincoln and Men of War-Times*, 180.

80. Isabel Wallace, *Life and Letters of General W. H. L. Wallace* (Chicago: R. R. Donnelley and Sons, 1909), 199.

81. John Y. Simon, ed., *The Papers of Ulysses S. Grant*, 5:36n11.

82. John H. Brinton, *Personal Memoirs of John H. Brinton* (New York: Neale, 1914), 159.

83. General Orders No. 21, April 25, 1862, in *The War of the Rebellion: A Compilation of the Official Records of the Union and Confederate Armies*, series 1, part 2, 10:621.

84. John Y. Simon, ed., *The Papers of Ulysses S. Grant*, 5:73n1.

85. U. S. Grant report of April 9, 1862, to Captain N. H. McLean, in *The Papers of Ulysses S. Grant*, ed. John Y. Simon, 5:35.

86. U. S. Grant to Henry W. Halleck, April 16, 1862, in *The Papers of Ulysses S. Grant*, ed. John Y. Simon, 5:52, 53n.

87. U. S. Grant to Julia Dent Grant, April 25, 1862, in *The Papers of Ulysses S. Grant*, ed. John Y. Simon, 5:73.

88. U. S. Grant to Julia Dent Grant, May 24, 1862, in *The Papers of Ulysses S. Grant*, ed. John Y. Simon, 5:130.

89. R. Steven Jones, *The Right Hand of Command: Use and Disuse of Personal Staffs in the Civil War* (Mechanicsburg, PA: Stackpole, 2000), 89.

90. Theodore G. Risley, "Colonel Theodore S. Bowers," *Journal of the Illinois State Historical Society* 12, no. 3 (1919): 407–11.

91. R. Steven Jones, *The Right Hand of Command*, 81.

92. H. W. Halleck to U. S. Grant, April 14, 1862, in *The War of the Rebellion: A Compilation of the Official Records of the Union and Confederate Armies*, series 1, part 2, 10:105–6.

93. John Y. Simon, ed., *The Papers of Ulysses S. Grant*, 5:48n1.

94. General Orders No. 39, April 17, 1862, in *The Papers of Ulysses S. Grant*, ed. John Y. Simon, 5:49n1.

95. General Orders No. 40, April 18, 1862, in *The Papers of Ulysses S. Grant*, ed. John Y. Simon, 5:50n1.

12

"[A] Strong Partisan, but Not a Traitor"

AFTER ARRIVING AT PITTSBURG LANDING on April 11, Henry Halleck began preparations for his advance on the rail hub of Corinth. *Advance* would be too kinetic a term: the massive Union force would be required to literally dig its way forward, entrenching as it went, erecting earthen breastworks, cautiously probing the enemy, and guarding against surprise attack. But first Halleck needed to consolidate the armies of Grant, Pope, and Buell; bring in fresh supplies; and reconstitute the troops who survived Shiloh. At the end of April, just before the first tentative step forward, Halleck saw fit to rearrange his vast army into right and left wings, a center, and a reserve unit. If there was a justification behind this rearranging, it was lost on William Sherman, who thought it due to Halleck having been "prejudiced by the rumors which had gone forth to the detriment of General Grant" following Shiloh.[1] Command of the right wing was given to Major General George H. Thomas, a division commander under Buell. Thomas's wing consisted of his old division plus the bulk of Grant's Army of the Tennessee. This arrangement rankled Grant, who felt superseded by Thomas. It probably marked the beginning of a "misunderstanding, a lack of good understanding, between the two generals that was never cleared up, and which operated greatly to the detriment of the service."[2] Halleck appointed Grant second in command, a position that came with an impressive title but no real responsibility, and Grant was able to retain his staff, notably the core of Rawlins, Lagow, and Hillyer.

Virtually ignored by Halleck, Grant watched the army inch toward Corinth, which he believed he could have captured in two days. "The movement," he later wrote, "was a siege from the start to the close."[3] Under the forced inactivity, he whiled away time smoking and watching others play cards, but he had not lost his sense of humor, which he used to needle the easily agitated Rawlins. Before leaving Galena, Rawlins's friends presented him with a splendid, long-tailed bay horse. One morning the bay appeared with its tail snipped to a two-inch stub. On seeing the damage, Rawlins raged that if he found the "enemy" who did this, he'd shoot him. Rawlins's outburst left Grant weak with laughter. Grant, who was a keen student of all things equine, offered Rawlins a different take on the matter: the bay's tail had been munched off, and the enemy was likely some irascible old army mule! Referring to Grant's own favorite cream-colored mount, Rawlins retorted, "Well, General, I hope that some night a mule will eat off the tail of *your* old yellow horse—and then see how you'll like it." For months afterward, when riding behind Rawlins's bay, Grant would convulse with laughter.[4]

Shortly after reorganization, Grant vented his frustration to Halleck: "It is generally understood through this army that my position differs little from that of one in arrest . . . I deem it due to myself to ask either full restoration to duty, according to my rank, or be relieved entirely from further duty."[5] Halleck was shocked that Grant had a beef: "I am very much surprised, General, that you should find any cause of complaint in the recent assignment of commands. You have precisely the position to which your rank entitles you." Moreover, he reminded Grant that when rumor and innuendo swirled around him, he had had his back: "For the last three months I have done every thing in my power to ward off attacks which were made upon you."[6]

On the day he wrote Halleck, Grant told Julia he had been "so shockingly abused that I sometimes think it almost time to defend myself."[7] Grant's staff were aware of his dissatisfaction. When they heard scuttlebutt that General David Hunter, commander of the Department of the South, might be relieved, they figured a transfer to the South Carolina coast and far beyond the easy reach of malicious newspaper correspondents was what Grant needed. Both Rowley and Lagow, unbeknownst to Grant, corresponded to Congressman Washburne, beseeching him to intercede on Grant's behalf. "Gen. Grant would be very much pleased to be transferred to a command on the coast," Rowley wrote, "as I have just heard him conversing upon the subject."[8]

The nadir was reached at the end of the Corinth campaign when Halleck casually informed Sherman that Grant had applied for, and was given, a thirty-day leave. This news alarmed Sherman, who knew "that [Grant] was chafing under the slights of his anomalous position." When Sherman rode up to Grant's camp, he saw Rawlins, Lagow, and Hillyer standing beside piles of office and camp chests that seemed to be waiting for someone to move them. Grant was inside his tent, bundling up letters. "Are you going away?" Sherman asked. Grant said yes and explained, "You know I am in the way here. I have stood it as long as I can, and can endure it no longer." Sherman immediately challenged his decision: you'd feel left out as the campaign moved along; something positive might happen to restore you to good graces; don't do anything rash until you talk to me again—these were arguments he used to dissuade Grant. Rawlins too held fast against Grant's despair. Grant had written his resignation, instructing Rawlins to send it to Washington, but Rawlins had "never seen the time when he felt it ought to go."[9]

A few days after their conversation, Grant sent Sherman a note saying it was his intention to stick it out. Sherman believed he had talked Grant out of leaving.[10] And Rawlins could bury the resignation letter.

—⁊⁊⁊—

Sherman was proved right: Grant held tight, and something positive happened. The summer of 1862 saw Grant's fortunes pivot—while Rawlins, simultaneously, became increasingly valuable to Grant.

At the end of May, Beauregard, yielding to the inexorably encroaching Federal army, evacuated Corinth, and fell back to Tupelo. That left Memphis, Tennessee, exposed. It was captured on June 6 after a brisk naval firefight. Just days thereafter, Halleck rescinded his reorganization order, returned Grant to command of the Army of the Tennessee, and dispatched him to occupy Memphis. On the nineteenth, Rawlins issued the order announcing Grant would be headquartered there "until further notice."[11] Dubbed the "Charleston of the West," Memphis was the South's sixth largest city and a busy river port. For the first time, Grant faced the responsibility of being the occupier of a major population center. Fortunately, he had in Rawlins an adjutant who "has become so perfectly posted in the duties of the office that I am relieved entirely from the routine."[12] Rawlins would use his administrative knack to address a host of unforeseen challenges attendant to occupying a fiercely secessionist city, as well as changes to Grant's personal staff.

Grant, staff, and a cavalry escort left Corinth on June 21 and arrived two days later in Memphis after a hot, dusty ride. About twenty miles outside Memphis, the party stopped to rest under some shade trees off the road. Only after arriving in Memphis did they learn that a detachment of Confederate cavalry under Colonel William Jackson had come within three-quarters of a mile of their resting spot.[13]

In the time it took to set up initial headquarters at the Hunt-Phelan home on Beale Street, Grant and staff received a swift introduction to how fervently Memphians embraced the Confederate cause. In dispatches to Halleck, Grant decried that "secessionists [are] governing much in their own way" and that "there is great disloyalty manifested by the citizens of this place."[14] To rein in the secessionist governing system and address citizens' disloyalty, Grant and Rawlins made some staff changes. On June 24, Rawlins issued an order appointing Chief of Staff Webster the commander of the post at Memphis. To Webster fell the responsibility of making "all needful rules and regulations for the Government of the City . . . subject to the approval of the general commanding." The same order announced that Colonel Hillyer, still discomfited by the bloodshed he witnessed at Shiloh, was appointed provost marshal for the military district.[15]

In response to citizens' complaints and to prevent unrest, Rawlins released an order on June 24 forbidding Federal troops from trespassing on private grounds, making unauthorized seizures of private property, or leaving camp without permission. Offenders would be brought before the provost marshal.[16] Hillyer clashed with the editors of the *Memphis Avalanche* over an editorial about mistreating civilians. Finding the editorial "exceedingly objectionable," he decreed that "no criticism of the acts of the military authorities of the United States will be permitted in the press of Memphis." Soon after, the paper ran another editorial that impudently advised the provost marshal to put in writing, swear to, and sign all information leading to arrests. That was enough for Hillyer. On July 1, he suspended publication of the *Avalanche*.[17]

Grant and Rawlins were united in confronting threats within and without. Confederate units under William Jackson and Jeff Thompson prowled beyond Memphis. Grant complained of the "spies and numbers of the Southern Army [that] are constantly finding their way in and out of the city in spite of all the vigilance." He worried saboteurs would set fire to the city.[18] To crack down on guerilla activity, Rawlins issued general orders on July 3 stipulating that losses sustained by the federal government would be compensated through the seizure of rebel sympathizers' personal property; and that persons acting as guerillas and not in uniform would not be treated as prisoners of war.[19] A week later, an even stronger edict was issued by Provost Marshal Hillyer. His harsh Special Orders No. 14 required that within five days, all families or persons must leave Memphis who are in the "so-called" Confederate army, in the employ of the Confederate government, or who claim allegiance to the Confederacy. Hillyer's order incensed Jeff Thompson, who wrote a scathing reply to Grant warning him to "beware of the curses and oaths of vengeance ... against the persecutor of helpless old men, women, and children."[20]

Besides these challenges, there was another that had more serious implications. The Treasury Department had instituted policies to facilitate trade and bolster local merchants in order to foster a positive attitude toward the Yankee occupiers. As one historian put it, "If under Federal control trade could be restored and necessities of life be made available, many would probably renew their allegiance to the Union."[21] Merchants and speculators, some Jewish, arrived from the North to partake in the liberal trading environment. They came bearing desperately needed supplies such as flour, pork, and salt as well as hard currency in order to purchase cotton. In short order several things happened: the price of cotton increased, Northern speculators stood to make a bundle, many of the food supplies were funneled to Confederate forces, and Rebel sympathizers used the incoming gold and silver to purchase munitions that could be turned against Federal troops. Greedy speculators also tried to sneak contraband cargo past inspectors. On July 6, Rawlins authorized seizure of the steamer *Saline*, which was used in unlawful trade with the enemy.[22] Managing this tricky trade situation later bedeviled Sherman and Hurlbut, who succeeded Grant as Union commanders in Memphis.

Grant, Rawlins, and staff were not three weeks in Memphis when Halleck was ordered to report to Washington, DC, and become general in chief of the Union armies. On receiving this news, Halleck summoned Grant to Corinth. Grant, unsure of the proper way to respond to this stunning turn of events, telegraphed, "Am I to repair alone or take my staff?" To Grant's ingenuous query, Halleck sent a coolly straightforward reply: "This place [Corinth] will be your Head Quarters. You can judge for yourself."[23]

Just before returning to Corinth, Grant's staff underwent another change. Colonel Lagow received orders from Rawlins appointing him acting inspector general for the District of West Tennessee in addition to duties as aide-de-camp.[24] In this capacity, Lagow would check the orderliness of military camps, quality of equipment, troop readiness, and anything contributing to morale and effectiveness.

—◦◦◦—

Grant and staff arrived in Corinth on July 15. The next day Halleck issued a field order appointing Grant as his replacement. Halleck may have had misgivings about Grant, but the order pronounced Grant commander of the District of West Tennessee to "include the Districts of Cairo and Mississippi; and that part of Alabama which may be occupied by the troops of his particular command, including the forces heretofore known as the Army of the Mississippi."[25] That Army of the Mississippi, formerly commanded by John Pope, was now headed by Brigadier General William Rosecrans.

With Grant now responsible for a sprawling district and Sherman taking command at Memphis, Federal occupiers faced a substantial (and growing) enemy. After Corinth fell, General Beauregard was removed and his replacement, General Braxton Bragg, now led more than fifty thousand men. Bragg's divisions stood to be augmented by troops from the west under Earl Van Dorn and Sterling Price. If only the Yankee occupiers could focus attention squarely on the military threats, without the distractions posed by the avaricious speculators and traders.

Only ten days into his role in Memphis, Sherman wrote Rawlins that he had been busy handling citizens' questions. He was also disgusted by the frenzied exchange of gold and essential commodities like salt for cotton, placing blame on a convenient religious minority:

> I found so many Jews & Speculators here trading in cotton and secessionists had become so open in refusing any thing but Gold that I have felt myself bound to stop it. This Gold has but one use, the purchase of arms & ammunition. . . . In like manner so great was the demand for salt to make Bacon, that many succeeded in getting loads of salt out for cotton. Salt is as much contraband of war as Powder. . . . If we permit money & salt to go into the Interior, it will not take long for Bragg & Van Dorn to supply their armies with all they need to move. Without money, Gold Silver & Treasury notes, they cannot get arms & ammunition . . . & without salt they can not make Bacon & Salt Beef. We cannot carry on war & trade with a people at the same time.[26]

Sherman's outrage was hardly news to Rawlins, who had acted five days earlier to stop the gold for cotton trade. On July 25, Major Rawlins issued a sternly worded General Orders No. 64 that addressed the abuses in the trading system and warned of severe punishment to violators. This order was intended to prohibit speculators after August 1 from purchasing cotton with gold or silver, and using instead US Treasury notes—acceptable for local trade but useless to Confederate agents for purchasing guns, powder, and ammunition from foreign entities—as the preferred medium of exchange:

The attention of the Major General Commdg, having been called to the fact of persons within this District, sympathizing with the Rebellion, who have Cotton for sale, refusing to receive U. S. Treasury notes in payment therefor, or any thing other than Gold and Silver, which is paid them by Speculators whose love of gain is greater than their love of Country, and the Gold and Silver thus paid, indirectly affording aid and comfort to the enemy, renders necessary the publication of the following orders: From and after the 1st day of August, 1862 Gold and Silver will not be paid within this Dist. by Speculators for the products of the Rebel States. U. S. Treasury notes are a legal tender in all cases, and when refused, the parties refusing them will be arrested, and such of their crops as are not actually required for the subsistence of their families, stock, &c. may be seized and sold by the nearest Quarter Master for the benefit of whom it may concern.... Any Speculator paying out Gold and Silver in violation of this order will be arrested and sent North, and the property so purchased seized and turned over to the proper Dept. for the benefit of the Government. A strict enforcement of this order is enjoined upon all officers in this Dist.[27]

Much to Sherman's chagrin, this order was annulled by authorities in Washington. Secretary of War Stanton and new general in chief Halleck feared the cotton supply in the North could dry up if hard money was no longer available to purchase it. On August 15, Rawlins telegraphed both Rosecrans and Sherman that the restrictions on gold were lifted.[28]

Order No. 64 illustrates how Rawlins and Grant applied a creative solution to a complex problem by eliminating gold for cotton transactions. The order appears to reveal clues into the working relationship developing between the two: that is, how Rawlins was becoming more "perfectly posted" in his role and tackling problems Grant found wearisome. Perhaps it was Rawlins who called Grant's attention to the problem and suggested Treasury notes be used for trade. The order itself, with its verbose and convoluted sentences, indicates Rawlins's authorship, whereas Grant's written orders were known for clarity and succinctness. But often orders were collaborative efforts, with Grant sketching out a rough draft and Rawlins taking over from there.[29] The contempt expressed in the order for those who love profit more than country seems consistent with Rawlins's deep patriotic feelings, and the punishments for violators reflect Rawlins's often uncompromising approach.

⟞⟋⟋⟋⟍

The first few weeks back in Corinth were taxing ones for Rawlins. He witnessed an ugly incident while riding with Grant to a sulfur spring south of Corinth. A musket went off inside a house, followed by a mother and daughter fleeing out the door. They were chased by a Union soldier who had fired the shot and appeared intent on assaulting them. Responding instinctively, Grant jumped from his horse, disarmed the soldier, and used the gun to knock him unconscious. Seeing the scoundrel stretched out, Rawlins said, "I guess you have killed him, General." "If I have," Grant replied, "it has only served him right."[30] Such incidents as well as a painful medical condition were trying Rawlins's self-control. Augustus Chetlain recalled he visited headquarters one day in early summer and found Rawlins alone reading a letter from their mutual Galena friend, Reverend Aratus Kent. The reverend heard reports Rawlins was using profane language. Rawlins admitted Kent was right, but after slamming his fist on a table, he barked to Chetlain, "It is very kind in the old Christian man to write this, but I'll be _____ if any army like this can be run without swearing."[31]

In mid-August, Rawlins underwent surgery to prevent a carbuncle from turning into a fistula.[32] Rawlins was probably suffering from a perianal abscess, which appears as a boil and may develop into a fistula. In Rawlins's case, it could have been caused by the horseback rides between Corinth and Memphis.[33] Following surgery, Rawlins was confined to bed until Grant ordered him home. On the twenty-second, he received a twenty-day leave, and Bowers filled in for him.[34]

Rawlins had been absent from home for eleven months. The return to the farm in Guilford was a welcome opportunity to see his children and parents, and to congratulate his sister, Laura, on her marriage on July 3 to Jeremiah Sheean, younger brother of David, Rawlins's former law partner. Sheean and Rawlins had dissolved their partnership in January when it appeared that Rawlins's staff appointment would continue indefinitely. The triumphant Galena homecoming was capped off with a grand supper party on Friday, August 29, at the De Soto House feting Rawlins and the Lead Mine Regiment's Colonel John E. Smith, who was on furlough.

Sixty of Galena's notables turned out for the Friday event. Rawlins took the dais and spoke for an hour; his remarks, as the newspaper reported the next day, served as an "utter demolition of the infamous slanders on Maj. Gen. Grant" in circulation after Shiloh. He took pain to shatter two pernicious rumors, attesting that Grant was "one of the most temperate men in his habits that he ever knew" and that Grant had hastened to Pittsburg Landing as soon as possible after the battle commenced.[35]

The newspaper story, however, did not mention whether Rawlins had been nettled by or closely queried about other events reported in that same day's edition of the *Galena Daily Advertiser*. The breaking story occupied hardly a square inch, scant initial coverage for what would be one of the most contro-versial episodes to occur in Illinois during the war.

Among the few snippets of information Galena residents learned was that US Marshal J. Russell Jones had, on the twenty-eighth, placed Madison Y. Johnson and David Sheean under arrest for disloyalty. The pair was to be taken to Fort Lafayette. The paper claimed, "These men have been conspicu-ous leaders against the Government in its attempt to put down the rebellion." It went on to explain, not quite accurately, that "the arrest was just a few days after Bradner Smith made an affidavit leading to the arrest of Nicholas Roth for discouraging enlistments. Johnson and Sheean were Roth's lawyers who instigated him to bring suit against Smith for $10,000."[36]

With Bradner Smith being the uncle of his deceased wife and Sheean his closest friend, John Rawlins found himself entangled in the fray.

Newspaper readers across the river in Dubuque received more details, and an eye-popping allegation, about the arrests thanks to a Galena source who identified himself only as "X." As X told it, "Their unique crime consists . . . in having been employed as counsel by two persons who have been confined in the County Jail for several weeks, charged with discouraging enlistments. . . . It is doubtless through the representations of these men, against whom suits were brought, and the influence of . . . E. B. Washburne . . . who is now at Washington, that [Sheean and Johnson were] arrested." X went on to ful-minate against "those [e.g., Washburne?] who have the ear of the Secretary of War [and who are] using their influence for the purpose of gratifying their ma-lignant personal and political spite against those [i.e., Sheean and Johnson?] who are loyal and true to the Union, and better patriots than their accusers."[37]

Sheean had been arrested, without warrant, at his law office on August 28 by George Webb, a deputy of the United States Marshal at Chicago, and J. Russell Jones, who was a confidant of Washburne's. The day before, Jones had received telegraphic orders from the secretary of war as issued by Judge Ad-vocate Levi C. Turner to arrest Sheean and Johnson for unspecified "disloyal practices" and "convey them to and place them in Fort Lafayette N. York."[38] Webb told Sheean to "fire up to go" so as to be ready to board a train to Chi-cago. While in Webb's custody and waiting at the Galena depot, Sheean saw a few acquaintances who expressed astonishment at his arrest. Sheean told them that it was the work of Washburne, who was then in Washington.[39]

Sheean's destination was Fort Lafayette, a prison in New York Harbor. It was the repository for political opponents deemed disloyal to the war effort. It is not known whether Rawlins made last-ditch efforts to intercede on behalf of Sheean, but it seems unlikely, because X indicated Sheean's friends were intentionally kept ignorant about actions to be brought against him.[40]

—–⁓⁓⁓–—

What trouble had Sheean gotten into? In the summer of 1862, a fresh infantry regiment, the Ninety-Sixth Illinois, was forming in Jo Daviess County, and recruits were being offered enlistment bounty enticements. On August 11, while a crowd gathered at the Galena recruiting station, a burly, half-tipsy Irishman, Bernard Donnelly, was spouting that he would not enlist unless he received his bounty money upfront. He blathered that he had acquaintances who enlisted and then were stiffed for the bounty. In the crowd was S. W. McMaster, a Republican and former business associate of Washburne's, who warned Donnelly, "You will be arrested if you keep up this talk, discouraging enlistments."[41] Donnelly's unpatriotic griping incensed Daniel S. Harris, who slugged the Irishman and knocked him down. Harris and his brother, Robert, both influential Galena businessmen, dragged the bloodied Donnelly to the county jail, where he was taken into custody by Deputy Sheriff John C. Hawkins.[42] After sobering up, Donnelly retained Sheean for legal representation.

Sheean applied for a writ of habeas corpus, but Judge Benjamin Sheldon of the circuit court refused on the ground that, as he heard the situation described, Donnelly, by discouraging enlistments, had violated a recent decree authorizing the arrest of such violators.[43] Judge Sheldon was following an order issued on August 8 by Secretary of War Stanton stipulating "that all U. S. marshals . . . or chiefs of police of any town, city, or district . . . are authorized and directed to arrest and imprison any person or persons who may be engaged, by act, speech, or writing, in discouraging volunteer enlistments, giving aid and comfort to the enemy, or in any other disloyal practice against the United States."[44] Undeterred, Sheean informed Sheldon that whereas his client was jailed without a complaint filed against him, he would file a trespass suit for $10,000 in damages against the Harris brothers and Deputy Hawkins for falsely arresting and imprisoning his client.[45] Soon thereafter, the Harris brothers confronted Sheean on the courthouse steps and threatened that if he didn't drop the suit, he would also find himself behind bars.[46] During the quarrel, the Harris brothers grabbed Sheean, who then acted as if he were drawing a weapon from his pocket. The brothers began shouting, "Murder!"

which aroused the court clerks, who ran outside to break up the scuffle.[47] Sheean, showing he would not be bullied, pursued the suit.

While Sheean encountered frustration and intimidation in his defense of Donnelly, another incident was brewing that would bring Madison Johnson into the fray. A bizarre squabble between Bradner Smith and Nicholas Roth, a recently discharged Union officer, coincidentally came to a head on that same Monday, August 11. On that day, Smith filed an affidavit that Roth was discouraging his friends from enlisting. Roth had been a lieutenant in a company of the Twelfth Illinois before being discharged in June for a rheumatic condition.[48] On returning to Galena, his patriotic enthusiasm appeared to have soured because townsfolk heard him making disparaging remarks about abolitionists and the war. There was a history of bad blood between Smith and Roth that escalated that Monday into a shouting match in a saloon. Smith accused Roth of cowardice at Shiloh; Roth retaliated by calling Smith an abolitionist who made money staying home and out of the fight.[49] Smith's affidavit, however, was reason enough for the sheriff to take Roth into custody. To gain his release, he engaged Madison Johnson, who, on the twelfth filed a suit on Roth's behalf for ten thousand in damages against Bradner Smith.

Two weeks later on August 27, Stanton issued his order to US Marshal Jones to have Johnson and Sheean arrested for "disloyal practices" and transported to Fort Lafayette. Both were stunned that defending their clients could be construed as disloyalty. Ironically, three days earlier Sheean and Johnson had demonstrated at least a modicum of loyalty by volunteering in a home militia unit commanded by wealthy lead miner Hezekiah Gear. Sheean was to head Gear's staff, and Johnson was appointed regimental judge advocate.[50]

It is doubtful that disloyal practices led to the attorneys' incarcerations; rather, "their positions as spokesmen for the Galena Democracy appears a more fundamental cause for the arrests." By late summer 1862, the political bipartisanship that flourished in northwest Illinois after Fort Sumter had eroded. The Democrats were spoiling for a fight come November. They sensed a chance to succeed in state and congressional elections by exploiting voters' trepidation about the implications of possible emancipation, exasperation with military setbacks, and disgust with crackdowns against political dissenters. Quite simply, Sheean and Johnson were political threats. Shortly before his arrest, Sheean had advocated for the organization of county Democratic clubs that would stand against Republican abolitionists, whom they believed were the "instigators and abettors of the rebellion."[51] The Republican *Galena*

Gazette reacted by warning, "Let those who are disseminating such doctrines be marked as enemies of their country."[52]

For years, Johnson and Sheean had been thorns in Washburne's Republican hide. During the 1858 election, Johnson led a personal crusade against Washburne and his antislavery agenda by attacking two Washburne men, one a candidate for the Illinois House and the other a state senator up for reelection.[53] While serving as Rawlins's legal apprentice, Sheean had taken political potshots at Washburne. In December 1856 at a De Soto House post-presidential-election victory celebration, Sheean paid tribute to the Democrats of Galena for helping defeat Frémont, and he chortled that Washburne had suffered "a rebuke of which Galenians will ever be proud."[54] Given their antagonistic relationship, Sheean suspected that Washburne was approached by the Harris brothers to induce Stanton to send the telegram ordering his arrest.[55] The Washburne complicity theory in the Sheean-Johnson cases gained traction with the public, thanks to its inclusion in one influential postwar book that vividly recounted examples of Lincoln administration overreach: "Washburne had the ear of the 'Government.' He could direct its right arm, the Secretary of War. Armed with such influence and a certified transcript of the trespass suit, he departed for Washington on his devilish errand. The foregoing telegram was sent back the day after his arrival."[56] Despite newspaper reports[57] placing him in Washington when the telegram was sent, "That Washburne's complicity was enlisted as these accounts charge, available evidence does not firmly establish. . . . If he bore any responsibility for the arrests, he had covered his tracks with uncommon care."[58]

—◦◦◦—

Rawlins returned to Corinth from his leave about September 12, still feeling the effects of surgery and unable to ride a horse.[59] Before he left Galena, hundreds of townsfolk had signed a petition that on September 11 was sent to Stanton requesting a "speedy examination" for Sheean and Johnson. An accompanying cover letter intriguingly attributed their arrests "to the misrepresentations of a political enemy."[60] Eager to help his friend, Rawlins requested a brief leave in October to perform a fact-finding mission in Galena about the Donnelly case, Sheean's role in it, and particulars about his arrest.

Fortified with more information, Rawlins, from Grant's new headquarters at Jackson, Tennessee, penned a long letter on October 30 to Stanton. Rawlins also solicited letters attesting to his own good character, honesty, and patriotism from Grant, Generals John Logan and Stephen Hurlbut, Lt. Colo-nel Maltby of the Forty-Fifth Illinois, and ADC Rowley. Rawlins made copies of the documents and mailed them to his brother Lemmon in Guilford Town-ship.

Rawlins devoted part of the letter to speak as character witness. He praised Sheean as "a gentleman in every sense of the term" but acknowledged that he is known to be "a strong partisan, but not a traitor, unless all men who disagree with the Administration on political questions are to be regarded as such." Rawlins's challenge was how to defend his friend to Stanton using language that would not compromise the truth. In a carefully worded summation for the defense, Rawlins wrote, "That he [Sheean] desires the restoration of the Union, and the maintenance of the Constitution, I have no doubt; but differs with me and others as to the best mode of attaining so desirable and end." This was a tactful way of getting around the fact that Sheean was no War Democrat.[61]

Rawlins also shared his theory for why Sheean was arrested. Of course, he couldn't suggest that Washburne inappropriately used his influence with the secretary to order the arrest, so he blamed the Harris brothers. It was getting revenge, pure and simple, for the trespass suit Sheean brought against them. "The suit," Rawlins argued, "was instituted by him for no other purpose than to vindicate what he considered to be the rights of his client, and to teach the defendants in the suit that they could not constitute themselves a court, and take the law in their own hands, and unmercifully beat a man, who from what I can learn, is equally loyal as themselves."

Rawlins argued that the Harris brothers were no enthusiastic supporters of those who served their flag. When a petition had been circulated in Galena calling for appropriating monies to induce men to enlist in the Forty-Fifth Regiment, Jasper Maltby approached Robert Harris for his signature, but "he pre-emptorily refused to sign it notwithstanding his loud protestations of opening the Mississippi river." To Rawlins, this was bitter irony, given the Harrises' longtime investments in the steamboat business. Moreover, after the recent call from Washington for more volunteers, Daniel Harris, "instead of sending his son into the army, sent him to California, and none of the family are in the war!"

Rawlins concluded the letter by beseeching the secretary "that the trial of Mr. Sheean, if he is to have one, be brought on for hearing at an early day, or he be released from arrest and imprisonment."[62]

In Grant's accompanying letter, he stood behind Rawlins: "From the firing of the first gun at Fort Sumpter to the present hour his heart and soul has been in favor of a vigorous prossecution of this war. Before entering the service no man made more strenuous efforts to encourage enlistments. I refer you to the Hon. E. B. Washburn for any information that you may want as to the standing of Maj. Rawlins."[63] General Hurlbut endorsed Rawlins extravagantly: "His loyalty is undisputed—his integrity of purpose and character for veracity and manliness [regarded] so highly that the fullest credit may be given to his statements."[64]

When Stanton failed to reply, Rawlins contacted Washburne, hoping to secure his help in obtaining Sheean's release.[65] Whatever Rawlins's plea, it failed to move Washburne.

———

Rawlins's sense of urgency was well founded. No formal charges had been preferred against either Sheean or Johnson; they were in legal limbo. Moreover, shortly after entering Fort Lafayette, their fortunes took a turn for the worse. One of the prisoners in the unit was Lewis Ballard, incarcerated as a felon rather than a political prisoner. In his diary entry of September 2, Sheean noted he had had a discussion with Ballard, whom he described as "an abolitionist of the craziest kind."[66] Barely a day after the three had come into contact, Ballard submitted a sworn affidavit testifying to having heard Sheean and Johnson utter treasonable threats against the government and words of sympathy for secessionists. Ballard further stated Johnson revealed himself to be a member of the Knights of the Golden Circle, a secret cabal of Confederate sympathizers. When news broke about Sheean and Johnson's alleged seditious disclosures, Republican newspaper editors in northern Illinois had a field day. Sheean, and no doubt Rawlins, were aghast. Suspecting that Ballard was playing the role of informer, Sheean wrote Judge Advocate Turner to clarify that "on the evening of my arrival here [Fort Lafayette] Ballard and myself engaged in a discussion upon 'Abolitionism,' which may have been the conversation alluded to. I know not what Ballard has reported to you but anything I said to him I am ready to admit at any time."[67]

If securing Sheean's release for disloyal practices was not proving difficult enough, adding treason to the mix sent the odds soaring against him. With prospects of trials dimming and usual avenues for redress blocked, the Galena city council in December agreed that Governor Yates be petitioned to arrange the return of Sheean and Johnson to Illinois for trial. While rescue efforts were afoot in Galena, Darius Hunkins, a former Galena alderman, railroad entrepreneur, and close associate of Madison Johnson, was in Washington during the last week of November attempting to put his War Department connections to work. He met with Stanton and Levi Turner but made no headway with them.

Hunkins tried a different method: a direct appeal to Washburne. Hunkins met with Washburne on December 10 and presented him with a petition to sign and circulate among congressional Republicans. Washburne, on deliberation, backed away from it. Hunkins and Washburne met again on December 11, and following that meeting, some unexpected—even odd—events unfolded. For one, a letter strangely dated December 10 was presented to Stanton. Odder still, the letter was written in Washburne's hand but signed by Hunkins.[68] This Washburne-Hunkins hybrid letter reads in part, "I [Hunkins] now desire that they may be released. As the friend of both the parties and acting for them in this behalf I pledge myself if they are released they shall deport themselves as good, loyal and peaceable citizens and that they shall do no act of hostility to the government nor to the prejudice of any persons connected therewith."[69] Essentially, Hunkins promised Stanton that Sheean and Johnson would behave if set free. Then most unexpectedly, two days later Stanton discharged the attorneys. What prompted Washburne to participate in the release of these political nemeses whose arrest he may have facilitated?

The answer may never be known. Perhaps Washburne had been rattled by November's midterm election results. Although he had been voted another term in Congress, the Sheean and Johnson brouhaha appeared to have hurt his popularity locally—he had garnered only 37 percent of the Galena vote.[70] Another explanation—probably one Johnson told about his arrest that appeared in *American Bastile*—had Hunkins approaching a friend who was also personally close to Washburne. Hunkins told this friend a story, knowing he would blab it to Washburne, about "terrible excitement" back in Galena. Dangerous emotions were being stirred up because there was a belief among Sheean's and Johnson's friends that Washburne was standing against their releases. More ominously, Washburne's personal safety, the friend allegedly warned, might be at risk if the two were not immediately discharged. When Hunkins and Washburne met on December 11, a shaken Washburne is said to have asked, "What can I do?" Hunkins suggested writing a letter to Stanton. After some back-and-forth about the authorship of the letter, Hunkins said,

"I do not know how to address these officials. You write it, and I will sign it, and take it to the Secretary of War." Shortly after Hunkins delivered the letter, Washburne allegedly sidled into Stanton's office, and the discharges were authorized.[71]

On the face of it, the letter Hunkins had signed and delivered to Stanton was no more persuasive or contained any more assurances than the long letter Rawlins sent six weeks earlier in behalf of Sheean. That Hunkins's letter sprung the two lawyers suggests that it had help from Washburne.

———

Within ten days after being released, Sheean and Johnson were waving to cheering crowds as their train chugged toward Galena. They received enthusiastic welcomes even in outlying hamlets like Scales Mound and Council Hill, "but it remained for the unterrified Democrats of Jo Daviess County to crown the glory of this most magnificent expression of the public joy in Galena, where these 'honorably discharged' and now triumphant victims of lawless oppression are best known and most justly appreciated."[72] A massive celebration was planned in Galena for December 23, but rain depressed the turnout. Nonetheless, when the attorneys alit from their railcar, they were mobbed by a cheering crowd and treated to a display of fireworks and blazing torches.[73] The friendly embraces and bonfires were appreciated, but they could not soften the hard feelings Sheean would harbor against Washburne, a man he referred to as "that contemptible piece of humanity."[74]

Rawlins, writing from Holly Springs, Mississippi, on New Year's Day 1863, sent his friend a congratulatory letter on learning of his release:

> Let me assure you nothing has occurred in a great while that has pleased me more than to know, as I now do, that one whom I have known from earliest recollection has been restored to liberty, and the rights which every American citizen is entitled to enjoy; feeling as I do that your arrest was but the result of the personal malice of ——— seeking a revenge their cowardly and craven souls failed to find in their attempt at personal violence against you. . . . I am as firm to-day in the support of my Government and yours as ever. I believe that if the war is properly conducted it must finally end in the triumph of the government established by our fathers, and whether it ends in one year or ten, I am for its vigorous prosecution; but to the arrest of loyal citizens and imprisonment without trial I am opposed and shall be opposed to the end of life.
>
> I will in a few days be troubling you to attend to my private affairs. Write me on receipt of this. Give my love to all the folks and my friends.[75]

Playing it safe, the publisher of the letter expunged the name(s) of those Rawlins thought responsible for the "personal malice" against Sheean. Rawlins reveals his views to seeing the war through to the country's reunification but not at the expense of obliterating due process and free speech—perspectives that were consistent with most Galena Democrats' criticism of "the administration's police state methods."[76]

Despite rejoicing in his friend's freedom, by year's end of 1862, Rawlins and Sheean were astride markedly diverging career paths. Perhaps neither of the friends could notice how they were veering apart. His four months in federal captivity only made Sheean more cynical and hardened his antipathy toward the Lincoln administration. To that welcoming crowd at Galena's train station, Sheean lashed out against Lincoln, Stanton, and the war and abolition: "I come back firm in every opinion heretofore held, and adhere to every sentiment expressed by me concerning this war. You all know I never believed in it and never gave it aid, for I believed it to be an abolition war. . . . I am opposed to its prosecution now when *you all know and see* that abolition is the main object for which it is waged by this infernal administration.[77]" In coming months, Sheean and Johnson would emerge as two of the most vociferous Copperheads in Illinois and would work strenuously against the Republican Party. Until beyond the 1864 election, Sheean, who shunned federal military service, would remain an unyielding, outspoken defender of the Democratic Party's peace faction.[78]

On the other hand, Rawlins never deviated from a belief that the war must be vigorously prosecuted or from his resolve to seeing it to the finish. His commitment to aiding Grant to prosecute that war was only strengthening. In late October, Grant petitioned the War Department for Rawlins's promotion to lieutenant colonel.[79] When a response from Washington was not quickly forthcoming, Grant pressed Washburne to exert his influence on Rawlins's behalf. One wonders how Rawlins reacted to this ironic twist. To Washburne, Grant praised Rawlins's commendable service: "His merit would entitle him to a Brigadier General[']s commission."[80] Just days later, Grant announced that Rawlins was appointed chief of staff in addition to his duties as AAG at the rank of lieutenant colonel; Colonel Webster, the former chief, was recommended for promotion to brigadier general and made superintendent of military railroads supplying Grant's forces.[81] Thus in mid-November, Rawlins was established as the right-hand man to the general who would become the favorite of Abraham Lincoln, a man whom Sheean loathed.

On November 13, 1862, Grant initiated a benevolent program for coping with the influx of escaped slaves into the Union lines. Rawlins was integral to this program as the issuer of Grant's special orders appointing Chaplain John Eaton of the Twenty-Seventh Ohio as the program's administrator. Eaton was to take charge of the fugitive slaves coming and establish a camp for them "where they will suitably be cared for and organized into companies and set to work picking, ginning and baling cotton" and provided with medical care and rations.[82] A month later, Rawlins's general order expanded the "contrabands'" job responsibilities to include working on steamboats, railroad gangs, and "in any way where their service can be made available."[83] The thirty-three-year-old Eaton proved an effective and compassionate manager.

As the year ended, Sheean protested that abolition had become an object of the war while orders being issued through Rawlins in Tennessee were crippling the institution of slavery.

NOTES

1. William T. Sherman, *Memoirs of General William T. Sherman by Himself* (New York: D. Appleton, 1875), 1:250.

2. Henry Stone, "Major-General George Henry Thomas," in *Papers of the Military Historical Society of Massachusetts*, Vol. X, *Critical Sketches of Some of the Federal and Confederate Commanders*, ed. Theodore F. Dwight (Boston: Houghton, Mifflin, 1895), 178.

3. U. S. Grant, *Personal Memoirs of U. S. Grant* (New York: Charles Webster, 1885), 376.

4. Albert D. Richardson, *A Personal History of Ulysses S. Grant* (Boston: D. L. Guernsey, 1885), 255.

5. John Y. Simon, ed., *The Papers of Ulysses S. Grant* (Carbondale: Southern Illinois University Press, 1973), 5:114.

6. H. W. Halleck to U. S. Grant, May 12, 1862, in *The War of the Rebellion: A Compilation of the Official Records of the Union and Confederate Armies*, series 1, part 2, 10:182–83.

7. John Y. Simon, ed., *The Papers of Ulysses S. Grant*, 5:116.

8. William R. Rowley to Elihu Washburne, May 24, 1862, quoted in Mark Washburne, *A Biography of Elihu Benjamin Washburne: Congressman, Secretary of State, Envoy Extraordinary* (self-pub., Xlibris, 2001), 2:149.

9. John Eaton, *Grant, Lincoln and the Freedmen* (New York: Longmans, Green, 1907), 43.

10. William T. Sherman, *Memoirs*, 1:255.

11. John Y. Simon, ed., *The Papers of Ulysses S. Grant*, 5:143.

12. U. S. Grant to Julia Dent Grant, June 9, 1862, in *The Papers of Ulysses S. Grant*, ed. John Y. Simon, 5:140.

13. U. S. Grant, *Personal Memoirs of U. S. Grant*, 1:389. In the *Memoirs*, Grant refers to a "General Jackson" as the cavalry officer who came close to capturing the party. The officer was almost certainly William "Red" Jackson, who was only a colonel at the time. See Ezra J. Warner, *Generals in Gray* (Baton Rouge: Louisiana State University Press, 1959), 152.

14. U. S. Grant to H. W. Halleck, June 24, 1862, in *The War of the Rebellion: A Compilation of the Official Records of the Union and Confederate Armies*, series 1, part 2, 17:29–30; U. S. Grant to H. W. Halleck, June 27, 1862, in *The War of the Rebellion: A Compilation of the Official Records of the Union and Confederate Armies*, series 1, part 2, 17:41.

15. Special Orders No. 118, June 24, 1862, in *The War of the Rebellion: A Compilation of the Official Records of the Union and Confederate Armies*, series 1, part 2, 17:30–31.

16. John Y. Simon, ed., *The Papers of Ulysses S. Grant*, 5:151n4.

17. Ibid., 181–82n.

18. U. S. Grant to H. W. Halleck, June 27, 1862, in *The War of the Rebellion: A Compilation of the Official Records of the Union and Confederate Armies*, series 1, part 2, 17:41.

19. John Y. Simon, ed., *The Papers of Ulysses S. Grant*, 5:190

20. Ibid., 192–93n.

21. Joseph H. Parks, "A Confederate Trade Center under Federal Occupation: Memphis, 1862 to 1865," *The Journal of Southern History* 7, no. 3 (1941): 292.

22. John Y. Simon, ed., *The Papers of Ulysses S. Grant*, 5:196n.

23. Ibid., 207n.

24. Ibid., 268n2.

25. Special Field Orders No. 161, July 16, 1862, in *The War of the Rebellion: A Compilation of the Official Records of the Union and Confederate Armies*, series 1, part 2, 17:101.

26. John Y. Simon, ed., *The Papers of Ulysses S. Grant*, 5:240n.

27. Ibid., 238–39n.

28. Ibid., 240–41n.

29. E. B. Long, "John A. Rawlins: Staff Officer Par Excellence," *Civil War Times Illustrated* 12, no. 9 (1974): 45.

30. Albert D. Richardson, *A Personal History of Ulysses S. Grant*, 264.

31. Augustus L. Chetlain, *Recollections of Seventy Years* (Galena, IL: Gazette, 1899), 98.

32. U. S. Grant to Julia Dent Grant, August 18, 1862, in *The Papers of Ulysses S. Grant*, ed. John Y. Simon, 5:328.

33. Jack D. Welsh, *Medical Histories of Union Generals* (Kent: Kent State University Press, 1995), 398.

34. U. S. Grant to Julia Dent Grant, August 22, 1862, in *The Papers of Ulysses S. Grant*, ed. John Y. Simon, 5:328, 328n5.

35. *Galena Daily Advertiser*, August 30, 1862.

36. Ibid., August 29, 1862.

37. *Dubuque Herald*, August 30, 1862.

38. U. S. Military Telegraph L. C. Turner to J. R. Jones, August 27, 1862, National Archives and Record Service, Turner-Baker Papers, Record Group 94, Turner Files, Case File 205.

39. David Sheean diary entry for August 28, 1862. Diary in possession of private collector.

40. *Dubuque Herald*, August 30, 1862.

41. S. W. McMaster, *60 Years on the Upper Mississippi: My Life and Experiences* (Rock Island, IL, 1893), 197.

42. *The History of Jo Daviess County Illinois* (Chicago: H. F. Kett, 1878), 421.

43. John A. Marshall, *American Bastile: A History of the Illegal Arrests and Imprisonment of American Citizens During the Late Civil War* (Philadelphia: Thomas W. Hartley, 1871), 452.

44. *The War of the Rebellion: A Compilation of the Official Records of the Union and Confederate Armies*, series 3, August 8, 1862, 2:321.

45. John A. Marshall, *American Bastile*, 453.

46. *The History of Jo Daviess County Illinois*, 421.

47. John A. Rawlins to Edwin Stanton, October 30, 1862, National Archives and Record Service, Record Group 94, Turner-Baker Papers, Turner Files, Case File 205.

48. Special Field Orders No. 116, Headquarters, Department of the Mississippi, June 20, 1862, Military Service Record of Nicholas Roth, National Archives and Records Service, Washington, DC. Roth, one of "Galena's First Offering," enlisted on April 18, 1861, during the courthouse meeting presided over by Grant. See *The History of Jo Daviess County Illinois*, 376–77.

49. Gene Edwin Arnold, "Without Due Process: Madison Y. Johnson and the Civil War" (master's thesis, DePaul University, 1967), 146–48. In his report following Shiloh, Captain James Huginin of the Twelfth Illinois said, "All my officers and men behaved handsomely; all fought bravely." Huginin singled out Roth for his battlefield performance; *The War of the Rebellion: A Compilation of the Official Records of the Union and Confederate Armies*, series 1, part 2, 10:157–58.

50. Kenneth N. Owens, *Galena, Grant, and the Fortunes of War* (DeKalb: Northern Illinois University Research Series, 1963) 41–42.

51. Ibid., 43.

52. *Galena Gazette*, August 12, 1862.

53. Gene Edwin Arnold, *Without Due Process*, 70–81.

54. *Galena Courier*, December 4, 1856.

55. *The History of Jo Daviess County Illinois*, 421.

56. John A. Marshall, *American Bastile*, 453.

57. The *Galena Gazette* of September 3, 1862, mentioned Washburne was absent at Washington. Congress was not in session at this time.

58. Gene Edwin Arnold, *Without Due Process*, 260.

59. U. S. Grant to Julia Dent Grant, September 14, 1862, in *The Papers of Ulysses S. Grant*, ed. John Y. Simon, 6:43.

60. Petition sent to Edwin Stanton, September 11, 1862, National Archives and Record Service, Record Group 94, Turner-Baker Papers, Turner Files, Case File 205.

61. J. A. Rawlins to Edwin Stanton, October 30, 1862, National Archives and Record Service, Record Group 94, Turner-Baker Papers, Turner Files, Case File 205.

62. Ibid.

63. U. S. Grant to Edwin Stanton, October 30, 1862, in *The Papers of Ulysses S. Grant*, ed. John Y. Simon, 6:220.

64. S. A. Hurlbut to Edwin Stanton, October 30, 1862, National Archives and Record Service, Record Group 94, Turner-Baker Papers, Turner Files, Case File 205.

65. James Harrison Wilson, *The Life of John A. Rawlins*, 102. A search during October 2016 of the Elihu B. Washburne Papers, Book 27, at the Library of Congress, covering correspondence from July to December 1862, failed to turn up that letter.

66. David Sheean diary entry for August 28, 1862. Diary in possession of private collector.

67. D. Sheean to L. C. Turner, September 10, 1862, National Archives and Record Service, Record Group 94, Turner-Baker Papers, Turner Files, Case File 205.

68. Gene Edwin Arnold, *Without Due Process*, offered the results of a document analysis by a handwriting examiner who concluded that the letter was written by Washburne; see 369–72.

69. D. Hunkins to Edwin Stanton, December 10, 1862, National Archives and Record Service, Record Group 94, Turner-Baker Papers, Turner Files, Case File 205.

70. Kenneth N. Owens, *Galena, Grant, and the Fortunes of War*, 47.

71. John A. Marshall, *American Bastile*, 527.

72. *Galena Democrat*, December 26, 1862.

73. Ibid., December 24, 1862.

74. Ibid., December 26, 1862.

75. *Portrait and Biographical Album of Jo Daviess County, Illinois* (Chicago: Chapman Brothers, 1889), 192–93. While Rawlins rejoiced in Sheean's release, he had been worried about the health of two-year old Emily, who was in the care of his parents. Writing on December 20, 1862, from Oxford, Mississippi, to his Galena friend Enos Ripley, Rawlins said, "My little ones East are well, the one with my mother I fear never will recover" (U. S. Grant Presidential Library, Mississippi State University, Series 2, Box 10, Folder 66). This may be one of the "private affairs" Rawlins wished Sheean to attend to.

76. Kenneth N. Owens, *Galena, Grant, and the Fortunes of War*, 46.

77. *Galena Democrat*, December 26, 1862.

78. Gene Edwin Arnold, *Without Due Process*, 294, 325.

79. U. S. Grant to Lorenzo Thomas, October 27, 1862, in *The Papers of Ulysses S. Grant*, ed. John Y. Simon, 6:203.

80. U. S. Grant to E. B. Washburne, November 7, 1862, in *The Papers of Ulysses S. Grant*, ed. John Y. Simon, 6:275.

81. General Orders No. 6, November 11, 1862, in *The Papers of Ulysses S. Grant*, ed. John Y. Simon, 6:294–95.

82. John Y. Simon, ed., *The Papers of Ulysses S. Grant*, 6:315–16n.

83. Ibid., 316n.

13

"You Countermanded Such an Order
Two Weeks Ago"

THE TIME SPANNING RAWLINS'S OPERATION, Galena recuperation, and the arrest and first weeks of incarceration of his former law partner coincided with a stretch in late summer and fall 1862 that Grant would regard as his "most anxious period of the war."[1] Grant's Army of the Tennessee was on the defensive, holding captured territory, guarding rail and communication lines, and fending off Rebel raiders. Its units were scattered from western Tennessee across northern Mississippi, with Sherman in Memphis, Rosecrans east at Corinth, and General Edward Ord in between at Jackson, Tennessee. It was also depleted: Grant was obliged to send three of Rosecrans's divisions north to reinforce Buell. Ten days after Halleck's taking of Corinth, Buell had been ordered eastward to capture Chattanooga, but less than three months later, he struggled to intercept a Confederate force under General Braxton Bragg— he replaced Beauregard after Corinth—that had invaded Kentucky and was menacing Louisville. Grant was being checked by two independent Confederate commands, each with about fifteen thousand troops, which he hoped to prevent from consolidating. Mississippi-born Earl Van Dorn led one that operated toward Vicksburg, and Sterling "Old Pap" Price commanded the Army of the West. They were to occupy Grant's attention and minimize the help he could send against Bragg.

On September 13, Price moved into northeast Mississippi and struck the far eastern end of Grant's line at Iuka, a town on the Memphis and Charleston Railroad twenty miles east of Corinth. Price's intentions were of critical concern because Halleck and Grant worried he might slip away and join Bragg. In Iuka, a large quantity of supplies and cotton was guarded by a small Union garrison under Colonel Robert Murphy. That day Price's cavalry probed the Union defenses but were chased away. However, Murphy was outnumbered and withdrew the next morning, leaving Iuka to Price and a cache of supplies he had failed to destroy. Murphy's withdrawal incensed Rosecrans, who demanded his arrest. Court-martial proceedings were swiftly initiated, a move with which Rosecrans was in full agreement: "I think extreme fright and want of judgement of Col. M so manifest," he wrote, "as to need no comment."[2]

Once apprised of Price's presence at Iuka, Grant devised a pincer movement to vanquish him. Ord, accompanied by Grant—Rawlins remained behind at Corinth—would be positioned northwest of Iuka and launch the attack. Rosecrans's two divisions aggregating about nine thousand would sweep in from the southwest. Price's army would be sandwiched between. The two-pronged operation started badly because Rosecrans was delayed getting to his staging area. The plan was for Ord to begin the attack, but it needed modification now that Rosecrans wouldn't be in place until early afternoon on the nineteenth. According to the revised plan, once Ord heard Rosecrans's guns to the south, he would pitch his own two divisions into the fight. Early in the morning on the nineteenth, Grant sent his ADC, Clark Lagow, and Colonel Lyle Dickey, the chief of cavalry, to deliver to Rosecrans the new plan of attack. Lagow and Dickey found him at a farmhouse several miles south of Iuka. After a lunch, they rode with Rosecrans to the head of his column and watched the engagement against Price escalate into a raging battle. Lagow and Dickey headed back to report to Grant that a battle was on. However, rough terrain and nightfall slowed their progress. At one point, Lagow's horse, with him on it, tumbled over a creek bank. Then they got lost. After arriving at dawn, they discovered that just hours before, Grant had been informed Rosecrans and Price were fighting a savage battle a few miles distant. The noise of that battle never reached Grant because an atmospheric anomaly, an acoustic shadow, had muffled the sounds.[3] Ord had not heard the battle either, leaving Rosecrans to carry on the fight by himself.

That was not Grant's only surprise. Rosecrans had been loath to split his force, so his two divisions covered only one of the two roads leading south out of town, giving Price an opening for his overnight retreat. The Yankees attempted a pursuit on September 20, but they were so exhausted that Rosecrans, with Grant's approval, called it off, leaving Price to hook up with Van Dorn. There was the consolation that he had been prevented from joining Bragg. In his report of the battle, Grant conceded his side suffered a defeat because Price was not destroyed. That report contained nary a complimentary word about Rosecrans's performance at Iuka.[4]

Price's escape stoked criticism of Grant. Why hadn't he and Ord attacked and bagged Price? Was the lack of coordination with Rosecrans due to Grant's drinking? On the other hand, Rosecrans was praised for having given Price a thrashing despite being outnumbered. As Dabney Maury, one of Price's brigadiers allowed, "At Iuka Rosecrans struck us a heavy blow. Grant failed to cooperate fortunately, and we got back to Tupelo considerably worsted."[5] Moreover, Rosecrans's haughty attitude didn't mesh well with his being subordinate to Grant. Might there be a clashing of egos or jealousy between the camps of the generals? Something unconstructive was brewing, as a Rosecrans biographer noted: "The aftermath of Iuka produced a lifetime of bad blood between Grant and Rosecrans."[6]

—◦◦◦—

Tensions between Grant and Rosecrans escalated following Van Dorn's decision shortly after Iuka to retake Corinth, the defense of which Grant entrusted to Rosecrans. With his and Price's combined forces, on October 3, Van Dorn unleashed his attack on Rosecrans and after a day of heavy fighting closed within a third of a mile of Corinth. Van Dorn felt confident he could finish the job the next day, but on the fourth, Price's furious charge was repulsed. By 2:00 p.m., Van Dorn had had enough, and the Confederates hastily withdrew. Rosecrans did not begin his pursuit until the next morning. It was Iuka all over again: Rosecrans won a battle, failed to apply the coup de grâce, but was praised by the press for pummeling the Confederates—to Grant's chagrin.[7] As some consolation, Grant received a congratulatory note from Lincoln. Poor roads, unhelpful guides, and heavily laden wagon trains contributed to the slow pace of Rosecrans's chase. Three days later, Grant called off the pursuit, claiming later he did so because Rosecrans might have had to fight a reinforced Van Dorn on the latter's choice of battleground.[8] Rosecrans was bitterly disappointed. He argued that given the cool weather and fields of corn to feed his men, "If Grant had not stopped us, we could have gone to Vicksburg."[9]

As Grant's most prominent staff member, Rawlins hardly could have avoided becoming tangled in this clash between generals. This was especially so because of Rawlins's concern that Grant was again threatened by false accusations. A correspondent of the *Cincinnati Commercial* who was close with

Rosecrans's staff ran stories suggesting Grant was drunk at Iuka. On October 19, Colonel Mortimer Leggett of the Seventy-Eighth Ohio wrote Rawlins, warning that "the minions of a newly fledged Major Genl"—Rosecrans had just been promoted to that rank—were making "irresponsible assertions, and mysterious insinuations, to attempt to awaken & deepen, former prejudices against [Grant]." Leggett surely knew Rawlins would not be passive should lies or others' ambitions threaten Grant. "Major Genl. Rosecrans is undoubtedly an excellent officer," Leggett wrote, "but the evidence is such, that I cannot rid my mind of the conviction that he must be, at least, *privy* to the whole devilish scheme.... But I fear that the inordinate ambition of Rosecrans, leads him to seek the downfall of Grant, hoping that thereby he may succeed to the command of the department." Leggett implored Rawlins to intervene: "It would seem that a friendly note to Gen Rosecrans from you would bring the subject sufficiently before him, to induce his sense of justice to repair a *wrong* which at least he has permitted[.] For Heaven's sake do *something* in the matter."[10]

Rawlins had already tried to do something. Both Rawlins and McPherson had approached Julia Grant, who was staying in a house that served as headquarters at Jackson, Tennessee. McPherson was quite direct: "We want to reach the General's ear through you. In justice to General Grant—in fact, in justice to ourselves—General Rosecrans ought to be relieved." But Rawlins had beaten McPherson to the punch. "General [*sic*] Rawlins already mentioned this to me this morning," she said, "and I have already spoken to the General about it." However, Grant dismissed the idea, believing Rosecrans would "come around all right."[11]

After the Iuka battle, Rawlins received a lengthy letter from Colonel Robert Murphy in which he defended his conduct. Despite Rosecrans's contempt for Murphy's alleged cowardice, Rawlins endorsed Murphy's letter, noting Grant's opinion "that he was justified in his action in the evacuation of Iuka." Murphy was acquitted of the charges and returned to duty. Rosecrans disapproved of the verdict.[12]

On October 22, Rosecrans griped to Halleck that some on Grant's staff were poisoning their relationship. "I am very sorry to say that after the battle of Iuka," Rosecrans confided to Halleck, "there has been the spirit of mischief among the mousing politicians on Grant's staff to get up in his mind a feeling of jealousy." Those staff members were well aware that praise was heaped on Rosecrans for having given a licking to Price and Van Dorn at Iuka and

Corinth. The politicians are unnamed but likely included Rowley and Rawlins, who had the strongest connections to Congressman Washburne. "I am sure these politicians will manage matters," he went on, "with the sole view of preventing Grant from being in the background of military operations." The thought that a staff could be so dedicated to boosting Grant, a man whom Rosecrans believed "lacks administrative ability," contributed to his requesting to be "relieved from duty here if I can be assigned to any other suitable duty."[13] Secretary of War Stanton swiftly complied with Rosecrans's reassignment request.[14] He replaced Buell, who failed to demolish Bragg on October 8 at Perryville, Kentucky. Rosecrans's departure seemed welcome news for Grant because, as Hillyer told Sherman, "Rosecrans has been ordered to Cincinnati to receive further orders. This is greatly to the relief of the general [i.e., Grant], who was very much disappointed in him."[15]

—◈—

During this "anxious time," Grant was fortunate to have in Rawlins a staff member who was providing service of meritorious value.[16] Rawlins kept track of and responded to an avalanche of details ranging from the mundane to critically urgent. He orchestrated the transfer of headquarters from Grand Junction to La Grange, Tennessee, instructing his assistant, Joe Bowers, to "move every thing belonging to Hd Qrs including Printing Press to this place."[17] As the point person at headquarters, he was the recipient of incoming messages and reports as well as the issuer of orders to subordinates in the field. Incoming messages included status reports such as the one on September 18 from General Hurlbut, whom Rawlins ordered to move his command from Memphis to Bolivar, Tennessee. Hurlbut's fact-filled report detailed the pace and route of his march.[18] Rawlins also received intelligence regarding enemy activities. For example, from Memphis, Sherman alerted Rawlins on September 12 to several reports of enemy movement, including one that had John Villepigue, one of Van Dorn's brigadiers, moving up to Holly Springs, Mississippi.[19]

The numerous orders emanating from Rawlins (or from Grant through Rawlins) included an urgent one to General McPherson assigning him command of two brigades and ordering him to proceed "with all possible dispatch" to Rosecrans at Corinth just as Van Dorn was mounting his attack there.[20] In a similar vein, on October 8 Rawlins sent General Hurlbut a telegram pressing him to send out a force to repair railroads in order to supply Rosecrans who at that moment was pursuing Van Dorn.[21]

There was the never-ending problem of tightening troop discipline—an issue fixed in Rawlins's mind after the thwarted assault against two women by a soldier outside of Corinth. On November 7, Rawlins issued orders holding officers accountable for plundering their men committed while on the march.[22]

The never-ending flow of communications wasn't limited to military exigency. There were also the human dimensions of warfare to consider. Following the Corinth battle, Rawlins received medical updates on the condition of Brigadier General Richard Oglesby, who had been seriously wounded by a musket ball that lodged in a vertebrae. Rawlins issued orders granting Oglesby a leave of absence and sending him home to Decatur, Illinois, to convalesce.[23] In November, Rawlins issued Grant's order providing for families within the limits of the department lacking sufficient clothing and food.[24]

There were tedious details that sapped Rawlins's energy and diverted his attention like the box of books that was to be sent to Grant in early November. Rawlins was distracted trying to locate the box and have it shipped from Columbus, Kentucky, to Jackson, Tennessee.[25]

Rawlins's hard work and commitment were rewarded with his promotion in November and expanded duties as chief of staff while retaining his role as assistant adjutant general. Grant requested the promotion shortly after Stanton elevated him to command of the Department of the Tennessee. This department encompassed the territory north to Cairo, south to northern Mississippi, Forts Henry and Donelson, and the portions of Kentucky and Tennessee west of the Tennessee River.[26] Surely, one of Rawlins's prouder moments was issuing Grant's order announcing the composition of his department staff, including himself as lieutenant colonel. The staff, now numbering seventeen, included those of the "old guard"—Webster, Lagow, Hillyer, Riggin, Rowley—and a newcomer, a young, bright West Point graduate, First Lieutenant James Harrison "Harry" Wilson, appointed chief of topographical engineers.[27]

—◦◦◦—

Wilson reported to Grant's headquarters at La Grange, Tennessee, on November 8. This was their first time meeting, although Rawlins had known his maternal grandfather in Galena. Seated alone at his desk, Rawlins swung around to greet Wilson: "General Grant is absent at Memphis, but will be back shortly. I'm Major Rawlins, his adjutant; I am glad to see you, lieutenant; damned glad to see you." The greeting sounded genuine. "We've been looking for you for several days. We need you here. I know all about you." Wilson wondered whether Rawlins had investigated into his character, perhaps checking with McPherson, Wilson's close friend, who had hoped to have his services as engineer. Wilson had heard positive words about Rawlins: "a man of good sense, simple manners, and great independence" was how Rawlins had been described.[28]

If he didn't know already, what Rawlins would learn about Wilson, who hailed from Shawneetown, Illinois, was how closely matched their views and temperaments were. Wilson believed in the sanctity of the federal union and regarded secession with contempt. Neither he nor Rawlins supported slavery, but they tolerated it because the Constitution sanctioned its existence. Like Rawlins, Wilson was dogmatic and humorless, and he embraced temperance and shunned carousers. And like Rawlins, he developed a strong bond with Grant. Although Wilson could clash with others who vied for Grant's attention, his relationship with Rawlins remained close—he never regarded the modest, unassuming Rawlins as a threat. They were so close that near the end of his life, Rawlins appointed Wilson his literary executor.[29]

At this initial meeting, a trusting Rawlins laid his cards on the table. "I want to be friends with you," he told Wilson. "Indeed, I want to form an alliance, offensive and defensive, with you." What Rawlins meant would be explained in this and subsequent conversations. It was a slow day at headquarters, so Rawlins could give Wilson the lowdown on the army, the prominent brass, the staff officers, and Grant. He also confessed to Wilson he was deficient in military science and unschooled in the technical side of war or military administration. "As there were no other West Point men on the field staff and but few in that army," Wilson recollected Rawlins admitting, "he would necessarily and frequently have to lean not only upon my book knowledge, but possibly upon my observation and experience."[30]

Rawlins presented a frank appraisal of the staff. Captains Theodore Bowers, his assistant, and William Rowley came in for praise for their bravery and patriotism. But the higher-ranking aides-de-camp—Colonels Hillyer, Lagow, Riggin, and George Ihrie, the last appointed a month after Shiloh—Rawlins characterized as "rounders" and possessed of little character. Not only were their services mostly useless, Rawlins complained, but the examples they set and the influence they wielded around headquarters were detrimental. Rawlins now sought Wilson's help in getting rid of them! This stunning appeal signaled the emergence of an offensive alliance.[31] Rawlins revisited these issues for Wilson's consideration on another occasion: "I am told you don't drink, but you should know there are lots of men in this army, some on Grant's staff, who not only drink themselves but like to see others drink, and whenever they get a chance they tempt their chief, and I want you to help me clean them out."[32] After Wilson became acquainted with the staff, he was in agreement with Rawlins's appraisals.[33]

The scoop on the staff was interesting, but more intriguing to Wilson was Rawlins's perspectives on Grant. Rawlins ticked off a half dozen of Grant's greatest attributes, "good sense," "courage," and "unshakable self-reliance" among them, which added up to him being "in all ways easily ahead of the best of his subordinates." But all this was of little consolation to Rawlins when newspapers or "one of his ambitious generals" overplayed Grant's intemperance. Rawlins assured Wilson that Grant's "habits" were not as bad as the press insinuated, but they were of enough concern that friends should unite to "stay him from falling." Rawlins hoped to enlist Wilson's help in this endeavor.[34] To illustrate what he meant, Wilson said Rawlins produced a document, a pledge, in Grant's handwriting, which could avert future indiscretions.[35] The pledge Rawlins had extracted from his chief was a supportive intervention—precisely of the sort friends in a defensive alliance devise.

When Wilson reported for duty, the colonels were skating on thinning ice. On November 20, Rowley wrote Washburne to complain about them: "Gen Grant has four Cols on his staff[.] 3 appointments by Gen Halleck[:] Lagow Regan [sic; Riggin] & Hillyer and I doubt whether either [sic] of them have gone to bed sober for a week[.] the other Col Ihrie . . . is not much better than the rest." In a follow-up four weeks later, Rowley amplified his concerns: "I fear [General Grant] will hardly have the heart to cut loose from the four Colonels. It is *very* important that it should be done. You can perhaps realize the necessity of it. Rawlins rote [sic] me last night that he would write you immediately upon the subject and state some facts. I hope that when I am called back from Columbus to find fewer loafers about head Quarters."[36]

Rowley was perceptive: Grant tried to avoid the discomfiture of sacking these men—he even kept them busy with soft deployments like transporting prisoners—especially Hillyer, an old friend from St. Louis whose wife was close to Julia. While Rowley was triangulating Washburne into the conflict, Grant was helping Hillyer order a new and larger uniform. Since joining the staff, Hillyer had gained thirty-three pounds.[37] It would take a year before Rawlins was rid of the quartet. However, Rawlins would be without Lagow for about four months. Injured after his horse fell on him at Iuka, Lagow was issued orders by Rawlins to return to his home in Palestine, Illinois, to recover.[38]

—✦—

Wilson joined the staff at a propitious moment. Grant's depleted forces had been strengthened, and he decided it was time to take the offensive. On October 26, he offered a proposal to Halleck: "With small re-enforcements at Memphis I think I would be able to move down the Mississippi Central road and cause the evacuation of Vicksburg and to be able to capture or destroy all the boats in the Yazoo River."[39] He envisioned an overland route through the middle of the state as a first step to clearing out Vicksburg. Although Halleck did not respond to this bold idea, Grant pressed forward. He concentrated forces, two divisions under Major General McPherson and three under Brigadier General Charles S. Hamilton, around Grand Junction, Tennessee, right on the Mississippi border where he would follow the Mississippi Central Railroad southward. The first objective would be Holly Springs, fifteen miles south of Grand Junction, a good place for a supply and munitions depot as the troops encroached deeper into Mississippi.

After occupying Grand Junction on November 8, the expedition moved out to confront Van Dorn's replacement, John Pemberton, a Philadelphian who shifted allegiance after marrying into a Virginia family. Despite an undistinguished record, Pemberton had risen rapidly in rank to lieutenant general. Electing to avoid a firefight, Pemberton evacuated Holly Springs on November 13, leaving the town to Grant.

About this time, Wilson shared with Grant and Rawlins news gleaned from a meeting he had had a month before in Washington, DC, with another former Shawneetown resident, Major General John McClernand. McClernand, formerly one of Grant's divisional commanders, had clashed with him over issues of authority. Chronically uncomfortable in a subordinate role, McClernand in August asked to be relieved and sent to Illinois to raise troops. He had been bucking since early summer for an independent command, and these troops might be used to fulfill that desire. A crony, Illinois Governor Richard Yates, interceded on his behalf with Stanton to arrange the transfer, and since the end of August, McClernand was posted in Springfield, Illinois, where he determinedly recruited fresh troops and organized units. Soon after returning to Illinois, he was again beneficiary of Yates's clout. Yates summoned McClernand to Washington, where in late September Yates provided him with invaluable access to the administration. McClernand met with Treasury Secretary Chase and Lincoln, explaining to both his bold proposal for an army-navy operation to open the Mississippi River and capture Vicksburg. They were receptive to the plan.

McClernand boasted to Wilson about his proposal to raise troops for taking Vicksburg; about the support he was receiving from Stanton and Lincoln; how Grant's "bad habits" were proving to be to McClernand's advantage; and how, if successful, McClernand would be awarded command of his own department. He even enticed Wilson with a plum assignment on his future staff. Wilson listened attentively and offered his opinion that Halleck would probably favor Grant for the job of taking Vicksburg.[40]

Lincoln and Stanton were sufficiently persuaded by McClernand's plans. On October 21, he received from Stanton confidential orders to begin the process of raising troops and mounting a Mississippi River expedition:

> Ordered, That Major-General McClernand be, and he is, directed to proceed to the States of Indiana, Illinois, and Iowa, to organize the troops remaining in those States and to be raised . . . and forward them . . . to Memphis, Cairo, or such other points as may hereafter be designated by the general-in-chief [i.e., Halleck], to the end that, when a sufficient force not required by the operation of General Grant's command shall be raised, an expedition may be organized under General McClernand's command against Vicksburg. . . .
>
> The forces so organized will remain subject to the designation of the general-in-chief, and be employed according to such exigencies as the service in his judgment may require.[41]

Perhaps the orders left McClernand so elated that he failed to appreciate Stanton's nuanced language: he was not assigned an independent command, just command of an "expedition"; Grant controlled the force until he no longer required it; and Halleck, who put little stock in politician-generals like McClernand, could deploy the forces elsewhere as need arose. These stipulations would soon come into play.

Wilson shared another detail from his meeting with McClernand: that he "had been specially authorized to organize and command an expedition for the specific purpose of capturing Vicksburg and opening the Mississippi."[42] There had been already some speculation in the press regarding the purpose behind McClernand's raising troops, so Wilson's disclosure didn't come as a surprise to Grant and Rawlins. Of course, no one at headquarters knew of Stanton's confidential orders to McClernand. However, Wilson's news was shocking enough given that "this was the first authentic information received at Grant's headquarters in regard to the scope of McClernand's instructions."[43] Wilson's report would have only confirmed Rawlins's opinion about McClernand's "ambition, his jealousy, and his disposition to intrigue with the politicians in Washington."[44]

———⁓———

Reports about McClernand forwarding troops to Cairo and Memphis, locations within Grant's departmental purview, left Grant and his staff wondering how McClernand's maneuverings might affect the overland incursion now underway. On November 10, Grant sought guidance from Halleck regarding this rumored independent operation. "Am I to understand that I lay still here while an Expedition is fitted out from Memphis or do you want me to push as far South as possible?" he asked Halleck. "Am I to have Sherman move subject to my order or is he & his forces reserved for some special service?" Halleck replied, "You have command of all troops sent to your department, and have permission to fight the enemy where you please."[45] In effect, Halleck reassured Grant that he, not McClernand, had authority over troops in his departmental jurisdiction.

Anxious to accelerate his campaign, Grant notified Sherman in Memphis that Halleck had given him clearance to drive south and "fight the enemy my own way." He wanted Sherman to move with three divisions, if possible, to Oxford, Mississippi, where their forces would be combined.[46] The strategy was for Sherman to wrest Vicksburg away from Pemberton while Grant kept other Rebel units from reinforcing Pemberton. Sherman left Memphis on November 26 with three divisions totaling eighteen thousand men, and he reached the Tallahatchie River a few miles north of Oxford on December 2.

Sherman was not to stay there long. Grant got wind that McClernand's move downriver was "inevitable," and "desiring to have a competent commander in charge," he ordered Sherman on December 8 to return with one of his divisions to Memphis. Time was of the essence. As Grant explained, "I feared that delay might bring McClernand, who was his senior and who had authority from the President and Secretary of War to exercise that particular command—and independently. I doubted McClernand's fitness."[47] Sherman arrived in Memphis four days later.

Meanwhile, McClernand was beside himself in Springfield. He had done the heavy lifting of organizing and sending southward regiments for the operation he believed he was sanctioned to command. Now he waited anxiously for the order unbinding him from Springfield. It came on December 17 from Secretary of War Stanton. "The operation being in General Grant's department," Stanton explained, "it is designed to organize all the troops of that department in three army corps, the First Army corps to be commanded by you, and assigned to the operation on the Mississippi under the general commanding the department."[48] Not only was McClernand's dream of independent command crushed, he was again subordinate to Grant. Ordered to proceed to Memphis, McClernand arrived on the twenty-ninth and found a dispatch from Grant placing him in command of the Thirteenth Corps. He also found Memphis devoid of the regiments he had raised and sent there. Sherman had left with them nine days before, taking them downriver to strike Confederates occupying the Chickasaw bluffs, which formed part of Vicksburg's protective bulwark.

In late October, a jaunty newspaperman appeared at Grant's Jackson, Tennessee, headquarters. The man was Sylvanus Cadwallader, a recent hire by Wilbur Storey, editor of the *Chicago Times*. Cadwallader's mission was to obtain the release from the Alton, Illinois, military prison of Warren Isham, a reporter for the *Times* and Storey's brother-in-law. Isham had caused turmoil in Washington when in August he submitted a bogus story about a fleet of British-built ironclad gunboats arriving in Mobile Bay. An unamused Grant ordered Isham's arrest. Cadwallader would pass as a correspondent to establish a connection with Grant. One of the first he met at headquarters was John Rawlins, to whom he presented his letters of introduction and credentials in order to obtain permission to work within the lines. Rawlins was polite and acquainted Cadwallader with the staff. Thus began their close friendship. Not only would Cadwallader, like Harry Wilson, serve as a lifelong champion of Rawlins's service to Grant and country, but he would name a son Rawlins to honor that friendship.[49]

Cadwallader set about establishing good relationships with headquarters staff and ranking line officers. He strove to be respectful, which included no eavesdropping or freeloading in camp. He ingratiated himself with the chief of cavalry, Lyle Dickey, who introduced him to Grant. Cadwallader appealed to Grant's tender instincts, explaining Isham's punishment was sufficient and how his family suffered without his income. Grant was moved and authorized

Isham's release. Later, Dickey persuaded Cadwallader to tag along on the ensuing overland campaign that was underway. During that troop advance, Cadwallader was invited to join Grant and staff at their breakfast table in a Bolivar, Tennessee, hotel where Hillyer was cracking up everyone with stories about the practical jokes being played on the green recruits of the 124th Illinois by the camp veterans. From this morning, Cadwallader's relationship with Rawlins and Grant steadily progressed to where he became a fixture at headquarters and one of the foremost correspondents of the war.[50]

As Cadwallader joined the army's advance, he was distressed to witness callous depredations—burning buildings, robbing houses, stealing horses and mules—perpetrated by the Federal troops during their march. He filed a blistering, fact-filled report back to the *Times*. However, he quickly second-guessed his decision to send that dispatch, fearing Grant or others might retaliate, given the *Times*'s notorious copperhead slant. Hoping to avoid Rawlins's disparaging eye, Cadwallader made himself scarce around headquarters for a while. He need not have been so apprehensive.

One evening Grant spied Cadwallader and summoned him into his office. He had no objections to the story, didn't believe in censorship, and would ban correspondents only if their dispatches contained untruths or speculation. The shameful behavior of the troops, Grant allowed, was difficult to prevent but was in flagrant violation of a set of orders, which he showed to him.[51] Rawlins had recently issued just such orders to address the chronic problem.

In Special Field Orders, No. 1, circulated on November 7, Rawlins addressed the vandalism occurring on the march, and warned "Such acts are punishable with death by the Articles of War and existing orders." He stipulated that "in future marches all men will be kept in the ranks, and regimental commanders held accountable for their good conduct." That this order had teeth was soon discovered by men of the Twentieth Illinois, who broke into a store in Jackson, Tennessee, and caused over $1,200 in damages. Rawlins assessed that amount against the regiment's officers and enlisted men and ordered two officers mustered out of the service for neglect of duty.[52]

―∾∾∾―

If Grant and his staff had bad months before, December 1862 was probably the topper. There was, of course, the anxiety engendered by the drama at Memphis. Could Sherman move quickly enough to evacuate the troops deposited there before McClernand arrived? Grant's plan during the overland campaign to "make a real attack" against Pemberton was thwarted by the latter's prefer-ence to hang back and avoid a pitched battle.[53] Then in mid-December, the Confederacy's premier cavalry fighter, Nathan Bedford Forrest, tore up miles of railroad track, destroyed Grant's Tennessee supply line, severed telegraph lines, and frustrated Union pursuers. While Forrest wreaked destruction in Tennessee, the demoted Earl Van Dorn raided Grant's massive supply depot at Holly Springs. He attacked on December 20 and found its unprepared gar-rison quick to surrender. The loss of hundreds of thousands of dollars' worth of food and ammunition was magnified when it was realized that the Holly Springs commander was second-chance recipient Colonel Robert Murphy, who had capitulated to Price at Iuka.

Theodore "Joe" Bowers, Rawlins's assistant, was at the depot making a roll of the troop strength and supplies there. He was awakened by angry threats against the sentry guarding his door. Clad in only his drawers, Bowers de-manded to know the intruders' business. He received a shocking response: "Come out here, you Yankee _ _ _ _, and we'll show you!" While distract-ing his capturers' attention, Bowers tossed his roll into the fireplace. Rawlins feared that Bowers was forced to destroy all the papers and records stored at the depot.[54] Hauled before Van Dorn, the Rebel general ordered Bowers be given a parole. He refused, assuming friendly forces would soon retake the town. To show his appreciation, Grant presented Bowers with an inscribed sword.[55]

With the supply base gone, a thoroughly vexed Grant—no doubt doubly infuriated by the fact that Julia, who had been staying in Holly Springs, nar-rowly escaped capture by Van Dorn's staff officers—was forced to suspend his overland campaign and fall back. Less than three weeks later, Rawlins issued Grant's order dismissing Murphy from service for having "failed to make any preparations for resistance or defense or show any disposition to do so."[56] De-cember ended with a disastrous thud. Sherman carried out his operation to move down river with four divisions and assail Vicksburg from the north. On the nineteenth, he wrote Rawlins, confidently predicting, "You may calculate on our being at Vicksburg by Christmas."[57] But on the twenty-ninth, Sher-man's frontal assaults against the Confederate defenders of the Chickasaw Bluffs were repeatedly repulsed. It was sheer slaughter.

In the middle of these stinging setbacks can be added Grant's issuance of General Orders Number 11. To say these orders generated controversy is an un-derstatement. Reactions to it reverberated from headquarters to Washington and back, causing a boilover between commander and chief of staff. The source of trouble was the chronic problem of traders' eagerness to profit from cotton, and on this point Rawlins and Grant were in fundamental agreement: both "abominated cotton buyers as a class."[58]

The grab for cotton in west Tennessee and Mississippi only intensified, and traders required a staggering degree of oversight. Speculators hounded authorities for permits, and these authorities scrambled to abide by trading policies that seemed to change daily. Writing from Grant's supply depot before its capture, a *Chicago Tribune* correspondent reported, "If ever a community were . . . afflicted with a disgusting moral malady, it is the crowds of speculators and vagrants which have congregated at Holly Springs to deal in cotton—they have 'cotton' on the brain—every one of them."[59] It seemed that almost everyone, civilian and military, hankered for a piece of action—and some people profited handsomely, including enterprising crewmen of Union vessels patrolling the river channels. Because of the peculiar interpretation of international law concerning the capture of naval vessels, prizes could be taken where they were found. This legal loophole caused the crews of federal gunboats in the Mississippi Valley to focus on capturing cotton, which could be lawfully divided as a naval prize. Many naval officers and crew members of western gunboats amassed fortunes.[60] Some among this avaricious multitude were familiar faces.

One such face belonged to J. Russell Jones, the US marshal who had arrested David Sheean. While trolling for cotton, Jones stopped to pay respects to Grant and fellow Galenians. It is not known whether Rawlins had a choice word or two for Jones, but it wouldn't have flustered him. Jones was having too high a time lining his pockets. As Cadwallader Washburn mentioned to his brother, "Saw Russ Jones in Grant's Boat. He will go down to Vicksburgh. He told me that he . . . made about $15,000 down at Oxford."[61] Jesse Grant took a steamboat south to visit his son, arriving during the height of the McClernand drama in the company of three new business partners. They were the Mack brothers, Henry, Harmon, and Simon—and they happened to be Jewish. They planned to buy cotton and split the profits with Jesse in return for him influencing his son, the general, to make all the necessary permits appear. When Grant understood the crux of this plan, he angrily dispatched the Mack brothers northward without permits.[62]

Shortly thereafter, a fuming Grant had Rawlins issue the soon-to-become notorious General Orders No. 11:

The Jews, as a class violating every regulation of trade established by the Treasury Department and also Department orders, are hereby expelled from the Department.

Post Commanders will see that all of this class of people be furnished passes and required to leave, and any one returning after such notification, will be arrested and held in confinement until an opportunity occurs of sending them out as prisoners, unless furnished with permits from headquarters.

No passes will be given these people to visit headquarters for the purpose of making personal application for trade permits.[63]

—◦◦◦—

The anxious weeks dealing with sniping critics, an insolent subordinate, marauding enemy raiders, inscrutable government trading policies, and Jesse's scandalous appeal for favoritism left Grant so frazzled that he lashed out. As historian Stephen Ash surmised, "The Jews thus became for Grant and his harassed officers a convenient symbol of all the frustrations and annoyances with which they were contending."[64]

Rawlins, acting like an attorney to prevent his client from making incriminating disclosures, counseled against posting the order. Rawlins was one of few who could give Grant his unvarnished opinions. "You countermanded such an order two weeks ago," Rawlins reminded him, referring to a similar order issued by Colonel John DuBois at Holly Springs. In crude language, DuBois had set about expelling from the town "All Cotton-Speculators, Jews and other Vagrants." Grant rebuffed Rawlins's logical argument. "Well, they can countermand this from Washington if they like," he snapped, "but we will issue it anyhow."[65]

Grant had singled out Jews earlier for discriminatory treatment. In November, he issued orders to General Hurlbut and Colonel Joseph Webster to restrict the movement of Jews. Webster, the superintendent of railroads, was to instruct his conductors "that no Jews are to be permitted to travel on the Rail Road southward from any point."[66] Moreover, antisemitic sentiments were also expressed by Grant's subordinates. For example, Brigadier General Alvin Hovey complained that "unprincipled sharpers and Jews" were supplying the enemy; Sherman reported to Rawlins that he refused to respect new permits being issued to "swarms of Jews."[67] But because General Orders No. 11 came from Grant, the racist content would find a way to leak out of his department.

Some of the most significant leaking was done by an understandably aggrieved Jewish businessman, Cesar Kaskel in Paducah, who appealed directly to Lincoln. Ironically, Lincoln was preoccupied with his proclamation to free the slaves while Grant was intent on expelling the Jews.[68] On January 3, Kaskel met with Lincoln and showed him a copy of the order, which appalled him. The next day, Halleck telegraphed Grant: "A paper purporting to be General Orders, No. 11, issued by you December 17, has been presented here.... If such an order has been issued, it will be immediately revoked."[69]

Luckily for Grant, the uproar against the order was not long-lasting. Democrats in the House and Senate put forward resolutions to condemn the order, but they were quickly tabled. Reliable Elihu Washburne led the fight in the House to table. What lingered, however, was speculation regarding Grant's motive behind the order. Historian John Y. Simon provided a psychoanalytical explanation utilizing the defense mechanism known as displacement: unable to muster the courage to give his domineering father the boot, Grant expelled the Jews instead.[70] Bertram Korn cited sources to support his contention that authorities in Washington directly commanded Grant, or otherwise prompted him, to issue the order. Korn came to this conclusion "even through [sic] no such dispatch or messages . . . appear in any known collections of war documents."[71] On the other hand, historian Jonathan Sarna doubts any such order came from Washington. He cites testimony from a telegraph officer who was in the White House when General Orders No. 11 was issued, claiming that there were in Washington only three men (presumably Lincoln, Stanton, and Halleck) who had authority to so order Grant, and none of them is known to have done so.[72]

During the run-up to the 1868 presidential election, Grant's candidacy revived questions about the expulsion order, and Rawlins offered his own explanation for what actuated Grant to issue it. Rawlins's explanation appeared in the June 23 issue of the *New York Herald* as a measured response to Lewis N. Dembitz of Louisville, Kentucky, a Jew and ardent Republican:

> The most stringent orders had previously been published forbidding persons going or coming through our lines, limiting traders to certain boundaries and prohibiting the passage of corn South or the payment of it for Southern products. Persistent violators of these orders by persons principally of the Jewish race were the subjects of constant reports by many of General Grant's subordinates, some of whom had even issued orders expelling them from the lines but which General Grant had promptly revoked. . . . At length, on the evening of December 17, 1862 . . . the mail brought from Washington a large number of complaints, officially referred to him by the General-in-Chief of the army, against this class of persons for violations of the above mentioned orders. The

general felt, on reading them, that some immediate action was demanded of him. He realized to the full extent the critical condition of military affairs and judged, whether wisely or unwisely, that to meet the exigency action must be immediate, thorough and in a form not to be evaded. The order you refer to was the result....

The idea that it was issued on account of the religion of the Jews cannot be seriously entertained by any one who knows the General's steadfast adherence to the principles of American liberty and religious toleration.[73]

Thus, Rawlins explained that the complaints Halleck sent compelled Grant to take swift action. But is Rawlins, perhaps, only giving a partial explanation? If his account of the complaints is true, would they provide Grant with reason enough to feel justified in taking punitive action, especially if the inclination to do so was already in place? Given the disgust Grant felt that day toward the Jews, it would seem that a last straw, like a sheaf of complaints arriving from Washington, could have precipitated a full-scale blow-up. On the same day he issued "The Order," December 17, he wrote an angry letter to Christopher Wolcott, assistant secretary of war, railing against "Jews and other unprincipled traders." Grant told Wolcott that he had "instructed the Commdg Officer at Columbus to refuse all permits to Jews to come South, and frequently have them expelled from the Dept. but they come in with their Carpet sacks in spite of all that can be done to prevent it."[74]

Two other points Rawlins made in his reply to Dembitz bear comment. Korn takes Rawlins to task for coming to Grant's defense in such a way as to "misrepresent an essential phrase of The Order." Was Rawlins drawing on a hazy recollection when he said the order was written "leaving all persons not justly amenable to its terms to be relieved on their individual application"? This was not Grant's intent, because his order stipulated, "No passes will be given these people to visit headquarters for the purpose of making personal application for trade permits." The second point is Rawlins's assurance that a tolerant man such as Grant would not use religion as a basis for issuing an order of expulsion. However, what the order likely exposed was how Grant shared the prevailing antisemitic and racial stereotypes. The national outpouring of disapproval to General Orders No. 11 taught him a lesson about tolerance and American liberties. Julia later wrote that he felt the disapproval was deserved and that "he had no right to make an order against any special sect."[75] Bertram Korn commended President Grant because he later "came to bury the prejudice which expressed itself in The Order" by appointing Jews to a number of public offices. He also made diplomatic efforts to address the persecution of Jews in Romania and Russia.[76]

—◊◊◊—

The tribulations caused by troublesome subordinates, cotton traders, slaves flooding into Union lines, and hostile newspaper editors needed to be set aside. Sherman's costly setback at Chickasaw Bluffs needed to be processed and surmounted. Eyes were to be focused, Rawlins would remind Grant, on one prize, the prize Grant informed Halleck about only days into the new year: "I will start for Memphis immediately and will do everything possible for the capture of Vicksburg."[77]

NOTES

1. Ulysses S. Grant, *Personal Memoirs* (New York: Charles L. Webster, 1885), 1:395.

2. John Y. Simon, ed., *The Papers of Ulysses S. Grant* (Carbondale: Southern Illinois University Press, 1977), 6:177n3.

3. Ibid., 177–78n8.

4. U. S. Grant to J. C. Kelton, October 22, 1862, in *The Papers of Ulysses S. Grant*, ed. John Y. Simon, 6:168–76.

5. Dabney H. Maury, *Recollections of a Virginian in the Mexican, Indian, and Civil Wars* (New York: Charles Scribner's Sons, 1894), 160.

6. William M. Lamers, *The Edge of Glory: A Biography of General William S. Rosecrans, U.S.A.* (New York: Harcourt, Brace and World, 1961), 117.

7. U. S. Grant to Elihu B. Washburne, November 7, 1862, in *The Papers of Ulysses S. Grant*, ed. John Y. Simon, 6:275.

8. Ulysses S. Grant, *Personal Memoirs*, 1:419.

9. William S. Rosecrans, "The Battle of Corinth," in *Battles and Leaders of the Civil War*, ed. Robert Underwood Johnson and Clarence Clough Buel (1887; repr., New York: Thomas Yoseloff, 1956), 2:755.

10. John Y. Simon, ed., *The Papers of Ulysses S. Grant*, 6:166–67n.

11. John Y. Simon, ed., *The Personal Memoirs of Julia Dent Grant* (New York: G. P. Putnam's Sons, 1977), 104.

12. John Y. Simon, ed., *The Papers of Ulysses S. Grant*, 6:177n3.

13. W. S. Rosecrans to H. W. Halleck, October 22, 1862, in *The War of the Rebellion: A Compilation of the Official Records of the Union and Confederate Armies*, series 1, part 2, 17:286–87.

14. Edwin M. Stanton to Maj. Gen. Rosecrans, October 23, 1862, in *The War of the Rebellion: A Compilation of the Official Records of the Union and Confederate Armies*, series 1, part 2, 17:291.

15. William S. Hillyer to William T. Sherman, October 29, 1862, in *The War of the Rebellion: A Compilation of the Official Records of the Union and Confederate Armies*, series 1, part 2, 17:307.

16. U. S. Grant to Elihu B. Washburne, November 7, 1862, in *The Papers of Ulysses S. Grant*, ed. John Y. Simon, 6:275.

17. John Y. Simon, ed., *The Papers of Ulysses S. Grant*, 6:256n4.

18. S. A. Hurlbut to John A. Rawlins, September 18, 1862, in *The War of the Rebellion: A Compilation of the Official Records of the Union and Confederate Armies*, series 1, part 2, 17:226.

19. W. T. Sherman to John A. Rawlins, September 12, 1862, in *The War of the Rebellion: A Compilation of the Official Records of the Union and Confederate Armies*, series 1, part 2, 17:215–16.

20. John Y. Simon, ed., *The Papers of Ulysses S. Grant*, 6:111n1.

21. Ibid., 137n1.

22. Special Field Orders No. 1, November 7, 1862, in *The Papers of Ulysses S. Grant*, ed. John Y. Simon, 6:266.

23. John Y. Simon, ed., *The Papers of Ulysses S. Grant*, 6:144–45n4.

24. General Orders No. 6, November 11, 1862, in *The Papers of Ulysses S. Grant*, ed. John Y. Simon, 6:294–95.

25. John Y. Simon, ed., *The Papers of Ulysses S. Grant*, 6:449.

26. Special Orders No. 159, October 16, 1862, in *The War of the Rebellion: A Compilation of the Official Records of the Union and Confederate Armies*, series 1, part 2, 17:278.

27. General Orders No. 6, November 11, 1862, in *The Papers of Ulysses S. Grant*, ed. John Y. Simon, 6:294–95. After removing General Webster as chief of staff, Grant appointed him superintendent of military railroads; ADCs Lagow, Hillyer, Riggin, and Rowley were given additional duties as acting inspector general, provost marshal general, superintendent of military telegraphs, and mustering officer, respectively.

28. James Harrison Wilson, *Under the Old Flag* (New York: D. Appleton, 1912), 133, 135.

29. Edward G. Longacre, *From Union Stars to Top Hat: A Biography of the Extraordinary General James Harrison Wilson* (Harrisburg, PA: Stackpole, 1972), 32–33, 38.

30. James Harrison Wilson, *Under the Old Flag*, 1:133, 135.

31. Ibid., 136, 138.

32. Ibid., 137.

33. Ibid., 140.

34. Ibid., 136, 137.

35. James Harrison Wilson, *The Life of John A. Rawlins* (New York: Neale, 1916), 100. Rawlins believed in the power of abstinence pledges, but whether he induced Grant to write and sign one, as Wilson claimed, is an open question. Dana said that "at the beginning of the war he gave him [Rawlins] his word of honor not to touch a drop as long as it lasted." But Dana did not indicate whether this was a written or verbal pledge or how and from whom he learned of it. See Charles A. Dana, *Recollections of the Civil War* (New York: D. Appleton, 1902), 73. Perhaps the intervening years distorted Wilson's memory of the event. Just three weeks before Wilson's arrival, an abstinence pledge in Hillyer's handwriting had been drawn up and signed by him, Rowley, Lagow, and Rawlins: "We pledge our honor that from the time of signing this paper until the 14th day of November we will altogether abstain from the use of any intoxicating liquor." Under his signature, Rawlins added a commitment to uphold this pledge "forever and may my children curse me if I deviate." On the reverse, Rawlins penned a poignant endorsement: "This pledge signed by me shall never be broken. Teach my boy its great value, tell him his father was never a drunkard, but signed this that he might exert a proper influence on those with whom and under whom he

served his country, that this influence has shed light upon the American name." See Pledge of Abstinence, October 14, 1862, William Hillyer Papers, Box 1, 1862 Military Papers, in the Albert and Shirley Small Special Collections Library, University of Virginia.

36. John Y. Simon, ed., *The Papers of Ulysses S. Grant*, 7:32n1.

37. U. S. Grant to Richardson, Spence and Thompson, December 15, 1862, in *The Papers of Ulysses S. Grant*, ed. John Y. Simon, 7:45.

38. John Y. Simon, ed., *The Papers of Ulysses S. Grant*, 6:295n1.

39. U. S. Grant to H. W. Halleck, October 26, 1862, in *The War of the Rebellion: A Compilation of the Official Records of the Union and Confederate Armies*, series 1, part 2, 17:296.

40. Richard L. Kiper, *Major General John Alexander McClernand: Politician in Uniform* (Kent, OH: Kent State University Press, 1999), 135–36; James Harrison Wilson, *Under the Old Flag*, 1:119–21;

41. Edwin M. Stanton, October 21, 1862, in *The War of the Rebellion: A Compilation of the Official Records of the Union and Confederate Armies*, series 1, part 2, 17:282.

42. James Harrison Wilson, *Under the Old Flag*, 1:145.

43. James Harrison Wilson, *The Life of John A. Rawlins*, 103.

44. James Harrison Wilson, *Under the Old Flag*, 1:138.

45. U. S. Grant to H. W. Halleck, November 10, 1862, in *The War of the Rebellion: A Compilation of the Official Records of the Union and Confederate Armies*, series 1, part 1, 17:469; H. W. Halleck to U. S. Grant, November 11, 1862, in *The War of the Rebellion: A Compilation of the Official Records of the Union and Confederate Armies*, series 1, part 1, 17:469.

46. U. S. Grant to William T. Sherman, November 14, 1862, in *The War of the Rebellion: A Compilation of the Official Records of the Union and Confederate Armies*, series 1, part 2, 17:347–48.

47. Ulysses S. Grant, *Personal Memoirs*, 1:428–30.

48. Edwin M. Stanton to Major General McClernand, December 17, 1862, in *The War of the Rebellion: A Compilation of the Official Records of the Union and Confederate Armies*, series 1, part 2, 17:420.

49. Benjamin P. Thomas, ed., *Three Years with Grant as Recalled by War Correspondent Sylvanus Cadwallader* (New York: Alfred A. Knopf, 1961), xii; Rawlins Cadwallader, born in 1866, became a highly respected obstetrician.

50. Ibid., 10–14, 16–18.

51. Ibid., 21–22.

52. Special Field Orders, No. 1, November 7, 1862, in *The War of the Rebellion: A Compilation of the Official Records of the Union and Confederate Armies*, series 1, part 2, 17:326–27; Special Field Orders, No. 6, November 16, 1862, in *The War of the Rebellion: A Compilation of the Official Records of the Union and Confederate Armies*, series 1, part 2, 17:349–50.

53. U. S. Grant to H. W. Halleck, December 8, 1862, in *The War of the Rebellion: A Compilation of the Official Records of the Union and Confederate Armies*, series 1, part 1, 17:474.

54. J. A. Rawlins to Enos Ripley, December 20, 1862, U. S. Grant Presidential Library, Mississippi State University, Series 2, Box 10, Folder 66.

55. Albert D. Richardson, *Personal History of Ulysses S. Grant*, 280–82.

56. Special Orders, No. 4, January 8, 1863, in *The War of the Rebellion: A Compilation of the Official Records of the Union and Confederate Armies*, series 1, part 1, 17:516.

57. December 19, 1862, in *The War of the Rebellion: A Compilation of the Official Records of the Union and Confederate Armies*, series 1, part 1, 17:603.

58. Benjamin P. Thomas, ed., *Three Years with Grant as Recalled by War Correspondent Sylvanus Cadwallader*, 22.

59. *Chicago Tribune*, December 18, 1862.

60. E. Merton Coulter, "Commercial Intercourse with the Confederacy in the Mississippi Valley 1861–1865," *Mississippi Valley Historical Review* 5, no. 4 (1919): 392.

61. C. C. Washburn to Elihu Washburne, January 28, 1863, in Mark Washburne, *A Biography of Elihu Benjamin Washburne Congressman, Secretary of State, Envoy Extraordinary*, 2:233.

62. Bruce Catton, *Grant Moves South* (Boston: Little, Brown, 1960), 352–53.

63. General Orders, No. 11, December 17, 1862, in *The War of the Rebellion: A Compilation of the Official Records of the Union and Confederate Armies*, series 1, part 2, 17:424.

64. Stephen V. Ash, "Civil War Exodus: The Jews and Grant's General Orders No. 11," *The Historian* 44, no. 4 (1982): 509.

65. Albert D. Richardson, *Personal History of Ulysses S. Grant*, 275; John Y. Simon, ed., *The Papers of Ulysses S. Grant*, 7:9n1; U. S. Grant to J. V. DuBois, December 9, 1862, in *The Papers of Ulysses S. Grant*, ed. John Y. Simon, 7:8.

66. U. S. Grant to S. A. Hurlbut, November 9, 1862, in *The Papers of Ulysses S. Grant*, ed. John Y. Simon, 7:283; U. S. Grant to Joseph Webster, November 10, 1862, in *The Papers of Ulysses S. Grant*, ed. John Y. Simon, 7:283n.

67. Report of Brigadier General Alvin P. Hovey, December 3, 1862, in *The War of the Rebellion: A Compilation of the Official Records of the Union and Confederate Armies*, series 1, part 1, 17:532; W. T. Sherman to J. A. Rawlins, July 30, 1862, in *The War of the Rebellion: A Compilation of the Official Records of the Union and Confederate Armies*, series 1, part 2, 17:141.

68. Jonathan D. Sarna, *When General Grant Expelled the Jews* (New York: Schocken, 2012), 11.

69. H. W. Halleck to U. S. Grant, January 4, 1863, in *The War of the Rebellion: A Compilation of the Official Records of the Union and Confederate Armies*, series 1, part 2, 17:530.

70. John Y. Simon, ed., *The Papers of Ulysses S. Grant*, 7:53 note.

71. Bertram W. Korn, *American Jewry and the Civil War* (Cleveland: Meridian, 1961), 140.

72. Jonathan D. Sarna, *When General Grant Expelled the Jews*, 46.

73. *New York Herald*, June 23, 1868.

74. U. S. Grant to C. P. Wolcott, December 17, 1862, in *The Papers of Ulysses S. Grant*, ed. John Y. Simon, 7:56.

75. John Y. Simon, ed., *The Personal Memoirs of Julia Dent Grant*, 107.

76. Bertram W. Korn, *American Jewry and the Civil War*, 145–46.

77. U. S. Grant to H. W. Halleck, January 9, 1863, in *The Papers of Ulysses S. Grant*, Vol. VII, ed. John Y. Simon, 7:204.

James Dawson Rawlins, father of John.

The History of Jo Daviess County, Illinois
(Chicago: H. F. Kett, 1878).

Emily Smith Rawlins, first wife of John.

Galena and U. S. Grant Museum,
Galena, IL.

A Henry E. Henning photo of a beardless John Rawlins, as he appeared in 1861.

Galena and U. S. Grant Museum, Galena, IL.

William Rowley, Galena neighbor of Rawlins and member of Grant's staff.

Galena and U. S. Grant Museum, Galena, IL.

Courtroom in Jo Daviess County Courthouse,
scene of April 1861 speech.

Galena and U. S. Grant Museum,
Galena, IL.

Grant and Staff in Cairo, IL, October 1861.
Surrounding Grant, clockwise from top left:
Clark Lagow, John Rawlins, William Hillyer,
and Dr. James Simons.

Facing, Brigadier General John Rawlins.

National Archives photo no. 111-BA-1611
(Brady Collection).

John Rawlins (*seated second from left*), Ely Parker
(*seated second from right*), and others at City Point, Virginia.

Library of Congress Prints and Photographs Division,
Washington, DC.

Facing, John Rawlins; wife, Emma; and daughter Jennie
outside their log hut at City Point, Virginia.

Library of Congress Prints and Photographs,
Washington, DC.

Rawlins, Grant, and Theodore "Joe" Bowers at City Point.

Library of Congress Prints and Photographs,
Washington, DC.

Grant and staff on April 12, 1865, captured in a Matthew Brady photograph
taken shortly after their return from Appomattox; Ulysses Grant (*seated*)
is flanked to his right by John Rawlins and on his left by the gray-bearded
Brevet Major General Marsena Patrick, provost marshal general.

Photo No. 111-B-13, National Archives Collection.

A late image of a gaunt John Rawlins.

Library of Congress Prints and Photographs,
Washington, DC.

Grenville Dodge surveying party: *Back row (left to right)*:
Lt. J. W. Wheelan, Lt. Col. J. K. Mizner (commanding escort),
Dr. Henry C. Terry, John E. Corwith; *front row (left to right)*:
David Van Lennep (geologist), John R. Duff, Gen. Dodge,
John Rawlins, Major William Dunn.

Rawlins Statue in Rawlins Park, Washington, DC.

Photo by Melissa A. Winn.

14

"I Am Surprised, Col. Duff, at Your Discourteous and Unmilitary Remarks"

JOHN RAWLINS BEGAN 1863 ON a high note: his friend was out of prison, and he had been promoted to lieutenant colonel and appointed chief of staff while retaining duties as assistant adjutant general. Moreover, Grant sang Rawlins's praise to Halleck—"absolutely indispensable" was how Grant described him.[1] Grant's star could only ascend after a dismal December. Despite the Holly Springs debacle, the abandonment of his advance through central Mississippi, and blowback from the order expelling Jews, he faced January undeterred. His sights were trained on Vicksburg, but there would be no replicating the overland strategy, which he said would be seen as a "backward movement."[2] Instead of following a rail line, the Union army would take the river road. Grant signaled in a January 13 letter to McPherson his intent "to command the expedition down the river *in person* [italics added]."[3] This would be *his* expedition, not McClernand's. To facilitate this move, Rawlins was already dispatching orders directing troop deployments.

On January 30, Rawlins issued the order announcing Grant's assumption of command. It assigned McClernand and his Thirteenth Corps to the Mississippi's west bank. A stunned McClernand complained that Grant's order "conflicts with the order of the Secretary of War, made under the personal direction of the President, bearing date October 21, 1862."[4] McClernand's belief he had been entitled to independent command had just been shaken.

On January 16, Grant, Rawlins, and Wilson left Memphis on a four-day excursion that included visiting McClernand's and Sherman's troops encamped near Vicksburg at Young's Point and Milliken's Bend. On the sixteenth, Grant huddled with Sherman, McClernand, and his naval commander, Rear

Admiral David Dixon Porter, at Napoleon, Arkansas.[5] A convivial Grant encouraged Rawlins and Wilson to participate in the collaborative discussion about all aspects of the upcoming campaign.[6] During the trip, Grant learned that his army and navy commanders doubted McClernand's fitness to command, a finding he shared with Halleck after returning to Memphis.[7]

Rawlins and Grant had one week in Memphis to make final preparations and entrust the continued occupation of the city to Hurlbut. Before they left again for Young's Point, Dr. Edward Kittoe, a Galena physician and surgeon on the medical staff, recollected an incident in which Grant couldn't resist teasing his chief of staff for his propensity to burst into profanity:

> I was smoking a cigar with the General in his room when a dispatch arrived which provoked Gen. Rawlins, the chief of staff, and which Rawlins read to the General, and with some pretty rough oaths urged him to take summary measures with a prominent General who had, I believe, disobeyed or transcended orders. The General, in his good-humored way turned to me and asked: "Do you know what I keep Rawlins for?" I replied no, unless it was on account of his valuable services. "I'll tell you what for. I never swear myself, so I keep him to do it for me when occasion needs."[8]

One of Rawlins's last acts before boarding the headquarters steamer, *Magnolia*, was to issue, for the sake of troop discipline, Special Orders No. 26, which decreed, "The bars on all boats in Government service in this department will be closed, and no spirituous, vinous, or malt liquors will be allowed to be sold on boats or in the camps. Card-playing and gaming is also strictly prohibited."[9]

Considering the challenge facing the Army of the Tennessee, it would need all the discipline it could muster: after the four-day visit that included consulting with his chief lieutenants, Grant wrote Halleck that taking Vicksburg, protected by fortified bluffs, would require time and a large force.[10] Confederate defenders had constructed a fearsome array of batteries atop the hills stretching northeast to Haynes' Bluff overlooking the Yazoo River southward to Warrenton, Mississippi, about five miles south of Vicksburg. The city's flanks were protected by natural defenses—swamps, bayous, serpentine channels—that restricted infantry movements.

Grant and staff returned to the Vicksburg vicinity, landing at Young's Point, Louisiana, on January 28. That day Grant, accompanied by McClernand, Sherman, McPherson, Rawlins, Wilson, and others, performed a reconnaissance of an incomplete canal dug across the base of a narrow peninsula, known as DeSoto Point, that jutted into the Mississippi River across from Vicksburg.

The peninsula's location meant that vessels attempting to steam past Vicksburg had to twist around a hairpin turn while being exposed to artillery fire. The canal, known as the Williams cut-off, was begun the previous summer by Brigadier General Thomas Williams, who thought if it were dug deep and wide enough, Union ships could pass through the mile-wide peninsula and bypass enemy batteries. However, falling river water and illnesses shut down the project. Now the canal looked like a soggy ditch, perhaps a rod wide and a dozen feet deep.

Rawlins and Harry Wilson paired off and rode to the southern end of the canal. Wilson expressed serious misgivings about its feasibility. While standing at the canal's edge and watching water trickle through, Rawlins also had doubts. "What's the use of a canal unless it can be dug at least fifty feet deeper?" Rawlins asked. "This ditch will never wash out large enough in all the ages to admit our steamboats." The two friends sat down on a felled cottonwood. Here, Wilson said he gave Rawlins his frank opinion regarding the options for capturing Vicksburg. According to Wilson, there were but three: turn it by the left through the Yazoo Pass, land troops at the wharf and carry the city by direct attack, or run boats past the batteries and march troops below the city. Rawlins was intrigued by this third option but thought it risky: wouldn't the lightly armored gunboats and transports be vulnerable to artillery fire? Wilson replied he had seen such daring naval maneuvers work while at Port Royal, South Carolina. There, he witnessed Union gunboats steam around the harbor's fortifications while sustaining surprisingly little damage.

After considering this option, the friends found themselves agreeing on a related topic: that the Vicksburg campaign should not be abandoned; to do so would "be fatal to Grant and sure to be greatly discouraging to the country." While riding back to the *Magnolia*, Rawlins contemplated Wilson's argument for running the batteries. "Wilson, I believe you are right," Rawlins concluded, "and I shall advise Grant to carry your plan into effect at once."[11]

—✧—

Rawlins's earliest opportunity to "advise" his chief likely occurred two days later at headquarters. Grant hosted his corps commanders and engineers to mull over options for mounting an offensive. At a lull in the discussion, Rawlins summoned his courage to put a fresh idea before the West Pointers.

"Wilson and I have a project of our own for taking Vicksburg," he began. Except Wilson wasn't in the room; he had been ordered to Helena, Arkansas, to head an engineering project to reduce a levee at a place on the Mississippi called Yazoo Pass, thereby causing the flooding water to carve a channel large enough to allow vessels through the pass.

General Sherman's curiosity was mildly aroused, and he asked, "What is it?"

Rawlins had suddenly put himself on a limb, but he plunged ahead. "Why, not to dig a ditch, but to use the great one already dug by Nature—the Mississippi River; protect our transports with cotton bales, run them by the batteries at night, and march the men down the Louisiana shore, ready to be ferried across."

Sherman, who once had been thought crazy for ideas he held about how to win the war, sputtered in disagreement. "What! These boats? These transports? These mere shells? They wouldn't live a minute in the face of the enemy's guns."

Grant listened intently to this exchange but stayed silent.[12] It was a plan he himself had in mind if all else failed. He often withdrew into a small office on the *Magnolia*, thinking deeply about how to foil the Vicksburg defenses. But he was not ready to reveal, even to his closest staff, the cards he might play. Reflecting back to this critical period in his *Memoirs*, Grant said, "I had in contemplation the whole winter the movement by land to a point below Vicksburg from which to operate."[13] However, incessant rains and high water afforded no dry footing for infantry movement. Until the ground solidified in spring, Grant committed his troops to conduct a "series of experiments"—five major canal projects and expeditions through flooded bayous—that might lead to the high ground east of the Mississippi or bypass Vicksburg's defenses. Although Grant expressed little confidence in these experiments, he hoped one might pan out. There was time to give them a try. At worst, the projects would keep the troops busy, mollify an impatient public, perhaps lighten the mood of the critical press, and give Pemberton pause to wonder what he was planning.[14]

In his biography of Rawlins, Wilson gave Rawlins (and himself) substantial credit for Grant's running of the Vicksburg batteries: "Each of the other possible plans [i.e., the 'experiments'] received the preference over his; but as each in turn proved abortive, it strengthened him correspondingly in the advocacy of and the ultimate success of the one which he [Rawlins] brought forward. He lost no opportunity thereafter of advocating it, and finally, when every other plan had been tried and failed, he had the satisfaction of seeing Grant openly adopt this one and carry it through to a brilliant conclusion."[15] Yet Grant acknowledges neither Rawlins nor Wilson in his *Memoirs*. It is hard to imagine that Grant would not have conceived of the same plan, especially in light of the success achieved the previous summer by David Farragut. Following his capture of New Orleans, Farragut carried out an operation against Vicksburg, running his boats past and under the Confederate guns. That Rawlins or Wilson can lay claim to Grant's having adopted the plan is, in the word of one scholar of Grant's Civil War staff, "spurious."[16] Although it is not known how greatly Rawlins (or Wilson) influenced Grant, it seems more likely Rawlins's role was as a "persistent advocate" for the idea.[17]

—◦◦◦—

Grant wasted no time employing Sherman's troops on the first experiment, enlarging the canal started by General William at DeSoto Point. They were assisted by runaway slaves pressed into work details. Rawlins monitored the progress, optimistically informing Wilson on February 16, "I have great hopes of the 'Canal' here. In ten days it ought to be completed."[18] Twelve days later and with the work unfinished, Rawlins's enthusiasm had hardly dimmed, as he conveyed to Wilson: "The river has risen very much and impeded the work on the Canal here considerably, but we shall be able to resume it tomorrow. It is bound to succeed as a canal. You know I have taken large stock in its success."[19] Despite strenuous physical efforts and two steam-powered dredging machines, sickness, flooding, and Rebel shelling doomed the project before March was out.

While work began at the Williams canal, another project, the Yazoo Pass Expedition, a combined army-navy operation, got underway. It held promise as the one experiment that might succeed. Brigadier General Leonard Ross led a division of over four thousand troops, and Lieutenant Commander Watson Smith, a cautious seaman in delicate health, commanded the flotilla. Harry Wilson, to his self-satisfaction, was Grant's choice as supervising engineer, thus assuring that Rawlins maintained an interest in the expedition's progress. Wilson and Rawlins would exchange a close correspondence over its six-week duration.

On February 3, Wilson launched the expedition with a bang by detonating a charge to cut the levee at the Yazoo Pass. The pass lay opposite and below Helena, Arkansas, and far above Vicksburg. It was hoped the resulting flooding would spill into the Yazoo tributaries and allow a flotilla of ironclads, gunboats, and troop transports to proceed through the pass; wend a circuitous route through the Coldwater, Tallahatchie, and Yazoo Rivers; and get the infantry onto high ground east of Vicksburg and above the Rebel batteries north of Vicksburg at Snyder's Bluff. The next day, a delighted Wilson described to Rawlins how results exceeded expectations: "About 7 o'clock, after discharging a mine in the mouth of the cut, the water rushed. . . . By 11 p.m. the opening was 40 yards wide, and the water pouring through like nothing else I ever saw except Niagara Falls. Logs, trees, and great masses of earth were torn away with the greatest ease."[20]

The flotilla progressed slowly through tortuous waterways that the pesky Rebels often obstructed with felled trees. In the bayous, the cautious Watson Smith appeared to Wilson to be out of his element. Wilson was too brazen to keep to himself his criticism of Smith. At headquarters, Rawlins cheered Wilson on: "Every one here is delighted with your success, in getting into the Coldwater, for whatever light we may hope for in the movement against Vicksburg comes from that direction." And Rawlins acknowledged Wilson's frustration with Commander Smith, "I wish to God I were with you. I could at least sympathize with you."[21]

On March 11, Smith's flotilla approached a hastily constructed fortification—cotton bales shored up with mounds of sand and earth—erected near the point where the Yalobusha and Tallahatchie Rivers meet to form the Yazoo. The Confederates dubbed it Fort Pemberton and armed it with light guns. Smith's gunboats had scant room to mass their fire and took a drubbing from the Rebel artillery. Unable to reduce the fort, Smith was forced to withdraw to Helena.

During the middle of the fight, Wilson wrote Rawlins, complaining, "Smith, you doubtless have understood by this time, I don't regard as the equal of Lord Nelson. . . . Commodore Smith is entirely responsible for the detention at this point and the consequent failure of the expedition, and responsible for no other reason than his timid and slow movements." After the expedition was stymied, Wilson unleashed more anti-Smith diatribe to Rawlins: "His Excellency Acting Rear-Admiral Commodore Smith left to-day for a more salubrious climate, very sick, giving his opinion that the present force of iron-clads could not take the two rebel guns in our front. . . . We have thrown away a magnificent chance to injure the enemy, and all because of the culpable and inexcusable slowness of the naval commander . . . I can't begin to give you an idea of my disgust."[22]

A third project was simultaneously underway. Above Vicksburg and close to the Arkansas-Louisiana border lay Lake Providence, a small landlocked body of water. A levee separated the lake from the Mississippi. By reducing that levee, a flood of water might create a channel through a maze of bayous and rivers to allow naval vessels to bypass the Vicksburg defenses and emerge miles below. McPherson had the engineering credentials to merit the assignment. He put an infantry division to work, but the need for dredging and removing cypress stumps that clogged the channel proved too much to overcome. Two other attempts to turn Vicksburg's flanks fizzled. The canal cut at Duckport, Louisiana, between Milliken's Bend and Vicksburg failed due to falling river water. The Steele's Bayou Expedition was thwarted when an alert enemy felled trees to block Porter's vessels.

The ill-fated experiments failed to discourage Grant who expected little to be gained by them. Rainy weather was a hardship on the troops; outbreaks of measles and smallpox added to their woe. Grant chose to look on the bright side: "the loss of life was much less than might have been expected."[23] However, as Grant's soldiers and sailors sloshed through the bayous, detractors within and critics without questioned his competence and leadership.

Criticism of Grant commonly coursed through private back channels. This was the hidden communication meant to malign Grant's character that Rawlins was powerless to prevent. About all Rawlins could do was to make sure that Grant minimized the amount of ammunition critics could use against him. One source of such clandestine trouble was Brigadier General Charles S. Hamilton, a classmate of Grant's at West Point, who now commanded a division in Hurlbut's corps. The previous year in the East, he succeeded in aggravating George McClellan, which resulted in his transfer west. As the Vicksburg campaign developed, Hamilton schemed for higher command, and he and Hurlbut were at each other's throats. In late January, Hamilton wrote privately to Wisconsin Senator James Doolittle, accusing Hurlbut of a drinking problem and also backstabbing Grant. "Grant's a drunkard," said Hamilton. "He tries to let liquor alone—but he cannot resist the temptation always." In mid-February, an infuriated Hurlbut requested that Rawlins assign Hamilton elsewhere before Hurlbut had him arrested. Grant thankfully accepted Hamilton's resignation on March 28.[24]

Another covert critic was Cadwallader Washburn, who participated in the foiled Yazoo Pass expedition. He griped to Elihu about Grant's mishandling of the campaign: "The matter on Yazoo Pass would have been a splendid success had Genl. Grant properly availed himself of it. I am thoroughly disgusted. The truth is Grant has no plans for taking Vicksburg and is frittering away time and strength to no purpose. . . . I wish you could come down and go to Vicksburg and see for yourself so you could write the President."[25] The letter reached Elihu in Galena, where he was recuperating from an injury. Alarmed by his brother's stinging criticisms, Elihu forwarded the letter to Treasury Secretary Chase, who shared it with Lincoln. Its revelations provoked Lincoln to send Washburne on a fact-finding mission to Vicksburg.[26]

Two weeks later, Cadwallader sent Elihu another disquieting letter bemoaning the situation at Vicksburg. "This campaign is badly damaged. . . . All Grant's schemes have failed. . . . He is surrounded by a drunken staff." However, Cadwallader pointed to the one redeeming exception on the staff: "Rawlins is a good man."[27]

⸺◦⸺

During winter newspapers reported about appalling working conditions under which illness-ravaged soldiers labored. The *New York Times* of February 13 reported, "The rise of water, the immense quantity of rain that has turned this portion of the 'bottom' into a fathomless abyss of mud, and the severe fatigue duties required of our soldiers in digging canals and building levees, will show the origin of much of the sickness in the camps; but there is no explanation why the mortality is so fearful—no reason why our men should be packed like hogs in narrow pens, and left to die in filth, darkness and neglect." Perhaps coincidentally, Rawlins two days later, sent an urgent order to General Hurlbut at Memphis to send all surgeons and assistant surgeons he could spare because many of the surgeons with Grant in the field were incapacitated by illness. In the same order, Rawlins complained that hospital accommodations in Memphis for sick troops were inadequate and must now be "pushed with all possible dispatch."[28]

Grant regarded reports such as those by the *Times* as unfounded. He wrote Washburne, attempting to set the record straight: "The [ill] health of the command is a subject that has been exagerated [*sic*] by the press. . . . Really our troops are more healthy than could possibly have been expected with all their trials."[29]

Even when Grant tried to deal generously with the press, he took a pummeling. In early February, Hurlbut banned the circulation of the anti-war *Chicago Times* among the troops of his command. Sylvanus Cadwallader, a *Times* correspondent, conferred with Rawlins about the suppression, arguing that any paper that was allowed to be published should be allowed to circulate in the US armies. Rawlins agreed but knew Grant had the final say. Grant soon revoked that order, claiming it only gave the paper more notoriety. But when Joseph Medill, the editor of the rival *Chicago Tribune*, learned about the revocation, he sent Washburne a blistering letter castigating Grant for allowing the *Chicago Times* "to breed mutiny and demoralization" among his troops. Medill told Washburne that his paper had held back criticizing Grant "on your account," but "could have made him stink in the nostrils of the public like an old fish."[30]

When threats to Grant were palpable, Rawlins needed little prodding to act. He had the opportunity to block a potentially treacherous situation that came to his attention in March. A lead player in this emerging scenario was William Kountz, the river transport officer who had worked for McClernand in late 1861. Kountz had leveled absurd charges of intoxication against Grant, an action that almost resulted in Rawlins coming to blows with Kountz. Now over a year later, McClernand and Kountz would refresh their relationship just when McClernand believed Grant had foiled his dream of leading the campaign down the Mississippi. McClernand still might realize that opportunity if a smear campaign succeeded against Grant.[31]

In late January, Kountz corresponded with Secretary of War Stanton and had a meeting with him in Washington. Following this meeting, Kountz wrote to McClernand indicating Stanton ordered him to report to McClernand for "specal [sic] duty" and adding a tantalizing postscript: "Stanton is evedently [sic] your friend. I have some thing to say to you which I will not put on paper."[32] The friendship reference no doubt assuaged McClernand's battered feelings. Shortly after Kountz joined McClernand, the latter wrote Lincoln a letter of introduction of sorts regarding his new superintendent of river transportation: "Permit me to present to you Capt Kountz an honest and riliable [sic] gentleman. I would add more but he must embark." On the reverse, Kountz penned his own message to Lincoln: "On the 13th of March 1863 Genl. Grant I am informed was Gloriously drunk and in bed sick all day. If you are averse to drunken Genls I can furnish you the Name of officers of high standing to substantiate the above."[33] Kountz was back to his old tricks.

Rawlins had no knowledge of Kountz's slanderous postscript to Lincoln, but Rawlins did learn that Kountz was near Vicksburg with McClernand. On March 16, Rawlins shot McClernand a blunt order: "If W. J. Kountz, late

Quartermaster is at Milliken's Bend you will please cause to be ascertained by what authority he is there and on what business and report the same to these Headquarters." McClernand responded, "Captain Kountz left there going up the river. I think I understood that he had been at Dept Head Quarters—He left on [the steamer] city of Memphis."[34] Rawlins had intervened at the opportune moment to counter Kountz.

Just three weeks after Kountz left, Stanton would send his own investigator to Vicksburg to report about the true situation there. Rawlins ensured this suspect observer received a warm welcome.

—∿∿—

By the end of March, the efforts to dig or blast alternative routes past Vicksburg were proving impracticable. Grant would soon opt for the simpler but riskier plan of marching troops down the Mississippi's west bank to well south of Vicksburg, running vessels past the enemy's artillery gauntlet, and using the vessels to ferry troops to the east bank. The simpler plan came as a relief for the editor of the *Galena Daily Advertiser*, who struggled to explain Grant's complex strategies: "There have been so many Pass Expeditions inaugurated to circumvent Vicksburg that we are somewhat confused in the attempt to define them. . . . Neither do we know precisely how many have been tried and abandoned as unserviceable, or if all have not been."[35]

On March 29, Grant ordered McClernand to move his Thirteenth Corps south from Milliken's Bend to New Carthage, Louisiana, about twenty miles southwest of Vicksburg, which would be the staging area for ferrying troops across the river. To keep Pemberton guessing, Sherman would remain behind and use his corps to make demonstrations north of Vicksburg. Leading the way and facing only token Confederate resistance, McClernand's men built bridges over bayous and laid roads as they went, making slow but steady progress. By April 6, the first of McClernand's divisions reached New Carthage.

April 6 was also the day that Charles Dana, Stanton's "special commissioner," arrived at Grant's Milliken's Bend headquarters. Dana, former editor of the *New York Daily Tribune*, was there on the pretense of making visitations "to investigate and report upon the condition of the pay service in the Western armies."[36] However, his mission—as everyone at headquarters knew—was to report to Stanton about Grant's military situation, information that could help Stanton and Lincoln "to settle their minds as to Grant, about whom at the time there were many doubts, and against whom there was some complaint."[37]

This was not the first time Dana had met Grant and Rawlins; he sat between them at a July 4, 1862, dinner in Memphis. Coincidentally, Grant was under a cloud at that time too, following Shiloh.

In anticipation of Dana's arrival, the staff officers conferred, and Rawlins explained procedures for receiving him. Rawlins insisted Dana needed to be placated while details of the upcoming campaign were developed. For Rawlins, "the paramount object was to keep Dana quiescent until Grant could work out the next phase of the campaign and then present it as a *fait accompli*."[38] Some staffers objected to coddling Dana. Lieutenant Colonel William Duff, the Scottish-born chief of artillery, regarded him as a government spy and thought he deserved to be thrown into the river. Instead of profanely rebuking Duff, Rawlins's response was reasonable and composed: "I am surprised, Col. Duff, at your discourteous and unmilitary remarks. He should not be left in a moment's doubt as to the cordiality of his reception. He is entitled to as much official recognition as Mr. Stanton, or any other high public functionary. I shall expect you to see that a tent is always pitched alongside Gen. Grant's, for Mr. Dana's use as long as he remains at headquarters—that sentries are placed in front of it—that orderlies are detailed for his service—and a place at mess-table specially reserved for him."[39]

Rawlins confided in Wilson the need to bring Dana into their circle. This would entail being completely forthcoming about plans for the upcoming campaign and to demonstrate their confidence in Grant's ability to succeed with it. Absent that confidence, it was feared Grant might be relieved and Mc-Clernand elevated to command. The two staff officers became near constant companions of Dana, sharing meals with him, chatting into the evening, and taking him on inspection tours. Under this arrangement, Dana got to know Grant too and became an ally and supporter. Rawlins's handling of Dana was a masterstroke. By choosing cordiality over confrontation and openness over suspiciousness, the result, as Wilson later wrote, was that "Dana did all in his power to remove the prejudice against Grant from the minds of those high officials [i.e., Stanton and Lincoln], and to build up in its place a feeling of respect and confidence."[40]

An opportunity arose that brought Dana into the fold. Soon after arriving, he attended a meeting in Grant's headquarters that included Porter, McPherson, Frank Blair, Sherman, Wilson, and Rawlins. Here, Grant laid out his new plan, but the reception to it was lukewarm. Sherman didn't like the idea of a river operation; he preferred the overland thrust through the state of Mississippi. With Porter, he also expressed reservations about putting Mc-Clernand's corps in the vanguard and allowing him to lead the attack against the enemy at Grand Gulf. Grant was not swayed. He reminded the attendees that McClernand was his senior corps commander, and perhaps more importantly, he had embraced the plan from the beginning.[41] After the meeting, Wilson, Rawlins, and Dana candidly discussed Grant's plan and Sherman's reservations.

On April 8, Sherman, in a long letter to Rawlins, laid out his own recommendations for an operation against Vicksburg. Sherman acknowledged that this missive might be interpreted by some as a letter of protest. Fortunately, despite his misgivings, he would apply himself to ensure the operation's success. Rawlins advised Grant to put Sherman's letter aside unanswered. The initial agitation engendered by Grant's plan soon dissipated, and as Dana noted, in the ensuing days all "became more sanguine that the new project would succeed."[42]

—–⁓⁓–—

By helping to win over Dana and in so doing burnishing Grant's image within the Administration, Rawlins performed a remarkable feat on Grant's behalf, coming as it did during a time when critics scoffed that he was bogged down before Vicksburg. Three months after Dana's arrival, Grant would be heralded as the foremost commander in the West. It was also evident that, after eighteen months at Grant's side, Rawlins was hitting his stride and proving an invaluable fixture at headquarters. However, after carefully observing Rawlins, Dana's appraisal of him, written just after the surrender of Vicksburg, credits him mostly for being a watchdog over Grant. In a July 13 letter to Secretary Stanton, Dana, in keeping with his observer's role, provided several insightful and frank personality profiles of the men on Grant's staff. In Dana's estimation,

> Lieutenant-Colonel Rawlins, Grant's assistant adjutant general, is a very industrious, conscientious man, who never loses a moment, and never gives himself any indulgence except swearing and scolding. He is a lawyer by profession, a townsman of Grant's, and has a great influence over him, especially because he watches him day and night, and whenever he commits the folly of tasting liquor hastens to remind him that at the beginning of the war he gave him [Rawlins] his word of honor not to touch a drop as long as it lasted. Grant thinks Rawlins a first-rate adjutant, but I think this is a mistake. He is too slow, and can't write the English language correctly without a great deal of careful consideration.[43]

Dana's early take on Rawlins is short on unabashed praise but contains elements of truth. Rawlins was an industrious, efficient toiler, but this was much to Grant's benefit. When constituting his staff, Grant did so without great forethought. He offered jobs to those who had shown him kindness— and then hadn't the heart to dismiss them when they proved inefficient or too fond of alcohol.[44] Back in the summer of 1861, the choice of Rawlins would prove providential, especially when stacked against Dana's appraisal of two of Grant's notorious "colonels": "There are two aides-de-camp with the rank of colonel, namely Colonel [Lagow] and Colonel [Riggin], both personal friends of Grant's. [Lagow] is a worthless, whisky-drinking, useless fellow. [Riggin] is decent and gentlemanly, but neither of them is worth his salt so far as service to the Government goes."[45]

Rawlins's strengths were not flashy and consisted of old-fashioned work ethic values: loyalty, patriotism, conscientiousness, indefatigability, sobriety, and steadfastness. Simply put, he could be relied on. One example from May 1863 reveals the contrast between him and the colonel Dana termed "worthless." On May 24, Rawlins issued Special Orders No. 139, assigning Lagow to deliver a large contingent of Confederate prisoners to Island No. 10 above Memphis. At Memphis, the Federal troops guarding them were to return to Young's Point, Louisiana, while Lagow took a fresh set of guards for the final leg of the trip. On the twenty-ninth, General Hurlbut informed Rawlins that Lagow had just arrived in Memphis and that Hurlbut had ordered him to send down the prisoners' guards once they had been relieved. To Hurlbut's surprise, he learned that "Col. Lagow does not appear to have paid any attention to this duty or to have taken any care of the officers and men under his charge nor even to have known how many men constituted the Guard."[46] No doubt when Rawlins learned of Lagow's derelict duty—negligence that Rawlins would never countenance—he let loose with plenty of "swearing and scolding." If Rawlins had had his say, Lagow would have been cashiered, but regarding personnel matters, he could only advise Grant who made the final decisions.

Rawlins watched over Grant for understandable reasons. Consider the story told by Mary Livermore, a member of a Sanitary Commission group visiting Grant and his staff on board the *Magnolia*. Her brief audience with him left the noteworthy impression that "the clear eye, clear skin, firm flesh, and steady nerves of General Grant gave the lie to the universal calumnies, then current, concerning his intemperate habits and those of the officers of his staff. Our eyes had become practised in reading the diagnosis of drunkenness."[47]

If this good-hearted matron was sizing up Grant for signs of intemperance, imagine how those with axes to grind against him might exploit a moment of indulgence.

Grant was also the subject of one of the sketches Dana sent to Stanton:

> Living at headquarters as I did throughout the siege of Vicksburg, I soon became intimate with General Grant . . . Grant was an uncommon fellow—the most modest, the most disinterested, and the most honest man I ever knew, with a temper that nothing could disturb, and a judgment that was judicial in its comprehensiveness and wisdom. Not a great man, except morally; not an original or brilliant man, but sincere, thoughtful, deep, and gifted with courage that never faltered; when the time came to risk all, he went in like a simple-hearted, unaffected, unpretending hero, whom no ill omens could deject and no triumph unduly exalt.[48]

Rawlins knew this about Grant—and more. He knew that Grant was a specially gifted military leader poised to accomplish something historic, perhaps force the turning point of the war. Just days before Grant announced his new plan, he received a letter from Halleck urging him to fix his eyes on Vicksburg. Rawlins was almost certainly aware of the contents of this letter. Halleck wrote, "The great object on your line now is the opening of the Mississippi River, and everything else must tend to that purpose. The eyes and hopes of the whole country are now directed to your army. In my opinion, the opening of the Mississippi River will be to us of more advantage than the capture of forty Richmonds."[49] To fulfill this destiny, Rawlins understood Grant needed to be prevented from inflicting damage on himself or allowing others to stain his reputation. To not watch "day and night" exposed the country to too great a risk.

Assuming the role of vigilant other was in keeping with Christian temperance ideals. Reverend Lyman Beecher, whose sermons were well-known to temperance advocates, implored his followers to be proactive in sustaining one another against the use of liquor: "Will you not watch over one another with keener vigilance . . . and draw tighter the bands of brotherly discipline?"[50] It is possible Rawlins shouldered this burden because he believed he was almost uniquely fit for it. One learns that from a telling letter Rawlins wrote his fiancée, Emma Hurlburt, in November 1863 following a night of drinking and revelry: "Today, however, matters have changed, and the necessity of my presence here made almost absolute, by the free use of intoxicating liquors at Headquarters, which last night's developments showed me had reached to the General commanding. I am the only one here (his wife not being with him) who can stay it in that direction and prevent evil consequences resulting from it."[51] Wife Julia was regarded as a moderating influence on her husband, and Rawlins attributed similar powers to himself.

What led Rawlins to believe he had this influence? Dana's thumbnail profile provides two clues. First, he never allowed himself any "indulgence." When Rawlins laid down a policy of no tolerance for alcohol, he did not speak as a hypocrite. Second, there was Rawlins's naturally confrontational style. No one who spent so much time with Grant, other than Rawlins, had the grit to take him to task. The confronting was motivated out of the best of intent—for Grant's good and out of devotion to him. Rawlins was also convinced that disciplinary methods, such as banning alcohol in camp or extracting a pledge from Grant, were necessary to curb his access to and appetite for drink. Of course, by dint of his reputation as Grant's abstemious monitor, Rawlins's presence assured those who entrusted Grant with greater military responsibilities.

Dana was critical of Rawlins's writing skills and less than first-rate performance as an adjutant. Rawlins could not match Grant's clarity of writing style. In fairness, few could. In his later life, Sherman attempted to set the record straight about who wrote out the orders. "[Grant] would sit down and scribble off an order easier than he could tell another what he wanted. If anyone came along and remarked to him, 'That was a clever order Rawlins put out for you today,' Grant would say right out, 'I wrote that myself.' I presume I have 150 orders and memoranda all in his own hand. . . . He knew what was wanted and so sent me word. . . . He remembered the most minute details and watched every point."[52] Historian Bruce Catton marveled at Grant's growth as a writer and as a general who was sure of his purpose: "I think that . . . early in the winter of 1863 Grant's dispatches become recognizable. The reader can identify them without looking for the signature; suddenly, Grant's writing became unmistakably Grant. Here, in the midst of barren acres of official jargon, are things written by a man who knows exactly what he is doing and what he wants to say."[53] The reports may have been written by Grant, but they were checked by Rawlins, who might perform a rewrite where necessary, "adhering as closely as possible to Grant's original reports, but making them conform to the facts as they were understood at headquarters."[54] For example, Rawlins assisted in the preparation of Grant's report of the Vicksburg campaign, which Grant probably began drafting before the city's capitulation. Rawlins copyedited the draft, corrected errors, added names and dates, and inserted figures where needed.[55]

Years after Rawlins's death, Sherman spoke critically about his differences with Grant, such as over the men he chose as close associates, including his staff officers: Grant "did not have about him near his person officers of refinement and culture; his staff at Shiloh was inferior—Rawlins, Lagow, Hillyer, etc., and when he was at the White House he had as intimates men I could not have tolerated."[56] At Shiloh, Rawlins had just over half a year's experience on staff, and he would grow into his staff role. Over time, Grant came to trust Rawlins implicitly and to assign him greater responsibilities, including placing him in temporary command at Vicksburg after it capitulated, when Grant left for a conference in New Orleans—a decision acquiesced to by Sherman. Dana later became a strong advocate for Rawlins, and in his memoirs his opinion about Rawlins differed markedly from the 1863 sketch. Regarding Rawlins, Dana later said, "He had a very able mind, clear, strong, and not subject to hysterics. He bossed everything at Grant's headquarters. He had very little respect for persons, and a rough style of conversation. I have heard him curse at Grant when, according to his judgment, the general was doing something that he thought he had better not do. But he was entirely devoted to his duty, with the clearest judgment, and perfectly fearless. Without him Grant would not have been the same man."[57] There will be more said about Dana's efforts to attribute to Rawlins a substantial amount of Grant's successes.

—⁓—

While McClernand's troops were pushing on foot toward New Carthage, where they would be brought across the river, Grant and Admiral Porter considered how to run the naval vessels past the batteries. The moonless night of April 16 was chosen for the run. Seven gunboats, three transports laden with supplies, and a steam ram began their descent shortly before 10:00 p.m. An observation party was assembled on Grant's command steamer, moored a safe distance away. Julia and two of the young Grant boys were on hand, as were Rawlins, Dana, and Wilson, select senior generals, and a few wives, McClernand's recent bride included. Following dinner, the party was witness to one of the most remarkable spectacles of the war: the little flotilla's heroic attempt to pass through a curtain of plunging artillery fire.

The Federal vessels' boilers were protected with water-soaked hay and cotton bales. For added protection, coal barges were lashed to the vulnerable starboard sides. Engine noises were minimized. However, it was impossible to prevent detection, and once alerted, the Confederate defenders lit barrels of tar and torched abandoned houses to illuminate the river. As the vessels glided through the four-mile gauntlet, they were subjected to ninety minutes of shelling. Through the awful firestorm, Harry Wilson held one of the Grant sons on his lap, comforting him as best he could. In her memoir, Julia recollected the fearful cannonading, the river cloaked with smoke, and the surreal return to normalcy. "The smoke cleared away," she later wrote, "and the katydids and the frogs began their summer songs."[58] Late that night, Grant rode down to New Carthage to inspect the condition of the flotilla. To his relief, he discovered only one boat, a transport, had been lost, and there had been no fatalities.

Another run past the batteries was scheduled several days later. Six troop transports had to be spirited to New Carthage, and each towed two barges crammed with coal, food, forage, and medical supplies. Most of the civilian crew members declined to serve on these unarmed transports, so volunteers were sought from army units. One of those volunteers was none other than Clark Lagow. Rawlins issued Grant's order placing him in command of this fleet and assigning him to the *Tigress*, Grant's old headquarters steamer.[59]

This second run began late on April 22. Lieutenant Colonel William Oliver of the Seventh Missouri, in command of the *Tigress*, reported that a shot to the stern smashed a four-foot gash in its hull. Oliver ordered the crippled steamer to the Louisiana shore, barely reaching it before sinking. All the terrified crew survived.[60] Another army volunteer, Charles Evans of the Lead Mine Regiment, served as pilot of the *Anglo Saxon*, although he had never before steered a steamboat. When a shot disabled the boat's rudder, it veered directly in front of an enemy battery. Miraculously, after receiving thirty hits, not a man was lost.[61]

Despite the loss of one transport and six barges, this fleet also coasted on to New Carthage. The essential elements, the infantry and naval vessels, were now in place to effect a crossing of the Mississippi. At New Carthage, a shaken Lagow collected reports from the commanders of his transports and submitted them to Grant, who never publicly commended him for carrying out this hazardous assignment.[62]

―∿∿∿―

It turned out there was no suitable site for disembarking on the Mississippi side opposite New Carthage. The Federal troops were forced to mosey farther south about twenty miles to a ramshackle Louisiana hamlet known as Hard Times. From Hard Times, the crossing was to be made at Grand Gulf,

Mississippi, which first had to be cleared of eight thousand Confederates under Brigadier General John Bowen, Pemberton's most able subordinate, who would demonstrate during the Vicksburg campaign "remarkable talents as an outstanding combat leader with an uncanny feel for defensive-offensive tactics."[63] Admiral Porter's gunboats were to blast Bowen and his defenders into submission.

Arriving in time for the martial display was Elihu Washburne who, as Lincoln had urged, was there to follow up on his brother's pessimistic reports. Rawlins accompanied Washburne to Hard Times, and Grant invited him to observe Porter's bombardment and then cross to Grand Gulf with the troops. Washburne was not the only Illinois visitor. Also on hand was Governor Yates, eager to see how his citizens in uniform were faring. Fellow Illinoisan John McClernand, never shy about gaining political points, ostentatiously received the governor with a fifteen-gun salute and invited him to review a brigade. Dana, in his informer role, tattled to Stanton that the salute was performed despite the fact "that positive orders had repeatedly been given to use no ammunition for any purpose except against the enemy."[64] Yates came south bearing a barrel of whiskey to treat the soldiers. Before his return home, Yates bestowed the barrel's leftover contents to Colonel Duff and Sylvanus Cadwallader.[65]

On April 29 at about 8:30 a.m., Porter's gunboats began shelling the Confederates at Grand Gulf. However, the Rebels gave better than they got. After absorbing a four-hour shellacking, Porter withdrew his vessels, necessitating another crossing plan. A detained slave familiar with the local geography recommended the troops be disembarked at Bruinsburg, Mississippi. This involved marching down to a Louisiana plantation landing from which McClernand's and some of McPherson's men were finally ferried to the Magnolia State. By noon on April 30, most were ashore. After struggling four months to achieve this goal, Grant expressed an intense feeling of relief: "All the campaigns, labors, hardships and exposures from the month of December previous to this time that had been made and endured were for the accomplishment of this one object."[66]

―⁓―

From Bruinsburg, the Federals would move eastward, with the town of Port Gibson about twelve miles distant the first objective. But there was a four-hour delay getting started. Through an oversight that ultimately could be blamed on McClernand, the troops' food supply had run out, and more rations had to be ferried over. This delay gave General Bowen time to evacuate Grand Gulf and shift his troops to the Port Gibson area. McClernand's four divisions and one of McPherson's made their way across roads that ran through a forbidding terrain of ravines, heavy timber, and canebrakes.

In the earliest hours of May 1, McClernand's advance line bumped into Confederate skirmishers, and some brisk volleys were exchanged. But the battle did not erupt until dawn. The Confederates put up a spirited defense and made hard counterattacks, but McClernand had too much size advantage. Grant, along with Yates and Washburne, watched McClernand chase the enemy off the field in what proved to be a costly fight for both sides. Although Bowen and his small force escaped, the Illinois politician-general turned in a mostly competent performance.

It was a good enough performance, thought Rawlins and Wilson, to use as the opportunity for Grant to give McClernand some congratulatory due. They urged their commander to strike up better relations with him. Grant declined, contending that by holding the brigade review for Yates, McClernand delayed the river crossing. Grant was also sore that McClernand, against orders, expended too much artillery ammunition during the battle. Moreover, the staff officer who delivered those orders got from McClernand an earful of abuse that was reported back to Grant. Despite the effort by Rawlins and Wilson to forge a more harmonious relationship between the two generals, Grant became more watchful of McClernand and met with him as infrequently as possible.[67]

Grant and his staff reached Port Gibson about 8:00 a.m. on May 2. After they rode down to the South Fork of Bayou Pierre, a stream running by the town, they discovered the retreating Confederates had destroyed the suspension bridge over it. Grant told Wilson and Rawlins to see that it was rebuilt. As chief engineer, Wilson called on McClernand for a brigade to use as a construction gang. After repeated pleas, McClernand finally detached a brigade that reported at noon. Eager to help in any way, Rawlins wielded an axe and scavenged wood from barns and fences. At 4:30 p.m., the bridge was completed, and troops began moving across. Around 9:00 p.m., the leading edge of the Federals arrived at the North Fork, some eight miles above. Here, the suspension bridge had sustained enough fire damage to make it unsafe for artillery or cavalry to cross. A company of pioneers performed the repairs while Rawlins worked through the night to procure timber. Repairs were completed at 5:30 a.m.[68]

Grant wrote Sherman about the good news: the Port Gibson battle had been won. Bridges had been built. The Army of the Tennessee was on the move. In the letter, Grant's confidence was on display: "The enemy is badly beaten. . . . The road to Vicksburg is open. All we want now are men, ammunition, and hard bread."[69] However, the fact was the army was deep into Mississippi and facing unknown challenges. Come what may, Rawlins would be beside his commander tending to reports, processing orders, being alert to threats, and doing his part as adviser and choreographer of an invading army on hostile soil.

At this propitious moment, Grant and Rawlins could take additional consolation from the fact that they were on the road to Vicksburg in part because two potential sources of conflict had been appeased. The War Department "mole," Charles Dana, was won over to Grant's side, and Congressman Washburne had nothing but glowing words after his two-week sojourn with the army. Washburne's return to Galena on May 16 merited a column in the local paper. He called the running of the batteries "one of the boldest and most successful movements of the war." He rated the Battle of Port Gibson as "a most brilliant and substantial victory." And he brought back a message from the general himself: "Tell my friends in Galena that I considered the biggest half of my work in taking Vicksburg done when I landed my army safely at Bruinsburg and got a foothold on the Mississippi shore."[70]

NOTES

1. U. S. Grant to Henry W. Halleck, December 14, 1862, in *The Papers of Ulysses S. Grant*, ed. John Y. Simon (Carbondale: Southern Illinois University Press), 7:28.

2. U. S. Grant, *Memoirs* (New York: Charles L. Webster, 1885), 1:443.

3. U. S. Grant to James B. McPherson, January 13, 1863, in *The Papers of Ulysses S. Grant*, ed. John Y. Simon, 7:28.

4. General Orders No. 13, January 30, 1863, in *The War of the Rebellion: A Compilation of the Official Records of the Union and Confederate Armies*, series 1, part 1, 24:11; John A. McClernand to U. S. Grant, January 30, 1863, in *The War of the Rebellion: A Compilation of the Official Records of the Union and Confederate Armies*, series 1, part 1, 24:12.

5. Michael D. Hammond, "Arkansas Atlantis: The Lost Town of Napoleon," *The Arkansas Historical Quarterly* 55, no. 3 (2006): 214.

6. James H. Wilson, *The Life of John A. Rawlins* (New York: Neale, 1916), 106.

7. U. S. Grant, *Memoirs*, 1:440; U. S. Grant to Henry W. Halleck, January 20, 1863, in *The Papers of Ulysses S. Grant*, ed. John Y. Simon, 7:234–35.

8. *The Ulysses S. Grant Association Newsletter* 10, no. 3 (April 1973): 18. It is not known to which "prominent General" Kittoe refers. Perhaps Kittoe's recollection was off a few days, because a letter sent by General McClernand on January 30 would have caused Rawlins

to spout profanity. McClernand was upset with Grant for ordering him to move the camp of the Fifty-Fourth Indiana beyond the limits of the camp hospital. Grant's order was a simple measure to deal with a trivial issue, which was likely the result of a personality conflict between the regiment's colonel and the hospital surgeon. However, McClernand took umbrage with Grant's order and fired an impertinent response:

> The enforcement of your order will be the subversion of my authority. . . . I understand that orders are being issued from your Head Quarters directly to Army Corps Commanders, and not through me. As I am invested, by order of the Secretary of War, endorsed by the President . . . with the command of all the forces operating on the Mississippi river, I claim that all orders affecting the condition or operations of these forces should pass through these Head Quarters. . . . If different views are entertained by you, then the question should be immediately referred to Washington, and one or other, or both of us relieved.

Given McClernand's insolent tone, it is not surprising that also on January 30, Rawlins issued General Orders No. 13, announcing Grant would assume command of the Vicksburg expedition; see John Y. Simon, ed., *The Papers of Ulysses S. Grant*, 7:265–67n.

9. *The War of the Rebellion: A Compilation of the Official Records of the Union and Confederate Armies*, series 1, part 3, 24:15.

10. U. S. Grant to Henry W. Halleck, January 20, 1863, in *The Papers of Ulysses S. Grant*, ed. John Y. Simon, 7:234.

11. James Harrison Wilson, *Under the Old Flag* (New York: D. Appleton, 1912), 155–58.

12. Albert D. Richardson, *Personal History of Ulysses S. Grant* (Boston: D. L. Guernsey, 1885), 294.

13. U. S. Grant, *Memoirs*, 1:460.

14. Ibid., 444, 446.

15. James H. Wilson, *The Life of John A. Rawlins*, 115.

16. R. Steven Jones, *The Right Hand of Command: Use and Disuse of Personal Staffs in the American Civil War* (Mechanicsburg, PA: Stackpole, 2000), 106.

17. J. M. Shaw, "The Life and Services of General John A. Rawlins," in *Glimpses of the Nation's Struggle* 3, ed. Edward D. McNeill (New York: D. D. Merrill, 1893), 389.

18. J. A. Rawlins to James H. Wilson, February 16, 1863, Wyoming State Archives, Bender Collection, James H. Wilson Papers, Microfilm Reel 61b.

19. J. A. Rawlins to James H. Wilson, February 28, 1863, Wyoming State Archives, Bender Collection, James H. Wilson Papers, Microfilm Reel 61b.

20. James H. Wilson to John Rawlins, February 4, 1863, in *The War of the Rebellion: A Compilation of the Official Records of the Union and Confederate Armies*, series 1, part 1, 24:373.

21. James H. Wilson, *The Life of John A. Rawlins*, 112.

22. James H. Wilson to John Rawlins, March 15, 1863, in *The War of the Rebellion: A Compilation of the Official Records of the Union and Confederate Armies*, series 1, part 1, 24:380; James H. Wilson to John Rawlins, March 18, 1863, in *The War of the Rebellion: A Compilation of the Official Records of the Union and Confederate Armies*, series 1, part 1, 24:385–86.

23. U. S. Grant, *Memoirs*, 1:458.

24. John Y. Simon, ed., *The Papers of Ulysses S. Grant*, 7:308n; U. S. Grant to Lorenzo Thomas, March 28, 1863, in *The Papers of Ulysses S. Grant*, ed. John Y. Simon, 7:481–82.

25. C. C. Washburne to Elihu Washburne, March 28, 1863, in Mark Washburn, *A Biography of Elihu Benjamin Washburne: Congressman, Secretary of State, Envoy Extraordinary* (self-pub., Xlibris, 2001), 240.

26. Ibid., 241.

27. C. C. Washburn to E. B. Washburne, April 11, 1863, in Mark Washburn, *A Biography of Elihu Benjamin Washburne*, 242.

28. John Y. Simon, ed., *The Papers of Ulysses S. Grant*, 7:394n1.

29. U. S. Grant to E. B. Washburne, March 10, 1863, in *The Papers of Ulysses S. Grant*, ed. John Y. Simon, 7:410.

30. Ibid., 316, 318n.

31. Brooks D. Simpson, *Ulysses S. Grant: Triumph over Adversity* (Boston: Houghton Mifflin, 2000), 176.

32. John Y. Simon, ed., *The Papers of Ulysses S. Grant*, 7:275n; William J. Kountz to John McClernand, February 25, 1862, McClernand Papers, Abraham Lincoln Presidential Library.

33. John Y. Simon, ed., *The Papers of Ulysses S. Grant*, 7:275n.

34. Ibid.

35. *Galena Daily Advertiser*, April 4, 1863.

36. Charles A. Dana, *Recollections of the Civil War* (New York: D. Appleton, 1902), 22.

37. Ibid., 21.

38. Brian Holden Reid, "The Commander and his Chief of Staff: Ulysses S. Grant and John A. Rawlins, 1861–1865," in *Leadership and Command: The Anglo-American Military Experience since 1861*, ed. G. D. Sheffield (London: Brassey's, 1997), 26.

39. Sylvanus Cadwallader, *Three Years with Grant*, ed. Benjamin P. Thomas (New York: Alfred A. Knopf, 1961), 61.

40. James H. Wilson, *The Life of John A. Rawlins*, 122.

41. Charles A. Dana, *Recollections of the Civil War*, 32–33.

42. James Harrison Wilson, *Under the Old Flag*, 1:160–61; William T. Sherman, *Personal Memoirs*, 3rd ed. (New York: Charles L. Webster, 1890), 1:317; Charles A. Dana, *Recollections of the Civil War*, 33.

43. Charles A. Dana, *Recollections of the Civil War*, 72–73.

44. R. Steven Jones, *The Right Hand of Command*, 122.

45. Charles A. Dana, *Recollections of the Civil War*, 74.

46. John Y. Simon, ed., *The Papers of Ulysses S. Grant* (Carbondale: Southern Illinois University Press, 1979), 8:243n, 250n2.

47. Mary A. Livermore, *My Story of the War* (Hartford, CT: A. D. Worthington, 1889), 310–11.

48. Charles A. Dana, *Recollections of the Civil War*, 61.

49. H. W. Halleck to U. S. Grant, March 20, 1863, in *The War of the Rebellion: A Compilation of the Official Records of the Union and Confederate Armies*, series 1, part 1, 24:22.

50. Lyman Beecher, *Six Sermons on Intemperance* (New York: American Tract Society, 1833), 97.

51. J. A. Rawlins to Emma Hurlburt, November 16, 1863, transcribed copy in the Rawlins file, Chicago History Museum.

52. Bruce Catton, *Grant Moves South* (Boston: Little, Brown, 1960), 392.

53. Ibid., 528n6.

54. J. M. Shaw, "The Life and Services of General John A. Rawlins," 389.

55. John Y. Simon, ed., *The Papers of Ulysses S. Grant*, 8:508n.

56. Lloyd Lewis, *Sherman: Fighting Prophet* (New York: Harcourt, Brace, 1958), 607.

57. Charles A. Dana, *Recollections of the Civil War*, 62.

58. John Y. Simon, ed., *The Personal Memoirs of Julia Dent Grant* (New York: G. P. Putnam's Sons, 1975), 112.

59. Special Orders No. 111, April 21, 1863, in *The War of the Rebellion: A Compilation of the Official Records of the Union and Confederate Armies*, series 1, part 3, 24:216–17.

60. Report of William S. Oliver, April 24, 1863, in *The War of the Rebellion: A Compilation of the Official Records of the Union and Confederate Armies*, series 1, part 1, 24:565–67.

61. *Galena Daily Advertiser*, May 11, 1863.

62. R. Steven Jones, *The Right Hand of Command*, 109.

63. Edwin C. Bearss, "John Stevens Bowen," in *The Confederate General*, ed. William C. Davis (National Historical Society, 1991), 1:111.

64. C. A. Dana to E. M. Stanton, April 25, 1863, in *The War of the Rebellion: A Compilation of the Official Records of the Union and Confederate Armies*, series 1, part 1, 24:81.

65. Sylvanus Cadwallader, *Three Years with Grant*, 66.

66. U. S. Grant, *Memoirs*, 1:480–81.

67. James Harrison Wilson, *Under the Old Flag*, 1:174–76.

68. Albert D. Richardson, *Personal History of Ulysses S. Grant*, 308–9; Report of J. H. Wilson, May 30, 1863, in *The War of the Rebellion: A Compilation of the Official Records of the Union and Confederate Armies*, series 1, part 1, 24:128–29.

69. U. S. Grant to W. T. Sherman, May 3, 1863, in *The War of the Rebellion: A Compilation of the Official Records of the Union and Confederate Armies*, series 1, part 3, 24:268–69.

70. *Galena Daily Advertiser*, May 18, 1863.

15

"You Have *Full* Control of Your Appetite"

WITH GRAND GULF IN FEDERAL hands, Grant and Rawlins spent several days aboard Admiral Porter's flagship writing dispatches and orders. Grant was anxious to stockpile supplies in Grand Gulf should it prove infeasible for the army to subsist off the Mississippi countryside. One of Rawlins's orders named Hillyer to superintend the disbursement of incoming supplies.[1] This was a curious appointment given that just days earlier, Hillyer had submitted his resignation, citing a need to attend to his law and real estate businesses. His resignation came a year after witnessing the bloodbath at Shiloh.[2] While the resignation was being processed, Grant pushed Hillyer hard—despite Hillyer suffering from paralysis in his right arm—urging him to bring up wagonloads of supplies and ammunition because "every days delay is worth two thousand men to the enemy."[3]

As paperwork increased, Wilson suggested Rawlins lighten his burden by adding a military secretary. Wilson recommended Captain Adam Badeau, then on the staff of Brigadier General Thomas Sherman (no relation to William T. Sherman), who was taking part in the Port Hudson operation farther down the Mississippi. Badeau was short, was stoop shouldered, wore glasses, had little military aptitude, and could barely mount a horse. He was a former New York newspaper reporter who wrote about art and literature and spread society gossip under the pseudonym Vagabond. On the day Badeau received orders to report to Grant's headquarters, he was wounded in the left foot. A lengthy recuperation followed, and he was not to join the staff until February 1864.[4]

In their few days in Port Gibson, Grant and staff were headquartered in a small house. Port Gibson, with its stately homes and attractive gardens bursting with roses and lilies, greatly impressed the Yankee Midwesterners. Plums and peaches were ripening in local orchards, and the soldiers gorged on strawberries. The well-stocked smokehouses had not gone unnoticed by the blue-clad troops—this when Grant contemplated cutting loose from his supply line and living off the countryside.

Young Fred Grant accompanied his father on the campaign, which was becoming the most exciting field trip a twelve-year-old could imagine. Ulysses wrote Julia that the boy was "enjoying himself hugely" and had been unfazed by the whistling bullets during the Port Gibson battle.[5] After the battle, he was seen astride his horse among members of the general staff, outfitted with his father's sword hitched to his waist by a broad yellow belt.[6] Fred was a hit with the soldiers, to whom he was a link to the normalcy back home. Even Rawlins was so amused by Fred's assuming the role of amateur soldier—a part that he played while uncomfortably close to the action—that he dubbed him the "Veteran."[7]

From May 3 through May 7, while Grant and Rawlins grappled with the logistics of bringing forward rations, ammunition, and wagons to carry them, Sherman's corps marched down from Vicksburg. Two divisions, minus Frank Blair's, would be ferried over to Grand Gulf on the seventh. Also, Grant had decided to abandon the idea of coordinating with Nathaniel Banks, who was floundering to wrest Port Hudson, Louisiana—the other river city that blocked Federal control of the Mississippi—from Confederate hands. Grant's sole focus was on the Confederate forces opposing him and seizing Vicksburg.

On the eleventh, Grant's three corps were moved to the positions from which they would advance at dawn the next day. McClernand's corps was on the left, angling mostly north toward the rail line connecting Vicksburg and Jackson. McPherson, on the right, marched eastward toward the town of Raymond, about sixteen miles west of Jackson. Sherman, in the center, supported the corps on each of his flanks. Grant was interposing his three corps between Vicksburg and Jackson and threatening both. Recent reports indicated that Joseph E. Johnston, a full general, had just arrived to command all Confederate forces in Mississippi. Johnston was headquartered in the Bowman House, Jackson's best hotel, awaiting reinforcements and cobbling together a fighting force. He wanted Pemberton to abandon Vicksburg and unite with him to fight Grant. This placed Pemberton, now the subordinate, in a difficult spot because he was also ordered by Jefferson Davis to hold Vicksburg at all cost. Pemberton cautiously moved about two-thirds of his army eastward to encounter the invaders, leaving the reserve behind at Vicksburg. He wasn't sure where Grant was heading or what his intentions were. Perhaps he might demolish Grant's trailing supply line—but Pemberton was unaware that that option eluded him. Grant, also on the eleventh, decided to detach from his Grand Gulf supply base and mostly live off the land. Communication ties with Grand Gulf would also be curtailed, with the result, as Grant informed General Halleck, "You may not hear from me again for several days."[8]

About two miles west of Raymond, around 11:00 a.m., McPherson's corps bumped into enemy opposition. It was a brigade just summoned from Port Hudson and commanded by John Gregg, a fierce Texan and member of the Provisional Confederate Congress, who preferred fighting over politicking. Gregg was unaware he was confronting about one-third of Grant's force, but his brigade held for three hours before succumbing to superior numbers. Rawlins and Wilson noted that Gregg's retreat was not toward Vicksburg but east toward Jackson to reinforce Johnston. The two staffers galloped off to inform Grant. With this information, Grant decided to turn east and confront the enemy now threatening his rear at Jackson; then he would concentrate on Pemberton. Grant verbally instructed Wilson to order McPherson to push ahead early the next day to nearby Clinton on the rail line connecting Vicksburg and Jackson. The evolving plan had the corps of McPherson and Sherman converging on Jackson on the fourteenth, while McClernand hung back at Bolton Depot, on the rail line almost midway between Vicksburg and Jackson, in order to check Pemberton's eastward advance.

Wilson, now accompanied by Dana, met with McPherson at dusk and repeated Grant's order. McPherson, quite out of character, upbraided Wilson, arguing he didn't expect his men to do all the fighting, and he declined to venture forth without support. A shocked Wilson returned with Dana, got Grant to write the order, and delivered it to McPherson about midnight. Despite Grant's insistence on haste, McPherson dallied and didn't get to Clinton until midafternoon on the thirteenth.[9]

Around the time Wilson handed the written order to McPherson, Grant was stepping into the tent shared by artillery chief William Duff and Sylvanus Cadwallader. He wearily asked for a drink, and Duff extracted a canteen from beneath his pillow. It was whiskey remaining from Yates's gift barrel. Grant complained of fatigue—perhaps the report of McPherson's querulousness was a last straw on top of other issues—and needed a tonic to ease his exhaustion. As he knocked back a measure, Duff offered a toast: "Success to our campaign, and confusion to the whole Confederacy." After one or two more drinks, Grant retired for the night. Duff recommended the incident be kept among themselves. Cadwallader said he learned later that Duff had supplied Grant with drinks on other occasions, something Rawlins suspected but had not proved.[10]

On the morning of the fourteenth, McPherson's and Sherman's corps sloshed through rain to reach Jackson, dispersed its outnumbered defenders, and captured the Mississippi capital. Joe Johnston, who had been quartered in the Bowman House since his arrival twenty-four hours before, barely had time to evacuate his few thousand troops, which now had been eliminated as a threat. Grant, his staff, and the two corps commanders celebrated victory and indulged themselves for a night in the hotel's posh amenities. In the morning, Wilson settled the sixty-five-dollar bill by giving the hotel keeper a Confederate one-hundred-dollar note. The fellow had expected payment in sounder currency. "Oh," he said. "If you pay in Confederate money, it will be ninety-five dollars."[11]

Sherman was to stay in Jackson on the fifteenth, wrecking anything of military value, while McPherson took his corps westward to close on McClernand at Bolton Depot. Grant and Rawlins left Jackson and rode west some eight miles to the town of Clinton, also on the Vicksburg-Jackson rail line and midway between Jackson and Bolton Depot. The scattered divisions comprising the corps of McPherson and McClernand were coalescing in the Bolton and Clinton areas.

Early on May 16, Grant, while in Clinton, received a tip that Pemberton's force had been seen coming eastward and were just west of Bolton. An engagement was in the offing, and Grant aimed to get the better of it. Armed with this intelligence, Grant and his staff took to their mounts for an eight-mile dash to Bolton Depot in anticipation of the fight. Rawlins strained to keep up with a masterful horseman like Grant during a ride that required "leaping logs, brush, or whatever came in their way."[12]

Grant and Rawlins arrived at the front around 7:30 a.m.

—◦◦◦—

If central Mississippians were expecting summer's arrival, it checked in on the sultry sixteenth of May. As Pemberton edged east, he came into contact with advance elements of blue-clads. Expecting a fight that should prove as hot as the weather, Pemberton chose a formidable defensive position across Champion Hill, a prominence rising sixty to seventy feet south of the rail line and just west of Bolton. Heavy skirmishing broke out around 10:00 a.m. An hour later, the fighting intensified as one of McClernand's division commanders, Alvin Hovey, drove up the incline against the left of the Confederate line, swept aside the defenders, and captured eleven of their guns. However, Pemberton summoned John Bowen's division from the center of the line to lead a furious counterattack against Hovey. The hard-pressed Hovey was reinforced by two of McPherson's divisions under "Black Jack" Logan and Marcellus Crocker. Both sides took turns pushing the other back in what turned into a brawl. Around 4:00 p.m., the Confederate left gave way under pressure applied by Logan. Pemberton's battered troops were forced to retreat toward Vicksburg. On the evening of May 16, they were in a defensive position at the Big Black River, about twelve miles east of Vicksburg.

Two aspects of the Champion Hill battle bear comment. First, with the exception of Hovey's division, the rest of McClernand's corps was virtually uninvolved in the fight. If they had been brought forward, Pemberton might have been cut off. Grant rued this lost opportunity, commenting, "McClernand, with two divisions was within a few miles of the battlefield before noon, and in easy hearing. I sent him repeated orders by staff officers fully competent to explain to him the situation. . . . Had McClernand come up with reasonable promptness, or had I known the ground as I did afterwards, I cannot see how Pemberton could have escaped with any organized force."[13]

Also, the battle was remarkable for its ferocity and terrible carnage, the images of which were etched on the memories of the survivors. One recalled how the tall magnolia trees on the hill, in full bloom, had many of their limbs amputated by the hail of shot and shell, and that on a single oak tree, two hundred bullet marks could be counted.[14] General Hovey, a participant at Shiloh, was moved to report, "It was, after the conflict, literally the hill of death; men, horses, cannon, and the debris of an army lay scattered in wild confusion. . . . I never saw fighting like this."[15] Almost four thousand killed and wounded, blue and gray, covered the battleground.

After the fighting ceased, Charles Dana and Rawlins rode onto the battlefield. They encountered General Logan, who was still so gripped by the day's furor that he declined to believe his side had won. Dana and Rawlins continued their ride over to where the fighting had been severest. There, dead and wounded of both sides lay intermingled. To their surprise, a badly wounded elderly Confederate hoisted himself to an elbow and implored, "For God's sake, gentlemen, is there a Mason among you?"

Rawlins dismounted and knelt beside the dying man. The member of the Galena Miners' Lodge responded, "Yes, I am a Mason." Feeling secure that his last wishes would be honored, he gave Rawlins some letters and a keepsake. Would he pledge to convey them to his wife in Alabama? Rawlins was moved to tears by the man's plight and soon kept his promise to return these precious objects.[16] Grant, Rawlins, and the rest of the staff overnighted at a nearby farmhouse, sleeping under the porch. However, it was a fitful sleep. The house was full of wounded Confederate soldiers, including one in a raving delirium due to brain trauma.[17]

Rawlins was up at dawn on the seventeenth, a Sunday, and was soon in the saddle, riding west with Grant and Dana in pursuit of Pemberton, who the night before had retreated to a prepared position at the Big Black River. On arriving at the Confederate defensive line at 7:00 a.m., they found it to be an intimidating presence: rifle pits, artillery placements, abatis, and fronted by a swampy bayou with chest-deep water. This had the makings of a hotly contested fight under a broiling sun. Then the unexpected happened. Two of McClernand's divisions that had not partaken in the Champion Hill fight and that were now perched on the right of the Union line began making menacing actions. Suddenly, a Union brigade broke loose from that group and sprinted forward, pitching into the muddy bayou water and emerging against the blazing rifles of the Confederate defenders. It was Michael Lawler's brigade. The burly Irishman, a farmer from Shawneetown, Illinois, had shed his tunic and urged on his men. Lawler's audacity spurred the advance of other units across the Union front. As the Confederate defenders staggered back, Pemberton issued an order to withdraw. The demoralized Rebel remnant—only about one-third remained of the twenty-three thousand Pemberton took into action a week before—retreated to Vicksburg. Their parting act of defiance was to destroy bridges across the Big Black.

Ironically, this Union victory might never have happened. Rawlins recounted later that before Lawler's charge, an officer had ridden up to Grant bearing an order from Halleck. Written six days earlier, it ordered Grant to withdraw immediately and march south to join Banks's operation against

Port Hudson. Grant blithely ignored these stale orders. The battle might have turned tragic for Grant because "Veteran" Fred had foolishly joined in the pursuit of the retreating Confederates. Rawlins revealed at an 1864 holiday get-together with the Grants that Fred was grazed by a ball to his left thigh. He was taken to a field surgeon, who found "that the ball had only clipped out a little piece of flesh." The incident was far enough in the past that Rawlins could quip, "He was not damaged enough to have joined the ranks of the disabled."[18]

Wilson was pressed into constructing three bridges to enable the corps of McPherson and McClernand to cross the Big Black. One was cobbled together from timber torn from a railroad trestle, another fashioned out of cotton bales, and the third from planks ripped from barns and cotton gins. Crews toiled through the night in illumination from torches and bonfires. A sleep-deprived but uncomplaining John Rawlins demonstrated his willingness to pitch in, riding with Dana and Wilson from site to site, encouraging the crews and lending a hand where needed.[19]

—◦◦◦—

The Army of the Tennessee moved swiftly to pin the Confederates behind their intimidating Vicksburg fortifications. By late evening on May 18, the city was invested—Sherman on the north of the Union line, McPherson to the east, and McClernand on McPherson's left. Grant, believing the enemy was reeling from its string of defeats, wasted no time trying to deliver a knock-out punch. He launched an all-out assault at 2:00 p.m. on the nineteenth. The assault over difficult terrain was not well coordinated and met stiff resistance from revived Rebel defenders. The little ground the attackers purchased came at a cost of over nine hundred casualties. Undeterred, Grant ordered a renewed attack on the morning of May 22. It too failed despite a sacrifice of three thousand killed and wounded. The May 22 fiasco, however, did result in two consequential outcomes: it convinced Grant that laying siege to Vicksburg was his most viable path to victory, and it placed General John McClernand on the lip of a slippery slope down which he would slide to his abrupt dismissal—a result Rawlins would heartily endorse.

Around 11:15 on the morning of the twenty-second, McClernand requested Grant to have McPherson make a diversion to take enemy pressure off him, but Grant declined, telling McClernand to use his men who were held in reserve.[20] In another dispatch sent at noon, McClernand confidently reported, "We have part possession of two forts, and the Stars and Stripes are floating over them. A vigorous push ought to be made all along the line."[21] Grant doubted this claim, but Sherman counseled him that McClernand's request ought to be acknowledged. Grant relented and sent one of McPherson's divisions to reinforce McClernand, and he ordered McPherson and Sherman to renew their attacks. These efforts resulted only in burgeoning the Union casualty lists. Some thought McClernand exaggerated the gains he had made within the enemy forts. Dana, for example, telegraphed Stanton the next day that "McClernand's report was false, as he held not a single fort, and the result was disastrous."[22] Sylvanus Cadwallader—if his eyewitness account of the assault is valid—claimed that a few of McClernand's men reached the Confederate earthworks but never established footing in them. Cadwallader said he related his account to Grant and Rawlins, who probed him about it. As the details emerged, Rawlins became livid and let loose a string of execrations, whereas Grant's face revealed "the grim glowering look of disappointment and disgust."[23] A furious Grant complained to Halleck that "General McClernand's dispatches misled me as to the real state of facts, and caused me much loss. He is entirely unfit for the position of corps commander, both on the march and on the battlefield."[24]

The mood that evening at Grant's headquarters was especially tense. Many of the corps and division commanders were present, and they were not favorably inclined toward McClernand. Rawlins captured the anger boiling inside everyone when he told Joe Bowers to make an entry in the record book charging a thousand lives "to that _____ McClernand." Rawlins used his choicest profanity to put an exclamation point on his feelings.[25]

McClernand might have adopted a lower profile at this point, but that was not in this politician's makeup. Two weeks later, with the siege firmly established, Grant ordered McClernand to send troops to reinforce crossings on the Big Black River. The order was delivered by Lieutenant Colonel Wilson, who found himself the object of McClernand's misdirected rage: "I'll be God damned if I'll do it—I am tired of being dictated to—I won't stand it any longer, and you can go back and tell General Grant!" After his initial astonishment abated, Wilson reminded him of the consequences of disobeying the order. Then he fired a warning shot across McClernand's bow: "And now, General, in addition to your highly insubordinate language, it seems to me that you are cursing me as much as you are cursing General Grant. If this is so, although you are a major general, while I am only a lieutenant colonel, I will pull you off that horse and beat the boots off of you!" On his return, Wilson related the incident to Rawlins and Grant. The latter reassured him, "I'll get rid of McClernand first chance I get."[26]

That chance materialized in mid-June. On May 30, McClernand issued an order—a congratulatory letter, really—to his Thirteenth Corps regarding their recent battlefield heroics. In part it read, "On the 22d, in pursuance of the order from the commander of the department, you assaulted the enemy's defenses in front at 10 a.m., and within thirty minutes had made a lodgment and planted your colors upon two of his bastions. This partial success called into exercise the highest heroism, and was only gained by a bloody and protracted struggle; yet it was gained, and was the first and largest success achieved anywhere along the whole line of our army. . . . How and why the general assault failed, it would be useless now to explain."[27] The order slipped into newspapers and then into the hands of McPherson and Sherman, who felt it was a rebuke of the efforts made by their corps. Sherman complained to Rawlins, calling McClernand's statements "a catalogue of nonsense—such an effusion of vain-glory and hypocrisy" and accusing him of engaging in "his process of self-flattery."[28] Because such a communiqué violated Grant's stipulation that official publications needed headquarters approval, McClernand was vulnerable.

On June 18, Rawlins issued Special Orders No. 164, announcing, "Major General John A. McClernand is hereby relieved from the command of the 13th Army Corps. . . . Major General E. O. C. Ord is hereby appointed to the command."[29] Ord was returning to field duty after recovering from a battle wound. Rawlins gave a copy of the order to Wilson to deliver to McClernand. Because the hour was late, Rawlins told him to wait until morning, but Wilson insisted on delivering it immediately lest Grant might rescind it. Wilson arrived at McClernand's headquarters about 2:00 a.m. and, after saluting, said, "General, I have an important order for you which I am directed to deliver into your hands and to see that you read it in my presence, that you understand it, and that you signify your immediate obedience to it." On reading the order, McClernand exclaimed, "Well, sir! I am relieved! By God, sir, we are both relieved!"[30]

McClernand was gone from the Army of the Tennessee, but he was not exiting quietly. He bombarded Lincoln with missives in which he argued his case. He wrote Stanton requesting an investigation of Grant's conduct.[31] On returning near the end of June to his Springfield, Illinois, home, McClernand was greeted like a hero and serenaded by bands.[32] Governor Yates liberally interceded on his behalf with Lincoln, suggesting McClernand be returned to his former command and crowing, "He has been received by the people here [Springfield] with the greatest demonstrations of respect, all regretting that he is not now in the field."[33] Grant and Rawlins had ample reason to be concerned these accolades might encourage McClernand to stir up trouble. In July, Rawlins would be sent on a sensitive mission to prevent matters from getting out of hand.

—⁓—

Following the unsuccessful assaults, the Army of the Tennessee constructed a semicircle of entrenchments that were cinched tighter every day, blocking Pemberton from receiving supplies, munitions, and reinforcements by land or water. Grant's headquarters was situated on a bluff at the top of the semicircle within Sherman's sector. For most of the siege, he and his staff lived in open-flap tents meant to catch the occasional breeze that offered scant relief from the muggy heat. Feelings ran optimistic at headquarters that Pemberton would soon surrender—a realistic prediction considering his thirty thousand troops were poorly nourished and outfitted. Grant liked to hold strategy discussions in his tent at this time of the campaign. Sherman, it was said, presented himself as "brilliant and trenchant," whereas McPherson gave the impression of being "politically critical and intellectual." Rawlins, true to his nature, "would break in occasionally with some blunt and vigorous opinion." While taking in his subordinates' views, Grant sat "impassable and dumb in his camp-chair, smoking," but his passive posture belied how the discussion stimulated his common sense and boosted confidence in his judgments.[34]

Yet Grant was by no means smugly confident. He fretted about the intentions of Joe Johnston, who was said to be assembling a sizable force at Canton, a hard day's march north of Jackson. The fear was that Johnston might spring an attack at Haynes' Bluff on the Yazoo River's east bank, twelve miles northeast of Grant's headquarters. In anticipation, Grant dispatched troops and patrols to check a possible enemy incursion. These Union forces were sent toward the towns of Satartia on the Yazoo River some forty miles beyond Haynes' Bluff and Mechanicsburg, about four miles southeast of Satartia. Brigadier General Nathan Kimball's division, just arrived from Memphis, was dispatched on June 3 to Satartia. Kimball immediately sent ominous reports to Rawlins regarding estimates, likely exaggerated, of enemy strength thereabouts. Kimball was so alarmed that he deemed it prudent to fall back to Haynes' Bluff.[35] To

Grant, the situation was threatening enough to warrant an in-person investigation. On June 6, he and Dana embarked on the *Diligence*, a small steamer to head up the Yazoo River. They departed from Haynes' Bluff about 7:00 p.m. Before departing, Dana dashed off a brief note to Stanton that "Grant was ill and went to bed soon after he started."[36]

Grant's departure on the *Diligence* capped a week of escalating drama at headquarters. Since at least May 31, Grant had been suffering from an indeterminate illness that led him to seek treatment from Dr. Charles McMillan, Sherman's medical director. Perhaps Grant was suffering from migraines, an affliction that had tormented him for years. If so, the wine McMillan prescribed might have exacerbated the problem.[37] It certainly aggravated Rawlins. Perhaps Grant was sickened by the muggy heat. Admiral Porter had gotten so overheated that he had begged off meeting with Grant on May 31, the same day Grant complained of feeling ill.[38]

Rawlins had noticed Grant showed signs—impaired decision making and trouble expressing thoughts in writing—that he took as evidence of drinking. If Rawlins was only leery, the box of wine he discovered on June 5 before Grant's tent removed all doubt. That evening, Grant socialized with a group of gentlemen, empty wine bottle in their midst. An unnamed captain recently assigned to duty at headquarters, so it was later revealed, had smuggled some boxes of wine through the lines to entertain a party arriving in camp to visit Grant. It was one of these boxes that Rawlins found. Rawlins learned the identity of the smuggler, descended on his tent, extracted a confession, and ordered him away from Grant's army.[39]

That evening as he repaired to his tent, Rawlins felt compelled to directly address the drinking issue. While bent over his desk, he knew that to him, and to him alone, fell the responsibility of pressing on his superior the enormity of the risks at stake. No one else had the audacity or the leverage to confront Grant because no one believed more in him than Rawlins. A message, earnestly expressed, must be conveyed to Grant. It needed to sound an alarm and appeal to his sense of honor and desire to succeed. There needed to be a balance between sincere support for his commander and the challenge Rawlins felt he must lay down in order to implant backbone into his intervention. Rawlins summoned that voice within and began committing it to paper. As night progressed into morning, the message took shape, the complex themes were articulated just so, and what emerged might be the most eloquent person-to-person temperance address of the Civil War:

The great solicitude I feel for the safety of this army leads me to mention what I had hoped never again to do—the subject of your drinking. This may surprise you, for I may be (and I trust I am) doing you an injustice by unfounded suspicions, but if an error it better be on the side of his country's safety than in fear of offending a friend. I have heard that Dr. McMillan, at Gen. Sherman's a few days ago, induced you, notwithstanding your pledge to me, to take a glass of wine, and to-day, when I found a box of wine in front of your tent and proposed to move it, which I did, I was told you had forbid its being taken away, for you intended to keep it until you entered Vicksburg, that you might have it for your friends; and to-night, when you should, because of the condition of your health if nothing else, have been in bed, I find you where the wine bottle has just been emptied, in company with those who drink and urge you to do likewise, and the lack of your usual promptness of decision and clearness in expressing yourself in writing tended to confirm my suspicions.

You have the *full* control of your appetite and can let drinking alone. Had you not pledged me the sincerity of your honor early last March that you would drink no more during the war, and kept that pledge during your recent campaign, you would not to-day have stood first in the world's history as a successful military leader. Your only salvation depends upon your strict adherence to that pledge. You cannot succeed in any other way. As I have before stated, I may be wrong in my suspicions, but if one sees that which leads him to suppose a sentinel is falling asleep on his post, it is his duty to arouse him; and if one sees that which leads him to fear the General commanding a great army is being seduced to that step which he knows will bring disgrace upon that General and defeat to his command, if he fails to sound the proper note of warning, the friends, wives, and children of those brave men whose lives he permits to remain thus imperilled will accuse him while he lives and stand swift witnesses of wrath against him in the day when all shall be tried. If my suspicions are unfounded, let my friendship for you and my zeal for my country be my excuse for this letter; and if they are correctly founded, and you determine not to heed the admonitions and the prayers of this hasty note by immediately ceasing to touch a single drop of any kind of liquor, no matter by whom asked or under what circumstances, let my immediate relief from duty in this department be the result. I am, General, your friend,

John A. Rawlins[40]

Satisfied he had struck the right balance, Rawlins made copies, and late in the afternoon of June 6, he hand-delivered one to Grant. Grant, Dana, and a small cavalry escort had ridden out toward Haynes' Bluff, where Rawlins caught up with them. Before boarding the *Diligence* for Satartia, Dana recalled that Grant pocketed the letter.[41] It is not known what immediate reactions either Grant or Rawlins shared about the contents of the letter. However, Rawlins's intervention apparently worked to good effect, because Rawlins had written on a retained copy an undated endorsement saying, "This is an exact copy of a letter to the person addressed, and delivered at its date about four miles from our headquarters in rear of Vicksburg. Its admonitions were heeded and all went well."[42]

Neither Rawlins nor Grant would live to witness how one's letter and the other's inspection trip would turn into a controversy that has lingered for over a century.

—◦∿◦—

Rawlins's June 6 letter to Grant and his undated endorsement were first made public in a long letter written by newspaper correspondent Henry Van Ness Boynton, an old nemesis of both Grant and Sherman. Boynton's letter, entitled "Grant's Liquor Drinking," appeared in the January 23, 1887, *New York Sun*, Charles Dana's paper. It was sensational front-page news. By revealing episodes of "Grant's yielding to his old habits at several critical times during the war," Boynton wanted to show how close the country came to disaster. "This secret chapter cannot be longer concealed," he wrote, "and it must henceforth be recognized as a part of the truth of history." As one example, Boynton lifted extracts from a February 19, 1863, letter sent to Treasury Secretary Chase by Boynton's crony, Murat Halstead, editor of the *Cincinnati Commercial*. Halstead shared with Chase information he was given by a correspondent at Vicksburg who complained that the Federal army was demoralized, sick, and commanded by "the foolish, drunken, stupid Grant." Now, to corroborate the charges laid out in Halstead's letter, Boynton released Rawlins's missive, which may have been furnished to him by a Rawlins family member.

Besides disparaging Grant, Boynton had another agenda: to elevate Rawlins's stature and give him long-deserved due. Boynton melodramatically wondered "what terrible possibilities" would have befallen the nation if Rawlins hadn't intervened. He praised Rawlins as one who "stood guard for the country, a sentinel of unceasing vigilance, a friend of unflinching courage, and a patriot of sterling mould." But perhaps more significant, Rawlins was "the man who rescued Grant, and made possible the successes and the greatness of his subsequent career." Boynton also advanced the notion that "the two men formed one complete, though by no means perfect character."[43] Although it is true that Rawlins possessed certain complementary or compensatory personal qualities and that he could advise, persuade, or remonstrate with Grant, few today would credit him with his commander's achievements.

Five days later, the *Sun* ran an editorial, no doubt written by Dana, that piggybacked on Boynton's letter. The editorial, "Gen. Grant's Occasional Intoxication," began with the argument that Lincoln was right to promote Grant because his "seasons of intoxication were not only infrequent" but timed so as not to interfere with important military movements. As an example, Dana revealed his own experience with Grant on the "excursion up the Yazoo" toward Satartia. The Satartia trip, the editorial claimed, was one such time when the campaign had entered a "dull period." (Dana was wrong on these points: the trip was not an excursion, and Grant embarked on it to investigate a possibly serious military situation.) Dana also mentioned that Rawlins delivered his "admirable" letter to Grant prior to his boarding the steamer. Then Dana unloaded his own sensational clincher: Once aboard, Grant is said to have proceeded "getting as stupidly drunk as the immortal nature of man would allow; but the next day he came out as fresh as a rose, without any trace or indication of the spree he had passed through."[44] Thus, we have Dana taking the incongruous position of lauding Grant for responsibly timing his bouts of intoxication but ridiculing him for being intoxicated.

Dana, ten years later and just before his death, revised his story. In this second version, Grant was "ill" and took to bed shortly after leaving Haynes' Bluff. The general's steamer was close to Satartia when it met two gunboats coming downriver. The gunboats' officers reported that since General Kimball had pulled back, the area was no longer safe. Dana ordered *Diligence* to turn around, but only after consulting Grant, who said he was too ill to make the decision. The next morning back at Haynes' Bluff, Grant presented himself for breakfast "fresh as a rose, clean shirt and all, quite himself." He may have been fresh, but he was under the impression the boat was docked at Satartia.[45] Had Grant been ill, or was Dana coyly hinting he was drunk? What accounts for the discrepancies in the two versions? Had Dana mellowed in his last months? Was he sparing the Grant family further embarrassment? No firm answers have been forthcoming.

In response to Boynton, Sylvanus Cadwallader chimed in with his own piece, "Grant and Rawlins," which appeared in February 1887 in the St. Louis *Globe-Democrat*.[46] He chastised Boynton for opening "a mournful chapter in history, which millions of patriotic hearts sincerely hoped had been closed forever by the death of Gen. Grant." And he denounced the "traducers of Gen. Grant" who wanted to show that "the glorious reputation he confessedly achieved was due to the advice, support and maintenance given him by others, and by the control sometimes notably exercised over him by Gen. Rawlins." Then, rather disingenuously, Cadwallader proceeded to make that exact argument, calling Rawlins "the source and inspiration of Gen. Grant's brilliant achievements."

According to Cadwallader, it is no exaggeration that without Rawlins, Grant would have been nothing. This applied not only to Grant's military accomplishments but even to his character. Regarding the former, Cadwallader claimed, "He had such implicit faith in Rawlins' judgment that he distrusted his own plans if they did not commend themselves to Gen. Rawlins." Moreover, Grant "never adopted the plan for a campaign, nor moved an army, or changed a corps, a corps commander, nor any commissioned officer, without the full consent of Gen. Rawlins." As for the latter, Cadwallader said Rawlins was known to have been "the power behind Grant, even greater than Grant himself." Perhaps more remarkable is Cadwallader's assessment of Grant's makeup: "Grant's was a dual existence, composed of Grant-Rawlins, with the Rawlins element in all emergencies strongly predominating."

Was Cadwallader's disappointment with Grant's memoirs a factor in compelling him to regard Grant a midget in comparison to Rawlins—as well in constructing his own controversial version of Grant's trip to Satartia?

—◦◦◦—

Not too long before writing "Grant and Rawlins," Cadwallader had read Grant's two-volume memoirs. Cadwallader was stunned, as were many who knew Rawlins, as to why Grant had made few references to Rawlins in the entire work. The longest reference to Rawlins covers about a page and includes a notable passage: "He was an able man, possessed of great firmness, and could say 'no' so emphatically to a request which he thought should not be granted that the person he was addressing would understand at once that there was no use pressing the matter. General Rawlins was a very useful officer in other ways than this. I became very much attached to him."[47] That Grant deemed Rawlins "useful," but in ways never specified, galled Cadwallader.

The Rawlins-Cadwallader relationship had been so thick that Cadwallader and his wife even shared a home in Georgetown with Rawlins and his second wife in 1866, the year that the Cadwalladers' son, whom they named Rawlins, was born. Thus, it is understandable that Cadwallader felt Rawlins had been betrayed by Grant. Just a week after his *Globe-Democrat* piece was published, Cadwallader expressed his deep disappointment and anger in a revealing letter to Harry Wilson, his good friend and a Rawlins advocate: "You may partly appreciate but can never wholly understand my feelings when I had read through to the end. At first my surprise was stupefying, but those soon gave way to indignation at the cold, hard, heartless fact that [Grant] could have written such a book at such length, and dismissed R[awlins] from history (as far as he could do it) with a single commonplace paragraph. . . . Time has tempered my anger, and I am trying to charitably attribute it to human infirmity, without thinking bitterly of Gen. Grant. But it is not easy to do, and he has lost a place in my heart to which nothing can ever restore him."[48] Whether time tempered Cadwallader's anger is debatable, because seventeen years later, he still harbored strong feelings about needing to defend Rawlins by laying bare Grant's imperfections, and he shared those feelings again with Wilson: "My intimate acquaintance with Grant's intemperate habits was not revealed to everyone till the war was over, and concealment no longer necessary. From that day to this when Rawlins's vindication made it necessary to tell some plain truths about Grant. I have taken the ground that Grant was large enough to bear some faultfinding, and strong enough to bear the burden of all imperfections which could be laid upon him. . . . But justice to [Rawlins] will require much plain speaking in the matter of intoxicants.[49]" Cadwallader, while hoping to bring about justice to Rawlins, would tell some tall tales about Grant's intemperate habits.

Like Dana and Grant, Cadwallader wrote his own personal memoirs, except that after he finished them in 1896, they sat for decades, unpublished and mostly forgotten. Historian Benjamin Thomas resurrected Cadwallader's handwritten manuscript and published it in greatly edited form as *Three Years with Grant*. Cadwallader shared the raw manuscript with James Wilson. During their exchanges of correspondence over the years, Rawlins's two old friends traded jaundiced views about former comrades, speculated about what happened to Rawlins's large cache of letters and documents after he died in 1869, and wondered who provided Boynton with Rawlins's June 6 letter.[50] They also shared similar attitudes vis-à-vis Grant and Rawlins, as Wilson indicated to Cadwallader: "There is no difference between you and me as to the proper theory about Grant and the historical treatment which should be accredited to him in connection with his relations with Rawlins. I agree fully with you that Rawlins was at least one half of Grant."[51]

If Cadwallader used his book of reminiscences to vindicate Rawlins by telling some "plain truths" about Grant, he did so in a sensational and controversial version of the Satartia trip, or what is often referred to as Grant's "Yazoo Bender." It's a story that has been embraced by some serious scholars and discredited by others.[52] In Cadwallader's version, he placed himself aboard the *Diligence* returning from his own reconnaissance trip to Satartia when he encountered Grant—Cadwallader made no mention of Dana being present—on another steamboat en route to Satartia. Grant requested a transfer to the *Diligence* and ordered it to turn about and head back to Satartia. Cadwallader noticed that not only had Grant been drinking (he was "stupid in speech and staggering in gait"), but he was determined to keep at it. Cadwallader's account contains such highlights as his locking a drunken Grant in a stateroom on the *Diligence*; Cadwallader throwing whiskey bottles overboard, undressing Grant, and fanning him to sleep; Grant commandeering a horse at the Chickasaw Bayou landing and riding pell-mell over bridges, past guards, and through soldiers' camps before Cadwallader overtook him and seized the reins; and Cadwallader summoning an ambulance to have the wobbly Grant hauled back to headquarters. There they were supposedly met by Colonel Riggin and a fuming John Rawlins. Cadwallader feared Rawlins would excoriate him if he thought he was to blame, but Rawlins is to have suppressed his anger and said, "I want you to tell me the exact facts—and all of them—without any concealment. I have a right to know them, and I will know them." Cadwallader related that he told Rawlins the whole sordid story, for which he received Rawlins's thanks and a promise there would be no "disagreeable consequences" for what he had done.[53]

All this makes for entertaining reading, but as Bruce Catton concluded, "It is extremely hard to see how the Cadwallader story can be classed as anything but one more in the dreary Grant-was-drunk garland of myths."[54] Other historians call Cadwallader's account "concocted" and state that he "lied and lied in the extreme."[55] Unfortunately, Cadwallader contributed to shaping the perception of Grant as a pathetic inebriate. The story can be exploded for a variety of reasons. For example, Michael Ballard found no evidence in soldiers' letters and diaries that support Cadwallader's tale of a drinking spree or a wild ride through the soldiers' camps. Surely, such an event would have been recounted in detail for the folks back home.[56] Also, Rawlins's endorsement appended to the June 6 letter that his "admonitions were heeded and all went well" does not correspond with the angry Rawlins that Cadwallader said he encountered after bringing Grant back to headquarters.

Despite collaborating in 1868 on a friendly biography of Grant, Dana and Wilson also came to regard him with disappointment. In the early days of Grant's first presidential term, Dana expected to be appointed collector of customs for the Port of New York. Rawlins even expressed his approval of Dana for the job. However, Grant gave the plum to Moses Grinnell, a former congressman. Despite being passed over, Dana's dismay with Grant arose more from the scandals that rocked his administration. One *Sun* editorial mourned the fact that the country was "passing through an epoch of public corruption without precedent in its history, and almost in the history of free governments."[57] When Grant in his later years came to financial ruin, Dana opposed Congress granting him a pension.

Wilson too became critical of the corruption and shady politicians that threatened to bring down Grant. Wilson's younger brother, Bluford, who served as solicitor of the Treasury Department, was involved in investigating and prosecuting the culprits involved in the Whiskey Ring fraud. By the end of Grant's first term, his and Wilson's relationship had fractured, and the two men eventually parted company.

As Dana and Wilson became estranged from Grant, both did their part to elevate Rawlins's stature, even sometimes promoting him above Grant. But neither did so by resorting to the belittling tactics Cadwallader employed. At the time Rawlins was appointed secretary of war, Dana's *Sun* applauded the choice, declaring Rawlins "is a man of high moral and intellectual qualities. He knows what his present position requires and will be more than equal to all its duties."[58] Just six years earlier, Dana thought it a "mistake" to regard Rawlins as even "a first-rate adjutant."[59] How much Rawlins had grown in such short time! Wilson frequently heard Dana "express the opinion that had Rawlins lived and retained his influence, Grant's civil career would have been as creditable as his military career."[60] This fits with Dana's summation of Rawlins that "without him Grant would not have been the same man."[61]

Given Wilson's lasting friendship with Rawlins and his falling away from Grant, it is not surprising that Wilson's biography of Rawlins is positively biased toward him. In Wilson's estimation, Rawlins shored up Grant's makeup: Rawlins's "highest function was in protecting Grant from himself as well as from others, in stimulating his sense of duty and ambition, and in giving direction and purpose to his military training and aptitudes. It was Rawlins, more than any other man, who aroused Grant's sensibilities and gave his actions that prompt, aggressive, and unrelenting character which so distinguished them." And according to Wilson, it was Rawlins who self-effacingly became alloyed with Grant to bond into something greater: "In fact it has been frequently and truthfully said that the two together constituted a military character of great simplicity, force, and singleness of purpose, which has passed into history under the name of Grant." This was Wilson echoing Boynton's claim that the two melded into one complete character. Moreover, Wilson argued that Rawlins provided Grant with the ingredients essential to his success: "it seems to be certain that Rawlins . . . furnished him with qualities and characteristics which Grant did not possess at all, or which he possessed in a limited degree, and without which, either from Rawlins or from some other source in whom he had confidence, it would have been impossible for him to succeed as he did."[62]

In effect, with claims such as these, Wilson was being unfair to both Grant and Rawlins. As Wilson biographer Edwin Longacre concluded, Wilson's "deep friendship with Rawlins and his checkered association with Grant caused him to paint a less than wholly accurate picture of those men's relationships. Specifically, he helped perpetuate the myth of a commanding general almost totally dependent on his adjutant's temperance, prudence, and probity to stabilize and strengthen his character. Later historians, failing to recognize the bias in Wilson's viewpoint, accepted such assertions as fact."[63] Rawlins was not the source of Grant's success but a contributor to it. Rawlins gave unstintingly of his service, was able to offer frank advice, consistently had the good of Grant at heart, provided input regarding campaign planning, and could intervene to prevent his commander from being imposed on. Perhaps Adam Badeau had the most accurate perspective on how Rawlins might have reacted to being regarded as the complement to Grant: "It did not take Grant and Rawlins to make Grant, as some have said who knew neither intimately. Rawlins himself would have been the first to repel the pretension. He was simply an earnest, able man who devoted himself absolutely to serving his country, and for him this was synonymous with serving Grant."[64]

—∞—

Two issues related to the Satartia discussion bear further scrutiny. The first deals with the June 6 temperance letter Rawlins allegedly delivered to Grant. Julia Grant commented about this letter after she learned that John Shaw read it before an audience in late 1891. She believed that Rawlins kept a copy of it for less than honorable intentions: "*If* such a letter was *ever sent*, General Grant *must* have felt that *devotion alone prompted such a letter*, but how could Rawlins have kept this letter? To me, it looks very like making a record for the future."[65] Bruce Catton agreed, lauding her for her perspicacity. "And as Julia remarked," Catton surmised, "the preservation of this letter looks very much as if this devoted defender of Grant's reputation had been trying to make a record. . . . [Rawlins] was known as the keeper of Grant's conscience, and he did what he could to build up his own reputation. With a defender like Rawlins, Grant had no need of any enemies."[66] To Catton, this looked much like Rawlins applying his lawyerly skills to create a paper trail on his behalf. However, it is not known for what purpose Rawlins retained a copy, but it was almost certainly not to disparage or undercut Grant. If he was establishing a record, Rawlins, a man who harbored deep self-doubt due to his deficient background, could have been demonstrating how he was indispensable to Grant.

The second issue concerns the mystery of why Rawlins is so infrequently referenced in Grant's *Memoirs*. Writing to an old Grant friend during the aftermath of the Boynton letter brouhaha, William Sherman said the reason was that "some of Rawlins's flatterers gave out the impression that he, Rawlins, had made Grant, and had written most of his orders and dispatches at Donelson, Shiloh and Vicksburg—Grant disliked being patronized—and though he always was most grateful for all friendly service he hated to be considered an 'accident.'"[67] Sherman's explanation fits with chatter in certain circles at that time unfairly crediting Rawlins for having "supplied Grant with brains."[68] Grant historian John Simon conjectured the reason was Grant tired of hearing Rawlins mentioned as his conscience, his shadow, or the "genius behind Grant's success."[69] E. B. Long allowed that it is not known whether Grant's slighting Rawlins was a conscious omission or due to faulty recollection. Like Simon, he surmised that Grant's reluctance to credit Rawlins was to squelch the whispers that he was Grant's protector.[70] And so the mystery persists.

After the *Diligence* returned Dana and Grant to Haynes' Bluff on the morning of June 7, Grant asked him to accompany a detail of cavalry to the Satartia area to investigate whether Johnston was making an advance. Dana endured an exhausting scouting ride that found no evidence of Johnston moving his command. Over the next three weeks, Grant sought intelligence about Johnston's intentions, but the wary Confederate made no effort to assist Pemberton.[71] Meanwhile, several divisions of reinforcements were coming Grant's way. And it seemed that daily the Union besiegers inexorably tightened their grip and edged closer to the Vicksburg defenses. By mid-June, the Federals had closed within twenty-five yards of the Confederate line. Now Grant felt confident enough to boast to his father, "I have the enemy closely hem[m]ed in all round. . . . I do not look upon the fall of Vicksburg as in the least doubtful."[72]

NOTES

1. Special Orders, No. 120, April 30, 1863, in *The Papers of Ulysses S. Grant*, ed. John Y. Simon (Carbondale: Southern Illinois University Press, 1979), 8:137n.

2. John Y. Simon, ed., *The Papers of Ulysses S. Grant*, 8:219n.

3. U. S. Grant to William Hillyer, May 5, 1863, in *The Papers of Ulysses S. Grant*, ed. John Y. Simon, 8:162.

4. *The Ulysses S. Grant Association Newsletter* 3, no. 1 (October 1965).

5. U. S. Grant to Julia Dent Grant, May 3, 1863, in *The Papers of Ulysses S. Grant*, ed. John Y. Simon, 8:155.

6. S. H. M. Byers, *With Fire and Sword* (New York: Neale, 1911), 66.

7. Horace Porter, *Campaigning with Grant* (New York: Century, 1897), 363.

8. U. S. Grant to Henry W. Halleck, May 11, 1863, in *The Papers of Ulysses S. Grant*, ed. John Y. Simon, 8:196.

9. James Harrison Wilson, *Under the Old Flag* (New York: D. Appleton, 1912), 1:198–99.

10. Sylvanus Cadwallader, *Three Years with Grant*, ed. Benjamin P. Thomas (New York: Alfred A. Knopf, 1961), 70–72.

11. James Harrison Wilson, *Under the Old Flag*, 1:203.

12. S. H. M. Byers, *With Fire and Sword* (New York: Neale, 1911), 72.

13. U. S. Grant, *Personal Memoirs*, 519–20.

14. S. H. M. Byers, *With Fire and Sword*, 81–82.

15. Report of Alvin P. Hovey, May 25, 1863, in *The War of the Rebellion: A Compilation of the Official Records of the Union and Confederate Armies*, series 1, part 2, 24:44.

16. Charles A. Dana. *Recollections of the Civil War* (New York: D. Appleton, 1902), 53–54.

17. Albert D. Richardson, *Personal History of Ulysses S. Grant* (Boston: D. L. Guernsey, 319–20.

18. Horace Porter, *Campaigning with Grant*, 364.

19. James Harrison Wilson, *Under the Old Flag*, 1:205–6.

20. John A. McClernand to U. S. Grant, May 22, 1863, in *The War of the Rebellion: A Compilation of the Official Records of the Union and Confederate Armies*, series 1, part 1, 24:172; ibid., U. S. Grant to John A. McClernand.

21. Ibid., John A. McClernand to U. S. Grant, May 22, 1863.

22. Charles A. Dana to E. M. Stanton, May 23, 1863, in *The War of the Rebellion: A Compilation of the Official Records of the Union and Confederate Armies*, series 1, part 1, 24:86.

23. Sylvanus Cadwallader, *Three Years with Grant*, 92.

24. U. S. Grant to H. W. Halleck, May 24, 1863 in *The War of the Rebellion: A Compilation of the Official Records of the Union and Confederate Armies*, series 1, part 1, 24:37.

25. William L. B. Jenney, "Personal Recollections of Vicksburg," in *Military Essays and Recollections* (Chicago: Dial, 1899), 3:261.

26. James Harrison Wilson, *Under the Old Flag*, 182–83.

27. John A. McClernand, General Orders No. 72, May 30, 1863, in *The War of the Rebellion: A Compilation of the Official Records of the Union and Confederate Armies*, series 1, part 1, 24:161.

28. W. T. Sherman to J. A. Rawlins, June 17, 1863, in *The War of the Rebellion: A Compilation of the Official Records of the Union and Confederate Armies*, series 1, part 1, 24:162–63.

29. John Y. Simon, ed., *The Papers of Ulysses S. Grant*, 3:385n.

30. James Harrison Wilson, *Under the Old Flag*, 1:185–86.

31. John A. McClernand to E. M. Stanton, June 27, 1863, in *The War of the Rebellion: A Compilation of the Official Records of the Union and Confederate Armies*, series 1, part 1, 24:166–67.

32. Richard L. Kiper, *Major General John Alexander McClernand: Politician in Uniform* (Kent: Kent State University Press, 1999), 273.

33. R. Yates, O. M. Hatch, and J. K. Dubois to A. Lincoln, August 6, 1863, in *The War of the Rebellion: A Compilation of the Official Records of the Union and Confederate Armies*, series 1, part 1, 52:431; Richard Yates to Abraham Lincoln, June 30, 1863, in *The War of the Rebellion: A Compilation of the Official Records of the Union and Confederate Armies*, series 1, part 1, 24:167–68.

34. Jacob Dolson Cox, *Military Reminiscences of the Civil War* (New York: Charles Scribner's Sons, 1900), 5.

35. John Y. Simon, ed., *The Papers of Ulysses S. Grant*, 8:316–17n.

36. C. A. Dana to E. M. Stanton, June 6, 1863, in *The War of the Rebellion: A Compilation of the Official Records of the Union and Confederate Armies*, series 1, part 1, 24:94; Charles A. Dana, *Recollections of the Civil War*, 83.

37. American Migraine Foundation, accessed June 6, 2017, https://americanmigraine-foundation.org/understanding-migraine/alcohol-and-migraine/.

38. William T. Sherman to U. S. Grant, June 2, 1863, in *The Papers of Ulysses S. Grant*, ed. John Y. Simon, 8:300n.

39. Edward D. Neill, ed., *Glimpses of the Nation's Struggle, Third Series: Papers Read before the Minnesota Commandery of the Military Order of the Loyal Legion of the United States, 1889–1892* (New York: D. D. Merrill, 1893), 396–97.

40. *New York Sun*, "Grant's Liquor Drinking," January 23, 1887.

41. *New York Sun*, "General Grant's Intoxication," January 28, 1887. This editorial was likely written by Dana himself, who was editor of the *Sun* at the time.

42. *New York Sun*, "Grant's Liquor Drinking," January 23, 1887.

43. *New York Sun*, January 23, 1887; William T. Sherman, in a February 4, 1887, letter to his former aide-de-camp John E. Tourtelotte, said he had seen Boynton's letter and referred to him as "a Coyote, or hyena, scratching up old forgotten scandals"; Ronald L. Fingerson, "A William Tecumseh Sherman Letter," *Books at Iowa* 3, no. 1 (November 1965): 35.

44. *New York Sun*, January 28, 1887.

45. Charles A. Dana, *Recollections of the Civil War*, 83.

46. *Globe-Democrat*, St. Louis, February 11, 1887.

47. Ulysses S. Grant, *Personal Memoirs of U. S. Grant* (New York: Charles L. Webster, 1885), 256.

48. S. Cadwallader to J. H. Wilson, February 18, 1887, James Harrison Wilson Papers, Container 5, Library of Congress.

49. S. Cadwallader to J. H. Wilson, August 31, 1904, James Harrison Wilson Papers, Container 5, Library of Congress.

50. Cadwallader at one time thought a Rawlins family member furnished Boynton with the letter or a copy; see S. Cadwallader, *Three Years with Grant*, 115. However, later Cadwallader was perhaps not so sure, and he tried pressing Boynton to reveal the name of his source. Boynton declined to do so; see S. Cadwallader to J. H. Wilson, August 31, 1904, James Harrison Wilson Papers, Container 5, Library of Congress. John M. Shaw, a Galena lawyer and acquaintance of Rawlins, said he had a copy of the letter in his possession, which he read during his address on December 8, 1891, before the Minnesota Commandery, Military Order of the Loyal Legion of the United States. Lucien B. Crooker of Mendota, Illinois, formerly of the Fifty-Fifth Illinois and a member of the Illinois state legislature, claimed to have seen a copy of the endorsed letter (at some unspecified point in time) in the possession of Rawlins's Galena neighbor, General John E. Smith. Rawlins is said to have left many of his papers in Smith's care when Rawlins accompanied Grant to the eastern theater in 1864; see L. B. Crooker, "Grant and Rawlins," *The Nation* 57, no. 1481 (November 16, 1893): 369–70.

51. J. H. Wilson to S. Cadwallader, September 8, 1904, James Harrison Wilson Papers, Container 5, Library of Congress.

52. Two early doubters of the veracity of Cadwallader's story were Gordon Parks, "*Three Years with Grant as Recalled by War Correspondent Sylvanus Cadwallader*: An Appraisal," *Wisconsin Magazine of History* 40, no. 1 (1956): 50–56; and Kenneth P. Williams, "Letter to the Editor," *American Heritage* 7, no. 5 (1956): 107–9. Two more recent and compelling criticisms of the story are those by Michael B. Ballard, *Grant at Vicksburg: The General and the Siege* (Carbondale: Southern Illinois University Press, 2013), 43–63; and Brooks D. Simpson, "Introduction to the Bison Books Edition," in *Three Years with Grant as Recalled by War Correspondent Sylvanus Cadwallader*, ed. Benjamin P. Thomas (Lincoln: University of Nebraska Press, 1996), v–xix.

53. *Three Years with Grant as Recalled by War Correspondent Sylvanus Cadwallader*, ed. Benjamin P. Thomas (Lincoln: University of Nebraska Press, 1996), 102–10.

54. Bruce Catton, *Grant Moves South* (Boston: Little, Brown, 1960), 464.

55. Brooks D. Simpson, *Ulysses S. Grant: Triumph over Adversity* (Boston: Houghton Mifflin, 2000), 207; Michael B. Ballard, *Grant at Vicksburg*, 63.

56. Michael B. Ballard, *Grant at Vicksburg*, 56–57.

57. *New York Sun*, February 17, 1872.

58. *New York Sun*, March 12, 1869.

59. Charles A. Dana, *Recollections of the Civil War*, 73.

60. James Harrison Wilson, *The Life of Charles A. Dana* (New York: Harper and Brothers, 1907), 388.

61. Charles A. Dana, *Recollections of the Civil War*, 62.

62. James Harrison Wilson, *The Life of John A. Rawlins* (New York: Neale, 1916), 61–62.

63. Edward G. Longacre, *From Union Stars to Top Hat: A Biography of the Extraordinary General James Harrison Wilson* (Harrisburg, PA: Stackpole, 1972), 285–86.

64. Adam Badeau, *Military History of Ulysses S. Grant* (New York: D. Appleton, 1881), 2:191n.

65. John Y. Simon, ed., *The Personal Memoirs of Julia Dent Grant* (New York: G. P. Putnam's Sons, 1975), 114.

66. Bruce Catton, "Introduction," *The Personal Memoirs of Julia Dent Grant*, ed. John Y. Simon, 4–5.

67. W. T. Sherman to A. H. Markland, July 23, 1887, Abraham Lincoln Presidential Library, Springfield, IL, SC 1383.

68. James Harrison Wilson, *The Life of John A. Rawlins*, 62.

69. John Y. Simon, cited in Michael B. Ballard, *Grant at Vicksburg*, 54.

70. E. B. Long, "John A. Rawlins: Staff Officer Par Excellence," *Civil War Times Illustrated* 12, no. 9 (1974): 43.

71. Charles A. Dana, *Recollections of the Civil War*, 83–85.

72. U. S. Grant to Jesse Root Grant, June 15, 1863, in *The Papers of Ulysses S. Grant*, ed. John Y. Simon, 375–76.

16

"Rawlins Especially Is No Ordina[ry] Man"

THE SECOND HALF OF JUNE brought personnel changes that were to Rawlins's satisfaction. McClernand was out as commander of the Thirteenth Corps, replaced by Major General E. O. C. Ord, a regular army man who would not cause much drama. Having ousted McClernand, Grant, in a telegram to Halleck, bluntly justified his decision: "I should have relieved him long since for general unfitness for his position."[1] Clark Lagow, whom Rawlins had long dismissed as a worthless "rounder," left on sick leave, and Grant doubted he would return.[2] Hillyer too was gone; his departure was expected, but he left in such a rush that he failed to bid Grant farewell, sending an apology only after arriving at his St. Louis home. He blamed the "excruciating" pain in his right arm for his abrupt behavior, and he added he had seen McClernand in St. Louis looking "very abject" and "cut down," which elicited no sympathy at headquarters.[3]

One of the new arrivals was Captain Ely Parker. Soon after the war began, Parker traveled to Washington to offer his services as an army engineer to Secretary of State William Seward. But Seward rebuked Parker's offer, lecturing the proud Seneca chieftain, "The fight must be settled by the white man alone" and advising him to "go home and cultivate your farm." Finally, Seward's wrong had been corrected. Parker was the recent recipient of a commission and assigned to Brigadier General John E. Smith's division in McPherson's corps as assistant adjutant general and engineer. In October he would join Grant's staff.[4] It is curious that with Hillyer gone and Lagow on leave that Rawlins expressed no formal objection to Parker's joining the staff despite no doubt being aware of accusations in Galena regarding his "dissipations."[5]

Also joining Grant's staff was thirty-two-year-old Captain Cyrus Comstock, the new chief engineer. Comstock was transferred from the Army of the Potomac, and he came with a fancy pedigree. He graduated from West Point at the top of his class and then served on its faculty. The Massachusetts-born Comstock was said to possess "somewhat the air of a Yankee schoolmaster, buttoned in a military coat."[6] He was one of the bright, professionally trained officers who would assume prominent roles on staff. Against men like these, Rawlins, the coarse, haphazardly educated Westerner, would feel uncomfortably inferior.

Despite staff turnover, a war still needed to be waged. Headquarters deemed the end was drawing near for the Vicksburg defenders. Rebel deserters told of scant rations and plummeting morale. To further erode that morale, Rawlins issued orders forbidding all conversation, exchange of newspapers, and "other friendly intercourse between our pickets and those of the enemy's."[7] Grant felt that one robust blow, artfully applied, might break the enemy defenses. That blow was being prepared underneath McPherson's section of the line. Logan's division of McPherson's corps had the men, including those of the Lead Mine Regiment, who could tunnel and dig, and they were burrowing beneath the Confederate fortifications. Once completed, the tunnel was packed with explosives. These were detonated midafternoon of June 25, creating a cavity large enough to accommodate two regiments. Union troops poured into the breach, but despite fierce fighting that lasted into the night, the Confederate line held. At one point during the fighting, McPherson's AAG sent a desperate message to Rawlins: "Find it impossible to hold [this] point without great sacrifice of life. Have withdrawn men, and have opened with artillery. Think we shall yet hold it."[8] Another mine was exploded on July 1, with middling results. Besides doing some damage to the Confederate works, it succeeded in blowing six men into the Union lines. McPherson declined this time against a subsequent assault.

—∽∾∽—

Grant told Dana a day later he would storm Vicksburg on July 6 if Pemberton had not yet surrendered, but that proved unnecessary. At 10:00 a.m. on July 3, General Bowen and an aide rode out under a truce flag and were met by General A. J. Smith. Bowen carried a letter from Pemberton calling for an armistice and the formation of a commission to discuss surrender terms. Grant's written counteroffer was for unconditional surrender, but he told Bowen he would meet Pemberton between the lines that afternoon at 3:00 p.m., if he desired.

At three o'clock, Grant, Rawlins, and Wilson were standing in the shade of a small oak tree within a few rods of the enemy line. On this sultry afternoon, they could see threatening clouds to the west and south that might bring a cooling rain. Generals Logan, Ord, A. J. Smith, and McPherson were also on hand. Pemberton, accompanied by Bowen and several aides, arrived twenty sweltering minutes late.[9] This meeting accomplished little. Grant stuck by the unconditional surrender terms spelled out in his letter, and Pemberton, hoping for more lenience, got testy. Before discussions broke down, Grant proposed sending Pemberton another letter later that night stipulating his final terms.

During the evening of July 3, Grant met with his senior military commanders and listened to their views. Most counseled paroling the Vicksburg garrison rather than sending them north as prisoners. The latter option would tie up steamboats, require a massive outlay of food and medicine, and mean pulling troops to guard thirty thousand Rebels. Better to let the parolees go home—where they were likely to remain, assuming they had had a bellyful full of war—and wait to be exchanged. Rawlins, in his advisory role, objected strenuously, arguing that many would return to Confederate service. Grant opted for parole.[10]

At 10:00 p.m., Grant sent Pemberton his revised terms: officers and men must sign paroles; beginning at 10:00 a.m. on the fourth, they were to march out of the lines, lay down arms, and stack their colors. Officers could keep one horse, their sidearms, and clothing. Enlisted men could keep the clothes on their backs. While he waited for Pemberton's response, Grant had Rawlins send a clever message to Ord and McPherson: "Permit some discreet men on picket to-night to communicate to the enemy's pickets the fact that General Grant has offered, in case Pemberton surrenders, to parole all the officers and men, and to permit them to go home from here."[11] This news would spread like wildfire, leaving Pemberton with a mutiny on his hands if he reneged on a surrender deal.

But there was no reason to worry. Fred Grant, who shared a tent with his father, recollected that after midnight, an orderly appeared bearing a dispatch. "W-e-e-e-ll," Grant said after reading it, "I'm glad Vicksburg will surrender tomorrow."[12]

Word of Vicksburg's imminent capitulation created feverish excitement in the Federal ranks and provided reason for festivities. The superintendent of steamboats, George Graham, telegraphed Rawlins on July 3 requesting permission for his crewmen to celebrate the fourth by firing cannon at sunrise and sunset and having a reading of the Declaration of Independence—and, by the way, could Rawlins send a copy of same early in the morning? Rawlins telegraphed, "I will if I can find one." Sunrise on July 4 came and went, with Graham still awaiting word of the surrender. He telegraphed Rawlins again: "Boys very uneasy along the river[.] Cannot you send me glad tidings something that I can depend upon for Fourth of July?" Rawlins reassured him. "Vicksburg will probably be surrendered at 10 o'clock today, the terms have not yet been fully settled, will be by nine o'clock. Will send you word." Rawlins ended his telegram with advice for Graham: "Don't go off half-cocked."[13]

—◆◆◆—

Rawlins's time estimate was accurate. At 10:00 a.m., Grant and staff were at the front near the oak tree where the previous day's meeting occurred. They watched as Confederate soldiers filed out, stacked arms, and deposited cartridge boxes and knapsacks. A party of Union officers rode inside the Confederate line about one-half mile down the Jackson road to meet Pemberton. The interview took place in a once quaint house, now in sad disorder but surrounded by lush grounds; it had been headquarters of one of Pemberton's division commanders. The conquering Yankees were treated to a cool reception. Grant was forced to stand for most of the formalities. When he requested a glass of water, Wilson recollected that "a member of the Confederate staff merely told him where he could find it."[14]

While Grant and Pemberton concluded their interview, Logan's division marched along the Jackson road, bands playing and colors waving, eager to garrison the captured city. At the forefront was the Lead Mine Regiment. Its flag, the one presented by the ladies of Galena in 1861, now begrimed and battle-torn, was hoisted atop the Vicksburg courthouse.[15]

Grant and staff repaired to the riverfront to hail Admiral Porter and the men of the navy. En route, Rawlins would have witnessed the destruction inflicted on the town during the bombardments: shattered trees, cratered streets, buildings pockmarked by shell fragments. But there was hardly time to devote to ceremony or gawking. So much needed attention. That afternoon, Grant dispatched Lt. William Dunn to Cairo to wire the surrender news to Halleck. Ink was hardly dry on the surrender papers when Grant sent Sherman on a mission to seek out and destroy Johnston, thereby eliminating him as a threat. There were thousands of parolees to process, generating paperwork that would take a week to complete. Regarding paperwork, Grant and Rawlins were finishing a detailed report, started some weeks before, of the Vicksburg operations covering the time up to the investment of the city. Grant wrote the substance of the report, and Rawlins, assisted by Bowers, copyedited and fact-checked. This report was sent to Halleck on July 6. Issues abounded regarding policies toward and treatment of the emancipated slaves. Grant wrote McPherson about delaying trying to enlist captured, able-bodied Black men, but Grant stressed, "I want the negroes all to understand that they are free men" and should not be coerced to go off with their former owners.[16] Even General Logan, the southern Illinois Democrat, protested to Rawlins about "the manner in which Confederate officers are permitted to intimidate their servants in presence of officers appointed to examine said servants."[17] And there was the flow of well-wishers who sought an audience with the victorious general. One visitor complimented Grant on his "brilliant strategy," but he modestly replied, "Oh, I don't know much about that. I had as many men as I wanted, and simply pounded away till I pounded the place down."[18] If Grant was downplaying his success, others were displaying gratitude and celebrating.

General in chief Halleck hastily recommended Grant's appointment as major general in the regular army, thereby fixing his career at that rank.[19] Lincoln's letter to Grant contained both appreciation and an apology: "I write this now as a grateful acknowledgement for the almost inestimable service you have done the country. I wish to say a word further. . . . When you got below, and took Port Gibson, Grand Gulf, and vicinity, I thought you should go down river and join Gen. Banks; and when you turned Northward East of the Big Black, I feared it was a mistake. I now wish to make the personal acknowledgement that you were right, and I was wrong."[20] When the news of Vicksburg's surrender reached New York City, flags were raised over hundreds of businesses, atop municipal buildings, and from ships' masts. In City Hall Park, a crowd lustily cheered as a brass cannon fired off thirty-five rounds.[21] The townsfolk in Galena celebrated too. A half-mile procession with bands and banners wound through town. Whenever a speaker mentioned Grant's name, there was "unbounded applause, and the enthusiasm at times was intense." Bonfires and fireworks illuminated the evening sky. "Not only were the houses and hills lighted up, but every *heart* was lighted up with joy."[22]

Grant generously allowed others to reap the benefits of his success. In late July, he wrote adjutant general of the army, Lorenzo Thomas, requesting promotions for fourteen officers, vaulting Rawlins from lieutenant colonel to brigadier general. He put in a special plug for Rawlins: "Lieut Col. Jno. A. Rawlins has been my Assist Adjutant General from the beginning of the rebellion. No officer has now a more honorable reputation than he has won, and I think I can safely say that he would make a good Corps Commander. This promotion I would particularly ask as a reward of merit."[23] Grant slathered it on liberally on behalf of his trusted friend: Rawlins had no experience even drilling troops on a parade ground. Halleck, on August 10, forwarded the recommendation for Rawlins's promotion to Stanton for approval.[24] Although Rawlins had his brigadier's star, his promotion was not confirmed by the Senate until April 14, 1864.[25]

Another beneficiary of these heady times was Rawlins's nineteen-year-old brother, James. He was serving in the Lead Mine Regiment when Grant, on August 11, recommended him to Lorenzo Thomas for appointment to the Military Academy: "Private Rawlins is on detached service as Mail Messenger and is now some place between here and Cairo with the Mail. He is under twenty years of age, is a young man of good character and I would be pleased to have him one of those appointed to a Cadetship. He has been in the service since the organization of the 45th regiment in 1861 and I will venture has never been so much as reprimanded since that time."[26] That summer, Grant recommended twelve men for appointment to the USMA. That James Rawlins was atop the list demonstrates how much Grant held John Rawlins in esteem and appreciated his service. James made his brother proud by passing the entrance examination.[27]

The promotions and adulation were well deserved. After all, Grant had captured an entire army (the second he had bagged), and he did it by orchestrating a textbook campaign requiring coordination between army and navy and fighting (and winning) five battles. Grant solved a tricky logistical problem by ferrying troops across river after his navy ran the Vicksburg batteries and managing to keep them supplied. Moreover, he handled such dicey issues as providing for former slaves who, after pouring into the lines, encountered incidents of abuse; balancing the avaricious aims of cotton traders with the government's desire to grab that valuable commodity; and thwarting a powerful politician-general pushing his agenda. For his part, Rawlins served admirably as Grant's sounding board and point person. He kept abreast of reports of hostile contact, culled through intelligence reports of enemy troop movement, and responded to requests from the field ranging from supplying artillery pieces to sending out telegraph operators. He also transmitted a spate of field orders to commanders to ensure their units were properly positioned. Historian Michael Ballard summed up what the commander and his chief of staff together achieved: "With the assistance of Rawlins, Grant managed to deftly resolve most all issues that confronted him."[28]

—⟡—

Following the surrender came a period of relative inaction, but tasks still needed to be accomplished, such as finding a proper headquarters for the Army of the Tennessee. On July 5, as Grant's cavalry escort sauntered through Vicksburg in search of that place, they rode past an entrance gate flanked by a bevy of women, one of whom made insolent faces at the Yankee captain. His attention darted past her to a magnificent mansion set on attractive grounds. "This will suit us," he concluded and began taking possession. The mansion was the residence of widow Anne Lum and, until the day before, the headquarters of General Pemberton. Now Grant, joined later by Julia, Rawlins, and other officers, would occupy the first floor while the Lum family moved upstairs. The mansion boasted a view of the Mississippi River, an assortment of outbuildings, and two shelters dug into a hillside in which the family sought refuge during bombardments.[29]

A portion of July was spent dispersing troops from Grant's command. Sherman was sent against Johnston's army toward Jackson, Mississippi; and Ord's Thirteenth Corps was to report to General Banks at New Orleans. Banks, another politician-general—he had risen to Speaker of the House of Representatives—was fresh from accepting the surrender of Port Hudson, Louisiana. Shortly thereafter, he proposed cooperating with Grant on a joint operation to capture Mobile, Alabama. The idea intrigued Grant enough that he told Halleck, "It seems to me that Mobile is the point deserving the most immediate attention." On August 1, Banks was in Vicksburg conferring with Grant about the Mobile operation, and on the same day Grant sought permission from Halleck to visit Banks in New Orleans. Grant would return Banks's visit in early September, but by then the Union high command no longer made Mobile a priority.[30]

Another issue requiring attention was the disposition of wounded and sick Confederate prisoners. Much to Rawlins's chagrin, after Lagow returned from his leave of absence, Grant assigned him to supervise the transporting southward of a steamboat full of prisoners.[31]

About the third week of July, Grant, Rawlins, and Bowers wrapped up for Halleck the final report of the Vicksburg campaign. It was sprinkled with withering criticisms of McClernand's generalship. For example, Grant expressed dissatisfaction with McClernand's failure to arrive at Champion's Hill "until the enemy had been driven from the field," and with his plea for reinforcements during the May 22 assault that resulted only in "the increase of our mortality list fully 50 per cent, without advancing our position or giving us other advantages."[32] No doubt Grant intended the latter jab as a rejoinder to the claim McClernand made in his own report, submitted a month earlier, in which he attributed his failure in the assault to the delay in reinforcements coming to him.[33] As far as McClernand's campaign report was concerned, Grant told Washington it was full of inaccuracies and demonstrably "pretentious and egotistical."[34]

This comparatively quiet postsurrender interval gave Grant and Rawlins the opportunity to address fallout from McClernand's removal. McClernand may have felt "cut down," as Hillyer reported, but being wounded made him more dangerous. He had already protested to Stanton, accusing Grant of "personal hostility" toward him and requesting an investigation of Grant's conduct from Belmont to the May 22 assault.[35] Now was the time to ascertain how Grant's handling of McClernand's dismissal had gone over with Lincoln and his administration. Was there a need to do damage control at the Executive Mansion? Perhaps an emissary from the Army of the Tennessee might be sent to Washington who could cogently present Grant's side of the case. John Rawlins began preparing for that mission.

—✧—

Before Rawlins left Vicksburg, Grant dispatched a letter introducing him to President Lincoln:

> Col. Rawlins goes to Washington now by my order as bearer of the reports of the campaign just ended, and rolls, and Paroles, of prisoners captured. Any information desired of any matter connected with this Department, from his official position, he can give better probably than any other officer in it.
>
> I would be pleased if you could give Col. Rawlins an interview and I know in asking this you will feel relieved when I tell you he has not a favor to ask for himself or any other living being. Even in my position it is a great luxury to meet a gentleman who has no "axe to grind" and I can appreciate that it is infinitely more so in yours.[36]

This looked innocent enough: Rawlins endorsed as the man best prepared to answer questions about the successful campaign just concluded. Moreover, Grant promised that Rawlins would make no trouble—no doubt welcome news to a chief executive who too often had listened to generals backstabbing other generals or currying him for favors.

Rawlins was an excellent choice as emissary. Even if he showed partiality toward Grant, his perspective could not be dismissed as a political grudge: Rawlins was known to be a War Democrat like McClernand. Rawlins could present a gripping story of how the operation unfolded and what it cost the Confederacy—a narrative that would underscore the wisdom of entrusting the Mississippi River campaign to Grant. Rawlins could use his lawyerly skills and loathing for McClernand to weave a convincing case for why he had to be relieved.

Rawlins left Vicksburg on July 22 on a steamboat that traveled northward at an agonizingly slow rate. This gave him time to rehearse how he might handle the most important undertaking yet entrusted to him. While on this leg of the journey, Rawlins discovered that steamboat operators were gouging soldiers headed home on leave.[37] It is likely that an enraged Rawlins, as soon as he could, telegraphed headquarters complaining about this unfair practice, because on July 30, Bowers issued orders establishing rules for protecting military personnel "against the exorbitant charges . . . daily practiced by steamboats of this Department."[38] Families in Galena received word about the popular order fixing rates for officers and men traveling the lower Mississippi. Now enlisted men would be charged no more than one-half cent per mile anywhere south of Cairo.[39]

Rawlins exchanged the steamboat salon for a seat in an Illinois Central railcar. About one hundred miles outside Chicago on July 27, the train jumped the track. He was in the car that suffered the most damage. Luckily, the accident left him more terrified than hurt. He readily admitted to Grant a few days later, "I came nearer being killed than ever before in my life."[40] The stack of paperwork he was carrying to Washington—the final version of the report on the Vicksburg campaign and a carton two feet deep containing lists of the Confederate parolees—came through intact. While changing trains in Chicago, Rawlins bumped into Edward Beebe, a Galena businessman and, like Rawlins, a former alderman, who informed people at home that Rawlins was slightly injured but able to continue to Washington.[41] After arriving in Baltimore on July 30, Rawlins telegraphed Colonel John Kelton, Halleck's adjutant, requesting permission to proceed to Washington. On receiving it, he boarded a car for the short trip and an initial meeting with the general in chief.

After his audience with Halleck, Rawlins dashed a letter to Grant in which he gloated how famously the meeting went, even waggishly referring to Halleck as "Brains," the sobriquet hung on him for being more introspection than action. There was nothing to report but good news, and Halleck seemed to bend over backward to accommodate. "It is worth a trip here to see how delighted they are over your successes," Rawlins gushed. "There is nothing left undone by them to make me feel that I am here properly."[42] Halleck even urged Grant to send him recommendations for promotions. Sherman, McPherson, and George Thomas could fill brigadier general vacancies in the regular army. Moreover, Halleck complained to Rawlins that whereas Grant's army racked up battlefield victories, the promotions went to the Army of the Potomac. There was more glorious news. Rawlins could report that "they have finally concluded to hand McClernand out to grass."[43] The next day, the thirty-first, Rawlins planned to meet with Lincoln and several of his cabinet, including Secretary of War Stanton.

If Rawlins hoped to neutralize any trouble McClernand might cause, Lincoln and cabinet hoped to draw out from Rawlins details about his commanding general, the hero of the hour. Except for Halleck and Congressman Washburne, hardly anyone in Washington knew firsthand anything about Grant. Also, he was being mentioned to replace George Meade as commander of the Army of the Potomac. This was a job Grant would have strenuously declined, and Rawlins no doubt knew his feelings. While Rawlins was returning to Vicksburg, Grant wrote Charles Dana that "it would cause me more sadness than satisfaction to be ordered to the command of the Army of the Potomac." Dana shared this letter with Lincoln and Stanton, who for now spared Grant from being thrust as an outsider into that army's command.[44]

Rawlins's meeting lasted nearly two hours. Details of it and the impression he made were chronicled that day by the secretary of the navy, Gideon Welles, in his famous diary. Welles was taken—even entertained—by Rawlins's "frank, intelligent and interesting description of men and account of army operations." What proved Rawlins's winning gambit was to transparently present himself. Welles was won over by Rawlins's character, "his honest, unpretending, and unassuming manners," especially his "absence of pretension, and . . . unpolished and unrefined deportment."

Welles knew Rawlins was in Washington because Grant "evidently sent him here for a purpose." That purpose was to provide "statements in regard to

McClernand which show him an impracticable and unfit man . . . an obstruction to army movements and operations." Welles recognized that Rawlins was prejudiced against McClernand, "but with such appearance of candor, and earnest and intelligent conviction, that there can be hardly a doubt McClernand is in fault, and Rawlins has been sent here by Grant in order to enlist the President rather than bring dispatches. In this I think, he has succeeded." It was reminiscent of attorney John Rawlins making a cogent and sincere summation to a jury, and he pulled off a triumph. McClernand might fuss or fume, but he would no longer vex Grant.[45]

With that crucial business completed, Rawlins left that day to return to Vicksburg. He could hardly have been faulted if he had elected to tarry a day to sightsee—it was his first visit to the nation's capital—but wasn't that just like Rawlins to deny himself frivolity? Or perhaps he had more appealing attractions to attend to in Vicksburg.

—∘∾∘—

When Rawlins returned to Vicksburg in mid-August, he was thrust into the middle of distractions arising from the fact that staff shared a dwelling with a civilian family. There was at that time, in the employ of the Lum family and residing at the mansion, a twenty-two-year-old Connecticut-born governess, Miss Mary Emeline "Emma" Hurlburt. She had moved to Vicksburg shortly before hostilities broke out. As "a most attractive picture of health and beauty," her presence did not go undetected by the military personnel.[46] Grant was one of the first to make her acquaintance. One day she, Grant, and Wilson were engaging in conversation in the drawing room when Grant was called away. He asked Wilson to keep her company until he returned. This was no imposition for Wilson, who may have had romantic designs toward her.[47] While they chatted, a bouquet of flowers arrived for her, but it came with no card or explanation. It was the second such mystery bouquet sent by the same admirer, who, it was later learned, was a married colonel on Grant's staff. It was up to chief of staff Rawlins to keep this from blowing into a scandal. He admonished the married admirer and set about reestablishing propriety at headquarters.[48]

Emma was the person from the mansion household who was most often enlisted to ask favors of the headquarters officers. Usually the request was for horses to draw the carriage, because the Lums' horses had been pressed into Confederate service. The young officers eagerly served as carriage drivers, so it could be argued Emma was hardly being an imposition. This arrangement rankled Rawlins, and he groused to Grant, while Julia was present, that he thought it improper for a US soldier "to act as a coachman for a bunch of rebel women."

Rawlins's emphatic denunciation amused Grant: "What is it all about? Who is doing it, Rawlins, and why do you permit it? You are chief of staff."

"Well, you see, General," Rawlins replied, "these women ask a favor, not a very great one, I admit, and the fellows are glad to make their positions as comfortable as possible, but I for one do not believe it is just the thing."

"Nor do I," Grant agreed. "That is not what they are here for, surely."

As Rawlins was to leave, Julia looked reproachfully at him, and he returned a smile to her: "This is war, Mrs. Grant, war in earnest, and we must not forget it."[49]

He might have to confront Miss Hurlburt about keeping a subdued profile around staff, but this required a delicate verbal exchange he was not accustomed to performing. However, circumstances intervened that forced Rawlins to postpone this tricky, albeit not wholly unwelcome, confrontation. Late in August, Grant accepted Banks's invitation to visit him at New Orleans. Rawlins and Wilson strenuously argued against this idea. Rawlins was adamant that Grant's place was in Vicksburg with his army. Furthermore, the operation against Mobile had been shelved. Rawlins's concern magnified when he learned two bad influences, Colonels Riggin and Duff, would accompany Grant.

Just before embarking for New Orleans on August 31, Grant composed an intimate letter to Elihu Washburne expressing relief that Halleck and Dana had helped sidetrack his transfer to the Army of the Potomac. He closed the letter with news that Rawlins and Jasper Maltby received promotions to brigadier general. Then he singled out Rawlins for extended praise. In perhaps no other communication does Grant so candidly remark about Rawlins's competency and uniqueness, as well as his sterling reputation as a staff officer:

> Rawlins & Maltby have been appointed Brigadier Generals. These are richly deserve[d] promotions. Rawlins especially is no ordina[ry] man. The fact is had he started in this war in the Line instead of in the Staff there is every probability he would be to-day one of our shining lights. As it is he is better and more favorably know[n] than probably any other officer in the Army who has filled only staff appointments. Some [m]en, to[o] many of them, are only made by their Staff appointments whilst others give respectability to the position. Rawlins is of the latter class.[50]

In his absence, Grant unofficially left the army in Rawlins's hands. Both Sherman and McPherson were amenable to the arrangement, with Sherman figuring that if he were to assume the reins, "it would confuse the record." If an emergency were to arise, Rawlins would have Sherman issue an order.[51] During Rawlins's two and a half weeks as interim commander, there was but one significant military event. Frederick Steele, commanding a division in Sherman's Fifteenth Corps, moved against Little Rock, which he captured on September 15. Communications occurred between General Hurlbut and Rawlins regarding sending reinforcements to Steele; Rawlins, in turn, tapped McPherson, who forwarded John E. Smith's division to Steele.[52] On completion of his brief term, Rawlins self-assuredly summed up the state of army affairs in a telegram to Halleck's adjutant: "Everything here is quiet. The health of the troops is good."[53]

As Rawlins could have predicted, trouble struck in New Orleans. On September 4, Grant had been invited to witness a troop review in a New Orleans suburb. The review was followed by a luncheon at which wine was served. Grant rode back to the city on a feisty borrowed mount. The horse was panicked by a locomotive whistle and toppled over onto Grant. Miraculously, Grant suffered no broken bones, but his left side was so badly bruised that he was unable to walk. Rumors circulated he had been drinking, and Rawlins suspected the worst. Moreover, in a letter to Wilson, Rawlins indicated sarcastically that no one had informed him of Grant's injury: "No one of his *highly intelligent* staff has deemed the matter of sufficient importance to write me one word nor even as much as send a verbal message. The General I understand is at Carrollton and I suppose his staff are in New Orleans enjoying hugely the time the General's indisposition from injuries gives them. In the meantime, however, matters here move on as smoothly as could be desired."[54]

On the fourteenth, Grant was lifted onto a steamboat for the two-day trip back to Vicksburg. Julia was soon at his side at headquarters. Rawlins was relieved she was available to boost her husband's spirits, yet he fumed because the trip had been unnecessary. Julia found her husband battered and bruised, but she marveled at John Rawlins's glowing appearance.

—⁂—

After attending to her bedridden husband, Julia, on the day of her return, encountered Dr. Henry Hewit, who had been checking on the general. "Do you see any changes about headquarters?" the surgeon inquired of Julia.

"No," she said as she scanned her surroundings. "What is it?"

"What? No change in anyone?"

"Oh, why yes," she replied. "I think General Rawlins is looking splendidly. Has he consented to let you take him in hand?"

Hewit was delighted that Julia caught on so quickly. "I know your woman's wit would see it at a glance. Oh, you know how it was when you left. Those ladies upstairs were 'rebel women.' Rawlins could not stand to see Uncle Sam's soldiers and uniforms degraded, but Lord bless you, my dear lady, all that is changed. Soldiers, uniforms, and chiefs of staff even are sacrificed!"

Now confused, Julia asked Hewit, "What does it all mean and how did it happen?"

Hewit gave a hearty laugh and explained, "Well, you know how Miss Hurlburt made her petition for any favor always so modestly, with burning cheeks and downcast eyes. One morning she came down wearing a little blue apron, the same she has on this morning, with her pretty hands thrust into the pockets; well, to make a long story short, the pockets in that apron were too much for Rawlins. He simply surrendered unconditionally, and since then we and they all ride as much as we like and so does the Chief of Staff."[55]

It was more than apron pockets that precipitated Rawlins's unconditional surrender, as he revealed in a letter to Wilson: "I myself, all sedate, sober, and sad, as I have been towards the fair ones, have had excited within me a feeling of deepest friendship for her. Whether it is those ringlets, things I have always loved, her laughing nature and rich good sense withal, which has most to do with enrolling her name on memory's scroll, even to be recurred to with pleasure." Rawlins could not resist letting Wilson know, "I am not surprised at the interest you manifested toward Miss Hurlbut."[56]

Wilson, who had been on an inspection assignment, returned to Vicksburg on September 21, and besides finding Grant hobbling on crutches, he also saw how smitten Rawlins was by Emma Hurlburt, and how she too was enamored of the dark-haired and earnest brigadier general. The attraction and affection between the two erupted so intensely that by the end of September, they were engaged, and Emma was planning to leave for her parents' home in Connecticut. Emma, like John, was born into a family of limited means. Her father, Stephen Ambler Hurlburt, was in business in Danbury, the nation's hat manufacturing capital, cutting fur for hats—rabbit and South American nutria, mostly. Her parents were of plain New England stock and unsophisticated cultural background, deficient in social graces. However, while growing up, Emma so availed herself of an education and formative relationships that she lifted herself above her parents' humble level. Her charm, modesty, and "very unusual beauty" also worked to her advantage.[57]

The love-struck Rawlins confided in Wilson that at times he felt unsure where he stood with Emma. Such misunderstanding would not be unexpected, given that "they . . . had been thrown together by circumstances over which neither had full control." While Rawlins struggled to find his bearings in this whirlwind courtship, he let Wilson know he was "doubtful of his fate." To improve his chances, he resisted urges to unleash his temper and use foul language. As if to compound that doubt, he would find her at times to be "uncertain, coy, and hard to please."[58] These mixed signals left Rawlins confused. If she showed uncertainty or hesitancy, John might attribute it to some sorrowful residue from past romantic experiences. She confided to him in a letter early during their engagement that "in previous affairs of the affections [she] had always some regrets"—but none in theirs, she hastened to add.[59]

If, as Wilson reported, "the course of love did not run smoothly," it is tempting to speculate that that love got snagged on the sharp edges of the expectations John soon laid down on Emma. For one, he pressured her to get right with him on politics. It is possible that Emma's months in the Deep South provided her a different slant on the war. If so, John was adamant about asking her to "Conform your actions & serious conversation to the support of my political sentiments and the cause in which I am engaged. . . . If you cannot accede to this request, don't say that you cannot, but let it pass as though it had not been written."[60] There was also the issue of Emma becoming the stepmother of three young children. Rawlins's daughter Emily, who had been ill during the summer, lived with John's parents in Guilford Township. The two older children were in Goshen, with their grandmother and an aunt. Rawlins desperately hoped to consolidate his children at his parents' and wanted Emma to live there too, in admittedly "most humble circumstances," until the war ended. Exchanging a Southern mansion for a ramshackle cottage in the woods required a huge adjustment.[61] Moreover, Emma would have to become reconciled to the fact that her betrothed still held tender feelings for his first wife, Emily. John had visions that Emma would keep alive the memories of Emily in his three children: "There is a still sweet whisper in my heart, coming from the 'echoless shores'—from the one who has gone on before us Emma, *commendating* [sic] *of her whom* I have *chosen* to be the *mother of my children*, and saying that they should be brought together that they may be taught to love *her* and *one another*." Emma faced the daunting prospect of being the woman in between John and the one whispering to him from across the infinite divide.[62]

While Grant was incapacitated in New Orleans and Rawlins occupied the commander's chair in Vicksburg, General Rosecrans used his Army of the Cumberland to achieve a stunning victory. On September 9, after a period of clever maneuvering, Rosecrans ousted Braxton Bragg's Army of Tennessee from the strategic city of Chattanooga—a feat Rosecrans accomplished by shedding hardly a drop of blood. Bragg withdrew into north Georgia near the town of LaFayette. There, Bragg concentrated his forces and awaited reinforcements. Believing, erroneously, that Bragg was in full retreat, Rosecrans pushed his corps forward. The two armies collided in northwest Georgia on September 18, where fighting during the next two days occurred near a small stream, Chickamauga Creek. On September 20, the Confederates exploited a gap in the Union line and drove most of the Federals from the field and back toward Chattanooga. Rosecrans himself was among the retreating mass— trying to rally his demoralized army, he later would claim. That army might have been annihilated had it not been for the defensive stand George Thomas made on a prominence known as Snodgrass Hill.

Less than two weeks before, Rosecrans had been the triumphant occupier of Chattanooga. Now Bragg had him bottled up there, with the Tennessee River to Rosecrans's back and Bragg occupying high ground, Missionary Ridge and Lookout Mountain, outside of the city. Supplies into Chattanooga were choked off, and the Army of the Cumberland was in danger of being starved into submission. The Union high command recognized the crisis and readied reinforcements to rescue Rosecrans. News of the Chickamauga disaster eventually reached Vicksburg. Grant was handicapped because telegraphic communications between Washington and his Army of the Tennessee went only so far as Cairo. To speed delivery of his dispatches, Grant sent Harry Wilson to Cairo, where he sent telegrams to Washington and hustled replies back to Vicksburg. On October 10, Wilson brought to Grant an order from Halleck dated October 3 summoning Grant to Cairo as soon as he was able. It appeared that Grant would be on a mission to rescue Rosecrans.[63]

On October 9, Rawlins wrote two letters to Emma, who was at home in Danbury. The first contained his suspicion that recent events would necessitate moving headquarters closer to the action, perhaps to Nashville. He surmised that if Grant took over operations in Tennessee, their December wedding might be delayed until January.[64] Rawlins also announced some welcome changes to the staff. Colonel John Riggin submitted his resignation, and surgeon Dr. Henry Hewit was reassigned. Riggin had long been a thorn in Rawlins's side, and Hewit was suspect too. Just before Shiloh, journalist Whitelaw Reid had written a scathing story, attacking Hewit for disloyalty and drunkenness. Now they were both gone, and Rawlins sniffed, "Of their withdrawal from Genl Grants staff I have no regrets and shall express none."[65] After Rawlins posted this letter, he must have received later that day an affectionate one from Emma, because he wrote a second time. Whatever Emma said left Rawlins in an intoxicated mood and prompted an outpouring of florid prose: "The lips of love never lisped sentiments of affection, nor pen in beauty's hand never traced for lover's eye, that which filled the heart with more real pleasure than that which your letter contains filled mine."[66]

The arrival on October 10 of Halleck's order meant the end of Rawlins's time in Vicksburg. The staff immediately began bundling records, headquarters supplies, and personal effects. In Grant's absence, General McPherson was placed in charge at Vicksburg. By nightfall Grant and Rawlins had vacated the Lum residence, and at 11:00 p.m. they boarded a steamer to Cairo, the first leg on a sometimes treacherous journey that would take them to Chattanooga.

NOTES

1. John Y. Simon, ed., *The Papers of Ulysses S. Grant* (Carbondale: Southern Illinois University Press, 1979), 8:385n.

2. U. S. Grant to Julia Dent Grant, June 15, 1863, in *The Papers of Ulysses S. Grant*, ed. John Y. Simon, 8:377.

3. W. S. Hillyer to U. S. Grant, June 30, 1863, in *The Papers of Ulysses S. Grant*, ed. John Y. Simon, 8:219–20n.

4. Arthur C. Parker, *The Life of General Ely S. Parker* (Buffalo, NY: Buffalo Historical Society, 1919), 102–3.

5. William H. Armstrong, *Warrior in Two Camps: Ely S. Parker Union General and Seneca Chief* (Syracuse: Syracuse University Press, 1978), 99. There were enough witnesses to Parker's periodic overindulgence to question the assumption that he was being judged in light of the racial prejudice of that era. As his biographer, Armstrong, concluded, "But as the witnesses mount, it is hard to escape the conclusion that Parker did on occasion conform to the stereotype" (100). James Wilson recounted that while he was engaged in a cavalry operation in June 1864, Parker appeared looking "somewhat under the influence of liquor." He asked Wilson for a squadron of cavalry. When Wilson inquired for what purpose, Parker, in all seriousness, said he wanted to capture Lee and bring him to Grant's headquarters; see James Harrison Wilson, *Under the Old Flag* (New York: D. Appleton, 1912), 1:452–53.

6. Theodore Lyman, *Meade's Headquarters, 1863–1865* (Boston: Atlantic Monthly, 1922), 81.

7. Special Orders No. 169, June 23, 1863, in *The Papers of Ulysses S. Grant*, ed. John Y. Simon, 8:410n.

8. *The War of the Rebellion: A Compilation of the Official Records of the Union and Confederate Armies*, series 1, part 3, 24:441.

9. William E. Strong, "The Campaign against Vicksburg," in *Military Essays and Recollections*, Papers Read Before the Commandery of the State of Illinois, Military Order of the Loyal Legion of the United States (Chicago: A. C. McClurg, 1894), 2:344.

10. Jean Edward Smith, *Grant* (New York: Simon and Schuster, 2001), 255, 255n; James Harrison Wilson, *The Life of John Rawlins* (New York: Neale, 1916), 152.

11 *The War of the Rebellion: A Compilation of the Official Records of the Union and Confederate Armies*, series 1, part 3, 24:460.

12. A. E. Watrous, "Grant as His Son Saw Him. An Interview with Colonel Frederick D. Grant about His Father," *McClure's Magazine* 2 (May 1894): 518.

13. John Y. Simon, ed., *The Papers of Ulysses S. Grant*, 8:470n.

14. William E. Strong, "The Campaign against Vicksburg," 3350–51; James Harrison Wilson, *Under the Old Flag*, 1:223.

15. *Galena Daily Advertiser*, July 21, 1863.

16. U. S. Grant to J. B. McPherson, July 5, 1863, in *The War of the Rebellion: A Compilation of the Official Records of the Union and Confederate Armies*, series 1, part 3, 1:479.

17. John A. Logan to John A. Rawlins, July 7, 1863, in *The War of the Rebellion: A Compilation of the Official Records of the Union and Confederate Armies*, series 1, part 3, 1:483.

18. Albert D. Richardson, *A Personal History of Ulysses S. Grant* (Boston: D. L. Guernsey, 1885), 341–42.

19. H. W. Halleck to E. M. Stanton, July 7, 1863, in *The War of the Rebellion: A Compilation of the Official Records of the Union and Confederate Armies*, series 1, part 3, 1:483.

20. Roy P. Basler, ed., *Collected Works of Abraham Lincoln* (Brunswick: Rutgers University Press, 1953), 6:326.

21. *The New York Times*, July 8, 1863.

22. *Galena Daily Advertiser*, July 13, 1863.

23. John Y. Simon, ed., *The Papers of U. S. Grant* (Carbondale: Southern Illinois University Press, 1982), 9:124–25.

24. Ibid., 125n.

25. As the Senate dragged its feet to confirm, Grant on February 20, 1864, submitted to Halleck a list of fourteen nominees in ranked order for promotion to brigadier general. Grant placed Rawlins's name at the top of that list. See John Y. Simon, *The Papers of U. S. Grant* (Carbondale: Southern Illinois University Press, 1982), 10:145–46.

26. Ulysses S. Grant to Lorenzo Thomas, August 11, 1863, Ulysses S. Grant Papers, SC 587, Abraham Lincoln Presidential Library, Springfield, IL; James S. Rawlins was admitted to the USMA on September 16, 1863. In the *Official Register of the Officers and Cadets of the U. S. Military Academy* of June 1864, Rawlins is ranked seventy-sixth in his class of eighty-three cadets. Results of his semiannual examination in January 1865 found him deficient in mathematics, and he was discharged from the academy on January 31, 1865; personal communication from Ms. Alicia Mauldin-Ware, USMA Archives Curator, no date.

27. John Y. Simon, ed., *The Papers of U. S. Grant*, 9:168n.

28. Michael B. Ballard, *Grant at Vicksburg: The General and the Siege* (Carbondale: Southern Illinois University Press, 2013), 172.

29. John Y. Simon, ed., *The Personal Memoirs of Julia Dent Grant* (New York: G. P. Putnam's Sons, 1975), 120; *Evening Post*, Vicksburg, MS, July 1, 1863, "Vicksburg Family Shared Their Home with U. S. Grant," University of Mississippi J. D. Williams Library, Archives and Special Collections, Newspapers (Box 57).

30. U. S. Grant to H. W. Halleck, July 24, 1863, in *The Papers of Ulysses S. Grant*, ed. John Y. Simon, 9:108–11; U. S. Grant to H. W. Halleck, August 1, 1863, in *The Papers of Ulysses S. Grant*, ed. John Y. Simon, 9:137–38.

31. John Y. Simon, ed., *The Papers of Ulysses S. Grant*, 9:59–60.

32. *The War of the Rebellion: A Compilation of the Official Records of the Union and Confederate Armies*, series 1, part 1, 24:53, 56.

33. Ibid., 155–56.

34. U. S. Grant to Lorenzo Thomas, July 19, 1863, in *The Papers of Ulysses S. Grant*, ed. John Y. Simon, 9:78–79.

35. John McClernand to E. M. Stanton, June 27, 1863, in *The War of the Rebellion: A Compilation of the Official Records of the Union and Confederate Armies*, series 1, part 1, 24:166–67.

36. U. S. Grant to A. Lincoln, July 20, 1863, in *The Papers of Ulysses S. Grant*, ed. John Y. Simon, 9:80–81.

37. Albert D. Richardson, *A Personal History of Ulysses S. Grant*, 342.

38. General Orders No. 49, July 30, 1863, in *The Papers of Ulysses S. Grant*, ed. John Y. Simon, 9:189.

39. *Galena Daily Advertiser*, August 14, 1863.

40. J. A. Rawlins to U. S. Grant, July 30, 1863, John A. Rawlins Collection, Chicago History Museum.

41. *Galena Daily Advertiser*, , July 29, 1863.

42. J. A. Rawlins to U. S. Grant, July 30, 1863, John A. Rawlins Collection, Chicago History Museum.

43. Ibid.

44. U. S. Grant to C. A. Dana, August 5, 1863, in *The Papers of Ulysses S. Grant*, ed. John Y. Simon, 9:146, 147n.

45. Gideon Welles, *Diary of Gideon Welles* (Boston: Houghton Mifflin, 1909), 386–87.

46. James Harrison Wilson, *The Life of John Rawlins*, 151.

47. Edward G. Longacre, *From Union Stars to Top Hat: A Biography of the Extraordinary General James Harrison Wilson* (Harrisburg, PA: Stackpole, 1972), 85. Writing to his intimate friend Adam Badeau shortly after Rawlins's second marriage, Wilson denied any strong affection for the former Miss Hurlburt: "Dana and [Baldy] Smith misinformed you about the 'old flame' business—I wasn't very spoony on Mrs. Rawlins." J. H. Wilson to Adam Badeau, January 13, 1864, Wyoming State Archives, Bender Collection, James H. Wilson Papers, Microfilm Reel 61a.

48. James Harrison Wilson, *Under the Old Flag*, 1:240.

49. John Y. Simon, ed., *The Personal Memoirs of Julia Dent Grant*, 120.

50. U. S. Grant to Elihu Washburne, August 30, 1863, in *The Papers of Ulysses S. Grant*, ed. John Y. Simon, 9:217–18.

51. Ulysses S. Grant, *Personal Memoirs of U. S. Grant* (New York: Charles L. Webster, 1885), 1:582.

52. John A. Rawlins to S. A. Hurlbut, September 13, 1863, in *The War of the Rebellion: A Compilation of the Official Records of the Union and Confederate Armies*, series 1, part 3, 30:594.

53. J. A. Rawlins to John C. Kelton, September 17, 1863, in *The War of the Rebellion: A Compilation of the Official Records of the Union and Confederate Armies*, series 1, part 3, 30:694.

54. James Harrison Wilson, *The Life of John Rawlins*, 154.

55. John Y. Simon, ed., *The Personal Memoirs of Julia Dent Grant*, 121.

56. John A. Rawlins to James H. Wilson, September 15, 1863, typescript of letter in the U. S. Grant Presidential Library, Mississippi State University, John A. Rawlins subject file, Series 2, Box 13, Folder 1.

57. Sylvanus Cadwallader to James H. Wilson, October 4, 1904, James Harrison Wilson Papers, Library of Congress, Container 5; James Montgomery Bailey and Susan Benedict Hill, *History of Danbury, Conn. 1684–1896* (New York: Burr, 1896), 237; James Harrison Wilson, *Under the Old Flag*, 1:240.

58. James Harrison Wilson, *Under the Old Flag*, 1:256.

59. John Rawlins to Emma Hurlburt, October 9, 1863, first of two letters to Emma written on that date, John A. Rawlins Collection, Chicago History Museum.

60. Ibid., second letter of October 9.

61. John Rawlins to Emma Hurlburt, November 2, 1863, John A. Rawlins Collection, Chicago History Museum. That Rawlins would allow his children and bride to live with his parents provides strong validation for David Sheean's claim that Rawlins's father, by the mid-1850s, had reined in his drinking. See David Sheean to J. H. Wilson, February 25, 1885, James Harrison Wilson: Correspondence File, S(1), Box 14, Series 2, Ulysses S. Grant Presidential Library, Mississippi State University Libraries.

62. John Rawlins to Emma Hurlburt, October 14, 1863, John A. Rawlins Collection, Chicago History Museum.

63. H. W. Halleck to J. H. Wilson, October 3, 1863, in *The War of the Rebellion: A Compilation of the Official Records of the Union and Confederate Armies*, series 1, part 4, 30:55.

64. John Rawlins to Emma Hurlburt, October 9, 1863, first of two letters to Emma Hurlburt written on that date, John A. Rawlins Collection, Chicago History Museum.

65. John Y. Simon, ed., *The Papers of U. S. Grant*, 5:62n; J. A. Rawlins to Emma Hurlburt, October 9, 1863. First of two letters to Emma Hurlburt written on that date, John A. Rawlins Collection, Chicago History Museum.

66. John Rawlins to Emma Hurlburt, October 9, 1863, second letter to Emma Hurlburt, John A. Rawlins Collection, Chicago History Museum.

17

"I Am the Only One Here . . .
Who Can Stay It in That Direction"

THE TRIP TO CAIRO, RAWLINS wrote Emma, was proceeding more quickly than expected—sixty miles beyond Memphis, and the steamer had not encountered a snag or sandbar.[1] On October 16, Grant and his staff arrived at Cairo, where a telegram from Halleck awaited, instructing Grant to report to the Galt House in Louisville, "where you will meet an officer of the War Department with your orders and instructions. You will take with you your staff, &c, for immediate operations in the field."[2] The next day, Grant's Louisville-bound train stopped in Indianapolis, and as it was leaving the station, word arrived that a special train from Washington had just pulled in carrying that War Department officer. It was none other than Secretary Stanton. Stanton, eager to finally meet Grant, entered his railcar compartment and enthusiastically pumped the hand of a bewhiskered gentleman. "How do you do, General Grant?" Stanton effused. "I recognize you from your pictures." The gentleman was Dr. Edward Kittoe of Galena, Dr. Hewit's replacement as Grant's personal physician. Rawlins, who knew Stanton from the July cabinet meeting with Lincoln, intervened and straightened out the introductions.[3]

Stanton got right to business. He informed Grant he was now in command of the new Military Division of the Mississippi, comprising the Departments of the Ohio, the Tennessee, and the Cumberland—virtually all the troops between the Alleghenies and the Mississippi. Stanton gave Grant the option of retaining Rosecrans as chief of the Army of the Cumberland or replacing him with George Thomas. Grant chose Thomas, and on the nineteenth he tapped Sherman to head the Army of the Tennessee.

Replacing Rosecrans required little deliberation. Rawlins believed it was a result of Grant's frustrating "experience with him in the summer and fall of 1862," specifically Rosecrans's performances at the battles of Iuka and Corinth. At the former, it was because of his "deviation from the entire plan and order of battle [that] the enemy was enabled to escape"; at the latter, his "tardiness of pursuit" allowed the Confederates to avoid greater losses.[4]

Grant and Stanton huddled together on the train discussing military and political matters before arriving in Louisville around 9:00 p.m. on October 18. Their meeting continued into the next day. On the evening of the nineteenth, Grant and most of his entourage attended a theatrical performance. Rawlins strongly disapproved and refused to participate in "a thoughtless and undignified proceeding." He allowed himself no foolish diversion or outlet for "dissipation." Fighting this rebellion was for Rawlins a full-time obligation, requiring serious expenditures of energy. As Wilson noted, "He seemed to think it rather a time for penance and prayer than for enjoyment." The awesome responsibilities Grant faced in his new district command seemed that evening in Louisville to weigh as much on Rawlins's shoulders as on Grant's. Rawlins expected some of the "heaviest details" would fall on himself.[5]

Rawlins penned these feelings to Emma in a letter from the Galt House. "Genl Rosecrans is relieved," he informed her hours after it happened. "This is now the most important command in the United States, involving immense labor, unceasing watchfulness and anxiety." Rawlins hardly exaggerated: Grant now commanded more troops than any general, and Chattanooga was, after Richmond and Atlanta, the choicest prize for Union forces. Rawlins expected coming events to take a toll on him, but that was the patriotic price to be paid: "In this new and important command of Genl Grant's, I see no relief from labor or exemption from danger, nor do I indeed desire it. My chiefest wish is to be where I can do the most in aiding the army of my country in conquering an honorable re-union of the states and restoring, as far as may be, the old order of things under the Constitution of our fathers."[6]

Therefore, instead of an evening of amusement at the theater, Rawlins, Wilson, and Bowers brainstormed ways of reconstructing the staff and filling vacancies with men who possessed "brains and respectability."[7] There would be an opportunity soon to oust one of its less respectable colonels.

It didn't take long for Rawlins to realize that the Chattanooga campaign would be fraught with danger and anxiety. After the theatergoers returned to the Galt House, Stanton emerged from his room agitatedly waving a telegram.

It was from Charles Dana, Stanton's War Department assistant, who was posted at Chattanooga to keep his eyes on Rosecrans—a role like the one he had played at Grant's headquarters. Dana was concerned about Rosecrans's mental stability and capacity to command. "General Rosecrans," Dana later wrote, "seemed to be insensible to the impending danger . . . [and] could not perceive the catastrophe that was close upon us." On the nineteenth, Dana wired the dire news, now in Stanton's fist, that Rosecrans, unless ordered to the contrary, planned to retreat from Chattanooga. After sending that telegram, Dana, as instructed by Stanton, ducked out of Chattanooga to travel to Louisville.[8]

Without hesitation, the new military district commander telegraphed his new Army of the Cumberland chief, "Hold Chattanooga at all hazards. I will be there as soon as possible." George Thomas, the imperturbable "Rock of Chickamauga," replied, "I will hold the town till we starve."[9]

—⁓—

"As soon as possible" began the morning of the next day. Grant and party—Rawlins, Wilson, Bowers, Dr. Kittoe, new assistant adjutant general Ely Parker, and a few orderlies—entrained for Nashville, the next leg on the roundabout and exhausting journey. Part of the evening in Nashville was spent listening to Tennessee military governor Andrew Johnson's overly long speech. Around 10:00 p.m., Charles Dana's Louisville-bound train arrived in Nashville and was met by Joe Bowers. Bowers told Dana his travel plans were now changed: he was to join Grant and his party on their way to Chattanooga.[10] Dana informed Grant about the dwindling supplies and deteriorating military situation in Chattanooga. After listening to Dana, Rawlins had a few moments to write Emma. Dana's concerns leaked into his letter. "The prospects of affairs here are not so cheering as I had hoped to find them," he told her. However, he quickly drew on that wellspring of confidence he had in Grant by reminding her (as much as himself) that Grant "wins success where others fail in the field." The love-smitten Rawlins closed with a plea for more letters that tell him "how much you love me and would like to see me."[11]

Rawlins predicted the Nashville to Chattanooga trek would take three days, one by rail and two on horseback. October 21 would be the last easy day of travel. Most of that day was spent on a Nashville and Chattanooga train making the one-hundred-mile southeasterly trip to the rail junction of Stevenson in northeast Alabama. At Stevenson, Grant was met by Major General

Oliver O. Howard, commander of one of the two corps from the Army of the Potomac sent west to help in lifting the siege of Chattanooga. Those two corps—Henry Slocum led the other—were headed by "Fighting" Joe Hooker and were concentrated there in Alabama's Appalachian foothills. Hooker too was in Stevenson, and when he heard of Grant's arrival, Hooker, claiming he felt unwell, invited Grant to call at his headquarters. It was a shocking breach of military etiquette. Rawlins bristled at Hooker's impunity: "General Grant himself is not very well and will not leave his car tonight. He expects General Hooker and all other generals who have business with him to call at once, as he will start overland to Chattanooga early tomorrow morning."[12]

Another general made a call. It was Rosecrans, fresh from being deposed from command, who was now in Stevenson, wending his lonely way north. In what must have been an uncomfortable tête-à-tête, Rosecrans apprised Grant of the situation at Chattanooga, even sketching out a plan for supplying the troops there. With business accomplished, Grant and his party, joined by General Howard, traveled ten miles further northeast by train to Bridgeport on the Alabama-Tennessee line. With the rail line beyond Bridgeport destroyed, this was where they overnighted. At sunrise on the twenty-second, Howard watched as Rawlins gently lifted his lame commander onto his horse, Old Jack.

With Dana as guide, the men on horseback followed the wagon road out of Bridgeport as it hugged the curve of the Tennessee River. This was the barely passable route used by teams carrying the trickle of provisions and supplies to Chattanooga. About fifteen miles beyond Bridgeport at Jasper, Tennessee, Dana and Wilson left the party for a more direct and difficult route to Chattanooga—too difficult for the suffering Grant. Wilson wanted to arrive in Chattanooga earlier to study the engineering challenges presented by the topography. Just east of Jasper, those remaining crossed the Sequatchie River and headed almost due north up the Sequatchie Valley. Here, rains had turned the road into sludge. Rawlins was appalled by the debris littering their path— broken wagons and carcasses of draft animals that had been worked or beaten to death. The mud got the better of Old Jack: he slipped and fell on Grant's sore left leg. Despite the difficulties, the riders got some distance beyond Jasper before making camp. The first day's ride was easy compared to conditions they would encounter on the twenty-third.

Back in their saddles, the riders took to the trail, following the meager path on its circuitous, inverted V-shaped route up and down a rocky escarpment called Walden's Ridge toward Chattanooga. The landscape barely supported vegetation. While picking his way along the rock-strewn trail, Rawlins was aghast that those supplying the Army of the Cumberland faced such logistical challenges. "The mountain road [is] the roughest and steepest of ascent and descent, ever passed over by army wagons and mules" was how he described it. "One riding over it, if he did not see with his own eyes they did get over, would not believe it possible for him to do so." He was shocked to encounter along the way loyal Union families that had been uprooted from their homes and were clinging to an uncertain existence. He movingly described their plight to Emma: "In crossing the mountains on our way here . . . amid a driving rain, we met Union families—refugees from their homes—mothers with little children in their arms, covered with only one thin garment, exposed to the beatings of the storm, wet and shivering with cold. I have seen much of human misery consequent on this war, but never before in so distressing a form as this." He had nothing but contempt for the secessionists who perpetrated this evil: "In all humanity or heaven there can be no voice of palliation or excuse for the authors of this rebellion. There will be joy in his Satanic's dominions when they die, for the chiefs of sinners will be knocking at its sin-charred doors for admittance."[13]

It was past 8:00 p.m. when the wet, weary, and hungry travelers crossed a pontoon bridge over the Tennessee River and entered Chattanooga. The trip ended at Thomas's headquarters, where Rawlins lifted an aching Grant from the saddle. Inside, Grant seated himself to one side of a fire, which caused his drenched uniform to steam. Thomas stood by the other side. Both looked uncomfortable, waiting for someone to speak. A puddle of water collected under Grant's chair. Smoke from his cigar drifted into the awkward silence that enveloped the room. Rawlins barely managed to conceal his rage as he watched this cool reception unfold. Just then Harry Wilson arrived at headquarters and noticed the uneasy atmosphere. Rawlins pulled him aside and said they had not been offered any assistance or sustenance and that Grant was too proud to request special hospitality. With that, Wilson broke the ice: "General Thomas, General Grant is wet and tired and ought to have some dry clothes, particularly a pair of socks and a pair of slippers. He is hungry besides, and needs something to eat. Can't your staff officers attend to these matters for him?"[14]

This nudge roused Thomas into sociability. Dry clothes were sent for, and a dinner of fried hardtack and salt pork served. Despite Thomas's recovery from his social gaffe, Rawlins, according to Wilson, never forgot this incident and held an unshakable grudge against him. Dana and Wilson also wondered about the tension evident between Grant and Thomas. They speculated Grant might still be sensitive about the events following Shiloh when Grant was in Halleck's doghouse and Thomas was given command of most of Grant's troops. Thomas might have felt miffed that he was now Grant's subordinate despite having held higher rank in the prewar army.[15]

Two noteworthy members of Thomas's senior staff were at the gathering. Horace Porter, the chief of ordnance and Wilson's friend from West Point, made his first acquaintance with Grant that evening. In the spring of 1864, he would be on Grant's staff. Chief of engineering Brigadier General William F. Smith was there to provide his insights and recommendations. He was known as "Baldy" despite having a headful of hair. It was his West Point nickname to distinguish him from the other Smiths in the army. Baldy Smith was a talented engineer and a man who rarely withheld his opinions—and it had cost him. In December 1862, he coauthored a letter to Lincoln highly critical of Ambrose Burnside's campaign plans. Smith's audacity resulted in his being stripped of corps command in the Army of the Potomac and the Senate refusing to confirm his promotion to major general.[16]

After dinner, there was amicable give-and-take conversation. Smith briefed Grant on the position of troops and state of affairs, after which Grant peppered Thomas and his staff with razor-sharp questions. "His questions showed from the outset that his mind was not only upon the prompt opening of a line of supplies," Porter recalled, "but upon taking the offensive against the enemy." Connecting Chattanooga with the supply base is what Grant called "opening up the cracker line." Before retiring, he scheduled a meeting with Thomas and Smith for the next morning, October 24, to inspect the lines and form an impression of the Confederate position.[17]

—⁓—

Grant and his staff, Smith, and Thomas trotted over the pontoon bridge and rode west of Chattanooga for less than two miles before stopping at the bank of the Tennessee River at a crossing point known as Brown's Ferry. Across the river, they spied a line of Confederate pickets. Brown's Ferry was situated on a vertical stretch of river as it made a hairpin turn just west of Chattanooga. It was connected by a decent road to Kelley's Ferry about eight miles almost due west. That connecting road passed through Cummings Gap, an aperture bisecting a prominence called Raccoon Mountain. Baldy Smith advanced the idea—and Thomas and Rosecrans may have devised elements of it—that if Brown's Ferry could be captured and a pontoon bridge thrown over the Tennessee River there, and if the enemy could be shooed off Raccoon Mountain, and if the eight-mile road between the two ferries could be secured, then a much more direct supply line to Chattanooga could be established. The food and supplies from the Bridgeport-Stevenson area could be transported to Kelley's Ferry and trucked over the "Cracker Line" to Brown's Ferry and thence into town. Achieving these objectives, according to Smith, required a two-pronged operation. Two brigades would move out of Chattanooga in the early morning, one aboard pontoon boats. These brigades would be responsible for securing the Brown's Ferry area, clearing the enemy from the road leading to Kelley's Ferry, and laying a pontoon bridge across the Tennessee. Hooker's two corps in Bridgeport and Stevenson constituted the second prong. Most of the divisions in these corps would be marched eastward to a point a few miles south of Brown's Ferry to provide protection for the newly opened supply line.

This plan required stealth and tricky coordination. Grant loved it and placed Smith in charge. Almost miraculously, the operation succeeded without a hitch. Just days after his reconnaissance near Brown's Ferry, Grant wrote Halleck that "Gen Thomas' plan for securing the river and south side road hence to Bridgeport has proven imminently successful. The question of supplies may now be regarded as settled."[18]

Late on the twenty-seventh, Rawlins wrote Emma the joyous news that the supply line was established. It placed him in such an unrestrained mood he began by describing that autumn night in words that wafted off the page: "To night is most beautiful, the full orbed Queen, (of the hour I write), looks down in regal splendors from her home above upon tens of thousands of slumbering Northmen, far from their happy homes of love – nor withholds she her rays of glory from the face of the sleeping Southron, as he in dreams revisits his once happy home, e're ambition's treacherous voice had summoned him away and left it to war's desolation." Then he got down to business: "To day the crossings were made and, as far as heard from, have been a success. Should the whole move result in the success it now promises, it will give us the use of the river to the foot of Lookout Mountain." And in a not unsubtle dig at Rosecrans and Thomas, he offered Grant as a contrast: "This movement, though talked of prior to his arrival, yet no one had ventured to carry it into execution. The moment he saw its importance, with promptitude & fearlessness of consequences, he ordered its execution. It is decisiveness and energy in action that always accomplishes grand results, & strikes terror to the heart of the foe. It is this, and not the conception of great schemes, that make military genius."[19]

———

With the threat of starvation lifted, some administrative issues could be addressed. Headquarters were established in the Lattner House, a two-story frame house on a bluff near the river. Rawlins and Colonel Duff set up a mess in a small house near headquarters and invited Sylvanus Cadwallader, who covered the campaign for the Chicago *Times*, to join them. For their first few days, before supplies caught up, they subsisted on bread and coffee.[20] On October 29, Charles Dana telegraphed Stanton with Grant's request for a promotion to brigadier general for Wilson.[21] Rawlins couldn't resist passing this news to Wilson a few days later.[22] His interim appointment arrived on November 17.[23] There was now time to train a new assistant adjutant general, one with the brains and respectability Rawlins sought. Private George K. Leet was serving in the Chicago Mercantile Battery when, at the end of July, Rawlins detached him for duty as a clerk at headquarters. Two months later, Rawlins requested that Leet be promoted to assistant adjutant general with the rank of captain and recommended him as "eminently qualified for the position."[24]

An item with Congressman Washburne needed preferential attention, and Rawlins was the best person to handle it. Washburne desired raising a cavalry regiment in Northern Illinois. Rawlins assured him that "nothing would gratify [General Grant] more than to have the regiment raised as you propose."[25] Rawlins was rising in Washburne's esteem: the congressman held the chief of staff up to his son, Gratiot, as a model. "It will just show what an Illinois boy can do," the father counseled, "who comes from General Grant's home."[26]

Health concerns were afflicting staff as well. Ely Parker had been ill with "fever and ague" during the entire journey from Vicksburg to Chattanooga, and at one point he was close to death. Parker lost thirty pounds and required weeks to regain his strength. While recuperating at Chattanooga, Parker had little to do, so Baldy Smith requested he share Parker's services. Parker and Smith were already acquainted, having served together in lighthouse construction and maintenance on the Great Lakes prior to the Civil War. Soon Captain Parker was an assistant adjutant for both Smith and Grant.[27]

The usually robust Rawlins also suffered from a persistent cough around mid-October. That rainy ride to Chattanooga had chilled him to the bone and left him exhausted. While he waited for this apparent cold to run its course, Rawlins assumed a reduced role at headquarters. Fortunately Rowley, Parker, and now Leet handled the lion's share of paperwork. As far as Grant assumed, nothing with Rawlins seemed amiss. Twice that fall in personal business letters to Russell Jones, Grant pronounced Rawlins "well."[28] But appearances belied how Rawlins felt. If he could grind it out a little longer—and the past two years had been an arduous grind—there was a blissful respite around the corner: a holiday wedding in Danbury. Time away from aggravations at headquarters, an escape from the southeast Tennessee gloom, and nights in Emma's embrace was the tonic he needed.

At headquarters, the situation with one of the chronic sources of aggravation was coming to a head. A November 1 telegram from Dana to Stanton carried the recommendation that Colonel Lagow be mustered out of service. Grant called him "worthless," and Rawlins wholeheartedly agreed.[29] Lagow may not have known it, but his staff days were numbered. His demise coincided with the arrival at headquarters of William Wrenshall Smith.

Smith was a successful Pennsylvanian merchant and banker and a first cousin to Julia Grant.[30] He subsequently became a favorite of her husband. In October, Grant had authorized a pass for Smith, who hoped to socialize some in Chattanooga and see a battle. Smith came well provisioned. He had packed jars of pickles and catsup, boxes of cigars for his cousin-in-law, and ten gallons of "fine" whiskey. On his way south, he had stopped at Grant's parents' house in Covington, where Grant's mother gave him a bottle of wine for her son. He arrived at headquarters on Friday, November 13, greeting Rawlins, who warmly welcomed him. They were conversing until Lagow rode up and pulled Smith away, insisting that he make quarters in his room, opposite Grant's, in the Lattner house.

Presently, Grant arrived and gave Smith a predinner earful about his recent financial investment decisions. After roast beef and potatoes, Smith joined Lagow and some of his friends—"pretty lively larks" is how Smith described them—for poker and cold punch. Around 11:00 p.m., Smith returned to headquarters to play euchre while Grant kibitzed. On Saturday night, Lagow and his whiskey-fueled friends threw what Smith disparaged as "quite a disgraceful party." At 4:00 a.m. an infuriated Grant had to break up the revelry. Later that day, Rawlins attended church services and read aloud from Scripture in "a fine strong voice," whereas Lagow was too humiliated to show his face at the mess table. Smith sensed Grant's considerable displeasure with Lagow and noted in his diary that "I am fearful it will result in his removal."[31]

—◦◦◦—

Rawlins got wind of Lagow's party and presumed the worst: that Grant had been there and gotten drunk. It renewed his suspicion that alcohol caused Grant's riding mishap in New Orleans. If that incident had put Rawlins on a heightened state of alert, Lagow's party dialed it up a notch. On the sixteenth, Rawlins unburdened himself to Emma. He felt in the middle of a quandary: should he take a leave for the wedding, or stay to protect Grant from the debauchery at headquarters? Under the circumstances, he was obligated to the latter: "Today, however, matters have changed, and the necessity of my presence here made almost absolute, by the free use of intoxicating liquors at Headquarters, which last night's developments showed me had reached to the General commanding. I am the only one here (his wife not being with him) who can stay it in that direction and prevent evil consequences resulting from it. I had hoped, but it appears vainly, his New Orleans experience would prevent him ever again indulging with this, his worst enemy.[32]"

The specter of those sinister "developments" shook a telling disclosure from Rawlins. A few sentences later, he divulged to Emma how "the blighting shadow of intemperance had hung like a pall" over his path through life. Because of this experience, he felt compelled to "prevent evil consequences" from befalling Grant. The letter reveals that not only did Rawlins believe Grant's New Orleans accident was alcohol-related, but the belief diminished Rawlins's confidence in Grant's capacity to manage himself. In Rawlins's view, he was the "only one here" who could "stay" Grant from drinking—an overestimated sense of his influence. It seems more accurate to regard Rawlins as the only one—the lone crusader—who would hazard to assert himself against Grant's drinking. Grant biographer Geoffrey Perret explained how this was so: "The entire staff, as well as most of Grant's division and corps commanders, was well aware of his drinking problem. McClernand tried to make capital out of it and one or two other officers expressed disgust at Grant's weakness, *but to the rest, it did not matter*" (italics added). Due to his family background and attitudes about drinking, Rawlins became the focal person most disturbed by Grant's use of alcohol and the one who came forward as his rescuer. Moreover, Rawlins was deceived if he thought he had the power to quash Grant's drinking. Rawlins could be intrusive, imploring, and admonishing, but ultimately,

Perret explained, Grant's drinking "was a release, but a controlled one, like the ignition of a gas flare above a high-pressure oil well."[33] With Grant possessing the capacity to exercise control over the timing of his drinking—if not as well the amount or the desire to drink—one feels sympathy for Rawlins, a man who suffered great anxiety for commander and country in his role of rescuer. In the final analysis, Rawlins had but two options regarding Grant's drinking. He cracked down on alcohol in camp and around headquarters. And he resorted to the recommendation of Reverend Lyman Beecher, who counseled, "Will you not watch over one another with keener vigilance—and lift an earlier note of admonition—and draw together the bonds of brotherly discipline?"[34] Neither option was foolproof.

Rawlins toyed with persuading Grant to bring Julia to headquarters to act in his stead while he slipped away to Connecticut. However, on that same Monday, he chose to pen another heartfelt letter imploring Grant to spurn alcohol for sake of country:

> I again appeal to you in the name of every thing a friend, an honest man, and a lover of his country holds dear, to immediately desist from further tasting of liquors of any kind no matter by whom asked or under what circumstances, not even under the delusive belief that it will aid you now to recover your wonted vitality and energy. . . . This very moment every faculty of your mind should be clear and unclouded, the enemy threatens your lines with immediate attack, Burnsides one of your Generals trembles where he stands, the authorities at Washington fear he will yield, they look to you to save him. Since the hour Washington crossed the icefilled Delaware . . . so much of weighty responsibility, has not been imposed by your Government upon one man as it has now imposed upon you. Nor has the man lived since then from whom so much is expected. Do you realise this? If so, you will drink not another drop of that which unmans you. Two more nights like the last will find you prostrated on a sick bed unfit for duty, this must not be. You only can prevent it, and for the sake of my bleeding country and your own honor I pray God you may.

Instead of delivering this patriotic pitch, Rawlins dropped the ball. He never gave the letter to Grant. Before filing it among his papers, he added the following endorsement: "This letter was written hastily with a view to handing to the one to whom it is addressed but on reflection it was not given to him, but I talked to him upon the subject to which it relates, with which had the desired effect."[35]

Did Rawlins talk to Grant? We have no evidence that he did; but the wording of the endorsement suggests that if he did, the talk was mostly one-sided and consisted of Rawlins lecturing Grant. Rawlins's reference to "two more nights like the last" implies that Grant had been heavily hungover on Sunday. Again, evidence does not support that accusation. On the evening of the fourteenth, before Grant broke up the party, he was in a strategy meeting with Thomas and Sherman, among others. William Wrenshall Smith noted this in his diary entry for that date: "A good many General officers with the General. The Head Quarters are very quiet, as much so as a private house."[36] Then on Sunday, Major General David Hunter arrived at headquarters on a War Department mission to inspect Grant's command. If Hunter had noticed anything amiss, he would have informed Stanton. In mid-December, he sent a letter to Stanton regarding his positive impressions of his weeks with Grant. "In fact, I saw [General Grant] almost every moment, except when sleeping, of the three weeks I spent in Chattanooga," Hunter wrote. "He is modest, quiet, never swears, and seldom drinks, as he only took two drinks during the three weeks I was with him."[37] On the morning of the sixteenth, a party that included Grant, Rawlins, Thomas, Sherman, and Baldy Smith ventured out to gauge the strength of the Confederate positions. If Grant suffered any ill effects of drink, they weren't apparent to Wrenshall Smith, who went along for the ride and noted, "Gens. Sherman and Smith went out to examine with their glasses while the balance of the party remained behind [in] the woods. Grant was in fine humor, and as he leaned against the fence, was telling us about the former great speculations in Real Estate in Chicago and Milwaukee."[38]

If Grant, as evidence suggests, took no part in that spree, then what is to be made of Rawlins's letter and its endorsement? Was Rawlins planting another "documentary record," as Bruce Catton conjectured about the June 6 Vicksburg letter, filing away "that unsent letter where future historians were bound to see it, and where it would spread an enduring stain on the reputation of the man to whom Rawlins was so devoted?"[39] There is another interpretation. Perhaps instead of besmirching Grant, Rawlins was attempting to provide cover for himself. If Rawlins was hedging that Grant might succumb to alcohol during a pivotal military operation, then the endorsed letter would be "proof" he had intervened. From the tone of both letters, it appears that Rawlins was becoming less confident Grant could maintain his sobriety—or learn from past mistakes. If Rawlins believed that, then in the precarious position as Grant's "stay," he could fear being shouldered with some of the blame. The endorsed letter might absolve him of much of that.

On November 18, Colonel Lagow tendered his resignation "on account of disability." Instead of dismissing him outright, Grant allowed him to simply walk away.[40] Wrenshall Smith saw Lagow the day before he left and wrote in his dairy, "He saw Gen Rawlins wanted him off the staff, and after the unfortunate spree that the General himself broke up, he says that he was treeted coldly by him. He to-day heard his resignation had been approved and sent to Washington for acceptance, and he resolved to go immediately. He went with sore, depressed spirits." During his visit, Smith developed a camaraderie with Lagow and was shocked by Rawlins's occasional callousness, such as his treatment of Lagow. "Rawlins acts, sometimes, ugly," he confided to his diary. "Like Gen Wilson, his sudden elevation [in rank], has spoiled him. But he is invaluable to the General and I hope he may always prosper, so long as he continues true to him."[41]

Others too were offended by some of Rawlins's behavior. Ely Parker resented that Rawlins often called Grant a "Damned old Skeeziks" and treated him "like a dog." At times Grant chided Rawlins for using profanity and reminded him he could speak forcefully without it. Rawlins would promise to stop but then mutter, "Damned old Skeeziks." Grant pretended not to hear. Nonetheless, Parker valued Rawlins's friendship and respected his ability.[42] Since their Galena days, Parker affably called Rawlins "Black John" for his dark complexion and black hair and eyes.[43]

Lagow's depressed spirits were lifted, at least temporarily, the next evening. He and Wrenshall Smith left Chattanooga together on December 1 for Bridgeport. There, Lagow found his old regiment, the Twenty-First Illinois, and hooked up with friends. While Smith retired at 10:00 p.m., Lagow was "indulging freely" and being "very boisterous." It was a while before Smith could fall asleep.[44]

To Rawlins's satisfaction, with Riggin, Hillyer, and Lagow gone, headquarters was cleansed of unwholesome influences. However, in what Rawlins must have regarded as an ironic turn, in March 1865 all three were brevetted brigadier generals for services rendered during the war.[45]

—◦◦◦—

With a reliable supply line, Thomas's Army of the Cumberland had become enough revitalized that by early November, an offensive could be initiated against Bragg and his Army of Tennessee. Grant was feeling reinvigorated too. All the exercise getting to Chattanooga seemed to have healed his sore leg, thus sparing Rawlins one additional duty. "I now walk without the use of a crutch or cane," he wrote Julia, "and mount my horse from the ground without difficulty."[46] But a number of hurdles—besides the fact Bragg held both a numerical superiority and the high ground—prevented Grant from taking the offensive. For one, the artillery could not be moved. Because of the earlier shortage of forage, draft horses were still understrength. Furthermore, Washington pressed Grant to send assistance to Ambrose Burnside, whose vulnerable Army of the Ohio around Knoxville kept the eastern Tennessee Unionists from being abandoned. That clamor intensified when it was learned that Bragg, on November 4, dispatched James Longstreet's corps toward Knoxville to assail Burnside. However, Grant was stymied until Sherman and his four divisions could arrive from Memphis. At least Sherman had his men moving smartly and was sending in progress reports. On November 8, he informed Rawlins that he and two of his divisions were in Fayetteville, Tennessee. "My troops are in fine condition, hardy and strong," Sherman boasted, "most of them having marched the whole distance from Memphis." Five days later, Sherman announced he had arrived at Bridgeport with his lead division just behind.[47]

By reducing his strength, Bragg provided Grant the opportunity to take the offensive. The concept was straightforward: smash Bragg while weakened, thus forcing him to recall Longstreet's corps and thereby relieving pressure on Burnside. The specifics called for Sherman to bring his divisions against the extreme right of Bragg's line on the north end of steep-sided Missionary Ridge, which lies east of town, stretches from north to south for about seven miles, and crests up to five hundred feet. In coordination with Sherman, Joe Hooker's divisions were to turn the Confederate left, anchored on Lookout Mountain. Meanwhile, Thomas's Army of the Cumberland was to occupy the Union center and be ready to charge ahead or aid Sherman or Hooker. Grant scheduled the assault for November 21, but bad weather prevented Sherman from getting into position, causing a delay of several days.

Because Grant received intelligence—including hearsay from two Confederate deserters—that Bragg might withdraw and join Longstreet, he wanted Thomas to conduct a reconnaissance in force in front of Missionary Ridge to corroborate these reports.[48] Around midday on November 23, Grant ordered Thomas to move forward from the center toward the Confederate line. A two-mile-wide plain, dotted with small hillocks, separated the Union line from the Confederates at the base of the ridge. In about the middle of the plain, Bragg had established a thin cordon of pickets manning rifle pits. Thomas readied three divisions in a massive martial display, and in early afternoon he moved them out, flags unfurled and bugles blaring. Suddenly, Union artillery pieces opened fire, and the blue-clads raced ahead. Wrenshall Smith thrilled to witness his first battle:

> At about 2½ oclock a long line of battle is formed more than a mile in length and just in front of us. The skirmishers move forward, and then, the whole line advances. As our skirmishers come near the enemys pickets, we see, distinctly, their rifles aimed, and the smoke, followed by the reports. It is like a piece of machenery—Then, in a few minutes, the long line become engaged in the woods and I for the first time hear the heavy roll of musketry. The enemy are driven from their first line of rifle pits and our troops get possession of the rising ground more than a half way to Missionary ridge.[49]

Smith was not the only excited witness to the bold Union thrust. On seeing the twelve-hundred-yard expanse of ground just gained, Rawlins, as General Howard recollected, seemed to beseech Grant not to allow the troops to be recalled after completing their reconnaissance. "It will not do for them to move back," Rawlins was heard to say. After drawing on his cigar, Grant gave the order: "Intrench them and send up support."[50] Shortly thereafter, Rawlins sent a dispatch to Sherman, informing him not only of Thomas's real estate grab, which included Orchard Knob, a one-hundred-foot hillock to be used as a Federal observation and command post, but also that Howard was advancing to form a junction with him. He also mentioned Thomas would hold the ground taken.[51]

The next day, November 24, Hooker and Sherman moved against the left (south) and right (north) ends of the Confederate line, respectively. Thomas, having demonstrated that Bragg wasn't going anywhere, stood pat in the center. Hooker sent a portion of his command across Lookout Creek and against the Confederate defenders on Lookout Mountain. The Federals worked their way upward over rocks, across chasms, and between fallen trees during intervals of fog and drizzle that obscured the fighting, much of it at close range, from Grant and staff observing from Orchard Knob. By day's end, Hooker had driven off the Confederates, who retreated eastward to Missionary Ridge. While Hooker was occupied on the left, Sherman brought his divisions across the Tennessee River intending to capture Tunnel Hill, the key to turning the right of Bragg's line. However, faulty reconnaissance and inexact maps caused Sherman to arrive at the wrong hill, one separated from the main ridge by a deep ravine. Thus delayed, Bragg had time to dispatch the peerless division of Patrick Cleburne to oppose Sherman.

Hooker and Sherman renewed their push the following day. But Hooker's advance toward Missionary Ridge was delayed because the retreating

Confederates burned a bridge across Chattanooga Creek. Though outnumbered, Cleburne had the topographic advantage and kept Sherman from making headway—and gaining glory—against the north end of the rebel line. That would leave it up to the methodical George Thomas.

—⁂—

On the cold, windy morning of November 25, Grant, Thomas, Baldy Smith, Wilson, Dana, Rawlins, and Fourth Corps commander Gordon Granger, from their vantage point atop Orchard Knob, observed Sherman struggling against Cleburne. As the morning progressed, the observers saw a troubling sight: enemy troops were moving along the top of Missionary Ridge to join the fight against Sherman. It was erroneously assumed by Grant and others that Bragg was drawing off troops from the center of his line to shore up the right. In truth, they were the men who yesterday had been driven off Lookout Mountain. The Orchard Knob observers were also exposed to a troubling sound: General Granger had appropriated several artillery pieces and amused himself hurling shells toward the Confederates and making a tremendous noise. Rawlins, displaying a bit of his "ugly" side, became "very much disgusted at the guerilla operations of Granger" and finally induced Grant to send him off to join his troops.[52]

Wilson claimed that he, Rawlins, and Baldy Smith huddled in the early afternoon to devise an idea for breaking the deadlock on the battlefield and easing pressure on Sherman. The idea was to have Rawlins suggest to Grant that he order Thomas to move forward in a demonstration to capture the line of enemy rifle pits at the base of the ridge. According to Wilson, Rawlins twice prodded Grant to present Thomas with the order. After the second prodding around 3:00 p.m., Grant, "with a blazing face and an expression of unusual determination," barked, "General Thomas, order Granger to turn that battery over to its proper commander and take command of his own corps. . . . And now order your troops to advance and take the enemy's first line of rifle pits."[53] Wilson's attempt to credit himself and Rawlins for getting Thomas into action seems suspect, given his adeptness at self-promotion.[54] In his memoirs, Grant mentioned no such incident and merely cited Hooker's delay and the pressure on Sherman as motivating him to give Thomas the order to charge.[55]

It was not until almost 3:30 p.m. that Thomas's four divisions were aligned, and the firing of six signal guns sent them off on a dash across the plain. Wrenshall Smith, who was with Grant and Rawlins on the Knob, was treated to another panoramic battle scene: "The roll of musketry from our lines (about two miles in length) and the reply from the enemies rifle pits near the foot of the ridge was terrific. As our men charged, the Graybacks broke from behind their protection and up the hill, our men following with chear upon chear and the cannon and musketry on top of the hill pouring shot and shell upon them."[56] If Thomas's men had been relegated to a role ancillary to Sherman, on this day of battle, they didn't show it. Once they overwhelmed the first line of rifle pits, the Federals, hardly pausing to draw a breath—and to the amazement of the Orchard Knob observers—began scrambling upward to the next line of defenders. They had little choice but to ascend the slope; to stop at the foot of the ridge would have left them exposed to enemy fire. Grant turned to Thomas and demanded to know who ordered the men up the ridge. Thomas slowly replied, "I don't know; I did not." Grant muttered something about somebody suffering if it did not come out well before turning to watch events unfold.[57]

He need not have worried. Enemy resistance melted against the irresistible Union surge. Yankees found the detritus of Bragg's army littering the crest—artillery pieces, muskets, knapsacks, blankets—and they whooped and hollered at the thousands of panic-stricken Rebels hightailing down the rear slope. Now it was time to pursue.

—◦◦◦—

After rising on Thursday the twenty-sixth, Rawlins informed Thomas that Sherman had already sent a division in pursuit at midnight, and that Howard's corps followed at 4:00 a.m. Now Rawlins told Thomas that Grant wanted him to "move in the direction of the Enemy . . . with all practicable dispatch."[58] After a late breakfast, Grant and staff made a foray to evaluate the results of the battle. Grant's small staff escort included Rawlins, aide-de-camp William Dunn, Dana, Wilson, Parker, short-timer Lagow, and tagalong Wrenshall Smith. The party stopped on top of Missionary Ridge to behold the winding Tennessee River, towering Lookout Mountain, and white tents dotting the landscape. Their ride eastward was slowed by the tangle of Union troops, escorted prisoners, and abandoned wagons choking the road. Along the way, a woman residing in a fine brick house accosted the party and appealed to Dunn to have her pigs protected from marauders. Half a mile past Chickamauga Station, the party met Sherman and his staff. After a round of consultation and map reading with Sherman, Grant and staff returned to Chattanooga, their path illuminated by a full moon, arriving at 1:00 a.m.[59]

At Friday's breakfast, Grant warned everyone to expect a long ride. It would prove a hard and dangerous ride as well. Rawlins knew Grant could spend hours on horseback and would cut through forest or cross any stream while on pursuit. The party moved along smartly in a southeasterly direction and toward the sound of artillery. A few hours out, they were in the midst of a clash between Cleburne's division and Hooker's pursuers where the Western and Atlantic Railroad passed through Taylor's Ridge at Ringgold Gap. Ely Parker recollected that "we rode for half a mile in the face of the enemy, under incessant fire of cannon and musketry—nor did we ride fast, but upon an ordinary trot."[60] As Rebel batteries blasted from Taylor's Ridge, Rawlins and Lagow, fearing the party would draw fire, rode ahead and found protection inside the railroad depot. They found Hooker inside too. When Grant arrived, he ordered several regiments to attack. While Rawlins and the other staff lunched in the depot, they watched the wounded being brought on stretchers to a nearby tavern. Early in the afternoon, after the fight broke off, Sherman arrived to confer with Grant and Hooker. Rawlins sent Parker and Dunn to locate quarters for the night. They found a house occupied by a family that included a fourteen-year-old girl who was "somewhat dumfounded" by the Yankees. The next morning, following a breakfast of pork and johnnycake and a confab with Sherman, the party turned back for Chattanooga, arriving after dark.[61] Having followed the Confederates about twenty miles into Georgia, Grant reluctantly called off the chase and turned attention to aiding Burnside.

———

The resounding defeat of Bragg's Army of Tennessee and the rescue of Burnside caused a grateful public and government to bestow honors on Grant and capitalize on his success. Democrats saw Grant as an attractive presidential candidate. Barnabas Burns, a prominent Ohio Democrat, approached Grant in early December about running as a War Democrat. Grant quickly rejected the idea, replying confidentially that he was focused on "crushing the rebellion" and not interested in being a candidate for office.[62] The powerful editor of the New York Herald, James Gordon Bennett, regarded Grant as a potential challenger to Lincoln. That possibility alarmed Elihu Washburne. Rawlins allayed his fears, assuring him that despite the outpouring of sentiment from sources like the New York Herald, such advocacy "gives [Grant] little concern; he is unambitious for the honor and will voluntarily put himself in no position nor permit himself to be placed in one he can prevent that will in the slightest manner embarrass the friends of the government in their grand effort to enforce its rightful authority and restore the Union of the States."[63]

Washburne proceeded to advance Grant's military prominence. In early December, he introduced in the House a bill to revive the rank of lieutenant general and confer it on Grant. A compromise bill—reviving the rank but without naming Grant the recipient—passed Congress and was signed into law on February 29, 1864.[64]

Washburne arranged for other, more symbolic honors for Grant. He introduced a resolution that passed through Congress and was approved by Lincoln for a gold medal to be struck bearing Grant's likeness. Joe Bowers was to obtain photographs of the general's profiles for the designer, John Antrobus, a Chicago-based artist. In January Washburne wrote Grant, "Mr. Lincoln has entrusted me with the whole duty of getting up the medal. It is much more of a job than I at first supposed. . . . I intend it shall be the finest medal ever got up in this country. . . . The whole cost of the medal will be between $4000.00 & $5000.00."[65]

During the summer of 1863, a petition was circulated requesting the board of supervisors of Jo Daviess County to appropriate funds for the purpose of purchasing a presentation sword for Grant.[66] On September 15, the board funded the manufacture of such a sword in the name of the people of the county. Actually, there was supposed to be two swords, one, for the general, nestled in a morocco leather presentation case, and the other to be framed and hung in the supervisors' room at the courthouse.[67] Washburne had a hand in this project too. He telegraphed Rawlins for the names and dates of the Chattanooga battles to be engraved on the sword,[68] and in late December he met with the owner of the Ames Manufacturing Company in Washington to get a progress update. The folks in Galena learned the sword would not be ready until February, but "it promises to be superior to anything of the kind ever got up in this country."[69]

Sylvanus Cadwallader, one of Rawlins promoters, touted him for his military genius and said later that Rawlins, at Chattanooga, "of all Grant's great campaigns . . . is unquestionably entitled to one-half that praise, for the strategy."[70] Rawlins was at Grant's side during the exhausting ride into Chattanooga and the pursuit of Bragg into Georgia, and he was exposed to enemy fire on several occasions. However, few would argue he had any significant hand in shaping campaign strategy. Moreover, as historian Steven Jones stated, "Rawlins was actually quiet during the Chattanooga campaign." Bowers and Rowley did the bulk of the correspondence and order writing—paperwork that Rawlins found onerous.[71] The credit was really due Grant. In his inspection report to Stanton, General Hunter expressed his conviction that if Grant had not replaced Rosecrans, "we should have been driven from the Valley of the Tennessee, if not from the State."[72] Hardly anyone in Galena would have thought differently. As the hometown newspaper boasted, "Not a very long time ago, a great many were disposed to look upon Gen. Grant as a very fortunate commander, but possessed of no military genius. But all, at last, are compelled to acknowledge his preeminent ability."[73]

NOTES

1. John Rawlins to Emma Hurlburt, October 14, 1863, John A. Rawlins Collection, Chicago History Museum.

2. H. W. Halleck to U. S. Grant, October 16, 1863, in *The War of the Rebellion: A Compilation of the Official Records of the Union and Confederate Armies*, series 1, part 4, 30:404.

3. James Harrison Wilson, *Under the Old Flag* (New York: D. Appleton, 1912), 1:260.

4. John Rawlins to Emma Hurlburt, November 23, 1863, John A. Rawlins Collection, Chicago History Museum.

5. James Harrison Wilson, *Under the Old Flag*, 1:260, 261, 262.

6. John Rawlins to Emma Hurlburt, October 18, 1863, John A. Rawlins Collection, Chicago History Museum.

7. James Harrison Wilson, *Under the Old Flag*, 1:262.

8. Charles A. Dana, *Recollections of the Civil War* (New York: D. Appleton, 1902), 127, 129.

9. U. S. Grant to G. Thomas October 19, 1863, in *The War of the Rebellion: A Compilation of the Official Records of the Union and Confederate Armies*, series 1, part 4, 30:490; G. Thomas to U. S. Grant, October 19, 1863, in *The War of the Rebellion: A Compilation of the Official Records of the Union and Confederate Armies*, series 1, part 4, 30:490.

10. Charles A. Dana, *Recollections of the Civil War*, 130–31.

11. John Rawlins to Emma Hurlburt, October 20, 1863, John A. Rawlins Collection, Chicago History Museum.

12. James Harrison Wilson, *Under the Old Flag*, 1:265.

13. John Rawlins to Emma Hurlburt, November 23, 1863, John A. Rawlins Collection, Chicago History Museum.

14. James Harrison Wilson, *Under the Old Flag*, 1:274.

15. James Harrison Wilson, *The Life of Charles A. Dana* (New York: Harper and Brothers, 1907), 282.

16. W. B. Franklin & W. F. Smith to A. Lincoln, December 20, 1863, in *The War of the Rebellion: A Compilation of the Official Records of the Union and Confederate Armies*, series 1, 21:868–70; Ezra B. Warner, *Generals in Blue* (Baton Rouge: Louisiana State University Press, 1964), 463.

17. Horace Porter, *Campaigning with Grant* (New York: Century, 1897), 4–6.

18. U. S. Grant to H. W. Halleck, October 28, 1863, in *The Papers of Ulysses S. Grant*, ed. John Y. Simon (Carbondale: Southern Illinois University Press, 1982), 9:335.

19. John Rawlins to Emma Hurlburt, October 27, 1863, John A. Rawlins Collection, Chicago History Museum.

20. Sylvanus Cadwallader, *Three Years with Grant*, ed. Benjamin P. Thomas (New York: Alfred A. Knopf, 1961), 137.

21. C. A. Dana to E. M. Stanton, October 29, 1863, in *The War of the Rebellion: A Compilation of the Official Records of the Union and Confederate Armies*, series 1, part 1, 31:73.

22. James Harrison Wilson, *Under the Old Flag*, 1:280.

23. John Y. Simon, ed., *The Papers of Ulysses S. Grant*, 9:324n.

24. John Y. Simon, ed., *The Papers of Ulysses S. Grant*, 10:161n2.

25. John Y. Simon, ed., *The Papers of Ulysses S. Grant*, 9:388n.

26. Mark Washburne, *A Biography of Elihu Benjamin Washburne: Congressman, Secretary of State, Envoy Extraordinary* (self-pub., Xlibris, 2001), 2:275.

27. William H. Armstrong, *Warrior in Two Camps: Ely S. Parker Union General and Seneca Chief* (Syracuse: Syracuse University Press, 1978), 59, 89.

28. Grant to J. R. Jones, November 17, 1863, and December 5, 1863, in *The Papers of Ulysses S. Grant*, ed. John Y. Simon, 9:406, 496.

29. C. A. Dana to E. M. Stanton, November 1, 1863, in *The War of the Rebellion: A Compilation of the Official Records of the Union and Confederate Armies*, series 1, part 2, 31:54.

30. John A. Carpenter, "Washington, Pennsylvania, and the Gold Conspiracy of 1869," *Western Pennsylvania Historical Magazine* 48, no. 4 (1965): 345.

31. William W. Smith, typescript of diary, Tennessee State Library and Archives, Ac. No. 89–177, Box S-26, p. 1, 2, 11, 12.

32. John Rawlins to Emma Hurlburt, November 16, 1863, John A. Rawlins Collection, Chicago History Museum.

33. Geoffery Perret, *Ulysses S. Grant: Soldier and President* (New York: Random House, 1997), 262.

34. Lyman Beecher, *Six Sermons of Intemperance*, 10th ed. (New York: American Tract Society, 1833), 97.

35. John A. Rawlins, unsent letter to U. S. Grant, November 16, 1863. William P. Palmer Collection of Civil War Manuscripts, Container 19, Folder 18, The Western Reserve Historical Society, Cleveland, OH.

36. William W. Smith, typescript of diary, 12.

37. David Hunter to E. M. Stanton, December 14, 1863, in *The War of the Rebellion: A Compilation of the Official Records of the Union and Confederate Armies*, series 1, part 3, 31:402.

38. William W. Smith, typescript of diary, 13.

39. Bruce Catton, *Grant Takes Command* (Boston: Little, Brown, 1968), 67.

40. John Y. Simon, ed., *The Papers of Ulysses S. Grant*, 9:476 note.

41. William W. Smith, typescript of diary, 38–39.

42. William H. Armstrong, *Warrior in Two Camps*, 94–95.

43. Ibid., 74.

44. William W. Smith, typescript of diary, 40.

45. Ezra B. Warner, *Generals in Blue* (Baton Rouge: Louisiana State University Press, 1964), 587, 588, 591.

46. U. S. Grant to Julia Grant, October 27, 1863, in *The Papers of Ulysses S. Grant*, ed. John Y. Simon, 9:334.

47. William T. Sherman to John Rawlins, November 8, 1863, in *The War of the Rebellion: A Compilation of the Official Records of the Union and Confederate Armies*, series 1, part 3, 31:90–91; William T. Sherman to U. S. Grant, November 13, 1863, in *The War of the Rebellion: A Compilation of the Official Records of the Union and Confederate Armies*, series 1, part 3, 31:139–40.

48. William B. Feis, *Grant's Secret Service: The Intelligence War from Belmont to Appomattox* (Lincoln: University of Nebraska Press, 2002), 184–85.

49. William W. Smith, typescript of diary, 19.

50. Oliver Otis Howard, *Autobiography* (New York: Baker and Taylor, 1907), 479.

51. John Rawlins to William T. Sherman, November 23, 1863, in *The War of the Rebellion: A Compilation of the Official Records of the Union and Confederate Armies*, series 1, part 2, 31:41–42.

52. Charles A. Dana, *Recollections of the Civil War*, 149.

53. James Harrison Wilson, *The Life of John A. Rawlins* (New York: Neale, 1916), 172–73.

54. R. Steven Jones, *The Right Hand of Command: Use and Disuse of Personal Staffs in the Civil War* (Mechanicsburg, PA: Stackpole, 2000), 182.

55. U. S. Grant., *Personal Memoirs* (New York: Charles L. Webster, 1884), 2:78.

56. William W. Smith, typescript of diary, 24–25.

57. Joseph E. Fullerton, "The Army of the Cumberland at Chattanooga," in *Battles and Leaders of the Civil War*, ed. Robert Underwood Johnson and Clarence Clough Buel (1887; repr., New York: Thomas Yoseloff, 1956), 3:725.

58. John A. Rawlins to George Thomas, November 26, 1863, in *The War of the Rebellion: A Compilation of the Official Records of the Union and Confederate Armies*, series 1, part 2, 31:45.

59. William W. Smith, typescript of diary, 26–30.

60. William H. Armstrong, *Warrior in Two Camps*, 90.

61. William W. Smith, typescript of diary, 30–37.

62. U. S. Grant to B. Burns, December 17, 1863, in *The Papers of Ulysses S. Grant*, ed. John Y. Simon, 9:541.

63. Mark Washburne, *A Biography of Elihu Benjamin Washburne*, 2:297–98.

64. John Y. Simon, ed., *The Papers of Ulysses S. Grant*, 9:523n3.

65. Ibid., 504n, 523n3.

66. *The History of Jo Daviess County* (Chicago: H. F. Kett, 1878), 417.

67. *Galena Daily Advertiser*, November 22, 1863.

68. John Y. Simon, ed., *The Papers of Ulysses S. Grant*, 9:491n.

69. *Galena Daily Advertiser*, December 29, 1863.

70. Sylvanus Cadwallader, *Three Years with Grant*, 140.

71. R. Steven Jones, *The Right Hand of Command*, 182.

72. David Hunter to E. M. Stanton, December 14, 1863, in *The War of the Rebellion: A Compilation of the Official Records of the Union and Confederate Armies*, series 1, part 3, 31:402.

73. *Galena Daily Advertiser*, December 3, 1863.

18

"I . . . Tremble at the Great Responsibility about to Devolve on Him"

WITH CHATTANOOGA SECURED AND KNOXVILLE holding, Grant turned his attention to where to carry the war next. He presented Halleck an intriguing, but ultimately disapproved, plan to capture Mobile by the end of January.[1] Meanwhile, John Rawlins planned for his wedding. He procrastinated asking Grant for a leave and even telling him about the wedding, although Rawlins suspected Julia had informed him. Finally, on December 7, he broached the subject with Grant, who freely approved a leave. He told Emma he would stop first at Goshen to retrieve his two older children, James and Jennie, and he requested that when he arrived at Danbury, he be met with as little ceremony as possible. He cautioned Emma not to expect him to be very social, given his discomfort among strangers.[2]

Rawlins's fellow officers chipped in $250 to purchase wedding gifts that included spoons, forks, creamer, a sugar bowl, and napkin rings.[3] On December 18, Rawlins left in the company of Dana, who was traveling to Washington to present Grant's Mobile plans to Lincoln and Stanton.[4] While Rawlins was en route to Danbury, the Lum mansion, where his romance had blossomed, was being razed, its site to become a Federal fort. After the war, Ann Lum wrote a desperate letter to Grant: "I am now almost dependent upon my children for the use of their homes . . . I do not ask as much for a favor, as I do for a simple act of kind and considerate justice. The Fort where my dear old home once stood is now abandoned . . . And it being all the land I own can you grant me an order . . . requiring the proper officers here to fill up the ditches and level the ground smoothly so that I may build there a simple cottage, in which I can pass the remainder of my days?"[5]

John and Emma married on Wednesday, December 23. After an obliga-
tory spell in Danbury, the newlyweds and two children headed west, spending a few days in Chicago. They stayed at the Sherman House,[6] a luxury hotel
on Randolph Street owned by the mayor, Francis Cornwall Sherman. The
Rawlinses may have gotten a deal, because the mayor's son, Colonel Francis
Trowbridge Sherman, was a brigade commander in Granger's Corps. While in
Chicago, John met J. Russell Jones, now a railroad executive and investment
adviser to Grant. Jones had commissioned artist John Antrobus, the designer
of the Grant medal, to paint two portraits of Grant. In the fall, Antrobus had
traveled to Chattanooga to make sketches for three-quarter and full-length
portraits. Jones urged Rawlins to visit Antrobus's studio, where crowds
flocked to glimpse the portraits. Jones effusively praised Antrobus's ability,
telling Grant the artwork was in a class by itself and that "Rawlins saw it & will
tell you all about it."[7] The portraits impressed Rawlins so that after returning
to headquarters, he told Washburne, "They are both very fine and the full size
one I regard as the finest likeness I ever saw. I am no judge of paintings but I
examined this one closely and compared it in my own mind with the General
& pronounced it like him."[8]

Inclement weather delayed the Chicago to Galena leg of the trip. Rawlins
had hoped to reconnect with friends, but his stay was so brief—he arrived
on January 8, delivered Emma and the children to his parents, and left on the
morning of the twelfth—that "few have had an opportunity to see and congratulate him upon his last gallant achievement." His return destination was
Grant's headquarters—recently established in Nashville for its centralized location—and on the trip, Rawlins was accompanied by William Rowley, who
had also been in Galena on leave.[9]

Rawlins reached headquarters late on the fifteenth, and in his next day's
letter to Emma, his health was a prominent topic. "I myself am still troubled
with my cold," he told her. Three months of coughing must have suggested
a more sinister condition. He also shared morbid excerpts from a letter that
Dana had written to Harry Wilson, no doubt based on Dana's impression of
Rawlins during their recent journey to Washington. "His appearance made
me somewhat anxious about him," Dana told Wilson. "I feared that his lungs
might be more seriously affected than I had supposed. His loss would be a
great misfortune, not only for his friends, but still more for the country." John
prefaced these disturbing disclosures with an incongruously lighthearted admonition for Emma: "Don't, however, indulge in Mr. Dana's foreboding as to

my health." But how could she not read these lines without feeling a chill for what the future might hold?[10]

—✵✵✵—

Back at headquarters, Rawlins was drawn into difficulties swirling about Adna Anderson, the superintendent of military railroads for Grant's military division. There were complaints about his inefficiency and foot-dragging. General Thomas was frustrated by a lack of food and forage due to rail transportation problems and blamed Anderson. He griped to Grant, "I have repeatedly urged [Anderson] to exert himself; his excuse is that cars are not unloaded properly on their arrival at Bridgeport and at waystations."[11] Rawlins was convinced of Anderson's ineffectiveness and had been urging Grant to replace him. On January 24, Grant was authorized to remove Anderson, and he speedily supplanted him with Colonel Daniel McCallum, a shaggy-bearded expert on managing railroad systems. The next day, Rawlins telegraphed Thomas to have McCallum report at once to Nashville headquarters. Rawlins's suspicions about Anderson were well founded because McCallum discovered an absence of records for railcars purchased, delivered, or contracted for.[12]

While the rail troubles simmered, signs in eastern Tennessee indicated that Rebels were mounting an operation against General John Foster, Burnside's replacement as commander of the Army of the Ohio. Grant pledged to come in person to facilitate the forwarding of supplies and reinforcements to Foster to meet the potential threat. Grant, accompanied by Rawlins and Baldy Smith, hurried off on January 21 for Chattanooga. To Rawlins's vexation, Foster's dispatches alternated hot and cold—one day Longstreet threatened, the next the threat seemed dispelled. Finally, Grant authorized Thomas to go to Foster's aid, if needed, and drive Longstreet from Tennessee.[13] Foster's tentativeness could have been due to his failing health. Before Christmas, Foster's horse fell on his leg and ruptured an old Mexican War wound. Now, Foster was in such excruciating pain that Grant requested he be replaced by Major General John M. Schofield, who commanded the Department of the Missouri at St. Louis.[14] To replace Schofield, Rosecrans would be reassigned to St. Louis.

After a few days monitoring the situation in eastern Tennessee, Grant and Rawlins returned to Nashville on January 25. Grant traveled on to St. Louis to see to his seriously ill son, Fred, and left Rawlins and Bowers to handle matters at headquarters. Fortunately, Fred's illness had abated, allowing Grant an enjoyable break from military duties. He attended a performance of the historical drama *Richelieu*, and his appearance electrified the audience.[15] The theater was followed by a banquet in his honor at the Lindell Hotel, an ornate architectural marvel that had recently opened. Between rousing speeches, the 250 guests regaled Grant with toast after flattering toast. Attendees pressed him for a speech, but he declined, sparing himself agonizing discomfort. Schofield, the new commander of the Department of the Ohio, sat to Grant's right and watched him exercise such self-control that he did not even sip wine. "I dare not touch it," he told Schofield. "Sometimes I can drink freely without any unpleasant effect; at others I cannot take even a single glass of light wine." This confession so impressed Schofield that he thought, "A strong man, indeed, who could thus know and govern his own weakness!"[16]

Rawlins, with jaundiced eye, read the news reports concerning his commander. In a letter to Emma, he sniffed, "To the theatre I never think of going . . . I attend to the various duties of my position with what abilities I possess and think of home."[17] To Rawlins, enjoying oneself at the theater was an unseemly diversion during national crisis. Rawlins's prudish attitude about the theater as a place of debauchery was common at the time. For example, Lincoln's pastor, Phineas Gurley, of Washington's New York Avenue Presbyterian Church, in a homily delivered after the assassination, expressed a belief many shared: "It will always be a matter of deep regret to the thousands that our lamented President fell in the theatre . . . Had he been murdered in his bed, or in his office, or on the street, or on the steps of the Capitol, the tidings of his death would not have struck the Christian heart of the country quite so painfully; for the feeling of that heart is that the theatre is one of the last places to which a good man should go."[18]

Rawlins saw the stories of the banquet and wrote Emma his reaction. He regretted Grant had come to this: parading himself before admirers and basking in adulation—then acting as if he disliked it. But Rawlins had never known him to decline a dinner party invitation. "You are fully aware of my fears in all this," he said. "I need not state them."[19] Certainly, Rawlins feared Grant might be plied with drink at these affairs, but his trepidation appeared to go beyond that relatively containable risk. A more serious question seemed to be: what effect might this have on Grant himself? Grant rose in rank and responsibility, Rawlins appreciated, due to his tenaciousness and clear-thinking—not through politicking, partying, or popularity. In important ways, this mirrored Rawlins's rise as well and constituted a bond he shared with Grant. Rawlins's success had been achieved through hard work, modesty, trustworthiness, and devotion to country and commander; one did not have to preen before the public or climb over the backs of others to earn promotions. Might Grant's clear focus become obscured by sycophantic newspaper headlines or overtures from political dealmakers? And if so, how would that impact their relationship?

Ten days elapsed before Grant returned to headquarters. Rawlins felt uneasy during his absence, especially with military affairs unsettled in East Tennessee. When Grant failed to arrive on February 3, a nervous Rawlins broke his promise not to swear. Headquarters was where that damned old Skeeziks belonged, and Rawlins did not appreciate his gadding about. Moreover, Rawlins, usually expecting the worst, was suspicious why Grant was postponed a day. When a clear-eyed Grant finally arrived, a relieved John Rawlins wrote to Emma, "I feared everything was not as it should be with him, but his appearance has agreeably disappointed me, and for once I have done him injustice in my thoughts."[20]

———

February began with speculation swirling around Grant's availability for public office. Rawlins, in a letter to Wilson, stood behind Grant's decision to avoid talk about the presidency:

> I cannot see a better course for us than that we have hitherto pursued, viz., attend strictly to our duties as soldiers, leaving the management and conduct of the canvass for the election of Chief Magistrate and civil officers to the people at home . . . . I cannot conceive how the use of General Grant's name in connection with the Presidency can result in harm to him or our cause . . . yet the matter is not in such a shape as to justify him in writing a letter declining to be a candidate for the Presidency. . . . To write a letter of declination now, would place him much in the position of the old maid who had never had an offer declaring she "would never marry;" besides it would be by many construed into a modest way to getting his name before the country in connection with the office, having as he always has, avoided public notice or newspaper talk relating to him. . . . Let the General but continue to be himself as now and heretofore . . . Military not civic honors best bedeck the soldier's brow.[21]

As for Grant's interest in seeking the presidency, Rawlins two weeks earlier had informed Washburne that although the *New York Herald* and other papers advocated him for the job, "he is unambitious of the honor."[22] This disclosure was surely a relief to Washburne and his fellow Republicans.

For most of February, Rawlins and Bowers helped prepare Grant's official report on the Chattanooga battles. Rawlins complained that working on it was "a very unpleasant and I might say thankless undertaking." What made it so was Grant's insistence on writing his own version, forcing Rawlins and Bowers to adhere closely to his copy.[23] Much of the work they performed was checking Grant's report against the orders he had written. Three weeks later, the report was submitted and seemed to satisfy Rawlins. He chirped to Wilson that it was written in Grant's "usual happy, narrative style, void of pomposity or parade."[24] No staff officer, including Rawlins, was cited by Grant in his report for special commendation; all simply received his "warmest thanks" for having "discharged faithfully their respective duties."[25]

February ended with Lincoln nominating Grant for the rank of lieutenant general, and March began with the Senate confirming his promotion. On March 3, Grant received telegraphic orders from Halleck to "report in person to the War Department as early as practicable."[26] Regarding the promotion, Grant took a wait-and-see attitude, writing Sherman the next day that he would not accept it if it meant being headquartered in Washington.[27] Rawlins was more emphatic. He wrote Wilson that with Grant's ability and experience, "we may hope high for the future of our country." Rawlins went further, allowing that the promotion placed Grant at the pinnacle of his country: "To merit by acts, not words, and receive the Lieutenant Generalcy of the armies of the United States, is to be more than President."[28]

On March 4, Grant left Nashville to report to Secretary Stanton, accompanied by Rawlins and son Fred. As he readied himself for the trip, Rawlins considered how ascendancy to such lofty rank brought with it equally lofty expectations for success and crushing responsibilities perhaps exceeding those shouldered by the president.

Sherman and Rawlins had strong, but greatly differing, reactions regarding the job Grant was to assume. Sherman wrote him a remarkable letter containing both praise and advice. Extolling Grant as "[George] Washington's legitimate successor," he also advised him, "Don't stay in Washington"—let Halleck contend with "the buffets of Intrigue and Policy." Sherman proposed instead that he and Grant lock arms and roll up the Confederacy west to east. "I now exhort you to come out West," Sherman implored him. "Here lies the seat of the coming Empire, and from the West when our task is done, we will make short work of Charleston, and Richmond, and the impoverished coast of the Atlantic."[29]

Rawlins feared following Grant to Washington would result in "ascending heights too far above the level of my plebian birth." As the army's ranking general, Grant deserved "an able and accomplished corps of staff officers." In this regard, Rawlins believed he did not measure up. "My military education is not such as to fit me for his chief of staff," he told Emma, "hence it becomes me to withdraw and allow one who is fitted for it to take the place." On the other hand, Rawlins regarded himself as Grant's constant "stay and support in his darkest hours . . . and braved with him the dangers of battle," perhaps reasons enough to "claim to retain the place." Leaving the service was Rawlins's idea alone; Grant had no compunction about retaining him as chief. This was the Galena Coal-Boy's fear of heights talking. Forces outside Rawlins's control were transporting him far from his geographic element to the epicenter of war and politics and yoking him to the supreme commander tasked with the awesome purposes of ending the former and navigating the latter. It was gazing from this precipice that prompted Rawlins to say, "I grow dizzy in looking from the eminence [Grant] has attained and tremble at the great responsibility about to devolve on him."[30]

—◦◦◦—

Rawlins had other reasons to tremble. Besides spinning in self-doubt about his scant military qualifications, he worried the Senate might not confirm his promotion to brigadier general. He had been waiting since August for them to act. Should the confirmation fall through, he told Emma, he might return to civilian life or take a lesser staff position.[31] Rawlins had some reason to worry because he would be in competition for the Senate's favor with another well-regarded staff officer, Rufus Ingalls, chief quartermaster of the Army of the Potomac, who, as a West Point graduate, had the training Rawlins lacked.

Rawlins's confirmation pessimism persisted despite friends' efforts to provide positive news and support. Some of that news came from Harry Wilson. Since January, Wilson had been temporarily assigned to the Cavalry Bureau in Washington to address problems such as contractors selling unsound horses to the government. He liked to brag this position gave him access to congressmen to whom he talked up Grant for lieutenant general and extolled Rawlins. While in Washington, Wilson boarded at the same house with Elihu Washburne. Washburne was keen on getting Grant promoted and providing for Rawlins's advancement in the process. Washburne had become convinced—and Dana and Wilson as Rawlins's advocates aided in that convincing—that "so long as Rawlins stood by [Grant] as guide, philosopher, and friend, the combination would continue to be successful."[32] It was a variation on the notion espoused by Wilson that Rawlins made up one-half of Grant. Wilson kept

Rawlins informed about his promotional efforts with congressmen, and this bolstered his confidence about being confirmed. As he wrote Emma, "Standing as I do in the near relation to General Grant, and the wholesome influence I am supposed to exercise for his good, which is not unknown personally to several gentlemen of great influence in Washington, and who are to be found both in Congress and in the War Department and belonging to both political parties, I do not fear the result."[33]

Rawlins's confirmation took a step forward when, on February 20, Grant submitted to Halleck fourteen names he recommended for a brigadier's star. Rawlins's name was atop the list.[34] In early April, Grant followed up with a letter to Henry Wilson, who chaired the Senate's Committee on Military Affairs. Grant pulled no punches requesting Rawlins's confirmation, stating, "He comes the nearest being indispensable to me of any officer in the service. But if his confirmation is dependent on his commanding troops, he shall command troops at once."[35] Not many, including Rawlins and certainly not Sherman, would have agreed with Grant's overgenerous estimation of his chief of staff.[36] But if a liberal application of grease was needed to squeeze Rawlins's overdue promotion through the Senate, then Grant was in a position to apply some. Grant gave Rawlins a copy of his letter to Senator Wilson, a small token but one that deeply touched Rawlins. He mailed it to Emma to save as a family heirloom. This letter was among several acts of kindness that Grant was lately bestowing on Rawlins. Bowers, Parker, and Rowley also sent ardent letters of support to Washburne. Bowers wrote, "Firmly impressed with the conviction that Gen. Rawlins confirmation is a matter of vital importance to the success of our arms, I beg of you, as the most influential man in Congress to spare no effort to secure his confirmation." Rowley eschewed the flattery and got to the point. Having read many accounts of others being confirmed, he told Washburne that Rawlins's snubbing "has induced me to think there must be a screw loose somewhere."[37]

Finally, on April 14 Rawlins received the propitious telegram from Washburne that the Senate had confirmed him. Just the day before, in an emotional letter to Emma, Rawlins tried not to despair. "The only poignant grief that pierces my heart is the effect a failure of my confirmation may have upon your mind," he told her. "If I go out of the service it is to strike hands with poverty and wrestle with existence."[38]

Questions about health also preyed on Rawlins's mind. February 13 was his thirty-third birthday, giving him pause to consider his progression from an impoverished childhood to (still poor) army general. "How full of anxiety and fears, of cherished hopes being disappointed my life has been," he shared with Emma. Yet he managed to realize most of his youthful dreams. He recounted his remarkable passage from laborer to lawyer to military figure and his participation in notable battles and campaigns. Domestic life has been happy, Rawlins admitted—before he digressed onto a macabre topic—but "not without sorrow, however, death having entered and for a while cast a gloom of sadness over my home."[39] The satisfaction derived from his achievements was tempered by memories of Emily wasting away—and perhaps by pondering how many more birthdays he had remaining.

The next day, he received photographs of himself and his new bride. He thought Emma's were "very good" and found her likeness "so sweet and pretty" that he pressed a kiss on it. His own appearance left him shocked. He called it "miserable." "I look in it sad and deathlike," he fussed to Emma, "yet I am not prepared to say it is not a correct picture, for perhaps it is." It occurred to him that he looked sorrowful in all his photographs and wondered whether others saw him as chronically miserable. However, inside he claimed to be happy. Because he felt the photo was untrue to his heart, he asked her to discard it.[40] Perhaps the arrival of this "deathlike" image, coming as it did so soon after Dana's pessimistic appraisal of his health, caused him to consider whether Emma's domestic harmony would be overshadowed by his death.

As winter ended, Rawlins became increasingly attentive to his health. He noted daily variations in the severity of his cough, hoping a couple days of milder coughing presaged improvement, and he monitored his appetite, as an indicator of robustness. With his cough having persisted for four months, he realized it was a serious matter, and he hoped his doctors were being honest with him.[41] In April he submitted to an opium regimen that precipitated debilitating headaches and lethargy.[42]

—–ↄↄↄ–—

Louisville was the first stop on the historic journey to Washington. On the evening of March 6, after registering at the Galt House, Rawlins accompanied Grant and other officers to the theater. Rawlins, who was "not at all delighted with having gone," went to satisfy Grant. During the performance, Rawlins felt "supremely disgusted . . . with the eagerness or willingness rather, of him we love to say is so modest and unassuming to acknowledge the notice people are taking of him."[43] In his next letter, his disgust seems to have been partially allayed, given his remark: "General Grant is getting on very quietly and I have hopes he will get on to Washington without a great deal of parade, which is more than I thought yesterday evening."[44]

From Louisville where they were joined by Lieutenant Colonel Comstock, it was on to Cincinnati by steamer and thence to Baltimore, where, while waiting for a connection to Washington, Rawlins figured time was overdue for a serious discussion with Grant about the post-promotion composition of his staff. Rawlins told him to organize it as he saw fit without regard for him. Besides, Rawlins added, he had misgivings about his health. His cough was little changed, and Dr. Kittoe's treatments provided little relief. If he failed to improve with the warmer weather, he would quit the service anyway. Grant would hear none of Rawlins's reasoning. Rawlins was deeply touched: "No man perhaps in the country is so great a friend to me, and to feel that I have this friendship is a great satisfaction."[45]

The traveling party's train pulled into Washington during the early evening of March 8. While Grant and Fred checked into the Willard Hotel—and generated a commotion among the throng in the dining room—Rawlins and Comstock tried hunting up Halleck, but he was neither in his office nor at the Georgetown mansion which he rented. That evening, Grant attended a reception at the Executive Mansion. Lincoln, pleased to finally meet him, vigorously shook his hand and introduced him to wife, Mary. Secretary of State Seward coaxed Grant to stand on a sofa, thereby giving the crowd a better glimpse of the hour's hero. Journalist Noah Brooks watched as the clamoring for Grant boiled over: "People were caught up and whirled in the torrent which swept through the great East Room. Ladies suffered dire disaster in the crush and confusion; their laces were torn and crinolines mashed."[46] Although Grant cringed while under this spotlight, Rawlins had to be appalled with how easily he allowed himself to be put on display. After suffering an hour of adulation, Grant, accompanied by Rawlins, met with Lincoln and Stanton in the Blue Room. There, Grant received instructions about the next day's ceremony at which he would receive the lieutenant general commission.

Rawlins, in the company of General Halleck, Illinois congressman Owen Lovejoy, and Lincoln's secretary John Nicolay, were on hand for the 1:00 p.m. ceremony in the cabinet chamber.[47] That evening Seward invited Grant to dinner, and Rawlins went along, although as he wrote Emma, "it is not my pleasure to do so." It would mean reverting to his role as monitor—a role that, like it or not, he played with more than a little success, for as he boasted,

"You know where I am wine is not drunk by those with whom I have any influence."[48]

—◦◦◦—

On a rainy March 10, Grant visited the Army of the Potomac headquarters at Brandy Station, sixty miles southwest of Washington. There, he met with Major General George Meade, that army's colorless but capable commander. He had just undergone a tense grilling by the Joint Congressional Committee on the Conduct of the War regarding his generalship at Gettysburg. Now, Meade was expecting to be replaced, perhaps by Sherman, but Grant surprised him with the assurance he planned to retain him. Although Grant intended to take the field with the Army of the Potomac, he would transmit orders for that army's movements to Meade, who would be responsible for executing them. It was an awkward arrangement but done to ensure that Meade had a semblance of independence of command.

Grant was back in Washington the next day. Eager to escape Washington, he declined a dinner invitation from the Lincolns. Rawlins, who had been pressuring Grant to wrap up affairs there, was also glad to leave. The Capital's overheated atmosphere presented the challenge of how to keep Grant grounded. In Rawlins's mind, the public's adulation and the administration's expectation for success were enough to unfetter anyone's passions and, as Rawlins might fear, thus lead one to act absent a full reservoir of tempering reason.

On the evening of March 11, Grant and Rawlins began their return to Nashville. The next day the War Department issued General Orders No. 98, detailing the new army organization. Grant was assigned command of the armies of the United States, and Halleck stepped down as general in chief to become army chief of staff headquartered in Washington. There, Halleck would be a first responder when political turmoil surfaced and the conduit for the avalanche of paperwork between Grant and the Union's other department commanders. The orders also specified that Grant would maintain a headquarters in the field. Rawlins would soon be announced as Grant's field chief of staff. Sherman was given Grant's previous job as commander of the Military Division of the Mississippi, composed of four departments, including the Department and Army of the Tennessee, now under command of James McPherson.[49]

Grant's promotion required a move to the eastern theater, as well as a change in John and Emma's domestic situation. In mid-February, Emma and the children had joined John in Nashville. For a few weeks, they domiciled there, but John expected that arrangement to soon end. "The new order of things will necessitate breaking up our little home at Nashville," he wrote her from Washington, "but not, I trust, before I see you again."[50]

—◦◦◦—

Back in Nashville on the fourteenth, Grant consulted with trusted subordinates for three days of strategy discussion with time for socializing and entertainment. Gathered about Grant were Rawlins, Sherman, McPherson, Phil Sheridan, Black Jack Logan, Gordon Granger, and Grenville Dodge. Dodge was a New Englander who had migrated in the early 1850s to Council Bluffs, Iowa. A civil engineer and early proponent of a transcontinental railroad, Dodge had helped rebuild rail lines to keep Grant's troops supplied, even providing him valuable intelligence about enemy movements. Dodge first met Rawlins and Grant after the battle of Corinth in fall 1862. While working with a railroad crew at Humboldt, Tennessee, he was ordered to report immediately to Grant. Still in work clothes, he hopped a southbound train. When the train stopped at Jackson, Tennessee, Rawlins came aboard looking for him. After accosting Dodge, Rawlins told him Grant was standing on the platform and waiting for him. Dodge protested that he couldn't meet Grant dressed as he was. "Oh," answered Rawlins, "we know all about you, don't mind that."[51]

No sooner had the generals assembled in Nashville than Grant hustled them to visit Tennessee's military governor, Andrew Johnson. Johnson burst into a tirade against the Rebels, slamming his fist onto a piano with such might that it reverberated through his house. "No rebel need hope for mercy from me!" he shouted. Everyone left much disgusted with Johnson's vulgar behavior. After returning to headquarters, Sherman proposed they attend the theater that evening.

Hamlet was playing in town. The generals occupied the balcony's first row but managed to remain unrecognized by the many soldiers in attendance. What transpired from that point could only have mortified Rawlins. The play, using Dodge's word, was being "butchered," much to the delight of the hooting audience. Sherman, an avid theatergoer, was so indignant at the actors' ineptness that he complained, "Dodge, that is no way to play Hamlet." Dodge could hardly keep Sherman restrained. During Hamlet's soliloquy over Yorick's skull, a soldier yelled, "Say, pard, what is it, Yank or Reb?" That brought the house down and signaled to Grant it was time for him and his generals to leave.

Sherman then proposed his second idea of the evening: an oyster supper. He sent Rawlins to find a suitable restaurant. Rawlins located a nice place, but there was only one small unoccupied table for the whole party. However, there was a larger table at which was seated a solitary diner. Rawlins asked the man to move to the small table, but he refused. Churning with disgust, Rawlins stormed out of the restaurant, followed by the generals. Sherman needled Rawlins, saying if they had to depend on him, they'd never get any oysters. Finally, Sherman asked a policeman for assistance, and he directed them to an oyster saloon run by a widow. Everyone got his oysters, but the party fell into such an engrossing conversation that at midnight their meals were only half eaten. The widow announced that a curfew order had gone into effect, and she had to close.[52]

On March 18, Halstead Townsend and Stephenson Napper, representing the citizens of Jo Daviess County, arrived bearing Grant's presentation sword. Its grasp and guard were adorned with the heads of Jupiter, Mars, Mercury, and Minerva, the pommel encircled by a ring of diamonds, and the cross-guard engraved "Jo Daviess Co. Ill., to Maj. Gen. Ulysses S. Grant, the hero of the Mississippi." Modestly accepting the sword, Grant promised he would use it "in the maintenance of our nationality, liberty and law so long as the Government and armies repose confidence in me."[53] The Nashville headquarters was shuttered the next day.

The first part of the journey to Washington brought the traveling party to Cincinnati. Grant stopped to visit his parents in Covington, Kentucky, and to hold strategy talks with Sherman. Grant envisioned a sweeping, coordinated effort to simultaneously engage the enemy on multiple fronts. Out west, Grant hoped to send Nathaniel Banks against Mobile. A small force under German-born Franz Sigel would patrol the Shenandoah Valley and keep reinforcements from there reaching Lee. An army comprised of two corps under Ben Butler was to move up the James River and pressure Richmond. It was risky entrusting these commands to these three political generals with questionable military capabilities, but with a presidential election looming, they had to be obliged. The centerpiece of Grant's plan was to work in tandem with Sherman, the former taking on Lee and the latter in Georgia pressing Joe Johnston, Bragg's successor. Both agreed that their purpose was vanquishing the Confederate armies rather than capturing territory.[54]

Rawlins parted from his family at Cincinnati, wishing Emma and the children a safe journey to his parents' home. He reached Washington on the evening of the twenty-second. The Grants were delayed because Julia wanted to swing through Philadelphia to buy new clothes. Rawlins was prepared to quickly establish the new headquarters at Culpeper Court House, Virginia. To his relief, headquarters would be in a roomy brick house instead of a drafty tent. When Grant showed up in the rain on the twenty-fourth, he invited Rawlins to take the house's other bedroom, appointed with featherbed and fireplace. Rawlins noticed both Grants had been showing considerable solicitude toward him. Two days before, he had written Emma about this: "I cannot tell the reason why unless it was that they thought my recent separation from you entitled me to sympathy. I certainly feel very kindly to them for their marked interest in my welfare. Be assured, there is nothing the General can do for me but he will do."[55] Perhaps they felt his evident decline in health warranted sympathy too. A few weeks later, Rawlins was the recipient of another gesture of Grant's kindness. He was presented with a silk sash, signed by Grant, and inscribed: "This sash, worn by me through all my battles and campaigns, from and including the surrender of Vicksburg, July 4th, 1863, is presented to Brigadier General John A. Rawlins, my chief of staff, in evidence of my appreciation as an officer and friend."[56]

Once headquartered at Culpeper, the reality of being transplanted to hostile territory took hold in Rawlins's consciousness. When he climbed into his featherbed that first night, he was only ten miles north of the Rapidan River, with Lee's Army of Northern Virginia just beyond. Rawlins approached the coming struggle with anticipation and hope. He anticipated being present at the battle that sealed Richmond's fate, an experience that meant attaining the summit of his ambition. And he fervently hoped he would have the stamina to withstand the ardors of the campaign.

—⁊⁊⁊—

The rain and overcast greeting Rawlins gave the desolate Virginia landscape an even more forbidding appearance. Three years of almost unrelenting warfare had left the countryside beaten down, exhausted. "Outside the town, not a house nor a fence, not a tree was to be seen for miles, where once all had been cultivated farm-land, or richly wooded country," Adam Badeau recollected. "This desert extended almost from Washington to the Rapidan."[57] The place and its people didn't sit right with Ely Parker, who felt no hospitality there. It was, he said, "an awful country—a d——d mean country," and he called the Virginians a "miserable spawn of humanity."[58]

By March 26, most of Grant's personal staff were present in this expanse of devastation. When Grant announced the composition of his staff,[59] there were familiar holdovers: Rawlins as chief of staff; Joe Bowers as Rawlins's assistant; Rowley as military secretary; and Ely Parker as assistant adjutant general. Cyrus Comstock, who steadily gained influence with Grant, was appointed senior aide-de-camp. George Leet was assigned, as per Rawlins's special orders, to duty in Washington at army headquarters.[60]

Among the newcomers was hobbling Adam Badeau, sufficiently recovered from his foot wound to join the staff as a second military secretary. Badeau was late to report because he had accompanied Julia Grant on her stay in Washington. Rawlins's first impression of Badeau was positive. "A very pleasant gentleman," he wrote Emma, "and I think I shall like him."[61] Grant dipped into his family to appoint as aide-de-camp Lieutenant Colonel Fred Dent, his brother-in-law and roommate at the Military Academy. The most notable additions were two aides-de-camp, Lieutenant Colonels Orville Babcock and Horace Porter. Both, like Comstock, were West Point graduates and brilliant students who opted for engineer corps duty. Twenty-eight-year-old Babcock had previously served on the staff of Nathaniel Banks. Porter, the son of a former Pennsylvania governor, had been on George Thomas's staff at Chattanooga, where he became acquainted with Grant, who eyed him for a spot on his own staff. However, in November Stanton called Porter to Washington to take a job in the Ordnance Department. Finally, in the spring Grant succeeded in recruiting Porter away from Stanton, and he reported to Culpeper at the end of April. Porter soon became one of Grant's favorites.

Grant's expanded responsibilities required a staff upgrade, and the West Pointers fit that need. Although their appointments increased professionalism, they also brought into sharp distinction the bifurcation between the regular army and volunteer staffers. Comstock, Babcock, and Porter had little affinity with the staff plucked from civilian life, and they were mostly unaware of how Rawlins's personal and professional relationships with Grant had steadily developed and what merits Rawlins brought to those relationships. Rawlins could acknowledge that the West Pointers' expertise could only have positive benefits, yet on measuring himself against them, he felt painfully inadequate. As the spring of 1864 advanced, there occurred a perceptible "drifting apart" between Rawlins and Grant. Rawlins became more reserved when voicing his views, and he began to feel his influence with Grant waning.[62]

To what that drift might be attributed is open to conjecture. Perhaps it came from Grant's need to rely less on others after experiencing a string of confidence-boosting successes. Perhaps Grant wearied of the Washington gossip that Rawlins kept him sober. If so, Grant could have been asserting his ascent was a result of intrinsic merits rather than critics' claims it was because of external factors like amazing good luck or facing inferior Confederate commanders. Moreover, as Rawlins became more protective of his health—in addition to opium, he was quaffing doses of bourbon and cod liver oil—he naturally drew into himself.[63]

—⁓—

A priority business item was conferring with Ben Butler at his headquarters at Fortress Monroe, at the tip of the Virginia Peninsula between the York and James Rivers. A small party consisting of the Grants, Rawlins, Comstock, and Congressman Washburne left Washington on March 31 aboard the *City of Albany*, arriving the next morning. Rawlins had sent Washburne a special invitation and urged him, "Come don't fail."[64] A zealous War Democrat, Butler was a rough political in-fighter. Because his appointment as major general occurred early in the war, he outranked almost all Union generals, yet he had little battlefield experience. Short, bald, and pudgy, he cut a poor military figure. His prominent feature was his eyes, severely crossed, lurking behind half-slit lids, and tucked above baggy pouches.

The conference went smoothly. Both Grant and Butler agreed how their roles in the pending campaign would unfold: the Army of the Potomac would focus on Lee, and Butler's Army of the James, operating in concert, would have Richmond as its "objective point." Butler would move his army up the James River and occupy City Point, situated at the confluence of the James and Appomattox Rivers between Richmond and Petersburg. Grant provided Butler with regular-army, battle-tested subordinates: Baldy Smith would command one wing, and Quincy Gillmore would be recalled from South Carolina with ten thousand troops to command the other.[65] Rawlins was initially impressed with Butler. He regarded Butler, along with Meade and Sherman, as a general Grant could trust, as one whose only ambition was to be in accord with orders given him.[66] Comstock's impression differed markedly: "Butler is sharp, shrewd, able, without conscience or modesty—over-bearing. A bad man to have against you in a criminal case."[67] The West Pointer, it turned out, came closer to accurately assessing Butler's makeup.

What Grant and Butler discussed differed from a more radical plan Grant proposed to Halleck just three months earlier. After Halleck invited Grant to share his views about future operations in the east, he asked Baldy Smith and Comstock to devise a plan. The pair, whom Grant held in regard, were experienced with the Army of the Potomac. In January, Grant shared their plan with Halleck. It called for drawing off a force of sixty thousand and shipping them to southeastern Virginia, where they would descend to Raleigh, destroying rail lines all the way, and then pivoting eastward to take Wilmington. To counter this incursion, Smith and Comstock reasoned, it would force the Confederacy to evacuate troops from Virginia and to operate along lines never anticipated. On January 15, both Smith and his ally Harry Wilson wrote letters to Assistant Secretary of War Dana pushing for the plan. As he had with Grant's plan to move against Mobile, Halleck rejected it, believing it best to defeat Lee's army "by attacking it between [Washington] and Richmond, on our shortest line of supplies."[68]

Baldy Smith grew sore when he realized that Grant, who was no longer duty-bound to Halleck, was not championing the plan to move an army into North Carolina, and he wrote a letter so informing Wilson. Wilson, in turn, shared it with Rawlins who passed it to Grant. Rawlins objected to Smith's plan because it violated his principle that an overwhelming force ought to be concentrated against Lee, a point he shared in an April 13 letter to Emma:

> You know my opinion of General William F. Smith, who has altogether a different plan from that of the General, and feels very badly that Grant don't fall into his views. General Wilson falls in with General Smith, and I believe from his talk, he thinks General Grant has adopted it. Fortunately however neither of these soldiers (and able soldiers they are too) know what the General's plans are. . . . Of one thing the country can be assured, the General does not mean to scatter his army and have it whipped in detail. No such calamity as this will happen to us, I am certain. If I ever have been of signal service to General Grant it has been in my constant, firm advocacy of massing large forces against small ones, in other words, of always having the advantage of numbers on our side.[69]

More disconcerting to Rawlins was how the letter revealed Smith's divisiveness and how it served "as an evidence of an improper desire on the part of its writer to exert a controlling influence over the plan of campaign in the East."[70] Rawlins supported Grant's decision to conduct what would be known as the Overland Campaign—the battles and maneuvering against Lee that culminated in the siege of Petersburg—where Lee's army was to be met head-on.[71]

Grant spent April acquainting himself with the Army of the Potomac, contemplating whether to cross the Rapidan above or below Lee, and ensuring coordination among the multipronged movements that would engage the enemy across several fronts. Grant explained his strategy in an April 4 message to Sherman: Banks was to conclude his expedition in Louisiana and take a combined command of twenty-five thousand (including five thousand from Rosecrans) to operate against Mobile. Butler was to move against Richmond on the south side of the James with thirty-three thousand men. The Army of the Potomac would be pitted against Lee. Sigel's command was to move in two columns, one starting from Beverly, West Virginia, and the other to strike the Virginia and Tennessee Railroad. As for Sherman, Grant said, "You I propose to move against Johnston's Army, to break it up and to get into the interior of the enemy's country as far as you can, inflicting all the damage you can against their War resources."[72] For his part, Sherman, through Rawlins, kept Grant apprised of his preparations and troop movements in his Military Division.[73]

During this month of preparation before the epic clash between the Armies of the Potomac and Northern Virginia, Rawlins attended to his health and business items. On the seventeenth, he confided to Emma he might have to quit the service to prevent permanent injury to his lungs, but he quickly added, "This, however, I do not seriously apprehend."[74] Rawlins seemed caught in denial, suppressing the awful thought that his cough was the bellwether symptom for the disease that had killed his wife. A day later, two army surgeons listened to his lungs and expressed satisfaction that nothing ailed them but chronic bronchitis that should yield to proper care, rest, and "good living." But at the end of April, Rawlins contemplated taking a leave once the campaign ended.[75]

At this same time, in the Army of the Potomac, a surgeon in the 121st New York, Dr. Daniel Holt, also worried about his ill health in letters to his wife. Holt would die from tuberculosis in 1868, just one year before Rawlins, so the progression of their illnesses is roughly comparable. Holt's situation provides insight into how Rawlins probably felt. In October 1864, Holt wrote his wife, "I shall try for [a transfer], as my health is very poor. My lungs are *very* sore and a cough distressingly severe is a constant attendant. I *must* leave the service soon, or die in it. There is no disguising the fact that I am daily running down. My friends advise the step, and I cannot look upon it with disfavor."[76]

For Rawlins, April meant toiling late at headquarters. Collaborating with Bowers, Rawlins finally completed the report of the battle of Belmont, an engagement that now seemed fixed to a quainter time. On the sixteenth, he worked on a letter to General Butler regarding policy for the exchange of prisoners. Butler had been serving as agent for their exchange, negotiating with his Confederate counterpart, Robert Ould. Butler kept Secretary of War Stanton apprised of those negotiations.[77] When Stanton invited Grant to offer input on the subject, Rawlins crafted a reply. One of the points Grant wished to emphasize was, "No distinction whatever will be made in the exchange between white and colored prisoners; the only question being, were they, at the time of their capture, in the military service of the United States." Grant stipulated the same treatment and conditions of release and exchange must apply whether the captured Union soldier was White or Black, a stipulation that Rawlins thought would bring at least a temporary end to exchanges.[78] This letter took on added importance in light of the appalling event five days earlier at Fort Pillow, north of Memphis on the Mississippi. There Rebels under Nathan Bedford Forrest attacked the fort's garrison and massacred African American soldiers while they surrendered. Rawlins regarded the massacre as "one of the most brutal and horrible acts of fiendishness on record."[79] An issue on which Grant and Rawlins were in accord was the desirability of bringing to the front troops now underutilized in rearguard duty. Rawlins assisted in transferring men from prison guard duty, as well as regiments of heavy artillery reserves who huddled unmolested in defensive positions outside of Washington.[80]

Grant also needed to prepare his staff for the upcoming campaign and to ensure they understood how he expected them to perform. On the night of May 3, the eve of the great movement against Lee, he gathered them in the front room of the headquarters house for their instructions. He collected his thoughts while putting a match to a fresh cigar. "I had no longer any hesitation in deciding to cross the Rapidan below the position occupied by Lee's army, and move to our left," he announced to the staff. This approach made it easier to supply the army and evacuate the wounded. After rising from his chair, Grant took a position next to a wall map and made a sweep of his arm to emphasize his next point. A key to victory was communicating his orders without delay to commanders in the field, and he invited the staff to talk freely with him, to grasp his thinking regarding the conduct of battle. "I expect to send you to the critical points of the lines to keep me promptly advised of what is taking place," he told them, "and in cases of great emergency, when new dispositions have to be made on the instant, or it becomes suddenly necessary to reinforce one command by sending to its aid troops from another, and there is not time to communicate with headquarters, I want you to explain my views to commanders, and urge immediate action." He was vesting in staff a stunning amount of responsibility, expecting them to induce the commanders to cooperate "without waiting for specific orders from me."[81]

With West Pointers on staff, Grant could more confidently send them into the field as his representatives or to act in his stead. There was a foreshadowing of this new approach in April when Grant sent Comstock to Nashville to brief Sherman about the details and expectations for the looming campaign. Moreover, Babcock was dispatched to Sigel's headquarters to help the German general get off on the proper foot.

Congressman Washburne, in the company of *New York Times* correspondent William Swinton, arrived at Culpeper Court House on May 3. Washburne was keen on accompanying the army as it opened its critical campaign. At headquarters, they found Grant and Colonel Comstock in the general's little room studiously reading the newspapers. Grant was happy to oblige, and he even arranged a pass for Swinton. Relations between Washburne and Grant and his staff seemed never more harmonious. Two weeks before, Brigadier General John E. Smith, the Galena jeweler and commander of a division in the Fifteenth Corps, proposed that a testimonial be gotten up for Washburne in appreciation for all he had done for his friends. A silver tea service might be appropriate, Smith suggested to Grant, who agreed and put in fifty dollars for himself, twenty dollars for Rawlins, and ten dollars for Rowley.[82] After a round of hearty welcomes, Grant briefed Washburne on the campaign's details. When Washburne's briefing ended, the Union advance was only hours from getting underway.

In early April, Grant recalled Wilson from the Cavalry Bureau and gave him command of one of the three divisions in Phil Sheridan's corps of cavalry. Now his division was chosen to lead the crossing of the Rapidan. To wish Wilson well, Rawlins, Porter, Babcock, and Badeau rode over to his headquarters during the afternoon of May 3. The friends dispensed plenty of good cheer, handshakes, and advice. But there was also an undercurrent of anxiety among the well-wishers, who preferred not to dwell on the peril Wilson might encounter.[83] The party returned to Culpeper headquarters, where in the evening staff received instructions about being Grant's proxies on the battlefield.

Grant, Rawlins, Washburne, Duff, and Rowley passed the last few hours of that day in the latter's tent in lively conversation. Washburne noted in his diary, "Our conversation turned on politics and war, discussions of individuals and the prospects of success, etc."[84] Washburne turned in a little before midnight. Minutes later and a few miles away, one of Wilson's brigades led by Colonel George Chapman forded the Rapidan and drove back a line of enemy pickets. That opened the way for the rest of Wilson's division and for Major General Gouverneur Warren's Fifth Corps following closely behind.[85]

NOTES

1. U. S. Grant to H. W. Halleck, December 7, 1863, in *The War of the Rebellion: A Compilation of the Official Records of the Union and Confederate Armies*, series 1, part 3, 31:349–50.

2. John Rawlins to Emma Hurlburt, December 3, 1863, and December 7, 1863, John A. Rawlins Collection, Chicago History Museum.

3. James Harrison Wilson, *Under the Old Flag* (New York: D. Appleton, 1912), 1:321.

4. Ibid., 316–17.

5. *Evening Post*, Vicksburg, MS, July 1, 1863, "Vicksburg Family Shared Their Home with U. S. Grant," University of Mississippi J. D. Williams Library, Archives and Special Collections, Newspapers (Box 57); John Y. Simon, ed., *The Papers of Ulysses S. Grant* (Carbondale: Southern Illinois University Press, 1982), 9:78n.

6. *Galena Daily Advertiser*, January 8, 1864.

7. John Y. Simon, ed., *The Papers of Ulysses S. Grant*, 9:542n.

8. Ibid., 543n.

9. *Galena Daily Advertiser*, January 11 and 12, 1864.

10. John A. Rawlins to Emma Rawlins, January 16, 1864, transcribed by J. H. Wilson, James H. Wilson Papers, Bender Collection, Wyoming State Archives and Historical Department, Microfilm Reel H-61a.

11. George H. Thomas to U. S. Grant, January 14, 1864, in *The War of the Rebellion: A Compilation of the Official Records of the Union and Confederate Armies*, series 1, part 2, 32:89.

12. John Y. Simon, ed., *The Papers of Ulysses S. Grant* (Carbondale: Southern Illinois University Press, 1982), 10:57 note.

13. U. S. Grant to G. H. Thomas, January 24, 1864, in *The Papers of Ulysses S. Grant*, ed. John Y. Simon, 10:64–65.

14. U. S. Grant to H. W. Halleck, January 27, 1864, in *The War of the Rebellion: A Compilation of the Official Records of the Union and Confederate Armies*, series 1, part 2, 32:229–30.

15. Bruce Catton, *Grant Takes Command* (Boston: Little, Brown, 1968), 114.

16. John M. Schofield, *Forty-Six Years in the Army* (New York: Century, 1897), 111.

17. John A. Rawlins to Emma Rawlins, January 31, 1864, transcribed by J. H. Wilson, James H. Wilson Papers, Bender Collection, Wyoming State Archives and Historical Department, Microfilm Reel H-61a.

18. P. D. Gurley, *The Voice of the Rod: A Sermon* (Washington, DC: William Ballantyne, 1865), 14–15.

19. John A. Rawlins to Emma Rawlins, January 31, 1864, transcribed by J. H. Wilson, James H. Wilson Papers, Bender Collection, Wyoming State Archives and Historical Department, Microfilm Reel H-61a.

20. John A. Rawlins to Emma Rawlins, February 4, 1864, transcribed by J. H. Wilson, James H. Wilson Papers, Bender Collection, Wyoming State Archives and Historical Department, Microfilm Reel H-61a.

21. James Harrison Wilson, *The Life of John A. Rawlins* (New York: Neale, 1916), 184–85, 187.

22. John A. Rawlins to Elihu H. Washburne, January 20, 1864, in James Harrison Wilson, *The Life of John A. Rawlins*, 387.

23. John A. Rawlins to Emma Rawlins, February 15, 1864, transcribed by J. H. Wilson, James H. Wilson Papers, Bender Collection, Wyoming State Archives and Historical Department, Microfilm Reel H-61a.

24. James Harrison Wilson, *The Life of John Rawlins*, 187.

25. U. S. Grant to J. C. Kelton, December 23, 1863, in *The War of the Rebellion: A Compilation of the Official Records of the Union and Confederate Armies*, series 1, part 2, 31:36. Although the report is dated December 23, 1863, it was not submitted until more than two months later; see John Y. Simon, ed., *The Papers of Ulysses S. Grant*, 9:567n1.

26. H. W. Halleck to U. S. Grant, March 3, 1864, in *The War of the Rebellion: A Compilation of the Official Records of the Union and Confederate Armies*, series 1, part 3, 32:13.

27. U. S. Grant to W. T. Sherman, March 4, 1864, in *The Papers of Ulysses S. Grant*, ed. John Y. Simon, 10:186–87.

28. James Harrison Wilson, *The Life of John A. Rawlins*, 187.

29. W. T. Sherman to U. S. Grant, March 10, 1864, in *The Papers of Ulysses S. Grant*, ed. John Y. Simon, 10:187–88.

30. John A. Rawlins to Emma Rawlins, March 5, 1864, transcribed by J. H. Wilson, James H. Wilson Papers, Bender Collection, Wyoming State Archives and Historical Department, Microfilm Reel H-61a.

31. John A. Rawlins to Emma Rawlins, February 9, 1864, transcribed by J. H. Wilson, James H. Wilson Papers, Bender Collection, Wyoming State Archives and Historical Department, Microfilm Reel H-61a.

32. James Harrison Wilson, *Under the Old Flag*, 1:346.

33. John A. Rawlins to Emma Rawlins, February 9, 1864, transcribed by J. H. Wilson, James H. Wilson Papers, Bender Collection, Wyoming State Archives and Historical Department, Microfilm Reel H-61a.

34. U. S. Grant to H. W. Halleck, February 20, 1864, in *The Papers of Ulysses S. Grant*, ed. John Y. Simon, 10:145–46.

35. U. S. Grant to H. Wilson, April 4, 1864, in *The Papers of Ulysses S. Grant*, ed. John Y. Simon, 10:259.

36. A month earlier, when Grant received orders to report for his confirmation, he wrote Sherman, expressing "my thanks to you and McPherson as *the men*, above all others, I feel indebted for whatever I have had of success"; U. S. Grant to William T. Sherman, March 4, 1864, in *The Papers of Ulysses S. Grant*, ed. John Y. Simon, 10:187.

37. John Y. Simon, ed., *The Papers of Ulysses S. Grant*, 10:260.

38. John A. Rawlins to Emma Rawlins, April 12, 1864, transcribed by J. H. Wilson, James H. Wilson Papers, Bender Collection, Wyoming State Archives and Historical Department, Microfilm Reel H-61a.

39. John A. Rawlins to Emma Rawlins, February 13, 1864, transcribed by J. H. Wilson, James H. Wilson Papers, Bender Collection, Wyoming State Archives and Historical Department, Microfilm Reel H-61a.

40. John A. Rawlins to Emma Rawlins, February 15, 1864, transcribed by J. H. Wilson, James H. Wilson Papers, Bender Collection, Wyoming State Archives and Historical Department, Microfilm Reel H-61a.

41. Ibid.

42. John A. Rawlins to Emma Rawlins, April 12, 1864, transcribed by J. H. Wilson, James H. Wilson Papers, Bender Collection, Wyoming State Archives and Historical Department, Microfilm Reel H-61a.

43. John A. Rawlins to Emma Rawlins, March 5, 1864, transcribed by J. H. Wilson, James H. Wilson Papers, Bender Collection, Wyoming State Archives and Historical Department, Microfilm Reel H-61a.

44. John A. Rawlins to Emma Rawlins, March 6, 1864, transcribed by J. H. Wilson, James H. Wilson Papers, Bender Collection, Wyoming State Archives and Historical Department, Microfilm Reel H-61a.

45. John A. Rawlins to Emma Rawlins, March 8, 1864, transcribed by J. H. Wilson, James H. Wilson Papers, Bender Collection, Wyoming State Archives and Historical Department, Microfilm Reel H-61a.

46. Noah Brooks, *Washington in Lincoln's Time* (New York: Century, 1896), 146.

47. Earl Schenk Miers, ed., *Lincoln Day by Day* (Washington, DC: Lincoln Sesquicentennial Commission, 1960), 245.

48. John A. Rawlins to Emma Rawlins, March 9, 1864, transcribed by J. H. Wilson, James H. Wilson Papers, Bender Collection, Wyoming State Archives and Historical Department, Microfilm Reel H-61a.

49. General Orders, No. 98, March 12, 1864, in *The War of the Rebellion: A Compilation of the Official Records of the Union and Confederate Armies*, series 1, part 3, 32:58.

50. John A. Rawlins to Emma Rawlins, March 9, 1864, transcribed by J. H. Wilson, James H. Wilson Papers, Bender Collection, Wyoming State Archives and Historical Department, Microfilm Reel H-61a.

51. Stanley P. Hirshson, *Grenville M. Dodge: Soldier, Politician, Railroad Pioneer* (Bloomington: Indiana University Press, 1967), 64.

52. Grenville M. Dodge, *Personal Recollections of President Abraham Lincoln, General Ulysses S. Grant and General William T. Sherman* (Council Bluffs, IA: Monarch, 1914), 139–41.

53. *The History of Jo Daviess County, Illinois* (Chicago: H. P. Kett, 1878), 418; *Galena Daily Gazette*, March 23, 1864.

54. John F. Marszalek, *Sherman: A Soldier's Passion for Order* (Carbondale: Southern Illinois University Press, 1993), 259.

55. John A. Rawlins to Emma Rawlins, March 22, 1864, transcribed by J. H. Wilson, James H. Wilson Papers, Bender Collection, Wyoming State Archives and Historical Department, Microfilm Reel H-61a.

56. *Galena Daily Gazette*, May 14, 1864.

57. Adam Badeau, *Military History of Ulysses S. Grant* (New York: Appleton, 1881), 40–41.

58. William H. Armstrong, *Warrior in Two Camps: Ely S. Parker Union General and Seneca Chief* (Syracuse: Syracuse University Press, 1978), 96.

59. General Orders, No. 155, April 8, 1864, in *The War of the Rebellion: A Compilation of the Official Records of the Union and Confederate Armies*, series 1, 32:820.

60. Special Orders No. 3, March 25, 1864, in *The Papers of Ulysses S. Grant*, ed. John Y. Simon, 10:220–21n.

61. Typescript of letter from John A. Rawlins to Emma, February 12, 1864, Ulysses S. Grant Presidential Library, Mississippi State University, Series 2, Box 10, Folder 66.

62. James Harrison Wilson, *The Life of John A. Rawlins*, 193–95.

63. John A. Rawlins to Emma Rawlins, April 18, 1864, transcribed by J. H. Wilson, James H. Wilson Papers, Bender Collection, Wyoming State Archives and Historical Department, Microfilm Reel H-61a. Although Rawlins claimed surgeons believed he suffered from chronic bronchitis, physicians treated consumption with cod liver oil, tonics and stimulants, a rich diet, warm clothing, and exercise. The oil and whiskey were taken usually after meals. One-half ounce of cod liver oil and one ounce of whiskey three times a day was typically prescribed; *Medical and Surgical History of the Civil War*, reprint (Wilmington, NC: Broadfoot), 6:828; Ron Chernow, *Grant* (New York: Penguin, 2017), 362.

64. John Y. Simon, ed., *The Papers of Ulysses S. Grant*, 10:241n.

65. U. S. Grant to B. F. Butler, April 2, 1864, in *The Papers of Ulysses S. Grant*, ed. John Y. Simon, 10:245–47.

66. John A. Rawlins to Emma Rawlins, April 23, 1864, transcribed by J. H. Wilson, James H. Wilson Papers, Bender Collection, Wyoming State Archives and Historical Department, Microfilm Reel H-61a.

67. Merlin E. Sumner, ed., *The Diary of Cyrus B. Comstock* (Dayton, OH: Morningside, 1987), 262.

68. U. S. Grant to Henry W. Halleck, January 19, 1864, in *The Papers of Ulysses S. Grant*, ed. John Y. Simon, 10:39–40; John Y. Simon, *The Papers of Ulysses S. Grant*, 10:18n; Henry W. Halleck to U. S. Grant, February 17, 1864, in *The Papers of Ulysses S. Grant*, ed. John Y. Simon, 10:110n.

69. John A. Rawlins to Emma Rawlins, April 13, 1864, transcribed by J. H. Wilson, James H. Wilson Papers, Bender Collection, Wyoming State Archives and Historical Department, Microfilm Reel H-61a.

70. James Harrison Wilson, *The Life of John A. Rawlins*, 207.

71. Ibid., 198, 209.

72. U. S. Grant to William T. Sherman, April 4, 1864, in *The Papers of Ulysses S. Grant*, ed. John Y. Simon, 10:251–53.

73. See, for example, *The War of the Rebellion: A Compilation of the Official Records of the Union and Confederate Armies*, series 1, part 3, 32:247–49, 410–11.

74. John A. Rawlins to Emma Rawlins, April 17, 1864, transcribed by J. H. Wilson, James H. Wilson Papers, Bender Collection, Wyoming State Archives and Historical Department, Microfilm Reel H-61a.

75. John A. Rawlins to Emma Rawlins, April 18, 1864, and April 29, 1864, transcribed by J. H. Wilson, James H. Wilson Papers, Bender Collection, Wyoming State Archives and Historical Department, Microfilm Reel H-61a.

76. James M. Greiner, Janet L. Coryell, and James R. Smither, ed., *A Surgeon's Civil War: The Letters and Diary of Daniel M. Holt, M.D.* (Kent: Kent State University Press, 1994), 266. Unable to provide for his family, Dr. Holt applied for a government pension in 1867, describing symptoms of "night sweats, coughing up blood and pus, and the formation of frequent abscesses"; ibid., 270.

77. B. F. Butler to E. M. Stanton, April 9, 1864, in *The War of the Rebellion: A Compilation of the Official Records of the Union and Confederate Armies*, series 2, 7:29–34.

78. U. S. Grant to B. F. Butler, April 17, 1864, in *The Papers of Ulysses S. Grant*, ed. John Y. Simon, 10:301–2; John A. Rawlins to Emma Rawlins, April 16, 1864, transcribed by J. H. Wilson, James H. Wilson Papers, Bender Collection, Wyoming State Archives and Historical Department, Microfilm Reel H-61a.

79. John A. Rawlins to Emma Rawlins, April 23, 1864, transcribed by J. H. Wilson, James H. Wilson Papers, Bender Collection, Wyoming State Archives and Historical Department, Microfilm Reel H-61a.

80. John Y. Simon, ed., *The Papers of Ulysses S. Grant*, 10:318–19n.

81. Horace Porter, *Campaigning with Grant* (New York: Century, 1897), 36–38.

82. U. S. Grant to John E. Smith, April 26, 1864, in *The Papers of Ulysses S. Grant*, ed. John Y. Simon, 10:356–57.

83. James Harrison Wilson, *Under the Old Flag*, 1:378.

84. Gaillard Hunt, *Israel, Elihu and Cadwallader Washburn* (New York: Macmillan, 1925), 207.

85. James Harrison Wilson, *Under the Old Flag*, 379.

19

"Smash 'Em Up! Smash 'Em Up!"

GRANT, RAWLINS, AND WASHBURNE LEFT Culpeper headquarters about 7:30 a.m. on May 4 on their way to a crossing of the Rapidan at Germanna Ford. They fell in with the Sixth Corps, commanded by "Uncle" John Sedgwick. Grant, wearing an unbuttoned uniform coat and accoutered with sword, spurs, and sash, was mounted on his large bay, Cincinnati. Rawlins, on Grant's left, was astride General Blair, named after Frank Blair, a corps commander in the Army of the Tennessee. Dressed in a black suit, Washburne cut a funereal figure. Soldiers wisecracked the general was bringing along an undertaker, a macabre joke that creepily presaged the slaughter of the next two days. Jokes aside, it seemed that nothing might diminish this glorious spring day. A brilliant sun reigned in the cloudless sky, foliage was budding, the air crisp and clean.[1] The threesome approached the Rapidan by way of the hamlet of Stevensburg, where the previous day Rawlins had visited a first cousin, Frances Virginia Rawlins Humes. Having learned that John was on duty nearby, she had managed to contact him and inquired whether they were relations.[2]

By the time Grant and Rawlins reached Germanna Ford at 11:15 a.m., most of Warren's Fifth Corps had crossed on pontoons; Sedgwick's corps was queued up behind. General Winfield Scott Hancock's Second Corps was crossing the Rapidan at Ely's Ford six miles east. The staff appropriated a deserted farmhouse situated a few hundred yards south of Germanna Ford as temporary headquarters. From its front porch, Rawlins watched the advance of the Sixth Corps while Grant wrote orders to General Burnside at Rappahannock Station to start his corps on a forced march to Germanna Ford. Near 1:00 p.m., an intercepted enemy communication told that Lee was alerted to the presence of the Army of the Potomac and moving men to initiate a confrontation. Grant wanted Burnside's independent Ninth Corps to be available for that contingency. However, Burnside's lead division would not arrive until 8:00 a.m. the next day.

The farmhouse lay on the edge of a thinly inhabited area, hardly over a hundred square miles, of tangled vegetation and second-growth forest, penetrated by few roads. The area's first-growth timber—walnut, hickory, ash, poplar—had been mostly cleared for tobacco cultivation or burned into charcoal (how ironic for John Rawlins!) for smelting the local hematite ore to produce pig iron.[3] This jungle was known as the Wilderness, an unforgiving place where a large army could become disoriented or jammed together and lose its manpower advantage. Grant hoped to pass through it quickly.

Headquarters staff spent the fourth at the farmhouse while the corps consolidated and their heavily burdened wagons caught up. Staff helped themselves to an informal dinner, grabbing mouthfuls as they dashed from task to task. Grant, Rawlins, and Washburne slept in the farmhouse's little garret. After a 4:00 a.m. breakfast, staff gathered around a large campfire, stoked not so much for heat but to engender feelings of camaraderie and conviviality.[4]

Around 8:15, one of Meade's staff delivered an urgent dispatch to Grant. "The enemy have appeared in force on the Orange pike," it warned, "and are now reported forming line of battle in front of Griffin's division, Fifth Corps." Meade added that he would respond with an order to Warren to attack "at once" with his entire force.[5] Grant, along with Rawlins and Washburne, rode down Germanna Road to Meade's headquarters, located near its junction with the Orange Turnpike. Germanna Road, the major north-south corridor through the Wilderness, stretched from the ford and ran in a mostly southerly direction. About four miles south of the ford, it intersected the Orange Turnpike, one of the two main east-west routes. Germanna Road terminated two miles farther south at the Orange Plank Road. The Orange Turnpike and Orange Plank Road were roughly parallel and separated at most points by two or three miles.

When they arrived at Meade's headquarters at 9:45, Warren had not yet taken the offensive. An hour later, word came that Lee was sending forward a force down the Orange Plank Road as well. Still there were no sounds of Warren attacking. Finally, around noon a rattle of muskets heralded heavy skirmishing developing along the front. An hour later, the Battle of the Wilderness erupted in earnest. A brigade of Charles Griffin's division of Warren's corps gained initial success driving back Confederates from Richard Ewell's corps. Within minutes of hearing the escalation in fighting, Grant, Rawlins and Washburne rode to the front. Rawlins soon encountered a stream of wounded staggering rearward. One of Meade's staff recalled it was not long before "the pike was a sad spectacle indeed; it was really obstructed with trains of ambulances and with the wounded on foot."[6]

On the return to Meade's headquarters, Grant's party met Warren. He told them that Griffin had been badly cut up. Ewell was reinforced and then counterattacked. At 2:45 p.m., Griffin, face flushed and barely containing his anger, barged into Meade's tent. The famously irascible Griffin barked that after having driven Ewell's troops three-quarters of a mile, he received no support and had to retire to his original position with great loss. Rawlins listened to Griffin's diatribe that bordered on insubordination. No general officer in the west would have resorted to such effrontery. Rawlins exploded and called for Griffin's arrest. Even the usually unperturbable Grant was aghast and echoed Rawlins. "Who is this General *Gregg*?" he asked Meade. "You ought to arrest him!" Meade tried to smooth Grant's feathers. "It's Griffin, not Gregg," he replied, "and it's only his way of talking."[7]

Near midafternoon, fighting on the Orange Turnpike slackened, although it sputtered on into evening. However, on the Orange Plank Road, three miles south, fighting was ratcheting up fast as Winfield Scott Hancock threw his divisions against a single division, Henry Heth's, of Rebel defenders. Heth's corps commander, Ambrose Powell Hill, brought forward Cadmus Wilcox's division to shore up Heth's flank just before it gave way. Hancock was getting reinforced too and might have broken the Confederate line had he more daylight. Hill's hard-pressed divisions held as darkness silenced the musket fire. But another fire erupted: gunfire had ignited mounds of dried leaves and spindly undergrowth, spawning an inferno that rapidly intensified. From inside the swelling, orange-tinged blackness came the bloodcurdling cries of the wounded who could not drag themselves to safety.

The consensus at Grant's headquarters tent that evening was that if the Army of the Potomac hadn't won the day, it had more than held its own. When Meade appeared, Washburne noted that even he "is in good spirits." Grant wanted Hancock to take the initiative as soon as possible on the sixth—5:00 a.m. was the stepping-off time—in order to demolish A. P. Hill before Lee's missing corps, Longstreet's, arrived on the battlefield. The staff was up at 4:00 a.m. and breakfasting thirty minutes later. While peering from the tent,

Washburne declared this Wilderness morning "clear and beautiful." There would be fifteen more minutes to relish the splendor of daybreak before a salvo of musketry defiled it.[8]

―――⁓⁓⁓―――

It was Hancock charging forward down Orange Plank Road, driving Hill westward a mile and a half by 7:00 a.m. Above Hancock on the turnpike, Warren and Sedgwick were occupying Ewell, who was thus prevented from sending help to Hill. Burnside was ordered to bring up his divisions and slide them between Warren and Hancock to plug a gap in the center of the Union line. However, the hapless Burnside became confused in the scrub pines and briar thickets. Porter and Comstock were dispatched to help orient him. Meanwhile, Hancock, sensing an opportunity to inflict a knockout blow against Hill—a KO virtually guaranteed if Burnside could lend his weight to the attack—seethed with rage as he waited for him to appear.

As if on cue, Longstreet's corps arrived in time to rescue Hill and arrest the Federal advance. By midmorning the reinvigorated Rebels had regained the ground lost. Then at 11:00 a.m., Longstreet unleashed a devastating roundhouse to Hancock's flank that threatened to roll up the Union line. Grant was stunned by the attack's success, and his alarm grew by the minute at Burnside's nonappearance. At 11:45, Rawlins sent an urgent dispatch to Burnside: "Push in with all vigor so as to drive the enemy from General Hancock's front, and get in on the Orange and Fredericksburg plank road at the earliest possible moment. Hancock has been expecting you for the last three hours and has been making his attack and disposition with a view to your assistance."[9] However, as the Rebels grew optimistic that the Army of the Potomac might retreat to the Rapidan by nightfall, there occurred a history-changing event that tipped the battle's outcome: Longstreet and one of his brigadiers, Micah Jenkins, were struck by friendly fire. Longstreet was seriously wounded; Jenkins took a fatal shot to the head. Uncertainty set in among the Confederate ranks, and their attack stalled. Hancock used the lull to regroup and to deploy Burnside's divisions that had finally arrived. The threat on the left of the Union line had been met. It would hold.

Hardly had fighting waned on the Union left when the Confederates overcame their reluctance to exploit the Federal's vulnerable right flank. Sedgwick had carelessly left it uncovered, and a Confederate brigadier, John Gordon, discovered that opportunity earlier in the day, but Gordon's superiors, mistakenly assuming Burnside was backing up Sedgwick, deflected his pleas to turn it. Finally, at 6:00 p.m., Ewell authorized Gordon to take the offensive. Were it not for nightfall and Sedgwick's timely reconfiguration of his line, Gordon might have succeeded. His audacious attack sent chills down the spines of Union officers—Army of the Potomac veterans who had been repeatedly thrashed by Bobby Lee—who now anticipated a collapse of the line or the liquefying of a lieutenant general's resolve. Reports of calamity on the right streamed back to Grant, who had spent much of the day near headquarters consuming a score of cigars and placidly whittling on twigs. After yet another panicked officer galloped up with dire news, Grant removed his ever-present cigar and gave him a famous dressing-down: "Some of you always seem to think [Lee] is suddenly going to turn a double somersault, land in our rear and on both of our flanks at the same time. Go back to your command, and try to think of what we are going to do."[10] Even faced with the threat of "overwhelming disaster," Rawlins watched as Grant "gave his orders calmly and coherently without any external sign of undue tension or agitation."[11]

But Grant's implacable exterior hid a welter of internal frustration and doubt. The fates of the Union and the Lincoln presidency, not to mention his own career, hinged on the right flank hanging on. Circumstances couldn't have been cast in more visceral relief. When the only outcomes totter between humiliating defeat or a heroic stand, the implications of those outcomes erupt as raw emotions before they can be thought through. At the end of the second day's fighting, after Gordon's brigade had been called back, after the fighting in Sedgwick's sector sputtered out, and after Grant had retired inside his headquarters tent, he released those emotions. Rawlins and Bowers stood by, ready to help but unsure how.

Grant and the staff awoke Saturday at 5:00 a.m. to a morning cloaked in fog and smoke. Some desultory artillery firing and skirmishing erupted, but on this day both armies did more maneuvering than fighting. At 6:30 a.m., Grant ordered Meade to prepare for a night march southeastward toward Spotsylvania Court House, twelve miles distant, putting the Army of the Potomac on a path to Richmond.[12] By midmorning, Hancock and Burnside reported that the Rebels appeared to be falling back; at 10:30, Hancock thought they had withdrawn from his front. Rawlins grabbed a moment to write Emma that on this morning, "after a very sanguinary battle," the army found itself "masters of the field, the enemy having withdrawn" but where "is not yet clearly ascertained."[13] In fact, Lee, who intuited that Grant's next move would be to advance, was withdrawing as well toward Spotsylvania, Grant's logical objective. It was a race to get there first.

When Wilson appeared at the headquarters tent Saturday morning, Grant gave him a cheery greeting. To Wilson, Grant seemed perfectly composed, even planning to take the offensive. Rawlins and Bowers were inside packing in anticipation of the army's move later that day when they pulled Wilson aside. Both maintained that "the situation the night before for a time seemed appalling." Rawlins disclosed that Grant's fortitude had been tested like never before. In the midst of all the uncertainty, Grant threw himself onto his cot and "gave vent to the greatest emotion." Only after it was established that the line held did he regain self-control.[14]

The order to press toward Spotsylvania was issued midafternoon. At 8:00 p.m., Grant, Washburne, and staff took to their mounts and started, as the congressman noted in his memo book, "onward to Richmond."[15] The rank-and-file infantrymen, however, were uninformed about the purpose of the march and assumed that after the inconclusive and bloody battle, they were withdrawing northward to lick their wounds. Army of the Potomac veterans had come to expect such pathetic behavior from their commanding generals. Therefore, it came as a shock that as the infantry columns filed onto the Brock Road and Orange Turnpike, they were bending south, not running from Bobby Lee but fixed on scrapping with him closer to Richmond. The troops hailed Grant, Horace Porter recalling, "Wild cheers echoed through the forest, and glad shouts of triumph rent the air."[16]

It was after 1:00 a.m. on Sunday that Grant and staff reached Todd's Tavern, about six miles from Spotsylvania Court House. Washburne overnighted inside the tavern on a blanket, and everyone else bivouacked outside and uncovered on the chilly ground. To their chagrin, they had wearily collapsed next to a pen once occupied by pigs and still reeking of their malodor—not what Rawlins desired for his ailing lungs. After breakfast, Meade and Grant established their respective headquarters two miles east of the tavern near a church. When a drum corps passed by Grant's, the musicians struck up a popular tune. Almost everyone caught on to their musical jest, and Rawlins shouted, "Good for the drummers!" Grant seemed perplexed and inquired, "What's the fun?" Someone told him they were playing the Negro spiritual "Ain't I Glad I've Got Out of the Wilderness," forcing Grant to admit, "Well, with me a musical joke always requires explanation. I know only two tunes: one is 'Yankee Doodle,' and the other isn't."[17]

The Confederates won the race to Spotsylvania. Wilson's cavalry division got there about 9:00 a.m. on the eighth and chased off a brigade of earlier arriving enemy cavalry. But Longstreet's infantry appeared and forced Wilson to abandon his position. Word of Wilson's retreat reached Grant's headquarters at Piney Branch Church at noon. Union infantry failed to come up on time to assist Wilson, a failure partially attributable to a communication breakdown between Meade and cavalry chief Phil Sheridan. Meade accused Sheridan of not following orders to clear his troopers out of the infantry's path, thereby slowing the foot soldiers' march to Spotsylvania. An outraged Sheridan blamed Meade for getting the infantry and cavalry mixed together.[18]

On this oppressively hot day, the Army of the Potomac, exhausted from a night march and the Wilderness fighting, maneuvered into place to confront Lee. Rawlins spent early afternoon preparing dispatches to Burnside. His Ninth Corps was still independent from the Army of the Potomac, and thus orders were sent directly to him. Rawlins precisely detailed the route Burnside was to follow to Spotsylvania, hoping to prevent a repeat of his disappointing performance in the Wilderness.[19] In midafternoon the Piney Branch headquarters was shuttered, and Grant, Rawlins, Washburne, and staff advanced closer to Spotsylvania Court House. What they would have seen was a portion of Lee's intimidatingly fortified defensive line, replete with sophisticated entrenchments, much of it concealed by dense woods. Around 4:30, Grant, Meade, and their staffs rode closer to the front to observe the heavy skirmishing. Theodore Lyman, an aide of Meade's, remembered they stopped in woods near the fighting. "There we sat on horseback," Lyman recollected, "while the bullets here and there came clicking among trunks and branches and an occasional shell added its discordant tone."[20] The fighting had dwindled when Grant and staff returned from the front at 7:30 p.m. and reported to Washburne that the enemy line hadn't been carried. Meanwhile, Rawlins sent Burnside an order to prepare to send two infantry divisions to Spotsylvania Court House.[21]

May 9 was spent preparing, getting troops in proper line of battle. Before 9:00 a.m., Rawlins dispatched another order to Burnside ensuring he followed the correct route: "Send out staff officers to learn and acquaint themselves with the roads leading from Piney Branch Church to the positions of Generals Warren and Sedgwick, near Spotsylvania, and to General Hancock at Todd's

Tavern." Rawlins further stipulated, "When the division receives orders to move it must be conducted by one of those staff officers who have familiarized themselves with the roads on which it is to move."[22]

An hour later, news arrived that General Sedgwick had been killed by a sharpshooter. In that day's letter to Emma, Rawlins bluntly stated that "the brave and heroic Sedgwick . . . was shot through the head, and died instantly." Except for that item of exceptional news, this letter was typical of the information he sent home: commentary about the campaign, descriptions of the movements of the armies—but few details regarding Grant's intentions, lest the letter fall into enemy hands—tallies of casualties, his optimism about the Union's ultimate success, and the occasional health update. Also in the May 9 letter, Rawlins confidently predicted that "with the superiority of numbers on our side, I think we can beat them notwithstanding their advantage of position."[23] This was a point of emphasis for Rawlins, who in March had expounded, "I believe more in the infallibility of numbers than in the infallibility of generals, no matter how great their reputation."[24] Grant was familiar with Rawlins's numbers refrain and how he favored the draft to restock depleted regiments. Of course, Grant grasped the importance of the North's numerical advantage, and because of it, he would take the offensive—attack, attack even if the enemy were protected by breastworks because each attack would deplete his thinning ranks—and become resigned to the fact that sustaining losses of life was a path to winning the war.[25]

—◊◊◊—

The attack on the tenth that held the most hope was led by Colonel Emory Upton in late afternoon against a portion of Lee's line known as the Mule Shoe. After arranging twelve regiments in an innovative four-line formation, Upton sped them across open ground and achieved a stunning breakthrough, but his support failed to arrive, causing Upton to fall back. Washburne accompanied Grant, Meade, and their staffs watched Upton's assault. "It was at its heighth [sic] just as the sun was going down," Washburne wrote in his memo book. "The roar of musketry and cannon and the cheers of our men as they rushed to the charge made an impression never to be effaced."[26] Besides an everlasting impression, their gallantry bought a thousand casualties.

The eleventh was a day of respite from the fighting. After Washburne breakfasted with Grant and several staff, all spent a few last minutes with him before the congressman departed for Washington. He had come to see the Army of the Potomac in action, but he left with a jumble of disturbing mental images that defied description. Two days before, he had written his wife Adele, "The imagination cannot paint all the horrors that are around us. It is war on the greatest scale the world has ever seen."[27] At 8:30 a.m. as his cavalry escort arrived, Washburne asked Grant to draft a message for Lincoln and Stanton, one to encourage them about the military situation. Grant obliged. He sat down at a table and, between puffs on his breakfast cigar, scratched out a dispatch of about two hundred words. It contained his proposition to "fight it out on this line if it takes all summer." The staff took turns reading the retained copy, not realizing, until newspapers later seized on those words, their "epigrammatic character."[28] Grant's resolve to "fight it out" must have resonated with Rawlins because in this day's letter to Emma, there was this similar conviction: "Our progress towards Richmond is slow, but we are on the way, and do not propose, unless some disaster overtakes us, ever taking a step backwards."[29]

In the afternoon, Grant told Meade that in preparation for the next day's assault, he would send staff officers to Burnside in order to "impress him with the importance of a prompt and vigorous attack."[30] Comstock and Babcock were chosen and ordered to spend all night with him. The next day, Burnside accused Comstock of complaining to Grant about his, Burnside's, slowness. By this time, Burnside may have been irritated by the overly solicitous treatment he had been receiving from Grant's headquarters. Comstock denied the charge, telling Burnside he reported to Grant only "what you were actually doing." In his diary on that day, Comstock complained that Burnside is "rather weak & not fit for a corps commander."[31]

—◦◦◦—

If Washburne had his fill of horrors, it was good he returned to Washington, because May 12 saw some of the war's ghastliest fighting. Attacking before dawn through rain and mud against the tip of the Mule Shoe, Hancock's Second Corps achieved stunning success, smashing through the Confederate entrenchments, capturing several thousand prisoners, and threatening to cleave Lee's line. There was premature celebrating at headquarters, with Rawlins eagerly anticipating word Lee had been cut in two.[32] But as Hancock pressed forward, a furious counterattack drove him back into the fortifications he had just overrun. The Sixth Corps, now led by Horatio Wright, was ordered to Hancock's aid and thrown against the western slant of the Mule Shoe, a plot of carnage that became known as the Bloody Angle. George Galloway, a private in the Sixth Corps, recalled the enemy's attempt to regain that portion of their line: "I cannot imagine how any of us survived the sharp fire that swept over us at this point—a fire so keen that it split the blades of grass all about us, the minies moaning in a furious concert as they picked out victims by the score."[33] Grant rode out with his staff to the front, and from several points they observed Wright's and Hancock's corps in action.[34] From dawn into night, fighting, all of it at close range or hand-to-hand, raged over these few acres of mud. Around midnight, Lee withdrew a half mile to a freshly constructed defensive line, leaving the Federals in possession of the corpse-strewn real estate parcel.

Once the Bloody Angle fighting had subsided, Charles Dana and Rawlins rode out to inspect the battlefield. The ground had been so cut up that they had to dismount and climb up a bank to the outer line of breastworks. With nightfall approaching, they peered over a fence and saw the ground covered with dead and wounded, the latter attended to by the relief corps. The rain-soaked earth had been worked into a pudding-like consistency. While witnessing this dreadful sight, they were astonished when a leg suddenly lifted from the mud. They called for the relief corpsmen to rescue the half-buried wounded man. Once extracted, he was taken to a hospital and apparently survived.[35]

The thirteenth was mostly quiet. Rawlins wrote Emma a brief letter, mentioning that "our losses have been very heavy" but sparing her the details.[36] At headquarters that day, Grant invited an exchange of views regarding the command structure that required sending field orders through Meade as an intermediary. The exchange quickly became a heated discussion. Some senior staff, Rawlins likely included, argued that the system was awkward and flawed: Meade had few responsibilities, field orders to corps commanders might become distorted during transmission, and Meade was positioned to receive neither credit for any successes nor blame for failure.[37] Moreover, although Rawlins respected Meade for his "soldierly qualities and great ability,"[38] he possessed a temperament that rubbed others wrong.

The problems in this arrangement were evident to General Andrew Humphreys, Meade's chief of staff: "There were two officers commanding the same army. Such a mixed result was not calculated to produce the best results that either singly was capable of bringing about."[39] The result hardly satisfied Meade, who complained to his wife, "If there was any honorable way of retiring from my present false position I should undoubtedly adopt it." Others on Meade's staff expressed discontent. Major James Cornell Biddle, of a prominent Philadelphia family and the Eastern elite Rawlins found threatening, castigated Grant as a "rough unpolished man" of only "average ability." As for Rawlins, Biddle thought him "one of the roughest, most uncouth men I ever saw" and scoffed that he knew "no more of military affairs than an old cat."[40]

Grant acknowledged the validity of the staff's arguments but declined to make changes. He felt it impolitic for an interloper from the West to remove an Eastern commander of the Army of the Potomac. Despite being relegated to an inferior position, Meade did not undermine Grant. Porter remarked that "General Meade manifested an excellent spirit through all the embarrassments which his position at times entailed."[41] Rawlins noted that Grant and Meade had demonstrated nothing but "the most cordial cooperation in all movements of the army."[42]

The Army of the Potomac rested on the thirteenth. Two days of chilly rain followed, adding to Rawlins's consternation about his health, bogging down supply trains, and stymieing Federal troop movement. Rawlins used this interlude to address domestic issues. After years in vibrant Vicksburg, Emma was discontented with life in isolated Guilford Township, where she and the three children were confined with John's parents. This troubled him enough to acknowledge "how different was the life I invited you from the one I had temporarily provided for you." Emma had put on a happy face, but John saw through it. "You have failed thus far," he wrote, "to convince mother and I you do not desire to live in the city rather than the country." To keep her happy, Rawlins made arrangements to have her and the children sent east. A member of the special staff—identified only as "Harry" in Rawlins's letter, but likely fellow Illinoisan Henry Janes, the assistant quartermaster—was to escort them. Rawlins regarded this as a temporary reprieve, and he pointedly instructed her to "assure father and mother that our home is in the West, and you intend returning to it in due course of time."[43]

With warmer and drier weather, Grant authorized a last assault, planned for predawn on the eighteenth and to be launched from the Mule Shoe against the Confederate left. Hancock and Wright were to attack entrenched defenders from Ewell's corps. The attack was delayed for several hours as the bluecoats got properly positioned. When they finally advanced in splendid formations against Ewell's front, they were met by a merciless artillery fire, including canisters of grapeshot, which tore through their ranks. It was a two-hour suicidal mission, resulting in hundreds of casualties.

Following this failed attack, more bad news arrived at headquarters. From the Shenandoah Valley came word that on the fifteenth, John C. Breckinridge's makeshift army, which included adolescent cadets from Virginia Military Institute, dealt Franz Sigel a stinging defeat at New Market. This upset Federal plans for securing the valley and allowed Breckinridge's small force to join Lee. It was also learned that on the sixteenth, General P. G. T. Beauregard pounced on Ben Butler's Army of the James at Drewry's Bluff, a strategic prominence about midway between Richmond and Petersburg. Butler hastily retreated behind his defensive line across a narrow neck of land, known as the Bermuda Hundred, jutting into the James River. Butler's defeat was a sour pill to swallow. If they had acted with alacrity, he and his corps commanders, Baldy Smith and Quincy Gillmore, were positioned over a week earlier to move successfully against either Richmond or the strategic rail center of Petersburg. Instead, their hesitant advance afforded Beauregard time to gather a sizeable army. With Butler bottled up on that thumb of land, Beauregard could transfer a portion of his army to Lee.

After sizing up Lee's formidable position at Spotsylvania, Grant decided to pivot to his left and maneuver southeasterly around Lee's right flank. The race this time was to Hanover Junction, just across the North Anna River and about twenty-four miles north of Richmond. The Army of the Potomac moved out late on May 20, but because Lee had the advantage of marching along interior lines, he reached the North Anna first and took possession of its south bank. Rawlins sent Emma the frustrating news that the enemy "succeeded in getting here about twelve hours in advance of us and throwing up rifle pits for defence. A few hours always suffice for an army acting purely on the defensive to fortify itself, and the fortifications make up greatly for inferiority of numbers."[44]

While the Federals skirted around Lee, Rawlins labored to bring medical assistance to four hundred Union soldiers, wounded during the Wilderness fighting, who fell into enemy hands. The Rebels insisted that a flag of truce order be issued by Grant before the wounded would be delivered.[45] On the twenty-first, Rawlins issued a Special Order to Dr. Edward Breneman to present himself under a truce flag to Confederate authorities for the purposes of retrieving the wounded or furnishing medical supplies.[46] The next day, Breneman wrote Rawlins that on the Orange Plank Road, he had met with a Confederate surgeon and cavalry captain who informed him that the wounded were comfortable but that supplies were becoming scarce. When Breneman tried to return, and while traveling under the truce flag, he was accosted near the Wilderness Tavern by a band of guerillas who, although clad in Confederate uniforms, acknowledged being under no authority. They took his horse and papers. He warned Rawlins about the presence of these plundering bands.[47] Rawlins acted on this advice and ordered General John Abercrombie to drive off the guerillas and evacuate the wounded.[48] In a few weeks, Assistant Surgeon Breneman would be assigned to headquarters to treat the staff.

On the twenty-third, Hancock captured a bridge over the North Anna and brushed aside Rebel opposition, and he crossed on the twenty-fourth. With its steep banks, swift current, and six-foot depth, getting across the river was a challenge. Further west, General Warren got the Fifth Corps over and then drove off a spirited challenge by troops from A. P. Hill's Corps. Aide Cyrus Comstock, in a revealing diary entry for the twenty-third, felt that Warren's and Hancock's corps might have accomplished more, but "some of the div[ision] commanders do not push vigorously—too fearful of losing men."[49] On the twenty-fourth, the Federals' right and left wings were over the river but miles out of contact with each other. However, the center of the line was vacant because Burnside had failed to cross. With his corps in this vulnerable position and Lee's men securely entrenched, Grant decided against attacking from either wing. He was resigned to yet another end run around the Confederate right so as to achieve an interposition between Lee and Richmond.

The twenty-fourth saw tension erupt between Grant and Meade. A dispatch from Sherman arrived at headquarters, and Charles Dana made the mistake of reading it aloud. When he read Sherman's wish that Grant might so inspire the Army of the Potomac as to make it do its share to win the war, Meade's eyes bulged. "Sir! I consider that dispatch an insult to the army I command and to me personally," he thundered. "The Army of the Potomac does not require General Grant's inspiration or anybody else's to make it fight."[50] That evening AAG Bowers issued Special Orders No. 25 assigning Burnside's Ninth Corps to the Army of the Potomac under Meade's command. Officially, the move was to achieve "greater efficiency in the administration of the army," but it would help soothe Meade's feelings.[51]

—◦◦◦—

After shifting around an impregnably positioned Army of Northern Virginia at the North Anna River, Grant edged further southward around Lee's right flank down near Totopotomy Creek and within ten miles of Richmond.

There on the twenty-ninth, he encountered the earlier-arriving Lee already dug in, artillery emplaced. After two days of standoff, the Army of the Potomac, sidling southward, crossed the Totopotomy with the goal being Cold Harbor, a hamlet at the intersection of several important roads. Just before crossing the creek and while riding at the head of the staff, Rawlins and Grant observed a teamster beating his horses with the butt end of a whip. Grant ordered the man tied to a tree. The incident so unsettled Grant that at an oyster dinner that evening, he lectured his headquarters personnel about treating horses with gentleness.[52]

Grant hoped to go on the offense at Cold Harbor before Lee could prepare earthworks, but the inevitable delays in deploying his troops forced a postponement until June 3. The delay proved catastrophic. It gave Lee time to prepare his seven-mile line—laid out mostly north to south, with the right protected against a flank attack by the Chickahominy River and the left stretching to Totopotomy Creek—replete with interlocking trenches and artillery positioned to sweep across the entire battle front.[53] On June 3, when sixty thousand blue-jacketed infantry attacked just after daylight, they were met with a maelstrom of fire. A Confederate artillery officer called it "inexplicable butchery" as "our infantry and our artillery fired at very short range into a mass of men twenty-eight deep, who could neither advance nor retreat, and the most of whom could not even discharge their muskets at us."[54] The fight's outcome was sealed after the first thirty minutes produced six thousand Federal casualties. Confederate losses were one-quarter of that.

The scope of the losses needed a while to sink in. Grant wired Halleck at 2:00 p.m., informing him, "Our loss was not severe nor do I suppose the Enemy to have lost heavily."[55] A day later, Rawlins called the battle "indecisive," estimating five thousand casualties and stating, "That of the enemy cannot be less, for each side attacked in turn from the fortified position of the other and was repulsed."[56] However, by the evening of June 3, as Porter recalled, Grant told headquarters staff he deeply regretted the assault, admitting "no advantages have been gained sufficient to the heavy losses suffered."[57] Cold Harbor transformed Rawlins's attitude toward the customary use of costly frontal assaults against prepared lines. On June 7, Rawlins and Wilson dined at Marlbourne, the abandoned plantation of Edmund Ruffin, the secessionist erroneously credited with firing the first shot at Fort Sumter. While they rode back to headquarters, Rawlins aired his vehement opposition to frontal assaults and criticized Cyrus Comstock whom, he believed, advised Grant to employ them.[58] To Rawlins, the futility of such assaults had been proven a year ago at Vicksburg.

The next day Rawlins, Dana, and Wilson continued the discussion. Rawlins and Dana favored the flanking movements, which were gradually forcing Lee to fall back—hardly the most brilliant or flashiest strategy but preferable to assaults that were decimating the army's ranks. Moreover, Rawlins and Dana decried "a certain baleful influence" at Grant's headquarters. Rawlins could no longer contain his emotion. With anger draining the blood from his face—a face, Wilson recollected, already pale from disease—Rawlins pointed a finger: it was Colonel Comstock who had gained Grant's confidence at his expense. The hotshot engineer was now driving the army to ruin by advocating sacrificial frontal assaults. Rawlins emphasized his opinion by mockingly reiterating Comstock's pet phrase, "Smash 'em up! Smash 'em up!" Rawlins and Dana urged Wilson to rejoin the staff and add his voice to theirs in opposition to this recklessness.[59] When Wilson expressed surprise that Rawlins had not countered Comstock's influence, both he and Dana said that the regular army staff officers had supplanted Rawlins and held sway over Grant.[60] Wilson counseled Rawlins to assert his opinions to Grant as before, but Wilson never learned whether he followed through.

─∾∾∾─

At that moment, a stunning change in strategy was about to be implemented. On June 5, Grant wrote Halleck that Lee's proclivity for fighting behind breastworks forced Grant to adopt a new plan. He would shift the Army of the Potomac south some fifty miles, cross the formidable James River, and thus be positioned to squeeze Lee's supply line.[61] There, he could join with Butler, seize the vital rail hub of Petersburg, and roll northward into Richmond.

This massive move had to be accomplished swiftly and stealthily. The plan would work only if the army could abandon its line at Cold Harbor unbeknownst to Lee. To facilitate the escape, Grant's engineers laid down corduroy roads and erected bridges. A vast supply train was organized, including thirty-five hundred cattle that would make the crossing. Ferry boats and pontoons were procured. To ensure a safe crossing, the Confederate vessels that patrolled the James had to be neutralized. On the thirteenth, Rawlins ordered Butler to deliver to Meade all ferries, pontoons, and bridging material and to have boats sunk at suitable points to obstruct the enemy's vessels.[62] A chief concern was finding an appropriate location to cross the James. On June 6,

Grant ordered Comstock and Porter to Butler's Bermuda Hundred headquarters to inform him of the details of the move and to select the best place for crossing. Their choice was Wilcox's Landing, which was, at twenty-one hundred feet, the narrowest point below City Point.

After dark on June 12, Baldy Smith's Eighteenth Corps was the first to peel from the Union line. Smith's Corps in late May had been detached from Butler in order to participate in the ill-fated Cold Harbor assault. Now, steamers would transport them around the York Peninsula and up the James River and return them to Bermuda Hundred. Because of their familiarity with the area, they were selected as the vanguard of the Union advance to seize Petersburg, believed to be lightly defended. Warren's Fifth Corps was next to slip away, followed by Burnside, Hancock, and Wright. The following morning, Lee discovered the works opposite him were empty. He was not sure where the Army of the Potomac had gone.

On the thirteenth, Rawlins's order hastened Smith along: "Send forward your troops, to Bermuda Hundred, as fast as they embark. . . . The object being, to get them to Bermuda Hundred at the earliest possible moment."[63] Also on the thirteenth, some advisers urged Grant to disembark the army ten miles east at City Point to further deceive the enemy. Rawlins was perhaps one of those trying to change Grant's mind. Grant rejected that plan as too risky and remained committed to Wilcox's Landing.[64]

This small incident, argued historian Brian Holden Reid, appears to reflect a decline in Rawlins's operational influence on Grant. Rawlins still provided valuable personal support and monitored political threats against Grant; however, his role in the planning of the James crossing was minor. Reid offered several explanations. With Grant as general in chief, Rawlins was responsible for keeping abreast of all Union armies operating in Virginia, Georgia, Tennessee, and beyond. In Virginia, Rawlins had to assist with coordinating troop movements, troubleshooting logistical glitches, and maintaining an up-to-the-minute correspondence flow—all done with an undersized staff. Reid made the evident point that Grant hardly needed any military advice. Since the summer of 1863, his confidence had increased, and the James operation, in terms of boldness and complexity, outshone the maneuver to get below Vicksburg and across the Mississippi. There was also the issue of Rawlins's declining health—a fact that was apparent to all by summer 1864. Writing to Julia shortly after the James operation, Grant added the sadly prescient remark, "The Staff are all well except Rawlins and he is as well as he ever will be."[65]

—◦∿◦—

Late in the afternoon of the thirteenth, the first Union troops arrived at Wilcox's Landing. Astonishingly, an enormous pontoon bridge for the James crossing was finished the next day. Even before the bridge was ready, troops were being ferried across. Correspondent Sylvanus Cadwallader had a panoramic view of the activity on the river: "Vessels and transports of every description, loaded with supplies, cast anchor and floated idly on the placid bosom of the James so far downward as the eye could reach."[66] That morning, Grant and Rawlins took a steamer to Bermuda Hundred to instruct Butler regarding the movement against Petersburg. Butler was told that Baldy Smith's corps would be arriving and that Butler should reinforce him. Smith, whom Grant held in esteem for his performance at Chattanooga, was to strike the enemy's Petersburg lines right after daylight on the fifteenth, before Lee could send troops to the rescue. Hancock's Second Corps, now being ferried across, would support Smith. Before leaving Bermuda Hundred, an optimistic Grant wired Halleck, "I will have Petersburg secured if possible before they get there."[67] A confident Rawlins could report to Emma, "Everything is progressing finely"—the weather was perfect, by dusk all of the army had come up, and supply trains were nearby.[68] Tomorrow, Union infantry should pour into Petersburg.

But not everything progressed so finely on the fifteenth. When by midafternoon no word had been heard from Smith, Rawlins was concerned the enemy was reinforcing, and Smith soon might find the Rebels too strong.[69] Rawlins had reason for concern. Unbeknownst to those at Grant's headquarters, Smith had spent the day reconnoitering and did not launch his attack until 7:00 p.m. He smashed through some thinly held outer defenses, captured a few artillery pieces, and then inexplicably halted, despite the way to Petersburg having been wide open. That brought relief to General Beauregard, who opposed Smith with a vastly outnumbered force.

When Hancock joined Smith on the sixteenth, the Confederates were outnumbered five to one. While the Federals dawdled, Beauregard shifted men into the trenches, creating enough firepower to repulse an uncoordinated assault during the early evening. Federal dysfunction on the seventeenth bought Beauregard more time. The next day, the Army of Northern Virginia began arriving, and Lee was on the scene by late morning. Petersburg held. Meade's aide Theodore Lyman summed up the disappointment: "If we only *could* have been a little quicker and more driving, we might have had Petersburg at a mouthful."[70] It would be a while before Grant and Rawlins learned how the opportunity to end the war had been squandered on the fifteenth.[71]

One positive outcome from Smith's attack on the evening of June 15 was provided by the fight displayed by the division of Brigadier General Edward Hincks. This untested division overwhelmed several Rebel batteries and captured their guns. Their success was unexpected because it was a division of United States Colored Troops, and every noncom in it was Black. "The colored troops, about 3,000, in the attack last night carried the strongest part of the entrenchments, losing in the assault about 500 killed and wounded," Rawlins wrote Emma. "They did nobly, and are entitled to be regarded as among the best of soldiers. You know I have ever had some misgivings of their efficiency, but seeing what they have accomplished, I doubt no longer."[72] Less than a week later, the man largely responsible for Rawlins changing his mind came to visit.

On the twenty-first, Abraham Lincoln arrived by steamer at the City Point wharf. After he greeted each staff member present, Grant suggested they circulate among the troops, including those of the bloodied USCT division. Lincoln had heard about their gallantry and was eager to see them. "I was opposed on nearly every side when I first favored the raising of colored regiments," he told Grant's party, "but they have proved their efficiency, and I am glad they have kept pace with the white troops in recent assaults."[73] Rawlins witnessed the Black soldiers applauding Lincoln and delivering "hearty hurrahs for the man whom they regard as their liberator." The event so moved Rawlins that he believed the cheers "went up to Heaven, I am sure."[74] On returning to headquarters, Lincoln regaled Grant and staff with his storehouse of anecdotes. What Lincoln and Grant may have discussed regarding strategy is unknown; Lincoln may have visited simply to solidify his relationship with Grant.[75]

—⚬⚬⚬—

After the abortive attempt to capture Petersburg, Grant's showdown with Lee soon evolved into a siege. The Union army erected their own intricately engineered and fortified lines opposite Lee's. Grant would gradually protract them southwestwardly to force Lee to spread his thinner ranks. The two railroads supplying Lee, the Weldon and the Southside, became early targets for destruction. On the twenty-second, Union forces reached the Weldon line, which ran south from Petersburg into North Carolina. However, the operation was repelled with heavy loss, including sixteen hundred captured. At about the same time, Harry Wilson led his cavalry division on a raid to destroy South-side track, but the raid became a harrowing operation his men barely survived. To pulverize Lee's lines, specialized heavy artillery was brought in. On the twenty-fourth, Grant, Rawlins, and Porter rode to Meade's headquarters to bring him the news that siege guns would be arriving by train and needed to be placed in proper position.[76]

During the siege's early days, Rawlins suffered from the stifling dust re-sulting from oppressive heat and lack of rain. Illnesses, brought on by fatigue, stress, and unsanitary conditions, felled many staff. Fred Dent was absent, no longer able to cope with rheumatism so debilitating that it compelled him to travel in an ambulance and so painful he could not turn over when lying on his back. William Rowley was so sick that he talked about resigning. In July, he would leave the army and return to Galena. Babcock, Porter, and Badeau all suffered bouts of ill health, and Bowers considered a leave to care for his ill mother. This left Rawlins, who was feeling chipper in comparison, believ-ing he was an indispensable presence at headquarters. Several incidents, each with political overtones, would soon occur that strengthened that belief.

In late June, Rawlins badgered Grant to write House Speaker Schuyler Colfax about eliminating the $300 commutation clause from the conscription act.[77] The clause allowed draftees to buy themselves out of the current draft lottery. Rawlins opposed commutation because of his devotion to maintain-ing an overwhelming numerical advantage. Average citizens thought commu-tation unfair—the buyout was an unskilled laborer's yearly wage—because it perpetuated the notion this was a rich man's war and a poor man's fight. To Rawlins's relief, Congress acted responsibly, and the March 1864 draft call was the last in which commutation was in effect.[78]

In mid-June, Jubal Early, who had replaced the disabled Richard Ewell as head of a fourteen-thousand-man corps, chased a marauding Federal army under David Hunter out of the Shenandoah Valley. Early then headed north, crossing the Potomac on July 6. Lee hoped that by shedding a sizeable chunk of his infantry, he might tempt Grant to make a costly frontal assault against his entrenched line.[79] Early's incursion was also intended to foment panic and thereby send a message to war-weary Northerners faced with a fall election. After he routed a collection of overmatched militia led by Lew Wallace at the Monocacy River near Frederick, Maryland, rattled refugees from Rock-ville, Silver Spring, and surrounding towns streamed into the capital, their worldly possessions crammed into wagons.[80] Lincoln too was unnerved and wired Grant on July 10 about Wallace's debacle, suggesting that Grant arrive at Washington with troops—although Lincoln fell short of ordering him to do so.[81] Instead of making a frontal assault against Lee or leaving City Point headquarters, Grant dispatched Wright's Sixth Corps to deal with Early. When Wright appeared, Early melted back into Virginia.

Grant told Halleck on July 9 that he was poised to go in person to Washington "if the President thinks it advisabl[e]."[82] Rawlins took strenuous issue with Grant on this point, arguing his place was before Petersburg, that he had dedicated himself to defeating Lee, and that Grant's running to Washington could be interpreted as "a faltering at least in his purpose." Rawlins figured there were plenty of troops in various commands around Washington and Baltimore who could get the job done against Early.[83] Moreover, if Grant absented himself, command would devolve onto Ben Butler, the most senior major general—and that could not be risked.

Where the Rebel raid succeeded was in exposing how the several military departments in the region failed to synchronize their efforts to repel the invaders. Too many Federal commanders found their hands tied by departmental barriers. In an urgent July 12 telegram to Grant, Dana laid this out plainly: "Nothing can possibly be done here toward pursuing or cutting off the enemy for want of a commander. General Augur commands the defenses of Washington, with McCook and a lot of brigadier-generals under him, but he is not allowed to go outside. Wright commands his own corps. . . . General Ord to command the Eighth Corps and all other troops in the Middle Department, leaving Wallace to command the city alone. But there is no head to the whole, and it seems indispensable that you should appoint one."[84] Later that day, Dana telegraphed Rawlins about the incompetent leadership on display: "Along this part of the lines there was no general commander—no real knowledge of what was in the front—nothing but wild imagination and stupidity. . . . I do not exaggerate in the least when I say that such a lamentable want of intelligence, energy and purpose was never before seen in any command."[85] Dana's communication to Rawlins on the fifteenth was dourer still: he alarmed Rawlins with his opinion that the results of the botched response against Early "are very likely to be the defeat of Mr. Lincoln & the election of Gen. McClellan to the Presidency."[86]

Should Lee threaten Maryland or Pennsylvania again, Grant proposed to Halleck on July 18 that four departments be merged into one and placed under one commander. Grant's initial choice was William Franklin, a crony of Baldy Smith.[87] A week later, Grant presented the reorganization idea to President Lincoln but hedged on committing himself to Franklin by proposing that Meade would make an equally good choice, thus allowing Hancock to head the Army of the Potomac. That same day, Grant dispatched Rawlins to Washington to provide Lincoln and Stanton with all the reasons for the changes.[88] Nothing was to come of the reorganization plan. Rawlins's trip became just a brief reprieve from the beastly conditions at the front.

Sandwiched between Rawlins's effort to intervene on the commutation vote and his appointment with Lincoln, a meeting occurred on June 29 between Grant, Butler, and Smith, the alleged results of which had Rawlins feeling he had failed his chief.

—⁓—

Smith claimed years later that he had recorded the particulars of that meeting in a July 30, 1864, letter to his senator, Solomon Foot of Vermont. The letter surfaced after Foot's death. According to Smith, Grant and Butler visited him at his headquarters tent that day. On arriving, Grant allegedly commented to Butler that a whiskey he had drunk recently at Butler's headquarters had done him some medicinal good, and he requested a nip from Smith. Maintaining that it would have been inappropriate to decline that request, Smith allowed his servant to pour Grant a drink, and he took a second one an hour later. When Smith noticed Grant's speech had been affected, he ended the meeting. Grant—who, Smith claimed, had to be helped onto his horse—returned to his headquarters "in the most disgusting state after having vomited all over his horse's neck and shoulders," an indelicate mishap not mentioned in the letter to Foot.[89] To his staff officer who had also witnessed the event, Smith remarked, "General Grant has gone away drunk. General Butler has seen it, and will never fail to use it as a weapon which has been put into his hands."[90] Butler, in his autobiography, vigorously denied the story: "But Smith knew, and all of the other officers under my command knew, that I drank no spirituous liquors in the field nor had any at my headquarters.... I never saw General Grant drink a glass of spirituous liquor in my life."[91]

Rawlins learned of the drinking from one of the staff the same day. He wrote Emma he regretted not accompanying Grant to the meeting, "and it was with misgivings I did so. Nothing but indisposition induced me to remain behind. I shall hereafter, under no circumstances, fail to accompany him."[92] The next day, Smith sent Rawlins a message describing the incident. "Your kind note of this date in regards to the General while at your headquarters yesterday is received," Rawlins replied. "I am thankful to you for your friendly forethought, and the interest manifested in his behalf. Yet 'tis only what one knowing your friendship for him might have expected. Being this timely advised of the slippery ground he is on, I shall not fail to use my utmost endeavors to stay him from falling."[93] Rawlins was probably not surprised that Smith was trying to curry favor with him at Butler's expense, because their contempt for each other was well-known. Both possessed notoriously difficult personalities, leading Comstock to remark, "I think neither could get on well with any one, much less with each other."[94] In fact, barely a week was elapsed since Rawlins had been caught in the blowback from a Butler and Smith squabble. On June 21, Butler sent Smith a smarmily sarcastic dispatch faulting him for the delay in getting his infantry columns on the march. That day they traded several messages, each bespeaking a lava-hot loathing of the other coated by a veneer of pseudopoliteness. Finally, Smith became so offended that he forwarded copies of this correspondence to Rawlins—with the request that he be relieved from duty in Butler's department.[95]

At the beginning of July, Smith wrote a lengthy letter to Grant in which, among other things, he appealed for a leave of absence to obtain relief from the Virginia heat, which was troubling his head. In May 1863, his surgeon had pronounced him susceptible to "congestion of the brain" when subjected to hot weather.[96] Smith should have ended his letter there, but as he freely admitted, "I had a bad habit of saying what I thought."[97] He went on to complain about "the sneers and false charges and snubbings" he received on returning to the Army of the Potomac. He closed the letter by insulting Butler and, by insinuation, Grant himself when he posed the question, "I want simply to ask you [i.e., Grant] how you can place a man [i.e., Butler] in command of two army corps, who is as helpless as a child on the field of battle and as visionary as an opium eater in council . . . when you have such men as Franklin and Wright available to help you[?]"[98]

At the time of Grant's alleged drinking at Smith's headquarters, Grant and Halleck were sharing options for what to do about Butler and Smith. Grant wondered whether the two might need to be separated and the more administratively inclined Butler shunted off "where there are no great battles to be fought."[99] But ousting the politically potent Butler during an election year might cost the incumbent president votes. On July 6, Grant thought he had a solution. He told Halleck to prepare an order giving Smith field command of the troops in Butler's department and letting Butler occupy the department's headquarters at Ft. Monroe.[100] Smith claimed that this arrangement came down in a July 7 order from Washington. Moreover, Smith said Assistant Secretary of War Dana had been sent to him by Grant with the message that Butler might be relieved and Smith placed in departmental command.[101]

On July 9, just before the order relieving Butler was to be put through, both Butler and Smith were at City Point headquarters to meet Grant. Butler saw him first and no doubt presented arguments to save his job. When it was Smith's turn, he unleashed for Grant's benefit a diatribe against Meade. "I tried to show him [i.e., Grant] the blunders of the late campaign of the Army of the Potomac," Smith said in his letter to Foot, "and the terrible waste of life that had resulted from what I had considered a want of generalship in its present commander."[102] Smith began his leave of absence the next day, surely feeling that he was in the catbird seat regarding departmental command. In truth, he had cooked his goose.

When Smith returned to City Point on July 19, he was met at the landing by a solemn-faced Rawlins, who said Grant wanted to see him. Grant gave him a double-barreled blast of shocking news. First, Butler was to remain in command of the department. Then, as Smith wrote Senator Foot, Grant said "that as I had so severely criticized General Meade, he had determined to relieve me from the command of the 18th Corps and order me to New York City to await orders."[103] Those orders never came. A disbelieving Smith pressed Grant repeatedly for the "real reason." Harassed beyond exasperation, Grant finally sputtered, "You talk too much."[104] But Smith was convinced there was only one sensible explanation for sparing Butler: "that General Butler went to General Grant and threatened to expose his intoxication if the order was not revoked."[105] Butler did not need a petty drinking episode to gain an upper hand. Lincoln and Stanton, as Badeau knew, had made it clear to Grant "that political considerations of the highest character made it undesirable to replace Butler: the administration needed all its strength, and could not afford to provoke the hostility of so important a personage."[106] The decision to relieve Smith, Rawlins said, was "because of his spirit of criticism of all military movements and men, and his failure to get along with any one he is placed under, and his disposition to scatter the seeds of discontent throughout the army." Rawlins had reached his own limit with Smith, vowing to cut support for him and siding with Grant.[107]

After Rawlins and Grant were deceased, Smith in 1887 penned a letter of reminiscences to his daughter in which he gave a peculiar reason for why he was relieved of his corps command. "I was sacrificed," he told his daughter, "because I was earnestly helping Rawlins to keep General Grant from becoming incapacitated by his vicious habits from using such capacity and experience as he had to the services of his country." Smith seemed to be intimating he was, in his mind, Rawlins's helpmate in managing Grant. If Smith were so dedicated to protecting Grant and aiding Rawlins, then his claim that courtesy compelled him to serve him liquor lacks credibility. In a similar vein, Smith recalled becoming acquainted with Rawlins in Chattanooga. He noted how Rawlins engaged in an "unceasing" watch over Grant, including ordering away from headquarters anyone who carried a flask of liquor. Smith said he counted himself as one of those "who were surest in aiding Rawlins" by abstaining from liquor.[108]

Smith's difficulty in toeing a socially appropriate line also tainted his relationship with Rawlins. Smith recounted another drinking episode involving Grant that took place on the evening of July 8. Smith, William Franklin, and Rufus Ingalls, all West Point acquaintances of Grant, were in a dining room at City Point hunting up drinks. Franklin pointed to a pitcher, tumbler, and glasses on the mantle as evidence Grant had been there earlier. Suddenly, Grant entered the room, and Smith felt greatly embarrassed by his presence. Ingalls gave Smith a whiskey while Grant went right to where the brandy was kept. The episode seemed to strike Smith as so sordidly unfitting that he became emotionally unglued. He said he "had to vent my anger on something" and chose the recent battle of Cold Harbor, where "I had been compelled to slaughter some thousands of men and for no good. I could not think on the subject without my eyes filling up. Franklin says I was very severe and I probably was."

The next day, Smith felt obliged to take this drinking matter to Rawlins. When he told Rawlins that he "*must*" put a stop to people plying Grant with liquor, Rawlins agreed, immediately suspected Ingalls, and began cursing him. Smith disclosed that he next responded perhaps too much out of place when he impulsively told Rawlins how the drinking episode impacted his relationship with Grant: "I have given up a life-long friendship because I did not think the friend [i.e., Grant] was the man to lead us through this war and I will support no one after I am convinced that we cannot win with him." Smith afterward admitted his remarks had been "impolitic" and "perhaps had a tendency to make Rawlins lukewarm when the fight against me was begun."[109]

—⁓—

Just before Rawlins left for Washington on July 25 to present Grant's ideas to Lincoln and Stanton, news arrived that General James McPherson had been killed outside of Atlanta on July 22. The loss of the well-liked and engaged-to-be-married commander of the Army of the Tennessee struck everyone hard, including Rawlins, who lamented, "McPherson, my friend, with whom I have shared the same blanket, messed at the same board, endured the fatigue of the march, the exposures of the storm and faced the dangers of battle. . . . I have not the command of language to do justice to his worth and fame."[110] Grant was visibly affected, recalling McPherson was an early member his staff "and seemed almost like one of my own family."[111]

Rawlins returned to City Point on July 28 and discovered that in his absence, Grant had "digressed from his true path." Here was another exasperating example of how he was saddled with the responsibility of guardian of his chief's habits. It triggered his guiding belief in his indispensability: "Owing to this faltering of his," he wrote Emma, "I shall not be able to leave here till the rebel movement in Maryland is settled and also the fate of Atlanta."[112] However, later that day, Rawlins was approached by Grant and Bowers and convinced to take a leave as early as August 1. To his credit, he listened to them. "All things considered," he wrote Emma, "I can perhaps as well be spared by that time as at any time thereafter."[113]

Rawlins was preparing for his leave when, on the morning of July 30, a mine was detonated under the Confederate line. In June Grant had endorsed the digging of a five-hundred-foot tunnel packed with explosives. If this scheme, undertaken by a regiment from Pennsylvania coal country, proved successful, it could obviate the need for a lengthy siege. The explosion blasted a huge gap in the enemy fortifications and excavated a gaping crater. Behind the cascading human debris, billowing smoke, and cloudbank of dust, the way into Petersburg had been blown open. Petersburg was ripe for the taking, except that Ambrose Burnside's divisions had been chosen to exploit the gap. And they failed. Lack of leadership from the bungling or unavailable division commanders caused confusion among the charging Federal infantrymen, many of whom dashed into the crater and could not clamber out. This allowed the Confederates to rush replacements into the line and repel the charge.

The shameful performance at the Battle of the Crater left the Army of the Potomac deflated. Grant was stunned. "It was the saddest affair I have witnessed in this war," he wired Halleck. "Such an opportunity for carrying fortifications I have never seen and do not expect to again have."[114] The staff also struggled to put the episode into a meaningful context. George Leet was sending periodic updates to William Rowley, who was home in Galena, and in one letter he shared Joe Bowers's reflections on the debacle: "Bowers . . . says, 'The plan, the strategy of the movement was the finest I ever saw; the execution of it the most disgraceful. The Staff . . . seemed to feel rather gloomy and it is not to be wondered at that they did feel so, for everything previous to the movement seemed to indicate that we would win a brilliant victory.'"[115] On August 3, Meade wrote a blistering report to Rawlins requesting that Grant relieve Burnside of duty.[116] However, by that date Rawlins was in Danbury, reunited with family.

NOTES

1. Horace Porter, *Campaigning with Grant* (New York: Century, 1897), 41–43.

2. "Letters of George Hume, of Virginia," *The William and Mary Quarterly*, 6, no. 4 (1898): 252; James Harrison Wilson, *The Life of John Rawlins* (New York: Neale, 1916), 427.

3. Sean Patrick Adams, *Iron from the Wilderness: The History of Virginia's Catharine Furnace* (National Park Service: US Department of the Interior, 2011), 2.

4. Gaillard Hunt, *Israel, Elihu and Cadwallader Washburn* (New York: Macmillan, 1925), 208.

5. G. G. Meade to U. S. Grant, May 5, 1864, in *The War of the Rebellion: A Compilation of the Official Records of the Union and Confederate Armies*, series 1, part 2, 36:403.

6. George R. Agassiz, ed., *Meade's Headquarters 1863–1865: Letters of Colonel Theodore Lyman from the Wilderness to Appomattox* (Boston: Massachusetts Historical Society, 1922), 90.

7. Ibid., 90–91.

8. Gaillard Hunt, *Israel, Elihu and Cadwallader Washburn*, 210.

9. J. A. Rawlins to A. Burnside, May 6, 1864, in *The War of the Rebellion: A Compilation of the Official Records of the Union and Confederate Armies*, series 1, part 2, 36:461.

10. Horace Porter, *Campaigning with Grant*, 70.

11. James Harrison Wilson, *Under the Old Flag* (New York: Appleton, 1912), 1:390.

12. U. S. Grant to George G. Meade, May 7, 1864, in *The Papers of Ulysses S. Grant*, ed. John Y. Simon (Carbondale: Southern Illinois University Press, 1982), 10:408.

13. John A. Rawlins to Emma Rawlins, May 7, 1864, transcribed by J. H. Wilson, James H. Wilson Papers, Bender Collection, Wyoming State Archives and Historical Department, Microfilm Reel H-61a.

14. James Harrison Wilson, *The Life of John A. Rawlins*, 215–16. Wilson's secondhand account of this event differs from Horace Porter's version. Porter recollected, "The general, after having given his final orders providing for any emergency which might arise, entered

his tent, and threw himself down upon his camp-bed. Ten minutes thereafter an alarming report was received from the right. I looked in his tent, and found him sleeping as soundly and as peacefully as an infant." See Horace Porter, *Campaigning with Grant*, 70–71. Wilson acknowledged the differences but thought Rawlins and Bowers "far more creditable," because their account showed a more human Grant, not someone "stolid and indifferent . . . without sensibility or emotion"; see James Harrison Wilson, *Under the Old Flag*, 1:391.

15. Gaillard Hunt, *Israel, Elihu and Cadwallader Washburn*, 214.

16. Horace Porter, *Campaigning with Grant*, 79.

17. Ibid., 82–83.

18. Gaillard Hunt, *Israel, Elihu and Cadwallader Washburn*, 215; Horace Porter, *Campaigning with Grant*, 83–84.

19. J. A. Rawlins to A. E. Burnside, May 8, 1864, 12:45 p.m., and 3:00 p.m., in *The War of the Rebellion: A Compilation of the Official Records of the Union and Confederate Armies*, series 1, part 2, 36:546–47.

20. George R. Agassiz, ed., *Meade's Headquarters 1863–1865*, 105.

21. J. A. Rawlins to A. E. Burnside, May 8, 1864, 7:30 p.m., in *The War of the Rebellion: A Compilation of the Official Records of the Union and Confederate Armies*, series 1, part 2, 36:547.

22. J. A. Rawlins to A. E. Burnside, May 9, 1864, in *The War of the Rebellion: A Compilation of the Official Records of the Union and Confederate Armies*, series 1, part 2, 36:547.581.

23. John A. Rawlins to Emma Rawlins, May 9, 1864, transcribed by J. H. Wilson, James H. Wilson Papers, Bender Collection, Wyoming State Archives and Historical Department, Microfilm Reel H-61a.

24. John A. Rawlins to Emma Rawlins, March 28, 1864, transcribed by J. H. Wilson, James H. Wilson Papers, Bender Collection, Wyoming State Archives and Historical Department, Microfilm Reel H-61a.

25. Ron Chernow, *Grant* (New York: Penguin, 2017), 407.

26. Gaillard Hunt, *Israel, Elihu and Cadwallader Washburn*, 218.

27. Ibid., 219–20.

28. Horace Porter, *Campaigning with Grant*, 97–98.

29. John A. Rawlins to Emma Rawlins, May 11, 1864, transcribed by J. H. Wilson, James H. Wilson Papers, Bender Collection, Wyoming State Archives and Historical Department, Microfilm Reel H-61a.

30. U. S. Grant to G. Meade, May 9, 1864, in *The War of the Rebellion: A Compilation of the Official Records of the Union and Confederate Armies*, series 1, part 2, 36:629.

31. Merlin E. Sumner, ed., *The Diary of Cyrus B. Comstock* (Dayton, OH: Morningside House, 1987), 266.

32. George R. Agassiz, ed., *Meade's Headquarters 1863–1865*, 114n.

33. G. Norton Galloway, "Hand-to-Hand Fighting at Spotsylvania," in *Battles and Leaders of the Civil War*, ed. Robert Underwood Johnson and Clarence Clough Buel (1887; repr., New York: Thomas Yoseloff, 1956), 4:171.

34. Horace Porter, *Campaigning with Grant*, 106, 108.

35. Charles A. Dana, *Recollections of the Civil War* (New York: D. Appleton, 1902), 196–97.

36. John A. Rawlins to Emma Rawlins, May 13, 1864, transcribed by J. H. Wilson, James H. Wilson Papers, Bender Collection, Wyoming State Archives and Historical Department, Microfilm Reel H-61a.

37. Horace Porter, *Campaigning with Grant*, 114.

38. John A. Rawlins to Emma Rawlins, May 28, 1864, transcribed by J. H. Wilson, James H. Wilson Papers, Bender Collection, Wyoming State Archives and Historical Department, Microfilm Reel H-61a.

39. Andrew A. Humphreys, *The Virginia Campaign of '64 and '65* (New York: Charles Scribner's Sons, 1883), 83n.

40. Gordon C. Rhea, *To the North Anna River: Grant and Lee, May 13–25, 1864* (Baton Rouge: Louisiana State University Press, 2000), 259.

41. Horace Porter, *Campaigning with Grant*, 115.

42. John A. Rawlins to Emma Rawlins, June 8, 1864, transcribed by J. H. Wilson, James H. Wilson Papers, Bender Collection, Wyoming State Archives and Historical Department, Microfilm Reel H-61a.

43. Typescript of letter from John A. Rawlins to Emma, May 14, 1864, Ulysses S. Grant Presidential Library, Mississippi State University, Series 2, Box 10, Folder 66.

44. John A. Rawlins to Emma Rawlins, May 26, 1864, transcribed by J. H. Wilson, James H. Wilson Papers, Bender Collection, Wyoming State Archives and Historical Department, Microfilm Reel H-61a.

45. E. D. W. Breneman to Thomas A. McPartlin, May 17, 1864, in *The War of the Rebellion: A Compilation of the Official Records of the Union and Confederate Armies*, series 1, part 2, 36:841.

46. John Y. Simon, ed., *The Papers of Ulysses S. Grant*, 10:462–63n.

47. E. D. W. Breneman to John A. Rawlins, May 22, 1864, in *The War of the Rebellion: A Compilation of the Official Records of the Union and Confederate Armies*, series 1, part 3, 36:136–37.

48. John A. Rawlins to J. J. Abercrombie, May 23, 1864, in *The War of the Rebellion: A Compilation of the Official Records of the Union and Confederate Armies*, series 1, part 3, 36:136.

49. Merlin E. Sumner, ed., *The Diary of Cyrus B. Comstock*. 269.

50. George R. Agassiz, ed., *Meade's Headquarters 1863–1865*, 126.

51. *The War of the Rebellion: A Compilation of the Official Records of the Union and Confederate Armies*, series 1, part 3, 36:169.

52. Horace Porter, *Campaigning with Grant*, 164–67.

53. Jean Edward Smith, *Grant* (New York: Simon and Schuster, 2001), 361.

54. Otto Eisenschiml and Ralph Newman, *The American Iliad* (Indianapolis: Bobbs-Merrill, 1947), 582.

55. U. S. Grant to H. W. Halleck, June 3, 1864, in *The Papers of Ulysses S. Grant*, ed. John Y. Simon (Carbondale: Southern Illinois University Press, 1982), 11:9.

56. Typescript transcription of letter from John A. Rawlins to Emma, June 4, 1864, Ulysses S. Grant Presidential Library, Mississippi State University, Series 2, Box 10, Folder 66.

57. Horace Porter, *Campaigning with Grant*, 179.

58. James Harrison Wilson, *The Life of John A. Rawlins*, 227.

59. James Harrison Wilson, *Under the Old Flag* (New York: D. Appleton, 1912), 444–46.

60. James Harrison Wilson, *The Life of Charles A. Dana* (New York: Harper and Brothers, 1907), 327.

61. U. S. Grant to H. W. Halleck, June 5, 1864, in *The Papers of Ulysses S. Grant*, ed. John Y. Simon, 11:19–20.

62. John Y. Simon, ed., *The Papers of Ulysses S. Grant*, 11:40n.

63. John A. Rawlins to William F. Smith, June 13, 1864, in *The Papers of Ulysses S. Grant*, ed. John Y. Simon, 11:39n1.

64. Adam Badeau, *Military History of Ulysses S. Grant* (New York: D. Appleton, 1881), 350; Brian Holden Reid, "The Commander and His Chief of Staff: Ulysses S. Grant and John A. Rawlins, 1861–1865," in *Leadership and Command: The Anglo-American Military Experience since 1861*, ed. G. D. Sheffield (London: Brassey's, 1997), 29.

65. Brian Holden Reid, "The Commander and His Chief of Staff," 29–30; U. S. Grant to Julia Grant, July 1, 1864, in *The Papers of Ulysses S. Grant*, ed. John Y. Simon, 11:151.

66. Benjamin P. Thomas, ed., *Three Years with Grant* (New York: Alfred A. Knopf, 1961), 218.

67. U. S. Grant to H. W. Halleck, June 14, 1864, in *The Papers of Ulysses S. Grant*, ed. John Y. Simon, 11:45.

68. John A. Rawlins to Emma Rawlins, June 14, 1864, transcribed by J. H. Wilson, James H. Wilson Papers, Bender Collection, Wyoming State Archives and Historical Department, Microfilm Reel H-61a.

69. John A. Rawlins to Emma Rawlins, June 15, 1864, transcribed by J. H. Wilson, James H. Wilson Papers, Bender Collection, Wyoming State Archives and Historical Department, Microfilm Reel H-61a.

70. George R. Agassiz, ed., *Meade's Headquarters 1863–1865*, 160.

71. Bruce Catton, *Grant Takes Command* (Boston: Little, Brown, 1968), 291.

72. John A. Rawlins to Emma Rawlins, June 16, 1864, transcribed by J. H. Wilson, James H. Wilson Papers, Bender Collection, Wyoming State Archives and Historical Department, Microfilm Reel H-61a.

73. Horace Porter, *Campaigning with Grant*, 219.

74. John A. Rawlins to Emma Rawlins, June 21, 1864, transcribed by J. H. Wilson, James H. Wilson Papers, Bender Collection, Wyoming State Archives and Historical Department, Microfilm Reel H-61a.

75. John Y. Simon, "Grant, Lincoln, and Unconditional Surrender," in *Lincoln's Generals*, ed. Gabor Boritt (New York: Oxford University Press, 1994), 177.

76. Edward G. Longacre, *From Union Stars to Top Hat: A Biography of the Extraordinary General James Harrison Wilson* (Harrisburg, PA: Stackpole, 1972), 134–42; Horace Porter, *Campaigning with Grant*, 225.

77 John A. Rawlins to Emma Rawlins, June 26, 1864, transcribed by J. H. Wilson, James H. Wilson Papers, Bender Collection, Wyoming State Archives and Historical Department, Microfilm Reel H-61a.

78. Peter Levine, "Draft Evasion in the North during the Civil War, 1863–1865," *Journal of American History* 67, no. 4 (1981): 816–34. Rawlins's friend, Sylvanus Cadwallader, had been drafted in late summer, but before he reported, he had furnished a substitute for himself; see John Y. Simon, ed., *The Papers of Ulysses S. Grant*, 12:200n.

79. R. E. Lee to J. Davis, July 11, 1864, in *The War of the Rebellion: A Compilation of the Official Records of the Union and Confederate Armies*, series 1, part 2, 37:595.

80. Margaret Leech, *Reveille in Washington* (New York: Harper and Brothers, 1941), 337.

81. Roy P. Basler, ed., *Collected Works of Abraham Lincoln* (New Brunswick: Rutgers University Press, 1953), 7:437.

82. U. S. Grant to H. W. Halleck, July 9, 1864, in *The Papers of Ulysses S. Grant*, ed. John Y. Simon, 11:198–99.

83. John A. Rawlins to Emma Rawlins, July 11, 1864, transcribed by J. H. Wilson, James H. Wilson Papers, Bender Collection, Wyoming State Archives and Historical Department, Microfilm Reel H-61a.

84. C. A. Dana to U. S. Grant, July 12, 1864, in *The War of the Rebellion: A Compilation of the Official Records of the Union and Confederate Armies*, series 1, part 3, 37:223.

85. C. A. Dana to J. A. Rawlins, July 12, 1864, in *The Papers of Ulysses S. Grant*, ed. John Y. Simon, 11:231n.

86. John Y. Simon, ed., *The Papers of Ulysses S. Grant*, 11:253n.

87. U. S. Grant to H. W. Halleck, July 18, 1864, in *The Papers of Ulysses S. Grant*, ed. John Y. Simon, 11:274.

88. U. S. Grant to A. Lincoln, July 25, 1864, in *The War of the Rebellion: A Compilation of the Official Records of the Union and Confederate Armies*, series 1, part 3, 40:436.

89. William F. Smith, *Autobiography of Major General William F. Smith 1861–1864*, ed. Herbert M. Schiller (Dayton, OH: Morningside, 1990), 110.

90. William Farrar Smith, *From Chattanooga to Petersburg under Generals Grant and Butler* (Boston: Houghton, Mifflin, 1893), 174–75. A variant of Smith's story appeared in a letter by General Isaac Wistar as a way of corroborating Smith's claim that Butler was obtaining damning information to use against Grant. Wistar, a brigade commander in the Army of the James, was relieved in May 1864. Wistar presented a statement from John Tucker, who was for several months in 1862 an assistant secretary of war. According to Tucker, when Butler learned he would be relieved and Smith given command of the Army of the James, Butler took Grant on visits to the various corps headquarters and induced him to partake there of "refreshments." These were the same commanders Rawlins had extracted promises from to keep liquor away from Grant. Once he had become visibly drunk in the presence of many witnesses, he was returned to his headquarters. As he was helped to dismount, Rawlins allegedly exclaimed, "'My God, there's the General drunk again after all the promises I got from the corps commanders,' or words to that effect." Wistar did not say from whom Tucker obtained this story. William Farrar Smith, *From Chattanooga to Petersburg under Generals Grant and Butler*, 192–93.

91. Benjamin F. Butler, *Butler's Book* (Boston: A. M. Thayer, 1892), 698.

92. John A. Rawlins to Emma Rawlins, June 29, 1864, transcribed by J. H. Wilson, James H. Wilson Papers, Bender Collection, Wyoming State Archives and Historical Department, Microfilm Reel H-61a.

93. John Y. Simon, ed., *The Papers of Ulysses S. Grant*, 11:207n.

94. Merlin E. Sumner, ed., *The Diary of Cyrus B. Comstock*, 278.

95. *The War of the Rebellion: A Compilation of the Official Records of the Union and Confederate Armies*, series 1, part 3, 40:299–301.

96. Jack D. Welsh, *Medical Histories of Union Generals* (Kent: Kent State University Press, 1996), 313.

97. William F. Smith, *Autobiography of Major General William F. Smith 1861–1864*, 111.

98. W. F. Smith to U. S. Grant, July 2, 1864, in *The War of the Rebellion: A Compilation of the Official Records of the Union and Confederate Armies*, series 1, part 2, 40:595.

99. U. S. Grant to H. W. Halleck, July 1, 1864, in *The War of the Rebellion: A Compilation of the Official Records of the Union and Confederate Armies*, series 1, part 2, 40:558–59.

100. U. S. Grant to H. W. Halleck, July 6, 1864, in *The War of the Rebellion: A Compilation of the Official Records of the Union and Confederate Armies*, series 1, part 3, 40:31.

101. William Farrar Smith, *From Chattanooga to Petersburg under Generals Grant and Butler*, 175.

102. Ibid., 176.

103. William F. Smith, *Autobiography of Major General William F. Smith 1861–1864*, 114–15n72.

104. Ibid., 116.

105. Ibid., 115n72.

106. Adam Badeau, *Military History of Ulysses S. Grant*, 2:246.

107. John A. Rawlins to Emma Rawlins, July 19, 1864, transcribed by J. H. Wilson, James H. Wilson Papers, Bender Collection, Wyoming State Archives and Historical Department, Microfilm Reel H-61a.

108. William F. Smith, *Autobiography of Major General William F. Smith 1861–1864*, 97, 108–9.

109. Ibid., 111–13.

110. John A. Rawlins to Emma Rawlins, July 23, 1864, transcribed by J. H. Wilson, James H. Wilson Papers, Bender Collection, Wyoming State Archives and Historical Department, Microfilm Reel H-61a. McPherson hoped to marry Emily Hoffman of Baltimore that spring. However, after assuming command of the Army of the Tennessee, he wrote his friend Brigadier General Elias Dennis that his request for a twenty-day leave had been denied, "and I do not know now when I shall be able to avail myself of it." J. B. McPherson to Elias Dennis, April 7, 1864, collection of the author.

111. Horace Porter, *Campaigning with Grant*, 245.

112. John A. Rawlins to Emma Rawlins, July 28, 1864, transcribed by J. H. Wilson, James H. Wilson Papers, Bender Collection, Wyoming State Archives and Historical Department, Microfilm Reel H-61a.

113. Ibid.

114. U. S. Grant to H. W. Halleck, August 1, 1864, in *The Papers of Ulysses S. Grant*, ed. John Y. Simon, 11:361.

115. George Leet to William Rowley, August 9, 1864. SC 1306, Abraham Lincoln Presidential Library, Springfield, IL.

116. G. G. Meade to J. A. Rawlins, August 3, 1864, in *The War of the Rebellion: A Compilation of the Official Records of the Union and Confederate Armies*, series 1, part 1, 40:172–76.

20

"The Nomination of General Rawlins Will Be Sent in Immediately and with Great Pleasure"

ON AUGUST 1, RAWLINS DEPARTED for Danbury on a sixty-day leave to benefit his health. John and Emma spent a few days in New York City visiting William Hillyer and his wife. Rawlins consulted a specialist there who attributed his cough to treatable chronic bronchitis.[1] At headquarters, Rawlins's absence was felt by everyone, and all hoped he would return recuperated. Grant himself "expressed no little anxiety about his illness."[2] Both Leet and Bowers maintained a steady correspondence with him, apprising him of military maneuvers and affairs at headquarters. Leet even sent Rawlins's pay drafts to Danbury. In one letter, Leet mentioned that in Washington, one day he had happened across Hillyer, who reported that Rawlins's health was improving. When Leet brought this news back to headquarters, "all were delighted to hear rich good tidings of you."[3]

While Rawlins was absent, Atlanta fell to Sherman on September 2, and that precipitated among the staff speculation about what Sherman would do next. It was known he contemplated the radical idea of detaching from his supply base and heading to Savannah or perhaps to Florida's Gulf Coast. On the twelfth, Grant chose Horace Porter to visit Sherman and bring his views back to headquarters. Sherman was unsure what his Confederate adversary, John Bell Hood, was planning. In July, the hard-fighting Hood replaced the defensive-minded Joe Johnston at the head of the Army of Tennessee. Although Hood had suffered heavily defending Atlanta, he was still dangerous. He might elect to harass Sherman or to give him the slip, head north, and threaten Tennessee and Kentucky. However, Sherman was not fixated on Hood. He told Porter he wanted to split off a portion of his army and combine that with scattered forces in the West. This amalgam of troops under George Thomas would deal with Hood, leaving Sherman with the sizeable remainder for a march to the sea.[4]

At the end of July, Early's corps was again operating north of the Potomac. He used the Shenandoah Valley as an access route for raids into Maryland, West Virginia, and Pennsylvania. A frustrated Grant selected Phil Sheridan to tackle Early. Given command of a revitalized Army of the Shenandoah, Sheridan started cautiously, but once he found traction, he dealt Early consecutive defeats at Winchester on September 19 and at Fisher's Hill three days later.

In mid-August, a meeting occurred at City Point between Grant and John Eaton, the chaplain who had been working strenuously on behalf of freed men and women. Eaton had been sent by Lincoln to get a sounding on Grant's political ambitions. After he expressed no inclination to become chief executive, their conversation drifted to another topic: the rumors circulating about Washington that Stanton might be replaced. If that position became vacant, Grant told Eaton, he favored Rawlins for it.[5] Also that summer, Grant's commissary of subsistence, Lieutenant Colonel Michael R. Morgan, took note of an uncanny prediction made by Mary Lincoln. After Lincoln's renomination, Julia Grant and Emma Rawlins called on Mary while she was visiting City Point. Mary prophesized that Ulysses would be the next person elected president and that John would be his secretary of war.[6] In late July, an editorial appeared in the *Galena Daily Gazette*: "The reported resignation of Mr. Stanton . . . gives us an opportunity to make a suggestion . . . which, if followed, would be worth to our army a power equal to two hundred thousand men. Had we the power for fifteen minutes we should occupy the first necessary part of that time in appointing Brig. Gen. John A. Rawlins Secretary of War. We know of no man in the United States . . . who would emphatically *fill* that office so well as he."[7] This hometown lobbying effort left Rawlins surprised and amused.[8] However, the barest of an idea was being floated. It didn't yet qualify as a trial balloon and perhaps was just an evanescent bubble.

———

When Rawlins returned to City Point on October 3, reactions to his health status were mixed. Wilson thought him "somewhat improved in strength and looks" but not looking fit for military work.[9] Porter was gratified to see that Rawlins, although not fully restored, appeared significantly recuperated, except for a troubling cough. However, when Rawlins was out of earshot, Grant expressed to Porter his own great concern: "I do not like that cough."[10] Bowers told Rowley, "Rawlins is stouter, fatter, heartier and in better health than I ever before saw him. He is not entirely rid of his cough, but is gradually loosing [*sic*] it."[11]

The more momentous topic around headquarters was Sherman's proposed march. Heated debates flared between factions among the staff. Rawlins used expletive-laced orations to express opposition to it. He argued that once separated from his base, Sherman would exhaust his supplies. Moreover, a sufficient opposing force might not be assembled in time to prevent Hood from marching north, perhaps to the Ohio River. Since meeting with Sherman, Porter had become a true believer. He countered that Sherman's army would find plenty of provisions in Georgia and that if Hood proved a threat, Sherman could detach troops that could be joined with others from sources like the Department of the Missouri. Grant listened attentively and felt amused by the vehemence of the debaters, who sometimes exceeded boundaries: Rawlins on one occasion was loudly haranguing a group into the wee hours when Grant emerged from his tent and yelled, "Oh, do go to bed, all of you! You're keeping the whole camp awake."[12]

To Porter, Rawlins expressed his earnest belief about the risks attendant to Sherman's plan and not being divisive. He was too devoted to Grant to foment dissent. Grant, according to Porter, was not dissuaded by others' opinions because this issue was "a purely military question about the advisability of which he really had no doubt in his own mind."[13] But Grant did have some doubts. He fretted about Hood's advancing into Tennessee and how a crisis would develop if Thomas could not deter him. It made sense to Grant to first demolish Hood, but Sherman thought that a waste of his time: let Thomas deal with Hood, while he strode through enemy territory and brought the Confederacy to its knees.[14] On October 11, Grant, with some reluctance, gave Sherman permission: "If there is any way of getting at Hood's army, I would prefer that, but I must trust to your own judgment."[15]

While debates about Sherman lingered at headquarters, Lee was reinforcing Early for a surprise attack against Sheridan, a last gamble, it turned out, for control of the Valley. At dawn on October 19, Early unleashed a surprise attack on the Federals bivouacked near Cedar Creek, Virginia. Sheridan had been in Washington the day before conferring with Halleck, and when the attack began, he was almost twenty miles away at Winchester. The jockey-size Sheridan put the spurs to Rienzi, his powerful gelding, jet-black and sixteen hands high.

When he got to the battlefield, he found his left flank turned and men streaming back in confusion. In a heroic burst of energy, Sheridan led a ferocious counterattack that wrecked Early's army and ended Confederate resistance in the Shenandoah. It was Sheridan's third pummeling of Early within a month. Sheridan's ride instantly became the stuff of legend, and Rienzi was rechristened Winchester.

That night Grant read to the staff Sheridan's battle report just after it came over the wire. Sheridan, never one to hide his light under a bushel, boasted, "I here took the affair in hand and quickly united the Corps [and] formed a compact line of battle just in time to repulse an attack of the enemy which was handsomely done at about 1 p.m. At 3 p.m. . . . I attacked with great vigor driving and routing the enemy." After the staff cheered the news, Rawlins distributed copies of the telegram to the senior commanders.[16]

—⁓⁓⁓—

In October, Hood's army was mending in northeastern Alabama and preparing to cross the Tennessee River. George Thomas would be facing Hood, and to augment his force, Grant and Rawlins looked west to the Department of the Missouri, where Rosecrans had been languishing since January. At that moment, Rosecrans was grappling with his Confederate nemesis, old Sterling Price, who in September had embarked on a campaign to rekindle the war west of the Mississippi, snatch Missouri from Federal control, and thereby swing voters away from Lincoln in November. Price's aggressiveness brought Rosecrans close to panic. He hastily cobbled together a force of citizen volunteers, Missouri militia, and US infantry. In truth, Price's army was poorly armed and accoutered, and during October it took one licking after another before limping into Arkansas.

Rosecrans managed to appropriate two infantry divisions commanded by Major Generals A. J. Smith and Joseph Mower. These divisions, which belonged to Sherman, had been detached earlier from him and sent to participate in the Red River expedition. Now they were being returned and earmarked for George Thomas. However, they veered into Rosecrans's bailiwick, and given the threat Price posed, he staked a quick claim to them. Sherman, who was not well informed of the situation in Missouri, was annoyed to have troops plucked from him.[17]

Meanwhile at headquarters, there was no sympathy for the reviled Rosecrans. Rawlins had been pressing Grant to remove him, maintaining he was doing nothing to defeat Price. Grant hardly needed convincing; he was waiting for a suitable replacement.[18] Both were sure that Rosecrans was hoarding troops in St. Louis. Trying to pry troops away from him was like pulling teeth, according to Grant, who told Halleck, "The only way any soldier can ever be taken from Gen. Rosecrans is by sending a staff officer directly to him to execute the order in person. I do not know that he has any troops to spare but it would be all the same if he had double the number he has."[19]

The staff officer chosen for that job was John Rawlins. "The necessity of reinforcing the Armies actually confronting the principle Armies of the enemy . . . is of such vital importance," Grant emphasized to Rawlins in writing on October 29, "that you are selected to go West as bearer of orders intended to accomplish this end." Rawlins was given the option of determining which of two orders to serve to Rosecrans: one called for the withdrawal of only A. J. Smith's command, and the other would withdraw Mower's as well. Rawlins was to see to the proper destination of the divisions: to Thomas if Hood was invading Tennessee, or otherwise to the trenches at Petersburg. When assigning Rawlins this task, Grant also pointedly reminded him of his support for Sherman: "I am satisfied on full and mature reflection that Sherman's idea of striking across for the sea coast is the best way to rid Ten. & Ky. of threatened danger and to make the war felt."[20] However, Grant was not wholly "satisfied." Two days later on November 1—Rawlins's second day on his trek west— Grant telegraphed Sherman: "Do you think it advisable now that Hood has gone so far north, to entirely settle him before starting on your proposed campaign? . . . If you can see the chance for destroying Hood's Army, attend to that first & make your other move secondary."[21] Sherman disagreed, arguing that by abandoning his plan, he would play into Jefferson Davis's hand and that Thomas was strong enough to tackle Hood.[22]

On October 29, Rawlins's instructions were changed in light of special orders Bowers wired to Rosecrans. Rosecrans was now to dispatch both Smith's and Mower's divisions to Thomas. Rawlins's presence at Rosecrans's headquarters was to ensure he followed those orders.[23] Rawlins left for St. Louis the next day. The first leg of the journey took him to Washington on a special boat, a trip he made in the company of Henry Halleck.[24] Rawlins reached St. Louis on November 3 and met the next day with Rosecrans. Expecting to spar with a recalcitrant Rosecrans, Rawlins instead found him remarkably compliant. The two divisions were already on the march toward embarkation points on the Mississippi. In fact, the situation was so well in hand that Rawlins thought it unnecessary to extend his visit. He even had spare moments to visit Julia Grant, who was in St. Louis at the time. Rawlins telegraphed Grant for permission to return by way of New York City to see his physician and spend a few days there with Emma.[25] On November 14, after arriving in Washington, Rawlins telegraphed he was returning to City Point on that day's mail boat.[26]

Two days later, Sherman's Army of the Tennessee departed Atlanta for the sea.

—◦◦◦—

Seventeen years after Sherman's march, Adam Badeau's three-volume biography of Grant was published. Volume three contains a stunning charge leveled against the long-deceased John Rawlins. Badeau accused Rawlins of "downright insubordination" against Grant. According to Badeau, Rawlins was so opposed to the planned march that, on his way to St. Louis, he first stopped at Washington to meet with Lincoln and Stanton, to whom he "forcibly" expressed his apprehensions of allowing Sherman to let Thomas contend with Hood.[27] In his memoirs, Grant in two coolly dismissive sentences made the same accusation: "I was in favor of Sherman's plan from the time it was first submitted to me. My chief of staff, however, was very bitterly opposed to it and, as I learned subsequently, finding that he could not move me, he appealed to the authorities at Washington to stop it."[28]

Many friends of both Grant and Rawlins were stunned by his accusation. Ely Parker, writing to fellow Galenian John C. Smith, said, "I have never entertained the thought that Grant in his heart ever believed Rawlins to have been disloyal or untrue to him either thoughtlessly or intentionally. . . . If Rawlins was opposed to Sherman's campaign to the sea, it was from conscientious motives and with no desire or intent to thwart Grant in his plans or wishes."[29] Absalom Markland, who knew both while overseeing the mail for the army, wrote Sherman that not only was Rawlins loyal to Grant but that "no man had more confidence in you and the success of your plans than did John A. Rawlins."[30] Sherman's reply piled on Rawlins: "I have further reason to believe that Rawlins went up to Washington about that date, Nov 1864." Sherman did not provide that reason. However, he suggested Rawlins had a motive for his treachery: "Rawlins especially in his later years was very sensitive & jealous of any body who seemed to share Grant[']s tremendous success"—that Rawlins was infuriated because Sherman was basking in limelight belonging to Grant.[31] Furthermore, Sherman believed that Rawlins feared he was going on a "wild-goose chase" because Rawlins was not fully informed, merely basing his opposition "according to the light he possessed."[32]

Rawlins's staunchest defenders, Sylvanus Cadwallader and Wilson, maintained he was not opposed to the march but advocated for its delay based on sound reasons. According to Cadwallader, what worried Rawlins was that Sherman was siphoning away men from Thomas, leaving him with an inadequate force to face Hood's advancing army.[33] In fact, Wilson, who had been assigned to command the cavalry under Thomas, informed Rawlins that Sherman had taken his pick of the army for his march and left Thomas with horseless cavalry and inferior infantry scattered over a wide territory.[34] General John Schofield, whom Rawlins later succeeded as secretary of war, after long consideration of Sherman's plans, arrived at the conclusion that "the opinion ascribed to General Rawlins, as opposed to General Grant's, was, in my judgment, the better of the two."[35]

Schofield believed Grant was correct in holding the view he expressed to Sherman as late as November 1 that Hood's army should have been his objective. But Sherman convinced Grant that he had given Thomas ample resources to handle Hood, and Grant, ever confident in Sherman, deferred to his judgment. When Schofield met with Sherman in October at Gaylesville, Alabama, he was surprised that Sherman "was going off to sea with five sixths of his army, leaving Thomas, with only one of his six corps, and no other troops then ready for field service, to take care of Hood until he could get A. J. Smith from Missouri, incorporate new regiments into the army and make them fit to meet the veteran enemy, remount his cavalry, and concentrate his garrisons and railroad guards in Tennessee!"[36] Moreover, it took a month before Smith's men joined Thomas. Sherman kept for himself the fittest troops, best cavalry mounts, and most of the wagon train because, as a biographer of George Thomas argued, he was "bound for glory" and needed to carry out a campaign he could not lose.[37]

There is no evidence that Rawlins met with authorities in Washington. Wilson defended Rawlins by suggesting that if he had, it would have been at their insistence, and if he were questioned by them, he would have been obligated to share his views.[38] One might conjecture that Rawlins divulged his opinions to Halleck while the two of them were traveling companions to Washington. Halleck himself had doubted the wisdom of Sherman's plan,[39] even characterizing it as madness to Senator Charles Sumner of Massachusetts.[40] Halleck would have been aware that Lincoln also harbored doubts. On October 12,

Stanton expressed Lincoln's uneasy feelings in a telegram to Grant: "The President feels much solicitude in respect to General Sherman's proposed movement and hopes that it will be maturely considered . . . a misstep by General Sherman might be fatal to his army."[41] If Halleck had passed along to Stanton or Lincoln Rawlins's reservations, then he might have been summoned to meet with them on his return from St. Louis.

—⁓—

Rawlins was only two days returned to City Point when Grant used the quiet time at the front to visit his family at Burlington, New Jersey—he left on November 17 with a retinue of staff that included Badeau, Comstock, and his telegraph operator Samuel Beckwith—and to treat Julia to a shopping excursion in New York. With Grant gone, a principal focus of Rawlins's attention was on the movement of Lee's army. Grant had been harboring the suspicion that Lee might evacuate his Petersburg lines and opt to fight Sherman. From Burlington, he wired Rawlins to alert him immediately if Lee should detach so that the Army of the Potomac would be prepared to follow.[42] Rawlins was also intent on monitoring the whereabouts of elements of Early's force as Lee closed down operations in the Valley. Rawlins wired Grant in New York that an agent of the Bureau of Military Information reported the return to Richmond of Joseph Kershaw's division, which had been detached to Early. The agent's information was firsthand: he operated a market stall in Richmond, and some of Kershaw's men robbed him.[43] Grant's date of return from New York City was not known, thus leaving Rawlins nervously anticipating he might be pressed to issue orders under his own signature. That was never a problem when in the West, but now with the armies in the East, such orders might be questioned.[44] While Rawlins bided his time at headquarters, he read the New York Herald's reporting of his chief's reception in New York City. Badeau (or perhaps Beckwith) implored the press to respect Grant's modesty by putting off announcing his presence there. Rawlins disgustedly clucked that this had the opposite effect: creating a clamor and preventing Grant from needed rest.[45]

The Union armies before Petersburg by this time had withdrawn into winter quarters. The tents around Grant's headquarters had been replaced by wooden huts outfitted with two bunks and an open fireplace at the rear. Grant returned on Thanksgiving Day, the twenty-fourth, in time for the luxury of turkey dinners and a celebration that even Rawlins allowed himself to appreciate. This period of relative inactivity allowed for another treat: visits from the wives. Grant wrote to Julia the next day imploring her to come to City Point and invite Emma Rawlins: "Gen. Rawlins would be pleased if you would do so and would regard it as a compliment."[46] But General Rawlins was not pleased with the proposal. "Now I would like very much to have you come," he told Emma, beginning on a cheery note before spoiling the whole idea, "were it not that I disapprove of having officers' wives in camp." How unseemly it would look, he maintained, to have the press report that in wartime, the commanding general and his chief of staff were hosting their wives. But, he hastened to add, these were simply his opinions, leaving the final say to her, "and whatever it is will meet with my concurrence and approval."[47] Apparently Emma was dissatisfied with John's response, because he reiterated his disapproval in a second letter, citing as reasons that "orders are against officers wives being with them in camp" and that everyone at headquarters should be ready to move if the enemy threatens. His views, he assured her, "are based upon firm principles which I trust will find in you a hearty support." In truth, Grant was opposed to having wives in camp, but he always bent the rule to accommodate Julia[48]—a point Rawlins would have known. By frowning on Emma's visit, it was the rule-bound John Rawlins applying principles like forswearing frivolity and doubling down on decorum that he used to transform the Coal Boy into a brigadier general. To his credit, he did not expressly forbid her from joining Julia Grant for a visit.[49]

As November faded into December, Rawlins scoured the Richmond newspapers for news of Sherman's progress, and he shared in the apprehension caused by Hood's unchecked advance into Tennessee. From this distance, Hood appeared a far more dangerous threat than he actually posed to Thomas. On November 30 at Franklin, south of Nashville, Hood incautiously threw his Army of Tennessee against an entrenched Federal force commanded by John Schofield. After badly mauling Hood, Schofield hastily withdrew to Nashville, where he joined Thomas, who was consolidating his army behind fortifications and readying his cavalry. Hood followed, drawing his depleted army up to Nashville's southern environs, where on December 2 he hunkered down, hoping to draw out Thomas. Hood's army was too played out to initiate an attack.

Grant wanted Thomas to take swift action and annihilate Hood. However, swift was not in "Slow Trot" Thomas's repertoire, and his methodical approach rankled Grant. On the eighth, he wired Halleck: "If Thomas has not struck yet he ought to be ordered to hand over his command to Schofield. There is no better man to repel and attack than Thomas—but I fear he is too cautious to ever take the initiative."[50] Then, a crippling ice storm socked in Nashville and further delayed Thomas. Meanwhile, Grant's patience was frayed. He prepared orders for Thomas's replacement and even departed for Nashville to expedite matters. He got only so far as Washington, where on the fifteenth he received news that Thomas had hit Hood with crushing blows. Following on the heels of Thomas's victory at Nashville came word that on the twenty-first, the small Confederate force defending Savannah bolted into South Carolina ahead of Sherman. Now with the exception of Lee's army at Petersburg, there was another item of unfinished military business occupying Grant's attention.

———

Wilmington, North Carolina, remained the last major Confederate port on the Atlantic seaboard. It was the destination of blockade runners supplying Lee's army. Protecting Wilmington twenty miles below at the mouth of the Cape Fear River was formidable Fort Fisher. Intelligence reports told of the fort's garrison having been reduced to confront the threat posed by Sherman. Grant saw the opportunity to strike Fort Fisher and close down the port. On November 29, Grant, Rawlins, and several other staff met with Ben Butler and Admiral David Porter at Fortress Monroe to discuss the logistics of an army-navy expedition to capture Fort Fisher. Grant intended to install Major General Godfrey Weitzel, one of Butler's subordinates, in field command of the two infantry divisions (about sixty-five hundred troops) and for Butler to handle organizational and administrative details. Butler appeared to be agreeable to this arrangement. He even proposed the intriguing idea of packing a vessel with explosives, detonating it close to the fort, and letting the infantry mop up. The shock of the blast, he argued, should reduce the fort to rubble. Grant was skeptical but allowed the experiment to go forward. Later, the old USS *Louisiana* was chosen as the sacrificial vessel and crammed with tons of gunpowder.

Instead of returning to City Point after the meeting, Grant overnighted in Norfolk and relaxed by attending the theater. All accompanied him except Rawlins. "To have gone there would have afforded me no pleasure," he confessed to Emma. "Besides in times like these I do not approve of those to whom the country looks for leadership and guidance through the terrible storm still swelling with unspent fury, going to such places. . . . The brave men in the front can't have this privilege, if they desired it, and I will not take the benefit of it though the privilege is mine. The looks of a thing is sometimes a great deal."[51] Here, Rawlins is declaring a choice: he is demonstrating the sincerity of his convictions and embracing the misery so many in the country were feeling. It is the stuff at his personal core: a penchant for sobriety, a distaste of affectation, an espousal of self-denial. Yet it also is an expression of his capacity for "feeling with"—an emotional solidarity with the war-widowed bride, the destitute families he encountered in East Tennessee, the escaped slave fleeing into Union lines—fostered during his days in grinding poverty in the Guilford woods. Now, ought his fellow officers admire him as an inspirational example or pity him as a killjoy?

Just before the troops were to embark for the expedition, Butler showed up at Grant's headquarters to declare his intention of accompanying Weitzel. Careful not to chafe Butler's feelings, Grant did not order him to remain behind, figuring he wanted only to be on hand to witness the gunpowder explosion.[52] However, Butler had no intent on being a passive observer: along the way, he usurped control from Weitzel. Bad weather and delays kept the expedition from taking offensive action until December 24, when the *Louisiana*'s cargo was exploded at 1:40 a.m. Cyrus Comstock, whom Grant had loaned to the expedition, noted that the explosion went off harmlessly "with much less noise than was expected." A massive bombardment by Porter's vessels also failed to damage the fort, and when Weitzel reported it could not be taken by assault, Butler suffered a total collapse of resolve. He ordered the troops to reembark and head back to Fortress Monroe. Colonel Newton Curtis, a brigade commander under Butler, implored Comstock to give him positive orders to try an assault. Comstock was sympathetic but powerless to authorize it.[53]

Grant was profoundly displeased with Butler's pathetic performance. On December 28, he wired Lincoln that the expedition proved "a gross and culpable failure" and hoped to discover whom to blame.[54] A week later, Grant asked Stanton to remove Butler—with Lincoln having won a second term, there were few political reasons to retain him—and on January 7, Halleck did so by issuing General Orders No. 1. Halleck stipulated that the order—a sensitive and highly newsworthy item—could not be published until Grant delivered it to Butler.[55] Butler was swiftly replaced by General Edward Ord.

Rawlins cautioned Sylvanus Cadwallader, who was at headquarters, not to broach the topic of Butler's removal until Grant spoke about it. After the evening dinner, Grant mentioned that he had been authorized to remove Butler but would wait until Sunday, the eighth, to have Horace Porter personally serve the order. Porter was late starting out and did not reach Butler until after noon. Meanwhile, Cadwallader jumped the gun with this scoop, sending off a dispatch to his paper, the *New York Herald*, on the 10:00 a.m. mail boat. It read in part:

> The news of the President's order, No. 1, series of 1865, removing Major General Benjamin F. Butler from the command of the Department of Virginia and North Carolina, is causing much comment; but so far as I can learn little or no animadversion. Whether rightfully or not, Gen. Butler has for months past been losing the confidence of the officers of the army, until very few will regret his departure outside of those who swarm around, and attach themselves to those in power. It has been Gen. Butler's misfortune to appoint too many of these selfish and irresponsible persons to official positions of trust and responsibility.

Butler soon realized that Cadwallader's dispatch had left before Porter served him the order—a serious military discourtesy. Butler was incensed. Later, when called to testify before the Committee on the Conduct of the War regarding the Fort Fisher failure, he used the opportunity to heap criticism on Grant and Admiral Porter.[56] In his autobiography, Butler presented his theory for what actuated Grant to have him removed. It was due, he said, to "the pressure [that] came from his West Point staff officers, who were trying in every way to have me vilified and abused. Grant had not, therefore, permitted that to be done, and yielded only under the pressure of ambition for the highest office which has caused so many next in position to murder their chief to attain his place."[57]

Several days after his removal, Butler wrote Rawlins a private letter that, under the gracious surface, simmered with resentment. As the link between Grant and Cadwallader, Rawlins was a logical target of Butler's animus. He began the letter informing Rawlins, "My enemies about your headquarters are very *bungling* in their malice." If he had been removed, as the *Herald* story said, to get rid of the "civilian generals," then, Butler cautioned, Grant should know that his real enemies lurk in the regular army ranks. These are the scoundrels who begrudge Grant's success, and as he warned Rawlins, "they seek to throw off those of the volunteers who would be his friends." And for the letter's recipient, Butler, whose major general rank was in the volunteer army, had some advice: "Now, my dear Rawlins, look after those stupid fellows a little or they will do mischief to their chief. They have already circulated a story that General Grant has always been opposed to me, and that I have been thrust on him for political reasons, so, if possible, to get a personal issue between me and the General."[58]

Soon after the Fort Fisher fiasco, a second expedition was gotten up, with Brigadier General Alfred Terry to lead the army contingent. Rawlins ordered Michael Morgan, the commissary chief, to Fortress Monroe to prepare transports for carrying rations, fuel, and water. Rawlins warned Morgan to keep the troops' destination a secret—to say only they are on the way to Savannah. When Morgan returned, Rawlins asked him, "I suppose you know where the troops are going?" to which Morgan replied, "Yes, to Savannah."[59] The second expedition left on January 6, but heavy seas delayed offensive operations. After a thunderous two-day naval bombardment and an infantry assault, the fort fell on January 15. Confederate Vice President Alexander Stephens called Fisher's capitulation "one of the greatest disasters which had befallen [the Confederate] cause from the beginning of the war."[60] In two weeks, Stephens and two other Confederate emissaries would be at City Point on a peace initiative.

—◦◦◦—

Rawlins and others at headquarters tried to make the best of the holiday season. Rawlins was amused by a brief biographical sketch of himself that ran in a pre-Christmas issue of *Harper's Weekly* that correctly complimented him on his modest nature but inaccurately reported he had been wounded in battle.[61] The fall of Savannah on December 22 helped offset some of the perturbing news that would come later about the Fort Fisher expedition. Grant, Rawlins, Cadwallader, and Bowers spent a bittersweet Christmas Eve before a fire, reminiscing about home and happier times and smoking a passel of cigars.[62] There was a welcome cease-fire on January 1, allowing Lee's army to celebrate the New Year. But illness was ravaging headquarters. Most of the staff was sick, with Badeau and Horace Porter taking leaves. Grant suffered from digestive woes and an attack of hemorrhoids.[63] Shortly into the new year, spirits brightened with the arrival of wives: Julia Grant, Mary Cadwallader, and Emma Rawlins (whom John could not dissuade) along with daughter Jennie.

The wives quickly bonded. On occasion, Mary Lincoln visited City Point. She usually kept to herself in her stateroom on the *River Queen*, rarely venturing ashore. On Mrs. Lincoln's first visit in January, the trio of wives conferred regarding the propriety of calling on her on board her steamer. Because none had ever met her, it was decided Julia was the most appropriate to make the first overture. However, Julia was met with such a frosty reception that Mary Cadwallader and Emma never risked paying their own respects.[64]

On January 27, Rawlins accompanied Grant, General Schofield, and Assistant Secretary of the Navy Gustavus Fox on a trip to Fort Fisher. On their return four days later to City Point, they found waiting three Confederate commissioners ready to enter into peace negotiations. Alexander Stephens was joined by R. M. T. Hunter, a member of the Confederate Senate, and John Campbell, Jefferson Davis's assistant secretary of war. While officials at Washington decided how to respond, a hospitable Grant lodged them in well-appointed steamer staterooms and invited them to the officers' mess.[65] Julia even had an audience with the commissioners regarding the plight of her brother, a civilian and ironically a fervent secessionist, who had been captured in Louisiana and was being held in a Southern prison.[66] On February 3, Lincoln and William Seward met with the commissioners for several hours at Hampton Roads. Due to the commissioners' intransigence on the issues of the restoration of the Union and abolishment of slavery, the talks quickly broke down.

On February 22, headquarters welcomed a fresh assistant adjutant general when Captain Robert Todd Lincoln reported. Robert finally got his wish to serve in uniform, but in a fashion: as a member of Grant's staff, his safety was virtually assured, and that mitigated his parents' fears.[67] Horace Porter recalled, "The new acquisition to the company at headquarters soon became exceedingly popular. He had inherited many of the genial traits of his father, and entered heartily into all the social pastimes at headquarters."[68] No one appeared aggravated that young Lincoln requested a leave a week into his new job to attend his father's inauguration.

While arrangements were underway to bring Robert on board, there was a flow of correspondence regarding a promotion for Grant's chief of staff. On February 21, former staff officer William Duff wrote Grant that a bill had just been introduced in the House to provide the commander of the armies a chief of staff with the rank of brigadier general in the regular army. As Duff explained, "The bill was framed by friends of yours & Rawlings [sic] who believed that nothing would gratify you more than to have the opportunity . . . of complimenting & rewarding one whose services had been so valuable."[69] Grant quickly copied Washburne on Duff's letter and told the Congressman he would be "delighted" if the act passed Congress. "It would also," Grant added, "reward an officer who has won more deserved reputation in this war than any other who has acted throughout purely as a staff officer."[70] Because so many knew of the strong affiliation between Grant and Rawlins as expressed in these communications, almost all of their mutual friends were perplexed that Grant's *Memoirs* were virtually devoid of commendation or positive sentiment toward Rawlins.

On March 3, Washburne alerted Grant that the chief of staff bill had passed, and that same day Grant sent Stanton a recommendation for Rawlins's appointment.[71] Stanton was only too happy to comply. Within three hours of receiving the recommendation, he wired Grant, "The nomination of General Rawlins will be sent in immediately and with great pleasure."[72] Just days earlier, Grant had recommended that brevet commissions be conferred on most of his staff, including Rawlins as brevet major general in the regular army.[73]

Rawlins's March 3, 1865, appointment as brigadier general in the regular army was the last such made during the Civil War.[74]

NOTES

1. James Harrison Wilson, *The Life of John A. Rawlins* (New York: Neale, 1916), 261.

2. Horace Porter, *Campaigning with Grant* (New York: Century, 1897), 273.

3. George K. Leet to John A. Rawlins, September 15, 1864, Ulysses S. Grant Presidential Library, Mississippi State University, Series 3, Box 24, Folder 30. Leet also mentioned his encounter with Hillyer in a letter to William Rowley, now resigned from the army and returned to Galena. In this letter, Leet expressed his more honest and pessimistic feelings: "Col. Hillyer, whom I saw just as I was leaving Willards . . . says [Rawlins] is improving fast and will soon be well. I sincerely hope his predictions may be fulfilled, but fear the news is too good to be true." George K. Leet to William Rowley, September 18, 1864, Abraham Lincoln Presidential Library, William Rowley Papers, SC 1306.

4. Horace Porter, *Campaigning with Grant*, 287–93.

5. John Eaton, *Grant, Lincoln, and the Freedmen* (New York: Longmans, Green, 1907), 189.

6. M. R. Morgan, "From City Point to Appomattox with General Grant," *Journal of the Military Service Institution of the United States* 41 (September–October 1907): 235.

7. *Galena Daily Gazette*, July 20, 1864.

8. John A. Rawlins to Emma Rawlins, July 24, 1864, transcribed by J. H. Wilson, James H. Wilson Papers, Bender Collection, Wyoming State Archives and Historical Department, Microfilm Reel H-61a.

9. James Harrison Wilson, *The Life of John A. Rawlins*, 261.

10. Horace Porter, *Campaigning with Grant*, 314.

11. George K. Leet to William Rowley, October 22, 1864, Abraham Lincoln Presidential Library, William Rowley Papers, SC 1306.

12. Horace Porter, *Campaigning with Grant*, 314–15.

13. Ibid., 316.

14. John F. Marszalek, *Sherman: A Soldier's Passion for Order* (Carbondale: Southern Illinois University Press, 1993), 295.

15. U. S. Grant to W. T. Sherman, October 11, 1864, in *The War of the Rebellion: A Compilation of the Official Records of the Union and Confederate Armies*, series 1, part 3, 39:202.

16. John Y. Simon, ed., *The Papers of Ulysses S. Grant* (Carbondale: Southern Illinois University Press, 1984), 12:327–28.

17. William M. Lamers, *The Edge of Glory* (Baton Rouge: Louisiana State University Press, 1999), 427.

18. John A. Rawlins to Emma Rawlins, October 20, 1864, transcribed by J. H. Wilson, James H. Wilson Papers, Bender Collection, Wyoming State Archives and Historical Department, Microfilm Reel H-61a.

19. U. S. Grant to H. W. Halleck, August 29, 1864, in *The Papers of Ulysses S. Grant*, ed. John Y. Simon, 12:103.

20. U. S. Grant to J. A. Rawlins, October 29, 1864, in *The Papers of Ulysses S. Grant*, ed. John Y. Simon, 12:363–64.

21. U. S. Grant to W. T. Sherman, November 1, 1864, in *The Papers of Ulysses S. Grant*, ed. John Y. Simon, 12:370–71.

22. Ibid., 371–72n.

23. John Y. Simon, ed., *The Papers of Ulysses S. Grant*, 364–65n.

24. John A. Rawlins to Emma Rawlins, October 30, 1864, transcribed by J. H. Wilson, James H. Wilson Papers, Bender Collection, Wyoming State Archives and Historical Department, Microfilm Reel H-61a.

25. Rawlins was likely a patient of Dr. John Hancock Douglas, the most prominent throat specialist in New York City. Dr. Douglas later treated Grant's throat cancer; Ulysses S. Grant III, *Ulysses S. Grant: Warrior and Statesman* (New York: William Morrow, 1969), 434.

26. John Y. Simon, ed., *The Papers of Ulysses S. Grant*, 12:366–68n.

27. Adam Badeau, *Military History of Ulysses S. Grant* (New York: D. Appleton, 1881), 3:156.

28. U. S. Grant, *Personal Memoirs* (New York: Charles L. Webster, 1884), 2:376.

29. Ely Parker to J. C. Smith, February 15, 1887, Papers of Ely Parker, SC 1143, Abraham Lincoln Presidential Library, Springfield, IL.

30. A. H. Markland to W. T. Sherman, July 19, 1887, A. H. Markland Papers, Abraham Lincoln Presidential Library, Springfield, IL.

31. W. T. Sherman to A. H. Markland, July 23, 1887, A. H. Markland Papers, Abraham Lincoln Presidential Library, Springfield, IL.

32. William T. Sherman, "The Grand Strategy of the Last Year of the War," in *Battles and Leaders of the Civil War*, ed. Clarence C. Buel and Robert U. Johnson (1887; repr., New York: Thomas Yoseloff, 1956), 4:257n.

33. Sylvanus Cadwallader, *Three Years with Grant*, ed. Benjamin P. Thomas (New York: Alfred A. Knopf, 1961), 254.

34. James Harrison Wilson, *The Life of John A. Rawlins*, 274.

35. John M. Schofield, *Forty-Six Years in the Army* (New York: Century, 1897), 323.

36. Ibid., 326.

37. Benson Bobrick, *Master of War* (New York: Simon and Schuster, 2009), 267.

38. James Harrison Wilson, *The Life of John A. Rawlins*, 279.

39. John F. Marszalek, *Sherman's March to the Sea* (Abilene, TX: McWhiney Foundation, 2005), 122.

40. Stanley P. Hirshson, *The White Tecumseh* (New York: John Wiley and Sons, 1997), 247. In correspondence with James H. Wilson, Absalom Markland shared his belief that

"it is sheer nonsense to say that Rawlins would have gone to Mr. Lincoln, or Stanton, for the purpose of interfering with the plans of Sherman which had been approved by Grant." Markland shared the belief that Halleck was against the plan: "the fact is that it is more likely that Halleck opposed the march, went to City Point to prevail of Genl Grant to oppose it and failed then returned to Washington to intervene with Mr. Lincoln against it." Absalom H. Markland to James H. Wilson, August 10 and August 12, 1887, from Washington, DC, Wyoming State Archives, Bender Collection, James H. Wilson Papers, Microfilm Reel 61b.

41. E. M. Stanton to U. S. Grant, October 12, 1864, in *The War of the Rebellion: A Compilation of the Official Records of the Union and Confederate Armies*, series 1, part 3, 39:222.

42. U. S. Grant to J. A. Rawlins, November 19, 1864, in *The Papers of Ulysses S. Grant*, ed. John Y. Simon, 13:10–11.

43. J. A. Rawlins to U. S. Grant, November 20, 1864, in *The War of the Rebellion: A Compilation of the Official Records of the Union and Confederate Armies*, series 1, part 3, 42:666.

44. John A. Rawlins to Emma Rawlins, November 21, 1864, transcribed by J. H. Wilson, James H. Wilson Papers, Bender Collection, Wyoming State Archives and Historical Department, Microfilm Reel H-61a.

45. J. A. Rawlins to Emma, November 23, 1864. transcribed by J. H. Wilson, James H. Wilson Papers, Bender Collection, Wyoming State Archives and Historical Department, Microfilm Reel H-61a

46. U. S. Grant to Julia, November 25, 1864, in *The Papers of Ulysses S. Grant*, ed. John Y. Simon, 13:26.

47. John A. Rawlins to Emma Rawlins, November 25, 1864, transcribed by J. H. Wilson, James H. Wilson Papers, Bender Collection, Wyoming State Archives and Historical Department, Microfilm Reel H-61a.

48. Julia Dent Grant, *Personal Memoirs*, ed. John Y. Simon (New York: G. P. Putnam's Sons, 1975), 146.

49. John A. Rawlins to Emma Rawlins, December 1, 1864, transcribed by J. H. Wilson, James H. Wilson Papers, Bender Collection, Wyoming State Archives and Historical Department, Microfilm Reel H-61a.

50. U. S. Grant to H. W. Halleck, December 8, 1864, in *The Papers of Ulysses S. Grant*, ed. John Y. Simon, 13:83.

51. John A. Rawlins to Emma Rawlins, November 29, 1864, transcribed by J. H. Wilson, James H. Wilson Papers, Bender Collection, Wyoming State Archives and Historical Department, Microfilm Reel H-61a.

52. Horace Porter, *Campaigning with Grant*, 337–38.

53. Cyrus B. Comstock, *The Diary of Cyrus B. Comstock*, ed. Merlin E. Sumner (Dayton, OH: Morningside House, 1987), 299.

54. U. S. Grant to A. Lincoln, December 28, 1864, in *The War of the Rebellion: A Compilation of the Official Records of the Union and Confederate Armies*, series 1, part 3, 42:1087.

55. Grant to E. M. Stanton, January 4, 1865, in *The Papers of Ulysses S. Grant*, ed. John Y. Simon, 13:223; H. W. Halleck to U. S. Grant, January 7, 1865, in *The War of the Rebellion: A Compilation of the Official Records of the Union and Confederate Armies*, series 1, part 2, 46:60.

56. Sylvanus Cadwallader, *Three Years with Grant*, 272–74.

57. Benjamin F. Butler, *Butler's Book* (Boston: A. M. Thayer, 1892), 852.

58. Ibid., 1130.

59. M. R. Morgan, "From City Point to Appomattox with General Grant," *Journal of the Military Service Institution of the United States* 41 (September–October 1907): 241.

60. Rod Gragg, *Confederate Goliath: The Battle of Fort Fisher* (New York: HarperCollins, 1991), 243.

61. *Harper's Weekly* 8, no. 415 (December 10, 1864).

62. Sylvanus Cadwallader, *Three Years with Grant*, 279.

63. U. S. Grant to Julia, January 1, 1865, in *The Papers of Ulysses S. Grant*, ed. John Y. Simon, 13:203; U. S. Grant to Julia, December 24, 1864, in *The Papers of Ulysses S. Grant*, ed. John Y. Simon, 13:203.

64. Sylvanus Cadwallader, *Three Years with Grant*, 282–83.

65. Ron Chernow, *Grant* (New York: Penguin, 2017), 466.

66. Julia Dent Grant, *Personal Memoirs*, 138.

67. Jason Emerson, *Giant in the Shadows: The Life of Robert T. Lincoln* (Carbondale: Southern Illinois University Press, 2012), 90–91.

68. Horace Porter, *Campaigning with Grant*, 338–89.

69. John Y. Simon, ed., *The Papers of Ulysses S. Grant* (Carbondale: Southern Illinois University Press, 1985), 14:31n.

70. U. S. Grant to E. B. Washburne, February 23, 1865, in *The Papers of Ulysses S. Grant*, ed. John Y. Simon, 14:30–31.

71. E. B. Washburne to U. S. Grant, March 3, 1865, in *The War of the Rebellion: A Compilation of the Official Records of the Union and Confederate Armies*, series 1, part 2, 46:803; U. S. Grant to E. M. Stanton, March 3, 1865, in *The War of the Rebellion: A Compilation of the Official Records of the Union and Confederate Armies*, series 1, part 2, 46:801.

72. E. M. Stanton to U. S. Grant, March 3, 1865, in *The War of the Rebellion: A Compilation of the Official Records of the Union and Confederate Armies*, series 1, part 2, 46:801.

73. U. S. Grant to Edwin M. Stanton, February 22, 1865, in *The Papers of Ulysses S. Grant*, ed. John Y. Simon, 14:15. Apparently the letter requesting Rawlins's brevet appointment was inadvertently destroyed, causing Grant to send another recommendation on his behalf a year later; U. S. Grant to Edwin M. Stanton, May 8, 1866, in *The Papers of Ulysses S. Grant*, ed. John Y. Simon (Carbondale: Southern Illinois University Press, 1988), 16:187. A brevet was an honorary promotion for gallant conduct or meritorious service (often broadly defined) that was functionally meaningless: it did not entitle its conferee to an increase in pay or authority, nor did it allow the conferee to wear the brevet rank. On March 13, 1865, the War Department conferred brevet promotions on hundreds of officers. "That they [the conferring of brevets] were overdone cannot be denied," remarked one historian; Ezra J. Warner, *Generals in Blue: Lives of the Union Commanders* (Baton Rouge: Louisiana State University Press, 1992), xvii.

74. Ezra J. Warner, *Generals in Blue: Lives of the Union Commanders*, 392.

21

"I Think *That* Will Do"

THE RAWLINS FAMILY—JOHN, EMMA, AND daughter Jennie—spent the winter of 1865 transforming their wooden hut at City Point into a home. At the same time, Emma and Julia Grant were establishing a friendship, even sharing concerns about what they should do when separated from their husbands during the critical movements against Richmond.[1] The approach of spring brought distinguished visitors to headquarters. Elihu Washburne and wife arrived for a visit on March 10. He carried in a morocco case the gold medal replete "with suitable emblems, devices, and inscriptions" that Congress had authorized in honor of Grant's victory at Chattanooga.[2] In a small ceremony the next evening aboard the *Mary Martin*, Washburne made the presentation, and Grant followed with a two-sentence speech. Earlier that day, Rawlins had telegraphed General Ord to round up some officers to flesh out the crowd.[3] Washburne desired to extend his visit to include trips to the captured cities of Wilmington and Charleston and then return to Virginia to witness Lee's capitulation. Edwin Stanton followed and spent two days conferring with Grant. On invitation from Grant, Lincoln arrived on March 24 accompanied by Mary and son Tad. The president fraternized during the day with the troops; in the evenings, before a toasty campfire and liberated from the pressures of Washington, he entertained with his inexhaustible store of anecdotes.[4] On the twenty-seventh, Sherman came up from North Carolina, and the next day aboard the *River Queen*, he attended a strategy session with Grant, Lincoln, and Admiral Porter. Grant presented the key issue: that the crisis of the war was about to be played out as he planned to maneuver without delay around Lee's left flank and block his escaping into the Carolinas.[5]

Of course, in the midst of the deliberations and socializing, a war was going on. Just a week before arriving on the *River Queen*, Sherman had inflicted a crippling defeat against Joe Johnston's collection of military commands at Bentonville, North Carolina. During Lincoln's visit, Lee unleashed a stealth attack on a portion of the Federal line anchored by a fortification known as Fort Stedman. The Confederates opened a huge escape hole, but the Union's Ninth Corps, under John Parke, Burnside's replacement, regrouped and plugged the gap. In a few hours, Lee lost five thousand irreplaceable men in this, his last offensive gasp. Grant, sensing this was a desperation gambit by Lee, was eager to launch an aggressive move westward (to his left) to overlap Lee's right flank and thereby block his escape. Grant knew whom he wanted to spearhead that move: Phil Sheridan.

The plucky cavalryman swung into army headquarters early on March 26, and the first to greet him was John Rawlins. Rawlins was demonstrably overjoyed to see him: he pumped Sheridan's hands and clapped him on the back. The hearty welcome was no surprise to Sheridan, who knew Rawlins as "a man of strong likes and dislikes" and who exhibited "marked feelings when greeting any one." Sheridan had been absent over a month, operating toward the Shenandoah Valley, where he had mopped up the remnants of Early's troops while destroying infrastructure. He had just been a few days refitting and resting his cavalry.[6]

With greetings over, Rawlins had troubling news for him. Grant, Rawlins said, had resolved to send him and his cavalry south to join Sherman. Rawlins, using his characteristically vehement language, disagreed completely with this plan. It was not Sheridan's choice either. He knew the war was coming to an end, and "I desired my cavalry to be in at the death."[7] Rawlins showed the disappointed Sheridan into Grant's quarters. Grant got down to business. He intended to begin on the twenty-ninth a movement to his left against Lee. Grant's written instructions called for Sheridan "in a certain event" to cut loose from the Army of the Potomac, join Sherman to defeat Johnston, and then return to address Lee. As Sheridan dejectedly turned to leave, Grant intercepted him and said he really had no plans to release him—it was a "blind" or cover should the operation he planned not succeed. Not even Rawlins had been informed of this. When Sheridan broke this news to him, Rawlins "manifested the greatest satisfaction."[8]

After breakfast on the twenty-ninth, Grant, Rawlins, and the rest of the staff prepared to board the train connecting headquarters with the front, eighteen miles off. Their mounts, having been readied, were led onto a stock car. Emma Rawlins and Julia Grant, the latter a recipient of Ulysses's affectionate farewell kisses, came to see off their husbands on what Julia recalled was "a glorious and bright morning." These two friends, since moving out of their winter huts, were now quartered aboard Grant's dispatch boat moored in front of headquarters on the James River. President Lincoln was on hand, looking, in the estimation of Horace Porter, serious and careworn. Lincoln shook each officer's hand as he boarded the car. Rawlins, last in line, shared his fervent wish with the president: "I hope we shall have better luck now than we have had." Lincoln replied, "Well, your luck is my luck, and the country's—the luck of all of us—except the poor fellows who are killed. Success won't do them any good. They are the only ones not to be benefited by it."[9] As the train slowly pulled away, commanding general and staff doffed their hats to salute the president, who, in a voice constricted with emotion, answered back, "Good-by, gentlemen. God bless you all! Remember, your success is my success."[10]

Sheridan's cavalry struck out that morning with orders to destroy portions of the Danville and Southside Railroads that supplied Lee. Going was slow because roads were softening with the spring thaw. On the evening of the twenty-ninth, Sheridan stopped at Dinwiddie Court House, a hamlet of shabby houses and a dilapidated tavern propped up by poles. Dinwiddie was situated just beyond the far western reaches of the Union line on a road leading to the strategic crossroads town of Five Forks, about four miles north. That night Sheridan, much to his satisfaction, received a dispatch from Grant, who told him, "I now feel like ending the matter." He instructed Sheridan to abandon the raid on the railroads and in the morning get around the enemy and on to his right flank.[11] With rain lashing against the rickety tavern, Sheridan and his staff sheltered inside. So much for the glorious and bright day.

A few miles away, Grant, Rawlins, and staff set up headquarters camp in a cornfield near Gravelly Run. With rain beating on his tent, Rawlins wrote a letter to Emma. Despite the grueling ride and his precarious health, he was energized by the import of the moment. "Sheridan has reached Dinwiddie Court House," he updated her, "and everything is ready for an advance early in the morning." He eagerly awaited tomorrow's rapidly unfolding developments: "The General feels like making a heavy push for everything we have hoped for so long, and I am not slow in seconding such feelings." The man in whom John Rawlins invested so much devotion and trust was poised to subdue the vaunted Army of Northern Virginia.[12]

—◦◦◦—

The rain fell unabated overnight, turning roads into paste. On the morning of the thirtieth, Grant sent a dispatch to Sheridan in which he backed off from his aggressiveness of the day before: "The heavy rains of to-day will make it impossible for us to do much until it dries up a little or we get roads around our rear repaired." He suggested using the time to deliver forage for the horses.[13] Sheridan, spoiling for a fight, rode to Gravelly Run for clarification. While Sheridan was on his way, Grant and Rawlins shared their opinions about the state of operations before a campfire. As Horace Porter recollected, Rawlins fretted about problems caused by the weather: he warned that while the army was stuck in place, Joe Johnston might come up in its rear; also, the delay was allowing Lee to make dispositions to defend his right flank. It might be better, Porter heard Rawlins claim, to fall back and start fresh later.[14] Grant later echoed Porter, writing in his *Memoirs* that Rawlins "had urged very strongly that we return to our position about City Point and in the lines around Petersburg."[15] The claims that it was Rawlins pressing for withdrawal seem of questionable validity given his avid support the day before for making a "heavy push" against Lee. Moreover, Porter's and Grant's versions do not match Sheridan's.

According to Sheridan's very different recollection, on arrival he found Grant and Rawlins debating whether operations should be temporarily suspended. Sheridan heard Rawlins making heated arguments against such a proposition. Grant, who was used to such boisterousness from his chief of staff, seemed to dismiss it by remarking, "Well, Rawlins, I think you had better take command." Not wishing to intrude on their debate, Sheridan ducked into the tent of Rufus Ingalls, where Grant found him a few minutes later and began agonizing about the "fearful plight" caused by the rain. It appeared necessary to suspend operations, he lamented—not that he wanted to, but because complaints about the impassable roads had swayed his opinion. Sheridan would hear none of this; he insisted that regardless of the weather, his cavalry, with a corps of infantry, could seize Five Forks and collapse Lee's right.[16] Sheridan's resolve reinvigorated Grant, and he ordered him to move against Five Forks.

Lee knew the strategic importance of Five Forks and had dispatched General George Pickett there with two infantry divisions and cavalry. After spirited fighting on the thirty-first, Sheridan was bursting with confidence and eager to take the initiative on the morrow. "We at last have drawn the enemy's infantry out of its fortifications," he told Horace Porter, "and this is our chance to attack it."[17] On April 1, Porter was under Grant's orders to attach himself to Sheridan and send progress bulletins every half hour. There was some holdup into the afternoon getting Warren's Fifth Corps divisions into position. However, momentum was building against Pickett throughout the day as evidenced by Porter's 2:00 p.m. dispatch to Rawlins: "The whole 5th Corps is now moving from here up to Five Forks & Gen. S. will attack the enemy with every thing . . . All are in excellent spirits and eager to go in."[18] At 4:00 p.m., Sheridan's attack formation was set, and the fight to overwhelm Pickett's entrenched position began. The combination of Sheridan's dismounted cavalry and Warren's infantry engulfed the Confederate line. The division led by Brigadier General Romeyn Ayres was at the point of attack, and "with fixed bayonets and a rousing cheer dashed over the earth-works, sweeping everything before them, and killing or capturing every man in their immediate front whose legs had not saved him."[19] Within three hours, Pickett had conceded Lee's right flank to Sheridan and the Union army. Once the Five Forks domino toppled, Petersburg and Richmond were fatally exposed.

Porter, eager to report the stunning victory, dashed back to headquarters, where he found Grant and most of the staff around a crackling campfire. As Porter broke the good news, everyone but Grant began celebrating. While the staff vented their excitement, Grant stepped into his tent to write several telegraph dispatches. When he rejoined the celebrants, he offhandedly remarked, "I have ordered an immediate assault along the lines."[20]

Rawlins reveled in Sheridan's "glorious victory," which he attributed to the fact that "the Lieutenant General has commanded in it himself and not permitted the spirit or, I might say, the genius of his orders, to be dampened by his *subordinate Commander*."[21] Rawlins was expressing his agreement with Grant's discontinuing the formality of sending orders through Meade. Now Grant was taking charge. There would be no delay in transmitting orders, no distortion of those orders as they moved along the chain of command.

———

Toward dawn a booming cannonade preceded the concentrated assault against the undermanned Confederate Petersburg works. The Federal Second, Sixth, and Ninth Corps burst through the Rebel lines, and by noon virtually all of the outer ring of defenses was in Union hands. To the west, Sheridan hit Lee's extreme right at Sutherland Station on the Southside Railroad, the last rail line to Petersburg from the south. Grant, accompanied by staff, ventured into the captured Petersburg fortifications and marveled at their intricacy. Awed by what had just been accomplished, Grant penned a letter to Julia, calling the morning's advances "one of the greatest victories of the war."[22] With circumstances turning so favorable, Grant invited Lincoln to drop down from City Point.

To save the remnants of his evaporating army, Lee began evacuating Petersburg late that evening—it would be formally surrendered early on April 3—and hoping to escape to the west. Jefferson Davis, his wife, and several of his cabinet were already aboard a special train bound for Danville, Virginia. Major General Godfrey Weitzel, a German American West Pointer, would soon occupy Davis's office in the Confederate Executive Mansion while his infantry corps, consisting mostly of African American troops, patrolled Richmond's streets.

Grant and Rawlins rode into Petersburg about 9:00 a.m. and were met by the president accompanied by his two sons. Lincoln sought out Grant and reached for his hand, "shaking it for some time, and pouring out his thanks and congratulations with all the fervor of a heart which seemed overflowing with its fullness of joy."[23] Lincoln spoke about dealing softly with the rebellious states, but there was little time for details. The race was on to overtake the Army of Northern Virginia. Grant and his retinue of staff camped on the night of April 3 at Sutherland Station, about nine miles west of Petersburg. Lee's retreating columns were spread out north of the pursuing Federals. The Confederates' objective was Amelia Court House thirty-five miles west of Petersburg and situated on the Richmond and Danville Railroad. There, they hoped to find a trainload of food and a rail connection to link with Joe Johnston.

Rawlins anticipated only a few hours of sleep. The war was morphing into a footrace, and the actors were rushing toward a climax whose outcome was hourly becoming more certain. There was hardly time for sleep and no excuse for fatigue. Despite the fatal illness incubating inside him, Rawlins felt unexpectedly energized. He yearned to see the job through, to celebrate the triumph of patriotism over sedition. As the last of Grant's original staff, as his collaborator during historic campaigns, as the friend who counseled his chief out of harm's way, John Rawlins was resolved to bear witness to the ceremony that ended this war.

On April 4, Rawlins encamped at Wilson's Station, having covered nine-teen miles that day. He wrote Emma that the "excitement of victory" was prov-ing a boon for his health. He also revisited the issue of Grant pondering the suspension of operations. "The decision of the General not to let Lee rest is a wise one," he told her. "I had feared he might not so decide but all is well now."[24] Rawlins's satisfaction was probably enhanced by his knowledge of a dispatch Grant sent to Sheridan that same evening. Grant alerted him that Lee was reportedly heading toward Farmville, a town on the Southside Rail-road well west of Amelia Court House by thirty miles, where supplies awaited him. Now, Grant urged Sheridan to intercept Lee at Farmville.[25]

When Lee's columns arrived at Amelia Court House on April 4, they found railcars containing ammunition but no food, thereby causing Lee a day's de-lay. That gave Sheridan the opportunity to tear up the tracks of the Richmond and Danville at Jetersville, about ten miles southwest of Amelia Court House. With the rail connection shattered, Lee would be forced further westward to find food and an escape route. His next logical destination was Farmville on the Southside Railroad, which led out to Lynchburg.

By dusk on April 5, Grant, Rawlins, and their small party had put in a full day in the saddle, covering twenty miles. They were a few miles east of Burke-ville, almost due south of Jetersville, where Sheridan was headquartered, when two of Sheridan's scouts arrived with a message from him. The message had been written on tissue paper, and to elude discovery, the tissue was folded into a tinfoil pellet, and the pellet tucked into a chaw of tobacco lodged in one of the scout's cheek. "I feel confident of capturing the Army of Northern Va. if we exert ourselves. I see no escape for Lee," Sheridan wrote. He added, "I wish you were here yourself."[26]

This was the invitation Grant hoped for, but he first checked with Rawlins. "What do you think of it?" he asked. "It looks well," Rawlins replied, "but you know Sheridan is always a little sanguine."[27] That was all the endorsement he needed. Grant and Rawlins selected fresh mounts and, without waiting for dinner, struck out northward with a party that included Horace Porter, a small escort, and the scouts as guides. The ride to Jetersville was through open coun-try, requiring them to regard road junctions and farmhouses as possible am-bush sites. About 11:00 p.m. they reached Sheridan's headquarters in a small log cabin set in a tobacco patch.[28] A dinner of chicken and beef rejuvenated Rawlins, and afterward Sheridan launched into profanity-laced descriptions of how he planned to snare Lee. Grant and party left around midnight to over-night at Meade's nearby camp.

The next day, April 6, Sheridan came close to delivering on his word. At Sayler's Creek west of Jetersville, he pounced on Richard Ewell's corps, in-flicting about two thousand battle casualties and capturing six thousand pris-oners. Sheridan bragged he had routed the Rebels "handsomely" and even captured six generals, including Ewell and Lee's eldest son, Custis. Sheridan could sense Lee's desperation. "If the thing is pressed," he added, "I think Lee will surrender."[29] The remnant of the Army of Northern Virginia fled west six miles to Farmville, where it hoped to find provisions. Later in the day, Grant, Rawlins, and Porter headed south to overnight near Burkeville.

Continuing their trek among the pursuing Union forces, Grant and Rawl-ins arrived at Farmville just before noon on April 7, mere hours after Lee had left. They commandeered a hotel, since stripped of furniture, for headquar-ters. Reports regarding the rapid military developments convinced Grant time had come to confront Lee with the inevitable. At 5:00 p.m., he composed a letter that began, "The result of the last week must convince you of the hope-lessness of further resistance on the part of the Army of Northern Va, in this struggle."[30] Brigadier General Seth Williams, Grant's adjutant general, was to take it to Lee under a truce flag. As he trotted in the enclosing darkness toward the Confederate lines, he was shot at and nearly hit, but he delivered the letter. Lee's response arrived after midnight. Although not yet ready to surrender his army, he was curious to learn "the terms you will offer on condition of its surrender."[31]

As the two commanders nudged negotiations forward, Seth Williams re-turned on the eighth with Grant's response: "In reply I would say that *peace* being my great desire there is but one condition I insist upon, namely: that the men and officers surrendered shall be disqualified for taking up arms again, against the Government of the United States, until properly exchanged."[32] While awaiting Lee's rejoinder, Grant and Rawlins, crossing to the north side of the Appomattox River, rode with the columns headed toward Appomattox Station, where Lee expected a trainload of provisions. It was there that the pursuit planned to intercept him and block his flight. The eighth was mostly devoid of hostile musket fire, a godsend for Grant, who suffered a wincingly se-vere migraine. Rawlins set up headquarters in the Clifton House, deserted by its owners but harboring a few servants. After dinner, Grant was treated with mustard plasters, a remedy thought to act as a counterirritant when applied to parts of the body such as the nape of the neck.[33] However, these blistering poultices provided no relief.

Grant and Rawlins claimed the lone bed upstairs, and the staff slept on the parlor floor. Around midnight, jangling spurs and a clanking saber heralded the delivery of a critical dispatch. The staff in the parlor strained to catch the news. Porter provided a candle while Rawlins unsealed the dispatch and, in his rich voice, read it loud enough for all to hear:

> GENERAL: I received at a late hour your note of to-day. In mine of yesterday I did not intend to propose the surrender of the Army of Northern Virginia, but to ask the terms of your proposition. To be frank, I do not think the emergency has arisen to call for the surrender of this army; but as the restoration of peace should be the sole object of all, I desired to know whether your proposals would lead to that end. I cannot, therefore, meet with you with a view to surrender the Army of Northern Virginia; but as far as your proposal may affect the C. S. forces under my command, and tend to the restoration of peace, I shall be pleased to meet you at 10 a.m. to-morrow on the old stage-road to Richmond, between the picket-lines of the two armies.
>
> *Very respectfully, your obedient servant,*　　　　　　　　R. E. Lee, General[34]

Rawlins took umbrage at Lee's seemingly disingenuous parry. "He did not propose to surrender," Rawlins snapped. "He now wants to entrap us into making a treaty of peace." Rawlins was focused on what looked like a clever ploy by Lee, and he delivered a lusty denunciation: "Now he wants to arrange for peace—something beyond and above the surrender of his army—something to embrace the whole Confederacy, if possible. No Sir! No Sir. Why it is a positive insult; and an attempt in an underhanded way, to change the whole terms of the correspondence."

Rawlins, in his touchy manner, was taking Grant to school, reminding him that his job was strictly a military one: negotiating peace terms was beyond his purview. It was only a month ago, Rawlins added, after the Confederate commissioners had tried to bargain for peace, that Lincoln, through Stanton, had explicitly directed Grant to have no conference with Lee unless it dealt with his surrender or other "purely military matter."[35] And to Lee's brazen claim that his situation had not yet risen to an emergency, Rawlins scoffed, "That emergency has been staring him in the face for forty-eight hours. If he hasn't seen it yet, we will soon bring it to his comprehension! He has to surrender. He shall surrender. By the eternal, it shall be surrender, and nothing else."

Grant let Rawlins air himself out and then calmly put the situation into a more indulgent perspective. "Lee was only trying to be let down easily," Grant countered. "Some allowance must be made for the trying position in which General Lee is placed. He is compelled to defer somewhat to the wishes of his government, and his military associates. But it all means perfectly the same thing. If I meet Lee, he will surrender before I leave."[36]

Following this exchange, Porter and Rawlins withdrew, allowing the pain-wracked Grant some rest. After breakfast at Meade's headquarters, Grant sent to Lee a toned-down reply. "As I have no authority to treat on the subject of peace the meeting proposed for 10 a.m. to-day could lead to no good. I will state however General that I am equally anxious for peace with yourself and the whole North entertains the same feeling. The terms upon which peace can be had are well understood. By the South laying down their Arms they will hasten that most desirable event, save thousands of human lives and hundreds of Millions of property not yet destroyed."[37] With this letter dispatched, Rawlins accompanied Grant on a ride to meet Sheridan, who was taking possession of Lee's supplies at Appomattox Station. Lee's emergency had arisen.

Just before noon on the ninth, one of Meade's staff, Lieutenant Charles Pease, overtook Grant and Rawlins as they were eight or nine miles east of Appomattox Court House. Pease handed Grant an urgent dispatch from Lee, who wished to know Grant's mind regarding surrender terms. After reading the dispatch, he handed it to his chief of staff: "Here, General Rawlins." Rawlins's black eyes scanned the lines and then riveted on Lee's last sentence: "I now ask an interview, in accordance with the offer contained in your letter of yesterday, for that purpose." With an almost undetectable smile, Grant asked, "Well how do you think that will do?" To which Rawlins replied, "I think *that* will do."[38] After conversing a few minutes with Rawlins, Grant composed his reply:

GENERAL,

Your note of this date is but this moment, 11.50 a.m. rec'd. in consequence of my having passed from the Richmond and Lynchburg road to the Farmville & Lynchburg road. I am at this writing about four miles West of Walker's Church and will push forward to the front for the purpose of meeting you. Notice sent to me on this road where you wish the interview to take place will meet me.

Very respectfully your obedient servant

U. S. GRANT
Lieutenant General[39]

Aide-de-camp Babcock, accompanied by Captain William Dunn, was chosen to take this document to Lee. Babcock and Dunn were among several staff who performed important but easily overlooked tasks during these hours at Appomattox.

After finding Lee resting by an apple tree one-half mile beyond Appomattox Court House, Babcock followed Lee and his aide, Lieutenant Colonel Charles Marshall, into the small town. It consisted of a square, the courthouse, and an assortment of homes, the stateliest being the brick McLean House, which was bordered by blooms of roses, violets, and daffodils and featured a flight of wide steps ascending to a spacious porch. Wilmer McLean allowed the esteemed officers the use of his parlor for their historic meeting. Grant arrived at 1:30 and found the three earlier arrivals waiting for him. Ord, Sheridan, Rawlins, and the rest of the generals and staff mingled outside until Babcock waved them in.

After some restrained socializing, Grant commenced drafting in pencil the surrender terms Lee reviewed and to which he recommended minor revisions. While the surrender document was being copied in ink, Grant presented his staff to Lee. Horace Porter noticed Lee's surprise on being introduced to the swarthy Ely Parker.[40] Lieutenant Colonel Theodore Bowers, who had ridden in that morning from Burkeville, was handed the copying job, but he was so rattled by the magnitude of the moment that he gave up after several tries. The task fell to Parker, he of the elegant handwriting. Coming to the topic of Lee's famished army, Grant directed Chief Commissary Morgan to issue them twenty-five thousand rations. On a small oval table, Grant signed the terms of surrender document, and Lee, sitting at a marble-topped table, signed the letter of acceptance. After final pleasantries, including the scheduling of a more private meeting between Lee and Grant the next morning, Babcock accompanied Lee and Marshall to their picket line. The momentous ceremony was over by 4:00 p.m.

Rawlins helped set up a very temporary headquarters camp near the McLean house, toward which Grant repaired after the meeting. But before he had gone very far, staff reminded him to share the earth-shaking news with Washington. Adam Badeau supplied the order book, and Grant, putting pencil to paper, informed Stanton that Lee had just surrendered. It was 4:30 p.m. After dinner, Grant expressed his desire to depart for City Point the next day after meeting Lee. There would be no time for staff to gawk at the remnants of the Army of Northern Virginia or fraternize with the erstwhile enemy.

Toward 10:00 a.m. the next day, Lee and Grant met on a slight elevation overlooking the camps of the armies. They conversed while mounted, with Grant's staff forming a semicircle behind him out of hearing range. Parker, as military secretary, remained at Grant's side in the event that, as the generals ironed out details, he would be ready to write orders.[41] One of Grant's aims was to encourage Lee to persuade the remaining Confederate armies to surrender. After conferring for about one-half hour, the generals tipped their hats in farewell. Lee rejoined his army while Grant headed to the McLean house, where he waited on the porch before embarking on the trip to City Point.

And that was how it ended. It is remarkable that a war preceded by angry, volatile invective concluded almost sotto voce. It is remarkable that a war that forever linked certain oddly named, unfamiliar locations—Chickamauga, Shiloh, Iuka, Spotsylvania—with incomprehensible violence would yield at its finish another of those strange-sounding places, Appomattox, and associate it with peace. It was a war that began for John Rawlins almost four years earlier to the day when he inspired the crowd at the Galena Court House with his incendiary rhetoric: "We will stand by the flag of our country, and appeal to the god of battles!" Now, he saddled his horse for a ride to Burkeville to catch the train that would return him to City Point.

—◦◦◦—

The headquarters staff left Appomattox during the afternoon of the tenth and, due to delays, did not reach Prospect Station, a stop on the Southside Railroad, until dark. A hearty dinner and campfire compensated for the muddy ground on which their tents were pitched. Elihu Washburne surprised Rawlins and Grant when he arrived at the station at 10:00 p.m.—a day late for Lee's surrender—on his way to the front. After spending the night sharing Grant's tent, Washburne left for Appomattox Court House protected by a cavalry escort. Grant's party continued on, and at Burkeville on the afternoon of the eleventh, they boarded a special train for City Point. Because the rail bed was in disrepair, cars jumped the track on three occasions, no doubt alarming Rawlins, who had escaped serious injury in such an accident. The sixty-mile trip to City Point took twelve hours.

Meanwhile at City Point, news of the surrender reached the wives. They thrilled to hear vessels on the James River tooting whistles in celebration. An excited Emma Rawlins took Julia's hands and exclaimed, "Are you not delighted that you did not go north when the General wanted you to? Now we will have the happiness of returning with our heroes." Because dispatches had announced that the "heroes" would be in time for a late dinner, Julia told the captain of the *Mary Martin* to prepare for as many guests as could be accommodated. Emma and Julia, along with the chief commissary's wife, Mrs. Morgan, after primping for dinner, assembled in the steamer's saloon and embraced each other while proclaiming, "Only think, the war is over, and General Grant is the victorious general!"[42] Unaware of the husbands' travel delays, the wives amused themselves playing the piano and waltzing with each other. After waiting until 4:00 a.m., they retired to their cabins but were awakened a few hours later when the party from the front arrived. The celebratory dinner now became breakfast.

The Rawlinses joined the Grants and other officers on the *Mary Martin* for a jaunt to Washington, arriving there on the sunny morning of the thirteenth. The brilliant blue skies served as a backdrop for a city festooned in bunting and reverberating with pealing bells and cannon salvos. There was an evening reception for Grant at Stanton's residence with handshaking and speechifying that carried into the late hours.

The next morning, Good Friday, Grant had a meeting with the president and cabinet. Julia implored him to return early enough so they could start that evening for Burlington, New Jersey, where their children attended school. As Julia recollected, around noon there was a knock on the Grant's Willard Hotel room door. An unsavory man, claiming to be a messenger from Mary Lincoln, told Julia of a theater invitation and to expect a call at 8:00 p.m. Taken aback by his sinister looks and discourtesy, Julia replied she and the general would not be in the city and therefore unable to accompany the president and first lady.

Perhaps two hours later, Julia and son Jesse joined Emma Rawlins and daughter Jennie for luncheon at a restaurant. After being seated, a quartet of men took a table opposite them. Julia seemed certain one of them was the suspicious messenger. A pale, dark-haired member of their party appeared too interested in what Julia and Emma were discussing. More strangely, he fiddled with his soupspoon, lifting it toward his mouth but never tasting it. Julia whispered to Emma, "Be careful, but observe the men opposite to us and tell me what you think." Mrs. Rawlins glanced at them and replied, "Since you called my attention, I believe there is something peculiar about them." Julia guessed they were John Mosby's partisan rangers, and she shuddered. "I believe there will be an outbreak tonight or soon. I just feel it, and am glad I am going away tonight." Not long thereafter, the dark-haired man, riding a black horse, made a pass close by the carriage carrying the Grants to the train depot. Julia was quite certain that the interloper was John Wilkes Booth.[43]

That evening, Booth enacted his assassination plot. Many struggled to comprehend this heinous crime. Stanton could hardly reconcile a now lifeless president with the one who had displayed a buoyant attitude at that day's cabinet meeting. He remarked how Lincoln on that morning seemed to be "more cheerful and happy than I had ever seen."[44] A disbelieving Phil Sheridan needed confirmation of the terrible news reaching him near Appomattox. "Is the reported assassination of President Lincoln and Secretary Seward, which reached here last night, true?" he inquired. Rawlins tersely replied, "The reported assassination of President Lincoln is true. He died yesterday morning at 7.22. His murderer is supposed to be J. Wilkes Booth, who is still at large."[45]

—⁓—

Despite the heavy gloom pervading Washington, the work of the government and its military moved forward. On the sixteenth, Stanton removed Henry Halleck as army chief of staff—thereby vacating the position for John Rawlins—and assigned him to Richmond to command the Military Division of the James. This was a time of crushing demands on both Grant and Rawlins. Grant's headquarters needed to be established at Washington, necessitating the transfer and consolidation of records. With the advent of peace, Grant undertook to shrink the armies to reduce strain on the US Treasury. Moreover, Grant began drafting his official report of the army operations since March 1864 that culminated in Lee's surrender. Rawlins, assisted by Ely Parker and George Leet, supplied him with facts, dates, and correspondence to flesh out the report. A draft was submitted to Stanton on June 20.[46]

In North Carolina, William Sherman was negotiating surrender terms with Joe Johnston. In the process, Sherman was also stipulating the terms under which the seceded states could be brought back into the Union. For example, under the agreement, the Rebels' weapons, instead of being confiscated, would be deposited in state arsenals. Moreover, once state legislators took oaths of allegiance, their existing state governments could be recognized; and Sherman's terms allowed for federal courts to be reopened. Unaware he had far exceeded his authority, Sherman was proud of the magnanimous features of the agreement, believing they would secure peace and facilitate reunification. When informed of the agreement's lenient terms, Stanton regarded them as dangerous concessions and broke everything to the papers. A blindsided

Sherman was raked over the coals of public opinion. Grant went to Raleigh to give support to his old friend and provided a steady presence when a second surrender agreement with Johnston was finalized.[47]

Sherman raged against Stanton's treatment of him—branding the Secretary "a mean, scheming, vindictive politician" to a group of his generals—and harbored hostility for years.[48] To Rawlins, he defended his decision to let the South down easy: "The South is broken and ruined, and appeals to our pity. To ride the people down with persecutions and military exactions would be like slashing away at the crew of a sinking ship." And Sherman got in a dig at Stanton: "I have no hesitation in pronouncing Mr. Stanton's compilation of April 22 a gross outrage on me, which I will resent in time."[49]

A month later, Sherman and Stanton crossed paths during the Grand Review of Union troops in Washington, a massive two-day victory march on May 23 and 24. The twenty-fourth was reserved for Sherman's western troops to parade before the crowds and pass in review of President Andrew Johnson and the cabinet. On the twenty-second, Sherman's men had completed the trek from North Carolina and were bivouacked across the Potomac. He announced his arrival in a bitter note to Rawlins: "Know that Vandal Sherman is encamped near the Canal Bridge half way between the Long Bridge & Alexandria to the west of the Road, where his friends if any can find him. Though in disgrace he is untamed and unconquered."[50] With "Black Jack" Logan at the head of Rawlins's beloved Army of the Tennessee, Sherman rode along wearing a corps badge presented to him by Logan. When Sherman reached the reviewing stand, he strode up the stairs and shook hands with Johnson, Grant, and all the cabinet members—except Stanton. When the secretary of war extended his hand, Sherman refused it and gained a morsel of revenge.[51]

With the Confederacy's armies capitulating during April and May, Grant cast his eyes southwestwardly to tensions brewing in Mexico. In 1862, the French propped up a puppet regime in Mexico and installed Ferdinand Maximilian at the head of the government, supplanting a democratically elected Benito Juarez. Not only were the French defying the Monroe Doctrine thereby, but during the war they had maintained a cozy relationship with the Confederate government. Grant regarded France's intervention in Mexican affairs as an act of hostility against the United States. In June he wrote President Johnson, "Rebels in arms have been allowed to take refuge on Mexican soil protected by French bayonets."[52] In fact, a throng of former Confederate politicians and generals—among the latter such Grant nemeses as Jubal Early,

Sterling Price, and John Pemberton—had fled below the border to find sanctuary. Grant favored a quick military strike to restore Mexico's rightful government, and to spearhead this strike, he turned to his most aggressive general, Phil Sheridan. Sheridan was in agreement with Grant about the political situation, and he found a sympathetic ear in Rawlins, who felt the French were violating the Monroe Doctrine. Sheridan also disclosed in a wire to Rawlins, "My own opinion is and has been that Maximilian should leave the country and that his establishment there was a part of the rebellion."[53] Moreover, as he told Rawlins in a personal letter, he looked forward to leading the military incursion: "I hope that I may have the pleasure of crossing the Rio Grande with [the cavalry columns] with our faces turned toward the city of Mexico."[54]

Grant's military solution to the problem was checked by Secretary of State Seward's preference for a diplomatic one. Seward's choice proved prudent and correct: Maximilian's reign ended two years later, before a firing squad of Juarez loyalists.

By the summer of 1865, an accumulation of stress—the fallout over Sherman's surrender gaffe, the weight of paperwork, the trauma of the assassination, tensions over Mexico—put Rawlins in need of distance from Washington. Besides the desire for recuperation, Rawlins also wanted to consolidate his family. It was time for him and Emma to return to Galena and reunite daughter Jennie with her siblings, Emily and James, who stayed with their grandparents. John Rawlins's Galena visit would precede Grant's by seven weeks.

—◆◆◆—

John Rawlins arrived in Galena on Friday, June 30, to a warm welcome. The local paper boasted, "He has come back famous, with the reputation of being one of the most complete military geniuses that the exigencies of war has developed." That adulation was followed by an appeal: "May [the pure air of Jo Daviess] invigorate his health, as it did in boyhood." The paper's references to his health were not only frequent, but some had ominous undertones.[55] A few days later, the *Gazette* declared, "Gen. Rawlins is enjoying the quiet luxury of his early home among the beautiful green hills of Jo Daviess. His health does not appear to be perfect but if the occasion demanded, we think he might break down a dozen strong men in another campaign through the wilderness. . . . The man whom Lt. Gen. Grant selected as his Adjutant General, and whom he kept close by his side all through the war, can be no ordinary character. . . . May his health improve as his labors lighten and may his life be long and happy."[56]

He kept a low profile on his parents' farm in order to reconstitute his health. Two weeks after he arrived, over a hundred of Rawlins's "friends and neighbors" drafted a letter requesting his presence at a public dinner; signees included Dr. Kittoe, William Rowley, J. C. Spare, and his former mentor, Isaac Stevens. The *Gazette* reported that Rawlins declined the dinner: "We regret that his health demands the caution referred to." Rawlins finally ventured into Galena on July 22. His condition appeared improved due to, the *Gazette* claimed, "rest, pure air, and he is in the best of spirits." The Rawlinses departed Jo Daviess County for the east on July 27.[57]

Hours after their departure, the Galena townspeople began preparations to receive General and Mrs. Grant. They had left Washington on July 24 for a tour that would take them up the East Coast, into Canada, and westward to Chicago and Galena. Eager Galenians formed a Committee of Arrangements in order to organize the gala reception. That committee met on the twenty-eighth and begat a host of subcommittees—Music, Banners and Flags, Street Decorations, Carriages, Fireworks, and others—to attend to the hundreds of details. The marshal for the day would be William Rowley.[58]

As a special train from Chicago chugged into Galena at 3:00 p.m. on August 18, a cannon volley signaled its arrival, and an estimated crowd of twenty-five thousand burst into shouts and wagged flags. Galena's former humble citizen was returned a conqueror! A "Triumphal Arch" had been erected in front of the De Soto House hotel, where Ulysses was joined by wife, Julia; father, Jesse; and aides Badeau and Babcock. Elihu Washburne's brief speech extended Grant "a cordial and affectionate welcome to your home." The congressman lavished praise on his favorite general, even managing a wobbly pun: "And when you poured your leaden hail into the rebels, it is no wonder they thought you *hailed* from the 'Galena Lead Mines' where the people *sell* that product in time of peace, but *give* it away in time of war." From 7:30 to 8:30 p.m., the Grants were given a reception at the post office, followed by fireworks. Houses across town were illuminated, bonfires blazed, and "music and dancing testified to the common joy."[59] The highlight of the visit occurred when Grant was bestowed with a furnished home on Bouthillier Street, purchased for $2,500 by some of the prominent citizens.

This was now the second house gifted to the Grants. The Union League of Philadelphia had recently presented him with an elegant, furnished residence on Chestnut Street. This set up a conflict of loyalties that caused Washburne much consternation. In mid-May, he wrote Grant a confidential letter that expressed how his Galena friends could feel betrayed: "The acceptance of the house in Philadelphia, and your removal into it, together with the impudent claim set up by the Philadelphia newspapers that you have taken up your permanent residence there and become a citizen of Pennsylvania, has created great uneasiness not only among your Galena friends but the people of the State, generally."[60] Grant hastily replied, offering Washburne an evasive apology and a qualified promise to make Galena, at least, his voting address, "never casting a vote elsewhere without first giving notice."[61]

After taking possession of the Philadelphia house, Julia performed an attic-to-cellar inspection. To her alarm, she discovered the house came with a large stock of rare wines and liquors. Unsure what to do with it, she discreetly sought Rawlins's advice. "Send for some responsible broker, or commission dealer, in such commodities," he instructed her, "have him dispose the entire stock at once; and put the money in your pocket."[62]

—◦◦◦—

After Rawlins returned with his family to Washington, he sent Grant a newsy personal letter—closing as "your friend"—that would have reached him just as he arrived in Galena. He was "taking things quite leisurely," he told Grant, and working only about four hours a day. He shared some good news regarding his health: the New York doctors had assured him his lungs were "sound," and he was feeling "as well as usual." However, something ghastly was embedded in between—an admission that the day before, he had "considerable bleeding of the throat."[63]

Grant penned a quick reply. He regretted that he had not written Rawlins earlier, inviting him to stay in Galena as long as needed to benefit his health. Now he insisted that Rawlins spend fall and winter there too—in his recently gifted home. "You will find it very comfortable and containing everything necessary for housekeeping," he wrote Rawlins.[64] One friend to another.

NOTES

1. John Y. Simon, ed., *The Personal Memoirs of Julia Dent Grant* (New York: G. P. Putnam's Sons, 1975), 148.

2. Mark Washburne, *A Biography of Elihu Benjamin Washburne: Congressman, Secretary of State, Envoy Extraordinary* (self-pub., Xlibris, 2001), 444–45.

3. John Y. Simon, *The Papers of Ulysses S. Grant* (Carbondale: Southern Illinois University Press, 1985), 14:132n.

4. Horace Porter, "Lincoln and Grant," *The Century Illustrated Monthly Magazine* 30, no. 6 October 1885): 943.

5. Horace Porter, *Campaigning with Grant* (New York: Century, 1897), 423.

6. Horace Porter, *Campaigning with Grant*, 411; P. H. Sheridan, *Personal Memoirs* (New York: Charles L. Webster, 1888), 2:126.

7. P. H. Sheridan, *Personal Memoirs*, 119.

8. U. S. Grant, *Personal Memoirs* (New York: Charles L. Webster, 1885), 2:436–38; P. H. Sheridan, *Personal Memoirs*, 2:129.

9. Albert D. Richardson, *Personal History of Ulysses S. Grant* (Boston: D. L. Guernsey, 1885), 467.

10. Horace Porter, *Campaigning with Grant*, 424–25; John Y. Simon, ed., *The Personal Memoirs of Julia Dent Grant*, 149.

11. U. S. Grant to Philip H. Sheridan, March 29, 1865, in *The Papers of Ulysses S. Grant*, ed. John Y. Simon, 14:253.

12. John A. Rawlins to Emma Rawlins, March 29, 1865, transcribed by J. H. Wilson, James H. Wilson Papers, Bender Collection, Wyoming State Archives and Historical Department, Microfilm Reel H-61a.

13. U. S. Grant to Philip H. Sheridan, March 30, 1865, in *The Papers of Ulysses S. Grant*, ed. John Y. Simon, 14:269.

14. Horace Porter, *Campaigning with Grant*, 425–26.

15. U. S. Grant, *Personal Memoirs*, 2:438.

16. P. H. Sheridan, *Personal Memoirs*, 2:144–45.

17. Horace Porter, "Five Forks and the Pursuit of Lee," in *Battles and Leaders of the Civil War*, ed. Robert Underwood Johnson and Clarence Clough Buel (1887; repr., New York: Thomas Yoseloff, 1956), 4:711.

18. Horace Porter to John A. Rawlins, April 1, 1865, in *The Papers of Ulysses S. Grant*, ed. John Y. Simon, 14:295.

19. Horace Porter, "Five Forks and the Pursuit of Lee," 4:713.

20. Ibid., 715.

21. John A. Rawlins to Emma Rawlins, April 2, 1865, transcribed by J. H. Wilson, James H. Wilson Papers, Bender Collection, Wyoming State Archives and Historical Department, Microfilm Reel H-61a.

22 , U. S. Grant to Julia Grant, April 2, 1865, in *The Papers of Ulysses S. Grant*, ed. John Y. Simon, 14:330.

23. Horace Porter, *Campaigning with Grant*, 450.

24. John A. Rawlins to Emma Rawlins, April 4, 1865, transcribed by J. H. Wilson, James H. Wilson Papers, Bender Collection, Wyoming State Archives and Historical Department, Microfilm Reel H-61a.

25. U. S. Grant to Philip Sheridan, April 4, 1865, in *The Papers of Ulysses S. Grant*, ed. John Y. Simon, 14:344.

26. Horace Porter, *Campaigning with Grant*, 454; John Y. Simon, ed., *The Papers of Ulysses S. Grant*, 14:348n.

27. Albert D. Richardson, *Personal History of Ulysses S. Grant*, 480.

28. Sylvanus Cadwallader, *Three Years with Grant*, ed. Benjamin P. Thomas (New York: Alfred A. Knopf, 1961), 312–13.

29. P. H. Sheridan to U. S. Grant, April 6, 1865, in *The War of the Rebellion: A Compilation of the Official Records of the Union and Confederate Armies*, series 1, part 3, 46:610.

30. U. S. Grant to Robert E. Lee, April 7, 1865, in *The Papers of Ulysses S. Grant*, ed. John Y. Simon, 14:361.

31. R. E. Lee to U. S. Grant, April 7, 1865, in *The War of the Rebellion: A Compilation of the Official Records of the Union and Confederate Armies*, series 1, part 3, 46:619.

32. U. S. Grant to Robert E. Lee, April 8, 1865, in *The Papers of Ulysses S. Grant*, ed. John Y. Simon, 14:367.

33. Peter J. Koehler and Christopher J. Boes, "A History of Non-drug Treatment in Headache, Particularly Migraine," *Brain: A Journal of Neurology* 133, no. 8 (2010): 2495.

34. R. E. Lee to U. S. Grant, April 8, 1865, in *The War of the Rebellion: A Compilation of the Official Records of the Union and Confederate Armies*, series 1, part 3, 46:641.

35. Edwin M. Stanton to U. S. Grant, March 3, 1865, in *The War of the Rebellion: A Compilation of the Official Records of the Union and Confederate Armies*, series 1, part 2, 46:802.

36. Sylvanus Cadwallader, *Three Years with Grant*, 319.

37. U. S. Grant to Robert E. Lee, April 9, 1865, in *The Papers of Ulysses S. Grant*, ed. John Y. Simon, 14:371.

38. Albert D. Richardson, *Personal History of Ulysses S. Grant*, 490.

39 U. S. Grant to Robert E. Lee, April 9, 1865, in *The Papers of Ulysses S. Grant*, ed. John Y. Simon, 14:372–73.

40. Horace Porter, *Campaigning with Grant*, 481.

41. William H. Armstrong, *Warrior in Two Camps: Ely S. Parker Union General and Seneca Chief* (New York: Syracuse University Press, 1978), 111.

42. John Y. Simon, ed., *The Personal Memoirs of Julia Dent Grant*, 152.

43. Ibid., 155–56.

44. E. M. Stanton to Charles Francis Adams, April 15, 1865, in *The War of the Rebellion: A Compilation of the Official Records of the Union and Confederate Armies*, series 1, part 3, 46:785.

45. P. H. Sheridan to U. S. Grant, April 16, 1865, in *The War of the Rebellion: A Compilation of the Official Records of the Union and Confederate Armies*, series 1, part 3, 46:794; J. A. Rawlins to P H. Sheridan, April 16, 1865, in *The War of the Rebellion: A Compilation of the Official Records of the Union and Confederate Armies*, series 1, part 3, 46:794.

46. U. S. Grant to Edwin M. Stanton, June 20, 1865, in *The Papers of Ulysses S. Grant*, ed. John Y. Simon, 14:164–206; the expanded, final report is in U. S. Grant, *Personal Memoirs*, 2:555–632.

47. John F. Marszalek, *Sherman: A Soldier's Passion for Order* (Carbondale: Southern Illinois University Press, 1993), 345–51.

48. Frederic Bancroft and William A. Dunning, ed., *The Reminiscences of Carl Schurz* (New York: McClure, 1908), 116.

49. W. T. Sherman to J. A. Rawlins, April 29, 1865, in *The War of the Rebellion: A Compilation of the Official Records of the Union and Confederate Armies*, series 1, part 3, 47:345.

50. William S. McFeely, *Grant: A Biography* (New York: W. W. Norton, 1982), 230.

51. John F. Marszalek, *Sherman: A Soldier's Passion for Order*, 356–57.

52. U. S. Grant to Andrew Johnson, June 19, 1865, in *The Papers of Ulysses S. Grant*, ed. John Y. Simon, 14:157.

53. P. H. Sheridan to J. A. Rawlins, June 13, 1865, in *The War of the Rebellion: A Compilation of the Official Records of the Union and Confederate Armies*, series 1, part 2, 48:866.

54. P. H. Sheridan to J. A. Rawlins, June 29, 1865, in *The Papers of Ulysses S. Grant*, ed. John Y. Simon, 14:259n.

55. *Galena Daily Gazette*, June 30, 1865.

56. Ibid., July 5, 1865.

57. Ibid., July 18, 1865; July 22, 1865; July 27, 1865.

58. Ibid., July 29, 1865.

59. Ibid., August 19, 1865.

60. Elihu B. Washburne to U. S. Grant, May 18, 1865, in *The Papers of Ulysses S. Grant*, ed. John Y. Simon, 15:86n.

61. U. S. Grant to Elihu B. Washburne, May 21, 1865, in *The Papers of Ulysses S. Grant*, ed. John Y. Simon, 15:85.

62. Sylvanus Cadwallader, *Three Years with Grant*, 120.

63 J. A. Rawlins to U. S. Grant, August 14, 1865, Morristown National Historical Park, Morristown, NJ.

64. U. S. Grant to J. A. Rawlins, August 20, 1865, in *The Papers of Ulysses S. Grant*, ed. John Y. Simon, 15:300–301

22

"Rather Late in the Day, but Better Than Not at All"

JOHN RAWLINS BROUGHT HIS FAMILY to Washington, where they shared a house in Georgetown with Sylvanus Cadwallader and his wife, Mary. Emma and Mary had become close over the winter at City Point. The wives alternated weeks as housekeepers, and the families made do with one table, one set of servants, and one horse and carriage. When the Hurlburts, Emma's working-class parents, would visit from Danbury, their unrefined behavior and unpolished table manners left an impression with the Cadwalladers.[1]

Rawlins had not been back a month when Grant, writing from Galena, recommended his appointment to brevet major general in the regular army—he had already been brevetted major general of volunteers on February 24.[2] While waiting Grant's return from summer touring, Rawlins provided magazine editor and academician Henry Coppée with records and reports for a biography he was writing of his former West Point acquaintance's recent military campaigns. Coppée credited Rawlins "for his invaluable assistance in furnishing materials."[3]

During spring and summer 1865, politicians and pundits pondered where Lincoln's successor, Andrew Johnson, stood on the looming issues. Both radical and conservative factions regarded him in their corner. Two Radical Republicans, Charles Sumner of Massachusetts and Ben Wade of Ohio, were convinced that Johnson was "thoroughly radical" and supported Black suffrage. Northern Democrats, on the other hand, pointed out Johnson still counted himself a "Jacksonian Democrat." That, they hoped, could bode well for a speedy reconciliation of the sections.[4] Both Rawlins and Grant tilted conservatively and were initially favorably disposed to Johnson, believing he would deal more benignly than punitively toward the South.[5] However, as Washington watched for Johnson to show his colors, Grant and Rawlins, when not resting and recuperating, were more focused on the Mexico situation and demobilizing the Union armies.

Maintaining over a million men in uniform was draining the US Treasury, so Johnson set Grant and Stanton to work at demobilization. Grant, with Rawlins's assistance, responded with such rapidity that on October 20, he could report that by stopping enlistments, mustering men out, and discharging the unfit, ranks had been depleted by about eight hundred thousand—and they would drop further.[6] Grant tasked Rawlins with being Sherman's point of contact for reducing forces within his Military Division of the Mississippi.[7] Rawlins worked with Meade, Sheridan, and Logan to obtain their plans for reducing troop levels or transmitting Grant's mustering out orders.[8] From Georgia, Harry Wilson informed Rawlins the mustering out plan was "producing a bad effect" on his troops and requested that he explain the policy being adopted.[9]

Johnson faced a problem much larger than demobilization: Reconstruction. Although Radical Republicans were initially confident that Johnson favored their fundamental conditions for a path to Reconstruction—that was, punishing the secessionists and enfranchising Blacks—it soon became evident that Johnson was hostile to the freed men and women and a zealous supporter of states' rights. In Johnson's view, the Southern states had never left the Union, and thus few conditions needed to be imposed on them to bring them back on equal footing—hence, no need to formally "reconstruct" the seceded states but merely to "restore" them.[10]

On May 29, 1865, Johnson issued two proclamations that initiated his Reconstruction plan. The first covered a liberal policy of amnesty and pardons for most former Confederates who took a loyalty oath, excepting high officials and wealthy Southern property owners (with taxable property valued over $20,000), who had to apply individually for pardons. The second described a process whereby North Carolina could reclaim its regular status in the Union. Johnson would appoint a provisional governor to arrange for the election of delegates to a convention charged with writing a new constitution. The North Carolina plan would be a model for several other ex-Confederate states. Although Johnson did not stipulate what the new constitution should include, he was clear only those who had been eligible voters at the time the state seceded and who had taken an oath of loyalty could vote for the delegates. Blacks were thereby barred from voting.[11] These proclamations appeared to augur for a quick restoration of the Southern states and delighted conservatives. As one Democratic newspaper applauded, "Mr. Johnson had set his foot down against permitting the negroes having anything to do with putting the State governments into operation."[12] Those in the Radical camp might find solace in the $20,000 clause that excluded the South's economically elite from having a dominant voice. It cast the proclamations, as historian Eric Foner put it, in "an aura of sternness."[13]

—⁓⁓⁓—

Days after the release of the proclamations, Grant attended an assembly at New York's Cooper Union on behalf of Andrew Johnson. Grant was aware that since the assassination, Northerners were backing Johnson, and his presence there would demonstrate his support for the president. At this early stage of Reconstruction, Grant and Johnson shared the goal of quickly demobilizing. Grant reported to Stanton that, after laying down their arms, Confederate soldiers had peaceably returned to their homes and that their "submission was perfect." Moreover, Grant boasted that since the end of hostilities, the number of troops left in Southern states to protect the freedmen has been reduced "in proportion as continued quiet and good order have justified it."[14] However, Grant's and Johnson's attitudes and outlooks on other issues revealed discrepancies. For example, whereas Grant favored going slow on enfranchising the freedmen lest it lead to racial tensions, the deeply racist Johnson bitterly opposed the idea, fearing it would trample the rights of Whites. Early in his presidency, Johnson exhibited a determination to punish the South and even to put Lee on trial "to make treason odious."[15] Grant favored a pardon for Lee, feeling there should be leniency toward the Confederacy's military leaders, but he was less benevolent toward its politicians: "The leaders in this rebellion have been guilty of the most heinous offence known to our laws," he told Stanton. "Let them reap the reward of their offence."[16] Both Grant and Johnson downplayed reports about violence perpetrated against Blacks in the Southern states, but for different reasons. Grant believed the freed people needed a period of protection while Whites adapted to the abolishment of slavery. Some violence would be expected as the adjustment process evolved. Grant was overly optimistic about Whites' capacity to transform their views on race. Johnson was not discomfited by such violence: intimidation was needed to reduce Blacks to their inferior status in society.[17]

Rawlins would have been familiar with these points of congruence and departure between his commanding general and the president. During the last half of 1865, Rawlins would also be exposed to conflicting narratives about the Reconstruction process and be faced with choosing what truth to draw from them. One of those narratives was espoused by President Johnson, who expressed confidence his efforts at Reconstruction were succeeding. Those efforts emphasized leniency toward the South. Where Johnson once preached retribution against Southern traitors, he now pushed for the reduction of Black occupation troops; distributed pardons to those wealthy ex-Confederates recently excluded from general amnesty, thereby qualifying them for office; returned confiscated land to former plantation owners; and allowed the raising of militia in several Southern states. These measures received support in some Northern circles and raised hope his leniency would pay off. A conflicting narrative emerged from stories about threats against Union loyalists residing in the South and former slaves. In late 1865, laws, known as Black Codes, were legislated in South Carolina and Mississippi to capriciously oppress Blacks and limit their economic opportunities. Vagrancy laws were enacted such that violation could result in freedmen being punished by performing involuntary plantation labor. Other Black Codes meted out unfair taxes and brutal retribution for arbitrary infractions.

In November, Grant wrote Meade, "In view of the peaceful conditions of the South I think now the number of interim posts held may be materially reduced in numbers and where regular troops are used they can generally be one and two company posts."[18] This was demobilization proceeding full speed. At the time, Meade was commander of the Military Division of the Atlantic, which consisted of six departments, one being the Department of South Carolina. Two days later, Meade sent a reply—and Rawlins surely would have been aware of it—reminding Grant of a recent report containing his department commanders' opinion that "the withdrawal of all military force would very likely be followed by a war of the races, and circumstances of recent occurrence in So[uth] C[arolin]a would seem to confirm this view." Were conditions "peaceful," or did they more resemble a tinderbox? Whose version was to be believed?

On the heels of Meade's reply, Rawlins received a letter from General Peter Osterhaus, the military governor of Mississippi, headquartered in Vicksburg, in which he expressed concern about the raising of militia companies in that state. The companies were forming in response to "the fear of negro insurrection." Osterhaus emphasized to Rawlins that he found no evidence of such a conspiracy against Whites. Rather, there was "the undeniable fact that a great number of murders are committed in almost every portion of the State where there are negroes, but in every case the latter class have been the victims and the Whites the aggressors."[19] Was Osterhaus's simply an anomalous report, or did it reveal serious exceptions to the notion of "perfect submission"? Rawlins, along with many others, had to wonder which stories to believe. Were the adjustments occurring in the South "normal"? Would a military presence be required in the South longer than expected? Was Johnson's conservative approach working?

Two quite different narratives describing the situation in the immediate postwar South appeared in late 1865. Johnson intended both to provide validation for his Reconstruction policies. The first was submitted by Radical Republican Carl Schurz. In June, Schurz wrote Johnson about his concerns regarding the North Carolina proclamation. To Schurz's surprise, Johnson summoned him to Washington and asked him to investigate conditions existing in the Gulf States. Johnson hoped to restore these states to their constitutional status quickly and wanted to know whether that could be done while maintaining the safety of the states' loyal Unionists and emancipated slaves. Johnson assured Schurz he expected a truthful rendering of conditions—and Schurz delivered. During his months of traveling, he sought out hundreds of various informants. Schurz discovered a consistent theme: informants believed that Blacks would not work without physical compulsion. Moreover, Schurz reckoned a large majority of the White population viewed emancipation as an unconstitutional overstep of power. Schurz learned of the violent efforts to coerce Blacks back onto plantations and of planters duping them with bogus work contracts. He saw evidence of Black men and women recuperating in hospitals from beatings and slashing. He received reports of ordinances intended to restrict Blacks' freedom of movement and county patrols to subjugate them. Young Whites whom Schurz interviewed thought "reunion" distasteful and hated Yankees. The reason for all of this, Schurz argued, could be placed on Johnson's policy to fast-track Southern states to self-governing status without addressing the realities of the new free labor system. Once these states realized they would regain full control over their affairs, they could treat Blacks with impunity. Naturally, the report strongly displeased Johnson, and he wanted to suppress it.[20]

To offset Schurz's findings, Johnson asked Grant to make another investigative trip to the South. Johnson figured he could capitalize on Grant's prestige and leniency toward ex-Confederates. On November 27, Grant, accompanied by Babcock, Badeau, and Comstock, left Washington on a fourteen-day journey to Richmond, Raleigh, Charleston, Atlanta, and other cities. Unlike Schurz, who mingled with a variety of informants, Grant was on a train much of the time and met mostly with politicians and former Confederate generals inclined to represent themselves as "anxious to return to self government, within the Union, as soon as possible."[21] When Grant presented his report at an Executive Mansion meeting, he left attendees with the impression that "people are more loyal and better-disposed than he expected to find them."[22] This was in sharp contrast to Comstock's experience in Charleston, where he heard that "the feeling between whites & negroes is bad, the negroes having no trust in the whites & the latter fearing a rising."[23] At the trip's end, Comstock concluded that "there is much bitter feeling still at the south ... that the government will have to exercise some control over the south for a year to come to secure the best treatment of the negro—& that keeping their numbers out of Congress till they have done everything necessary to secure the negroes well being, is the best way."[24] On this last point, Comstock expressed a moderate Republican view that the old rebel faction should be barred from assuming legislative power to safeguard the freedmen's gains secured by emancipation. Badeau summarized Grant's findings as being "in accordance with the expectations of the President, but very much to the disgust of ardent and bitter Republicans."[25]

Grant's report contained an important point on which he and Schurz agreed: "It cannot be expected that the opinions held by men at the South for years can be changed in a day," Grant said, "and therefore the freedmen require for a few years not only laws to protect them, but the fostering care of those who will give them good counsel and in whom they rely."[26] This need for protection seemed lost on Johnson and his supporters, who were more likely to seize on Grant's conclusion "that the mass of thinking men of the South accept the present situation of affairs in good faith."[27] The point was also overlooked by many Radicals who were dismissive of a report written by someone they believed was too cozy with Johnson.

To his credit, Grant read Schurz's report shortly after it appeared and recognized how he had erred. At a December 1868 soldiers' reunion, Grant admitted to Schurz, "I traveled as the general-in-chief and people who came to see me tried to appear to the best advantage. But I have since come to the conclusion you were right and I was wrong."[28] Taking that conclusion to heart, Grant began 1866 by implementing significant measures to protect the emancipated slaves.

—◦◦◦—

The rash of field reports of egregious White-on-Black violence and Schurz's comprehensive findings compelled Grant to shift from conciliation with the Southern states to protection of freed men and women. This shift soon became apparent to those in Congress.[29] On Christmas Day 1865, Grant ordered the generals overseeing Federal occupation troops in four departments to prepare as soon as possible "a report of all known outrages occuring [sic] within your command since the surrender of the rebel Armies committed by White people against the blacks and the reverse."[30] Less than two months later, Grant submitted the generals' findings to President Johnson. Two results stand out: forty-four Blacks were killed by Whites, and "the reverse" was zero. On January 12, Grant tasked division and departmental commanders with "protecting colored persons from prosecutions in any of said States charged with offenses for which white persons are not prosecuted or punished in the same manner and degree."[31] Later in the month, Grant sent Cyrus Comstock south on a fact-finding tour. In New Orleans he met with Generals Phil Sheridan and Edward Canby. The latter told him if occupation troops were withdrawn, "the negroes would be far worse off than before the war." In Texas, Comstock chatted with two bitter, unreconstructed "rebs," one of whom, he wrote in his diary, would have liked to have lynched him after Comstock shared his "moderate" view that "the negro must be treated like the white man."[32] Comstock's reports came to Grant through Rawlins, who was fully apprised of the information shaping the commander in chief's thinking.

Although keeping the peace and protecting lives were clearly military functions, there was a political dimension to Grant's orders, especially given the gulf between Johnson and the Republican-controlled Congress regarding the civil and political rights the freed slaves deserved and what pathway was required to reconstruct the states. During this time, Grant strove to display to the public a middle-of-the-road political posture and to leave it to others to guess how he leaned. Later in 1866, he sternly rebuked William Hillyer for saying he pledged to support Johnson. He reminded Hillyer he had no business speaking for him on political matters and preferred that people vote "without influence from me."[33] Staff Secretary Badeau explained this neutral position to Washburne: "we scrupulously abstain from an attempt at dabbling in personal politics. If you get a chance, won[']t you say so to Congressmen. . . . It is desirable, especially at this juncture, that we should not be represented as politicians, or partisans."[34] When Ohio Congressman Robert Schenck wrote Grant accusing Rawlins of backing the notorious Copperhead Clement Vallandigham against Schenck, Grant stoutly defended Rawlins, informing Schenck, "Whilst an officer of the Army he has not, nor will he, interfere with elections." Grant suggested that Schenck confused Rawlins with former Missouri congressman James Rollins.[35]

In the early postwar months, Grant and men closest to him harbored differing political proclivities. Babcock and Porter leaned most toward the Radicals, as did former staffer Harry Wilson.[36] Wilson also held a dislike for President Johnson that harked back to his time in Tennessee prior to Hood's invasion. Badeau and Rawlins held more conservative views that in coming months drifted leftward. While on his December Southern tour for Johnson, Grant met Wilson in Atlanta, where they had an evening of conversation. To Wilson, Grant described himself as "thoroughly conservative." He was critical of Johnson's judgment and statesmanship and also expressed distrust of Stanton and the Senate Radicals.[37] This put him in a vague political middle ground that left many in Washington wondering where he stood. Sherman, whom Rawlins highly respected, held the most conservative positions. Sherman was a critic of the Freedmen's Bureau, authorized by Congress in March 1865 to provide aid to freed slaves to help them attain self-sufficiency. He felt the bureau operated to force Black equality on disinclined Whites.[38] In January 1866, he warned Johnson about the Radicals' extreme views that could work against the South.[39]

Sherman was no doubt wary of two bills that were reported in January to the Senate. The first extended the life of the Freedmen's Bureau. The second, the Civil Rights Bill, provided some protections against the Black Codes. Republicans saw both bills as key elements in the Reconstruction process. Johnson vetoed the Freedmen's Bureau Bill in February and the Civil Rights Bill in March, claiming the latter, by granting Blacks full citizenship rights, discriminated against Whites. Obviously, Grant's report exposing Whites' murderous "outrages" against Blacks had no impact on Johnson. Historian Eric Foner called Johnson's veto of the Civil Rights Bill "the most disastrous miscalculation of his political career."[40] Congress in April overturned the veto, but Johnson's hard line had driven moderates—those who could countenance Blacks gaining civil equality but were not ready to grant them voting rights—from him and widened the split between the president and Congress.

Johnson followed his vetoes with an April 2 proclamation declaring the rebellion had come to an end—except in Texas—a decision that eviscerated military rule in the South. The Supreme Court in December would rule in *Ex parte Milligan* that military courts had no authority to try civilians in a jurisdiction if civil courts were functioning there. Due to Johnson's proclamation, Blacks faced arbitrary justice as meted out by Southern judges. White Southerners felt more emboldened. The proclamation caused confusion in the generals performing occupation duty. On April 3, Major General Alfred Terry, commander of the Department of Virginia, telegraphed Rawlins for guidance: "I have a very important case on trial before me, of a white man for the murder of a negro. I respectfully ask instructions whether this case should be completed or abandoned at once." George Thomas telegraphed Grant asking whether the proclamation abrogated martial law and restored the writ of habeas corpus.[41]

—◦◦◦—

On March 7, 1866, Colonel Theodore "Joe" Bowers was killed in a train accident. He was the first of Grant's "staff family" to die. Bowers had been accompanying Grant and son Fred on a West Point visit. On the return trip while Bowers retrieved a bag from the station agent's office, the train pulled away. He tried jumping onto the steps of the car in which Grant was seated but lost grip on the railing, fell onto the tracks, and was killed almost instantly. A shaken Grant ordered the body buried temporarily at West Point.[42] Sylvanus Cadwallader wrote Rowley that the news of Bowers's death hit him "like an earthquake." Rawlins requested that the journalist prepare a fitting obituary for the *United States Service Magazine*, edited by Henry Coppée.[43] In it, Cadwallader praised Bowers as an officer who "commanded the admiration and respect of everyone" and offered the plea: "May the turf rest lightly on his breast, and gentle winds forever chant his requiem."[44]

—◦◦◦—

Through spring and summer of 1866, Rawlins was at Grant's side during the unfolding of events that, in unknowable ways, would come to impact his views on Johnson's efforts at Reconstruction and on protecting the civil rights of the freed slaves. In July, Congress passed the Fourteenth Amendment—it would not be ratified until 1868—guaranteeing equal protection under the law for all persons born in the United States. Because it did not allow Black suffrage, it was a relatively moderate measure; however, Johnson tried to prevent its ratification.

In early May in Memphis and in late July in New Orleans, bloody rioting occurred that called into question Johnson's lenient Reconstruction policies. In Memphis on April 30, a minor incident exploded into three days of violence, consisting largely of city police indiscriminately attacking Blacks and torching their homes. Almost four dozen Black persons, including women and children, were killed. An investigative committee, headed by Elihu Washburne, was authorized by the House to conduct an inquiry. In his report, Washburne said a White mob "finding itself under the protection and guidance of official authority, and sustained by a powerful public sentiment . . . proceeded with deliberation to the commission of crimes and the persecution of horrors which can scarcely find a parallel in the history of civilized or barbarous nations."[45]

Twelve weeks later, violence erupted in New Orleans when a faction of Radicals attempted to convene a meeting to press for the enfranchisement of Blacks. Rioters, goaded by police, killed about forty of the Radical conventioneers. Johnson showed no empathy for the victims—he blamed the Radicals in Congress for instigating the slaughter—a position that did not play well in the North.[46] When Phil Sheridan, in command at New Orleans, gathered the facts, he telegraphed Grant: "It was no riot, it was an absolute massacre by the police which was not excelled in murderous cruelty by that of Fort Pillow."[47]

During this time, Rawlins would have observed Grant's growing discomfort with President Johnson's divisive approach as well as his effort to remain the obedient and nonpartisan military commander. Military secretary Adam Badeau remarked later that although Grant appeared to be in support of Johnson's views, "he was in reality doing more than all the country to thwart Johnson's designs."[48] Given a president indifferent toward the plight of Southern Blacks, Grant emerged as one of their most dependable protectors.[49] In this regard, Grant sent Johnson another report of racial crime statistics, this one from the Department of Alabama, showing a preponderance of violence perpetrated by Whites against Blacks.[50] It too failed to move Johnson. Following instances of deadly assaults against Freedmen's Bureau officers, Grant issued General Orders No. 44 on July 6, authorizing the arrest of those "charged with the commission of crimes against officers, agents, citizens and inhabitants of the United States regardless of color or when civil authorities failed to bring the perpetrator to trial."[51] A day later, Grant wrote Stanton that the victims of the Memphis attack were "helpless and unresisting negroes," and that the civil authorities permitted the perpetration of the attacks. Grant recommended arresting the leaders of the riot and holding them until civil courts could stage a fair trial.[52]

Rawlins was also taking note of Johnson's bald overtures to win Grant's favor. In late July, Johnson recommended Grant for promotion to full general. As the Senate was about to vote to confirm, Johnson engaged Rawlins in a "long & interesting interview." He asked Rawlins to take back to Grant the message that he, Johnson, had also forwarded the names of Sherman, Hancock, and Ord for promotions, a move that figured to please Grant.[53] Johnson also appointed Grant's father postmaster of Covington, Kentucky. Meanwhile, those on the political left looked for signs that Grant was with them. Wilson, for example, excitedly wrote to Washburne that newspapers were reporting that Grant was decidedly "for the Congressional Reconstruction policy. I hope & believe this to be true—for *he ought* to feel that way if any man should."[54] Likewise, many Radicals were heartened by Grant's issuance of General Orders No. 44.

—◦◦◦—

Rawlins's fluctuating health was an ongoing concern among staff. On May 11, Orville Babcock, who was on an inspection tour of the West, wrote Rawlins a long letter in which he floated an idea: "Why don[']t you take a trip to Santa Fe, New Mexico," he proposed. "The climate, the air, the sights will all do you good. I know you think you cannot leave your family. I think you are wrong. If you can come back well, your family will be infinitely better off. You can take Mrs. R. with you if wish though it will be rather rough for her. I advise you by all means to go for pleasure and for benefit of your health."[55] The next summer, an increasingly desperate Rawlins would head west to seek a cure.

—◦◦◦—

In August, Johnson, chafing from attacks by the Radicals and smarting over passage of the Fourteenth Amendment, itched to take his case to the people. He decided on a stump speech tour through the Northeast and west to St. Louis. Originally, he was to travel to Chicago only to lay a cornerstone at the monument, under construction, to Stephen Douglas. However, he fashioned he could turn the trip into a campaign tour for the fall elections. Johnson, hoping to boost crowd enthusiasm, pressured Grant to join the party. Because homage was to be paid to his political hero Douglas, Rawlins came along. Rawlins also wanted to ensure Grant displayed himself so as to gain favorable exposure.

Joining Grant and Rawlins were cabinet members William Seward and Gideon Welles and Assistant Postmaster General Alexander Randall. Military luminaries included Admiral Farragut and Generals George Custer and George Stoneman. The trip would cover two thousand miles over three weeks. Beginning on August 27, Johnson and his entourage traveled up the Eastern seaboard from Baltimore to Albany and thence across New York to Buffalo. During the West Point stop, Rawlins visited Cadet Fred Grant, who was hospitalized for an inflamed eyelid. At Auburn, New York, Grant wrote Julia he was weary of listening to repetitive political speeches.[56] With each westward stop, Johnson delivered the same speech and became more belligerent toward his political enemies. The tour, a debacle in the making, was soon derisively called "the swing around the circle."

Rawlins boasted to Emma of Johnson's avid reception in heavily Democratic New York City. He also expressed approval of Grant's agreeing to join the tour because it would "fix him in the confidence of Mr. Johnson, enabling him to fix up the Army as it should be, and exert such influence as will be of benefit to the Country." The exposure could prove beneficial and "do Grant good whatever may be his aspirations in the future."[57] At Buffalo, Rawlins wrote that the Democrats, apparently to his satisfaction, had a good chance to carry New York in November. Grant and Farragut, he thought, were earning the preponderance of cheers. Moreover, he told Emma that for someone who was uncomfortable making frequent speeches, "Grant was at first quite fidgety over the matter but has finally grown quite tranquil and seems to enjoy himself." Rawlins was enjoying himself as well by doing some socializing. Surgeon General Joseph Barnes procured a carriage and invited Rawlins for a ride to Niagara Falls. He also found Mrs. Farragut quite friendly and delighted in her caring words for his family. He confided to her, "We had a new babe"—a reference to the birth of a daughter, Mary, who would survive only briefly. But for Rawlins, socializing went only so far. Ever restrained, he drew the line at conspicuous gaiety, spurning attendance at that night's grand ball for a chance to retire early.[58]

On the Buffalo to Cleveland leg, the train had a refreshment car stocked with food and liquor. Cadwallader, who was also on the "swing," wrote later that Grant overindulged and had to be led into the baggage car and laid on empty sacks and rubbish piles. There, Cadwallader claimed, he and Rawlins alternated monitoring Grant all the way to Cleveland and protecting him from prying eyes.[59] This story was embroidered by Orville Browning, the secretary of the interior. Browning left a diary entry based on a verbal report from Postmaster Randall. Randall claimed Grant was "sick and drunk" and was attended to by Surgeon General Barnes, who himself was so inebriated that, while trying to take Grant's pulse, he tumbled on top of him. Gideon Welles also left a diary entry based on a secondhand report, a remark by Admiral Farragut's wife. Welles wrote that Grant had not been drinking until the party arrived at Buffalo, when "through the day until we reached Cleveland he became garrulous and stupidly communicative to Mrs. F. as she afterwards informed me."[60] At Cleveland, Grant was surreptitiously put on a steamer and taken to Detroit.[61] Perhaps the excess drinking was Grant's reacting to the stultifying speeches and grinding itinerary; or perhaps he suffered from a headache and self-medicated with alcohol. Perhaps Cadwallader's recollection was embellished, a point raised by Benjamin Thomas, the editor of his memoir, who noted, "Toward the end Cadwallader's reminiscences take on the garrulousness of old age."[62] There is no record of Rawlins leaving a catastrophic analysis of the event. Grant's account provides no clue. Writing to Julia from Detroit, he said merely, "Gen. Rawlins, Dr. Barnes and myself switched off from the party at Cleveland last night and came here by boat."[63]

In Cleveland, Johnson informed the crowd Grant was ill and unavailable. At this stage of the trip, Johnson had sunk to calling his political foes "hirelings and traducers" and exchanging insults with hecklers.[64] As the junket continued, Johnson followed one undignified speech with another, torpedoing chances for Democratic gains in the fall election. What Rawlins and everyone heard was a president who pandered to the Copperheads, championed the reintroduction of unapologetic Confederates into government, spurned civil rights for Blacks, and stood up for the agents of the violence in New Orleans. Given Johnson's vulnerability, Republicans might be interested in wooing Grant. Gideon Welles thought so. As the party reached Cincinnati, he noted "it became obvious [Grant] had begun to listen to the seductive appeals of the Radical conspirators."[65]

Although authorities in Chicago declined to welcome Johnson, the city was packed with visitors eager to greet the visiting luminaries. The *New York Herald* reported that "countless thousands" had descended on Chicago. Just past 10:00 a.m., Johnson climbed into the first carriage for the ride to the Douglas monument. Once it passed on ahead, "General Grant and his chief of staff General Rawlins, mounted the steps of the second one" as "applause swelled into a torrent that would have drowned the roar of Niagara itself." In contrast to the enthusiastic tumult in the streets, the solidly Democratic paper, in an adjacent column, ran Grant's summation of the whole affair: "I am disgusted with this trip. I am disgusted at hearing a man make speeches on the way to his own funeral."[66]

After the train made a whistle stop at West Junction in northern Illinois, Grant was accosted by a reporter while relaxing in the combined baggage and refreshment car. With Rawlins present, he told the reporter he would not do anything to associate himself with the president's political views. "He does not consider the Army a place for a politician," said the reporter, "and therefore will not permit himself to be committed to the support of either of the presidential parties."[67] This placed Grant in a tight spot: on one hand having been caught disparaging Johnson's grand tour, yet being quoted in another paper espousing political neutrality. After sending Julia a confidential letter dismissing Johnson's stump speeches as nothing but "a National disgrace," Grant quit the tour at the Cincinnati stop.[68] He and Rawlins escaped back to Washington.

What Rawlins had witnessed was Johnson's unraveling. Historian Albert Castel summed up the event: "In short, Johnson set out on the 'swing around the circle' to persuade the Northern people and ended up frightening and disgusting them."[69]

On October 25, Rawlins visited Interior Secretary Orville Browning, a nominal Republican and Johnson acolyte. The two engaged in a long conversation. "[Rawlins] thinks the country is in danger," Browning wrote in his diary entry for the day, "and came to talk with me upon public affairs."[70] Rawlins was not unique in seeing danger signs; many in both parties feared the worst. A month earlier, Johnson told Browning that "he had no doubt there was a conspiracy on foot among the radicals to incite to another rebellion, and especially to arm and exasperate the negroes in the South."[71] Republican candidates warned voters Johnson and his faithful could undo recent civil rights gains—and the carnage in Memphis and New Orleans proved how White Southerners might sabotage those victories.[72] Grant too was concerned about where Johnson's clashes with Congress might lead. As the "swing" concluded, he had written confidentially to Sheridan how he feared that Johnson "will want to declare the body itself illegal, unconstitutional and revolutionary."[73] Even as Browning and Rawlins conversed, there was the threat of violence in Maryland, where the Democratic governor sought to gain voting eligibility for thousands of former Rebels. To help the governor, Johnson wanted federal troops sent to Baltimore to keep peace.

During their talk, Rawlins told Browning, "He is heartily and entirely with the President in his political views."[74] If so, this was despite the embarrassing spectacles of the president trading insults with hecklers on the "swing" and returns from early voting states presaging a Republican landslide. Had Rawlins been unmoved by Johnson's racist rhetoric and willingness to empower unrepentant Southerners? Perhaps there were indications that Rawlins's support was wavering. Less than two weeks earlier, Harry Wilson wrote to Washburne, "Porter writes me that the 'swing around the Circle' completely cured Rawlins of his sympathy—and that he is *now* for the amendments. Rather late in the day, but better than not at all. . . . I think Badeau is cured also—& so we go!"[75] Wilson's claim would put Rawlins behind the ratification of the Fourteenth Amendment and its guarantees of citizenship for Blacks and equal protection under the law—and align him with Grant. Once the November election results were in, Grant exhorted Johnson to reconsider the Fourteenth Amendment, given that those who fought for the Union were in favor of it.[76] Johnson chose to ignore such advice. He remained firmly opposed to it, and Southern states—with Tennessee the exception—balked at ratification.

Rawlins shared with Browning a variety of opinions and impressions about Grant, as Browning's diary entry revealed: "[Rawlins] is annoyed, indeed provoked at Grant's reticence—says Grant is thoroughly conservative, but that he is not a politician or statesman—he knows how to do nothing but fight—would fail in other positions, but the radicals are anxious to use him as a candidate for the Presidency to promote their own ends, and he is a little unsettled about it—they were making some impression upon him—he was not a man of ability outside of the profession of arms, and was a man of strong passions and intense prejudices."[77] Grant intentionally adopted a shut-mouthed policy regarding politics. As he told Sherman, "No matter how close I keep my tongue each [political party] try to interpret from the little let drop that I am with them."[78] Grant may have kept his evolving political views so concealed that Rawlins was unaware how his frustration with Johnson's Reconstruction efforts was nudging him toward the Radicals' camp. In fact, by mid-autumn

1866, Johnson and many others suspected Grant would be his Republican opponent in 1868. The Grant whom Rawlins knew in Galena was of a conservative bent, and Rawlins was not likely to credit his superior with the capacity to make a significant political shift leftward. Likewise, in Rawlins's mind, Grant was a soldier, a fighter, and a safe bet to fail at anything else, especially the complex business of politics. Hence, Rawlins found Grant's reticence troubling: if he simply spoke up and showed his conservative stripes, the Radicals would desist from using him to their advantage. That the Radicals were leaving an impression on Grant seemed to Rawlins a troubling turn. Rawlins regarded Grant as someone at risk: one who could be swayed by applause and attention and who might need to be protected from his streak of vanity.

Another of the "public affairs" Rawlins and Browning discussed was the complex interplay afoot concerning Johnson, Grant, Sherman, and Stanton. In a letter written earlier in the year, Sherman expressed support for Johnson. Now steeped in political turmoil in October, Johnson considered turning to Sherman, another popular war hero, in order to gain traction with the public. Grant's cachet carried more value; however, Johnson was unsure of the strength of Grant's support and suspicious of his presidential ambition. Sherman might be a more reliable ally. Then there was Stanton. As he became more aligned with Congress, Johnson thought of replacing him—that was, if Stanton did not first resign. October events in Mexico allowed Johnson to put in motion a plan to elevate the friendlier Sherman at the expense of Grant and Stanton. With Benito Juarez's republican forces poised to oust Maximilian, Johnson wanted Grant to accept a mission to Mexico to observe the French withdrawal. Moreover, he instructed Grant to order Sherman to Washington. With Grant miles out of the picture, Johnson could slide in Sherman as his temporary replacement. Then, if Stanton vacated the War Department chair, Johnson had a replacement, William T. Sherman, at hand. Grant managed to see through Johnson's motives and refused the mission to Mexico. When Sherman discovered what was afoot, he refused to stand in during Grant's absence and would not partake in machinations against his friend. Sherman arrived in Washington on October 25—the same day Rawlins and Browning had their conversation—and met Grant that evening to discuss how they would foil Johnson's attempt to use them.[79]

"Sherman had more influence with [Grant] than any body else," Browning recalled Rawlins confiding to him, "and he thought it important Sherman should be here. In [Rawlins's] opinion Stanton ought to go out and Sherman be made Secy of War. He thought Sherman a great man—a statesman as well as a soldier—Grant was the soldier only."[80] If Browning captured Rawlins's intent, the chief of staff was decidedly out of tune with Sherman's loyalty to Grant and for his antipathy toward either assuming command during Grant's absence or for replacing Stanton. When Grant flatly refused the Mexico assignment—he argued that it would be inappropriate to fill a diplomatic role—Sherman volunteered to go in his stead.

—–∿∿∿–—

In April 1865 at Raleigh, a committee of officers submitted a plan to form "the Society of the Army of the Tennessee" to include as members every officer who had served honorably in it. The society's object was "to keep alive and preserve that kindly and cordial feeling" characteristic of that army.[81] John Rawlins was honored by being chosen the society's first president "in consideration of his eminent services to our country in connection with the 'Army of the Tennessee.'"[82] Rawlins, perhaps more than anyone, understood that "kindly and cordial feeling." An incident from October 1864 brought that into relief. At that time, Grenville Dodge was recovering from a head wound suffered in the Atlanta campaign, where he led a corps in the Army of the Tennessee. Rawlins invited Dodge to visit Grant's Army of the Potomac headquarters at City Point. While there, Dodge overheard officers criticizing fellow officers, even Grant. This backbiting was a new and troubling experience for Dodge. He shared his misgivings with Rawlins, who laughed and replied, "General, this is not the old Army of the Tennessee."[83]

With the society's inaugural meeting scheduled for November 14, 1866, at Cincinnati's Mozart Hall, Rawlins immersed himself that autumn in preparing his presidential address, one of his most important public utterances. When he advanced to the podium that evening, Rawlins dispensed for over two hours and in painstaking detail a chronological unfolding of the Army of the Tennessee's history. It began at Grant's Cairo headquarters of the District of Southeast Missouri, where Rawlins felt the army had germinated, and ended with the Grand Review in Washington in May 1865. In between was a recapitulation of prominent battles (e.g., Shiloh) and long-forgotten skirmishes (e.g., Medon Station). Rawlins relived the Vicksburg and Atlanta campaigns and the lifting of the Chattanooga siege. He called out the soldiers of the Army of the Tennessee for their bravery and patriotism, reminding the audience that on the first day at Shiloh, "Our men fought with a valor they never themselves excelled ... as soldiers, under the national flag, they were the superiors of any that dare raise a hand against it."[84] Rawlins recalled the ultimate sacrifices of C. F. Smith, W. H. L. Wallace, and James McPherson; and he reserved special encomiums for Sheridan, Thomas, Logan, and Ord.

As his speech wound down, Rawlins shifted course to Lincoln's Emancipation Proclamation and how it led to mustering Blacks into the army. "Whatever prejudice may have existed against their being elevated to the position of a soldier in the service of the United States," he proudly reminded them, "was overcome by your devotion to your country."[85] Rawlins next alluded to the fighting ability displayed by raw Black troops at Milliken's Bend on June 7, 1863. In that obscure battle, four Black regiments and a detachment from the all-White Twenty-Third Iowa resisted an attack by several Texas regiments. The hand-to-hand combat was some of the most vicious of the war. General Elias Dennis, who observed the battle, said, "It is impossible for men to show greater gallantry than the negro troops in that fight."[86]

From there, Rawlins moved on to the ratification of the Thirteenth Amendment abolishing slavery. Then, just before he concluded his speech, Rawlins revisited the message from the Declaration:

> In your burning patriotism the prejudice against race perished as that of party in the commencement of the contest: and you could read the Declaration of Independence as Jefferson wrote it, and see realized the grand truth "that all men are created equal; that they are endowed by their Creator with certain inalienable right; that among these are life, liberty, and the pursuit of happiness." That which was the subject of race under the law, was the equal of other races; and if, in the Providence of God, greater privileges ere to be extended to it, you could answer in your dead, "the sacrifice has been made, the lamb has been slain upon the altar, and the incense has risen to Heaven."[87]

Here, Rawlins embraced the core of the Fourteenth Amendment—equality of inalienable rights under law—that President Johnson scorned as prejudicial to Whites. Perhaps Harry Wilson was right about John Rawlins coming around late—but better than not at all.

At 9:30, the hungry assemblage followed the strains of music into the banquet hall and to the sight of boards groaning under an impressive feast. There were oysters prepared sixteen ways, from escalloped to champagne-baked, as well as galantine of pheasant, saddle of venison, roasted prairie chicken, and potted shoulder of lamb. Ice cream, vanilla and nectarine, and French coffee capped the dinner. An alcohol-averse John Rawlins led the veterans in nine official toasts. When he called for volunteer toasts, General William Belknap, who ironically would succeed Rawlins as secretary of war, proposed raising glasses to "the accomplished soldier, the able Adjutant-General, the able orator—The President of the Society of the Army of the Tennessee."[88] Rawlins modestly expressed thanks for the honor of the office.

After hoisting a final toast to Washington and Lincoln, Rawlins pronounced the banquet adjourned. Then he and his dear fellow officers of the venerated Army of the Tennessee departed the hall singing "Auld Lang Syne."

NOTES

1. S. Cadwallader to J. H. Wilson, October 4, 1904, James Harrison Wilson Papers, Library of Congress, Container 5.

2. U. S. Grant to E. M. Stanton, August 31, 1865, in *The Papers of Ulysses S. Grant*, ed. John Y. Simon (Carbondale: Southern Illinois University Press, 1988), 15:311. Unfortunately, it was not discovered until May 1866 that the board recommending this appointment did not receive Grant's supporting letter. Rawlins had inadvertently destroyed the letter when it went to be copied. The issue was corrected when Stanton, on May 9, 1866, wrote a letter ordering Rawlins's nomination for the brevet rank of major general in the regular army that Grant endorsed a day later; U. S. Grant to E. M. Stanton, May 8, 1866, in *The Papers of Ulysses S. Grant*, ed. John Y. Simon (Carbondale: Southern Illinois University Press, 1988), 16:187; John C. Kelton to U. S. Grant, May 9, 1866, in *The Papers of Ulysses S. Grant*, ed. John Y. Simon, 16:188 note. The War Department's official records indicate that Rawlins was brevetted major general, United States Army, dating to April 9, 1865, "for gallant and meritorious service during the campaign terminating with the surrender of the insurgent army under General R. E. Lee." Joseph P. Tracy, Adjutant General, to James H. Wilson, November 12, 1915, Wyoming State Archives, Bender Collection, James H. Wilson Papers, Microfilm Reel 61a.

3. Henry Coppèe, *Grant and His Campaigns: A Military Biography* (New York: Charles B. Richardson, 1866), 4.

4. Albert Castel, *The Presidency of Andrew Johnson* (Lawrence, KS: Regents Press of Kansas, 1979), 21–22.

5. James Harrison Wilson, *The Life of John A. Rawlins* (New York: Neale, 1916), 329.

6. U. S. Grant to E. M. Stanton, October 20, 1865, in *The Papers of Ulysses S. Grant*, ed. John Y. Simon, 15:357–59.

7. U. S. Grant to W. T. Sherman, August 21, 1865, in *The Papers of Ulysses S. Grant*, ed. John Y. Simon, 15:306.

8. George G. Meade to J. A. Rawlins, June 22, 1865, in *The Papers of Ulysses S. Grant*, ed. John Y. Simon, 15:214n; P. H. Sheridan to J. A. Rawlins, September 20, 1865, in *The Papers of Ulysses S. Grant*, ed. John Y. Simon, 15:299n; *The War of the Rebellion: A Compilation of the Official Records of the Union and Confederate Armies*, series 1, part 2, 49:1242; ibid., J. A. Rawlins to John A. Logan, June 19, 1865, in *The War of the Rebellion: A Compilation of the Official Records of the Union and Confederate Armies*, series 1, part 2, 49:1015–16.

9. J. H. Wilson to J. A. Rawlins, May 22, 1865, in *The War of the Rebellion: A Compilation of the Official Records of the Union and Confederate Armies*, series 1, part 3, 49:870.

10. Albert Castel, *The Presidency of Andrew Johnson*, 28.

11. Brooks D. Simpson, *The Reconstruction Presidents* (Lawrence: University Press of Kansas, 1998), 74–75.

12. Quote in Albert Castel, *The Presidency of Andrew Johnson*, 26–27.

13. Eric Foner, *A Short History of Reconstruction* (New York: Harper and Row, 1990), 85.

14. U. S. Grant to E. M. Stanton, October 20, 1865, in *The Papers of Ulysses S. Grant*, ed. John Y. Simon, 15:357, 358.

15. Adam Badeau, *Grant in Peace* (Hartford, CT: S. S. Scranton, 1887), 26.

16. U. S. Grant to E. M. Stanton, June 20, 1865, in *The Papers of Ulysses S. Grant*, ed. John Y. Simon, 15:165.

17. Brooks D. Simpson, *Let Us Have Peace: Ulysses S. Grant and the Politics of War and Reconstruction 1861–1868* (Chapel Hill: University of North Carolina Press, 1991), 116.

18. U. S. Grant to G. G. Meade, November 6, 1865, in *The Papers of Ulysses S. Grant*, ed. John Y. Simon, 15:398–99.

19. Peter J. Osterhaus to J. A. Rawlins, November 11, 1865, in *The Papers of Ulysses S. Grant*, ed. John Y. Simon, 16:53n.

20. Frederic Bancroft and William A. Dunning, ed., *The Reminiscences of Carl Schurz* (New York: McClure, 1908), 3:158–87, 202. That Schurz's report contains such rich observations might be due to his having had an unusual motivation to fulfill his mission. On his way to meet Johnson, Schurz stopped at the Philadelphia home of a friend, Dr. Tiedemann, whose wife practiced spiritualism. A séance was arranged for that evening to be led by Tiedemann's adolescent daughter, who had demonstrated skill as a "writing medium." Schurz requested the presence of Abraham Lincoln's spirit. When Lincoln's "spirit" was announced, Schurz inquired why Johnson had summoned him. "He wants you to take an important journey for him," was the written reply. Where would it take him? "He will tell you tomorrow." When Schurz asked if he should undertake the journey, the answer was, "Yes, do not fail." "Lincoln" had a bonus prediction for Schurz: he would become a senator from Missouri—a prophecy that Schurz, a resident of Wisconsin at the time, thought implausible, but one that later proved true. Frederic Bancroft and William A. Dunning, ed., *The Reminiscences of Carl Schurz*, 154–56.

21. U. S. Grant to Andrew Johnson, December 18, 1865, in *The Papers of Ulysses S. Grant*, ed. John Y. Simon, 15:436.

22. Gideon Welles, *Diary of Gideon Welles* (Boston: Houghton Mifflin, 1911), 2:397.

23. Merlin E. Sumner, ed., *The Diary of Cyrus B. Comstock* (Dayton, OH: Morningside House, 1987), 324.

24. Ibid., 326.

25. Adam Badeau, *Grant in Peace*, 33.

26. U. S. Grant to Andrew Johnson, December 18, 1865, in *The Papers of Ulysses S. Grant*, ed. John Y. Simon, 15:437.

27. Ibid., 434.

28. Joseph Schafer, ed., *Intimate Letters of Carl Schurz* (Madison, WI: Historical Society of Wisconsin, 1928), 457.

29. Ronald C. White, *American Ulysses: A Life of Ulysses S. Grant* (New York: Random House, 2017), 427; Brooks D. Simpson, *Let Us Have Peace*, 128.

30. U. S. Grant to George H. Thomas et al., December 25, 1865, in *The Papers of Ulysses S. Grant*, ed. John Y. Simon, 16:69–70n.

31. General Orders No. 3, January 12, 1866, in *The Papers of Ulysses S. Grant*, ed. John Y. Simon, 16:7–8.

32. Merlin E. Sumner, ed., *The Diary of Cyrus B. Comstock*, 331, 333.

33. U. S. Grant to William S. Hillyer September 19, 1866, in *The Papers of Ulysses S. Grant*, ed. John Y. Simon, 16:310.

34. Adam Badeau to E. Washburne, July 3, 1866, Washburne Papers, Library of Congress.

35. U. S. Grant to Robert C. Schenck, September 19, 1866, in *The Papers of Ulysses S. Grant*, ed. John Y. Simon, 16:311; U. S. Grant to R. C. Schenck, October 5, 1866, in *The Papers of Ulysses S. Grant*, ed. John Y. Simon, 16:321n.

36. Brooks D. Simpson, *Let Us Have Peace*, 150.

37. James Harrison Wilson, *Under the Old Flag* (New York: D. Appleton, 1912), 2:378.

38. John F. Marszalek, *Sherman: A Soldier's Passion for Order* (Carbondale: Southern Illinois University Press, 1993), 368.

39. Paul H. Bergeron, *Andrew Johnson's Civil War and Reconstruction* (Knoxville: University of Tennessee Press, 2014), 101.

40. Eric Foner, *A Short History of Reconstruction*, 113.

41. Alfred Terry to J. A. Rawlins, April 3, 1866, in *The Papers of Ulysses S. Grant*, ed. John Y. Simon, 16:149–50n; George H. Thomas to U. S. Grant, April 9, 1866, in *The Papers of Ulysses S. Grant*, ed. John Y. Simon, 16:150n.

42. *Harper's Weekly*, March 24, 1866. West Point became the permanent burial place of Bowers's remains.

43. Sylvanus Cadwallader to William Rowley, March 16, 1866, William Rowley Papers, Abraham Lincoln Presidential Library, SC 1306.

44. "Brevet Colonel Theodore S. Bowers, U.S.A.," *United States Service Magazine* 5, no. 4 (April 1866).

45. "Memphis Riots and Massacres," 39th Congress, 1st Session Report, No. 101, p. 5.

46. Hans L. Trefousse, *Andrew Johnson: A Biography* (New York: W. W. Norton, 1989), 258–59.

47. Philip H. Sheridan to U. S. Grant, August 2, 1866, in *The Papers of Ulysses S. Grant*, ed. John Y. Simon, 16:289n.

48. Adam Badeau, *Grant in Peace*, 47.

49. Ron Chernow, *Grant* (New York: Penguin, 2017), 572.

50. U. S. Grant to A. Johnson, March 14, 1866, in *The Papers of Ulysses S. Grant*, ed. John Y. Simon, 16:114.

51. General Orders, No. 44, July 6, 1866, in *The Papers of Ulysses S. Grant*, ed. John Y. Simon, 16:228.

52. U. S. Grant to E. M. Stanton, July 7, 1866, in *The Papers of Ulysses S. Grant*, ed. John Y. Simon, 16:233–34.

53. Ely S. Parker to U. S. Grant, July 26, 1866, in *The Papers of Ulysses S. Grant*, ed. John Y. Simon, 16:261n.

54. J. H. Wilson to E. Washburne, July 5, 1866, Library of Congress, Elihu Washburne Papers.

55. John Y. Simon, ed., *The Papers of Ulysses S. Grant*, 16:170n.

56. U. S. Grant to Julia Dent Grant, August 31, 1866, in *The Papers of Ulysses S. Grant*, ed. John Y. Simon, 16:306–7.

57. John A. Rawlins to Emma Rawlins, August 30, 1866, transcribed by J. H. Wilson, James H. Wilson Papers, Bender Collection, Wyoming State Archives and Historical Department, Microfilm Reel 61a.

58. J. A. Rawlins to Emma Rawlins, September 1, 1866, transcribed by J. H. Wilson, James H. Wilson Papers, Bender Collection, Wyoming State Archives and Historical Department, Microfilm Reel 61a.

59. Benjamin P. Thomas, ed., *Three Years with Grant as Recalled by War Correspondent Sylvanus Cadwallader* (New York: Alfred A. Knopf, 1961), 340.

60. Image 67 of Gideon Welles Papers, diaries 1866, June 18–Dec. 21, entry of September 17, 1866, https://www.loc.gov/resource/mss45054.mss45054-004_0008_0127/?sp=67 &r=0.354,0.294,0.654,0.376,0.

61. James G. Randall, ed., *The Diary of Orville Hickman Browning* (Springfield, IL: Illinois State Historical Library, 1933), 2:115.

62. Benjamin P. Thomas, ed. *Three Years with Grant as Recalled by War Correspondent Sylvanus Cadwallader*, 340.

63. U. S. Grant to Julia Dent Grant, September 4, 1866, in *The Papers of Ulysses S. Grant*, ed. John Y. Simon, 16:307.

64. Hans L. Trefousse, *Andrew Johnson: A Biography*, 263.

65. Gideon Welles, *Diary of Gideon Welles*, 2:592.

66. *New York Herald*, September 7, 1866.

67. *The United States Army and Navy Journal and Gazette of the Regular and Volunteer Forces*, September 22, 1866, 4:71.

68. U. S. Grant to Julia Dent Grant, September 9, 1866, in *The Papers of Ulysses S. Grant*, ed. John Y. Simon, 16:308.

69. Albert Castel, *The Presidency of Andrew Johnson*, 95.

70. James G. Randall, ed., *The Diary of Orville Hickman Browning*, 2:103.

71. Ibid., 94.

72. Brooks D. Simpson, *The Reconstruction Presidents*, 109.

73. U. S. Grant to Philip H. Sheridan, October 12, 1866, in *The Papers of Ulysses S. Grant*, ed. John Y. Simon, 16:330.

74. James G. Randall, ed., *The Diary of Orville Hickman Browning*, 2:103.

75. James H. Wilson to Elihu Washburne, October 13, 1866, Library of Congress, Elihu Washburne Papers.

76. Jean Edward Smith, *Grant* (New York: Simon and Schuster, 2001), 429.

77. James G. Randall, ed., *The Diary of Orville Hickman Browning*, 2:103.

78. U. S. Grant to William T. Sherman, January 13, 1867, in *The Papers of Ulysses S. Grant*, ed. John Y. Simon (Carbondale: Southern Illinois University Press, 1991), 17:14.

79. John F. Marszalek, *Sherman: A Soldier's Passion for Order*, 369–70; Brooks D. Simpson, *Let Us Have Peace*, 154–58.

80. James G. Randall, ed., *The Diary of Orville Hickman Browning*, 2:103–4.

81. *Report of the Proceedings of the Society of the Army of the Tennessee at the First Annual Meeting, Held at Cincinnati, O., November 14th and 15th 1866* (Cincinnati, OH: Author, 1877), 6.

82. Ibid., 7.

83. Grenville M. Dodge, *Personal Recollections of President Abraham Lincoln, General Ulysses S. Grant and General William T. Sherman* (Council Bluffs, IA: Monarch, 1914), 76–77.

84. Ibid., 39.

85. Ibid., 56.

86. Charles A. Dana, *Recollections of the Civil War* (New York: D. Appleton, 1898), 86.

87. *Report of the Proceedings of the Society of the Army of the Tennessee at the First Annual Meeting, Held at Cincinnati, O., November 14th and 15th 1866*, 57–58.

88. Ibid., 72.

23

"It Is Unquestionably the Platform
of General Grant"

AFTER SUCH GRATIFYING CAMARADERIE WITH the officers of the Army of the Tennessee in Cincinnati, Rawlins returned to Washington and a tension-filled winter. Except for Tennessee, the former Confederate states, goaded by Johnson, who was undeterred by the massive Republican electoral gains in Congress, resisted ratifying the Fourteenth Amendment. In December, the Supreme Court's decision in *Ex parte Milligan* threatened to dissolve military commissions and courts in the South, thus allowing unsympathetic local jurisdictions to try cases against freedmen and loyal Unionists. This ruling could exacerbate the intimidation these groups faced. Reports coming to Grant and Rawlins indicated that violence perpetrated against the Unionists and freedmen continued unabated.

Sheridan, for example, informed Grant about dangerous conditions in areas of Texas where "freedmen are shot and Union men are persecuted if they have the temerity to express their opinion. This condition exists in the northeastern counties of the State to an alarming extent."[1] A week earlier, Rawlins received a letter from Colonel Joseph Reynolds in Texas with the Twenty-Sixth US Infantry, saying Black troops in Brownsville had been shot at by drunken policemen.[2] General Ord reported to Rawlins that in Arkansas and Mississippi, Whites were "generally bitterly opposed to Negro suffrage, and unless the freedmen are protected ... [they] will [not] even present themselves at the polls."[3] These reports must have dismayed Rawlins, who in his address to the society declared that true Unionists embraced men of color who displayed devotion to country and that intimidation and a corrupt judicial system hardly represented Jeffersonian ideals. They alarmed Grant and compelled him to take corrective actions. On January 18, he wrote General Oliver Howard, commissioner of the Freedmen's Bureau, requesting "a list of authenticated cases of Murder, and other violence upon Freedmen, Northern or other Union men ... in the southern states for the last six months or a year." His purpose was to demonstrate that the courts in these states offered no personal security and therefore martial law needed to be declared in districts failing to provide protection.[4] Later in the month, Grant apprised Stanton of the problems in Texas, calling the situation "practically a state of insurrection" and recommending declaring martial law there.[5]

Tensions were escalating between Johnson and the Republican-dominated Congress, which was troubled by the violence and by efforts of recalcitrant Southerners to hold on to power. Before the winter of 1867 dissolved, Congress had passed two significant pieces of legislation and overrode Johnson's veto of them. In a move to protect Secretary of War Stanton, a Johnson adversary, the Tenure of Office Act blocked Johnson from removing Senate-confirmed cabinet members. The Military Reconstruction Act of 1867 partitioned the ten unreconstructed states (Tennessee exempted) into five military districts in which temporary military rule was established. It allowed the districts' commanders to set up military commissions, thereby undercutting the influence of the *Milligan* decision. The Reconstruction Act compelled each of the states to hold constitutional conventions to adopt new constitutions that eliminated race as a factor for voting. Moreover, on a state's ratification of the new constitution and the Fourteenth Amendment, Congress would seat its representatives. A second Reconstruction Act passed Congress on March 23. This bill, which remedied defects in the previous act, allowed the five district commanders to oversee the registration of voters. It too was vetoed by Johnson but quickly overridden.

Writing to Washburne, Grant expressed his approval of both bills and called Johnson's vetoes "ridiculous."[6] Lately when former secessionists asked Grant for advice, he counseled them to deal exclusively with Republicans in Congress and avoid being in league with Democrats who opposed the war. "The more you consort with them," Grant cautioned, "the more exacting the republicans will be, and ought to be." Moreover, he urged them to support suffrage for Blacks. That he was advising such a thing surprised Grant himself. As he told a friend, "I never could have believed that I should favor giving negroes the right to vote; but that seems the only solution of our difficulties."[7] With sentiments like these leaking out, Cyrus Comstock noted in his March 1, 1867, diary entry that "General [Grant is] getting more & more radical."[8]

Phil Sheridan, in command of the Fifth District (Louisiana and Texas), used his authority to clean house. On March 27, he removed the mayor of New Orleans for his role in the race riot, and for good measure he sacked Louisiana's attorney general and a district court judge. Grant felt Sheridan's actions defensible, writing him that "Congress intended to give district commanders entire control over the Civil government of these districts." However, Sheridan's bold moves amplified tensions with Johnson. Now, as Grant informed Sheridan, not only was the "White House" hostile to Congress's Reconstruction plans, but Johnson was of "a disposition to remove you from command."[9]

———❧———

With the coming of spring, John Rawlins wrestled with two critical issues: the states of his health and his politics. Regarding his health, Rawlins saw as his last option for a cure an extended trip to the arid elevations of the high plains and Rockies. He needed to dedicate himself to getting well, and this coming season would be the last time he could withstand such rigorous travel. He committed to the trip probably in early spring, and it was not an easy decision, given that Emma was pregnant with a second child and still recovering from the demise the previous year of their infant daughter. However, Grant was completely supportive of Rawlins's trip, writing Washburne in May, "He will soon start for the plains and I am strongly in hope he will return fully rested to health."[10] To justify his lengthy absence, Grant officially sent Rawlins on an inspection tour of the Military District of the Missouri, with Major William Dunn detailed to accompany him. On reaching the western edge of the Great Plains, Rawlins would be placed under the watchful eye of Grenville Dodge, the Union Pacific's chief engineer, who was exploring routes for the transcontinental railroad. In November, Dodge had been elected to Congress as a Republican from an Iowa district, but instead of heading to Washington, he favored scouting the topography of Wyoming and Utah.[11]

At this time, Rawlins's politics was undergoing a striking shift as he rethought his allegiance to Johnson and the Democrats. Likewise, Grant was aligning with congressional Republicans' designs for Reconstruction. During spring 1867, Rawlins worked on a powerful speech that would stake out his views (and presumably Grant's) on the recent Reconstruction actions. As he labored at it, Rawlins shared the emerging product with Grant, who joshed to J. Russell Jones that Rawlins's "hand is in a literary way."[12] Of course, Grant needed to be made privy to the speech's content because whatever Rawlins said would be scrutinized for clues about Grant's political sentiments. What

Rawlins wrought was a densely worded disquisition that began with a reca-pitulation of the establishment of slavery and continued into the constitution-ality of the Reconstruction Acts and the extension of voting rights to African Americans. He ended with the hope that such contentious issues would be soon settled, thus resulting in the withdrawal of military from the South, civil rights protected by laws, and the nation's resources made available for west-ern expansion. Rawlins's plan was to deliver the speech in Galena—one could hardly overlook the symbolic effect—before he embarked westward on his quest for a cure. He anticipated the speech would receive extensive newspaper coverage.

Rawlins left Washington on June 11 after bidding farewell to his family, now increased with the birth of a son, William. With an anticipated absence of four months and the new baby, Rawlins considered cancelling the trip, but Emma implored him to go. After a marathon forty-eight-hour train ride, Rawlins ar-rived in Chicago on June 13 and immediately wrote Emma he was safe and feeling well. Waiting for him in Chicago was Russell Jones. While they chat-ted in Jones's office, Jones was handed a telegram, and Rawlins absently asked if it was from Harry Wilson. No, it was not, Jones replied as he unexpectedly excused himself and slipped out of the room. Then an exhausted Rawlins fell into a deep but very brief sleep on the office sofa. Rawlins would learn momen-tarily that Jones had just read an urgent dispatch from Orville Babcock—and that the day before, Babcock had telegraphed this same heartbreaking news to Grant: "Genl Rawlins babe died this morning. Mrs Rawlins does not think it necessary for him to return—Every thing will be attended to."[13]

Rawlins was suddenly jostled awake, and Babcock's telegram was placed in his hand. "Oh Merciful God," he wrote Emma, "I have no words to express my grief. My sweet beautiful babe of whom I never thought in connection with death, was no more." Because the baby had appeared healthy, the news took him by complete surprise. Rawlins's first thought was to return to Washing-ton—he even sent a letter to Lovisa to that effect. However, Russell Jones and Judge Thomas Drummond, a former Galena lawyer and now on the US Dis-trict Court in Chicago, urged him to reconsider. Travelling to Washington and back, they argued, would add two thousand miles to his trip to the plains and likely wreck his health.[14]

A disconsolate Rawlins arrived in Galena on June 14 for a twelve-day stay. His appearance belied his emotional state, as the local paper reported he was "looking better than when we last saw him, and his many friends will be glad to learn that his health has improved."[15] He spent that night at William Rowley's residence. On the seventeenth, Rawlins received a letter signed by ninety-five prominent Galenians beseeching him to deliver an address "on the situation in the country." The venue would be the County Court House, the site of Rawlins's patriotic speech in April 1861. The next day, he acknowledged receipt of the letter, calling it "a pleasure to comply with your request."[16]

———

A crowd descended on the courthouse on Friday, June 21, to hear the former Coal Boy's lengthy address, which would have been an ordeal to deliver given his tubercular cough and disheartened emotional condition. Rawlins had honed his remarks to strike the right chords, and he was eager to know how they would be broadly received. He would be making two particularly important points. First, he would provide a short history of American slavery, to demonstrate that the institution and degradation of slaves were so embedded in the fabric of the Confederate states that legislation and edicts were required to protect the rights and liberties of the freedmen. Second, Rawlins presented a case that the requirements imposed by Congress on the former Confederate states for reestablishing their rights to representation were wholly appropriate.

Rawlins began by guiding his audience through examples of prewar legislation and the Dred Scott decision, whose effects were "to strengthen the title of the master and degrade the slave and free persons of his race." Lincoln's election, Rawlins maintained, "was held by the slave States as destructive of their rights in the Union and especially endangering their title to their slaves." Eleven of those states organized a government whose *raison d'être* was to keep enslaved and subjugated a race of people. Here, Rawlins quoted from Alexander Stephens's familiar "Cornerstone Speech." This new government, said the Confederacy's vice president, "is founded . . . upon the great truth that the negro is not equal to the white man; that slavery, subordination to the superior race, is his nature and normal condition."[17]

Rawlins continued his history lesson, detailing how a war was waged "upon the issues so clearly stated by Mr. Stephens." Once the salvos were fired on Fort Sumter, "the majesty and manhood of the nation was aroused to resistance—a resistance the magnitude and grandeur of which was only equaled by the good resulting from it to the human race." That good, he said, was embodied by the action taken by the District of Columbia to abolish slavery, by

Congress's passing a law granting freedom to slaves who fled into Union lines, by Lincoln's Emancipation Proclamation, and by the mobilization of two hundred thousand Black troops "who by their bravery and good fighting, proved the wisdom of the government."[18]

Rawlins reminded his listeners that on July 18, 1864, Lincoln invited Confederate authorities to offer any proposition that restored peace, reintegrated the Union, and ended slavery. Any such serious proposition, Lincoln said, would be met with liberal terms. This offer was ignored, and Rebel resistance hardened: their armies waged "bitter war" outside Richmond, and the government refused to regard captured Black soldiers as prisoners of war. Even as the Confederacy faced dire threats in early 1865, their commissioners at Hampton Roads, led by Alexander Stephens, refused to consider Lincoln's terms, which included abandoning slavery.[19] Once war ended and these Southern states failed to fill offices with loyal men and failed to offer citizenship and suffrage to emancipated Blacks, it led, quite rightly, to their representatives being barred from entering Congress. Congress, after finding that "the emancipated race was not afforded the equal protection of the laws with the governing class," passed the Civil Rights Act and proposed the Fourteenth Amendment. However, the Civil Rights Act was bitterly opposed and sparked intensified violence against Blacks, Union soldiers, and Freedmen Bureau officers. Military commanders in the South intervened when civil authorities neglected to properly deal with the perpetrators. Congress acted wisely to make ratification of the proposed amendment a prerequisite for the government of any seceded state to be recognized as legitimate, that is, republican in form. But only Tennessee, Rawlins pointed out, ratified it and offered voting rights to Blacks.[20]

Rawlins considered the question of extending all Constitutional rights and liberties to former slaves. The answer, to him, was self-evidently in the affirmative given that they are free and shed their blood for the Union. This was a remarkable declaration from a disciple of avowed Negrophobe Stephen Douglas. In a moving defense of this argument, Rawlins hearkened back to the days of the Revolution to convince his audience:

> In view of these facts, and the further fact that the representation the States had for them was used as a means to secure and perpetuate their enslavement, ignorance, and degradation, now that they are free . . . are they not entitled to representation to preserve that freedom . . . ? If their ancestors had been freed in the war for independence, and fought side by side with our revolutionary sires . . . what would our fathers have done? Why, sirs, they never would have questioned their right to representation. Shall we, their sons . . . refuse to . . . invest

the descendants of the enslaved race . . . with all the rights they would have had if their ancestors had all been free at the formation of the Constitution? When the compromise of human rights made by our fathers to secure the Union has been swept away by [those] . . . whose interest it was . . . to destroy the Union, will we any longer withhold from those whose liberties and human character were involved in that compromise the inalienable rights of man? No, we will restore to them these rights, as our fathers would were they living.[21]

Furthermore, near the end of his speech, Rawlins expressed his hope that all states would confer on Blacks the right to vote. Here, Rawlins's words soared to eloquent heights as he envisioned how universal suffrage would work for the common good of the nation and uplift the freedmen: "And the African, elevated from the degradation of slavery, rendered respectable by his voice in government, admitted to all sources of intelligence, inspired by the same love of freedom, speaking the same language and worshipping the same God, will rise rapidly in the scale of knowledge and the cloud of ignorance that now envelopes him will as rapidly pass away, and he will not fail 'to help keep the jewel of liberty in the family of freedom.'"[22]

Rawlins argued in favor of the Johnson-vetoed Military Reconstruction Acts, the first of which placed ten former Confederate states into five military districts. "That the use of military authority contained in these laws was necessary to enable the Government to perform its constitutional obligations," Rawlins concluded, "there is no doubt." The acts were regarded as temporary measures—and in Rawlins's estimation wholly constitutional—until these states adopted a new constitution, provided for protection of life and property, and ratified the proposed amendment giving the vote to all males regardless of race.[23]

Toward the back end of his speech, Rawlins diverged into foreign relations. He spoke with pride about the emergence of the United States as a force to be reckoned with by European powers. The Monroe Doctrine, he pointed out, "has been firmly established by the result of the war" and by frustrating France's designs on Mexico. Moreover, Rawlins alluded to England's "disposition to settle the claims for damages done our merchantmen by privateers fitted out in her ports in aid of the rebellion." Here, Rawlins referred to the damage inflicted on Northern shipping and trade by marauding Confederate cruisers such as the *Alabama*, *Florida*, *Georgia*, and *Shenandoah*, vessels built in England's shipyards and granted full privileges in British ports. Rawlins warned England that if proper restitution was not made, "it may become the duty of the people's representative to issue their writ in the form of a declaration of war for the seizure of her possessions in America in satisfaction of these claims, and thereby facilitate the departure of the last foreign power from this continent." By snatching North American territory from a European nation, Rawlins was spouting a conservative and muscular line. In the early months of the Grant administration, he would be a forceful influence among the cabinet for pursuing this foreign policy agenda.[24]

He ended his great speech by returning to the issue of liberalized voting rights, embracing the idea as a means of advancing globally the ideals of the founding fathers: "And if our experiment of manhood suffrage to all, without distinction of race, proves the success we believe it will, we may hope to see our republican principles engrafted upon all the other governments of the world, and the inalienable rights declared by our fathers in their Declaration of Independence, enjoyed by all mankind."[25]

—◊◊◊—

In his speech, Rawlins mentioned President Johnson by name only three times, and he offered no overt criticism of him. But there was no denying that Rawlins's robust support for Black suffrage and the Reconstruction Acts was in step with the Radicals. And for Republicans who were wagering that Grant would come around to their way of thinking, Rawlins's speech was a great comfort.[26] Although Rawlins had done the talking, most presumed that his speech was "supposed to reflect the views of the head of the Army."[27] This point was evident in an extract from the Chicago *Journal* reprinted in the *Galena Daily Gazette* of June 27: "What more was necessary to a full endorsement of Republicanism? Henceforth there can be no controversies on the sympathies of Gen. Grant. His actions have established the Radicalism of his loyalty, but this speech settles the question beyond dispute." The *Chicago Tribune* advanced the issue a few steps further by seeing in the speech the political implications: "This is the comprehensive platform embodied in the able speech of General Rawlins. It will meet with a hearty response from the whole American people. It is not open to doubt; each point is already stated and fortified with impregnable arguments. It is the platform of the army, it is the platform of the Republican party, it is, emphatically, and it is unquestionably the platform of General Grant."[28]

Rawlins was pleased with the speech and by the favorable reactions of the Chicago papers. His friends approved of it, and the local paper praised it as bearing "the unmistakable marks of statesmanship in every line."[29] Orville Babcock, writing to Washburne, took a more jaundiced view: "[The Republicans] are trotting [Grant] out too soon. Rawlins speech was most untimely and uncalled for. The Democrats look upon it as a bid from Grant, and many of them think—it was all gotten up by you and [Russell] Jones, and brought about in that way." If Rawlins was jumping the gun by exposing Grant's political sympathies as Babcock may have suggested, Grant would make a public break from Johnson later that summer.[30]

While concluding his Galena visit, Rawlins received touching condolence letters from Babcock and Horace Porter. On June 26, the day he was to leave, Rawlins received a $1,000 gift from the citizens of Galena. He wrote Emma that he would decide whether to let Russell Jones invest the money for him. He would do that deciding while on a train to Omaha, where he would arrive the next day to begin recuperation.[31]

—⁓⁓⁓—

Accompanied by Major Dunn and a banker friend from Galena, John Corwith, Rawlins met Grenville Dodge in Omaha. The next leg of the journey was a 370-mile train ride to the end of the Union Pacific line at Julesburg, Colorado, populated by some of the West's roughest escaped convicts, gamblers, carousers, teamsters, and assorted "bull-whackers."[32] Beyond Julesburg, travel continued overland with an escort of soldiers and Pawnee Indians. This was to be no rest cure for Rawlins; rather, in coming weeks it would test what remained of his stamina. On the fourth day out, Rawlins was getting into the swing of roughing it, raving about the best meal he had had in years: "antelope steak, coffee, cheese, not very good biscuit, canned pears and peaches."[33] Just before the Fourth of July, Rawlins and company were joined by Major General Christopher Columbus Augur, commander of the Department of the Platte; his staff; and part of his command. Augur was to establish a military post, Fort D. A. Russell, in southeast Wyoming for the protection of the Union Pacific laborers. Not far south of where the future post would be built, Dodge staked out the grid on Crow Creek that became the city of Cheyenne.

On the Fourth, there was a lively celebration as Augur and his staff joined Rawlins and Dodge's party. There were drinks, toasts, and patriotic speeches, including one by Rawlins.[34] Despite the opportunities for merriment, the soldiers and railroad men were on guard against Indian attack. Two members of a Mormon mule train were killed, forcing Augur to drive off their attackers; on July 6, one of the Pawnee scouts killed a Sioux, and an Arapaho, aided by his wife, performed the scalping.[35]

Over the next several days, Rawlins collaborated with Dodge as they studied the nearby terrain for a suitable location for that military post. Rawlins spent considerable time with Dodge and his crew studying maps and discussing possible lines and railroad affairs. Dodge came to rely on Rawlins, confiding in a letter home, "Gen. Rawlins has been of great help to me. He enters into the spirit of the matter; takes as much interest in our road as I do."[36] He also found himself developing a bond with Rawlins. "I like him very much," he wrote his wife, Anne, "but I can't say all are like him." Dodge was no doubt contrasting Rawlins with his consulting engineer, Colonel Silas Seymour, a fellow he regarded as deceitful and with whom he had a severe personality clash.

From the Cheyenne encampment, Rawlins could see the snow-topped mountains and feel "their icy breath upon us."[37] At an elevation of six thousand feet, a brilliant sun generated scant warmth, making an overcoat suitable during the day and three layers of blankets a requirement at night.[38] Despite the cold, Rawlins's health, in Dodge's estimation, seemed to be improving.[39] But any apparent improvement was only customary symptom fluctuation.

Around July 22, the party moved toward Fort Sanders, fifty-five miles northwest of Cheyenne. There, they received alarming news. A surveyor, Percy Brown, and his small soldier escort had been attacked by a party of Sioux. Brown was killed, causing Dodge to express uneasiness about their situation: "this Indian killing is getting to be terrific; stage stations attacked, trains and people generally."[40] From Fort Sanders, Dodge's team, minus one—Colonel Seymour, much to Dodge's satisfaction, was left behind—pushed on toward the Continental Divide. They were trekking through rugged territory, a country of "immense canyons, upland hills and perpendicular walls of stone" where "mountain piled on mountain."[41]

In camp on the Medicine Bow River, Rawlins's letter informed Emma about the constant Indian threat they faced and his desperate attempt to heal his aching lungs. He opened his shirt on a hot day and exposed his bare chest to the burning sun long enough to almost blister the skin. It was, he told her, the best counterirritant he could come by.[42] A counterirritant, often intense heat, was thought to stimulate the body's healing mechanism.[43] After traversing the Rattlesnake Hills, some sixty miles west of present-day Casper, Wyoming, the party passed through exceptionally dry country. Rawlins suffered from extreme thirst, necessitating a search for water. Dodge happened to find a spring running a generous supply and set up camp there. To Rawlins, that water was "the most gracious and acceptable of anything" so far on the march. He was so grateful that he told Dodge if there was to be anything named after him, he wanted it to be this spring of water. And so it was. Dodge announced, "We will name this Rawlins Springs." He would also lend the name of Rawlins to the future railroad station near the spring. As Dodge later noted, the Rawlins station "has grown now into quite a town and a division point of the Union Pacific Road."[44]

The party pushed westward from the spring toward the Continental Divide through a parched region of the Great Divide Basin known as the Red Desert. While perched on the rim of the basin, Dodge spied in the distance a group of men struggling to make their way east. It was a survey party under Thomas Bates, and they looked in great trouble. The exhausted men, without water for three days and tongues swollen, were rescued just in time.[45] On August 10, Rawlins covered thirty-eight miles, following a ridge over "very rough, rocky and tortuous road." Two days later after traveling twenty-nine miles, Dodge's party made a fine camp, except for thick clouds of mosquitoes.[46]

On August 19, Rawlins was at Fort Bridger. Here, he learned from newspapers that Grant had become secretary of war on an interim basis replacing Stanton. In a letter home, he surmised Grant took the job because he believed he could better manage the process of Reconstruction than someone inimical to it. However, as Rawlins saw it, Grant would face challenges: he had to maintain "a steady hand and clear head to keep out of the gulf that yawns between the President and the people." And there was the fact that "there is no friendship for the General with the President."[47] Rawlins could only conjecture about the political climate. He was virtually in the dark about goings-on in Washington since leaving Galena.

Around August 26, a weary Rawlins and the Dodge party approached Salt Lake City. Meanwhile, two thousand miles away, relations between Grant and Johnson had reached a critical point.

—◦◦◦—

Johnson long had wanted to part ways with Secretary of War Stanton, the lone voice of dissent on the cabinet. With Congress in recess during the summer, Johnson resorted to suspending Stanton and replacing him *ad interim* with Grant, a maneuver allowable under the Tenure of Office Act. On August 11, Johnson called Grant to the Executive Mansion to inform him of his new position; he would also remain as general in chief of the army. Johnson probably calculated that by having Grant on board, it would give the impression that he was in accord with the administration.[48] Also, by bringing Grant closer, it might hurt his standing with the Radicals and presumably weaken his attractiveness as a Republican nominee. Grant felt pressed to take this temporary appointment in order to protect his district commanders in the South from Johnson's interference.

That was a tangible threat. Johnson had reached his limit with the reform-minded Sheridan, who at the end of July, with Grant's approval, sacked James Throckmorton, the governor of Texas; in June, Sheridan had already disposed of Louisiana's Governor James Madison Wells. Johnson wanted to replace Sheridan with General George Thomas, but he declined the job for health reasons. Johnson next turned to General Winfield Scott Hancock, a conservative Democrat, to take command of Sheridan's Fifth Military District. On August 17, Grant wrote a strong letter of caution to Johnson about firing Sheridan and its effect on the country—what Rawlins referred to as the gulf between the president and the people. In a startling turn of events, at the end of August, Grant allowed the public release of that letter, setting off a storm of reactions. Grant was sending out a clear signal he was not in harmony with Johnson's methods for dealing with the South. He was hailed by some for coming out as a Radical and for confronting Johnson. The *Army and Navy Journal* heralded the publication of the letter, saying, "General Grant's protest against the removal of Sheridan must be regarded as the most extraordinary manifesto of our time. . . . In this letter of Grant's every word is golden."[49]

Less than two weeks later at a cabinet meeting with Grant in attendance, Johnson announced his intention to sack Major General Dan Sickles, who commanded the Second Military District encompassing the Carolinas. After three Federal soldiers had been murdered by four Carolinians, Sickles had them tried by a military commission despite a writ of habeas corpus issued in favor of the accused. Sickles refused to answer to the writ, and Stanton stood by him. Johnson was incensed that Sickles was superseding the civil courts.[50] Grant tried unsuccessfully to protect Sickles, and he was gone by August 27. To Grant, this was another point of conflict with Johnson, who was usurping the power Grant believed had been vested in him by Congress to oversee implementation of the Reconstruction Acts.

—◦◦◦—

Rawlins, Dodge, and party arrived at Salt Lake City on August 27. Rawlins was curious about Mormon life, and he wanted to visit some homes. Dodge knew a family living in a double house nearby, so they stopped in on the pretense of asking for milk. While the woman in the house went to fetch a glass, Dodge cautioned Rawlins about drawing her into a discussion of Mormonism. During their bland chat about crops and the countryside, a small boy came into the room. He was looking for something under the bed. "Jimmie, what do you want?" the woman asked. "I am after father's slippers. Mother says father is to stay with us this week." This episode left Rawlins aghast and "settled the question with [him] as to the method of their living."[51]

Rawlins and his fellow travelers lodged at Camp Douglas, three miles outside the city. For political reasons, Rawlins preferred to keep some distance from the Mormons. Polygamy was a contentious topic, and for years Republicans had fulminated against the practice. Rawlins did not want any indiscretion to taint Grant, if the latter had future political ambitions. Despite the efforts of the Mormon officials to pay Rawlins every courtesy and offer him opportunities to socialize, he remained diplomatically aloof.[52]

At Salt Lake City, Rawlins was greeted by fellow Galenian Augustus Chetlain, who, after being mustered out of the service, served there as assessor of internal revenue, having replaced another Galena general, John E. Smith. The visitors during their stay were treated with every kindness by both Chetlain and his wife. On the evening of the twenty-eighth, Rawlins and Dodge met Brigham Young and his favorite wife, Amelia Folsom, at the home of Franklin Head, superintendent of Indian Agencies. The sixty-six-year-old Young impressed Rawlins as appearing twenty years younger. The next day, Rawlins paid a visit to Governor Charles Durkee; John Titus, chief justice of the Utah Territorial Supreme Court; and Justice Thomas Drake. Those three returned the favor by calling on Dodge and Rawlins.[53]

Most of the visitors heard Brigham Young preach on Sunday, September 1. His sermon dealt with men's duty to marry, admonishing all men "to take one, two, three or a dozen wives as they wanted."[54] Dodge and Rawlins were unfavorably impressed with the practice of polygamy. To his wife, Anne, Dodge wrote, "As I look at the system here I cannot see anything but what is disgusting and abhorrent . . . all [women] appear to desire and wish polygamy was a relic of the past."[55] Rawlins also reported home, "Of the peculiar institution of these people, one has a more favorable idea from letter writing than from observation. My own views of them are far less favorable than others of General Grant's staff who have been here before me."[56]

⟶⟪⟫⟵

The seven-hundred-mile return trip to Fort Sanders in southeast Wyoming was to begin on September 4. The first major leg of the trip was a 150-mile trek to Soda Springs on the Bear River. Then it would be on to South Pass, southeast to Medicine Bow River, and finally due east to Fort Sanders. Dodge wanted to cover twenty-five miles per day.[57] He hoped to make Fort Sanders by October 1, but given the rugged mountain terrain, he feared it would be impossible to adhere to that schedule. Rawlins fell into the team's rigorous travel routine: arise at 4:00 a.m., eat breakfast, feed the animals, and break camp by 6:00 or 6:30. Then it was on the march and clambering up hills and mountains, scouting topography, pitching tents, building a campfire, and eating dinner at 6:00 p.m. After dinner around the campfire, Rawlins might entertain the party by reading aloud from a collection of poems before all turned in by 8:00 p.m.[58]

As Dodge drew closer to Rawlins, his respect for him only increased. "He is one of the purest, highest minded men I ever saw," Dodge wrote Anne. "You would like him; his ideas of right and wrong coincide with yours and he does not hesitate to make them known." Thus, it pained him to see Rawlins wearing down on the return journey. On reaching the west base of the mountains, Dodge realized that Rawlins was so fatigued he needed help traversing the steep landscape. Dodge's solution was to personally escort him ahead of the rest of the party to the evening's camp site to allow him extra time to rest. To Dodge, Rawlins's tragic fate was plain to see. "That he must die with that dread disease consumption," he told Anne, "seems too bad."[59] Tellingly, Dodge had floated that fatal word *consumption* and broached the tragic outcome, something that Rawlins, except perhaps in his most contemplative moments, was loathe to admit. Just eight days before Dodge's lament, Rawlins boasted to Emma, "I am in very good health except my cough and I think I am getting better of that all the time."[60]

Near marshy Gray's Lake, north of Soda Springs, the men saw numerous grizzlies, prompting Dodge to give orders not to follow or shoot them. When Dodge appeared at camp that afternoon, Rawlins and Dunn were missing. The cook said they left to tail a grizzly that had wandered by. A worried Dodge and a guide, Sol Gee, raced off to follow their trail. Soon, they heard two shots and next saw Rawlins and Dunn in panic sprinting toward them. A wounded grizzly was gaining on them fast. Dodge shot, but the bear kept charging. Gee held his ground until almost face-to-face with the bear before he fired and hit him between the eyes. Then to Dodge's shock, Rawlins, ever the stickler for rules, unleashed a profane outburst against himself and Dunn for having disobeyed his order. Rawlins's self-directed tirade escalated to the point where he even argued for his and Dunn's executions—but he did think Dodge should know that Dunn had been the instigator. As keepsakes, Dodge gave Rawlins the bear hide and Dunn the paws.[61]

On September 16, a snowstorm made passage difficult across the mountains on steep, poor roads that had to be built by a crew of pioneers working ahead. The snow continued in blinding intensity, leaving their mounts without feed. Dodge feared that at one point, their movement forward would be blocked by the mounting snow.[62] On September 21, 250 miles from Fort Sanders, the weather continued frigid, and each night meant camping in snow. Averaging a remarkable twenty miles a day, the party arrived in Fort Sanders on October 4. A two-day march brought them to Cheyenne. On October 9, Rawlins found himself at Pine Bluff Station, just west of the Nebraska border and at the end of the Union Pacific line. After four months of grueling travel, Rawlins was back in Galena on October 15.[63]

—◦◦◦—

Friends were initially encouraged by Rawlins's appearance and buoyant description of his health. Before heading to Guilford Township to spend a few days with his parents, he boasted he had just been more than thirty continuous days on horseback. Horace Houghton, the *Galena Gazette*'s editor, figured that was certainly "a good test of a man's power of endurance."[64] There were other exciting portents. Rawlins's arrival coincided with rumors leaking out of Washington that he would be recommended by Grant to fill the position of secretary of war on a permanent basis. However, as much as Houghton would have liked to see a favorite son elevated to the Cabinet, he waved off such talk: "We do not anticipate such a step on the part of Mr. Johnson, as Gen. R. would be no more agreeable than is Gen. Grant."[65]

With Rawlins's departure on the eighteenth to rejoin his family in Connecticut, his friends' earlier assessment of his vigor was recalculated downward: "His health, although considerably improved, is not as good as reports had lead [*sic*] his friends to hope."[66] In truth, although John Rawlins had spent weeks breathing the mountain air, eating wild game, engaging in manly activities, and even surviving a few close calls, he was not one whit improved.

NOTES

1. Philip H. Sheridan to U. S. Grant, January 25, 1867, in *The Papers of Ulysses S. Grant*, ed. John Y. Simon (Carbondale: Southern Illinois University Press, 1991), 17:39n.

2. Joseph J. Reynolds to J. A. Rawlins, January 19, 1867, in *The Papers of Ulysses S. Grant*, ed. John Y. Simon, 17:39note.

3. E. O. C. Ord to J. A. Rawlins, April 19, 1867, in *The Papers of Ulysses S. Grant*, ed. John Y. Simon, 17:143n.

4. U. S. Grant to O. O. Howard, January 18, 1867, in *The Papers of Ulysses S. Grant*, ed. John Y. Simon, 17:50n.

5. U. S. Grant to Edwin M. Stanton, January 29, 1867, in *The Papers of Ulysses S. Grant*, ed. John Y. Simon, 17:38.

6. U. S. Grant to Elihu B. Washburne, March 4, 1867, in *The Papers of Ulysses S. Grant*, ed. John Y. Simon, 17:76.

7. Albert D. Richardson, *A Personal History of Ulysses S. Grant* (Boston: D. L. Guernsey, 1885), 527.

8. Merlin E. Sumner, ed., *The Diary of Cyrus B. Comstock* (Dayton, OH: Morningside House, 1987), 344.

9. U. S. Grant to Philip H. Sheridan, April 5, 1867, in *The Papers of Ulysses S. Grant*, ed. John Y. Simon, 17:95.

10. U. S. Grant to E. B. Washburne, May 3, 1867, in Mark Washburne, *A Biography of Elihu Benjamin Washburne: Congressman, Secretary of State, Envoy Extraordinary* (self-pub., Xlibris, 2005), 175.

11. Stanley P. Hirshson, *Grenville M. Dodge: Soldier, Politician, Railroad Pioneer* (Bloomington: Indiana University Press, 1967), 152–53.

12. U. S. Grant to J. Russell Jones, June 3, 1867, in *The Papers of Ulysses S. Grant*, ed. John Y. Simon, 17:184.

13. Ibid., 184n.

14. John A. Rawlins to Emma Rawlins, June 13, 1867, transcribed by J. H. Wilson, James H. Wilson Papers, Bender Collection, Wyoming State Archives and Historical Department, Microfilm Reel H-61b.

15. *Daily Gazette*, Galena, IL, June 14, 1867.

16. Ibid., June 18, 1867.

17. "Speech of Major Gen'l John A. Rawlins, Chief of Staff U.S.A.," Washington, DC: The Union Republican Congressional Committee, 2.

18. Ibid., 3.

19. Ibid., 4.

20. Ibid., 5.

21. Ibid., 7.

22. Ibid., 13.

23. Ibid., 13.

24. Ibid., 15.

25. Ibid., 16.

26. Harold M. Hyman, ed., *The Radical Republicans and Reconstruction 1861–1870* (Indianapolis: Bobbs-Merrill, 1967), 392.

27. *The United States Army and Navy Journal and Gazette of the Regular and Volunteer Forces* 4, no. 47 (July 13, 1867): 742.

28. *Chicago Tribune*, June 24, 1867.

29. *Daily Gazette*, Galena, IL, June 24, 1867.

30. O. E. Babcock to Elihu B. Washburne, August 13, 1867, in *The Papers of Ulysses S. Grant*, ed. John Y. Simon, 17:291n.

31. John A. Rawlins to Emma Rawlins, June 26, 1867, transcribed by J. H. Wilson, James H. Wilson Papers, Bender Collection, Wyoming State Archives and Historical Department, Microfilm Reel H-61b.

32. Edmund B. Tuttle, *The Boy's Book about Indians: Being What I Saw and Heard for Three Years in the Plains* (New York: T. Whittaker, 1874), 52.

33. John A. Rawlins to Emma Rawlins, July 4, 1867, transcribed by J. H. Wilson, James H. Wilson Papers, Bender Collection, Wyoming State Archives and Historical Department, Microfilm Reel H-61b.

34. Grenville Dodge to wife, July 4, 1867 at Crow's Creek Crossing, Grenville Dodge Papers, Biographical Records, Vol. VI, State Archives of Iowa; Grenville M. Dodge, *How We Built the Union Pacific and Other Railway Papers and Addresses* (Council Bluffs, IA: Monarch), 24.

35. Stanley P. Hirshson, *Grenville M. Dodge*, 153; Grenville Dodge to his children, July 7, 1867, at Crow's Creek Crossing, Grenville Dodge Papers, Biographical Records, Vol. VI, State Archives of Iowa.

36. Grenville Dodge to wife, August 6, 1867, in camp west of North Platte, Grenville Dodge Papers, Biographical Records, Vol. VI, State Archives of Iowa.

37. John A. Rawlins to Emma Rawlins, July 4, 1867, transcribed by J. H. Wilson, James H. Wilson Papers, Bender Collection, Wyoming State Archives and Historical Department, Microfilm Reel H-61b.

38. Grenville Dodge to wife, July 15, 1867, at Cheyenne, transcribed by J. H. Wilson, James H. Wilson Papers, Bender Collection, Wyoming State Archives and Historical Department, Microfilm Reel H-61b.

39. Grenville Dodge to wife, July 11, 1867, at Crow Creek, transcribed by J. H. Wilson, James H. Wilson Papers, Bender Collection, Wyoming State Archives and Historical Department, Microfilm Reel H-61b.

40. Dodge Diary of 1867, July 24, 1867, in Grenville Dodge Papers, Biographical Records, Vol.VI, State Archives of Iowa.

41. Grenville Dodge to wife, August 3, 1867, at North Platte R. R. crossing, transcribed by J. H. Wilson, James H. Wilson Papers, Bender Collection, Wyoming State Archives and Historical Department, Microfilm Reel H-61b.

42. John A. Rawlins to Emma Rawlins, July 31, 1867, transcribed by J. H. Wilson, James H. Wilson Papers, Bender Collection, Wyoming State Archives and Historical Department, Microfilm Reel H-61b.

43. In 1858, Charles Sumner sought relief from the aftereffects of a brutal caning unleashed on him in 1856 by Congressman Preston Brooks. In Paris, Sumner consulted Dr. Charles Brown-Séquard, a specialist in spinal and nervous system disorders. To treat the "congestion about the brain" that was supposedly causing Sumner pain and weakness in his legs, the physician recommended a procedure called moxabustion. This involved

burning a ground herb on Sumner's bare skin as a counterirritant to offset the disease process within the damaged points in his spine. Sumner was exposed to six painful treatments. The procedure proved miraculously successful, allowing him to return to the United States in renewed health. It appears that Dr. Brown-Séquard affected a placebo cure for what was likely Sumner's posttraumatic stress disorder. See Allen J. Ottens, "A Brain That Has Lost Its Power," *Manuscripts* 62, no. 3 (2010): 101–8.

44. Grenville M. Dodge, *How We Built the Union Pacific and Other Railway Papers and Addresses*, 24–25.

45. Ibid., 112–13.

46. Dodge Diary of 1867, August 10 and August 12, 1867, in Grenville Dodge Papers, Biographical Records, Vol.VI, State Archives of Iowa.

47. John A. Rawlins to Emma Rawlins, August 19, 1867, transcribed by J. H. Wilson, James H. Wilson Papers, Bender Collection, Wyoming State Archives and Historical Department, Microfilm Reel H-61b.

48. Adam Badeau, *Grant in Peace* (Hartford, CT: S. S. Scranton, 1887), 88.

49. *The United States Army and Navy Journal and Gazette of the Regular and Volunteer Forces* 5, no. 1 (August 31, 1867): 21.

50. W. A. Swanberg, *Sickles the Incredible* (New York: Charles Scribner's Sons, 1956), 291.

51. Personal Biography of Major General Grenville Mellen Dodge, 1866–1869, Vol. III., Microfilm MS98, Reel 3, State Archives of Iowa, 661–62.

52. Ibid., 662.

53. Grenville Dodge to wife, August 30, 1867, at Salt Lake City, Grenville Dodge Papers, Biographical Records, Vol. VI, State Archives of Iowa; John A. Rawlins to Emma Rawlins, August 30, 1867, transcribed by J. H. Wilson, James H. Wilson Papers, Bender Collection, Wyoming State Archives and Historical Department, Microfilm Reel H-61b; Augustus L. Chetlain, *Recollections of Seventy Years* (Galena, IL: Gazette, 1899), 118–19, 132–33.

54. Grenville Dodge to wife, September 3, 1867, at Salt Lake City, Grenville Dodge Papers, Biographical Records, Vol. VI, State Archives of Iowa.

55. Grenville Dodge to wife, August 30, 1867 at Salt Lake City, Grenville Dodge Papers, Biographical Records, Vol. VI, State Archives of Iowa.

56. John A. Rawlins to Emma Rawlins, August 30, 1867, transcribed by J. H. Wilson, James H. Wilson Papers, Bender Collection, Wyoming State Archives and Historical Department, Microfilm Reel H-61b.

57. Grenville Dodge to wife, September 3, 1867, at Salt Lake City, Grenville Dodge Papers, Biographical Records, Vol. VI, State Archives of Iowa.

58. Grenville Dodge to wife, September 14, 1867, at Bear Mountain camp, and September 21, 1867, to wife at Sweet Water north of South Pass, Grenville Dodge Papers, Biographical Records, Vol. VI, State Archives of Iowa.

59. Grenville Dodge to wife, September 14, 1867, at Bear Mountain camp, Grenville Dodge Papers, Biographical Records, Vol. VI, State Archives of Iowa.

60. John A. Rawlins to Emma Rawlins, September 6, 1867, transcribed by J. H. Wilson, James H. Wilson Papers, Bender Collection, Wyoming State Archives and Historical Department, Microfilm Reel H-61b.

61. Grenville M. Dodge, *How We Built the Union Pacific and Other Railway Papers and Addresses*, 113–14; Personal Biography of Major General Grenville Mellen Dodge,

1866–1869, Vol. III., Microfilm MS98, Reel 3, State Archives of Iowa, 667–68. Rawlins later had the bear hide cured and displayed it in his office when secretary of war.

62. Personal Biography of Major General Grenville Mellen Dodge, 1866–1869, Vol. III., Microfilm MS98, Reel 3, State Archives of Iowa, 668.

63. Grenville Dodge to wife, September 21, 1867, at Salt Lake City, Grenville Dodge Papers, Biographical Records, Vol. VI, State Archives of Iowa; Dodge Diary of 1867, entries for September 16, 1867, October 4, 6, and 9, 1867, in Grenville Dodge Papers, Biographical Records, Vol.VI, State Archives of Iowa.

64. *Daily Gazette*, Galena, IL, October 18, 1867.

65. Ibid., October 14, 1867.

66. Ibid., October 18, 1867.

24

"This Will Not Do. It Is Not Enough."

LATER IN OCTOBER, THE RAWLINS family returned to their Georgetown residence at 78 Gay Street.[1] Rawlins's return meant becoming accustomed to Grant's new work routine: a few hours as interim secretary at the War Department in the morning, followed by a short walk to his duties at the old army headquarters office. His customary staff officers did not accompany him to the War Department. At this time, Rawlins was consulting one of Washington's foremost physicians, Dr. D. W. Bliss, former superintendent of Armory Square Hospital and one of the first doctors to be summoned to Ford's Theater to treat President Lincoln. Dr. Bliss sought to increase Rawlins's strength, putting him on a diet of raw beef, stale bread, fresh milk, and soft-boiled eggs—a diet which he fastidiously followed for two years.[2]

In the fall of 1867, while Rawlins had been wending his way back to Washington, events were taking intriguing turns. For one, the off-year elections had tilted the political landscape. To President Johnson's gratification, Democrats had scored sizeable gains, in part because of voters' reservations regarding the Republicans' eagerness for Black suffrage. On October 9, Orville Babcock conveyed his concern to Washburne: "No doubt now the Elections have gone as they have Mr. J. will be on the *Rampage* again."[3] Ironically, the Democrats' resurgence gave Radicals more impetus to promote presidential impeachment, an issue given a boost by Johnson's ouster of Stanton, Sheridan, and Sickles.

The election results produced another effect: Grant emerged as a more attractive Republican candidate. He supported Black suffrage, but with a less shrill voice, while his advocacy for a swift end to military oversight in the

South was a boon to conservatives. As a result, he tended to appeal to a broader spectrum of voters. Babcock's letter to Washburne followed on the heels of the latter's delivery of an important speech, which garnered national attention, to the Jo Daviess Republican convention. Washburne set out Grant's positions such as his belief in "impartial suffrage," denying he had any past sympathy with the Democratic Party and emphasizing his enforcement of the Reconstruction Acts. Washburne coyly added the disclaimer he was not speaking of Grant as a candidate for the presidency, per se, but was simply putting forth "his views, sentiments and convictions."[4] Given Washburne's status, the local press attached considerable weight to his remarks, rating them above the speech Rawlins had given ten weeks earlier at the court house. "When General Rawlins, Grant's Chief of Staff, addressed the citizens of Galena upon the condition of the country," the *Gazette* editorialized, "the speech was regarded as a semi-official declaration, but the statements of Mr. Washburne are still more authoritarian [*sic*]."[5]

Not all Republicans were happy the Democrats' gains were boosting Grant toward the nomination. Senator Charles Sumner had been plugging Chief Justice Salmon Chase, a politician who had always thirsted for the highest office. Sumner, a zealous abolitionist, had been sour on Grant since he submitted his positive 1865 report about conditions in the South. At a secret meeting in fall 1867 convened by Republican leaders that Rawlins and Babcock attended, Sumner warned the party would disintegrate if Grant, a political neophyte, were nominated. However, no one rose to second Sumner. Attendees were sworn to keep the meeting secret, but it is probable that Rawlins or Babcock alerted Grant to Sumner's opposition.[6]

As Grant became in the eyes of many (excluding Sumner) the Republicans' most viable candidate, his relationship with Johnson became fraught with questions about trust. In early October, Johnson called Sherman to Washington. The more conservative Sherman might be persuaded to replace Grant in the War Department, especially now that Johnson felt Grant "had gone over to the Radicals, and was with Congress."[7] However, Sherman told Johnson he was neither interested in the War Department nor amenable to influencing Grant. Johnson was growing worried about Grant's trustworthiness, especially as speculation surfaced that Johnson might be detained prior to a vote on impeachment and a Senate trial. Gideon Welles pressed Johnson to sound Grant out regarding his closeness to the Radicals. On October 12, Johnson ambled to the War Department to meet with Grant. Would he be willing to obey Johnson's orders if an effort were made to arrest him prior to any actions taken on impeachment? Grant responded in the affirmative—but if he should change his mind, he assured Johnson he would be given time to make any suitable arrangements.[8] Johnson and Grant probably also discussed at this meeting the question of how to respond if Congress, after it convened at the end of November, restored Stanton as secretary of war. Should that occur, Grant pledged he would leave the War Department in Johnson's hands or remain in the office pending a court ruling on the constitutionality of the Tenure of Office Act.[9]

—◦◦◦—

Three people who were keenly interested in boosting Grant for the presidency met in early November. They were John Forney, editor of the *Washington Daily Chronicle*; Chief Justice David K. Cartter of the Supreme Court of the District of Columbia; and Senator John Thayer of Nebraska. Forney was worried Johnson's pro-South policies were inflicting damage on the country. Cartter and Thayer proposed they all cooperate to make Grant the Republican candidate. To accomplish that, two things were needed: Grant's consent to run and evidence of his "approved Republican record." Forney was charged with researching Grant's political utterances since leaving Galena in 1861 and preparing a newspaper article from them.

Forney and Thayer took the finished article to Rawlins, who thought it should run the next day. But Forney tempered Rawlins's enthusiasm and counseled him to let Grant see it first. Following a lengthy consultation with his chief, Rawlins announced to Forney, "General Grant is quite pleased with your statement of his political record, and surprised that he proves to be so good a Republican." After the piece was printed, Rawlins assured Forney that the sentiments were Grant's but that "General Grant does not want to be President." Although Grant believed he could win two terms, he would face an unsettling question: "What is to become of him after his second Presidential term?" Rawlins reduced the issue to dollars and cents. "He is receiving from seventeen to twenty thousand dollars a year as General of the armies of the Republic—a life salary. To go into the Presidency at twenty-five thousand dollars a year for eight years is perhaps, to gain more fame; but what is to become of him at the end of his Presidency?" That would leave Grant without a salary at age fifty-five. What Rawlins expressed to Forney revealed two things about Grant: he still safeguarded his true political leaning and his years of financial hardship would guide his decision making.[10] Despite Grant's denials, a groundswell was building for his candidacy.

Before the year ended, more political blows would fall. On November 25, the House Judiciary Committee, based on an array of charges, recommended Johnson's impeachment by a 5–4 vote. At the end of December, Johnson sacked Major General John Pope, the commander of the Third Military District encompassing Alabama, Georgia, and Florida, and soon thereafter, he dismissed Edward Ord, the Fourth District (Arkansas and Mississippi) commander. Pope, who had aided Blacks to cast ballots during the October elections, had been attacked for this by Georgia's powerful Howell Cobb, a prewar Speaker of the House.[11] Pope's replacement was the apolitical George Meade, and Ord's was Brevet Major General Alvan Gillem, a Johnson crony.

At this time, Rawlins was alerted to an emerging humanitarian crisis in the seaboard districts of South Carolina. Brevet Major General Edward Canby, Sickles's replacement, reported the failure of the rice and cotton crops there, with the result that as many as thirty thousand Black citizens might face hunger. Canby felt compelled to help but saw grave dangers if interventions on behalf of the African Americans were too liberal. "If direct issues of food are made," he warned Rawlins, "we incur the risk of encouraging idleness, and its attendant vices, and of creating a proletarian population, that will look to the Government for relief, whenever misfortune, want of thrift, or idleness reduces them to want." Rather than making handouts, Canby argued for advancing loans that would be repaid with next year's crop. Canby felt these crop liens would protect the government against loss and teach these plantation laborers lessons about industry and morals.[12] Instead of endorsing what would have become an administrative headache, Rawlins simply authorized the Freedmen's Bureau "to issue sufficient rations to all classes of destitute persons, which will avoid much of the apprehended troubles."[13]

—⁂—

During the evening of Friday, January 10, 1868, Grant took the time to carefully study the Tenure of Office Act. He discovered that if the Senate overruled Johnson's suspension of Stanton, he would be restored to his position of secretary of war. Then to Grant's shock, he read that if he failed to relinquish the post to Stanton, he could face a stiff jail sentence or fine. Armed with these sobering facts, Grant met with Johnson in the afternoon of the eleventh to discuss how they would respond should the Senate, as anticipated, reinstate

Stanton. Their hour-long meeting could have been a case study of a communication breakdown—although exactly what positions each believed he was advocating have never been established—and it resulted in a misunderstanding that ultimately brought Grant into the White House.

Adam Badeau recollected that after Grant returned from this meeting, he was certain he had set forth "all the necessary notification to Johnson of his course."[14] What Grant believed he had given Johnson notification of was, "namely, that if the Senate refused to concur in the suspension of Mr. Stanton, my powers as Sec. of War, ad int. would cease, and Mr. Stanton's right to resume at once the functions of his office would under the law be indisputable, and I acted accordingly."[15] Grant would step aside, feeling bound by the Tenure Act until it might be found unconstitutional. What he was communicating was a reneging of his October pledge to hold on to the office and perhaps a signal to Johnson that he should choose someone else to defy Congress and thwart Stanton from reclaiming the War Department. Johnson, on the other hand, came away with the understanding that Grant would hold on to the office until a court ruling came down or until he, Johnson, could find a replacement for Grant. After an hour of wrangling, Johnson, believing no decision had been reached, suggested they continue discussion on Monday.[16]

That discussion never occurred. Rather, on Sunday the twelfth, Grant met with Sherman, who was back in Washington. Sherman endorsed Jacob Cox, the outgoing governor of Ohio, as a viable replacement for Stanton. Cox, a former division commander under Sherman, could be confirmed easily by the Senate. Moreover, Cox was only lukewarm about Black suffrage and had been a supporter of Johnson's Reconstruction politics. To Grant, working with Cox was preferable to chafing under the brilliant but irascible Stanton. Strangely, Johnson ignored this sensible compromise solution. Soon it became too late for him to settle on a fallback nominee, because on the thirteenth, the Senate voted to overturn Johnson's suspension of Stanton.

Grant arrived promptly at the War Department on the morning of Tuesday the fourteenth. He composed a brief letter informing the president that the Senate vote meant his functions as interim secretary had ceased. After handing over the office keys to acting adjutant general Edward Townsend, Grant tramped back to army headquarters, confident he had left sufficient time for Johnson to find a successor and for himself to pack up his papers before the War Department office became occupied. However, Grant had not figured on Stanton playing by different rules. The reinstated secretary swooped into the War Department later that morning, took possession of the keys, and established himself at his old desk. Alerted to this turn of events, an apoplectic Johnson told Grant to attend that afternoon's cabinet meeting.

Johnson, flanked by his cabinet, turned up the heat on Grant. He upbraided Grant for failing to meet with him on Monday, and he pressed Grant about defaulting on his promise to maintain possession of the War Department office, accusing him of duplicitous behavior. Grant countered by reminding Johnson he could have blocked Stanton by nominating Cox, and he offered an excuse that events—the Senate vote and Stanton's sudden appearance—happened so quickly. To Grant's consternation, portions of this confrontation with Johnson were leaked to a Washington daily, the *National Intelligencer*, and appeared in print on the fifteenth. The article declared that Grant and Stanton colluded to frustrate Johnson. There would soon be open warfare, with the president and his allies gunning for the general now forced to defend himself.

Early in the fray, William Hillyer, a Johnson acolyte, tried to pacify Johnson by informing him how his conversations with Grant and Rawlins on January 14 led Hillyer to conclude he was now "*fully satisfied that Gen Grant never had any conversation or collusion with Mr Stanton in regard to his (Stantons) restoration to the War office*, that Grant never expected that Stanton would resume the duties of the war office."[17] Johnson dismissed Hillyer's words of restraint. Instead, he decided to attack Grant by enlisting several loyal members of his cabinet to present their shared version of what transpired during that meeting on the fourteenth. As the *New York Tribune* reported, "all agreed that at that meeting Gen. Grant acknowledged that he had made an agreement with the President that he would give him timely warning of what he would do should the Senate reinstate Mr. Stanton in the War Department."[18] The *Army and Navy Journal*, however, sustained Grant: "Much bitter feeling has been indulged with regard to the General-in-Chief, and charges of duplicity even have been intimated against him in a part of the public press. So far from being true, these characterizations have not the shadow of a foundation. Beyond all question, the course of General Grant has been straightforward from the start. He made no pledges and declined to be the party to any controversy in which the Congress and the President chose to indulge."[19]

The *New York Herald* summed up how the warring factions faced off in this public clash: "According to the President's friends Grant has proved himself a deceiver, a trickster, a tool of Stanton and a willing instrument in the hands of the radicals to bolster up their failing fortunes. According to the other side, however, Grant is a much abused innocent and a worthy patriot, who has been maliciously misrepresented by Johnson men, who have inculcated unblushing lies, slanders and libels against his character."[20]

Grant and Johnson also sniped at each other in written communications. On the twenty-eighth, Grant wrote Johnson for instructions regarding when to obey orders from Stanton. As often happens when parties distrust each other, Grant wanted Johnson's instructions in writing "in consequence of the many and gross misrepresentations, affecting my personal honor, circulated through the press for the past fortnight, purporting to come from you." Then in this long letter, Grant presented the facts in the Stanton case and concluded with his version of the interchange during the cabinet meeting.[21] Replying on January 31, Johnson rejected Grant's version: "My recollection of what then transpired is diametrically the reverse of your narration." Furthermore, Johnson told Grant he had read his own account of the meeting's events to cabinet members who had been present, and "they, without exception, agree in its accuracy."[22]

Grant toiled over a rejoinder to Johnson before he showed a draft to Rawlins. Adam Badeau recollected what next transpired. "This will not do," Rawlins said. "It is not enough." Rawlins reworked passages of it, particularly those that contradicted and defied Johnson.[23] If Grant decided to come out punching, it was Rawlins who removed his gloves. In this reworked letter dated February 3, Grant rebuked Johnson, making clear that when he temporarily replaced Stanton or recommended Cox, he did so with the good of the country in mind, as opposed to the president acting to dispose of a cabinet member and usurp his office. The letter ended with Grant (and Rawlins) delivering a crushing haymaker to Johnson: "And now, Mr. President, where my honor as a soldier and integrity as a man have been so violently assailed, pardon me for saying that I can but regard this whole matter, from the beginning to the end, as an attempt to involve me in the resistance of law, for which you hesitated to assume the responsibility in orders, and thus to destroy my character before the country."[24] Grant, Badeau said, would have probably proceeded to "tranquilize the situation" and assume a subordinate position. But Rawlins would not allow that. He sensed that Grant's honor had been impugned and that time had come to break with Johnson. What Rawlins accomplished was to apprehend Grant's unexpressed reaction, his inchoate feelings about the president and the base deeds to which Johnson had tried to make him party. Badeau provided a breathtaking description of this moment of political reckoning: "But not a word was said by any one present of the political tendencies or results of the situation. Rawlins knew that he was expressing Grant's own sentiment, and Grant instantly perceived this fact—and acquiesced. I never in my intercourse with Grant saw another exercise so direct and palpable and important an influence with him. It was instantaneous and absolute."[25]

Rawlins's ability to apprehend Grant's unexpressed thoughts or emotions was, as Badeau explained, a distinctive hallmark of their relationship. "He seemed by nature utterly unobservant of the workings of his own mind," Badeau said of Grant, "and almost of the peculiarities of his own character." Rawlins was unique among those close to Grant in that he possessed the gift to read Grant's verbal and nonverbal cues and articulate their meaning or intent. Rawlins did not insert his own ideas into Grant; rather, "he got them all first from Grant; and having a greater faculty of expression would reveal them to him, or even impress them on their author." After describing Rawlins's art, Badeau added the enigmatic remark that Rawlins never discussed it—"he only exerted it; perhaps unconsciously."[26] What was this gift?

Rawlins had the ability to capture the feelings and meanings beyond Grant's ken and then give a concrete and fuller expression to them. Among members of the counseling professions, this skill is known as advanced empathy. Advanced empathy is based on an ability to perform abductive logic—to read clues or to select relevant facts and to weave them into a hypothesis or possible explanation. Thus, the psychologist who selects from various facts presented by the patient and arranges them into a plausible explanation for why he or she feels or acts a certain way is using abductive logic.[27] Rawlins probably honed these empathy skills while working as an attorney.

What would be the result of this seminal February 3 letter? As Badeau declared, "It made [Grant] a Republican. Rawlins knew this. I could see it in his face and detect it in his tone."[28] Rawlins, we might say, deduced that Grant's time had come. He had sensed that Grant was poised to break with Johnson. This, as Badeau understood, was "a stroke of political genius, for it also made any other candidate than Grant impossible for the Republicans."[29]

In early February, the House of Representatives requested all copies of correspondence between Grant and Johnson with the intent to make them public, and they began appearing in the press as soon as February 6. On the fourth, a clerk read aloud these bitter communications on the floor of the House. When the clerk finished reading the Rawlins-fortified February 3 letter, the House's most radical Republican, Thaddeus Stevens, was given cause to exult about

Grant: "He is a bolder man than I thought him. Now we will let him into the Church."[30]

Not only had Grant emerged as a leading Republican standard-bearer, but his letters, many thought, had fatally skewered Johnson. The *New York Herald* on February 6 could foresee his downfall: "Indeed with the declaration of war from General Grant against Mr. Johnson, his impeachment, conviction and removal from office have ceased to be impossibilities, and the necessity for his removal to the radicals is more urgent than ever."[31]

—◦◦◦—

Stanton's reinstatement so rankled Johnson that he struck back by naming another interim replacement, the aged Major General Lorenzo Thomas. On February 21, Thomas strode to the War Department and showed Stanton Johnson's order. Stanton refused to yield. When news of Johnson's defiant action reached Congress, the Republicans erupted in outrage. From the House floor, the infirm but feisty Thaddeus Stevens taunted his colleagues for their previous timid efforts to impeach Johnson. "What good did your moderation do you? If you don't kill the beast, it will kill you."[32] The march toward impeachment was on.

Meanwhile, Winfield Hancock, Sheridan's replacement, was asserting himself in Louisiana politics. Grant had been concerned about his moves to appoint conservatives to public offices and to discriminate against Blacks. In early February, Hancock sacked the New Orleans street commissioner, William Baker. Baker and his supporters claimed it was in retaliation for his hiring of Black street cleaners. Hancock followed by removing nine New Orleans aldermen, seven of whom were Black. All had been appointed by Sheridan. Grant and Rawlins intervened on Baker's behalf. Rawlins wrote Hancock on February 28 to disapprove of his firing and to order his reinstatement.[33] On February 21, Rawlins wrote Hancock a lawyerly worded interpretation of the case in which he revoked Hancock's order and reinstated the aldermen.[34] Under fire, Hancock asked to be relieved, and Grant assented.

Hancock was recalled to Washington, where he reported to Grant's headquarters as required. There, he registered with his signature and chatted with the staff, but he declined the customary interview with Grant. "Under existing circumstances it is probably as well," he explained to Rawlins, "and if you will notify the General that I have arrived in the city, and where my residence is, he will no doubt send for me if he desires to see me." Rawlins had Hancock's address, but Grant never asked for it.[35]

More disconcerting news from the South reached Grant's headquarters. In early March, he received two pieces of correspondence forwarded from General George Thomas. They were letters containing reports of depredations being perpetrated in Tennessee by an order known as the Ku Klux Klan. Because Tennessee had qualified as a "fully reconstructed" state, Thomas felt the military was not authorized to take counteractive measures. The reports of violence failed to move Johnson. On March 14, he wrote Grant, "It is not at this time deemed within the province of the Executive to give any instructions upon the subject to which these papers refer."[36]

Johnson was then distracted by other events. By March 3, the House had adopted eleven articles of impeachment against him—a move that Grant "heartily approved."[37] At the end of the month, his Senate trial would begin.

—◆◆◆—

In Columbus, Georgia, during the early morning of March 31, 1868, armed men wearing masks entered the residence of George W. Ashburn. Shots were fired, and Ashburn was killed. Ashburn was known locally as a scalawag for his service as a delegate to the state's Constitutional Convention and as an organizer of Republicans and Black voters. His murder, one of the first perpetrated by the Georgia KKK, attracted national attention.[38] Almost immediately, Grant ordered Meade, the district military commander, to investigate and mete out justice by a military court, if the civil courts proved unreliable.[39] Working fast, Meade requested the services of an experienced detective and made arrests. He retained, for a steep price, as counsel for the government Joseph Brown, the former governor of Georgia. The defendants had their own powerhouse legal team headed by Alexander Stephens and Henry L. Benning, a prewar associate justice on the state supreme court.

While Meade attended to the murder case, a sequence of historical events unfolded that spring and early summer in Washington, New York, and Chicago. On May 26, President Johnson survived a Senate impeachment trial by the barest of margins. Johnson's acquittal was too much for Stanton, who resigned as secretary of war. Major General John Schofield, despite misgivings and Grant's advice to decline the job, agreed to have his name put before the Senate, and he was confirmed as Stanton's successor on June 1.[40] At the Democratic convention in New York City in early July, a bitter Andrew Johnson watched as delegates abandoned him in favor of Horatio Seymour, the Copperhead wartime governor of New York. The November presidential election figured to be a mismatch with Seymour opposed by the Republicans' standard-bearer, Ulysses S. Grant, who in Chicago was the whirlwind nominee on the first ballot. Indiana's Schuyler Colfax, Speaker of the House, was picked as Grant's running mate. After four years of civil war and three more of sectional strife under Johnson, Grant's campaign slogan, "Let us have peace," resonated with a public eager for tranquility.

A month after accepting the nomination, Grant embarked on what was billed an inspection tour of the west that would take him to Denver. But the trip was more about Candidate Grant wanting relief from duties as general of the army and staying above the political fray. The tour was followed by a three months' sojourn in Galena lasting through the November election. That left Schofield assuming the functions of commander in chief. Badeau would join Grant in Galena in August, but until then, he fashioned a brief biography of Grant to be used during the campaign and handled the mountain of incoming correspondence. Rawlins remained in Washington until early October, transmitting orders in Grant's name and communicating with the political managers.[41]

With Grant out of town, Rawlins and Schofield monitored progress on the Ashburn murder investigation. On June 26, Meade telegraphed Schofield, recommending that a military trial seemed the most suitable way to bring justice in the Ashburn case. However, Meade was concerned that Georgia was close to complying with the conditions of the Reconstruction Acts and thus to regaining its rights as a state. When that happened, a military commission would no longer have jurisdiction over the case. Not wanting to see this case dismissed on a technicality, Rawlins, on Schofield's suggestion, consulted with Lyman Trumbull, who chaired the Senate Judiciary Committee. Trumbull in turn sought advice from several members of both the Senate and House Judiciary Committees. The consensus opinion was if a case was being heard before a military tribunal prior to a state's compliance with the requirements of the Reconstruction Acts, then the military's jurisdiction would continue to hold. Rawlins advised Meade, therefore, to allow the military trial to proceed. However, on July 21 the Georgia legislature adopted the Fourteenth Amendment, and military rule in the state ended. Meade closed down the trial and returned the prisoners to Columbus. The trial never resumed.[42]

Once Grant emerged as the Republicans' candidate, his issuance in December 1862 of General Orders No. 11 expelling Jews from his department was resurrected and erupted into a political crisis. A worried Joseph Medill, editor of the *Chicago Tribune*, wrote to Washburne about the potential loss of Jewish voters in Chicago and cities like St. Louis and Cincinnati. Medill was troubled that Edward Selig Salomon, an influential Chicagoan, had written to Grant about the expulsion letter but had received no response.[43] In fact, Grant disclosed he had received "hundreds of letters" about the order but admitted he did not answer them, believing it "better to adhere to the rule of silence to all questions." He preferred to permit "a statement of facts concerning the origin of the order" be given to one of the letter writers for publication.[44] That "statement of facts" was written by Rawlins to Lewis N. Dembitz, a Republican of Louisville, Kentucky, and it was published as an "explanatory letter" in the *New York Herald* on June 23, 1868.

In this letter, Rawlins attempted to provide context for the order. He reminded Dembitz that at the time, "military affairs were in a most critical condition" as the Vicksburg campaign unfolded. Prior to the issuance of No. 11, other orders had been published forbidding travel through the Union lines, restricting traders' movements, and banning corn from being sent south. According to Rawlins, there were "constant reports" that "persons principally of the Jewish race" were violating these orders. However, Rawlins denied there was any unseemly motive: "The idea that it was issued on account of the religion of the Jews cannot be seriously entertained by any one who knows the General's steadfast adherence to the principles of American liberty and religious toleration."[45]

In his zeal to defend Grant, Rawlins misrepresented a specific feature of General Orders No. 11. He answered Dembitz that the order went out to subordinates, "leaving all persons not justly amenable to its terms to be relieved on their individual application." Yet, as historian Bertram Korn pointed out, the order actually forbade this: Jews were not permitted to make an appeal and were not allowed to secure trading permits.[46] The *Herald* also published a rejoinder to Rawlins written by "A True Republican." This writer posed some telling questions for Rawlins. For example, "Did General Grant know that Jews only were apt to commit such offenses?" More pointedly, he asked Rawlins, "Was General Grant satisfied . . . that among those of other religious denominations crossing his lines there were none who would or might violate any of his orders or to reveal any of his plans to the enemy?"[47] In Korn's estimation, Rawlins's *Herald* letter, as well ones by Badeau and others on be-half of Grant, "were manifestly ineffectual."[48]

After completing his western tour, Grant arrived in Galena at 6:00 p.m. on Friday, August 7, initially planning to stay about two weeks. He was accompa-nied by Julia; three children; his father-in-law, Frederick Dent; his brother-in-law Frederick T. Dent; and two attendants. A crowd estimated at six thousand jammed the railroad depot, and a twelve-pound cannon atop a hill blasted a welcome. The cannon was supposed to be fired until 10:00 p.m., but cannoneer Lieutenant A. R. Richards was seriously injured—at first it was feared mor-tally—by a premature discharge. That failed to dampen the festivities as the Tanners' Club under General John C. Smith marched to Grant's east side resi-dence, where Schreiner's brass band performed a serenade. Following General Smith's welcoming speech, Grant addressed the assembled: "I shall be glad to see you at your homes and shall be pleased to greet you at mine whenever you can make it convenient to call."[49] The citizens heartily took him up on the invitation, and on the next Tuesday alone, one hundred visitors called.[50] A group of distinguished guests came to pay respects to the Republican nomi-nee. On the evening of August 21, naturalist Louis Agassiz, Senator Roscoe Conkling, and Congressman Samuel Hooper, among others, were hosted by the Grants.[51]

On August 18, Grant invited Adam Badeau and Cyrus Comstock to join him in Galena, where he thought Badeau would "find it pleasant here for a while." Grant, who had already decided to extend his stay, reminded Badeau to refer to Rawlins all the official business correspondence.[52] Unfortunately, Rawlins was in the midst of an alarming health setback. He was confined to bed after suffering two hemorrhages of the lungs on the seventeenth. Two days later, a telegram from Washington to Galena carried news that the in-trepid Rawlins had recovered enough from the bleeding to be at army head-quarters briefly on the morning of the nineteenth.[53] He attributed his attacks to lack of rest from anxiety over Emma's serious illness. The hemorrhages were frightening omens, leading him to confide in a former Galena acquaintance, "My own health is not so good I fear as I have been led to suppose it was. . . . I feel considerable fears as to the real condition of my lungs."[54]

Grant made side trips to Dubuque, Quincy, southwest Wisconsin, and a business trip to Chicago. Visitors from Wisconsin returned the call on Grant and found him at home in his library, reading newspapers, appreciating the absence of crowds, and "enjoying his inevitable cigar."[55] Badeau and Comstock had already joined him in Galena when Rawlins arrived at the end of September. He had been delayed due to Emma's lingering illness.[56] Rawlins's own health, always a concern to his hometown friends, was reported as "improving."[57]

A few states held elections on October 13 prior to the November national balloting. Indiana, Ohio, and Pennsylvania were crucial states to watch. The day before, Rawlins was anxiously anticipating these returns, predicting, "As goes any two of the states tomorrow, so will go the election for President."[58] The Western Union Company installed wires in the library of Washburne's residence to provide rapid dissemination of results. Although the day had been wet and chilly, the library's fireplace kept friends and guests warm. Badeau and Comstock had accompanied Grant to Washburne's home, and William Rowley and General Chetlain, on leave from his duties as assessor at Salt Lake City, dropped in later. The newspaper did not mention whether Rawlins joined the party that evening. The table in the library was covered with returns of previous elections so that comparisons could be made as results poured in. A young telegraph operator from Chicago "listened *erectis auribus*" while he caught the first clatter from the wires and then seized a pencil and began writing furiously. As fast as results came in, they were read aloud. "A glorious triumph in Pennsylvania," came a shout, and as the evening advanced, Grant's supporters turned gleeful, with Indiana, Ohio, and Nebraska also falling into line. "The business is settled," they agreed. "Galena has the next President, *sure*." Outside the congressman's home, the Lead Mine Band played patriotic tunes, obliging Grant to appear on the piazza and take a bow. By 1:00 a.m., a weary but very satisfied Washburne had bidden his last guest good night.[59]

—◦◦◦—

Rawlins wanted to do his part to ensure Jo Daviess County delivered votes for Grant. Even though Grant was Galena's favorite son, in 1864 the city's voters had preferred Democrat George McClellan over Lincoln. On October 31, just returned from a visit to his sister in Anamosa, Iowa, Rawlins delivered a campaign speech at a Guilford Township schoolhouse. Local Republicans worked until the last minute to deliver votes. On election eve, a Republican grand rally was held at the Galena Courthouse and presided over by Washburne, bidding for his ninth term in Congress. Rawlins, one of three speakers,

was received warmly by old friends, and his two-hour speech drew enthusiastic applause.[60]

In this speech, Rawlins worked to win over Democratic voters, making a
special appeal to recent veterans to vote to uphold the principles for which
they fought—principles, he would argue, were being trampled by the Democratic candidates. For example, he warned that the Democratic Party's program was "to enable the South to prescribe the terms upon which they would
live in the Union." Moreover, Rawlins blasted Horatio Seymour and his running mate, Francis Blair, specifically for their racial discrimination[61] and the
Democrats generally for their opposition to the Fourteenth Amendment. To
Rawlins, the amendment was wise and just and "so absolutely necessary to
meet the conditions of the country." In the political environment being generated by the Democrats, Rawlins denounced how duly elected state legislators
in Georgia had been expelled in violation of the Fourteenth Amendment and
how Klansmen were waging guerilla war in the South. Rawlins reminded his
audience Stephen Douglas, in contrast, had been a patriotic Democrat who,
after Sumter capitulated, urged his party to defend the Union and the Constitution.[62]

Rawlins closed with his wish that the United States be transformed into
"an ocean-bound Republic," as envisioned by Douglas. Rawlins saw potential
for this transformation inhering in the Fourteenth Amendment, where distinctly different states were now equal in rights and where distinctly different races were now equal before the law—"distinct as God made them, but
one as humanity." With a government so in harmony with creation, Rawlins
foresaw both Canada and Mexico seeking places within the United States. He
closed his speech with a bit of doggerel from an Irish tune of the day suggesting Grant too was in step with this territorial expansion:

In the world to-day no prouder name
Is borne on any breeze
And with Grant to steer the Ship of State
Our flag shall rule the seas.
No 'Dominion' shall be north of us,
And South of us no foe,
Our stars and stripes in the Canadas
And likewise Mexico.
For with President Ulysses
Will be few who care to fight,
May he rule the country he has saved,
And God defend the right.[63]

On November 3, election night, Washburne's elegant home was again prepared to receive telegraphic returns, which were expected to trickle in around 8:00 p.m. Grant arrived an hour before dinner. Washburne invited Rawlins to stay overnight. Many well-wishers dropped by to lend support as the popular vote count proved closer than expected. Grant, remaining ever imperturbable, left at 1:00 a.m. to make the short walk to his residence.[64]

Although Grant won only 53 percent of the popular vote, he received over 130 more Electoral College votes. On the evening of November 4, Galena celebrated Grant's victory with a torchlight parade, bonfires, serenades, and sparkling illuminations. With the Lead Mine Band, the Galena Tanners, and Dubuque's Germania Band in the lead, a procession of several thousand marched to Grant's residence, where they were met by fireworks and cheers. A thousand Roman candles exploded simultaneously, sending fireballs into the night sky and casting a red glow over the east side of town. Grant was coaxed to give a short speech. "I suppose it is no egotism to say that the choice has fallen upon me," was how he modestly summarized events. "I now take occasion to bid you good-bye, as I leave here tomorrow for Washington, and shall probably see but few of you again for some years to come." From there, the crowd paraded to Washburne's home to hail his reelection.[65]

NOTES

1. *Boyd's Directory of Washington & Georgetown* (Washington, DC: Boyd's Directory, 1867), 469.

2. *Daily Morning Chronicle*, Washington, DC, September 8, 1869.

3. Orville Babcock to E. B. Washburne, October 9, 1867, in *The Papers of Ulysses S. Grant*, ed. John Y. Simon (Carbondale: Southern Illinois University Press, 1991), 18:325.

4. *New York Herald*, October 7, 1867.

5. *Galena Daily Gazette*, October 7, 1867.

6. David Donald, *Charles Sumner and the Rights of Man* (New York: Alfred A. Knopf, 1970), 338–39.

7. Gideon Welles, *Diary of Gideon Welles*, October 8, 1867 (Boston: Houghton Mifflin, 1911), 3:232.

8. Gideon Welles, *Diary of Gideon Welles*, October 10 and October 19, 1867, 3:233–34.

9. See Albert Castel, *The Presidency of Andrew Johnson* (Lawrence, KS: Regents Press of Kansas, 1979), 157; Brooks D. Simpson, *Let Us Have Peace: Ulysses S. Grant and the Politics of War and Reconstruction, 1861–1868* (Chapel Hill: The University of North Carolina Press, 1991), 203.

10. John W. Forney, *Anecdotes of Public Men* (New York: Harper and Brothers, 1873), 1:285–87.

11. Peter Cozzens, *General John Pope: A Life for the Nation* (Urbana: University of Illinois Press, 2000), 293–94.

492 | GENERAL JOHN A. RAWLINS

12. Edward R. S. Canby to J. A. Rawlins, December 20, 1867, in *The Papers of Ulysses S. Grant*, ed. John Y. Simon, 18:62–63n.

13. J. A. Rawlins to E. R. S. Canby, January 4, 1868, in *The Papers of Ulysses S. Grant*, ed. John Y. Simon, 18:63n.

14. Adam Badeau, *Grant in Peace* (Hartford, CT: S. S. Scranton, 1887), 112.

15. U. S. Grant to Andrew Johnson, January 28, 1868, in *The Papers of Ulysses S. Grant*, ed. John Y. Simon, 18:117–18.

16. William S. McFeely, *Grant* (New York: W. W. Norton, 1981), 268.

17. William S. Hillyer to Andrew Johnson, January 14, 1868, in *The Papers of Ulysses S. Grant*, ed. John Y. Simon, 18:103n.

18. *New York Tribune*, January 18, 1868.

19. *Army and Navy Journal*, 5, no. 22 (January 18, 1868).

20. *New York Herald*, January 23, 1868.

21. U. S. Grant to Andrew Johnson, January 28, 1868, in *The Papers of Ulysses S. Grant*, ed. John Y. Simon, 18:116–18.

22. Andrew Johnson to U. S. Grant, January 31, 1868, in *The Papers of Ulysses S. Grant*, ed. John Y. Simon, 18:119–21n.

23. Adam Badeau, *Grant in Peace*, 114.

24. U. S. Grant to Andrew Johnson, January February 3, 1868, in *The Papers of Ulysses S. Grant*, ed. John Y. Simon, 18:124–26.

25. Adam Badeau, *Grant in Peace*, 114–15.

26. Ibid., 119. Badeau was of the opinion that only two people really understood Grant: himself and Rawlins; see Henry Adams, *The Education of Henry Adams: An Autobiography* (Boston: Houghton Mifflin, 1918), 264.

27. Allen J. Ottens, Gary D. Shank, and Richard J. Long, "The Role of Abductive Logic in Understanding and Using Advanced Empathy," *Counselor Education and Supervision* 34, no. 3 (1995): 199–211.

28. Adam Badeau, *Grant in Peace*, 115.

29. Ibid., 114.

30. Fawn M. Brodie, *Thaddeus Stevens: Scourge of the South* (New York: W. W. Norton, 1966), 333.

31. *New York Herald*, February 6, 1868.

32. Hans L. Trefousse, *Andrew Johnson: A Biography* (New York: W. W. Norton, 1989), 313.

33. John Y. Simon, ed., *The Papers of Ulysses S. Grant*, 18:137n; J. A. Rawlins to W. S. Hancock, February 28, 1867, in *The Papers of Ulysses S. Grant*, ed. John Y. Simon, 18:137–38n.

34. John Y. Simon, ed., *The Papers of Ulysses S. Grant*, 18:177–79n.

35. Glenn Tucker, *Hancock the Superb* (Indianapolis: Bobbs-Merrill, 1960), 288.

36. John Y. Simon, ed., *The Papers of Ulysses S. Grant*, 18:197n.

37. Adam Badeau, *Grant in Peace*, 134.

38. Elizabeth Otto Daniell, "The Ashburn Murder Case in Georgia Reconstruction, 1868," *Georgia Historical Quarterly* 59, no. 3 (1975): 299–300.

39. U. S. Grant to George G. Meade, April 2, 1868, in *The Papers of Ulysses S. Grant*, ed. John Y. Simon, 18:213.

40. John M. Schofield, *Forty-Six Years in the Army* (New York: Century, 1897), 418.

41. Ibid., 420; Adam Badeau, *Grant in Peace*, 146–47.

42. John Y. Simon, ed., *The Papers of Ulysses S. Grant*, 18:229–30n; Elizabeth Otto Daniell, "The Ashburn Murder Case in Georgia Reconstruction, 1868," *Georgia Historical Quarterly* 59, no. 3 (1975): 309.

43. Mark Washburne, *A Biography of Elihu Benjamin Washburne: Congressman, Secretary of State, Envoy Extraordinary* (self-pub., Xlibris, 2005), 3:250.

44. U. S. Grant to Isaac H. Morris, September 14, 1868, in *The Papers of Ulysses S. Grant*, ed. John Y. Simon (Carbondale: Southern Illinois University Press, 1995), 19:37.

45. *New York Herald*, June 23, 1868.

46. Bertram W. Korn, *American Jews and the Civil War* (Cleveland: Meridian, 1961), 277n62.

47. *New York Herald*, June 23, 1868.

48. Bertram W. Korn, *American Jews and the Civil War*, 133–34.

49. *Galena Evening Gazette*, August 8, 1868.

50. Ibid., August 12, 1868.

51. Ibid., August 22, 1868.

52. U. S. Grant to Adam Badeau, August 18, 1868, in *The Papers of Ulysses S. Grant*, ed. John Y. Simon, 19:24.

53. *Galena Evening Gazette*, August 18 and August 20, 1868.

54. J. A. Rawlins to Charles H. Rogers, August 27, 1868, in *The Papers of Ulysses S. Grant*, ed. John Y. Simon, 21:78n.

55. *Galena Evening Gazette*, September 27, 1868.

56. U. S. Grant to J. A. Rawlins, September 1868, in *The Papers of Ulysses S. Grant*, ed. John Y. Simon, 19:50.

57. *Galena Evening Gazette*, October 8, 1868.

58. John A. Rawlins to Emma Rawlins, October 12, 1868, transcribed by J. H. Wilson, James H. Wilson Papers, Bender Collection, Wyoming State Archives and Historical Department, Microfilm Reel H-61b.

59. *Galena Evening Gazette*, October 18 and October 16, 1868.

60. Ibid., October 28 and November 3, 1868.

61. The Democrats distributed campaign badges with the motto, "This is a White Man's Country: Let White Men Rule." Schomburg Center for Research in Black Culture, Photographs and Prints Division, New York Public Library, *Campaign badge supporting Horatio Seymour and Francis Blair, Democratic candidates for President and Vice-President of the Unites States, 1868,* retrieved from http://digitalcollections.nypl.org/items/62a9d0e6-4fc9-dbce-e040-e00a18064a66.

62. *The New York Times*, November 10, 1868.

63. Ibid.

64. Mark Washburne, *A Biography of Elihu Benjamin Washburne: Congressman, Secretary of State, Envoy Extraordinary*, 3:265–66; *Galena Evening Gazette*, November 7, 1868.

65. *Galena Evening Gazette*, November 5, 1868.

25

"And You Are Still My Adjutant"

AFTER THE ELECTION, RAWLINS TRAVELED alone to Washington, where he undertook a temporary nomadic existence while his home at Twelfth and M Streets was being prepared for occupation. The Grants invited him to stay with them in the meantime, but he declined, opting to sleep in his office, take some dinners with the Grants at their I Street house, and breakfast at the Willard Hotel. At Willard's, Rawlins could keep apprised of the political drift from the assortment of "editors . . . attaches of foreign journals, long-winded talkers, clerks, diplomats [and] mail contractors" who gathered there.[1] A hot topic of conjecture was the composition of Grant's cabinet. Rawlins already anticipated a plum position would fall to him. "In fact among those whom I have met the chief speculation is as to what I am to have," he wrote Emma two weeks before Christmas. "All seem to take it for granted that the General is going to do something very handsome, more than he has ever done for me, but what he intends of course none of them know."[2] Grant was holding his cards close to his vest, not dropping a clue about his cabinet plans to anyone including Rawlins, Washburne, or even Julia.

Due to health concerns, Rawlins delayed joining his family in Connecticut. On December 8, he underwent a painful procedure in which Dr. Bliss produced an ulcer or "issue" in his left arm.[3] Bliss likely applied a caustic to separate the skin, and into this open wound he inserted an "issue pea," a small globular object of an irritating substance such as orris root to prevent healing.[4] Rawlins was told the issue would drain mucus from the lungs and thus relieve his cough. Making issues in the skin was an old practice for treating consumption.[5] Unfortunately, as Bliss should have known, the appearance of thick mucus or pus indicates a more advanced stage of tuberculosis.[6]

Rawlins passed the holidays in Danbury, returning on January 6. The next day, he consulted Dr. Bliss, who apparently thought the issue a success, because he pronounced Rawlins's lungs "sound." Almost certainly Dr. Bliss was concealing the truth to sustain John's dwindling sense of hope. To bolster his health, Rawlins was taking saltwater ablutions twice daily and riding Jeff Davis, a black pony on loan from Grant, to and from dinner with Ulysses and Julia.[7] As the inauguration drew closer without Grant uttering a word about any handsome reward, Rawlins, feeling frustrated and dejected, retreated to Connecticut, wondering whether he need ever return to Washington. In Danbury, he received a telegram from Grant on February 15. It was Julia inviting Emma to be her houseguest for a few weeks. Rawlins wired back to accept the offer and to say he and Emma would leave on the seventeenth for Washington.[8]

On the evening of February 19, Harry Wilson and Russell Jones visited at Grant's home. After Grant read to them a draft of his inauguration speech, they settled into a wide-ranging discussion of people and places—but with the topic of cabinet choices off-limits. When Wilson inquired about what he planned for Rawlins, Grant replied that he was awarding him command of the Department of Arizona, where the climate could restore his health. Wilson informed Rawlins the next day about this plan, which to him was completely unsatisfactory. Rawlins thought he deserved the secretary of war post and urged Wilson to hastily impress this on Grant. This Wilson did on the evening of the twentieth, and Grant received Rawlins's appeal with no rancor or prevarication. "You can tell Rawlins he shall be Secretary of War," Grant said, stipulating Rawlins would have to be patient, because he had already asked General Schofield to stay on briefly. The news temporarily lifted Rawlins, but when Grant delayed confirming to him his intentions, his spirits sank. Dismayed, Rawlins contacted Grenville Dodge, who intervened on his behalf. Dodge accosted Grant and began as follows: "I have come, General, to have a square talk with you," and followed with his recommending Rawlins for the War Department. In short order, Grant conveyed to Rawlins his intent to nominate him as secretary.[9]

Dodge was not finished dispensing favors to Rawlins. Two weeks later, he presented the financially strapped Rawlins with the paid-off mortgage note on his Washington home. It was testimony to the great affection Dodge had

for Rawlins, a man whom he regarded as exceptionally patriotic and principled. Dodge self-effacingly allowed that he had arranged for this "through
the kindness of a few friends." In a touching tribute to Rawlins, Dodge told
him, "Allow me to say, I never performed a duty that gave me more pleasure or
satisfaction."[10]

—◦◦◦—

The morning of March 4, inauguration day, was overcast and chilly, but
crowds ignored the weather to line the streets and jostle for viewing locations.
Grant and Rawlins rode to the Capitol in a park phaeton drawn by two bay
horses and escorted by a company of the Fifth Cavalry. Vice President–elect
Schuyler Colfax rode behind in a second carriage. The lingering animus between Johnson and Grant was such that the outgoing president begged off attending the ceremony to finish paperwork. As Grant and Rawlins neared the
Capitol, the sun sliced through the clouds. Chief Justice Salmon Chase administered the oath of office, whereupon Grant, smartly attired in a tailor-made
black suit, delivered a brief address in which he focused mainly on the nation's
finances but also endorsed the ratification of the Fifteenth Amendment and
fair treatment for Native Americans.

The next day, Rawlins was on the Senate floor submitting Grant's first batch
of cabinet nominees. All six were confirmed that same day: Elihu Washburne
as secretary of state, Alexander T. Stewart as treasury, Adolph Borie as navy
secretary, John Creswell as postmaster general, Ebenezer Hoar as attorney
general, and Jacob Cox as secretary of the interior. General John Schofield
continued as secretary of war. The *New York Times* captured the feeling of the
moment: "The Cabinet appointed by Gen. Grant yesterday took everybody
by surprise."[11] Some were surprised and confounded by the choices. It was
widely thought Washburne, who had been bedridden all of February and even
close to death, was the recipient of the choicest cabinet position mostly by
virtue of his longtime benefaction of Grant. But some detractors pointed to
his ties with the rough-edged Northwest and doubted he had the refinement
needed for state. In a puzzling maneuver, Washburne resigned that week and
became Grant's choice as minister to France. Borie, who possessed no particular qualifications to head the navy, would resign four months later. Alexander
Stewart, one of the wealthiest Americans, abruptly stepped down from treasury after running afoul of an obscure law barring merchants or traders like
himself from occupying that post.

Something else stood out to the *Times* regarding Grant's choices: "The Cabinet is eminently and evidently one of the President's own selection. He has appointed the men who compose it because they suited him—not because they suited somebody else."[12] Rawlins also had been impressing on Grant that whomever he nominated should not be men who might become rivals. The last thing Grant needed, Rawlins counseled, was a cabinet member like Salmon Chase, Lincoln's secretary of the treasury, who had repeatedly operated at cross-purposes against him.[13] With Washburne expected to be an early departure from the State Department, Rawlins urged Grant to choose fellow Westerner James F. Wilson, a congressman from Iowa. However, Wilson scotched this idea, saying he did not have the personal fortune to help defray the expenses the salary would not cover.[14]

A second list of cabinet nominees went before the Senate on March 11. John Rawlins was named to replace John Schofield, the carryover from the Johnson administration. George Boutwell, a staunch Radical and leader of the impeachment effort, filled Alexander Stewart's vacancy. Grant's choice to replace Washburne at State was New Yorker Hamilton Fish, who possessed the pedigree that many thought Washburne lacked. Fish, a descendent on his mother's side of Peter Stuyvesant, was well educated and multilingual and had studied law in the office of Peter Jay, son of John Jay. The former congressman, governor, and senator possessed a magnificent estate, Glenclyffe, sited on a prominence affording a sweeping view of the Hudson River. He cast a striking but hardly handsome appearance with wispy mutton chops, a fleshy face sprouting a prominent nose, and thick wavy hair streaked with gray.

The three nominees were speedily confirmed by the Senate. At noon on Friday, March 12, during their first cabinet meeting, Boutwell and Rawlins were administered their oaths of office by David K. Cartter of the Supreme Court of the District of Columbia.

The press was generally favorably disposed toward Rawlins's appointment. The *Chicago Tribune* claimed his was "decidedly the best of the three appointments announced this morning" and called him "one of the invaluable men of the nation."[15] The *New York Tribune* lauded both Boutwell and Rawlins and said their selection "gives universal satisfaction." Regarding Rawlins, this paper said, "No other man in the country knows the army better than he; and the Cabinet is fortunate in having the benefit of his large experience and his ripe judgment."[16] Although the *New York Herald* believed that "[Rawlins's] fitness for the duties of the office is unquestioned," the paper struck an ominous tone by viewing him as "a temporary appointment because of [his] enfeebled and insufficient health."[17]

Shortly after confirmation, a delegation led by prominent Chicago attorney, J. Young Scammon, honored Rawlins with an address and resolution on behalf of all Illinoisans, proclaiming his appointment was fitting recognition for his war services. Rawlins expressed his gratitude and humility, "I shall exercise the best of my ability, fearing that then I shall bring far less in that position than ought to be brought there."[18]

Early into the Grant presidency, there was grumbling in some Republican circles that too many of Grant's family and Galena friends like Rawlins and Chetlain "had been let in a private way before the public door to the feast had been opened; that Washburne had staggered off with the *pièce de résistance*; that the Dents and Caseys had secured the pâtâs and the pastries; while Russell Jones and a few other Galenaites had moved upon the charlotte russes, and little but crust left for the after-comers."[19] In truth, Grant was generous with appointments to friends and those loyal to him, and he could uphold a friend past the point of propriety.[20]

Two immediate challenges gave Rawlins little time to relish his accession to the cabinet. One caused him wearisome annoyance because it required dealing with the crush of office-seekers descending on the new administration. He complained of the unrelenting pressure from petitioners requesting recommendations for government jobs.[21] The pressure was not confined to the War Department. As the *New York Sun* reported, all departments were crowded every hour of the day, and "Secretary Boutwell is literally overwhelmed with applications for clerkships, although there are no vacancies."[22] The other challenge required Rawlins to courageously order an administrative correction to ensure that "the General of the Army is subordinate to the Secretary of War."[23]

—⁓—

In December 1868, Grant met with Sherman in Chicago at a veterans' convention. There, the president-elect told Sherman he would nominate him for a fourth star and elevate him to general in chief of the army. Furthermore, it was Grant's intent to initiate an important change in the relationship between the secretary of war and the general in chief. Since James Madison's presidency, it had been the policy to keep the military's staff bureaus independent by placing them under the secretary of war. This arrangement sometimes resulted in commanding generals clashing with the War Department.[24] Grant himself went toe-to-toe with Secretary of War Stanton over whether bureaus should be outside the military chain of command. Almost three years before, Grant had lectured Stanton, "The entire Adjutant General's office should be under the entire control of the General in chief of the Army. . . . In short in my opinion the Gen. in Chief stands between the President and the Army in all official matters and the Secretary of War is between the Army, (through the General in chief,) and the President."[25] Besides the office of adjutant general under Brevet Major General Edmund Townsend referred to by Grant, there were six other bureaus each headed by a general: Andrew Humphreys, chief of the engineering corps; Dr. Joseph Barnes, surgeon general; Randolph Marcy, inspector general; Joseph Holt, the judge advocate general; Albert Myer, head of the signal corps; and Montgomery Meigs, quartermaster general. Sherman applauded Grant's intent to strip the secretary of war of authority over these bureaus, seeing it as an overdue fix to make the army more efficient.

Grant made good on his plan. On March 5, only hours into his presidency, he authorized outgoing Secretary of War Schofield to issue General Orders No. 11 subordinating the bureau and department heads to Sherman: "By direction of the President, General William T. Sherman will assume command of the Army of the United States. The chiefs of staff corps, departments and bureaus will report to and act under the immediate orders of the general commanding the army."[26] Most of the bureau chiefs resented losing independence and appealed to Congress, where they found support. Senator Sumner, never one to back down from Grant, recognized the inherent conflict in this order, denouncing it "as an act of revolution exalting the military power over the civil."[27] Grant, as he would learn, had acted before being apprised of the fact that the order ran counter to a host of federal statutes that had established these bureaus.

Rawlins, as Grant's chief of staff, would have supported the March 5 order. However, as secretary of war, he recognized that not only did it undercut his authority, but it had no legal foundation. After a few days at his post, he knew it was imperative to walk back the order "which virtually left the War Department under Sherman."[28] This required Rawlins to interpose himself between Grant and Sherman, two men who were as close as brothers. Probably no one besides Rawlins could have intervened. Secretary of the Interior Jacob Cox recognized that "no other man could be the successful intermediary between General Grant and his associates in public duty." Rawlins had earned that role by standing with Grant since Galena. But as Cox knew, Rawlins possessed more than loyalty: he had the ability to argue and to prove himself "as coura-geous to speak in time of need as Nathan the Prophet."[29]

Rawlins succeeded in convincing Grant his case was stronger than Sher-man's. Sometime before the evening of March 25, Grant made the hard de-cision. Sherman visited him that evening and just before leaving, Grant in-tercepted him and said, "I guess we have to revoke that order of Schofield's." Sherman was astounded. He reminded Grant that this was his order, the one he agreed to in Chicago. The next morning, Sherman dashed off a note to Grant, beseeching him, "Please do not revoke your order of March 5 without further reflection. It would put me in a most unpleasant dilema [sic] because the Army and country would infer your want of confidence." Sherman then met with Rawlins, just returned from a cabinet meeting, but he was too late to disengage what had been set in motion. Rawlins had already issued through the War Department Grant's rescission of the order: "All official business wh[ich] by law or regulations requires the action of the President or Secy of War will be submitted by the Chiefs of Staff Corps, Departments & Bureaux to the Secy of War." Rawlins showed Sherman the draft which, as he explained, could not be modified because "it had been passed on in [the] Cabinet and must stand." Rawlins explained that General Orders No. 11 had stripped him of certain powers and duties that by law devolved upon the secretary of war and that "it changed the Civil nature of the Departm[en]t of War."[30]

When Sherman later confronted Grant, the latter was plainly apologetic. "Rawlins feels badly about it," he explained. "It worries him, and he is not well." Sherman was not swayed. "But, Grant," he countered, "ought a public measure that you have advocated for years, and which he has known you were determined upon, to be set aside for such a reason?" Grant agreed in principle but felt circumstances justified his decision. "Yes, it would ordinarily be so," he replied, "but I don't like to give him pain now. So, Sherman, you'll have to publish the rescinding order."[31]

This episode over the revoking of General Orders No. 11 rankled Sherman for years. Even in his memoirs, he ranted against it: "Thus we were thrown back on the old method in having a double, if not a treble-headed machine. Each head of a bureau in daily consultation with the Secretary of War, and the general to command without an adjutant, quartermaster, commissary, or any staff except his own aides, often reading in the newspaper of military events and orders before he could be consulted or informed. This was the very reverse of what General Grant . . . seemed to want, different from what he had explained to me in Chicago."[32] It also cooled relations between him and Grant, though they remained polite to each other.[33] For the brief time Rawlins remained as secretary, he attempted to mollify Sherman's feelings by routing through army headquarters all the orders and communications affecting army discipline and organization.[34] To Sherman's bitter frustration, Rawlins's replacement, William Belknap, a former brigadier in Sherman's Army of the Tennessee, asserted even more authority over the army.[35] Despite the bruised feelings and impaired relationships, Rawlins had acted wisely, as the *Chicago Tribune* explained: "General Sherman's order putting all heads of bureaus on his staff proves to be the most remarkable of all late steps taken here in violation of well-known laws. There are twenty-seven distinct sections of the military laws which conflict with Sherman's order, as by them it is specially provided that the principal functions of the Quartermasters, Ordinance [*sic*], Paymaster, Surgeon General and Signal Corps shall be discharged under the direction of the Secretary of War."[36] Besides adhering to these laws, Rawlins also underscored the importance of maintaining civilian oversight of the military.

—⁓—

Early into the Grant administration, three thorny foreign affairs issues competed for attention. One, a carryover from Andrew Johnson and his secretary of state, William Seward, was a squabble between the United States and Britain over demands for restitution for damages inflicted during the war on US shipping by Confederate raiding vessels built or refitted in British shipyards. The demands were collectively known as the *Alabama* claims for the most notorious of the Confederate commerce raiders. The second erupted in October 1868 when rebel insurgents in eastern Cuba revolted against Spanish rule. Instantly, the new administration faced pressure to intervene on behalf of the insurgents. The third involved the clamor for annexing the independent nation of Santo Domingo.

Although Great Britain never recognized the Confederate States of America as a nation, Queen Victoria issued a proclamation of neutrality in May 1861 that thereby afforded the Confederacy wartime rights as a belligerent. Other European countries such as Spain and France followed Britain's lead. As a belligerent power, the CSA was allowed to use England's harbors, purchase arms, and contract with British shipbuilders to construct warships. Many in the North took offense at the queen's hasty proclamation of neutrality. Moreover, the Lincoln Administration argued the CSA was not entitled to belligerent status because the war was simply a domestic dispute. Britain's rejoinder was that the Union's naval blockade of Southern ports amounted to an act of war against a belligerent power—one that had a functioning government and army—not a loose conglomeration of insurrectionists. In effect, Lincoln's blockade had qualified the CSA for certain rights under international law. As the war progressed, scores of US merchant vessels were destroyed or captured by Confederate raiders such as the *Alabama, Georgia, Shenandoah*, and *Florida*. Insurance premiums on merchant ships flying the Stars and Stripes skyrocketed. Many across the North were outraged by the damage being inflicted and urged retaliation against England. Writing to Richard Cobden, a member of the British Parliament, Senator Sumner expressed concern: "I am very anxious, very anxious, on account of the ships building in England to cruise against our commerce." And he warned, "Our people are becoming more and more excited, and there are many who insist upon war."[37]

After the Civil War concluded, discussions with England over restitution proceeded slowly. The British foreign secretaries, Lord John Russell and Lord Stanley (who succeeded Russell in 1866), were not about to renounce their government's having taken a stance of neutrality, which precluded meaningful arbitration of damage claims. Some politicians thought the *Alabama* claims might be met through accession of British North American territory. William Seward, who had brokered the purchase of Alaska, had notions that a part of Canada and British islands in the West Indies might satisfy some of the claims. Charles Sumner cast covetous eyes on Canada, telling Samuel Gridley Howe, "I look to have that whole zone from Newfoundland to Vancouver."[38] And he thought the "zone" could be acquired peaceably through diplomatic pressure. Senator Carl Schurz enlisted the diplomatic assistance of Germany in facilitating the United States' annexing of Canada to settle claims. Secretary of State Fish prized Canada but believed it first must achieve its independence, and then its provinces would eventually fold into the United States.[39]

Others thought Canada might have to be grabbed by force, should the need arise. Zachariah Chandler of Michigan delivered to the Senate a long "warlike speech," in which he offered his solution to the controversies between the United States and Great Britain. He proposed that if Great Britain acknowledged being in the wrong and ceded Canada to settle the claims, there would be peace; "but if she does not, we must conquer peace." Chandler warned if negotiations were not peaceful "and England insists on war, then let the war be 'short, sharp, and decisive.'" He boasted that Michigan's sixty thousand veterans could capture Canada in thirty days.[40] During the Civil War, Grant worried that if England formally recognized the CSA as a nation, then war with England could not have been resisted. Grant said he would have dispatched Sheridan to Canada, which he could have taken in thirty days. To Grant, an advocate of expansionism, the fortuitous result would have been the withdrawal of England from North America.[41] In his platform speech at Galena in June 1867, Rawlins spoke about England's "disposition to settle the claims for damages" done by Confederate raiders. But he cautioned if England failed to make proper adjustments, "a declaration of war for the seizure of her possessions in America" might have to be issued, resulting in "the departure of the last foreign power from this continent."[42]

As one who broadly interpreted the Monroe Doctrine, Rawlins would have been pleased to see Britain compelled to exit Canada, as he and Grant were when the French abandoned their designs on Mexico. Rawlins was a more unabashed expansionist than Grant, having been infused with the spirit of Manifest Destiny that had been espoused by his political model, Stephen Douglas.

In August 1868, former Maryland Senator Reverdy Johnson arrived in England as minister at London. In December he entered into negotiations with the new British foreign secretary, Lord Clarendon. In the twilight of Andrew Johnson's presidency, an agreement was worked out, known as the Johnson-Clarendon Convention. Grant was not inclined to support this vestige of the previous administration. Moreover, there was thin public enthusiasm for it because it did not extract much compensation from the British. When the agreement went before the Senate on April 13, 1869, Sumner, who regarded himself as the foreign relations superior to Grant and Fish, savagely denounced it and the British, accusing them of causing billions of dollars in damages and for having doubled the length of the war. Sumner's motive was to angle for British North American territory as partial compensation. The Senate overwhelmingly rejected the agreement. Sumner's vitriol so incensed the British that the *Alabama* claims were not settled until two years later.

—⁓—

Cuba had been coveted by territorial expansionists well before the Civil War, especially those who hoped to bring it into the Union as a slave state. The Franklin Pierce administration had designs on Cuba, when in 1854, Secretary of State William Marcy instructed three of his diplomats to meet in

Ostend, Belgium, to consider means for persuading Spain to sell Cuba to the United States. The diplomats, all with a pro-South agenda, were James Buchanan, Pierre Soulé, and John Y. Mason, ministers to Great Britain, Spain, and France, respectively. Buchanan was assisted by his secretary, Daniel Sickles, a former New York State assemblyman. The ministers conspired to make an incautious overreach. In a document known as the Ostend Manifesto, they wrote that Spain should be made an offer for Cuba, but if it were refused, seizing Cuba by force might be necessary. The rationale for a possible invasion was blatantly racially motivated: to prevent Cuba from becoming "Africanized" and "a second St. Domingo with all its attendant horrors to the white race ... [and] to extend to our own neighboring shores, seriously to endanger or actually consume the fair fabric of our Union."[43] When the manifesto was made public, it proved an embarrassment to Pierce and triggered protests by antislavery groups. The manifesto was scuttled, but the taste for Cuba stayed in some politicians' mouths. In his annual messages of 1858 and 1859, Buchanan continued to press for its purchase from Spain.[44] In late 1858, just before sailing for Cuba, Stephen Douglas, advocating for national expansion, declared it was America's destiny to possess the island.[45]

Now, the incoming Grant administration faced difficult decisions following the revolt led by Carlos Cespedes that started in eastern Cuba in October 1868 against Spanish rule. By the end of the year, Cespedes's ragtag insurrectionists had inflicted surprising damage to the Spanish military. Fighting was, at times, beyond brutal, as riots and shootings erupted across Cuba. Prisoners were tortured. At a theatre on January 23, when audience members began singing a revolutionary hymn, Spanish volunteers and police fired into them, killing and wounding many.[46] The Cubans' plight aroused much sympathy in the United States, particularly from those who delighted in insurgents defeating an oppressor and thereby removing from the Western Hemisphere the footprint of another European monarchy—and ending the pitiless slavery system on the island. Many called for recognizing the insurgents as belligerents and intervening on their behalf; some of those interventionists hoped that once Cuba gained its independence, annexation would follow. Calls for action came from Congressmen John Logan of Illinois and Nathaniel Banks, chairman of the House Foreign Affairs Committee. Some came from influential newspaper editors James Gordon Bennett Jr. of the *New York Herald* and the *New York Sun*'s Charles Dana, former assistant secretary of war and one-time Grant promoter. Others came from within the administration, notably from Secretary of War Rawlins, who endorsed all the options, including risking hostilities with Spain.[47]

Cuba was an agenda item at the March 19 cabinet meeting, but discussion advanced cautiously. Interior Secretary Cox thought Spain should be treated delicately as she contemplated adopting a more liberal constitutional monarchy. Boutwell, of the Treasury Department, felt the millions in import duties derived annually from Cuba should be protected. Grant reminded everyone Spain had granted the Confederacy belligerent status. Fish thought Rawlins "seemed inclined to lean toward an easy recognition of the insurgents."[48] To Fish, this was an absurd idea because they "have no army—no courts, do not occupy a single town . . . [are] carrying on a purely guerilla warfare . . . Great Britain or France might just as well have recognized belligerency for the Black Hawk War."[49] Fish and Rawlins were also on opposite ends of the Cuban annexation issue. Although Rawlins favored its acquisition, Fish feared such a step ill-advised, given the Cubans' heterogeneous racial makeup and their unfamiliarity with US laws and institutions.[50] Fish favored independence for Cuba, not annexation.

At the Friday, April 6, cabinet meeting, the topic of recognizing the Cuban insurgency was discussed. Rawlins tilted toward "speedy action," whereas Attorney General Hoar strongly opposed such a move. Grant hesitated taking that step—despite Rawlins's urging and his own belief in the rightness of the insurgents' cause. What gave Grant pause was his worry such action might jeopardize negotiations with Great Britain over the *Alabama* claims. Also, by recognizing Cuban belligerency, the United States might appear hypocritical, because in 1861 it had protested England's proclamation of neutrality toward the Confederacy. Fish was relieved by Grant's decision.[51]

Fish attempted to avoid the Cuba topic during the April and May cabinet meetings lest Rawlins work himself into a lather on behalf of the insurgents and thereby influence Grant. While observing Rawlins, Fish came to regard him as, in some respects, the cabinet's most important member. He had Grant's ear and could rebuke and lecture him without causing offense. On the other hand, Fish thought Rawlins a danger to the State Department. Rawlins's thirst for territorial expansion, violent language, quick temper, and low regard for foreign powers were characteristics ill-suited for diplomacy.[52] Moreover, the cabinet was cleaving into two factions: Fish, Hoar, Boutwell, and Borie were opposed to intervening on the insurgent's behalf, whereas Rawlins, Creswell, and Cox favored immediate action. Grant vacillated between the two.

This split was displayed during an April meeting when Dan Sickles was under consideration as minister to Spain. Rawlins backed Sickles, who still coveted Cuba long after the Ostend Manifesto fiasco, and both sought Cuban independence as a step toward eradicating slavery from the Antilles. Rawlins had even visited Sickles in New York to pitch the job to him—a breach of etiquette, because the overture should have been made by the State Department. Sickles was reluctant to relinquish his army rank, a requirement for a diplomatic appointment; but Rawlins could arrange his retirement so he could make the transition.[53] Fish was opposed to Sickles and had long held him in low regard. Decades earlier, Sickles had paid a debt to Fish with a fraudulent five-dollar note. This small incident rankled Fish's strong sense of probity.[54] Therefore, when Sickles's name was brought up, Fish and Attorney General Hoar questioned whether his complicity with the Manifesto would hamper his effectiveness at the Spanish Court, whereupon Rawlins and Creswell piped up that they had favored the manifesto. After some silence, Grant announced he too was for it when it was issued, and that ended the discussion.[55]

Beyond the cabinet room, events regarding Cuba were moving apace. On March 25, at a pro-independence rally in New York's Steinway Hall, Charles Dana read resolutions that included providing Cuba with "every kind of assistance that other nations may be able to render."[56] Soon thereafter, the House passed a resolution expressing sympathy for the insurgents and encouraging Grant to recognize their belligerent rights. At the beginning of June, two young Americans were executed in Santiago by Spanish authorities. An irate Grant, no doubt prodded by Rawlins, sought Sumner's advice about issuing a proclamation according belligerency rights to the Cubans in language similar to that which Spain used eight years before on behalf of the Confederacy. However, Sumner advised him against such a step. Meanwhile, in several cities, including Washington and Boston, Cuban exiles and representatives of the insurgents organized into juntas to raise money, distribute propaganda, and lobby congressmen. At the New York junta, Carlos Cespedes installed Jose Morales Lemus, a Havana lawyer, as the minister to the United States from the Cuban "Republic." Around the country, filibustering expeditions were being raised to lend private military support to the insurgents. One prominent filibusterer, James Steedman, a former division commander under Sherman and old Douglas Democrat, reportedly visited Havana to connect with the insurgents. In New Orleans, Steedman was enlisting former Union and Confederate soldiers who lusted for money and adventure.[57] As spring advanced, tensions with Spain increased over the increase in filibustering expeditions attempting to aid the insurgents. Spanish naval vessels intercepted American ships indiscriminately, and both countries bolstered their naval presence. There were drumbeats for military action. The *New York Herald* berated Fish, calling him "a timid old fogy and utterly unfit for Secretary of State" because he feared war with Spain, a country of "limited power."[58] In contrast, Rawlins was regarded as "the aggressive spirit in the Cabinet" who "would not hesitate to recognize Cuban independence at the earliest possible moment."[59]

———

Amid escalating tensions, General Juan Prim, Spanish Council president, admitting his country was in dire financial circumstances, signaled Spain was willing to negotiate the sale of Cuba. Fish crafted in response a five-point proposal, received cabinet approval for it, got Morales Lemus on board, and by early July had Dan Sickles ready to carry it to Madrid. The proposal called for Cuba to issue bonds to pay Spain upward of $100,000,000 for her independence, with the United States, pending congressional approval, to guarantee the bonds using revenues from duties collected on Cuban imports. Among other provisions of the plan were an end to slavery on Cuba and an armistice to be in place during negotiations. By mid-July, a deal appeared in the offing for the sale of both Cuba and Puerto Rico for $150,000,000, to be guaranteed by the United States.[60]

While the cabinet contemplated a way for Cuban independence, John Rawlins sat on a secret he believed was known only to himself and a safe, select few. In the early days of the Grant administration, it is believed Rawlins had been approached by officers of the Cuban revolutionary junta in New York or Washington with a gift of bonds. They were worthless while Cuba was under Spanish rule but stood to appreciate as Cuba's fortune rose—an outcome more likely to occur if friends of Cuba could exert influence on her behalf. That this gift (or bribe) had been offered should not have taken a politically connected person by surprise, considering that hopeful Confederate agents once plied prominent Europeans with reams of junk bonds. Sometime during the spring of 1869, Don Mauricio López Roberts, Spanish minister to the United States, hired detectives to uncover parties who had been recipients of Cuban bonds. Roberts gave Fish a peek at his detectives' findings, and there on the list was Rawlins's name and a favor estimated at $20,000 or $25,000. Fish, too, sat on his own little secret.

A fuller story about these bonds emerged six years later when, in July 1875, Secretary of the Treasury Benjamin Bristow asked Fish if he knew about the $28,000 in Cuban bonds found among Rawlins's securities after his death. Bristow believed that Grant, as executor of the estate, ordered them destroyed. In turn, Fish shared his story about Rawlins and the detectives' list. Three months later, Grant mentioned to Fish and Navy Secretary George Robeson that shortly after Rawlins died, he had asked General John E. Smith to destroy the bonds. Later, when Grant inspected the safe, he found them still inside. Now Grant was unsure what to do with them. Fish said he thought it was inappropriate for Grant to be in the business of selling them. Fish also told Grant about Roberts and the list that contained Rawlins's name as well as those of congressmen, powerful newspapermen, and others of influence.[61]

To detractors of John Rawlins, that one so principled would succumb to financial temptation must have seemed the ultimate irony, or that notwithstanding his noble avowal of the Monroe Doctrine and desire to see a free Cuba, he "apparently had less lofty motives as well."[62] Strictly speaking, Rawlins needed no financial incentive to advocate for the insurgents against Spanish rule. However, in 1869, he was a man in desperate circumstances: he suspected his end was near, and he feared for his wife's health. During the summer of 1868, Emma had been in such precarious health that Rawlins described her to a former Galena friend as being "dangerously ill" and "slowly recovering."[63] She was pregnant during the first eight months of 1869—and it was probably a difficult pregnancy because the child, a girl, survived only days. At the time of John's death, Emma was "very sick" and in a "very weak condition."[64] Rawlins surely believed his three children could face life as orphans, leaving him susceptible to pitches that offered financial security for them—especially if such offers came from seemingly upstanding men like Jose Morales Lemus and Rawlins's personal physician, Dr. Bliss.

There was much about Morales Lemus that Rawlins could admire: in Cuba, he rose from humble beginnings, studied law, succeeded through luck and hard work, and established himself as an antislavery, reform-minded patriot.[65] Morales Lemus established close connections with Dr. Bliss. It was reported Bliss would be paid $2,000,000 in Cuban bonds if Congress passed a resolution of belligerent rights or any other law that modified US neutrality. Those bonds were alleged to have been deposited with the Safe Deposit Company of Washington by Jose Antonio Fesser, treasurer of the New York Cuban junta. Working with several lobbyists, Bliss was to recruit congressmen to accomplish his ends. Several resolutions were introduced in the House but not voted on. Newspaper correspondents in Philadelphia and Boston were said to have received large sums.[66] Only weeks before he died, Morales Lemus denied offering bribes in exchange for recognition of belligerent rights: "I wish to express publicly that neither I . . . nor any one acting under my authority, have ever attempted to use any such means of corruption."[67]

While writing his biography of Rawlins, Harry Wilson challenged the charge that Rawlins possessed the bonds. Horace Porter told Wilson the story of the bonds. Wilson, in turn, wrote John E. Smith for his version, and Smith denied there was truth to it. Wilson and Sylvanus Cadwallader, Rawlins's two biggest boosters, later exchanged correspondence in which they were agreed that the bond story was a hoax. Wilson said he believed Smith and would use quotes from his letter in the biography. Cadwallader's opinion was there was "no foundation for the Cuban bond story."[68] Wilson never specifically referred to the bond issue in the biography, although he did write that he heard "the innuendos and reflections" made against Rawlins. After doing his own investigations, he never found "the slightest fact upon which to base even a doubt as to his private or official character."[69] There appears enough evidence, however, that Cuban bonds were found among Rawlins's papers.[70]

—◦◦◦—

Although the clamor around Cuba drew more attention, developments progressed simultaneously regarding annexation of Santo Domingo (the Dominican Republic), which in 1865 achieved independence from Spain. Santo Domingo was desired for its natural resources and its location as a naval base by many politicians, including Andrew Johnson, William Seward, Nathaniel Banks, Ben Butler, and U. S. Grant, and a majority of its citizens favored annexation. Two US citizens, Joseph Fabens and William Cazneau, both aggressive promoters, were in league with Buenaventura Baez, the Santo Domingan president, to sell the annexation idea to the State Department, a deal in which Fabens and Cazneau figured to reap great financial gain. They demonstrated considerable astuteness by targeting Congressman John Logan, Admiral David Porter, and especially Rawlins, given his closeness to Grant.[71]

In July, Grant sent Orville Babcock, his personal secretary, to Santo Domingo solely on a fact-finding mission that included gauging public sentiment regarding annexation. The trip also placed him in a cozy relationship with Fabens and Cazneau that would reward him with "a financial motive to serve the annexationists."[72] Babcock was to receive one thousand acres of land "in case of annexation."[73] When Babcock returned to Washington in September 1869, after Rawlins's death, he presented to the Cabinet a draft of a treaty for the cessation of Santo Domingo. That Babcock went far beyond his authority embarrassed Grant and astounded Fish. Two months later, Babcock was returned to Santo Domingo where, in official capacity as an emissary, he worked out treaties for annexation and for leasing Samaná Bay for naval vessels. Despite Grant's lobbying efforts, on June 30, 1870, the Senate failed to ratify the annexation treaty.

—♦—

In the midst of heated rhetoric over Cuba and Santo Domingo, Rawlins looked forward to a respite in New England. Emma, confined in Danbury, was in her fifth month of pregnancy. The couple was no doubt anxious about augmenting their family after two unsuccessful attempts. But before he could leave, Rawlins faced the distasteful task of reducing the size of his clerical staff.[74]

On his return to Washington, Rawlins would become a pivotal player in launching the construction of one of the nineteenth century's significant engineering achievements: the Brooklyn Bridge. Detailed plans for the bridge had been worked through by its designer, John A. Roebling, who was assisted by his oldest son, Washington. In anticipation of final approval to begin construction, young Roebling had just completed survey sightings at the riverfront to pinpoint the precise locations for laying down the bridge.

The bridge had to comply with federal regulations stipulating it would not restrict or impede vessels navigating the East River. In Washington, officials raised the additional concern that the bridge might interfere with ship traffic to and from the Brooklyn Navy Yard. To review the details of the plan for the bridge, a panel was appointed by the Army's chief of engineers, Brigadier General Andrew Humphreys.[75] Humphreys was well-known to Rawlins as George Meade's chief of staff. Another former Army of the Potomac general, Henry Slocum, had serious interest in the approval of the plans considering he was Brooklyn's Democratic representative in Congress. Slocum helped run interference for the Roeblings, and he was suggested as a person who could move Humphreys along.[76] Slocum's political pull could come in handy because the Roeblings faced "very strong" opposition in Washington—"even Secretary Fish has put in personal influence against the bridge." Slocum met with Rawlins in early June and received from him a promise that "he would approve everything this week yet."[77]

As secretary of war, Rawlins's final approval was necessary before construction could begin, and he had familiarized himself with the engineering particulars. Rawlins had failed to honor his promise to secure approval by the end of the first week in June—but John Roebling was delayed until he could meet with his consultants on June 12 to get their go-ahead—because he had to accompany Grant to West Point to celebrate the class of '69 graduates. From West Point, Grant and his party traveled to Boston to attend the Peace Jubilee, a multiday musical extravaganza that featured one hundred firemen walloping blacksmith hammers against real anvils in a rendition of Verdi's "Anvil Chorus." Rawlins, instead, headed south, where on June 15 he met with Henry Slocum at the Brooklyn mansion of J. Carson Brevoort, a civil engineer, now engaged in public service endeavors. Rawlins told Slocum that Grant had left the bridge details to him, and he would settle the entire business once back in Washington.[78]

This time Rawlins delivered. On June 21, General Humphreys sent out word that Rawlins had approved of the bridge's plan and location, provided they met the conditions laid down by the US Engineers. One of the critical points, and one involving Rawlins's input, was the setting of the center of the span at a safely navigable height of 135 feet above flood tide.[79] The Brooklyn Daily Eagle of June 25 announced that the Federal government and the Board of US Engineers had given approval, "and the erection has become a fixed fact."[80]

At the end of June, Rawlins traveled alone to Gettysburg to attend the dedication ceremony of the Soldiers Monument sited on the apex of Cemetery Hill. The monument featured a statue of the Genius of Liberty atop a square twenty-five-foot base with an allegorical figure at each corner. Six years after the battle, Rawlins found the town and surroundings much returned to their former idyllic character. Grain was ripening under clear but sultry skies in fields remarkably free of the vestiges of war. The tranquility would have been complete if not for the crowds pouring into town. Hotel space was limited, but churches opened their doors to visitors, and tents were pitched on the battlefield for those desiring a more realistic experience.

At 10:00 a.m. on July 1, Rawlins participated in the processional march to the cemetery under a military escort commanded by General Humphreys. Rawlins shared the platform with an assemblage that included General Meade, Governor John Geary of Pennsylvania, Reverend Henry Ward Beecher, poet

Bayard Taylor, and Commissioner of Indian Affairs Ely Parker. The ceremony began with Reverend Beecher beseeching the Almighty to bless the president "and all that are associated with him in council and in administration." Following remarks by Meade, a passage was cleared from the platform to the base of the monument, where Meade, assisted by Rawlins, unloosed the veil covering the front of the monument, evoking applause from the thousands of onlookers. With Liberty exposed, a band struck up a patriotic air, followed by the firing of a salute.[81]

—◁◉▷—

In mid-July, Grant was eager to leave Washington's stifling heat for the breezy Jersey shore. Before leaving, he drafted a neutrality proclamation—no doubt due to the urging of Rawlins and that of Orville Babcock and Horace Porter as well—according recognition to the Cuban insurgents. Moreover, he chose language similar to that used by Spain to proclaim a stance of neutrality with regard to the Confederate States of America. Grant handed the document to a mortified Secretary Fish with instructions that if circumstances warranted, the proclamation could be issued while he vacationed. As July concluded, Sickles was reporting from Madrid that negotiations for the sale of Cuba were stalling, causing Fish to grow pessimistic that a settlement could ever be reached.

During the first week of August, Grant visited Fish at his Glenclyffe estate, where he was apprised of Madrid's hesitation. Grant's patience was growing thin, and Fish was convinced he was edging closer to recognizing Cuban belligerence.[82] On August 6, Grant and Fish traveled together to Newburgh, New York, where Fish gave a speech the next evening that was quoted by the *New York Herald*. "If the people of my own State and of the United States will be pleased to bear with my infirmities," Fish said, "I shall in all things defer to their better judgment, and believe that their judgment has confirmed them in the right." The *Herald*'s editorial staff seized on this disclosure that seemed out of place with Fish's stance against recognizing the insurgents. Was Fish finally acknowledging public sentiment was so strongly in favor of the insurgents that it was, at last, "his duty to conform to it"?[83] A few days later, the *Herald* published a report out of Cuba that the revolutionists had seized unnamed principal points on the coast and claimed to have the means to hold them against anything the Spaniards could mobilize against them. The insurgents were reported to be optimistic about their ultimate success, boasting "that if they were accorded belligerent rights by the United States they would have possession of the entire island outside of Havana in thirty days."[84]

Whether Grant based his decision on Fish's puzzling declaration to "defer" to the public's judgment or on the purported military gains made by the revolutionists or on reports that Spain would send thousands more troops to quash the rebellion, on August 14—right in the middle of tense diplomacy over the *Alabama* claims—he wrote Fish, "On reflection I think it advisable to complete the neutrality proclamation which I signed before leaving Washington, and to issue it if Gen. Sickles has not received an entirely satisfactory reply to his proposition to mediate between Spain and the Cubans."[85] But just before Fish was obliged to issue the proclamation—and much to his relief—he received on the same day a cable from Sickles announcing that negotiations with General Prim were revived and that Prim had presented four conditions for moving forward. The first of the Spaniard's conditions called for the insurgents to lay down their arms—a risk to which, Fish knew, they would never agree. However, Sickles's cable contained enough "satisfactory" news to allow Fish to defer issuing Grant's proclamation. After receiving Prim's dubious conditions, Fish worked fast, cabling Sickles to argue the case for Prim's declaring an armistice. Prim shot back a response rejecting an armistice and setting forth a revised six-step plan for the Cubans in which he again stipulated the rebels must first lay down their arms and disperse as preconditions to amnesty. The Cubans would not simply surrender and disband, and that caused Fish to inform Prim that the latest plan was "incompatible with any practicable negotiations" and implored him to grant an armistice. Fish waited for a reply, which by August 31 had not arrived.[86]

—◦◦◦—

The oppressive Washington heat was throttling Rawlins's diseased lungs. On July 17, Attorney General Hoar complained to his wife, "It is hot! hotter!! hottest!!! hottentot! hottentotter! hottentottest! more hottentotter! most hottentottest!" He also informed her that at the National Hotel, a temperature of 110 degrees was recorded.[87] That same day in Washington, Harry Wilson was at Rawlins's residence, where the emaciated secretary of war asked him to serve as his literary executor and do justice to his memory.[88] Wilson suggested Emma be brought into the room so she could be privy to her husband's dying wishes. Confronted with the harsh reality of his impending demise, she dissolved into tears but assured Wilson that when the time came, she would send him all the papers and records.[89] Rawlins could no longer ignore that his life was quickly expiring, but he could derive solace from knowing that besides his historical legacy entrusted to Wilson, there was a genetic one he and Emma would soon welcome into the world. Three weeks later, with Emma at her parents' home and about to give birth any day, Rawlins pulled himself away from his War Department desk and entrained for Danbury. He was so fragile that when he reached New York, his physician there, Dr. John Hancock Douglas, who fifteen years later would diagnose Grant's oral cancer, advised against continuing to Danbury. When Rawlins rejected that advice, Douglas insisted on accompanying him to Danbury. Rawlins would have none of that and refused his offer.

The Rawlinses welcomed a daughter, Violet, on August 17. Despite this blessed event, Rawlins's thoughts could not stray far from the grim calculus he faced and his hope that he could exert a deciding influence in choosing his successor in the War Department. Thus, on the nineteenth from Danbury, he wrote Grenville Dodge about his prospects for that post: "My health is much improved this summer, though for two weeks past I have been a little under the weather. And right here my dear Dodge if on that account I should have to quit if the President will allow me as they say he did Borie to suggest his successor it is clearly within the range of probabilities there might be more force given to the recent telegram that you were to be the person than some of the papers seem to give credence."[90] Rawlins hoped that on his return to Washington, he could meet both Dodge and Senator George Spencer in New York to plot a path for Dodge to succeed him. Spencer, a former Iowan who served under Dodge during the war and helped him get promoted, took advantage of Reconstruction politics to get elected as Republican in Alabama.

Suddenly, Rawlins's "much improved" health took a steep turn downward. He suffered a hemorrhage brought on, it was thought, by "the excitement and anxiety at Danbury."[91] A medical text of the day described a patient's experience of such an event: the hemorrhage may be preceded by a tickling in the throat, followed by a distinct cough "by which blood, frothy, or filled with air-bubbles, and of a bright arterial or vermilion color, is ejected," amounting "from several mouthfuls to a teacupful."[92] Rawlins rallied sufficiently to start for Washington, where the first cabinet meeting since July was scheduled for August 31, at a crucial time when Prim was complicating negotiations. In New York, Rawlins hemorrhaged again, but instead of resting there, he pushed ahead on a sweltering day to Washington. There he was laid prostrate by a third hemorrhage, from which he recovered a scrap of strength.

At noon on Tuesday, August 31, a ghastly vestige of John Rawlins appeared at the White House, much to the surprise and discomposure of those assembled: President Grant; Assistant Attorney General Walbridge Field; George Robeson, Borie's replacement at navy; Assistant Treasury Secretary William A. Richardson; Postmaster General John Creswell; Interior Secretary Jacob Cox; and Secretary of State Hamilton Fish.

—⁓—

Rawlins believed his attendance was of utmost urgency. With the Spaniards displaying recalcitrance, he felt it behooved him to stand firm for recognizing the Cuban belligerency. The day before, Rawlins's friend, Charles Dana, editor of the *New York Sun* and a strident voice among interventionists, urged the United States "at once to interfere in Cuba, and . . . to prevent the destruction of houses and plantations on the one hand, and the ferocious cruelties of the Spaniards on the other." For good measure, Dana berated the Grant administration for being "barren of great ideas" and "deficient in courage and character."[93]

The meeting was an historic contest between Rawlins and Fish, with the former drawing on the remnant of his physical reserves to passionately debate the case for according belligerent rights to the Cubans. So focused was Rawlins that it was reported he spoke "with a remarkable buoyancy of spirit"—as if oblivious to his physical condition.[94] Fish opposed that recourse as well as annexation and favored brokering negotiations after first establishing an armistice. After Rawlins delivered his long and lawyerly argument, he collapsed into his chair and begged Grant to consider the fervor he displayed in the context of their deep relationship: "I have been your adjutant, and I think you will excuse me for being earnest." Grant, acknowledging that bond, warmly replied, "Certainly, and you are still my adjutant."[95] For his part in this confrontation, Fish bore Rawlins no enmity; rather, he held his fellow cabinet member in respect. "I fear that his disease (consumption) has the entire mastery of him, and that he has not long to labor," Fish wrote shortly after the session. "He is a generous, high-spirited, and right-minded (impulsive) man, instinctively right in the direction of his impulses, even if occasionally extravagant."[96]

While Rawlins and Fish traded points and counterpoints, Grant was occupied putting thoughts to paper. When they finished, he nudged the paper toward Fish. On it were the terms Grant decided to offer Spain:

The United States are willing to mediate between Spain & Cuba, on following terms. Immediate armistice. Cuba to recompense Spain for public property &c. All Spaniards to be protected in their persons and property if they wish to remain on the island, or to withdraw with it, at their option. The United States not to guarantee except with approval of Congress. These conditions to be accepted by Sept. 25th or the United States to be regarded as having withdrawn all offer to mediate. As time progresses devastation depreciates value of property, and consequently of the sum that can or will be guaranteed.[97]

In effect, Grant was giving Spain a month—the date was extended to October 1—to agree to mediation. Perhaps beyond that date, Grant might issue a proclamation of neutrality. The president had tilted toward Fish. The terms were cabled to Sickles, but once they were disseminated to the Spanish public, they were met with fierce opposition.

—⁂—

The next day, Wednesday, Rawlins met with Grant at noon and then wrapped up business at the War Department in anticipation of Grant's departure that evening for Saratoga, New York. After returning to his residence in the afternoon, Rawlins sat on his sofa and was almost at once overcome by another hemorrhage.[98] Rawlins had already accepted an invitation for dinner on Thursday, September 2, at the home of General Giles Smith, a friend from the campaigns of Donelson through Chattanooga, who was assistant postmaster general. This meant Rawlins would have to forgo his prescribed regimen of raw beef, milk, and eggs. Ironically, Smith too had been hemorrhaging from the lungs, and he would succumb to tuberculosis in 1876.[99] Dr. Bliss called on Rawlins that same evening and admonished him that deviating from his diet could have serious consequences. Hours later, Rawlins suffered a terrible hemorrhage.[100] That was followed by another on Friday night that rendered him unconscious for five hours. Left almost incapacitated, Rawlins was removed to Giles Smith's residence. Friday night's attack was so violent he was not expected to survive. Dr. Bliss was summoned, but his medical interventions were limited to offering Rawlins an alcoholic stimulant. The liquor's revitalizing effect even surprised Bliss, who exclaimed to Smith, "General, he is going to live!" Incredibly, Rawlins initiated talk about needing to attend to some matters at the War Department. However, the next morning, intense coughing fits brought on a series of dangerous hemorrhages. Dr. Bliss, joined by Surgeon General Joseph K. Barnes, held vigils at Rawlins's bedside.[101]

NOTES

1. Carl Sandburg, *Abraham Lincoln: The War Years* (New York: Harcourt Brace, 1939), 174.

2. John A. Rawlins to Emma Rawlins, December 10, 1868, transcribed by J. H. Wilson, James H. Wilson Papers, Bender Collection, Wyoming State Archives and Historical Department, Microfilm Reel H-61b.

3. J. A. Rawlins to Emma, December 8, 1868, transcribed by J. H. Wilson, James H. Wilson Papers, Bender Collection, Wyoming State Archives and Historical Department, Microfilm Reel H-61b.

4. Henry Power and Leonard W. Sedgwick, *The New Sydenham Society's Lexicon of Medicine and the Allied Sciences* (London: Author, 1888), 3:600.

5. John Armstrong, "Pulmonary Consumption," in *Practical Illustrations Relative to Puerperal Fever, Scarlet Fever, Pulmonary Consumption, and Measles: A General View of the Pathology and Treatment of Chronic Disease, with Illustrations of the Utility of the Balsam of Copaiva in Inflammation of the Mucous Membrane*, 2nd American ed. (Philadelphia: J. Grigg et al., 1826), 101.

6. Sheila M. Rothman, *Living in the Shadow of Death: Tuberculosis and the Social Experience of Illness in American History* (Baltimore: Johns Hopkins University Press, 1994), 16.

7. J. A. Rawlins to Emma, January 8, 1869, and January 16, 1869, transcribed by J. H. Wilson, James H. Wilson Papers, Bender Collection, Wyoming State Archives and Historical Department, Microfilm Reel H-61b.

8. John Y. Simon, ed., *The Papers of Ulysses S. Grant*, 19:345–46.

9. James Harrison Wilson, *The Life of John A. Rawlins* (New York: Neale, 1916), 350–52; Stanley P. Hirshson, *Grenville M. Dodge: Soldier, Politician, Railroad Pioneer* (Bloomington: Indiana University Press, 1967), 173–74.

10. Grenville M. Dodge to J. A. Rawlins, March 8, 1869, James H. Wilson Papers, Bender Collection, Wyoming State Archives and Historical Department, Microfilm Reel H-61b.

11. *New York Times*, March 6, 1869.

12. Ibid. Grant was not above rewarding Galena friends with government appointments. Augustus Chetlain and J. Russell Jones were given diplomatic posts in Belgium, and Horace Houghton, editor of the *Galena Daily Gazette*, was appointed US consul to the Sandwich Islands.

13. Adam Badeau, *Grant in Peace* (Hartford, CT: S. S. Scranton, 1887), 164.

14. Ibid., 162.

15. *Chicago Tribune*, March 12, 1869.

16. *New York Tribune*, March 12, 1869.

17. *New York Herald*, March 12, 1869.

18. *Galena Evening Gazette*, March 29, 1869.

19. Hamlin Garland, *Ulysses S. Grant: His Life and Character* (New York: Doubleday and McClure, 1898), 392.

20. Ibid., 393–94.

21. John A. Rawlins to Emma Rawlins, March 19, 1869, transcribed by J. H. Wilson, James H. Wilson Papers, Bender Collection, Wyoming State Archives and Historical Department, Microfilm Reel H-61b.

22. *New York Sun*, March 29, 1869.

23. John A. Rawlins to Emma, March 28, 1869, transcribed by J. H. Wilson, James H. Wilson Papers, Bender Collection, Wyoming State Archives and Historical Department, Microfilm Reel H-61b.

24. Jean Edward Smith, *Grant* (New York: Simon and Schuster, 2001), 477.

25. U. S. Grant to Edwin M. Stanton, January 29, 1866, in *The Papers of Ulysses S. Grant*, ed. John Y. Simon (Carbondale: Southern Illinois University Press, 1988), 16:37.

26. John Y. Simon, ed., *The Papers of Ulysses S. Grant*, 19:143n.

27. James Harrison Wilson *The Life of John A. Rawlins*, 366.

28. John A. Rawlins to Emma, March 28, 1869, transcribed by J. H. Wilson, James H. Wilson Papers, Bender Collection, Wyoming State Archives and Historical Department, Microfilm Reel H-61b.

29. Jacob Dolson Cox, "How Judge Hoar Ceased to Be Attorney General," *Atlantic Monthly* 76, no. 454 (August 1895): 164.

30. John Y. Simon, ed., *The Papers of Ulysses S. Grant*, 16:144–45n.

31. Manning F. Force, *General Sherman* (New York: D. Appleton, 1899), 325.

32. William T. Sherman, *Memoirs*, 2nd ed. (New York: D. Appleton, 1889), 2:442.

33. John F. Marszalek, *Sherman: A Soldier's Passion for Order* (Carbondale: Southern Illinois University Press, 1993), 385.

34. Manning F. Force, *General Sherman*, 326.

35. Charles W. Calhoun, *The Presidency of Ulysses S. Grant* (Lawrence: University Press of Kansas, 2017), 531.

36. *Chicago Tribune*, March 30, 1869.

37. Manfield Storey, *Charles Sumner* (Boston: Houghton, Mifflin, 1900), 243.

38. Charles Francis Adams, *Lee at Appomattox and Other Papers* (Boston: Houghton, Mifflin, 1902), 154.

39. Alan Nevins, *Hamilton Fish: The Inner History of the Grant Administration* (New York: Dodd, Mead, 1936), 216, 223–24.

40. *New York Tribune*, April 20, 1869.

41. John Russell Young, *Around the World with General Grant* (New York: American News, 1879), 167.

42. "Speech of Major Gen'l John A. Rawlins, Chief of Staff U.S.A.," Washington, DC: The Union Republican Congressional Committee, 15.

43. M. W. Cluskey, *The Political Text-Book or Encyclopedia* (Philadelphia: Jas. B. Smith, 1860), 480.

44. James D. Richardson, *A Compilation of the Messages and Papers of the Presidents* (New York: Bureau of National Literature, 1897), 3173.

45. Damon Wells, *Stephen Douglas: The Last Years, 1857–1861* (Austin: University of Texas Press, 1971), 154.

46. *New York Times*, January 24, 1869.

47. Adam Badeau, *Grant in Peace*, 233.

48. Alan Nevins, *Hamilton Fish*, 125.

49. A. Elwood Corning, *Hamilton Fish* (New York: Lanmere, 1918), 86.

50. Charles W. Calhoun, *The Presidency of Ulysses S. Grant*, 181.

51. Alan Nevins, *Hamilton Fish*, 128–29.

52. Ibid., 136–37.

53. Adam Badeau, *Grant in Peace*, 387.

54. W. A. Swanberg, *Sickles the Incredible* (New York: Charles Scribner's Sons, 1956), 306.

55. *New York Herald*, August 9, 1869.

56. *New York Sun*, March 26, 1869.

57. *New York Times*, April 23, 1869; *New York Tribune*, April 30, 1869.

58. *New York Herald*, May 3, 1869.

59. *New York Tribune*, April 30, 1869.

60. Alan Nevins, *Hamilton Fish*, 194, 199.

61. Ibid., 921.

62. Charles W. Calhoun, *The Presidency of Ulysses S. Grant*, 181.

63. James Y. Simon, ed., *The Papers of Ulysses S. Grant* (Carbondale: Southern Illinois University Press, 1998), 21:78n.

64. *New York Times*, September 9, 1869.

65. Lisandro Perez, *Sugar, Cigars and Revolution: The Making of Cuban New York* (New York: New York University Press, 2018), 139.

66. *Washington Evening Star*, June 7, 1870.

67. *New York Herald*, June 7, 1870.

68. James H. Wilson to Sylvanus Cadwallader, September 8, 1904; Sylvanus Cadwallader to James H. Wilson, September 17, 1904; James H. Wilson to Sylvanus Cadwallader, September 24, 1904, Library of Congress, James Harrison Wilson Papers, Container 5.

69. James Harrison Wilson, *The Life of John A. Rawlins*, 361.

70. Charles W. Calhoun, *The Presidency of Ulysses S. Grant*, 626n3.

71. Alan Nevins, *Hamilton Fish*, 263.

72. Ibid., 275.

73. Charles W. Calhoun, *The Presidency of Ulysses S. Grant*, 215.

74. J. A. Rawlins to Emma, May 9 and May 14, 1869, James H. Wilson Papers, Bender Collection, Wyoming State Archives and Historical Department, Microfilm Reel H-61b.

75. David McCullough, *The Great Bridge* (New York: Simon and Schuster, 1972), 35.

76. Ibid., 87.

77. Washington Roebling to John A. Roebling, June 5, 1869, MC 654, Roebling Family Collection, Box 3, Folder 38, Special Collections and University Archives, Rutgers University Libraries, New Brunswick, NJ.

78. David McCullough, *The Great Bridge*, 88.

79. Ibid., 88–89; James Harrison Wilson, *The Life of John A. Rawlins*, 364.

80. *Brooklyn Daily Eagle*, June 25, 1869.

81. *New York Herald*, July 2, 1869.

82. Alan Nevins, *Hamilton Fish*, 236.

83. *New York Herald*, August 9, 1869.

84. Ibid., August 13, 1869.

85. U. S. Grant to Hamilton Fish, August 14, 1869, in *The Papers of Ulysses S. Grant*, ed. John Y. Simon, 19:234–35.

86. Alan Nevins, *Hamilton Fish*, 242–43.

87. Moorfield Storey and Edward M. Emerson, *Ebenezer Rockwood Hoar: A Memoir* (Boston: Houghton Mifflin, 1911), 215–16.

88. James Harrison Wilson, *The Life of John A. Rawlins*, 363.

89. James Harrison Wilson to David Sheean, August 24, 1904, James Harrison Wilson Papers, Box 22, Library of Congress.

90. John Y. Simon, ed., *The Papers of Ulysses S. Grant*, 19:260n.

91. *New York Herald*, September 8, 1869.

92. William Sweetser, *A Treatise on Consumption* (Boston: T. H. Carter, 1836), 48.

93. *New York Sun*, August 30, 1869.

94. *New York Herald*, September 8, 1869.

95. Alan Nevins, *Hamilton Fish*, 244.

96. Ibid., 246.

97. Memorandum of August 31, 1869, in *The Papers of Ulysses S. Grant*, ed. John Y. Simon, 19:238.

98. *New York Herald*, September 8, 1869.

99. Jack D. Welsh, *Medical Histories of Union Generals* (Kent: Kent State University Press, 1996), 309.

100. *Daily Morning Chronicle*, Washington, DC, September 8, 1869.

101. *New York Herald*, September 7, 1869.

26

"Sweet and Serene Be Your Slumber!"

VISITORS AT RAWLINS'S BEDSIDE WOULD have noticed his changed complexion during these last hours. His skin was of a smooth and fair appearance, and his face was the color and texture of old parchment, indicative of pulmonary distress. With his life ebbing, friends withheld the news that infant daughter Violet died on September 3. In Danbury, Emma's disconsolation was compounded by dispatches arriving every thirty minutes updating John's condition.

At Saratoga, New York, President Grant received on the morning of Saturday, September 4, two dispatches regarding Rawlins's condition. The earlier one noted that on the previous day, Rawlins had taken an ominous turn, but a later arriving telegram said he had revived and his condition had brightened. That optimistic news caused Grant to consider taking a visit with New York Senator Roscoe Conkling. However, at Sunday noon, another dispatch signaled a downturn in Rawlins's prospects. That settled the issue for Grant, who was now intent on hurrying to Washington. He left Saratoga with Horace Porter before 6:00 p.m. on Sunday for Albany in a private railcar compartment shared by Conkling and Justice Ward Hunt of the New York Court of Appeals.

On this Saratoga-to-Albany leg of the journey, Grant talked of little else than the close relationship he had with Rawlins. He told Conkling, "I could not feel the loss of a near and dear relative more keenly than the loss of General Rawlins." There was no special train available in Albany, so instead of waiting seven hours for the regularly scheduled train, he boarded the steamer *Vanderbilt* for New York City. From New York, he caught a train that passed through Jersey City and Wilmington, Delaware—where a dispatch awaited indicating that Rawlins was sinking rapidly—and finally to Baltimore, where a special train awaited to transport Grant to Washington.[1]

Despite the somber situation facing Grant, he used part of the trip to consider options to plug the looming gap in the War Department. Although Sherman would be named the temporary replacement, speculation abounded as to who would succeed Rawlins. Some names included Generals George Thomas, Grenville Dodge, Edward R. S. Canby, and even venerable Joseph Holt, secretary of war during the waning weeks of Buchanan's presidency.[2] Senator George Spencer thought Grant would select Dodge, who was Rawlins's preference.[3] However, Horace Porter used his proximity to Grant during the journey to talk up William Belknap for the job.[4] Grant would choose Belknap, who had a stellar record as a division commander under Sherman. Belknap served into Grant's second term until he resigned in the summer of 1876 after a scandal was uncovered involving kickback payments to him and his wife from the Fort Sill trading post.

Rawlins's visitors on Sunday, September 5, included cabinet members Fish, Robeson, Cox, and Creswell. With Creswell, he shared his frankest views about the course of Reconstruction and the Cubans' plight. Despite his frailty, Rawlins's mind overflowed with opinions as he engaged Creswell with "ideas wonderfully connected and practical."[5] Rawlins used Sunday to make final preparations. He dictated his will to Ely Parker, bequeathing the house at Twelfth and M Streets to Emma and the children, as well as land parcels in Cheyenne and Golden City in the Wyoming Territory. To son James, he left his law books—his only property remaining in Galena—currently in David Sheean's possession. Rawlins's last stipulation was the appointments of Emma and Ulysses Grant as the children's guardians and executors of his will.[6] Tellingly, Rawlins made no mention of any Cuban bonds in his will. Also that afternoon, Reverend Samuel A. Wilson of McKendree Chapel attended to his spiritual needs. At 3:00 p.m., Rawlins, who had been instructed in the Methodist faith, asked to be baptized. Three hours later, the minister returned to offer him communion.[7] At almost that same moment, Grant's train departed Saratoga for Albany.

For Monday's breakfast, Rawlins requested raw meat and, when served, remarked, "A king could fatten on that."[8] But even a ravenous appetite could not belie the gloomy warnings. His heart raced 110–115 beats per minute. Violent coughing fits produced bloody phlegm. By noon he was unable to move without aid. Meanwhile, Rawlins inquired repeatedly about Grant's time of arrival. Those at his bedside, which included Drs. Bliss and Barnes, Ely Parker, and John E. Smith, assured him Grant was expected any time. To endure until then, Rawlins asked for stimulants, and he was fed chicken broth.[9]

As the minutes counted down, Rawlins grew more impatient to see Grant. Dr. Bliss asked if he had a message for him, but Rawlins, perhaps resignedly, replied, "I would like to have seen him, but it's no matter."[10] During the early afternoon hours, dispatches conveying tributes of respect and affection reached the bedside. Secretary Cox read a message from Ebenezer Hoar, prompting Rawlins to say, "I am very grateful to the Attorney General for his love, and I wish you to say so to him."[11] About 3:00 p.m., a telegram from Sheridan arrived. "Will you please to give my love to Rawlins," it read. "All the officers here send their love to him." Despite being barely able to respire, Rawlins acknowledged the tender sentiments: "General Sheridan is very kind. I appreciate and am very grateful for his kindness. If the love of my friends could do it, I would soon be a healthy man."[12] Rawlins's dwindling remarks drifted to his family's welfare and the scant amount of property he could leave them. Indiana Senator Oliver Morton offered reassurances: "Give yourself no uneasiness about your family, General. The country will see they are well taken care of."[13]

To the end, Rawlins yearned to see Grant one more time. "Hasn't the old man come yet?" was his final question.[14] At 4:00 p.m., Rawlins uttered his last words: "Raise me up." Dr. Bliss obliged and tucked a pillow under his back. Rawlins lay still for ten minutes, when unexpectedly he lifted his head, his eyes became fixed, and he sank to the bed, expiring without a struggle. It was 4:12, Monday, September 6.[15]

———

An hour later, the special train carrying Grant and Horace Porter steamed into Washington. They were met at the station by Sherman, who accompanied them to Giles Smith's residence. At 5:25, their carriage drove up, and Grant, with Porter trailing, raced up the stairway and into the parlor where the body had been removed. There a "much affected" Grant stood transfixed as he gazed at the lifeless form of the man who had served him faithfully from Galena to the Executive Mansion.[16] A statement in the next day's *New York Times* captured the impact of that poignant moment on Grant: "To General Grant, the death of his townsman and friend, his constant ally and trusted counselor in war and peace, whose honest and intelligent advice was always asked, and always given, will be very great. It is doubtful whether he would feel more keenly the loss of any of his old companions in arms, than that of this constant sharer of his campaigns."[17]

Before leaving, Grant composed a letter and ordered it to be dispatched to Emma: "Your beloved husband expired at twelve minutes after four o'clock this afternoon, to be mourned by a family and friends who loved him for his personal worth and services to his country, and a nation which acknowledges its debt of gratitude to him." September 9 was suggested for the funeral procession and ceremony.[18] At the Giles Smith residence, Sherman supervised the removal of Rawlins's body, entrusting it to Alonzo Mann, the undertaker who had prepared Lincoln's remains for burial.[19] Then at precisely 7:00 p.m., the bells in Washington began tolling for two hours.[20]

Before dawn on Tuesday, Rawlins's prepared remains were placed in a white satin-lined coffin, which featured an oval glass plate affording a view of face and bust. The coffin was fitted on a nine-foot catafalque in the middle of a lower room in the War Department, where the public could pass through to pay respects and where Thursday's funeral service would be held. Three days later, just prior to internment and in the presence of Ely Parker, sculptor Fisk Mills, whose father had made life masks of Lincoln two months before the assassination, made a cast of Rawlins's face and took head and chest measurements for any future statue.[21]

Already there was a tug over a final resting place for those remains. On the seventh, brother Lemmon Parker Rawlins telegraphed from Galena that it was his and his parents' wish the body be brought home for burial. Illinois Governor John Palmer wired General John E. Smith with the offer to have Rawlins interred at Oak Ridge Cemetery outside Springfield. In addition, Danbury, Connecticut, was making claims on the remains.[22]

Precisely at that moment, there was another tug, of sorts, occurring—this one being exerted from inside the pages of one of the nation's most influential dailies, the New York Sun, owned by Charles Dana. Dana, as assistant secretary of war, had done much to promote Grant's military career, but since having been denied the plum patronage job of customs collector in New York, he turned on Grant and had become a harsh critic of what he regarded as the administration's timid posture toward Cuba. Just two days after Rawlins's death, under the heading "Apathy of the President," the paper printed a one-sentence, character-wrenching remark against Grant: "Today while Rawlins's corpse rested within two hundred yards of the White House, Grant did not feel interest enough to go and look at it." Moreover, elsewhere in the same issue, Dana tried to yank apart Grant's legacy in the annals of history with this contemptuous criticism based on his tardiness to reach Rawlins's bedside: "He had lingered too late in the lap of pleasure to receive the last blessing of his expiring comrade. Yet Rawlins was never missing when Grant wanted him. And it is probably safe to say today—with all the solemnity of history—*that had there never been a Rawlins, there would never have been a Grant*" (italics added).[23] What we see here is an early effort to attribute Grant's success to the contributions of his foremost staff officer. Later, other friends of Rawlins would strive to elevate him at Grant's expense.

—⟨⟨⟨—

The funeral service was set for 10:00 a.m. on Thursday in the War Department. Emma, who had been delayed due to her own illness, reached Washington early that morning accompanied by her parents, the three Rawlins children, brother-in-law James, and William Hillyer, among others. Carriages conveyed them to Willard's Hotel, where they were given rooms. Doors at the War Department opened at 8:00 to receive military, governmental, and foreign dignitaries; the general public was excluded. Sherman, Andrew Humphreys, Horace Porter, and George Leet represented the army. Ministers from Great Britain, the Netherlands, Belgium, Spain, and Brazil were among those attending. Henry Pinetro, secretary to Jose Morales Lemus, was the Cuban representative at the service. At 9:15, Grant arrived in the company of cabinet members Fish, Hoar, and Creswell. Emma, dressed in deep mourning, appeared fifteen minutes later and took her place at the head of the coffin, where she was steadied by Ely Parker.[24]

The service at the War Department was brief. After the concluding prayer by Reverend Hamilton, the cover over the coffin's glass plate was closed, and eight soldiers, followed by the pallbearers, carried the coffin through the north door to the waiting hearse. Minutes after 11:00 a.m., family and friends stood along Seventeenth Street for the carriages to take them to their position in the long funeral procession down Pennsylvania Avenue.

That procession followed proper protocol. At the head were various military and uniformed units: artillery batteries, mounted Metropolitan police, squadrons of cavalry, even a contingent of Mexican War veterans. Then came the officiating clergy, followed by the hearse. The hearse was topped by six black plumes and drawn by six gray horses, each led by a groom dressed in black. The eight soldiers who bore the casket flanked the hearse, which was trailed by Rawlins's riderless white horse, draped in black and led by two mounted cavalrymen. Trailing the hearse were the carriages carrying the sixteen pall-bearers that included Generals Oliver O. Howard, John E. Smith, Giles Smith, and Surgeon General Barnes. Next in line were the carriages transporting family, relatives, and friends, and behind them those of the president, cabinet, members of the Diplomatic Corps, Supreme Court justices, and senators and congressmen. Altogether over two hundred carriages and vehicles and a full marine band were bound for the Congressional Cemetery.[25]

Pennsylvania Avenue was packed with onlookers, the nimbler people climbing trees to get a better advantage. Stores were closed, and residences were draped in black. When the column reached the Wallach School, its twelve hundred students, all clad in white, greeted the hearse with a hymn:

> Sweet and serene be your slumber!
> Hearts for whose freedom ye bled,
> Millions, whom no man can number,
> Tears of sad gratitude shed.

By 12:15, the mourners had reached the cemetery, where the casket would be held temporarily in an ivy-covered brick vault owned by Thomas Blagden. Reverend Wilson began the brief ceremony by reading from Scripture. After casting a symbolic handful of earth on the casket, he offered prayers. Following Reverend Hamilton's benediction, the Beethoven Club sang a requiem:

> Sigh not, ye winds, as passing o'er
> The chambers of the dead ye fly;
> Weep not, ye dews,
> For these no more shall ever weep—shall ever sigh.

As the casket was being borne into the tomb, Emma slipped free of Parker's supporting arm, approached the casket, lifted her veil, and pressed a farewell kiss on it.[26]

Three volleys of musketry marked the conclusion of the ceremony and served as a signal for the mourners to return to their carriages. Emma, weakened by sickness and grief, returned with her family to their rooms at Willard's.

Washington's *Daily Morning Chronicle* of September 10 observed that not since President Lincoln's body passed through the streets of the capital had the city witnessed "such a universal and touching tribute to any of the great men who have since passed away." This was astonishing in that Rawlins never held national elective office and had toiled in roles mostly significantly ancillary to Grant. The paper concluded that this outpouring of respect and affection was due to the perceived purity of Rawlins's character, his generous nature, and the gentle manner in which he exercised the power of his offices—traits that resonated with all classes. In the days following Rawlins's death, the paper published anonymous letters by friends of Rawlins that spoke to the qualities that made him worthy of honor.

On September 7 and again on September 10, a writer identified as "Occasional" submitted two insightful letters that delved into Rawlins's character. In the first letter, the writer identified one of Rawlins's gifts as the ability to stay true to himself: "His convictions were sincere, though he never paraded them. His good sense was, perhaps, the salt of his nature. . . . Utterly indifferent to what we call fame, and really averse to politics as the world goes, he never talked about himself or became a party to the wild hunt for office so common to every inauguration." Three days later, Occasional praised Rawlins for focusing on making his War Department "a model of order and economy." Although a Democrat of the old school, "the rebellion cleared away all his pro-slavery prejudices" and brought forth a man who championed universal suffrage.[27] Thus, Rawlins proved a man of high standards who transcended his closeminded views about race.

"A Touching Tribute to the Late General John A. Rawlins, Secretary of War" was written by "E.," who probably was Ely Parker. E. said he was with Rawlins during the last hours, saw him baptized, felt his passion for the Cubans, and heard his words of affection for Governor Morton—incidents that, to E., demonstrated "not only the greatness of his mind, but the goodness of his heart." It was E.'s observation that "probably no public man was ever more loved and honored in this community than General Rawlins," feelings that "prevailed among all classes, high and low, rich and poor." And how to account for Rawlins's rapid rise from obscurity to distinction? In E.'s estimation it was because "he was no ordinary man."[28]

The folks in Galena also celebrated Rawlins's life and eulogized his memory. On the day of his death, his fellow Masons made an entry in their lodge's records: "His work was not done, yet his column is broken. The silver chord is loosed, the golden bowl is rent in twain; the dust has returned to the earth as it was, and the spirit to God who gave it."[29] On the nineteenth, Reverend S. A. W. Jewett delivered a funeral discourse at Galena's Methodist Episcopal Church, which was attended by Rawlins's mother, Lovisa, and sister, Laura Sheean. His father, James, who was rarely seen in town, begged off, making the lame excuse he had to care for two sons who were ill. Reverend Jewett marveled how Rawlins was able to lift himself from obscurity to power when, but "twelve years ago, he was scarcely thought of as more than an ordinary man."[30]

—◦◦◦—

The remembrance that would have meant the most to Rawlins occurred during the fourth annual meeting of the Society of the Army of the Tennessee held at Louisville in November 1869, where his fellow officers, once they glanced at his empty chair shrouded in black, were reminded of the true friend they had lost. Ely Parker consented to deliver the eulogy, in which he recounted what made Rawlins great. That greatness was not achieved by battlefield heroics or by sponsoring landmark legislation; rather, it emanated from his magnanimity and right-mindedness. As Parker recollected, no enlisted man ever received injustice from John Rawlins, and no officer who asked for help or counsel was ever turned away. Although he once regarded slavery as a necessary evil, Rawlins assisted Grant to bring about the "immortal truth of the Declaration of Independence."[31] In the cabinet, he was, as Parker affirmed, "on the side of right against wrong, freedom against oppression." To Rawlins, "the lowest, poorest and humblest individual had the same voice and weight in the affairs of the nation as the highest, wealthiest and proudest of the land."[32] It was to the oppressed that Rawlins was dedicated even to his end. He had told Parker that at the last cabinet meeting, he had made such a strenuous effort to secure recognition for the Cubans that "in his enfeebled condition he had over-exerted himself."[33] Parker concluded by communicating Rawlins's regrets that his poor health precluded his attendance at these reunions, but he wanted them to know, "He loved you all, and his spirit was always present with you upon every recurrence of these interesting occasions."[34]

The society's fourth toast of the evening, following ones to President Grant, the army and navy, and the Army of the Tennessee, was to John A. Rawlins, and all rose to lift their glasses in silence.[35]

—◦◦◦—

There were efforts to more permanently memorialize Rawlins. Three years before his death, Rawlins had been honored by having the District of Columbia's first Grand Army of the Republic's post named for him. The members of Rawlins Post worked for several years to facilitate the transfer of Rawlins's remains—including obtaining consent from relatives—from the Congressional Cemetery for reinternment in their ultimate resting place in Section 2 in Arlington National Cemetery. A ceremony to celebrate that event was held on February 7, 1899. He rests on a slope of the cemetery overlooking the Potomac River near the Arlington House mansion on the former estate of Robert E. Lee and near the burial sites of Admiral David Porter and Generals Sheridan and Doubleday.

On May 25, 1872, Illinois senator John Logan introduced a bill appropriating $10,000 for a Rawlins statue. Grant signed the bill into law, and by the end of the year, a three-member committee met to select a winning design from seven entries. Among the competing sculptors was Fisk Mills, who had cast Rawlins's death mask.[36] The winning design was submitted by Parisian-born Joseph A. Bailly. The eight-foot bronze statue, erected in 1874 in Rawlins Park at Eighteenth and E Streets N.W., depicts Rawlins in uniform atop a twelve-foot pedestal, holding in his right hand a pair of field glasses and a sword in his left. The statue was moved several times but in 1931 was returned to its original location. Historian James M. Goode regarded Bailly's sculpture as one of the better portrait statues in Washington and felt it possesses a "certain elegance and spirit."[37]

In early 1963, the residents of Rawlins, Wyoming, petitioned to have the statue moved there. Illinois congressman John Anderson got wind of the plan, which was endorsed by Wyoming senator Gale McGee. Anderson wrote Secretary of the Interior Stewart Udall that if the statue were relocated, the people of Galena and Jo Daviess County should be allowed "every opportunity to claim General Rawlin's [sic] statue before it be permitted to be sent to a far western community where there is considerable doubt the General ever even visited."[38]

―◦◦◦―

Immediately after Rawlins's death, there was concern for his family's welfare. Grant was reported to have been in favor of Congress appropriating funds to pay the family the salary for Rawlins's unexpired term as war secretary, about $28,000. Congress later authorized, and on May 11, 1870, Grant signed the legislation, paying out Rawlins's remaining salary to the executors of the estate.[39] Grant was also worried about the fate of Rawlins's children in light of Emma's lingering illness.[40]

Very soon after Rawlins's death, a group of merchants and bankers met in New York City and resolved to raise $50,000 in subscriptions on behalf of the family. In short order, the New York Stock Exchange pledged $5,000, and another $15,000 was subscribed on the spot by fifteen donors including Grant, financier Henry Clews, banker Moses Taylor, and New York City merchant H. B. Claflin. A six-person committee was appointed to raise the fund.[41] Jose Morales Lemus donated $20,000 in valueless Cuban bonds to the fund—they were unrelated to those discovered later in a safe—expressing in a letter to Emma that her husband's sympathy for the Cuban cause "filled the hearts of all patriotic Cubans with sincere grief for the untimely loss of such a noble and true friend."[42] The flood of such generosity on Emma's behalf galled Mary Lincoln, who complained to a friend, "I, the beloved wife of the great and good man whose life was sacrificed on his country's cause, have often to endure privations which I would not venture to whisper to anyone."[43]

—◦◦◦—

With Rawlins's passing, his widow and three orphaned children were left to mend their tattered lives. In 1870, Emma returned to Danbury, leaving the Washington house unsold. With the three children, she moved into a home on Balmforth Avenue that featured a mansard roof, basement laundry, and arched wooden front doors in the Italianate style. The house had been built the year before by Isaac Ives, uncle of composer Charles Ives, and was purchased by Grant with monies from the Rawlins fund, of which he was trustee, for a hefty $10,000.[44] Grant assumed a hands-on role in the financial details of the Rawlins family, seeing to it that the rent received from the house on Twelfth and M Streets would be disbursed to pay the children's educational expenses. He advised the house be rented because its value was now less than its purchase price. Throughout, Grant maintained due diligence over the fair disbursement of money across four individuals, a task made complex by necessarily portioning out income from bond interest and rent. The tricky arithmetic tripped up the mathematically inclined Grant, who on an occasion was forced to write out his own check to cover a mistake in his calculations.[45] He attended to even minute details such as giving Emma his approval to have gas fixtures installed in the Danbury house[46] and allowing her to transfer the furniture from the Washington house to Danbury.[47]

On January 29, 1872, Emma married Charles F. Daniels, a New York City music teacher. This marriage caused her to lose income derived from the fund, and she turned for advice to her attorney, William Hillyer, as to how the marriage would affect Grant's intentions regarding the children.[48] In the spring of 1872, the Rawlins children were enrolled in Connecticut boarding schools, the two girls at the Seaside Seminary in Southport and Jimmie at the Weston Boarding School. By the summer, Grant enlisted the help of William Rawlins, the children's uncle and now a practicing attorney, for their relocation to the west.[49] William would accompany the girls to the home of their aunt, Laura Rawlins Sheean, in Anamosa, Iowa, while Jimmie would stay with his paternal grandparents in Jo Daviess County. The children were not happy with this arrangement, with Jimmie expressing a desire to return east to attend school and voicing his sisters' preference to remain in the east.[50] In June 1873, the children were back in Goshen and living with their maternal grandmother and a spinster aunt. Shortly after their return, President Grant arrived in Goshen on a special train with the "especial object" of visiting a local farm to inspect horse stock. He also made a stop on the twenty-fifth to check on the Rawlins children.[51]

Almost immediately after remarriage, Emma's fortunes spiraled downward. Her health had been on the decline, and in fall of 1872, she informed Grant of her intent to travel to the west as recommended by her physician.[52] It would be a pitiful effort to seek a cure for the tuberculosis that had migrated from John to herself. Like her health, the marriage to Charles Daniels unraveled and resulted in Emma seeking a divorce in March 1874. Seven months later, she was in Cheyenne, where she passed away on November 6. Her remains were returned to Danbury for burial. In December, an uncle, Hiram Horton Smith, was appointed a guardian of the children.

Eighteen-year-old James "Jimmie" Bradner Rawlins's fortunes appeared on the upswing when Grant appointed him to West Point, and he enrolled on July 1, 1875, after passing the entrance exam. However, just weeks into his studies, he told Orville Babcock, Grant's personal secretary, of his intent to resign.[53] The news startled Babcock, who told Jimmie the president would be disappointed and urged him to reconsider. His promising career was cut short when, on July 12, 1876, he was officially dismissed from the academy—he had already resigned in January 1876[54]—for deficiencies in French and mathematics.[55] Health issues may have contributed to his academic demise. Grant quickly came to Jimmie's aid by writing a personal letter to financier Edwin D. Morgan, recommending Jimmie for a job.[56]

In 1879, Jimmie came under the care of former surgeon general William Hammond, who treated him for epilepsy. When he had last seen him ten years later, Hammond found that "his mind had measurably failed." Unable to sustain employment, Jimmie lived for a time in New Jersey with sister Jennie and worked for her husband. However, that job ended on September 1, 1896, inducing him to reach out to Harry Wilson for assistance in finding a position that might utilize his office skills.[57] Disabled by seizures and loss of vision likely caused by tubercular meningitis,[58] he was a resident for most of the last twenty years of his life at the Craig Colony for Epileptics in Groveland, New York. In 1898, he applied for a small government pension. Julia Grant supported his application by stating, "Jimmie's health was a source of great anxiety to General Rawlins," who feared he might be incapacitated for life. Jennie's supporting letter included the disturbing disclosure that when Jimmie was eighteen months old, he was confined in the cellar by his nurse, after which his health became impaired. Jimmie Rawlins passed away at the colony in 1917 at age fifty-nine.[59]

The youngest of the Rawlins children, Emily, also had chronic health problems. She passed away at age thirty-six in Newburgh, New York, leaving a ten-year-old daughter, Lucille, and husband, Dr. Wesley Wait, a prominent dentist.

Jennie married George Holman of New York City on September 6, 1882. Grant was expected to attend but only sent a congratulatory telegram.[60] The Holmans had three children. Their only son died at age thirty in Spokane, Washington, at the Payne Sanitarium, a facility treating insanity and nervous diseases.[61] Jennie and her brother, James, attended their father's 1899 reinterment at Arlington. By this time, James was completely blind, but he could hear the homage paid to his father: "He was supremely executive, the right arm of power, a steadfast citadel of strength to his trusting chief."[62]

NOTES

1. *Daily Morning Chronicle*, Washington, DC, September 9, 1869.
2. Ibid., September 8, 1869.
3. George E. Spencer to Grenville Dodge, September 9, 1869, in *The Papers of Ulysses S. Grant*, ed. John Y. Simon, 19:260n.

4. Horace Porter to William Belknap, October 10, 1869, in *The Papers of Ulysses S. Grant*, ed. John Y. Simon, 19:261n.

5. *Daily Morning Chronicle*, Washington, DC, September 7, 1869.

6. Widow's Certificate No. 167–018, John A. Rawlins, Brigadier General, US Volunteers: Case Files of Approved Pension Applications of Veterans Who Served in the Army and Navy Mainly in the Civil War and Later (1861–1934); Civil War and Later Pension Files; Records of the Department of Veteran Affairs, Record Group 15;National Archives Building, Washington, DC.

7. *Daily Morning Chronicle*, Washington, DC, September 10, 1869.

8. *New York Tribune*, September 7, 1869.

9. *Daily Morning Chronicle*, Washington, DC, September 7, 1869.

10. *New York Herald*, September 7, 1869.

11. The *New York Sun*, September 7, 1869.

12. Ibid.

13. *New York Herald*, September 7, 1869.

14. William H. Armstrong, *Warrior in Two Camps* (Syracuse: Syracuse University Press, 1978), 145.

15. *New York Tribune*, September 7, 1869; *Galena Evening Gazette*, September 7, 1869.

16. *New York Tribune*, September 7, 1869.

17. *New York Times*, September 7, 1869.

18. U. S. Grant to Mary E. Rawlins, September 6, 1869, in *The Papers of Ulysses S. Grant*, ed. John Y. Simon, 19:240–41.

19. *Washington Evening Star*, August 15, 1901.

20. *Galena Evening Gazette*, September 7, 1869.

21. *Daily Morning Chronicle*, Washington, DC, September 8, 1869; ibid., September 11, 1869.

22. *Galena Evening Gazette*, September 7, 1869; ibid., September 8, 1869.

23. *New York Sun*, September 9, 1869.

24. *Daily Morning Chronicle*, Washington, DC, September 10, 1869; *New York Herald*, September 9, 1869.

25. *Daily Morning Chronicle*, Washington, DC, September 10, 1869; *Galena Evening Gazette*, September 10, 1869.

26. *Daily Morning Chronicle*, Washington, DC, September 10, 1869.

27. Ibid.

28. *Daily Morning Chronicle*, Washington, DC, September 9, 1869.

29. *The History of Jo Daviess County Illinois* (Chicago: H. F. Kett, 1878), 515.

30. *Galena Evening Gazette*, September 21, 1869.

31. *Report of the Proceedings of the Society of the Army of the Tennessee*, Fourth Annual Meeting, Louisville, KY, 11/17 and 11/18/69 (Cincinnati: Author, 1877), 381.

32. Ibid., 383.

33. Ibid., 384.

34. Ibid., 386.

35. Ibid., 390–92.

36. *Washington Evening Star*, December 27, 1872. The *New York Times* editorialized on December 29, 1872, that the Rawlins statue was certain to be "a particularly bad one,"

given the makeup of the committee, which would deter competent sculptors from submitting models. The result was predicted to be a statue "to be made permanently hideous in marble."

37. James M. Goode, *The Outdoor Sculpture of Washington, D.C.* (Washington, DC: Smithsonian Institution, 1974), 466.

38. John B. Anderson to Stewart L. Udall, February 4, 1963, Galena-Jo Daviess County Historical Society, John A. Rawlins File.

39. John Y. Simon, ed., *The Papers of Ulysses S. Grant* (Carbondale: Southern Illinois University Press, 1998), 22:373n1. Emma's portion was used as a down payment on a house in Danbury; see U. S. Grant to William S. Hillyer, January 31, 1872, in *The Papers of Ulysses S. Grant*, ed. John Y. Simon, 22:372.

40. *Daily Morning Chronicle*, Washington, DC, September 8, 1869.

41. Ibid., September 10, 1869.

42. *New York Herald*, September 13, 1869.

43. W. A. Evans, *Mrs. Abraham Lincoln: A Study of Her Personality and Her Influence on Lincoln* (Carbondale: Southern Illinois University Press, 2010), 202–3.

44. *The News-Times*, Danbury, CT, January 29, 1984.

45. Orville E. Babcock to William D. Rawlins, January 2, 1873, in *The Papers of Ulysses S. Grant*, ed. John Y. Simon (Carbondale: Southern Illinois University Press, 2000), 23:219–20n.

46. Horace Porter to Mary E. Rawlins, September 6, 1870, Danbury, CT, Museum, John Rawlins File.

47. Ulysses S. Grant to William S. Hillyer, January 31, 1872, in *The Papers of Ulysses S. Grant*, ed. John Y. Simon, 22:372.

48. Mary E. Rawlins to William S. Hillyer, January 29, 1872, in *The Papers of Ulysses S. Grant*, ed. John Y. Simon, 22:378n.

49. Ulysses S. Grant to William D. Rawlins, July 30, 1872, in *The Papers of Ulysses S. Grant*, ed. John Y. Simon, 23:215–16.

50. Ulysses S. Grant to William D. Rawlins, June 18, 1873, in *The Papers of Ulysses S. Grant*, ed. John Y. Simon (Carbondale: Southern Illinois University Press, 2000), 24:144–45.

51. *Goshen Democrat*, June 26, 1873.

52. Ulysses S. Grant to William S. Hillyer, October 20, 1872, in *The Papers of Ulysses S. Grant*, ed. John Y. Simon, 23:264.

53. Orville E. Babcock to James B. Rawlins, October 15, 1875, in *The Papers of Ulysses S. Grant*, ed. John Y. Simon, 24:145n.

54. John Y. Simon, ed., *The Papers of Ulysses S. Grant* (Carbondale: Southern Illinois University Press, 2005), 27:22n.

55. "Academy Staff Records Book," "Cadet Admittance Book," and "Cadet Casualty Book," West Point, New York, US Military Academy.

56. Ulysses S. Grant to Edwin D. Morgan, January 30, 1876, in *The Papers of Ulysses S. Grant*, ed. John Y. Simon, 27:21.

57. James B. Rawlins to James H. Wilson, August 13, 1896, James Harrison Wilson Correspondence File, S (1), Box 14, Series 2, Ulysses S. Grant Presidential Library, Mississippi State University Libraries.

58. J. C. Ladenheim, *Grant's Keeper: The Life of John A. Rawlins* (Westminster, MD: Heritage, 2011), 218.

59. House of Representatives, 55th Congress, 2nd Session, Report No. 551 contained in Widow's Certificate No. 167–018, John A. Rawlins, Brigadier General, US Volunteers: Case Files of Approved Pension Applications of Veterans Who Served in the Army and Navy Mainly in the Civil War and Later (1861–1934); Civil War and Later Pension Files; Records of the Department of Veteran Affairs, Record Group 15; National Archives Building, Washington, DC.

60. *Goshen Democrat*, September 7, 1882.

61. *Spokane Daily Chronicle*, August 24, 1918.

62. *Evening Times*, Washington, DC, February 8, 1899.

Epilogue

ONLY HOURS AFTER RAWLINS'S FUNERAL ceremony, a newspaper report announced that William Hillyer planned to write John Rawlins's biography.[1] Moreover, the folks in Galena learned just days later that Hillyer's writing task would be facilitated by him "having in his possession a large collection of letters and documents which will enable him to enter into the details of the war record of the deceased."[2] This development must have stunned Harry Wilson, who believed that Rawlins intended for him to be the recipient of that collection. Over thirty years later, Wilson claimed in a letter to Sylvanus Cadwallader that a few weeks after Rawlins's death, he wrote Emma, reminding her of her husband's dying wishes to appoint him his "literary executor" and for Emma to turn over all of his papers to him "at the proper time." Emma wrote back, saying she recollected the arrangement Wilson described, but she said that Hillyer called on her right after John's death, stated that he wished to write her husband's memoir, and requested whatever papers she had. Thereupon, she said she fulfilled Hillyer's request by turning over to him all Rawlins's papers in her possession.[3]

Cadwallader was familiar with the trunks full of those papers, as was his wife. She and Emma—presumably when the Rawlinses and Cadwalladers shared a Washington residence—"spent hours in examining the contents of these trunks." He gave Wilson his frank opinion that Emma lied to him and that she and Hillyer "probably intended to use this material for their joint benefit." Rawlins, Cadwallader reminded Wilson, knew Hillyer's reputation "and would never have trusted him." Moreover, Cadwallader admonished Wilson for having made the "irreparable mistake" of not having taken immediate custody of the trunks before Rawlins died.[4] Curiously, a week later Cadwallader walked back his suspicions about Emma, writing Wilson that Hillyer may have imposed on Emma for the documents, "but I do not think she was in collusion with him to use the information for their mutual benefit."[5] Such inconsistencies require that one proceed with caution when relying on Cadwallader as a source.

Whatever happened to those papers once they left Emma's hands has remained a mystery. Historian John Y. Simon made a blunt assertion: "The disposition of the Rawlins papers upon the death of John A. Rawlins and their whereabouts constitutes one of the most perplexing problems for anybody in the Grant field."[6] Some of Rawlins's papers exist in various collections, and David Sheean provided Wilson with a trove of personal letters Rawlins sent to Emma. Wilson also had an assortment of Rawlins letters from their friendly correspondence. One explanation for the fate of the papers came from General John E. Smith, who, in his dotage, claimed he had come into possession of two army chests of Rawlins's correspondence just a day or two before the latter's death. Moreover, Smith said Rawlins had ordered him to immediately destroy all the documents, and Smith said he did this before Rawlins was even buried.[7] Smith's story is intriguing given his close, personal association to Rawlins—besides having been members of the same Galena Masonic Lodge, Smith was a witness to Rawlins's will—but he is not regarded as a reliable source.[8]

In a letter to Wilson, Cadwallader surmised that Hillyer took the papers to New York and that they later came into the hands of Hillyer's son, who gave them to Grant's son, Fred.[9] Wilson elaborated on this story, telling Cadwallader that on Hillyer's death, Wilson asked if any of Rawlins's papers in the family's possession could be turned over to him. As Wilson explained to Cadwallader, "I received a letter from William S. Hillyer, Jr., upon the death of his mother," who said he had found a collection of papers associated with Rawlins and Grant and that he had sent Grant the collection. Wilson speculated that Grant may have destroyed them or that they came into Fred's hands.[10] Wilson's story contains several apparent inaccuracies. Hillyer did not have a son who shared his name. Wilson may be referring to Ulysses Grant Hillyer. William Hillyer died in 1874, and his wife, Anna, died in 1896, leaving a twenty-two-year gap between when Wilson said he made his request and got a response. Moreover, Ulysses S. Grant predeceased Anna Hillyer by eleven years. Curiously, in a return letter to Wilson, Cadwallader confirmed this story: "I also wrote to W. S. Hillyer, Jr. . . . and received the same reply sent you." Cadwallader's guess as to the fate of the Rawlins papers was that either Grant or Fred had destroyed them.[11]

In the 1930s, archivists at the Library of Congress embarked on a search for some of the papers, "but the trail petered out disappointingly."[12] Dr. Michelle Krowl, the Civil War and Reconstruction specialist in the Manuscript Division of the Library of Congress, provided a synopsis of the division's search efforts to locate the papers. The details and results of those efforts are housed in the Manuscript Division's files and not open to researchers. Dr. Krowl's synopsis, she believed, describes the general parameters of the search without violating the privacy of any parties involved. In June 1933, J. Franklin Jameson, the Manuscript Division's chief, at the suggestion of the daughter of General John Logan, wrote Jennie Rawlins Holman to inquire whether the "considerable mass of papers" of John Rawlins might be in her possession or held by Dr. David Sheean of Montana. It is not known whether Jennie Holman responded to Dr. Jameson.[13] It is unlikely that the Rawlins papers are held by a member of the Sheean family, as suggested in a letter written by Galena attorney Louis Nack Sr. to John Y. Simon: "Mr. J. B. Sheean, who was a relative by marriage to General Rawlins and a very good friend of mine . . . spent many days in Washington trying to find the whereabouts of the Rawlins papers."[14] The relative referred to is undoubtedly James Benjamin Sheean (1863–1941), son of Rawlins's sister, Mary.

The search for the trove of Rawlins papers resumed in the 1960s. It was led by David C. Mearns, Manuscript Division chief, and Lloyd A. Dunlap, Civil War specialist. Mearns noticed that Lloyd Lewis, in his book *Letters from Lloyd Lewis*, mentioned having read Rawlins's letters at Chicago's Newberry Library. Staff at the Newberry told Mearns that Lewis's wife had transferred the letters to historian Bruce Catton. Mearns followed that lead, but there is no record of Catton's response. On February 28, 1968, a frustrated Dunlap wrote to E. B. Long,

> The John A. Rawlins papers continue to bother me. I have never completely convinced myself that somewhere, someplace, some of his papers did not exist. This is probably wishful thinking, but it led me to examine his will, in the faint hope it would shed some light on the question. His will was witnessed by Ely S. Parker, Jacob D. Cox, and Colonel John E. Smith, who, you recall, either did or did not destroy "two army chests" of papers. The curiosity is that the executor and guardian of his children was Ulysses S. Grant. What this means, I have no idea, but I thought you would be interested.

John Y. Simon told Dunlap he believed that the Rawlins papers Wilson and Cadwallader exchanged opinions about had been integrated into the Grant papers held by the Grant family and that whatever material not included with the Grant papers was lost. Dunlap responded to Simon that he thought the Federal Records Center in Suitland, Maryland, held Rawlins documents, but there is no record that Dunlap sought out these items.[15]

Recent inquiries into the location or relocation of the Rawlins papers have not borne fruit. For example, Will Hansen, curator of Americana at the Newberry Library, reported that, "I have not found any record here of papers of John Rawlins having been housed at the Newberry, or of their being transferred or deaccessioned."[16] Ms. DeAnne Blanton of the National Archives Reference Section expressed skepticism that the Rawlins papers were ever housed at the Federal Records Center in Suitland. During the 1960s, some archival records were stored at the Suitland facility because of overcrowding at the National Archives Building; however, it is unlikely that the Rawlins papers were sent there, "because no other 19th century War Department records were sent to Suitland."[17]

―⚬⚬⚬―

James Wilson took up the task of literary executor when, in 1884, he began writing Rawlins's memoir. At the outset, he sought the help of David Sheean in acquiring Rawlins's personal correspondence and information about his early years. Sheean, a Galena attorney, supported Wilson's efforts to memorialize his former law partner, hoping thereby "that justice may be done him in the part he acted with Gen. Grant in the war." In Sheean's opinion, there were few in Galena who did not believe that but for Rawlins "Gen. Grant would not possess the fame he has enjoyed."[18] However, intervening business and other writing pursuits—Wilson penned biographical works of "Baldy" Smith and Charles Dana—along with his return to military service in the Spanish-American War and the Boxer Rebellion caused him to put the Rawlins project aside until he returned to it in late 1903 with the intention "to put it through this time."[19] When Wilson later shared the raw manuscript with Sheean, the latter expressed a sense of satisfaction that Wilson's biography would set the record straight. "It will be a gratification to the friends of Rawlins to read this book," Sheean wrote, "and to many of them, it will be a confirmation of their own opinions of the relations of Grant and Rawlins."[20]

Sheean was deftly praising Wilson for producing a manuscript that, when published, would do justice to Rawlins by offering a long-overdue counterpoint to Grant's two-volume *Personal Memoirs*, a best seller when it appeared in print twenty years before. At the time, Rawlins's friends were stunned that, in the entire autobiography, Grant made but a few references to Rawlins—and one was a sharply worded accusation that he had schemed to prevent Sherman's march through Georgia. Shortly after reading the *Memoirs*, Cadwallader's bitter reaction was that Grant had "dismissed R[awlins] from history."[21] To former general and fellow Galenian John C. Smith, Ely Parker expressed his feeling that Grant was unappreciative of Rawlins's services: "It is much to be deplored that no competent person has yet undertaken to place Rawlins before the public in his true light. . . . No one could have been more true and loyal to his Chief and country than he, and yet he gets only faint praise from Grant in his Memoirs." Grant's accusation that Rawlins opposed Sherman's plan left Parker mystified and hurt, and he called it a "wicked thing . . . a grave and serious error which the true friends of both will never cease to regret."[22] John E. Smith expressed sad surprise that in the years following Rawlins's death, "his Memory should be so soon buried in Oblivion but it is a lamentable fact."[23]

The virtual omission of Rawlins from the *Memoirs* is puzzling considering Badeau's opinion that only Julia knew Grant better than Rawlins.[24] Moreover, the evidence shows, as historian E. B. Long pointed out, that Rawlins deserved much more credit in the *Memoirs* than he received.[25] Thus, friends of Rawlins such as Wilson, Parker, Henry Van Ness Boynton, and Cadwallader had a valid argument when deeming the treatment of him unfair. There is no certain explanation for why Grant gave Rawlins such short shrift. Perhaps, as Long surmised, Grant refrained from praising Rawlins because of his reputation as the one who protected Grant from his bad habits.[26] Perhaps by expanding on Rawlins's role in his path toward fame, Grant might be admitting his own weakness.[27] In this regard, Grant, in the *Memoirs*, stressed such eras of his life (e.g., the Mexican and Civil Wars) that best demonstrated his greatest strength, which was as a warrior; he had virtually nothing to say about himself as a politician or struggling farmer or businessman. There may also be a simple, straightforward explanation for saying so little about Rawlins: Mark Twain, who got Grant's *Memoirs* into print, explained that "General Grant's first order was to put in portraits of prominent generals, but he got so many letters from colonels and such, asking to be added that he resolved to put none in and thus avoid the creation of jealousies."[28]

Perhaps Grant made a conscious decision not to provide more ammunition for those, such as Charles A. Dana and James H. Wilson, who were touting Rawlins as the masterful man behind Grant's success. At the onset of Grant's presidency, Rawlins, according to James Wilson, was in favor of Dana's appointment as the collector of customs at New York City. Rawlins was so sure of Dana's chances for this juicy patronage job that he allegedly told Wilson he could share the news with Dana. Wilson assumed that Grant had settled on Dana, but that was not to be. Without explanation, the plum went to Moses Grinnell, a well-connected businessman. Compared to Dana, Wilson regarded Grinnell as "a gentleman of much less consideration."[29] Perhaps Dana was rankled that Grant passed him over because, as editor of the popular *New York Sun*, he became a frequent critic of President Grant. The *Sun's* torment of Grant probably reached a zenith in its issue of July 24, 1885—the day after Grant died—which featured a long biographical article about Grant. Although no author was credited, the piece was obviously written by Grant's former staff officer James H. Wilson.

Wilson took numerous critical swipes as Grant, such as blasting him, as general, for the enormous casualties sustained during the Overland Campaign because he was influenced by those who favored "smash up" assaults and, as president, for elevating to the cabinet too many unworthy and corruptible men. In contrast, Wilson was effusive in his praise of Rawlins, editorializing that he "exerted upon [Grant] as great an influence as Gneisenau or Müffling exerted over Blücher, or Berthier over Napoleon." By claiming that "Rawlins was . . . master of himself and of all his appetites and passions," Wilson intimated that Grant, in contrast, had little control over his drinking. The editorializing went to considerable length to exalt Rawlins as the key to Grant's military success:

> Grant has been credited, in military matters, at least, with unerring judgment as to men, and a keen insight into their motives, but in these faculties Rawlins was his superior. When the former deferred to the latter in regard to men or measures, the best results followed; when they differed, Rawlins was more frequently right than Grant and almost always secured the adoption of his views. . . . So long as Grant depended upon Rawlins, so long as his influence was dominant at Grant's headquarters, his career presented an unbroken series of successes. Although it was not Grant's habit to ask the advice of Rawlins, or of any one else, Rawlins always found a way to give it, if he thought it was needed; and if it was neglected, and to just the degree it was neglected, trouble generally followed, and the successes were less complete. If his vigilance was relaxed for one

moment, or if he was absent for a day, something was sure to happen to mar the favorable course of events; and this was not because Rawlins knew more than any one else or 'furnished brains' to Grant, but because his judgment was good and he would brook no nonsense or delay, and frowned with withering anger upon vice or vicious tendencies of every sort.

Moreover, according to Wilson, Rawlins could be credited with propping up Grant as chief executive, for the day of Rawlins's death marked the point where "Grant's political fortunes began to decline. Up to that time Rawlins had been the master mind in the Cabinet, as he had been on the staff." In summary, Wilson opined that "there can be no doubt as to the position [Rawlins] filled or the good influence he exerted. It is therefore safe to conclude that no consideration of Grant's career which neglects Rawlins as a potent factor can do justice to the truth."[30]

Wilson's praise of Rawlins reads remarkably similar to Van Ness Boynton's estimate of Rawlins that the *New York Sun* would run a year and a half later, when revealing the remarkable letter Rawlins composed at Vicksburg as an intervention to Grant's drinking. In that piece, Boynton credits Rawlins with having "supervised every act of Grant's military life, his personal and official conduct, and changed or controlled his conduct upon more occasions than any other or all other men."[31]

Tellingly, Wilson also made a point in his biographical piece about Grant to heap praise on Benjamin Bristow, Grant's third secretary of the treasury, who strove to break up the Whiskey Ring and thus "stem the tide of corruption." However, Wilson lamented, Grant turned against Bristow who withdrew from the Cabinet, leaving "the President to drift whithersoever chance or his stubborn adherence to unworthy friends might carry him."[32]

—◦◦◦—

The Whiskey Ring had been in operation for a number of years prior to Grant's time in the White House. Internal Revenue collectors and distillers collaborated in a wide-ranging cabal to evade millions in taxes on distilled liquors. The Ring had functioned with its usual impunity during the tenure of Grant's first two Treasury Department secretaries, George Boutwell and William Richardson. But the Ring's fortunes were due for a turn in early 1875 when Henry T. Yaryan, an Internal Revenue officer in the Midwest, traveled to Washington to present the details of the frauds to the solicitor of the treasury, Bluford Wilson, younger brother of Harry Wilson. Solicitor Wilson wasted no time relaying Yaryan's story to Treasury Secretary Benjamin Bristow, who had been on the job less than a year.

By spring 1875, the reform-minded Bristow and Wilson were accumulating reams of evidence against the Ring, which were presented to Grant in May. They had uncovered elaborate schemes to cheat the system—labeling whiskey as vinegar was one ploy—and fingered some high-echelon government officials that included John McDonald, an old acquaintance of Grant, who was a regional supervisor of internal revenue headquartered in St. Louis. Shockingly, Bristow would discover that the Ring's tentacles reached into the White House itself: he found cryptic telegrams attributed to Orville Babcock, Grant's secretary and member of his "kitchen cabinet," which appeared to alert McDonald to impending raids by Internal Revenue agents. That Babcock could be implicated was inconceivable to Grant. Bristow grew increasingly anxious to somehow convince Grant that Babcock—and even Horace Porter—was deeply involved in the fraud. Bristow and Bluford Wilson decided that Harry Wilson was the best choice to break the news to Grant. One evening, Wilson visited the White House and had his candid talk with the president. Rather than enlightening Grant, the talk had an unintended effect: it marked the beginning of the end of his relationship with Wilson.[33]

Convinced that Babcock was falsely accused, Grant believed that Bristow was really trying to implicate him, Grant, in the scandal in order to propel himself toward a run for president in 1876.[34] Later in the year, Grant, on Christmas Day 1875, angrily summoned Bluford Wilson to explain a swirl of rumors suggesting that prosecutors were considering indictments against his son, Fred, and brother, Orvil.[35] Some senators close to Grant, such as John Logan of Illinois and Matthew Carpenter of Wisconsin—both of whom had been suspected of accepting money from the Ring—were even calling for Bluford Wilson's dismissal.[36]

Although Babcock reeked of guilt, he was exonerated at trial on February 24, 1876, due in part to the prosecutors' largely circumstantial evidence against him and to the lengthy deposition Grant gave attesting to Babcock's sterling reputation. With their relationships with Grant strained beyond the limit, Bristow and Solicitor Wilson soon submitted their resignations. That summer Bluford Wilson testified before the House Whiskey Investigating Committee, saying that Grant was so certain of Babcock's innocence, he resented efforts to put him on trial, figuring the indictment was a conspiracy aimed at the White House. Wilson also made the claim that after Grant had obtained from

Bristow the evidence to be used against Babcock at trial, he turned it over to Babcock. Wilson's testimony left Grant seething.[37]

The Wilsons and Grant never reconciled. In the year after Grant left office, Harry Wilson received a letter from Sherman, who wrote that he had had a long talk with Fred Grant. When Sherman asked him how his father felt toward Wilson, Fred "said his father was not friendly to you, and your brother Bluford."[38] The rift in their relationship soon became a chasm, reaching a point where neither could tolerate the other's presence. In February 1881, Grant and some friends entered a New York City restaurant, where they encountered Harry Wilson and others at a table. Grant did an about-face and left.[39]

Harry Wilson would become seriously disillusioned by the corruption that had been allowed to percolate during Grant's terms as president. That disillusionment was made manifest in his support of reformer Benjamin Bristow to head the Republican ticket in 1876. Wilson was also unhappy with the treatment his brother had received at Grant's hands. Although Wilson's cordial relationship with Grant soured, his strong positive feelings toward John Rawlins seemed to magnify over time. Whereas Wilson had grown deeply jealous of some of Grant's later staff—Porter, Comstock, Babcock, and Badeau—who vied for the general's esteem, he felt no threat from the humble and less ambitious Rawlins.[40] These factors allowed Wilson to claim in his biography of Rawlins, "Rawlins was besides the only member of the Cabinet who actually knew the capacities and limitations of the President. . . . To those who knew what took place in government circles it was certain that the new Secretary of War wielded the same potent and controlling influence over the President, when he chose to exert it, that the Chief of Staff had wielded over the Commanding General."[41]

Wilson's biographical treatment of Rawlins never succeeded in elevating him to a revered status among historical personages. However, fueled by the rancor he harbored toward Grant, Wilson, along with others, contributed to creating a skewed rendering of Grant's accomplishments as president. Wilson's point of view was that if a healthy, vigorous Rawlins had been installed in the cabinet, "Grant's political career must have been much more successful than it was."[42] Wilson had also encouraged Cadwallader to publish his reminiscences from his stint as a newspaper correspondent at Grant's headquarters. Cadwallader hardly needed any goading to snipe at Grant. He had been so incensed by Grant's dismissal of Rawlins in his *Memoirs* that his first reaction after having read them was to believe Grant "deserved to be scourged from the face of the earth."[43] Cadwallader's account of Grant's "Yazoo bender" gave more impetus to the controversy over Grant's drinking and strengthened Rawlins's reputation as Grant's "conscience." That account has been essentially debunked "as a tall tale told to impress others, a story hard to reconcile with the available evidence."[44]

———

Rawlins would have blanched if he had known that one day he would be touted as the "master mind" of Grant's cabinet. And as someone who was cognizant of his shortcomings, he would never have wanted to be regarded as the influence behind Grant's military successes. So how might he have wished to be remembered? Perhaps the answer lies in a speech given at the 1886 Rock River Seminary reunion—a reunion that happened to coincide with the release of Grant's *Memoirs*—by prominent Chicago attorney H. O. McDaid. McDaid was chosen to pay tribute to the Amphictyons, the members of one of the school's literary societies whose rolls once included John Rawlins, whom McDaid singled out for special homage. "Rawlins! The friend of the 'Old Commander,'" McDaid declared, warming to his topic. "When Rawlins was laid to rest on the banks of the Potomac, no eyes were moist with sincerer tears than those of Ulysses S. Grant."[45] Rawlins was, foremost, Grant's friend. No one was truer or worked so selflessly for his benefit. He worked always for Grant's benefit—and consequently for the nation's as well—never scheming to undo him or upstage him. If Rawlins were too intrusive regarding Grant and alcohol or too emphatic in stating an opinion, it was as a demonstration of the esteem he had for Grant and his loyalty toward him. To be known for being the one whose friendship had most deeply touched Grant might have been all that John Rawlins could have asked.

McDaid added that what Rawlins accomplished was "to round out, into complete symmetry, the character and military genius of U. S. Grant."[46] He helped enhance the former, as Grant biographer Ron Chernow noted, by performing as the intermediary for a chief who could be taciturn and inhibited; and he burnished the latter by "sometimes questioning Grant's tactical moves where others feared to tread."[47] He did this always as an ancillary, standing to the side and respectfully behind Grant. Joe Bowers, when he urged Congressman Washburne to push for Rawlins's promotion to brigadier, probably best summed up Rawlins's preferred annotation in the historical registry: he served as "Grant's associate and adviser in all his battles and Campaigns."[48]

How will the people of John Rawlins's native state choose to remember him? Seminary alumnus McDaid had his ready answer: "Illinois is proud of her son. Time alone will reveal to her the debt of gratitude which she owes to the intellectual, the brave, the devoted John A. Rawlins."[49]

Such are the attributes of no ordinary man.

NOTES

1. *Daily Morning Chronicle*, Washington, DC, September 10, 1869.

2. *Galena Evening Gazette*, September 16, 1869.

3. James H. Wilson to Sylvanus Cadwallader, September 8, 1904, James Harrison Wilson Papers, Box 5, Library of Congress.

4. Sylvanus Cadwallader to James H. Wilson, September 17, 1904, James Harrison Wilson Papers, Box 5, Library of Congress.

5. Sylvanus Cadwallader to James H. Wilson, September 24, 1904, James Harrison Wilson Papers, Box 5, Library of Congress.

6. John Y. Simon to Louis Nack, September 25, 1974, John A. Rawlins Subject File, Series 2, Box 13, Folder 2, Ulysses S. Grant Presidential Library, Mississippi State University Libraries. In April 1864 while at Culpeper Court House in Virginia, Rawlins sent to Emma "a trunk full of valuable letters and papers," which he begged her "to keep most carefully"; see Wilson's paraphrased note of J. A. Rawlins to Emma, April 27, 1864, Wyoming State Archives, Bender Collection, James H. Wilson Papers, Microfilm Reel 61b.

7. John E. Smith to Sylvanus Cadwallader, May 8, 1895, Sylvanus Cadwallader Papers, Library of Congress.

8. Cadwallader told James Wilson that Smith had several other versions of the fate of Rawlins's papers, including his belief that they were in actually in Cadwallader's possession and that Emma had taken the most important documents to Danbury; see S. Cadwallader to J. H. Wilson, August 31, 1904, James Harrison Wilson Papers, Container 5, Library of Congress.

9. Sylvanus Cadwallader to James H. Wilson, August 31, 1904, James Harrison Wilson Papers, Container 5, Library of Congress.

10. James H. Wilson to Sylvanus Cadwallader, September 17, 1904, James Harrison Wilson Papers, Container 5, Library of Congress.

11. Sylvanus Cadwallader to James H. Wilson, September 17, 1904, James Harrison Wilson Papers, Container 5, Library of Congress.

12. E. B. Long, "John A. Rawlins: Staff Officer Par Excellence," *Civil War Times Illustrated* 12, no. 9 (1974): 46.

13. Dr. Michelle Krowl, personal email communication to the author, January 25, 2017.

14. Louis Nack to John Y. Simon, September 27, 1974, John A. Rawlins Subject File, Series 2, Box 13, Folder 2, Ulysses S. Grant Presidential Library, Mississippi State University Libraries.

15. Dr. Michelle Krowl, personal email communication to the author, January 25, 2017.

16. Will Hansen, personal email communication to the author, February 8, 2017.

17. DeAnne Blanton, personal email communication to the author, March 1, 2017.

18. David Sheean to James H. Wilson, January 10, 1885, James Harrison Wilson: Correspondence File, S (1), Box 14, Series 2, Ulysses S. Grant Presidential Library, Mississippi State University Libraries.

19. James H. Wilson to David Sheean, December 22, 1903, James Harrison Wilson Papers, Box 22, Library of Congress.

20. David Sheean to James H. Wilson, October 13, 1904, James Harrison Wilson Papers, Container 22, Library of Congress.

21. Sylvanus Cadwallader to J. H. Wilson, February 18, 1887, James Harrison Wilson Papers, Container 22, Library of Congress.

22. Ely Parker to J. C. Smith, February 15, 1887, SC 1143, Manuscripts Department, Abraham Lincoln Presidential Library, Springfield, IL.

23. J. E. Smith to S. Cadwallader, May 8, 1895, Sylvanus Cadwallader Papers, Library of Congress.

24. Adam Badeau, *Grant in Peace* (Hartford, CT: S. S. Scranton, 1887), 404.

25. E. B. Long, "John A. Rawlins," 43.

26. Ibid., 43.

27. Ron Chernow, *Grant* (New York: Penguin, 2017), 953.

28. Albert Bigelow Paine, *Mark Twain's Notebook* (New York: Harper and Brothers, 1935), 183.

29. James Harrison Wilson, *The Life of Charles A. Dana* (New York: Harper and Brothers, 1907), 407.

30. *New York Sun*, July 24, 1885.

31. Ibid., January 23, 1887.

32. Ibid.

33. William S. McFeely, *Grant* (New York: W. W. Norton, 1981), 408.

34. Allan Nevins, *Hamilton Fish: The Inner History of the Grant Administration* (New York: Dodd, Mead, 1936), 800.

35. Charles W. Calhoun, *The Presidency of Ulysses S. Grant* (Lawrence: University Press of Kansas, 2017), 519.

36. Allan Nevins, *Hamilton Fish*, 801.

37. Ross A. Webb, *Benjamin Helm Bristow: Border State Politician* (Lexington: University Press of Kentucky, 1969), 255–57.

38. W. T. Sherman to J. H. Wilson, December 24, 1878, in *The Papers of Ulysses S. Grant*, ed. John Y. Simon (Carbondale: Southern Illinois University Press, 2005), 28:474n.

39. Edward G. Longacre, *From Union Stars to Top Hat: A Biography of the Extraordinary General James Harrison Wilson* (Harrisburg, PA: Stackpole, 1972), 245.

40. Ibid., 109.

41. James Harrison Wilson, *The Life of John A. Rawlins* (New York: Neale, 1916), 358–59.

42. Ibid., 380–81.

43. S. Cadwallader to J. H. Wilson, February 18, 1887, James Harrison Wilson Papers, Container 5, Library of Congress.

44. Brooks D. Simpson, Introduction to the Bison Books edition of *Three Years with Grant*, ed. Benjamin P. Thomas (Lincoln: University of Nebraska Press, 1996), xv.

45. Isabel Wallace, *Life and Letters of General W. H. L. Wallace* (Chicago: R. R. Donnelly and Sons, 1909), 7.

46. Ibid., 7.

47. Ron Chernow, *Grant*, 671.

48. T. S. Bowers to E. H. Washburne, April 9, 1864, in *The Papers of Ulysses S. Grant*, ed. John Y. Simon (Carbondale: Southern Illinois University Press, 1982), 10:260n.

49. Isabel Wallace, *Life and Letters of General W. H. L. Wallace*, 7.

INDEX

of a soldier, 308; on Rawlins's temperance letter, 291–92; telegram inviting Rawlinses to Washington, 495; before Vicksburg, 265; visit in Cairo, 133

Grant, Orville, 65, 83, 85

Grant, Simpson, 44, 65

Grant, Ulysses S., correspondence: to Dana on commanding the Army of the Potomac, 306; to Emma on Rawlins's death, 524; to father-in-law on going to war, 84; to father on the war and his staff, 83, 90, 292; to Halleck on Battle of the Crater, 388; to Halleck on McClernand's fitness to lead, 280; to Johnson on firing Sheridan, 468; to Johnson on Stanton case, 482–83; to Johnson resigning as secretary of war, 480; to Julia about loneliness, 65; to Julia on his frustration, 99, 113–14, 195; to Julia on his health, 329; to Julia on promotion, 108; to Julia on Rawlins, 88, 188, 379; to Julia on staffing, 90; to Julia on the war, 148, 418; to Lee on surrender, 420, 422; to Lincoln on the Overland Campaign, 372; to Lincoln to introduce Rawlins, 304–5; to Lorenzo Thomas regarding a military position, 96; to McClernand on drunkenness in the army, 102; to McPherson on taking command to Vicksburg, 250; on promotion of Rawlins, 408; to Rawlins offering his Galena home for recuperation, 430; to Stanton on Lee's surrender, 423; to Stanton on Sheean, 206; to Walcott on Jews and traders, 232; to Washburne on position, 98; to Washburne on Rawlins, 4, 308; to Wilson on promotion of Rawlins to brigadier general, 346

Grant, Ulysses S., death of, 541

Grant, Ulysses S., description, skills, and character: antisemitism and stereotyping, 232; and barroom altercation (Galena), 66; biographies and studies of, vii, viii, xi; calmness in the face of disaster, 368; effect of seeing wounded soldiers,

157; gratitude at field commander's gift to, 165; indomitable will, xii–xiii; initiative, 100, 130–31; public speaking, 84–85; rare venting of emotion, 369, 389n14; Rawlins on change in character of, 86–87; as related by Rawlins to Wilson, 222; response to compliments, 301; self-control, xiii, 326, 342; Sherman on abilities of, 292; singleness of purpose, 333–34; sociability, 488; as storyteller, 66–67; strength of character, xii–xiii, 66; on treatment of horses, 377; writing style, 123, 264. *See also* alcohol, consumption of; theatrical performances

Grant, Ulysses S., *Memoirs*: Belmont campaign in, 128; incomplete picture of Grant in, 540; on McClernand in, 120; Rawlins's biography as counterpoint to, 540; on Rawlins's call for delay before Petersburg, 416; Rawlins's sparse presence in, xiii, 4, 5, 254, 287, 292, 408; on telegraph operator with possible Rebel sympathies, 162; on Vicksburg strategy, 253

Grant, Ulysses S., military career: assigned command of the armies of the United States, 349; on Buell's approach, 147; command in Jefferson City, 99–100; command of the Twenty-First Illinois, 93n35, 97–98; complaints, criticism, and hostility toward, 136–37, 256–58; confirmation and invitation to Rawlins, 88, 89; confusion in Ironton, 98–99; decision to reenter the military, 83; demonstrations in western Kentucky, 142; disgust with Johnson, 447; dismissal of Butler, 405–6; expressions of thanks to Sherman and McPherson, 360n36; frustration with clerical duties under Yates, 95–96; frustration with forced inactivity, 113–14, 194–95; frustration with McClernand, 277; gifts of homes to, 429–30; honors in St. Louis, 341–42; hospitality to negotiators, 408; importance of the Union's

ALLEN J. OTTENS is Professor Emeritus of Counselor Education and Supervision, Northern Illinois University. He worked as a psychologist at several university counseling centers. He is also a past president of the Manuscript Society. He has had a lifelong interest in the Civil War and Abraham Lincoln. He, his wife, and their green-cheek conure, Cisco, live in northern Illinois.